THEOLOGY AFTER POSTMODERNITY

Theology after Postmodernity

*Divining the Void—A Lacanian Reading
of Thomas Aquinas*

TINA BEATTIE

OXFORD
UNIVERSITY PRESS

OXFORD
UNIVERSITY PRESS

Great Clarendon Street, Oxford, OX2 6DP,
United Kingdom

Oxford University Press is a department of the University of Oxford.
It furthers the University's objective of excellence in research, scholarship,
and education by publishing worldwide. Oxford is a registered trade mark of
Oxford University Press in the UK and in certain other countries

Published in the United States of America by Oxford University Press
198 Madison Avenue, New York, NY 10016, United States of America

British Library Cataloguing in Publication Data
Data available

Library of Congress Control Number: 2013938326

ISBN 978-0-19-956607-5

As printed and bound by
CPI Group (UK) Ltd, Croydon, CR0 4YY

For Dave

My soul yearns and pines
For the courts of the LORD.
My heart and my flesh
cry out for the living God.
(Psalm 84:3)

Contents

Part V—Embodying Desire

Acknowledgements

This book began life as a very different project. In 2001 I had published a book on Marian theology and Irigarayan psychoanalytic theory, based on my doctoral thesis.[1] My next project was a continuation of this earlier research, being a critical exploration of the representation of sexual difference in the work of various feminist theorists and Catholic theologians, focusing primarily on Hans Urs von Balthasar.[2] I had then intended to start a completely new field of research, in order to write a book on theology, human rights, and women's rights. That was six years ago, and I decided to begin by reading Thomas Aquinas's account of natural law in the *Summa theologiae*. Gradually, I found myself thrilling to what I was discovering. Themes of desire and grace, embodiment and goodness, wisdom and reason, creation and participation, glistened and came to life as I read. Strange worlds hovered into view—angels and demons, phantasms and incubi, supernatural presences creating a sense of disorder and wonder around the edges of Thomas's pedantic Aristotelianism. Shimmering through it all, appearing and disappearing, enigmatic, mystical, elusive, was Thomas's maternal Trinity. With Jacques Lacan's help, I went in quest of this maternal, relational Other of Thomas's One God, and this book is an account of that tortuous theological quest. It is not the book I had intended to write.

However, this means that these three books constitute a single body of work. Not only that, but although this is the last chronologically, it is the first in terms of what I now see as the theological archaeology of my writings—a consequence perhaps of allowing psychoanalysis to play such a significant role in my theological explorations. I have been digging back through layers of meaning so that, in the words of T. S. Eliot, I have indeed arrived at where I started, 'and know the place for the first time'. If I were to write these books again I would change relatively little, but I would write this one first. I say this because if readers want to know where my ideas would go from here, they would go next to *New Catholic Feminism* where I explore the violent implications of a certain kind of Thomism for modern theology, while suggesting possible reconfigurations of the maternal ecclesiology and sacramental expressiveness of the Catholic liturgical tradition. Finally, *God's Mother, Eve's Advocate* proposes a Marian theology of the redemption of the female body in

---

[1] Tina Beattie, *God's Mother, Eve's Advocate: A Marian Narrative of Women's Salvation* (London and New York: Continuum, 2002).
[2] Tina Beattie, *New Catholic Feminism: Theology and Theory* (London and New York: Routledge, 2006).

terms of an Irigarayan understanding of sexual difference. I am less confident now than I was then about the theological potential of Irigaray's understanding of sexual difference, for reasons that will become clear in this book. Nevertheless, my overall understanding of the centrality of Mary's role for a theology of the incarnation capable of accommodating all bodies and all of creation within its expansive vision remains unchanged.

The end is indeed where we start from. The Christian story starts in the body of the earth in Genesis and in the body of the Mother of God in the Gospel of Luke, and the risen Christ is reborn from the womb of the earth on Easter Sunday. However, we shall not understand the significance of these beginnings until we arrive at the ending.

Lists of acknowledgements risk ending up like Oscar acceptance speeches, and this one certainly would if I listed the many people whose ideas, support, and friendship have sustained me along the way and shaped my thinking. I have had to sacrifice a vast hinterland of research in order to remain within manageable boundaries, and this has meant excluding many theologians and theorists to whom I am deeply indebted. Although I profoundly disagree with her theological liberalism, Rosemary Radford Ruether's book *Sexism and God-Talk* changed the way I read and understood theology during my undergraduate years.[3] The reflections that bear fruit in this book would not have been possible without the ongoing influence and friendship of Professor Ursula King, who supervised my doctoral research and continues to be a rich source of theological reflection for me—although I suspect she might find this present book altogether too dark. In particular, Fergus Kerr and Marcus Pound have helped me more than I can say in my grappling with Thomas and Lacan respectively, and I am deeply grateful to them. They would both distance themselves from some of the ideas expressed here, but their guidance has been indispensable at times when I have felt myself lost amidst the complexities and obscurities of my chosen sources. Eliana Corbari has awakened me to the neglected significance of medieval women's vernacular theologies, and her insights have been helpful in identifying a number of questions to do with theological language, particularly in my reading of Catherine of Siena. Sarah Jane Boss, George Ferzoco, Karen Kilby, Gerard Loughlin, Thomas Lynch, Carolyn Muessig, Jean Porter, Marika Rose, and Janet Martin Soskice have been sources of conversation, illumination, and inspiration, and all of my PhD students have contributed to my thinking, particularly Andrew Cooke and Phillip Taliadoros in their work on aspects of Thomism. I am grateful to the Arts and Humanities Research Council (AHRC) for funded research leave while I was working on this book, and to the University of Roehampton for providing a supportive research culture in

[3] See Rosemary Radford Ruether, *Sexism and God-Talk—Towards a Feminist Theology* (London: SCM Press, 1993).

difficult and challenging times. Lizzie Robottom and Tom Perridge of Oxford University Press have been constructive, patient, and endlessly supportive throughout the long gestation period and repeatedly extended deadlines of producing this book.

Dave has been there, in ways that have made all this possible. To him, and to our expanding family of adult children and their partners, I owe whatever I have learned of love's endurance and fecundity.

Introduction

THE END OF DESIRE

Desire, its means, and its ends. Desire is the beginning and end of all human life—the energy behind every action, the love within every act of compassion, the urge within every act of violence. Our hearts yearn for the living God, and this makes us the most mysterious of creatures, even to ourselves—the most wondrous and the most dangerous of species. Desire inspires the best and the worst we are capable of, and it confuses us as to the nature of both. It flows through the furrows of the imagination between heaven and hell, populated by angels and demons, home to dreams and nightmares, to the brightest of hopes and the most dreadful of horrors. It is the medium wherein the souls of our medieval forebears swam in an oceanic creation of porous boundaries and teeming spirits. Today, it is the buried labyrinth deep within the Freudian soul, wherein God lies unconscious amidst our banished faith and our futile hopes.

Do we need another book about the theology of desire? Sexuality and gender, desire and its discontents, bodies and their appetites, women and their experiences, men and their abuses—have we not done all these subjects to death? What more is there to say that has not already been said in every possible way and from every possible theological perspective?

This book is a long and winding journey through the labyrinths of desire. It seeks to render desire strange and troubling before the complacent gaze of liberal theologies, and to unsettle the androcentric certainties of their conservative counterparts. It follows the road less travelled through the theology of Thomas Aquinas, with Jacques Lacan as its unreliable guide. Hence its meandering gaze across the surface of the making of the western soul, from the rise of the medieval universities to the postmodern condition in which the ancient Aristotelian paradigms are dissolving. Hence its plunging beneath the surface into alien worlds, where some visceral ooze of desire is home to creatures of the deep, to life forms that have evolved to flourish far below the flattened landscapes of our modern minds, eluding the sterile glare of rationalism, fleeing from the softened gaze of romanticism. This is another book about desire. It is a book about the cost of becoming modern. It is a book about the cost of losing our souls, and the grace of finding them again.

SEEKING GOD IN THE LABYRINTHS OF LANGUAGE

Even after the so-called death of God, Christianity continues to shape the western soul and its desires in profound and unacknowledged ways, and through this to have a continuing influence on the formation of western values and institutions and on our personal and social relationships. In this book I am particularly concerned with the ways in which enduring ideas about God, nature, and gender are encoded deep within our linguistic structures and meanings, so that language becomes the Trojan horse wherein an unexamined religious legacy visits itself upon us in dark intimations of violence and fear, and in fragile epiphanies of grace. My argument is that God, nature, and gender are tethered together within our system of language, so that a shift in the meaning of any one results in a shift in the meaning of the other two. Not only does this help to account for the violence with which religious traditions react to any proposed change in sexual meanings and relationships, it also suggests that we shall not find the resources to bring about the necessary transformation in our attitudes to nature until we are willing to address the environmental crisis in the wider context of the meanings our culture inscribes upon nature and gender in the name of its unconscious but not quite dead God.

With Lacan, I argue that the sexual relationship has explicitly or implicitly been the ontological lens through which western thinkers have viewed the whole order of creation and the processes of being and becoming within it. Even though ancient sexual mythologies have yielded to the more rationalizing agendas of modern science, they retain their power to fuel violent pornographic fantasies and insatiable romantic yearnings, while continuing to inscribe the relationship between mind and matter, reason and nature, bodies and souls, within a dualistic framework that sustains a culture of exploitation, alienation, and subtle but pervasive forms of oppression. All this has been thoroughly explored and criticized by contextual, liberationist, environmental, feminist, and postmodern theologies over the last forty years or so, but I seek to show why a Lacanian approach suggests that such theologies remain too deeply implicated within the systems that they seek to criticize. Lacan unsettles our claims to knowledge, calls into question the values and visions that have been inspired by the Christian theological tradition, and seeks to discover the nature of its truth. In allowing him to guide me, I am groping my way through the fog of theology towards the mysterious absence of the incarnate Other of Thomas's One God.

Lacan seeks to liberate our desire from an unspeakable abyss, and Thomas seeks to direct it towards an unsayable plenitude. It is not easy to tell them apart. Although I resist Lacan's nihilism, he offers a path of purgation and purification of theological desire, a way of asking God to free us from God, in the words of Meister Eckhart's prayer. My aim is to go beyond Lacan—to knowingly dupe Lacan in my reading of him perhaps—to a retrieval of an incarnational theology that can be bodily expressed and realized within the structures of a world that will remain divided, wounded, and violent until the redeeming grace of God finally gives us the joy that is the deepest desire of every human heart. This means abandoning the myth of progress with its empty rhetoric and bitter failures, but it does not mean abandoning the eschatological hope of the Christian faith, nor does it mean giving up on the struggle for justice. However, the political struggle for justice is not unique to Christians. The task that uniquely belongs to Christian theology is neither ethical nor political, but doctrinal and sacramental. It is to ask how the core doctrines of the Christian faith can reveal their truthfulness anew within the changing conditions and challenges of the times within which we find ourselves, and the ideas that we encounter within the irreducible and graced diversity of created material beings.

SETTING THE CONTEXT

Although Lacan has had a significant influence on various forms of critical theory in the English-speaking academic world, he has had less influence on theology, with the exception of thinkers such as Clayton Crockett,[1] Marcus Pound,[2] and contributors to two collections of essays—*Lacan and Theological Discourse*,[3] and more recently, *Theology after Lacan*.[4] Generally, however, postmodern theologians have been more ready to engage with thinkers such as Jacques Derrida and Emmanuel Levinas than with Lacan, and when Lacan does feature he is often filtered through the interpretations of Lacanian theorists such as Luce Irigaray, Julia Kristeva, and Slavoj Žižek.[5]

---

[1] Clayton Crockett, *Interstices of the Sublime: Theology and Psychoanalytic Theory* (New York: Fordham University Press, 2007).

[2] Cf. Marcus Pound, *Theology, Psychoanalysis and Trauma* (London: SCM Press, 2007).

[3] Edith Wyschogrod, David R. Crownfield, and Carl A. Raschke (eds), *Lacan and Theological Discourse* (Albany NY: State University of New York Press, 1989).

[4] Clayton Crockett, Creston Davis, and Marcus Pound (eds), *Theology After Lacan* (Eugene OR: Wipf and Stock, forthcoming).

[5] Cf. Kevin J. Vanhoozer (ed.) *The Cambridge Companion to Postmodern Theology* (Cambridge and New York: Cambridge University Press, 2003); Graham Ward (ed.), *The Blackwell Companion to Postmodern Theology* (Malden MA and Oxford: Blackwell Publishing, 2005).

However, in recent years a growing number of scholars have begun to explore the profound influences that medieval theology has had on the shaping of twentieth-century French thought. There is now a strong case to be made for reading Lacan as a strange kind of Thomist—or perhaps as a Thomist who renders Thomas strange. Bruce Holsinger refers to the 'omnivorous medievalism'[6] of Lacan's seventh seminar, and he suggests that 'Lacan's truly bizarre understanding of the nature and purpose of ethical reflection cannot be fully understood apart from its historical rootedness in the courtly, theological, and philosophical cultures of the European Middle Ages.'[7] Julia Kristeva asks, 'Lacan a Thomist? As Marx was a Hegelian? The one without God, the other without absolute Spirit?'[8] Erin Labbie suggests that Lacan, who was deeply influenced by the work of his theological contemporary, French Thomist Étienne Gilson,

> struggled to articulate a form of Thomistic inquiry that also accounted for his own lack of faith in God. Lacan's Thomism is clearly a perverted form of belief in the combination of faith and reason, in love and being, that exists without God as the primary cause that is so central to Aquinas.[9]

These various scholars all recognize the ways in which Lacan was influenced by Thomism, but so far there has been little attempt to bring Thomas and Lacan into close theological conversation. The only book I am aware of that does anything remotely similar to what I am attempting here is François Regnault's little-known *Dieu est Inconscient: Études Lacaniennes autour de Saint Thomas d'Aquin.*[10] I have been guided by Regnault in some of what follows, although my engagement with Lacan is less comprehensive than Regnault's, since I seek to address specific questions to do with the linguistic representation of nature, gender, and God as these emerge in the encounter between Thomas and Lacan.

I have situated Lacan in the context of theologians associated with the *ressourcement* movement of 1950s French Catholicism, particularly Gilson, because it is clear that these thinkers had a formative influence on the development of his thought.[11] Ultimately, however, I have focused as far as possible on Thomas's own texts rather than on his Thomist interpreters, for

---

[6] Bruce W. Holsinger, *The Premodern Condition: Medievalism and the Making of Theory* (Chicago and London: University of Chicago Press, 2005), p. 60.

[7] Holsinger, *The Premodern Condition: Medievalism and the Making of Theory*, p. 61.

[8] Julia Kristeva, *Tales of Love*, trans. Leon S. Roudiez (New York: Columbia University Press, 1987), p. 183.

[9] Erin Felicia Labbie, *Lacan's Medievalism* (Minnesota: University of Minnesota Press, 2006), p. 18.

[10] François Regnault, *Dieu est Inconscient: Études Lacaniennes autour de Saint Thomas d'Aquin* (Paris: Navarin, 1985).

[11] Cf. Marcus Pound, 'Lacan's Return to Freud: A Case of Theological *Ressourcement*?', in Gabriel Flynn and Paul D. Murray (eds), *Ressourcement: A Movement for Renewal in Twentieth-Century Catholic Theology* (Oxford: Oxford University Press, 2012), pp. 440–56.

reasons that will become clear as this book unfolds. I have already written about the ways in which a certain trend in modern Catholic theology, deeply influenced by Hans Urs von Balthasar, has gone down the road of a highly romanticized form of sexual essentialism, which has its roots in a retrieval of the gendered ontologies of Thomas's Greek philosophical world view.[12] More liberal forms of modern Thomism elide gender altogether as a significant feature of Thomas's thought, so that some of the most interesting questions that Lacan brings to a postmodern reading of Thomism are not evident if one relies on twentieth-century Thomists, whether conservative or liberal.[13]

A similar problem arises with bringing a Thomist theological perspective to bear on Lacan. English-speaking Lacanian theorists do not generally acknowledge the extent to which his work is influenced by his early Catholicism and his ongoing engagement with Catholic thinkers, and their interpretations tend to be highly secularized in ways that distort some of Lacan's more interesting insights with regard to the role of religion and theology in the formation of the unconscious. Lacan was an atheist, but he was an atheist who knew how fundamentally important the question of God is, and who sought to show the extent to which the secular soul remains haunted by the effects of Christianity's dead God. That is why he refers to God as unconscious—a point to which I shall return repeatedly.

So this book is in many ways a rogue voice with regard to its positioning within existing theological and theoretical paradigms. I hope that it will be of interest to both Thomists and Lacanians, and I hope also that it will show why questions of gender and sexuality are among the most important of all the questions we should be asking ourselves today, for they touch on every aspect of our relationships with one another, with nature, and with God. There is much here that is tentative, opaque, and at times impenetrable. Partly, this is a consequence of engaging with a thinker as deliberately obtuse as Lacan, while also struggling through the medieval intricacies of the *Summa theologiae*. Partly, it also has to do with a gradual change in my own theological style and concerns during the several years it has taken me to write this.

I have found myself increasingly interested in creativity, art, and literature as expressions of theological desire, and I have a growing conviction that these creative forms of expression are trustworthy heirs to the Christian theological tradition. Academic theologians, driven by the bureaucratic and utilitarian policies of modern universities and, if they are Catholic, increasingly bullied into silence and timidity by the authoritarianism of the official magisterium,

---

[12] See Tina Beattie, *New Catholic Feminism: Theology and Theory* (London and New York: Routledge, 2006).

[13] For an excellent overview of twentieth-century Thomism, see Fergus Kerr, *After Aquinas: Versions of Thomism* (Malden MA and Oxford: Blackwell Publishers, 2002). See also Kerr, *Twentieth-century Catholic Theologians: from Neoscholasticism to Nuptial Mysticism* (Oxford and New York: Blackwell Publishing, 2007).

can no longer allow themselves to be possessed by the imaginative and playful spirit of prayer and wonder which is the essence of all true theology. Readers of this book will discern a tension between an urge for literary creativity that longs to break free of the constraints and conventions of modern scholarly texts, and a respect for the rigours of academic scholarship which demand that experimental hypotheses and radical ideas are rooted in the deep loam of textual study and intellectual reflection and analysis.

In the hopes that this book might appeal to readers with neither Thomist nor Lacanian expertise, I have tried to avoid over-simplification while achieving some clarity of style with regard to the sometimes anachronistic terminology of Thomas's philosophy, and the wilful obscurantism of Lacanian psychoanalysis. So, for example, I have decided not to engage with Lacan's attempt to use mathematical equations and diagrams to illustrate his ideas, in his quest to find a relatively value-free form of expression for his theories. In my view, these more often than not only add to the difficulty of rendering Lacan coherent and intelligible in dialogue with other discursive frameworks and concerns. Nor do I think that any theologian should value the gratuitous obscurity of postmodern discourse, which is altogether different from the sometimes unavoidable complexity of the language and ideas with which theology must concern itself. I hope this book will show why I believe that Lacan is of fundamental significance for the task of contemporary theology, but that does not preclude a selective engagement with his theories.

Although I do not engage directly with their ideas, this book shares a number of common concerns with two significant works of feminist theology—Elizabeth Johnson's *She Who Is*[14] and Catherine Mowry LaCugna's *God for Us*.[15] Like both of these theologians, I ask how feminist insights might contribute to a renewed appreciation of the relevance of Thomas Aquinas (Johnson) and the doctrine of the Trinity (LaCugna) for contemporary theology and the practice of the Christian faith. However, those familiar with their work will also recognize that my methods and approaches are very different from theirs, and this difference is I think primarily focused on the question of women's experience as a theological resource. In what follows I make no direct appeal to women's experience—apart from the last chapter where I draw on personal experience to offer an imaginative account of what the resurrected body might be. The appeal to experience is one aspect of feminist theology that I find most problematic, and the other is the tendency sometimes to use that as a way of positioning God before the horizon of woman, so that the divine mystery dissolves in the shadowy Feuerbachian

---

[14] Elizabeth Johnson, *She Who Is: The Mystery of God in Feminist Theological Discourse* (New York: Crossroad, 1992).

[15] Catherine Mowry LaCugna, *God for Us: the Trinity and Christian Life* (San Francisco: HarperSanFrancisco, 1993).

projections of women's experience in the case of liberal feminist theologies, and in the linguistic subjectivities of postmodern feminisms.[16] While the latter strategy is one that a quasi-theological theorist such as Luce Irigaray might advocate—the turn to a feminized Feuerbachian God to challenge the androcentrism of the dominant Christian understanding of God—I do not believe it is a method that can take Christian theology very far along the path of mystical unknowing, and if that is not the path that theology is treading, then it is on a path to nowhere.

To say this is not to deny that, in different ways, Johnson, LaCugna, and many other feminist theologians take seriously the phenomenological and ontological questions that arise with regard to interpreting experience, nor is it to deny their subtle and careful endeavours to protect the mystery of God from psychological reductiveness. However, their understanding of the human remains defined within the parameters of a certain normative humanism—an experiencing individual knowingly and responsibly positioned within the time and space of her own life—and this is what I am calling into question.[17]

A partial explanation for this might be that many liberal/liberationist theologies are marked by the spirit of optimism that suffused Catholicism after the Second Vatican Council. Although the feminist and liberationist theologies that began to emerge in the late 1960s were in many ways unprecedented in their critical and often highly acute analysis of the Christian theological and ethical tradition, they were marked by a certain progressive optimism about the future. Today, the shadows have lengthened in the Church and the world, and we look back on the failure of that forward-looking era to make good on its promises. We see how easily liberationist movements have been overwhelmed by the onslaught of neo-liberal economics and religious conservatism, exacerbated first by the collapse of the Soviet Union and the apparent triumph of the homogeneous and brutal political and economic ideology of neo-liberalism, and later by the rise of violent Islamist extremism which has

---

[16] For an interesting debate between these different liberal–political and postmodern linguistic influences on feminist theology, see Emily R. Neill, Marla Brettschneider, Regula Grünenfelder, et al., 'Roundtable Discussion: From Generation to Generation: Horizons in Feminist Theology or Reinventing the Wheel?', *Journal of Feminist Studies in Religion*, Vol. 15, No. 1 (Spring, 1999), pp. 102–38. Although somewhat out of date, this discussion addresses issues which remain crucial to debate about the methods and concerns of feminist theology. For an essay that addresses similar critical questions to those which concern me here, see Jenny Daggers, 'On Playing with the Boys', ESWTR Journal Conference Papers for the 14th International Conference, Salamanca, 24–28 August 2011, *Feminist Theology: listening, understanding and giving answer in a secular and pluralist world.*

[17] For a nuanced critique of the appeal to experience in feminist theology, see Serene Jones, 'Women's Experience Between a Rock and a Hard Place: Feminist, Womanist, and *Mujerista* Theologies in North America', in Seth Kunin (ed.), *Theories of Religion: A Reader* (New Brunswick NJ: Rutgers University Press, 2006), pp. 397–410.

been used to underwrite the militaristic violence and increasingly repressive laws of many western democracies. This is the context within which my own feminist theological struggle is played out, and I am aware that it might sometimes appear as a bleak contrast to more optimistic forms of feminism. Nevertheless, hope is not optimism, and if this is not an optimistic book, it is a book about hope. Optimism defers the being of the here and now in anticipation of a better tomorrow. Hope plunges into the being of the here and now to take hold of life and refuse to let it go, no matter how deadly the forces that are ranged against it. Optimism is a closing down of the here and now in order to concentrate on the future. Hope is a breaking open of the here and now to discern the eternal coming into being of the future within it.

In drawing attention to the unreliability of our interpretations of experience as a basis for theological reflection, I am not denying that our bodily experiences of the world are of the utmost importance—on the contrary, my argument in this book is that they matter absolutely, but they often challenge or call into question what we understand or think we know in terms of experience. I am suggesting that we do not know ourselves, we are unreliable witnesses and interpreters of our own experiences, and none of us quite adds up to the self that we think we are. My quest is not for a theology that validates truth against the unreliable benchmark of women's experience, or indeed of any human experience, but rather for the opening up of a mystical space, illuminated by the doctrines and traditions of the Catholic faith, wherein all benchmarks disappear in the sublime encounter between the bodily human and the incarnate God.

In addition to a range of feminist theologians and theorists, there are other theologians whose work also involves considerable overlap with my own and who are implicitly part of the conversation that follows. These would include, for example, the contributors to the collection of essays in the volume *Queer Theology*, edited by Gerard Loughlin.[18] In the end, however, in deciding to go with Lacan and to follow where he might lead through the pages of the *Summa theologiae* and beyond, I have allowed him to influence my choice of secondary sources. I regret the omission of so many others whose murmured presences I hope might still be detected.

MAPPING THE TERRAIN

I have structured this book in such a way that those unfamiliar with the writings of either Lacan or Thomas will find sufficient background and explanation to guide them through some of the more dense and multifaceted

---

[18] Gerard Loughlin (ed.) *Queer Theology: Rethinking the Western Body* (Malden MA and Oxford UK: Blackwell Publishing, 2007).

encounters between the two. The first four chapters introduce their thought in the context of language, desire, and God. Chapter 1 offers an overview of the main contours of Lacan's psychoanalytic theory, and Chapters 2, 3, and 4 identify key themes in Thomas's theology in terms of reason and revelation, nature and grace, language and meaning, desire and God.

Beginning with Chapter 5, the second part of the book considers the ways in which medieval philosophy and theology established the foundations of western culture through the rise of the universities and the dissemination of Aristotelianism through all the levels and structures of society. Chapter 5 offers a broad sketch of the most significant aspects of Platonic and Aristotelian cosmology, as these pertain to Thomas's account of gender and the role of woman in creation. In Chapter 6 I consider how this influences Thomas's understanding of law and the social order, and in Chapter 7 I focus on his representation of contemplation, angels, and demons. This allows me to explore how the social, theological, and psychological aspects of the self were woven together in the making of Thomas's world by way of Platonic as well as Aristotelian influences, which Lacan suggests still shape the western soul in subliminal and significant ways today. With this in mind, I conclude this section in Chapter 8 by analysing the foundational role that the medieval universities played in the ongoing formation of western social and sexual hierarchies, and the Lacanian implications of this in terms of sexuality, language, and power.

Part III marks the transition to modernity. Chapter 9 is another broad overview, in which I engage with a number of secondary sources, including Charles Taylor's influential book, *A Secular Age*,[19] to navigate a Lacanian path from the medieval world to secular modernity by way of the Reformation, the Enlightenment, and the scientific revolution. In Chapters 10 and 11, I focus on Lacan's complex analysis of the relationship between Kantian ethics and Sadean violence, in order to evaluate the impact of the rise of rationalism on the formation of modern values within dualistic philosophical parameters stripped of their theological content. In Chapter 12 I return to Thomas to ask how some of these themes might be identified in his theology, so that the medieval encounter between Aristotelian rationality and Christian concepts of revelation, sin, and redemption are shown to be a fertile seedbed for the making of the modern soul as revealed by psychoanalysis. From this perspective, Thomas is read as a liminal figure, straddling the wide boundary between two epochs (the medieval and the modern), so that he lends himself to numerous different interpretations which sometimes contradict or call into question one another's claims.

---

[19] Charles Taylor, *A Secular Age* (Cambridge MA: Harvard University Press, 2007).

In Part IV, I consider the changing significance of the female body in Lacan's thought, relating this again to Thomas's theology. In Chapter 13 I focus mainly on Lacan's *Seminar VII*, to show how he maps the female body according to ideas of lack and the death wish, so that an ancient dread still clings to the female flesh as the Freudian 'horror of nothing to see'. In Chapter 14, I turn to *Seminar XX* to discover a different way of configuring the relationship between female *jouissance*, the sexual relationship, and the God of Greek philosophy and Christian theology. This is the seminar in which Thomist influences are most evident in Lacan's thought, and it allows me to begin to tease out the differences between the One God of Thomas's Aristotelianism, and the relational, trinitarian God of Christian revelation. This leads to an analysis in Chapter 15 of Lacan's revision of his earlier association of the female body with lack and the death drive, to show how it becomes instead a site of incarnational revelation with regard to the body and desire for God.

In Part V, I turn to a Lacanian reading of the doctrine of creation *ex nihilo*, and this constitutes the beginnings of my reconstruction of Thomas's theology around different configurations of being in relation to matter, form, and God. In Chapter 16 I consider Thomas's interpretation of Exodus 3 from a Lacanian perspective. In Chapter 17 I engage with a debate about Thomas's reading of Exodus 3 published in the journal *Modern Theology* between Richard Kearney, John Caputo, and John Manoussakis,[20] in order to argue that postmodern theology is not radical enough in its engagement with either continental philosophy or with Thomas's theology. I suggest that closer attention to Thomas's neglected theological insights and alternative interpretative possibilities might offer a way beyond postmodern nihilism to a fuller account of being than can be found either in postmodern theology or in its philosophical conversation partners. In Chapter 18 I focus on the maternal Trinity who is everywhere and nowhere in Thomas's writings, and I ask what it might mean for theology to develop a different Thomism, not now in terms of Greek philosophy but in terms of the maternal, relational, and incarnate love of God materialized in creation as the wisdom of God at play in the world. In Chapter 19 I turn to the writings of Catherine of Siena, to ask how her mystical theology might be interpreted as a different Thomist voice, giving expression to the surplus *jouissance* that was produced in the making of Thomas's theology. Finally, I conclude with a reflection on the role of memory and imagination in enabling us to explore the enigma of the doctrine of the resurrection of the body.

---

[20] See Richard Kearney, 'God Who May Be: A Phenomenological Study'; John D. Caputo, 'Richard Kearney's Enthusiasm: A Philosophical Exploration on the God Who May Be'; John P. Manoussakis, 'From Exodus to Eschaton: On the God Who May Be', all three essays appear in *Modern Theology*, 18:1 (January 2002), pp. 75–107.

Readers will notice that for much of this book I avoid the use of inclusive language. The subject throughout is masculine and, although it is not always clear-cut, I have tried to be discerning as to when it might be appropriate to use 'she' instead of 'he'. This is because I am calling into question what is at stake in the construction of sexual difference, the gendering of subjectivity, and the ways in which gendered language has its taproot in the deepest and most mysterious absences and desires within the human soul. To change the gendering of language requires the most radical transformation of the soul, and that is a question of redemption, desire, and the body's grace. So, because for different reasons both Thomas and Lacan regard the subject as masculine, I use the masculine pronoun when they do. They were both clear that what they said of 'he' did not necessarily include 'she', for 'he' is what 'she' is not. For Thomas, that is 'his' perfection, for Lacan it is 'his' fatal flaw. To elide this difference in order to give the semblance of inclusivity would be to betray my whole quest to understand what is at stake in this copulative construction of language and being.

I also tend to use the word 'soul' more often than might be acceptable to readers accustomed to secular interpretations and translations of psychoanalysis. However, as Bruno Bettelheim argues,[21] English translations of Freud's work are seriously misleading insofar as they consistently eliminate references to the soul in the German texts (*die Seele*), and choose instead words such as 'mental apparatus', 'mental organization', or 'mind'. Referring to the *Standard Edition of the Complete Psychological Works of Sigmund Freud*, Donald Capps argues that

> This translation misses Freud's point that treatment concerns the very core of one's being, and that the 'pathology' being addressed is the loss of one's soul. What Freud wanted precisely to challenge was the 'medicalization' of the language of treatment, where emphasis is placed on 'psychiatric' or 'personality' disorders, and to restore its original Greek sense of soul-sickness.[22]

Freud insisted repeatedly that the concern of psychoanalysis was not the mind but the soul, understood not in a religious sense, but still admitting of far more mystery, fragility, and obscurity than our modern understanding of 'mind' implies.

Finally, I should point out that I do not in this book engage with Lacan's idea of the *sinthome*, a word that Lacan borrows from the sixteenth-century spelling of the French word for 'symptom', as a title for his 1975 seminar on

---

[21] Bruno Bettelheim, *Freud and Man's Soul* (London: Pimlico, 2001).
[22] Donald Capps, 'Enrapt Spirits and the Melancholy Soul: The Locus of Division in the Christian Self and American Society', in Richard K. Fenn and Donald Capps (eds), *On Losing the Soul: Essays in the Social Psychology of Religion* (Albany NY: State University of New York Press, 1995), pp. 137–69, 138–9.

James Joyce.[23] Although Lacan uses the word as an obscure allusion to St Thomas, it adds little of relevance to the themes in this book that are not already covered in earlier seminars, particularly *Seminar VII* and *Seminar XX*, which form the main focus of much of what follows, although *Seminar XVII* also features significantly.

My quest in what follows is not to explain and to rationalize but to tremble and to wonder, to reopen the theological imagination to mysteries beyond its ken, and to kneel in awe before the majesty and mystery of creation and its creator. I have been guided by both Thomas and Lacan with regard to the elusive relationship between language, desire, the material world within which we belong, and the unattainable Other who calls to us in and through language from beyond all the horizons of time and space with a persistent, unnameable sense of loss and longing. Ultimately, however, this is a book that seeks to explore what it might mean to say with the psalmist,

> My soul longs, yes, even faints
> For the courts of the Lord;
> My heart and my flesh cry out for the living God.
> (Psalm 84:3)[24]

---

[23] See Jacques Lacan, *Le Séminaire livre XXIII, Le sinthome* (Paris: Seuil, 2005). There is no published English translation, but see *The Seminar of Jacques Lacan, Book XXIII, Joyce and the Sinthome, 1975–1976*, trans. Cormac Gallagher, available at 'Jacques Lacan in Ireland': <http://www.lacaninireland.com/web/wp-content/uploads/2010/06/Book-23-Joyce-and-the-Sinthome-Part-1.pdf>.

[24] Quotation from *The New King James Version*, Thomas Nelson, Inc., 1982.

Part I

Being and Desire

1

Language About the Abyss

The seminars of Jacques Lacan stage a mimesis of the psychoanalytic encounter, exploiting the instability of meaning in order to call into question philosophical claims to truth.[1] When an interlocutor suggested to him that 'What you say is always decentered in relation to sense, you shun sense', Lacan responded: 'This is perhaps precisely why my discourse is an analytic discourse. It's the structure of analytic discourse to be like that.'[2] Jacques-Alain Miller writes of Lacan's lecturing style, 'Who speaks? A master of wisdom, but a wisdom without resignation, an anti-wisdom, sarcastic, sardonic. Everybody is free to find their own way into his ideas.'[3]

Lacan's 'anti-wisdom' operates across multiple boundaries of philosophy, literature, science, theology, and psychoanalysis, but in adopting Thomism as one of his many sources, he invites comparison between his style and that of Thomas Aquinas. Thomas is a vast presence in the making of the western mind. As the greatest genius of medieval Aristotelianism, his quest to marry philosophy with theology and reason with revelation makes him a pioneer in the systematization and rationalization of knowledge and the rise of humanism, which would become the defining hallmarks of modernity.

If Thomas might be recognized retrospectively as a founding father of modernity, Lacan can be read as an anti-modern mischief maker, a gnomic figure who sets himself the task of undoing what Thomas began, stripping away the masks of reason and humanism to reveal the complex dynamics of desire and dread, love and loathing, that constitute the hidden underside of the modern subject. Thomas builds the edifice of the human around the goodness and mystery of God at the heart of creation, but Lacan asks what happens to

---

[1] Cf. Malcolm Bowie, *Lacan* (Fontana Modern Masters; London: Harper Collins, 1991), pp. 11–16.

[2] Jacques Lacan, *The Other Side of Psychoanalysis, The Seminar of Jacques Lacan, Book XVII*, ed. Jacques-Alain Miller, trans. Russell Grigg (New York and London: W.W. Norton & Co. Ltd, 2007), p. 146.

[3] Jacques-Alain Miller, Frontispiece to Jacques Lacan, *Le Triomphe De La Religion Précédé De Discours Aux Catholiques* (Paris: Éditions du Seuil, 2005).

the human when there is no God and when creation itself is a product of language encircled around a void (the Lacanian real).

Pitting himself against the apparent self-assurance of modernity's rational, knowing subject and the political structures that sustain him (the subject is, according to Lacan, necessarily masculine), Lacan refracts modern man's identity through the prism of otherness and desire in order to bring to light the darker aspects of his soul which have been driven underground in the making of the modern mind. In an expansive application of Freudian psychoanalysis to wider philosophical, theological, and political questions, he seeks to throw the masculine subject into disarray through the invocation of a threatening and seductive feminized otherness that undergirds the laws, truths, and values of the modern symbolic order, penetrating beyond every image that presents itself in the mirror of identity and truth, to the tain of fantasy. Rejecting any form of ego psychology that would reconcile the troubled soul to the social and political status quo, Lacan seeks instead to expose the human condition as a comic tragedy, and to present psychoanalysis, not as a cure but as a route to living and loving truthfully and ethically with the insatiability of desire.

With these preliminary comments in mind, I sketch a broad overview of Lacan's psychoanalytic theory to set the scene, in preparation for the more detailed analysis to follow.

THE HUMAN CONDITION—UNIVERSALITY, DESIRE, AND RELIGION

Lacanian psychoanalysis can be read both as a universal theory about the human condition, and as an insight into the making and unmaking of the western subject in the transition from late medieval humanism to postmodernity's abandonment of the humanist project. Erin Labbie, who describes Lacan as a medievalist, refers to his 'theological investment in the potential for knowing the unknowable'.[4] Lacan's real, like Thomas's God, is a truth claim that requires an act of faith and a context of interpretation, in which linguistic and textual sources are sifted, analysed, and debated in terms of different possibilities of meaning foregrounded against a real that is unknown and unknowable. Labbie argues that Lacan's 'methodologies follow those established by the medieval scholastic scholars who sought to determine the potential for the human subject to know and to represent real universal categories', and she

---

[4] Erin Felicia Labbie, *Lacan's Medievalism* (Minnesota: University of Minnesota Press, 2006), p. 4.

compares the claim to universality invested in Lacan's real, with a Thomist approach to questions of faith and reason:

> The question of Thomism is always one of a balance between faith and reason. This is precisely what is at stake in believing the unconscious exists. Whether we speak of what came before Freud or what happens after Freud makes little difference to the necessity of a certain degree of faith in the understanding of the unconscious. . . . Either the unconscious exists, and it has always existed, or it does not exist and it has never existed.[5]

Labbie situates Lacan in the context of medieval debates about nominalism ('a belief that language refers only to itself') and realism, which attributes a capacity of language to signify 'a greater category outside of itself'.[6] Like Thomas's God, Lacan's real is a universal, ahistorical truth that transcends its contextual interpretations, but it can only be approached from within the historically variable conditions of language and meaning that cultures and religions make available to the knowing linguistic subject, and therefore it is also invested with a certain contingency.

For Thomas, it is the desire for God that is ontological and universal, not the particular ways in which that desire manifests itself. To be human is to experience a lack that awakens a desire for God through the desirable things of the world, and this is where Lacan is an atheist Thomist. No matter what culture or era we belong to, even if we belong to a culture that has declared God to be dead, we cannot escape the desire for the Other that haunts the human soul through all the material objects it encounters. Lacan also insists that the relationship to the real and the configurations of desire are subject to religious interpretations that play a defining role in the acquisition of subjectivity and the formation of culture, and these vary across history and societies.[7]

Many post-Christian theorists and philosophers treat 'religion' as a uniform category cut off from its theological moorings and its diverse cultural and historical contexts, leading them to believe that the bracketing out of religious perspectives has little impact upon secularism's knowledge, institutions, and discursive encounters. However, Kenneth Reinhard and Julia Lupton argue that Lacan insists upon a more thorough-going analysis of the formative effects that religious discourse has on the shaping of subjects and identities, even in post-religious modernity. They argue that,

> in Lacan's strong formulation, . . . religious discourse *supposes us* – supports and underwrites our very structures of being, subjectivity, and social interaction. That is, the secular subject is *produced* by the religious discourses that precede and

---

[5] Labbie, *Lacan's Medievalism*, p. 4.

[6] Labbie, *Lacan's Medievalism*, p. 6.

[7] Cf. Kenneth Reinhard and Julia Reinhard Lupton, 'The Subject of Religion: Lacan and the Ten Commandments', *Diacritics*, 33/2 (2003), pp. 71–97.

continue to speak through it; the challenge for the contemporary critic is not to silence or debunk those discourses, but rather to bring the modern subject to assume responsibility for their enunciation.[8]

This entails a greater understanding of the extent to which religions are not a subset of cultures but rather produce cultures, so that only by knowing the religious traditions within which cultures take the forms they do, can we hope to enunciate responsibly with regard to religious discourses. In western culture, this requires acknowledgement of what Reinhard and Lupton refer to as the 'epochal divide' by way of which monotheism establishes western subjectivity 'as a set of discursive ruptures or cuts which continue to scar and brand the modern subject beyond their secular abrogation. . . . The laws, narratives and symbols of monotheism continue to undergird key fantasies of personhood, nationhood, and neighbourhood in the modernity that purports to have supplanted them.'[9]

This is Lacan's particular concern. He holds that monotheism—originally that of the Hebrew Bible, and later that of Christianity (and, one could add, Islam)—ruptures the relationship between human consciousness and the material world in a dramatic and unprecedented way, so that it ushers in a more radical sense of alienation, prohibition, and transgression than one finds in more pantheistic or polytheistic religions. The gradual shaping of western consciousness through the long history of Jewish and Christian monotheism and its aftermath provides the central focus of Lacan's psychoanalytic theory.[10]

Lacan seeks to offer a psychoanalytic explanation for the universality of desire, while rejecting the idea of a transcendent Good or God as its focus. The real—the ultimate object of Lacanian desire—is, as we shall see, a vortex that threatens to suck the self into an abysmal and formless void, because it has lost its divine referent and nothing can or should claim to replace that absent God, even though scientific modernity crams the emptiness with illusory claims to knowledge.

This is why Lacan presents his account of language and socialization as ontological, albeit in a way that unravels all previous philosophical ontologies.[11] He uses the neologism 'hontology' to suggest the shame (*la honte*) that human

---

[8]   Reinhard and Lupton, 'The Subject of Religion: Lacan and the Ten Commandments', p. 71.

[9]   Reinhard and Lupton, 'The Subject of Religion: Lacan and the Ten Commandments', p. 71.

[10]   In this book, I include only a brief engagement with Judaism on the question of monotheism and creation *ex nihilo* (see Chapter 16), and I exclude any engagement with Lacanian scholars of Islam. However, both of these are important in terms of a comprehensive appreciation of Lacan's significance for theology. Lacanian approaches to Islam are an underdeveloped but significant area for further research. Cf. Fethi Benslama, *Psychoanalysis and the Challenge of Islam*, trans. Robert Bononno (Minneapolis MN: University of Minnesota Press, 2009), and Christian Jambet, *La Logique Des Orientaux* (Paris: Seuil, 1983).

[11]   Cf. the discussion in Jacques Lacan, *The Four Fundamental Concepts of Psychoanalysis: The Seminar of Jacques Lacan, Book XI*, trans. Alan Sheridan (New York: W.W. Norton, 1981), pp. 29 ff. See also Justin Clemens, 'Love as Ontology: Psychoanalysis against Philosophy', in Christine Kerslake and Ray Brassier (eds), *Origins and Ends of the Mind: Philosophical Essays on Psychoanalysis* (Leuven: Leuven University Press, 2007), pp. 185–200.

being conceals.[12] To be human is to inhabit a linguistic and social world that conceals at its heart an unspeakable desire. We might note in passing how close this is to a Christian account of original sin. To be human is to experience a deep sense of shame, associated with but more primal than the sexual relationship, which cannot be explained by way of anything that we ourselves have done or attributed to any personal guilt. We inherit it as part of the human condition.

'SHADOWS OF WHAT IS NOT'—LANGUAGE AND DESIRE

According to Lacan, this 'hontology' is rooted in the disjunction between the animality of the living organism with its instincts and needs, and the conscious self who has no language for that for which he (or she?) yearns above all else. This yearning translates into the uniquely human demand that our needs be met by another person who loves unconditionally. Whether we express this in terms of the biblical expulsion from Eden or in terms of the Oedipus complex, we could say that there is a dim perception in human consciousness that we have been forcibly cut off from some original fullness of being, and we spend our lives longing for a return. Lacan associates this with the act of separation from the mother that initiates the child into language and culture, so that the lost maternal relationship manifests itself as an insatiable and negated demand for love within the prohibitions and taboos of the socio-linguistic order. In theological terms, this would mean that all language about God is either an expression of or a disguise for the forbidden oedipal desire for the maternal body and the paternal law that prohibits this desire. For Lacan, this constitutes the peculiar tragedy of the human condition, setting us apart from all other species whose hunger can be satisfied through the meeting of their physical needs, and it blights all our relationships with a volatile inadequacy.

As we shall see when we consider Lacanian ethics, this sets in motion a deadly dynamic of expectation and frustration, projection and failure, which thwarts our attempts at happiness and sows the seeds of violence and hatred in our relationships with one another. This is particularly true of secular modernity, in which the veneer of rationality, the optimistic laissez-faire of liberalism, and the seductions of consumerism, deprive us of the means to acknowledge and address our proclivity towards violence and the restlessness of our desire, in ways that might enable us to find more sustaining and sustainable ways of living with ourselves and others.

---

[12] Cf. Lacan, *The Other Side of Psychoanalysis*, p. 180.

Slavoj Žižek suggests that 'For Lacan, language is as dangerous to humanity as the horse was to the Trojans: it offers itself to our use free of charge, but once we accept it, it colonizes us.'[13] Our entry into the symbolic order that constitutes society is a process of expulsion as well as inclusion, of separation as well as socialization. Even as language offers the individual an identity and weaves him into society (to reiterate, the socialized subject is always, for Lacan, masculine), it refuses to accommodate those aspects of the self that would threaten the functioning of the social order, and these are expelled to the margins and beyond. In Freudian terms, these are the animality of our physical drives and the intense feelings of incestuous desire and violence associated with the pre-oedipal relationship.

The formation of culture is therefore a sacrificial and traumatic process, predicated upon the prohibition of the mother–child relationship, the repression of desires associated with that primal, imagined source of nurture, comfort, and pleasure, and the murderous mimesis this engenders in the relationship with the father. According to Lacan, the apparent universality of the incest taboo justifies his claim that the oedipal account of human development is not unique to any particular culture or era—it is the process by way of which culture itself is formed.[14] The intrusion of the paternal symbolic order into the union between mother and child is experienced as castration, since it cuts the individual off from its primal sense of wholeness and bliss and thrusts it into the linguistic order of society as a masculine subject who must conceal the castrating wound by pretending to possess the phallus. This, as we shall see later, is true for anybody, whatever their biological sex, who lays claim to subjectivity. To forfeit that position—to enter society marked by the lack or the not-all of the one who is visibly or knowingly castrated—is to occupy the position of a woman.

This is the main focus of Luce Irigaray's critique of Lacan—his insistence that the sacrifice of the maternal relationship is the pre-condition for the emergence of culture premised upon the paternal law, in a way that renders female subjectivity impossible. According to Irigaray, this sacrificial economy with its violent and repressive attributes is the symptom of a patriarchal or phallocentric culture in which the maternal body, the female subject, nature, and desire are elided from the linguistic order as bearers of meaning, in a way that perpetuates the trauma of separation which Lacan posits as fundamental to the construction of the linguistic subject as masculine. What would happen, Irigaray asks, if we sought a non-sacrificial form of socialization through the affirmation of

---

[13] Slavoj Žižek, *How to Read Lacan* (London: Granta Books, 2006), pp. 11–12.
[14] There has been much debate among anthropologists about the meaning of incest, its universality and its social function. See Arthur P. Wolf and William H. Durham (eds), *Inbreeding, Incest, and the Incest Taboo: The State of Knowledge at the Turn of the Century* (Stanford CA: Stanford University Press, 2004).

embodiment, fecundity, desire, sexual difference, and the maternal relationship? I have discussed these questions extensively in my earlier work and, although references to Irigaray are relatively sparse in this book, the questions she poses to Lacan are fundamental to my Lacanian reading of Thomas.[15]

Because desire is generated by the insatiable demand for unconditional love beyond the meeting of any physical need, it can never achieve its object—for Lacan, there is no such object. The subject is coiled in language around a void, preyed upon and played upon by desire, and the love that we crave beyond any material satisfaction of need haunts every object of desire with a relentless insufficiency. We encounter an anamorphic capacity in the object which produces a sense of alienation, a distant awareness of the emptiness at its heart. It becomes the *objet a*, pointing beyond itself to an imperceptible Other that renders it incapable of offering the satisfaction we crave.[16]

Explaining this elusive quality of the *objet a*, Žižek quotes a passage from Shakespeare's *Richard II*, in which Bushy tries to allay the Queen's anxieties over the King's departure:

> Each substance of a grief hath twenty shadows,
> Which shows like grief itself, but is not so;
> For sorrow's eye, glazed with blinding tears,
> Divides one thing entire to many objects;
> Like perspectives, which rightly gazed upon
> Show nothing but confusion, eyed awry
> Distinguish form: so your sweet majesty,
> Looking awry upon your lord's departure,
> Find shapes of grief, more than himself, to wail;
> Which, look'd on as it is, is nought but shadows
> Of what is not.[17]

---

[15] See Tina Beattie, *God's Mother, Eve's Advocate: A Marian Narrative of Women's Salvation* (London and New York: Continuum, 2002), and *New Catholic Feminism: Theology and Theory* (London and New York: Routledge, 2006). Irigaray and Lacan rarely refer to one another by name, although her work is Lacanian through and through, and her influence is I think detectable in his later seminars, particularly *On Feminine Sexuality—The Limits of Love and Knowledge: Encore, 1972–1973, The Seminar of Jacques Lacan, Book XX*, ed. Jacques-Alain Miller, trans. Bruce Fink (New York and London: W.W. Norton & Company, 1999). Irigaray's most substantial critique of Lacan can be found in her three early books—Luce Irigaray, *Speculum of the Other Woman*, trans. Gillian C. Gill (Ithaca NY: Cornell University Press, 1985); *This Sex Which Is Not One*, trans. Catherine Porter with Carolyn Burke (Ithaca NY: Cornell University Press, 1985); *An Ethics of Sexual Difference*, trans. Carolyn Burke and Gillian C. Gill (London: The Athlone Press, 1993).

[16] Cf. Jacques Lacan, *The Ethics of Psychoanalysis 1959–1960: The Seminar of Jacques Lacan, Book VII*, trans. Dennis Porter (London and New York: Routledge, 1999), pp. 134–7. See also Žižek, *How to Read Lacan*, pp. 66–9.

[17] Žižek, *How to Read Lacan*, pp. 68–9, quoting *Richard II*, II, ii, 14–24.

Žižek explains the Lacanian relevance of this as follows:

> the object-cause of desire is something that, viewed from in front, is nothing at all, just a void: it acquires the contours of something only when viewed at a slant. . . . This is *objet a*: an entity that has no substantial consistency, which in itself is 'nothing but confusion', and which acquires a definite shape only when looked at from a standpoint slanted by the subject's desires and fears – as such, as a mere 'shadow of what is not'.[18]

The sense of otherness that haunts every object of desire and condemns us to inhabit a world of shadows and ghosts is the manifestation of the real as lack. This is what language seeks but cannot find in its quest for the perfect 'fit' between self and other, word and flesh, desire and object. It infects language with a complex insufficiency to perform as we intend it to, so that Lacanian linguistics exposes a continuous slippage between the chain of signifiers and some surplus meaning—the signified—although the relationship between them is not free-floating. Language derives some stability, not from the objects to which it refers, but from certain master signifiers that act as 'quilting' between different layers of meaning, so that the linguistic surface tugs at something hidden to which it is connected, which is inaccessible to consciousness. In order to mean what we say and say what we mean, we have to conceal even from ourselves the impossibility of doing that, for the meanings we inhabit are constructed over an inaccessible absence—an 'it' at the heart of things, beyond the conscious 'I' who speaks.

The real, the Lacanian Other, this nameless 'Thing' that resists us even as it compels us, is what Alenka Zupančič refers to as 'the *remainder of the signifier itself* which retroactively establishes the dimension of the Thing'.[19] This is not some pre-symbolic excess, but rather the surplus produced by symbolization which, 'in its very perfection and completeness, produces a surplus which "undermines" it from within by engendering impasses. To paraphrase Hegel: the remainder is the bone of spirit itself, not something external that spirit has not been able completely to devour'.[20]

Lacan claims universality for his theory because, wherever we find the linguistic subject (that is, wherever we find a socialized human being), we also find this linguistic surplus. As Marcus Pound explains it, 'the real is both universal, always at stake, evident in language, yet remains intangible and dependent upon language'.[21]

---

[18] Žižek, *How to Read Lacan*, pp. 68–9, quoting *Richard II*, II, ii, 14–24.
[19] Alenka Zupančič, *Ethics of the Real* (London: Verso, 2000), pp. 190–1 (italics as given).
[20] Zupančič, *Ethics of the Real*, p. 191.
[21] Marcus Pound, 'Lacan's Return to Freud: A Case of Theological *Ressourcement*?' in Gabriel Flynn and Paul D. Murray (eds), *Ressourcement: A Movement for Renewal in Twentieth-Century Catholic Theology* (Oxford: Oxford University Press, 2011), pp. 440–56, 446.

Although the real is primarily associated with the maternal relationship in the pre-linguistic stage of life, it is not only, or not even, a memory of physical origins. It is a forbidden fantasy borne within language, which reveals an unspeakable lack. Language itself produces the lack, as a vase can be said to produce the emptiness it contains.[22] To quote Pound, 'the real is not simply outside language, but the very heart around which language wraps itself: it is "something strange to me, although it is at the heart of me"'.[23] The real is a longing that dare not and indeed cannot speak its name—it has no name—but it derives its haunting power from that very namelessness. Language circulates around it but cannot penetrate its abysmal depths. It is before and beyond any 'I'. It is non-being, a formlessness that lures the subject towards love and abjection,[24] in the dual interplay of the desire for love (*eros* or the Freudian pleasure principle), and the drive towards oblivion (*thanatos* or the Freudian death drive). It is the before and beyond of the womb and the tomb which mark the beginning and end of the torment of being.

Lacan's real can thus be explained as a psychoanalytic hypothesis which seeks to account both for religious faith and for otherwise inexplicable traumas, neuroses, and psychoses associated with the intrusion of an alien and abysmal otherness into the consciousness of the speaking subject. In medieval theology, this would be explored in terms of the relationship between 'form and matter'/'soul and body' that was mediated by desire for God and distorted by the effects of sin. Lacan attributes it to the rupture between the animality of the human body and the linguistic capacity of the human soul which remains insurmountable, no matter how vigorously science seeks to banish its mysterious otherness by its totalizing claims to knowledge, and no matter how intensely modern secularism seeks to break free of its theological inferences. With this in mind, I want to consider briefly how Lacan's changing interpretations of the Oedipus complex inform his understanding of language and the formation of culture.

CASTRATION AND THE OEDIPAL FATHER

Lacan focuses on the structural rather than the chronological significance of the Oedipus complex. Observing that 'it is from speech that analytic experience

---

[22] Cf. Lacan, *The Ethics of Psychoanalysis*, pp. 119–21. Lacan borrows the metaphor of the vase from Heidegger—which in English translations of Heidegger is usually rendered as 'jug'.

[23] Marcus Pound, *Theology, Psychoanalysis and Trauma* (London: SCM Press, 2007), p. 46, quoting Lacan, *The Ethics of Psychoanalysis*, p. 71.

[24] Julia Kristeva uses these terms in her reading of Freud and Lacan. Cf. Julia Kristeva, *Powers of Horror: An Essay on Abjection*, trans. Leon S. Roudiez (New York: Columbia University Press, 1982). See also *Tales of Love*, trans. Leon S. Roudiez (New York: Columbia University Press, 1987).

receives its instrument, its frame, its material, and even the background noise of its uncertainties', he claims that 'it is the whole structure of language that psychoanalytic experience discovers in the unconscious'.[25] The speech of the analysand is an encrypted language of mourning for the lost mother and the plenitude and satisfaction associated with that body (not 'her' but 'it', because it precedes the onset of awareness of sexual difference that comes with language). The language of the unconscious reveals the fantasized longing for a perfect and all-fulfilling union between self and the maternal Other which would reach into the well of loneliness and fill it with love, erasing the wound of separation and healing the primal act of castration that births us into a world of individuation but also of desolation.

Lacan's early analysis of the paternal role in the formation and support of the speaking subject is informed by his critical reading of Freud's two late works on the metapsychology of religious origins—*Totem and Taboo* and *Moses and Monotheism*.[26] He reads *Totem and Taboo* as the founding myth of modernity, 'perhaps the only myth that the modern age was capable of'.[27] Seeking to explain the claim to reality that is invested in such psychoanalytic theories, Žižek writes:

> the murder of the primordial father and other Freudian myths are in a way *more real than reality*: they are 'true', although, of course, they 'didn't really take place' – their spectral presence sustains the explicit symbolic tradition.... This foreclosed ('primordially repressed') myth that grounds the rule of *logos* is thus not simply a past event but a permanent spectral presence, an undead ghost that has to persist all the time if the present symbolic frame is to remain operative.[28]

The 'spectral presence' suspends the speaking subject in language while concealing the void around which his desire circulates. Because the absent father maintains his prohibitive power, he becomes the god to which the subject is answerable: the Other before whose desire our own desire is accountable, and the absent law-giver who underwrites the authority of the law.

However, as Žižek points out, the murdered father in *Totem and Taboo* is not the same as the murdered Moses of *Moses and Monotheism*.[29] The former is an orgiastic tyrant, more akin to the Yahweh God of *Moses and Monotheism*

---

[25] Lacan, 'The Instance of the Letter in the Unconscious or Reason since Freud', in *Écrits*, trans. Bruce Fink (New York and London: W.W. Norton, 2006), p. 413. See also Russell Grigg, *Lacan, Language and Philosophy* (Albany NY: State University of New York Press, 2008), pp. 37–53.

[26] See Sigmund Freud, 'Totem and Taboo' and 'Moses and Monotheism', trans. James Strachey, in Albert Dickson (ed.), *The Origins of Religion*, The Penguin Freud Library 13 (London, New York, Victoria, Toronto and Auckland: Penguin Books, 1990).

[27] Lacan, *The Ethics of Psychoanalysis*, p. 176.

[28] Slavoj Žižek, *The Fragile Absolute—or, Why Is the Christian Legacy Worth Fighting For?* (London and New York: Verso, 2000), pp. 64–5.

[29] See Slavoj Žižek, *The Ticklish Subject: The Absent Centre of Political Ontology* (London and New York: Verso, 2000), p. 317.

than to the rational God of Aten associated with the murdered Moses. The murdered father therefore appears variously as a domineering, unpredictable, and vengeful god who must be obeyed, and as a rational and benign god who brings order to the world. In Lacanian terms, the former is the father of the real and the latter is the father of the symbolic, both of which exert their lingering influences on the western soul long after it has ostensibly declared its gods to be dead. The symbolic derives its veiled authority from the threat of castration invested in the father of the real so that, as we shall see, Lacan argues that the modern social order is underwritten by a deadly threat that has its roots in this primordial tyrannical force, which the transition from religious to secular culture buries deep in the psyche but does not eliminate.

Perhaps in response to his feminist critics (although he never acknowledges their influence), from the late 1960s Lacan became increasingly critical of Freud's interpretation of the Oedipus complex, seeing in it Freud's unacknowledged desire to reinstate the father beyond religion. Increasingly it is the maternal rather than the paternal relationship and the otherness of desire associated with feminized *jouissance* that interests Lacan in his later work. As we shall see, these shifts and ambiguities with regard to maternal and paternal relationships in Lacan's interpretation of the Oedipus complex are vital for a Lacanian reading of Thomas.

LANGUAGE AND THE EMPTINESS OF DESIRE

Once we gain some insight into the implications of Freud's discovery of the unconscious for our understanding of subjectivity, identity, and otherness, we are able with difficulty and sustained endeavour to attend to a way of speaking beyond the ideologies, assumptions, and beliefs that present themselves as truth, in order to discern a more troubling and enigmatic truth about the human condition and the institutions we inhabit. Through psychoanalysis a linguistic otherness is revealed as a potential site of achieving a negotiated freedom: 'It is by touching, however lightly, on man's relation to the signifier . . . that one changes the course of his history by modifying the moorings of his being.'[30] In psychoanalysis, 'it' speaks. As the analysand is released from the expectations and demands of society by the listening presence of the analyst, another way of speaking emerges that is redolent with the desires, memories, and terrors of an imagined and abandoned past. This enables us to see through the ideological construct of the dutiful, rational subject which the modern socio-symbolic order produces to serve its commands and sustain its

---

[30] Lacan, 'The Instance of the Letter in the Unconscious', p. 438.

institutions, and to seek instead a reanimation of the desiring self which occupies an intermediate space of fluidity between the real and the symbolic.

This is a fragile and unformed self, a dream or an aspiration of a self that is free to sway and to play, to seek and to mourn, within the currents of desire. It is the earliest and most elusive object of desire, since it is the desiring self I encounter in the mirror as the object of the mother's desire—an apparently integrated and unified other that I recognize as myself only with difficulty, because it contradicts the flux and fragmentation of intuitions and feelings, of bodily satisfaction and need, to which I am prey. This aporia between the coherence and stability of the external image and the inchoate fluidity of the psyche constitutes the dynamic terrain of the imaginary, wherein the unconscious finds its voice in the circulation of yearning and desire between self and other.

The imaginary is a no-man's land, its borders dissolving into the mute horrors of the real on the one side and vigorously policed by the symbolic on the other. To allow desire to move freely in this space of the in-between, one must understand the polarities of the soul between which it operates. This entails coming to terms with the ultimate futility of desire in order to resist the hollow threats and empty promises by which the symbolic retains its power to direct and control our desire, while avoiding being sucked into the abyss of the real with its mute and all-consuming demands and drives.

For as long as we remain ignorant of the dynamics of language and desire, for as long as we allow ourselves to be persuaded that there is an other— human or divine, sexual or maternal, mortal or immortal—capable of satisfy- ing our desire by a process of infinite deferral or nostalgia, we remain captive to the enveloping power of the symbolic order and its subterranean forces. Psychoanalysis presents an alternative to this totalizing structure encoded within the symbolic as its annihilating other, by enabling us to live our desire within 'the subjective realization of being-toward-death':

> Symbols . . . envelop the life of man with a network so total that they join together those who are going to engender him 'by bone and flesh' before he comes into the world; so total that they bring to his birth, along with the gifts of the stars, if not with the gifts of the fairies, the shape of his destiny; so total that they provide the words that will make him faithful or renegade, the law of the acts that will follow him right to the very place where he is not yet and beyond his very death; and so total that through them his end finds its meaning in the last judgment, where the Word absolves his being or condemns it – unless he reaches the subjective realization of being-toward-death.[31]

It is through an acceptance of the emptiness at the heart of desire—the void around which desire circulates—that the individual can rediscover some less-than-all

---

[31] Lacan, 'The Function and Field of Speech and Language in Psychoanalysis', p. 231.

relationship to the other which is the pre-condition for any ethical or loving relationship and any capacity for enjoyment and satisfaction.

This means recognizing that language emerges as the product of separation, for it is only when the rupture between self and (m)other appears that communication becomes both possible and necessary. This is why language cannot create a bridge—or, more appropriately, a tunnel—to the real. It can only echo across the void, and in that echo psychoanalysis hears it calling to the nameless other, a voice of mourning and desire within which the analysand might discover an ephemeral and elusive enjoyment (*jouissance*). That is why Lacan repeatedly insists that 'the unconscious is structured like a language'. The desiring other of the symbolic 'I' manifests itself as a fragmented and dissipated voice, encoded within language but gabbling semi-coherently through the gaps and fractures in meaning to reveal a traumatic sense of dislocation, yearning, and loss. It emerges as the lining of language, the underside that appears when the tightly woven fabric of a coherent structure of meaning which provides the subject with his linguistic cloak begins to fray and come apart at the seams, revealing what lies beneath.

But according to Lacan, it is language that lies, and truth is beneath. Malcolm Bowie refers to Lacan's 'truth-intoxicated writing', which at times betrays his insistence on the elusiveness and instability of the truth we seek.[32] One might ask if this passion for truth is the lingering legacy of Lacan's Catholic upbringing, whose influence manifests itself again and again in his work even as he struggles against it.

The truth discovered in psychoanalysis is an unravelling of the self through confrontation with the otherness that is its underside. This other speaks from the site of the excess that language produces, the inchoate detritus discarded by language's ordered coherence, in the interstices where the otherness within seeps and speaks through the structures of language. It emerges when the analyst offers himself or herself in the place of the Other and thus releases the desire of and for the Other that constitutes the unconscious.

The speech of the analysand reveals the existence of nothing other than speech itself, and it is in the discovery of the nothingness within and beyond language that a paradoxical truth emerges: 'Even if it communicates nothing, discourse represents the existence of communication; even if it denies the obvious, it affirms that speech constitutes truth; even if it is destined to deceive, it relies on faith in testimony.'[33]

Thus language is the onion skin that constitutes the subject. If we peel it away to find the core of the self—the 'real me'—we discover only more and more layers of the same, until eventually we are left with nothing at all to speak of. The function of language is not referential but evocative, revelatory, and

---

[32] Bowie, *Lacan*, p. 116.
[33] Lacan, 'The Function and Field of Speech and Language in Psychoanalysis', p. 209.

constitutive of the world: 'the function of language in speech is not to inform but to evoke'.[34] Speech is an evocation—perhaps one could say an 'invocation'—of meaning in the other to whom it is addressed.

Referring to Lacan's claim that the unconscious is structured like a language, Žižek writes,

> The unconscious is not the preserve of wild drives that have to be tamed by the ego, but the site where a traumatic truth speaks out. Therein lies Lacan's version of Freud's motto *Wo es war, soll ich werden* (Where it was, I am to become): not 'The ego should conquer the id', the site of the unconscious drives, but 'I should dare to approach the site of my truth.' What awaits me 'there' is not a deep Truth that I have to identify with, but an unbearable truth that I have to learn to live with.[35]

The 'unbearable truth' that Lacan tracks through the labyrinths of psycho-analysis is a futile hare's chase, with language pursuing desire along an elusive and fragmented trail, deceptive, misleading, and disjointed, incapable of being gathered together into a teleological whole that might give direction and meaning to life. But this is also where Lacan invites us to search for the real truth of the human condition. In his 1955 paper titled 'the Freudian thing', Lacan speaks as the voice of truth:

> Whether you flee me in deceit or think you can catch me in error, I will catch up with you in the mistake from which you cannot hide.... [T]he most innocent intention is disconcerted once it can no longer conceal the fact that one's bungled actions are the most successful and that one's failures fulfill one's most secret wishes. In any case, doesn't my escape – first from the dungeon of the fortress in which you think you are most sure to hold me by situating me not in yourselves, but in being itself – suffice to prove your defeat? I wander about in what you regard as least true by its very nature: in dreams, in the way the most far-fetched witticisms and the most grotesque nonsense of jokes defy meaning, and in chance – not in its law, but rather in its contingency.[36]

The task of the analyst is to guide the analysand towards an acceptance of this predicament as the inescapable truth of what it means to be human. We need to abandon our fantasies of plenitude and union, if we are to experience love and joy at all within the always partial and always unsatisfying relationships that life offers us. In *Seminar XX*, Lacan explains this in terms of a love that guides the other to accept and endure lack as the condition of loving at all, beyond the narcissistic and consuming infantile demands that masquerade as

---

[34] Lacan, 'The Function and Field of Speech and Language in Psychoanalysis', p. 247.

[35] Žižek, *How to Read Lacan*, p. 3. See also Lacan, 'The Instance of the Letter in the Unconscious'.

[36] Lacan, 'The Freudian Thing, or the Meaning of the Return to Freud in Psychoanalysis', in *Écrits*, pp. 341–2.

love but that seek the absorption or annihilation of the other in the quest to satisfy desire (see Chapter 15).

This is an important theme to which we shall return, but it alerts us to the complex relationship between desire and the drives according to Lacan—a relationship that undergoes significant changes in the development of his thought.

LOVE AND LACK

Lacanian desire is neither need nor the drives, although it has something in common with both. Needs are capable of satisfaction, and the drives are associated with the capacity for enjoyment that comes from a libidinal drive associated with a particular bodily source of pleasure. Desire, however, is aroused and sustained by the impossibility of pleasure or satisfaction, rooted in the insatiable need for unconditional, all-sustaining love, which is why its object is the *objet petit a*, the constantly elusive and anamorphic other that is its cause, on condition that it remains unattainable. So, the drive might awaken desire for some particular object, but desire is surplus to the drive and remains active in its restless quest, even when the drive is capable of bringing enjoyment that can briefly tranquillize desire.[37]

The analyst must accompany the analysand through and beyond the transference which projects onto the other the narcissistic demand of and for an all-sustaining love, to a renunciation of the object. Only by accepting lack through a recognition of the limits of desire and its capacity for gratification does love become possible: 'Love . . . can be posited only in that beyond, where, at first, it renounces its object.'[38] This entails acceptance of the necessary act of separation, acceptance of lack as the condition by way of which love might mediate between the desire and the drive, in a way that has particular implications for the sexual relationship:

> any shelter in which may be established a viable, temperate relation of one sex to
> the other necessitates the intervention . . . of that medium known as the paternal
> metaphor. The analyst's desire is not a pure desire. It is a desire to obtain absolute
> difference, a desire which intervenes when, confronted with the primary signifier,
> the subject is, for the first time, in a position to subject himself to it. There only

---

[37] Cf. Lacan, *The Four Fundamental Concepts of Psychoanalysis*, pp. 174–86. See also the discussion in Elisabeth Roudinesco, *Jacques Lacan and Co: A History of Psychoanalysis in France, 1925–1985*, trans. Jeffrey Mehlman (Chicago: University of Chicago Press, 1990), pp. 145–6; Charles Shepherdson, 'Lacan and Philosophy', in Jean-Michel Rabaté (ed.), *The Cambridge Companion to Lacan* (Cambridge and New York: Cambridge University Press, 2003), pp. 116–52.

[38] Lacan, *The Four Fundamental Concepts of Psychoanalysis*, p. 276.

may the signification of a limitless love emerge, because it is outside the limits of the law, where alone it may live.[39]

Again, we must discuss this in more detail, but central to Lacan's theory is (a) the insistence that the paternal separation of the child from the mother is necessary for the formation of culture, and that consequently (b) sexual identity is formed around possession or lack of the phallus in terms of the symbolic positioning of the self as male or female. This construction of sexual difference in terms of (illusory) male perfection and female lack is essential for my analysis of Thomas and requires much more detailed analysis. However, we should note at this stage that, in Lacan's account, it is when each sex can acknowledge the lack in the other, when the impossibility of all-fulfilling love between self and other is accepted, that an ethical relationship of sexual love becomes possible.

LACAN'S UNCONSCIOUS GOD

Hegel's influence is clear in Lacan's understanding of desire and otherness. The Hegel whom Lacan encountered primarily through the scholarship of Alexandre Kojève and Jean Hyppolite is, to quote Bowie, 'the supremely resourceful poet of an otherness that haunts consciousness and finds endless echoes and analogues in the public sphere'.[40] But for Lacan, Hegel's concept of *Aufhebung*, by way of which consciousness progressively transcends or sublates the conflict between self and other through their reconciliation within the concept (*Begriff*), advancing towards an ever more unified form of absolute mind as the endpoint of history, is yet one more example of 'philosophy's pretty little dreams'[41] of an ultimate singularity and unity of meaning and purpose, which belies the fragmented reality of the human condition.

Lacan disrupts the Hegelian system by removing its metaphysical orientation and by resisting its teleological thrust. He denies the reconciling move in the Hegelian synthesis and positions desire, not before the other as object but before the Other as lack. The closer one comes to it the more elusive it becomes, whether as the absent Other of the symbolic order which is both exempt from and crucial to the power of the law or as the absent Other of the real which resists all attempts at articulation while constituting the void of the self around which language circulates.

---

[39] Lacan, *The Four Fundamental Concepts of Psychoanalysis*, p. 276.
[40] Bowie, *Lacan*, p. 80.   [41] Lacan, *On Feminine Sexuality*, p. 86.

Moreover, while Hegel's vision is ultimately focused at the macrocosmic level of law, politics, and the state, Lacan offers a microcosmic insight into the workings of the individual human soul in its struggle with the interwoven dynamics of desire, alienation, and death. His ethical project follows Freud in its focus on 'the sick individual' and 'the powers that derive from the know-ledge of good and evil'.[42] In captivity to finitude and entrapped in language, the analysand must discover his or her ethical and existential significance in relationship to those epiphanies of desire which offer a fragile vitality capable of sustaining life in the face of its own futility and inevitable decomposition.

Lacan thus opens up pathways of thought that short-circuit the Hegelian dialectic, not through overcoming it but through frustrating its relentless logic by bringing into linguistic play the dynamism of desire and the *jouissance* or enjoyment of the body. The drive towards the singularity of the One, epitom-ized not only in Hegel's rational Absolute but in all forms of philosophical and theological monotheism that seek a unified point of truth as the ultimate goal of human existence, deceives us into believing that there is a perfect object capable of satisfying our desire. We seek this in and beyond every other object of desire, because it holds out the seductive promise of restoring us to a sense of wholeness and bliss associated with the phallic body, which is also the maternal body. This promise beckons to us elusively through all the tangible and attainable material objects that surround us, rendering them unreal and inadequate in the face of the insatiability of our desire. Modern atheism does nothing to liberate us from this delusion, for it continues to dupe us with its scientific belief in an objective world accessible to the rational mind, within which to ground our claims to truth and knowledge. The man of science no longer seeks an infinite God but an infinite knowledge which will overcome forever the darkness and ignorance of the mind. Richard Dawkins typifies this attitude when he declares himself 'thrilled to be alive at a time when humanity is pushing against the limits of understanding. Even better, we may eventually discover that there are no limits'.[43] The phenomenal success of Dawkins' book, *The God Delusion*, and the cult of scientific atheism that it has fuelled, suggests how persuasive this fantasy of scientific plenitude has become in modern western society. However, according to Lacan, the scientific quest for total understanding of everything is as misguided as the religious quest that it replaces.

It is the lingering effects of monotheism on the western soul that lead Lacan in his later work to say that God is not dead but unconscious. Freudian psychoanalysis exposes the continuing power of modernity's absent God so that modern atheism is founded not on the death of God but on the uncon-sciousness of God: 'The true formula of atheism is not God is dead—even by

---

[42] Lacan, *The Ethics of Psychoanalysis*, p. 106.
[43] Richard Dawkins, *The God Delusion* (London: Bantam Press, 2006), p. 374.

basing the origin of the function of the father upon his murder, Freud protects the father—the true formula of atheism is God is unconscious.'[44]

We should note what is being suggested here. Freud does not argue away faith by seeking logically to demonstrate the non-existence of God, as modern scientific atheism attempts to do. Rather, Freud seeks to explain how the idea of God comes about, by attributing it to the different emotional attachments to and reactions against the father figure in the oedipal stages of development. Thus the Father God 'exists' not as a metaphysical being or a cause of the universe but as a product of the human soul, upon which the modern symbolic order is parasitic in order to justify its power and shore up its laws, even in the absence of a divine legislator. Lacan came to see Freud's emphasis upon the paternal role in this psychological process as evidence of Freud's own attachment to the primacy of the father in the formation of religion and culture. We might ask if the increasing emphasis on the maternal role in Lacan's later work marks the difference between his French Catholicism with its potent Marian influences, and Freud's secular Jewishness interpreted through the patriarchal lens of early twentieth-century Protestant culture.[45] Either way, even if Lacan eventually calls into question Freud's patriarchal interpretation of the Oedipus complex by focusing more on the maternal role in the formation of the psyche, he makes no attempt to distance himself from the essentially atheistic implications of Freud's theory.

God is a function of language, an explanation that no longer suffices to channel desire or to command obedience in modern society. Lacan thus resists any appeal to a philosophical or theological ethics justified by a transcendent and ultimate good: 'The question of the Sovereign Good is one that man has asked himself since time immemorial, but the analyst knows that it is a question that is closed. Not only doesn't he have that Sovereign Good that is asked of him, but he also knows there isn't any.'[46]

However, we continue to be positioned before an unknowable Other whose commands and prohibitions govern our desire—whose desire determines the conditions of our own desiring. Lacan, following Hegel (but not all the way), insists that desire is subservient and responsive to the desire of the Other. My own desire is dominated by the futile attempt to discern what the Other is

---

[44] Lacan, *The Four Fundamental Concepts of Psychoanalysis*, p. 59. See also the discussion in Mark C. Taylor, 'Refusal of the Bar', in Edith Wyschogrod, David R. Crownfield, and Carl A. Raschke (eds), *Lacan and Theological Discourse* (Albany NY: State University of New York Press, 1989), pp. 39–53.

[45] See Élisabeth Roudinesco, *Jacques Lacan: An Outline of a Life and History of a System of Thought*, trans. Barbara Bray (Cambridge: Polity Press, 1999). See also Rael Meyerowitz, *Transferring to America: Jewish Interpretations of American Dreams* (Albany NY: State University of New York Press, 1995), which includes a helpful evaluation of charges that Lacan was anti-Jewish. See also Paul Roazen, *The Trauma of Freud: Controversies in Psychoanalysis* (New Brunswick: Transaction Publishers, 2002), Chapter 8, 'Lacanianism', pp. 149–80.

[46] Lacan, *The Ethics of Psychoanalysis*, p. 300.

asking of me and to satisfy its demands in order to be loved, in order to experience that blissful state of union that is associated with the phallic mother. If I know what It wants of me I can make It love me, and then I shall be complete. If this is how monotheism acquires its grip on the human soul, its effects endure long after the abandonment of Christianity as the organizing focus of western culture. The question of how this maternal desire relates to the Father God of the Christian tradition is the central focus for much of what follows in my reading of Thomas.

ON NOT HAVING IT ALL

In a consumerist culture, the quest for happiness becomes a tyrannical force which makes us believe we can and must have it all. Having it all is what joy demands of us.[47] The recuperation of our capacity for joy entails letting go of this consuming and consumerist fantasy. According to Lacan, there is no Other that wants us to have it all, and there is no 'all' to be had. It is the very condition of becoming human that we experience and learn to live with lack. The politics of envy, acquisitiveness, and insatiable desire upon which the advertising industry feeds is dependent upon the lingering effects of Christian theology on the western soul, with its promises of deferred plenitude. For Lacan, the solution is not a return to faith but a more radical acceptance of the cost of atheism. We must settle for less in order to enjoy more. Only by evacuating the soul of its hidden oedipal gods and hauntings of terror and muffled desires, might the self learn to accept and express its inconsolable longings and its epiphanies of joy. This attempt to go beyond the death of God proclaimed by Nietzsche to a more radical purgation of desire is for Lacan the ultimate goal of psychoanalysis: 'The pinnacle of psychoanalysis is well and truly atheism, provided one gives this term another sense than that of "God is dead," where all the indications are that far from calling into question what is at play, namely the law, it is consolidated instead.'[48]

I want to leave Lacan for now, in order to bring Thomas onto the scene as a medieval precursor to Lacanian psychoanalysis, invoked by Lacan at various stages in his theory. This means bearing in mind a cluster of questions that emerge in staging an encounter between Thomas and Lacan: who or what is Lacan's God, and why is a journey through theological desire essential if we are

---

[47] See for example the film and television commercial for the BMW X3 at <www.youtube. com/watch?v=0-vnFlFc8OU> [accessed 2 July 2012]. An irony of consumer choice is that one is exposed to advertising slogans wherever one goes, but these are protected by copyright rules which prevent the slogan being quoted here!

[48] Lacan, *The Other Side of Psychoanalysis*, p. 119.

to arrive at a point of acceptance in which desire becomes liveable, without the consolations of divine or sexual union as its goal? But I also turn that question around, in order to ask why a journey through Lacan's God may be necessary for the rehabilitation of theological desire as the only condition within which the Christian life can be lived as a loving expression of faith in an incarnate God. That is the direction towards which this whole book is moving, through and beyond Lacan and through and beyond Thomas, but only by way of the strange path that opens up before us in the encounter between the two.

So I turn now from Lacan's unconscious God who prevails over the post-modern soul with a quixotic and pervasive potency, to the God of medieval theology. To what extent does Thomas's God correspond to Lacan's real? How does Thomas's understanding of language, desire, and God relate to Lacan's defiant post-Catholic rebellion and its fragile linguistic hypotheses based on the psychoanalytic encounter? According to Lacan, this encounter is where the human soul, forsaken by God and abandoned by modern society, expresses its desolation and longing in the attentive presence of the one who has ears to hear, silence to keep, and time to listen—that is, the psychoanalyst. Might a postmodern Thomism enable the Church to hear, to keep silent, and to listen to the expressions and confessions of desire wherein God might still have something to say to those whose heart and flesh cry out to the living God?

2

Knowing the World in God

In this chapter, I position Thomas Aquinas's *Summa theologiae*[1] in relation to the overall quest of this book—to discover what kind of theological language might suffice for the challenges that postmodernism sets before us with regard to knowledge, and the crises that loom before us in the disintegration of modernity's values and institutions, not least with regard to questions of embodiment, gender, and nature. I set aside the latter questions for now, but they are the direction in which I am moving as I stage an encounter between Thomas and Jacques Lacan, as the prelude to a more detailed exploration of Thomas's understanding of the relationship between God and the world in terms of language, knowledge, and desire.

Thomas and Lacan share the age-old philosophical question of how to account for the aporia between human consciousness and matter, whatever terminology we use to express this duality. Whether we use Thomas's philosophical language of form and matter, or more recent terms such as consciousness or mind in relation to the body or materiality, the problem remains the same. Even if we couch our questions in the language of evolution rather than theology or philosophy, we are still left with the question as to how an animal species jumped the evolutionary tracks and acquired a capacity to reflect upon its existence within a world of which it is a part and to whose laws it is subject, so that we are able to imagine different modes of existence, to remember and to anticipate, and to exercise a certain freedom in relation to the laws of nature both in terms of our moral lives and in terms of our technological and creative abilities. Beyond all the inadequate responses of the behavioural sciences, the mystery refuses to go away. The problem of consciousness might reinvent itself

---

[1] I have consulted the Latin version and several English translations of the *Summa theologiae*. Quotations are from the Benziger Brothers edition of 1947, translated by the Fathers of the English Dominican Province. The Latin text and the Benziger edition are available online at the website of the Dominican House of Studies, Priory of the Immaculate Conception at <http://dhspriory.org/thomas/>. Sometimes, for the sake of clarity, I have used an abbreviated version of a quotation or a section from Timothy McDermott's *Summa Theologiae: A Concise Translation* (London: Methuen, 1992). In these instances I include the reference to McDermott after the reference to the relevant section of the *Summa theologiae*.

in different guises and different theories, but it remains one of the fundamental mysteries of what it means to be human.

'METAPHYSICAL AMPHIBIANS'—THE PARADOX OF THE HUMAN SPECIES

For Thomas as for Lacan, questions such as these focus with particular intensity on certain epistemological puzzles. Given the mystery that encompasses us (God/the real), how and what can the human know, enmeshed as we are within the ostensibly irreconcilable duality of mind/matter, spirit/body, consciousness/corporality? What does it mean to be human in the gap that opens up between objects and otherness in our ways of perceiving, experiencing, and knowing the world? Timothy McDermott points out that, for Thomas, the distinction between spirit and matter is 'one of the great divisions which cuts across creation'.[2] Given this, Thomas asks how we account for human understanding, since 'nothing material is actually understandable'.[3] What is the relationship between mind and matter, since 'being aware is exactly the opposite of being material'?[4]

We could situate Thomas's preoccupation with angels in the context of this dilemma.[5] To a modern reader, his extensive ruminations on angels might seem like an example of esoteric medievalism that is irrelevant to modern forms of enquiry, but the disembodied, immediate knowledge of God that constitutes angelic ways of knowing provides Thomas with a foil for thinking through the problem of how humans know, and this is highly relevant to a Lacanian reading of Thomas. Thomas is wrestling with the complexity of a life form—the human—that is both material and immaterial, animal and spiritual, as opposed to angels which are purely spiritual, and non-human life forms which lack a spiritual capacity—although they are naturally encompassed within the creative love of God. To use Eleonore Stump's phrase, human souls are 'metaphysical amphibians'[6] because they exist 'on the borderline between corporeal and separated [that is, purely spiritual] substances'.[7]

As we shall see, Thomas seeks to address these enigmas by way of an Aristotelian epistemology in which experience of the world is internalized, processed, and redirected towards the world and God as volitional activity

---

[2] Timothy McDermott, 'Introductory Comment', in Timothy Mcdermott (ed.), *Summa Theologiae: A Concise Translation* (London: Methuen, 1992), p. 106.
[3] ST I, 79, 3. McDermott, 'Introductory Comment', p. 122.
[4] ST I, 84, 2. McDermottt, 'Introductory Comment', p. 130.
[5] See ST I, 50–64.
[6] Eleonore Stump, *Aquinas* (London and New York: Routledge, 2003), p. 17.
[7] Thomas Aquinas, *Quaestio disputata de anima*, quoted in Stump, *Aquinas*, p. 17.

through various passive and active capacities of the soul. Having said this, we also need to be aware that much of Thomas's understanding of Aristotle was filtered through various commentaries and works ascribed to Aristotle, which also bore significant Platonic and Neoplatonic influences.[8] So, although Thomas probably had little direct knowledge of Plato's writings, he became increasingly aware in the later years of his life of the extent to which Plato as well as Aristotle was a significant resource for Christian theological reflection. This sometimes results in inconsistencies in Thomas's understanding of the unity and being of God and the effects that flow from that in the order of creation, and I shall suggest later that this presents a particular challenge for feminist interpreters of Thomas.

By reading Aristotle and his medieval interpreters from the perspective of Christian theology and scripture, Thomas introduces into Greek thought a fundamental personal mystery (God), as the ontological source and *telos* of human desire, and a haunting darkness that afflicts our desire (sin), both of which touch the human in every aspect of his or her being in the world. This means that knowing truthfully is contemplative rather than propositional, to such an extent that the more truthfully we know, the more conscious we become of the mystery of which we are a part. This explains why we might trace the structuring of consciousness revealed in psychoanalysis back to Thomas's influence—in particular, the disjunction between the rationality and order of the symbolic, the volatile unknowability of the real, and the omnipresence of desire which pervades human existence with an inescapable sense of alienation and otherness. The doctrine of the resurrection of the body also presents Thomas with a significant challenge in reconciling Aristotle's concept of the intellect with the Christian understanding of the soul, but we must come back to that later.

THOMISM AND LACANIAN ATHEISM

In seeking to read Thomas from a Lacanian perspective, we might also read Lacan as being engaged in a sustained struggle to articulate an atheist response to his French Thomist interlocutors of the 1950s, bearing in mind his childhood Catholicism and his unrelenting preoccupation with the question of God. Lacan's criticism of modern atheism has much in common with the criticism offered by Catholic theologians such as Étienne Gilson, Henri de

---

[8] Cf. Patrick Quinn, *Aquinas, Platonism, and the Knowledge of God* (Aldershot: Avebury, 1996). See also Wayne John Hankey, 'Aquinas, Plato, and Neoplatonism', in Brian Davies and Eleonore Stump (eds), *The Oxford Handbook of Aquinas* (Oxford and London: Oxford University Press, 2012), pp. 55–64.

Lubac, and Jacques Maritain, with the existential Thomism of Gilson being an enduring influence on Lacan's thought.

De Lubac offers an extended critique of 'atheist humanism', which he contrasts with 'coarsely materialist atheism' and 'an atheism of despair'.[9] De Lubac attributes atheist humanism to the influence of thinkers such as Auguste Comte, Ludwig Feuerbach, Karl Marx, and Friedrich Nietzsche. This atheism provides a response to '*the* human problem' by an ostensibly positive move: 'Man is getting rid of God in order to regain possession of the human greatness that, it seems to him, is being unwarrantably withheld by another. In God he is overthrowing an obstacle in order to gain his freedom.' But, argues de Lubac, this means that 'Modern humanism . . . is built upon resentment'.[10] We have seen how Lacan seeks what we might call an atheist *via media* by reopening the pathways of ateleological desire, navigating precipitously between an atheism of despair (which is over-invested in the death drive), and humanist atheism which is over-invested in the symbolic and prey to the resistance and resentment to which de Lubac refers.

But perhaps we can position Lacan more closely in relation to 1950s existential Thomism if we consider how Jacques Maritain, writing in 1952, describes what he refers to as positive and negative atheism. Maritain describes two contrasting forms of negative atheism. On the one hand, there is 'shallow and empirical' atheism, like that of seventeenth-century *libertines*, which 'digs a hollow in the center of the universe of thought which has taken shape through the centuries around the idea of God, but it does not bother about changing that universe; it is merely concerned with making us live a comfortable life, enjoying the freedom of doing exactly as we please'.[11] He contrasts this with negative atheism which

> can be lived at a profound and metaphysical level: in which case the hollow it creates at the heart of things extends to and lays waste our whole universe of thought; the freedom it claims for the human Self is absolute independence, a kind of divine independence that this Self, like Dostoievsky's Kirilov, has no better way of affirming than by suicide and voluntary annihilation.[12]

Over and against this, Maritain contrasts 'positive atheism', which is

> an active struggle against everything that reminds us of God—that is to say, antitheism rather than atheism—and at the same time a desperate, I would say

---

[9] Henri De Lubac SJ, *The Drama of Atheist Humanism*, trans. Edith M. Riley, Anne Englund Nash, and Mark Sebanc (San Francisco: Ignatius Press, 1995), p. 24.

[10] De Lubac SJ, *The Drama of Atheist Humanism*, pp. 24–5.

[11] Jacques Maritain, *The Range of Reason* (New York: Charles Scribner's Sons, 1952), Chapter 8.1, available online at the Jacques Maritain Center website: <http://maritain.nd.edu/jmc/etext/range.htm> [accessed 9 May 2012].

[12] Maritain, *The Range of Reason*.

heroic, effort to recast and reconstruct the whole human universe of thought and the whole human scale of values in accordance with that state of war against God.[13]

This is the post-war theological milieu within which Lacan first cast himself as an unholy fool, seeking to thwart the Thomism of his Catholic contemporaries while simultaneously seeking to avoid aligning himself with those forms of atheism that they criticized, by using psychoanalysis to excavate the unconscious gods upon which such atheisms were parasitic. We must return to that point, but I now approach Thomas himself, to begin to pose to him the questions with which Lacan confronts us. Implicit in my reading of Thomas is an orientation towards the Thomism of *la nouvelle théologie* of 1950s French Catholicism, to which I shall refer from time to time.

REASON, REVELATION, AND WONDER

Thomas begins the *Summa theologiae* by insisting upon the primacy of revelation over reason with regard to the knowledge of God, because philosophy is inadequate to the task of knowing the truths of God.[14] Sacred doctrine, revealed by God, is the science against which the science of philosophical theology must measure its claims,[15] for it constitutes the principles according to which reasoning about God is possible. But this also means that Christian doctrine, establishing its claims not upon 'the natural light of human reason'[16] but upon divine revelation, is superior to all other sciences, insofar as all other ways of knowing are positioned within the overarching vocation to God that is the meaning of human existence. Moreover, because doctrine originates in God and 'treats chiefly of those things which by their sublimity transcend human reason',[17] it is the most certain form of knowledge and entirely free from error, even though the limitations of human understanding might obscure its clarity and its certainty.

But there is also for Thomas a subtle distinction between knowing and comprehending: we can know God, but this does not amount to comprehension.[18] While philosophical reflection can provide us with limited but truthful knowledge about the world and with the knowledge *that* God is, only the self-

---

[13] Maritain, *The Range of Reason*.

[14] ST I, 1. See also the discussion on faith in ST II-II, 1.

[15] We must remember that the word 'science' (*scientia*) is used by Thomas to refer to all forms of human knowledge, and not in the more restrictive sense associated with modern scientific discourse.

[16] ST I, 1, 5.   [17] ST I, 1, 5.   [18] Cf. ST I, 12, 1.

revelation of God in the Christian scriptures and the person of Jesus Christ can tell us *who* God is and the true meaning of the world. These different ways of knowing have the same source in God, so they serve to complement one another: there can be no fundamental conflict between the demands of faith and the demands of reason. Rather, 'we have a more perfect knowledge of God by grace than by natural reason'.[19] This is why Thomas is able to say repeatedly and in different ways that 'grace perfects nature'.[20] He also argues that 'faith presupposes natural knowledge, even as grace presupposes nature'.[21] Ostensibly then, there is no possible conflict for Thomas between grace and nature, faith and reason, providing we struggle to free ourselves of the distorting effects of sin upon our ways of knowing and desiring, and providing we accept the finitude of all mortal knowing with regard to the things of God.

Thomas's account of our human capacity for meaning-making and coherence in a material world derives from the nature of being that derives from the being of God and which all beings have in common.[22] This constitutes the '*ens commune*'—being in general or 'the communion in being'.[23] Humans have a unique capacity for a relationship with God, since we are made in the divine image and therefore endowed with rational intellects, but as animals we are also immersed within the being of the world. Here it is worth briefly referring to Thomas's widely debated five ways for proving the existence of God.[24] Given the primacy of revelation over reason with which Thomas begins the *Summa theologiae*, we must read the five ways not in terms of propositions about the existence of God that would convince a closed philosophical mind that God logically must exist, but as reflections on the mystery of being which might guide an awakened consciousness towards the ways in which God is manifest in creation.

Thomas has already insisted that it is futile to seek to prove the existence of God by way of reasoned argument to those who reject the possibility of divine revelation,[25] so his proofs do not stand alone independently of revelation, but are rather ways of showing how the Christian faith in God is consistent with

---

[19] ST I, 12, 13.   [20] Cf. ST I, 62, 5.   [21] ST I, 2, 3.

[22] See Thomas Aquinas, *Commentary on the Metaphysics*, 'Prologue', trans. John P. Rowan, html-edited by Joseph Kenny OP (Chicago, 1961) at <http://dhspriory.org/thomas/Metaphysics.htm> [accessed 3 July 2012].

[23] Cf. Fergus Kerr, *After Aquinas: Versions of Thomism* (Malden MA and Oxford: Blackwell Publishers, 2002), p. 68.

[24] See ST I, 2, 3. There is a vast range of commentaries and interpretations of Aquinas's five ways. The most relevant interpretation for my purposes here is Étienne Gilson, *The Christian Philosophy of St Thomas Aquinas*, trans. L.K. Shook SCB (London: Victor Gollancz Ltd, 1961), pp. 59–83. As we shall see in a later chapter, Gilson's interpretation had a profound influence on Lacan's struggle with the puzzle of being.

[25] See ST I, 1, 8.

the demands of philosophical reason, providing the latter is already charged with a sense of wonder about the mystery of being. In other words, they are a way of illustrating what can be known of God through creation in a manner that preserves God's absolute transcendence, but which also presupposes the intelligibility of the world. Debates about nominalism and Cartesian scepticism have not yet entered the scene: Thomas does not even think to ask *if* we know. Rather, given *that* we know, he is asking *how* we know and *how much* we can know, in a world in which 'things disclose their intelligibility'[26] to human intelligence.

Maritain suggests that Thomas's philosophical proofs need to be read from the perspective of a medieval culture in which a sense of the wonder of being was 'an atmosphere too habitual to be regarded as a surprising gift'.[27] Thomas takes for granted an intuition that modernity resists, an ontological and erotic intuition that still has the capacity to awaken us to perceive, 'in an enigmatic but inescapable manner', the 'tremendous fact, sometimes exhilarating, sometimes disgusting and maddening: *I exist*'.[28] For modern consciousness, this pervasive sense of the mystery of being is not habitual but comes in a 'sudden flash of intuition' in which we become aware that 'this solid and inexorable existence, perceived in anything whatsoever, implies... some absolute, irrefragable existence, completely free from nothingness and death'. Maritain explains what this experience amounts to:

> When it takes place, I suddenly realize that a given entity – man, mountain or tree – exists and exercises this sovereign activity to be in its own way, in an independence of me which is total, totally self-assertive and totally implacable. And at the same time I realize that I also exist, but as thrown back into my loneliness and frailty by this other existence by which things assert themselves and in which I have positively no part, to which I am exactly as naught.[29]

We are touching on a significant Lacanian theme here, and we shall return to explore this in more detail in a later chapter. However, by the time of *Seminar XX* in the early 1970s, Lacan was gnawing away at the mystery of being with a persistence that I suspect can be attributed to the unrelenting hold that existential Thomism had on his thought. In *Seminar XX* he returns to a question that is central to Thomas: 'How can being know?'[30] He situates this in the context of an enquiry into the relationship between love and the Oneness of being which is Thomist through and through: 'Then what matters in love?... Love, is it about

---

[26] Kerr, *After Aquinas*, p. 68.

[27] Maritain, *The Range of Reason*, Chapter 7.1.

[28] Maritain, *The Range of Reason*, Chapter 7.1.

[29] Maritain, *The Range of Reason*, Chapter 7.1.

[30] Jacques Lacan, *Le Séminaire de Jacques Lacan, Livre XX: Encore (1972–1973)* (Paris: Éditions du Seuil, 1975), p. 176.

making one? Is Eros a tension towards the One? People have been talking about nothing but the One for a long time. There's something of the One' (*Y a d' l'Un*).[31] We shall tease out all this later.

We also need to bear in mind that Thomas's *Summa theologiae* was written as an exercise in theological education, for students who found themselves confronted by the philosophical debates and conflicting theories that animated European thought in the aftermath of the rediscovery of Greek philosophy through its Jewish and Muslim interpreters. Thomas is seeking to give those in his own theological community the confidence to participate in these debates, while also cautioning them against excessive confidence in claiming to understand the divine mystery. In this, he is as relevant for theologians today as he was for those of the thirteenth century.

THE FIVE WAYS

In setting out his five ways, Thomas begins by denying that the existence of God is self-evident, because one cannot admit the opposite of a self-evident truth, whereas it is possible to deny that God exists. He also challenges Anselm's ontological argument which says that, if 'God' signifies that than which nothing greater can be conceived, then 'existence' is a predicate of 'God' because it is greater to exist actually as well as mentally, so if we can conceive of God mentally then that entails the actual existence of God. But for Thomas, for a proposition to be self-evident the essence of the subject must necessarily include the predicate, as in the claim 'Man is an animal'.[32] But with God, (a) we cannot know God's essence, and (b) the predicate of existence is the same as the subject. In other words, whereas the relationship between subject and predicate is not normally reversible—we could say that gold glitters but all that glitters is not gold—God and existence mean one and the same thing (a point to which we shall return). Moreover, although the human desire for happiness implies a natural disposition towards God since God is our human beatitude, this also fails as an argument that necessitates the existence of God. The awareness that there is a perfect good which we desire in order to be happy does not necessarily translate into desire for God, because many people seek happiness through other means, such as the acquisition of wealth or the pursuit of pleasure.[33] Again, we are very close to Lacan's Thomism here, the only difference being that, for Thomas, the perfect happiness we seek is to be found in a post-mortem union with God, while for Lacan there is no such consummation of desire in this life or any other.

[31] Jacques Lacan, *Encore*, p. 13.   [32] ST I, 2, 1.   [33] See ST I, 2, 1.

Having denied that the existence of God can be proved deductively in terms of formal semantics, Thomas still wants to insist that we can speak meaningfully of God through reasoning about creation. His five ways are not proofs of existence, so much as grammatical rules which govern what we can and cannot say meaningfully about God or, in the words of Cornelius Ernst, he sets out 'to show how one might *go on* speaking of God in the ordinary world',[34] despite the ultimate mystery of which we speak.

Thomas turns to Aristotle's idea of an unmoved mover and interprets it in terms of a creator God in order to argue that the existence of God can be inductively demonstrated through our knowledge of the laws that govern the material world. With Aristotle, Thomas understands all phenomena in terms of relationships of cause and effect, and potentiality and actuality. In order for creation to become (i.e. to actualize its potential for existence), there must be a prior being—an actual existent—in which it originates. Although we cannot know the being of God from the being of the world (we do not necessarily know a cause from its effects), we can nevertheless know that such being must be in order for the world to be. It is this wondering about the cause of the world—this primal wonder which issues forth in a 'why?' before and beyond every possible answer—that is the precondition for understanding what the five ways are intended to do. They are unlikely to gain any purchase at all, let alone serve as proofs, for modern minds mired in the hubris of rationalism and desensitized to the intimations of the eternal within the matter of the cosmos.

It is superfluous to my purpose here to offer a more developed analysis of the five ways, but this brief summary suggests why, for Thomas, philosophy can come to know something truthful but partial about God inductively through its rational observation of existent phenomena, providing it is open to wonder. However, deductively it is scripture, not logic, which tells us about the existence of God in the form of a self-revealing mystery. Truthful language about God is therefore predicated on the revelation of God in creation (the language of reason), and on the revelation of God in scripture and in the person of Jesus Christ (the language of faith).

THE BEING OF GOD

To appreciate the significance of Thomas's understanding of the being of God (and Lacan's understanding of Thomas), we have to go beyond ontotheology—the

---

[34] Cornelius Ernst, 'Metaphor and Ontology in *Sacra Doctrina*', in Fergus Kerr and Timothy Radcliffe (eds), *Multiple Echo* (London: Darton, Longman and Todd, 1979), p. 74. For more on the linguistic interpretation I am offering here, see Nicholas Lash, *Holiness, Speech and Silence: Reflections on the Question of God* (Aldershot UK and Burlington VT: Ashgate Publishing Ltd, 2004); Kenneth Surin, *The Turnings of Darkness and Light: Essays in Philosophical and Systematic Theology* (Cambridge: Cambridge University Press, 1989), p. 53.

modern idea of God as a singular Being over and beyond a multitude of beings (a proposition that generates much contemporary debate between atheists and theologians)—and appreciate that the being of God is best understood as a verb rather than a noun. As we have already seen, Thomas argues that in God, unlike in any created being, existence and essence are one and the same.[35] This means that God's creative and sustaining activity as an expression of the divine love is one with the being of God, so that God is pure act [*purus actus*].[36] This is what Thomas means by the divine simplicity—a perfection of all modes of being and doing in the three-in-one God beyond all human understanding, which is the source from which everything else that is comes to be. God is the eternal activity of being which generates and sustains all being in a continuous, dynamic expression of love that constitutes the being of creation, so that, to quote McDermott, 'the being of the world is the doing of God'.[37] So, argues Thomas,

> The activity by which God maintains things is no new activity, but the continued act of giving them existence, an act which is not a process in time.... Before things existed God had the power not to give them existence, and thus not to make them. So, in the same way, after they have been made, he has the power to cut off the inflow of existence, so that they cease existing; that is, he has the power to annihilate them. But there is no point in him doing it. For his goodness and power are shown better by eternally maintaining both spirits and matter in existence.[38]

Thomas's God is, suggests Fergus Kerr, 'sheer existing ... the activity of sheer being'.[39] Gilson refers to 'the privileged role [Thomas] attributes to *esse* in the structure of the real'.[40] He argues that, with Thomas, we need to 'pass beyond the identification of God's substance with his essence and posit the identity of his essence with His very act-of-being.... God is His essence, and His essence is the act itself of being; He is, therefore, not only His essence but His act-of-being'.[41] Given Gilson's influence on Lacan during the formative years of the 1950s, we begin to see why this idea of being as the eternal activity of doing finds considerable resonance with Lacan's concept of the real as a turbulent, unknowable influence on human consciousness.

If we are to translate this into philosophical arguments about the existence of God in terms of cause and effect, we need to recognize that Thomas's arguments are not about the chronology of creation but about the fundamental conditions

[35] ST I, 3, 4. See also ST I, 44, 1.
[36] Cf. ST I, 25, 1 and in numerous other places throughout the *Summa theologiae*.
[37] McDermott (ed.), *Summa Theologiae*, p. xxxi.
[38] ST I, 104. McDermott, *Summa Theologiae*, pp. 154–5.
[39] Kerr, *After Aquinas*, p. 189.
[40] Etienne Gilson, *The Christian Philosophy of St. Thomas Aquinas*, trans. L. K. Shook (London: Victor Gollancz Ltd, 1961), p. 91.
[41] Gilson, *The Christian Philosophy of St. Thomas Aquinas*, pp. 91–2.

that are necessary in order for there to be something rather than nothing—in order for time, space, and differentiated beings to exist at all. All of Thomas's theology of creation is predicated upon the impossibility of being without the being of God, and God is the first cause because all being emanates from and is held in being by the divine being. If God were to cease the sustaining activity of being in creation, 'all nature would collapse'.[42] Thomas's God is, in the words of Gilson, 'not the supreme carpenter of Paley or the supreme watchmaker of Voltaire, but the infinite act of self-existence, by whom all the rest is, and as compared with whom all the rest is as though it were not'.[43] But because God creates outside of time and space, our conceptual capacities fail us since there is no possibility of us understanding what that means.

The fact that all life originates in God means that all life participates in and is dependent upon God, even though God remains outside of creation and is therefore not related to creatures. 'God is in all things,' says Thomas,[44] and 'as the soul is whole in every part of the body, so is God whole in all things and in each one.'[45] In other words, there is godliness in creatures even though there is no creatureliness in God,[46] so that the world is inherently graced with a natural capacity for goodness—a concept that would later be rejected both by the Protestant reformers and by their Kantian progeny, and later by Barthian theologians. It is this creaturely capacity to manifest the beauty and goodness of God that arouses the desire of all living beings for their creator through the things of creation: 'Whatever good anything wants, be it in a rational, animal or natural and unconscious way, God is the ultimate goal sought, for nothing is good or desirable except by having some likeness to God.'[47] Again we can see why, for Lacan, the negation of God opens up a lack at the heart of the object of desire, and leaves us with a dilemma that no amount of rationalization or gratification can resolve. There is an otherness that haunts our desire and, even if we no longer call that God or attribute divine characteristics to it, it does not go away. In order for atheism to be true to itself, it must face up to and accept the futility of desire—and yet desire nevertheless.

'A TEXT IS NOT A THING OF THE WORLD'—THE GRAMMAR OF CREATION

Before we can consider Thomas's understanding of desire from a Lacanian perspective, we must attend more closely to the ways in which the function of

---

[42] ST I, 104, 1. Aquinas is quoting Augustine (*Gen. Ad lit.* viii, 12).

[43] Etienne Gilson, *God and Philosophy*, Powell Lectures on Philosophy at Indiana University, ed. W. Harry Jellema (New Haven: Yale University Press, 1941), p. xvi.

[44] ST I, 8, 1.   [45] ST I, 8, 2.   [46] Cf. ST I, 4, 3. See also ST I, 28, 1.

[47] ST I, 44, 4. McDermott, *Summa Theologiae*, p. 85.

language informs not only the style and method of Thomas's theology, but also its substance. Although Thomas's theology does not explicitly present itself as a theory of language, an attentive reading enables us to see how much of Lacan's understanding of the relationship between desire, language, and knowledge is influenced by Thomism. The centrality of language is attributable not only to the content of Thomas's theology, but also to the context in which he worked in the emergent milieu of Europe's universities.

With the rise of the universities and the emergence of the natural sciences, Christian thinkers were beginning to observe and study the material world according to its own rules, in a more systematic and informed way than had been the case before. 'Nature' therefore began to enter Christian consciousness in a way that created a hairline crack in the order of knowledge, even though it would be several centuries before natural theology and later secular science would topple biblical revelation from its place of pre-eminence in the hierarchy of truth.[48] The catalyst for these innovations in Christian thought was the rediscovery of a formidable source of knowledge that had been largely lost to western Christianity during the so-called 'dark ages': the mathematics and philosophy of the ancient Greeks, particularly that of Aristotle, had re-entered western Europe by way of Muslim and Jewish translators and scholars.[49]

However, the medieval *Summa* was not a work of natural science, but a textual interpretation of the whole material and spiritual world as understood in the context of God's creation and the redemption of the world in Christ. As François Regnault points out, the scholastics acquired their knowledge of the world by going from one library to the next, and the proof to which they appealed in resolving their debates 'rests in the authority of a text, and not in that of a thing of the world, for a text is not a thing of the world'.[50] Nevertheless, texts were still regarded as reliable commentaries on the world, for the world itself could be read as a text—an orderly and interrelated assemblage of material signs which invited interpretation as the work of the author of creation.

Comparing the medieval *Summae* with Descartes' *Meditations*, Regnault observes that 'The *Summa* originates directly from the power of the world,

---

[48] Cf. Amos Funkenstein, *Theology and the Scientific Imagination from the Middle Ages to the Seventeenth Century* (Princeton NJ and Chichester UK: Princeton University Press, 1986); Edward Grant, *The Nature of Natural Philosophy in the Late Middle Ages* (Washington DC: The Catholic University of America Press, 2010); David C. Lindberg, *The Beginnings of Western Science: The European Scientific Tradition in Philosophical, Religious, and Institutional Context, Prehistory to A.D. 1450* (Chicago: University of Chicago Press, 2008 (2nd edition, first published 1992)).

[49] Cf. Richard E. Rubenstein, *Aristotle's Children: How Christians, Muslims, and Jews Rediscovered Ancient Wisdom and Illuminated the Dark Ages* (New York and London: Harcourt Brace International, 2003).

[50] François Regnault, *Dieu Est Inconscient: Études Lacaniennes autour de Saint Thomas d'Aquin* (Paris: Navarin, 1985), p. 23.

while the *Meditation* originates indirectly, secondary to reason.'[51] Unlike the authors of the *Summae*, Descartes regarded himself to have been deceived both by the books he had been made to read at university and by his own travels. In other words, while the scholastics trusted the intelligibility of the world and the capacity of texts to interpret the world truthfully, Descartes trusted nothing but his own rationality. That is a significant difference between the medieval soul and the modern mind, and it is a question to which we must return, for it is also central to Lacan's understanding of the modern subject.[52] We should, however, note here the importance and the subtlety of what Regnault is suggesting. Thomas is not studying the world, but is interpreting the world according to authoritative texts (primarily the Bible, secondarily the great theological writers of the Catholic tradition, and thirdly Aristotle and other thinkers of the pre-Christian, Islamic, and Jewish worlds). Again, this invites comparison with Lacan's method, as Erin Labbie suggests.[53] Like Thomas, Lacan is not concerned with the observation and study of material objects, but in the ways in which these are encrypted in language and open to different interpretations and linguistic nuances.

In seeking to join the philosophical debates of their non-Christian contemporaries, and in seeking to explain creation in terms of philosophical systems of thought, Christian thinkers began for the first time to construct a systematic account of their faith according to the conventions and grammatical rules of philosophical enquiry, in a way that also required introducing a distinction between philosophy and theology, reason and revelation. Anton C. Pegis provides an account of the medieval milieu in which this was played out, and the following quotation suggests why this endeavour can be seen as an important early step in the formation of humanism that Lacan seeks to deconstruct by way of psychoanalysis:

> For centuries Christian thought had learned, and had meditated deeply on, the grammar of the love of God. But in the presence of Greek philosophy, those who had hitherto spoken the language of supernatural devotion were called upon to learn in addition the natural language of reason seeking to understand the world and itself. . . . [W]hereas early mediaeval thought lived on the mysteries of the ways of God to man, the thirteenth century inaugurates the era when the Christian reason sought to discover and to trace the ways of man to God.[54]

Here, we see the beginnings of a rift between the language of faith and revelation and the language of philosophy and reason. With hindsight, we could argue that

---

[51] Regnault, *Dieu Est Inconscient*, p. 22.

[52] For a critique of the influence of the Cartesian turn to the subject on modern theology, see Fergus Kerr, *Theology after Wittgenstein* (Oxford and New York: Basil Blackwell, 1988).

[53] See Erin Felicia Labbie, *Lacan's Medievalism* (Minnesota: University of Minnesota Press, 2006).

[54] Anton C. Pegis, 'Introduction', in Pegis (ed.), *Basic Writings of Saint Thomas Aquinas: God and the Order of Creation*, Vol. 1 (Indianapolis IN: Hackett Publishing Company, 1997 [1945]), p. xxxvi.

Thomas's *Summa theologiae* was a significant influence in initiating this process (although he may have been appalled to know that). It has had a formative influence on the shaping of western thought, not only through Catholic theology, but also through its influence on our understanding of law and politics, and because he was the greatest Christian interpreter of Aristotle, whose categories of knowledge continue to give the western university and therefore the structuring of western knowledge its disciplinary boundaries and discursive conventions. In other words, the postmodern assault on truth, the dissolution of disciplinary boundaries and categories of knowledge in the academy, and the dismantling or calling into question of institutions of authority and all forms of hierarchy, can be seen as bringing to an end the era of western history that began with Thomas and his contemporaries.[55]

In seeking to weave together a coherent account of the relationship between revelation and reason, theology and philosophy, the eternal and the temporal, God and the world, metaphysics and materiality, Thomas's *Summa theologiae* has a chiastic structure in which the question of God as revealed in scripture and creation (Part I) focuses in on and traverses the question of human knowing and living in the world (Part II, subdivided into two parts), and fans out again into the incarnation of God in Christ and the human capacity to respond to and worship God in the sacraments (Part III, which was unfinished at the time of Thomas's death). The human might therefore be described as the chiasmus or the crossing point between God and creation, first since in the incarnation God became human, and second since it is through the human that the sanctifying power of the things of creation are acknowledged and offered back to God in the sacraments of the Church. To quote Regnault on the structure of the medieval *Summae*:

> By this cycle of emanation and return, the *Summa* mimics reality in its entirety. It is therefore no longer the sum of the parts, for there is a particular order to the whole. This is also why the *Summa*, which sets out to summarise a compendium of questions, arrives at the stage where it constitutes an exhaustive and systematic presentation, a system of the world.[56]

In content, style, and structure, then, Thomas's *Summa theologiae* enacts what it sets out to explain. Its content constitutes the dialectical working out of a series of propositions about God and the world, but the text repeatedly reminds us of the inability of language to name or communicate the divine mystery. Stylistically, therefore, Thomas knowingly positions his knowledge before the creaturely unknowing of author and reader alike, so that the text occupies a position analogous to the world in being written and read against a

---

[55] For more on this, see Alasdair MacIntyre, *God, Philosophy, Universities: A Selective History of the Catholic Philosophical Tradition* (Lanham MD and Plymouth UK: Sheed & Ward, 2009).
[56] Regnault, *Dieu Est Inconscient*, pp. 27–8.

background of divine mystery. Structurally, Thomas takes his reader on a narrative journey that stages a textual mimesis of creation. The reader/creature finds herself in a world in which God is already mentally intuited and scripturally revealed (Part I); she seeks to position herself materially in that world through observation of its laws and through attentiveness to the dynamics of her own desire (Part II), and she finds that this process draws her to recognize and worship the God of creation through the incarnation of God in Christ and the sacramental worship of the Church (Part III).[57] It is the latter which gathers up creation into revelation, and manifests the activity of supernatural grace which brings nature to perfection through the sanctification of reason by faith. Inclusive language is appropriate here, because this epistemology is that of the human species and not only of the educated man.

BEING HUMAN—'A CROWD OF HOBBLED ANGELS'

This enactment of the world within a text shows just how acutely aware Thomas is of the extent to which language constitutes the world of human understanding. To quote Brian Davies, 'For Aquinas, the model for human understanding is talking... And talking, for him, is the deployment of symbols which have significance for us as creatures that belong to a material world.'[58] Language is the communicative ability by way of which we as a species make sense of the world, but this also involves negotiating the complex terrain of our own materiality. Our souls remain hidden from others (but not from God), by a double barricade: we can decide to keep our thoughts private through the will, but our bodies also make our souls opaque unless we decide to make them known, not only through our actions, but more importantly through the meanings we attribute to ourselves in speech: 'when we wish to make ourselves known, we go out as it were by the door of the tongue to show what we really are'.[59] Thomas has recourse to angels to elucidate the ways in which bodiliness obscures and inhibits our communicative capacity, whereas angels, lacking bodies, are able to communicate directly—soul to soul—if they desire to do so.[60] To quote Kerr, 'We turn out to be a crowd of hobbled angels, each isolated "behind the wall of the body", like a hermit in a moated grange.'[61]

---

[57] Cf. Pamela M. Hall, *Narrative and the Natural Law: An Interpretation of Thomistic Ethics* (Notre Dame and London: University of Notre Dame Press, 1994).

[58] Brian Davies, 'Introduction', in Thomas Aquinas, *On Evil*, trans. Richard Regan (New York: Oxford University Press, 2003), p. 44.

[59] Gregory, *Moral. ii*, quoted in ST I, 107, 1.

[60] ST I, 107, 1.

[61] Kerr, *Theology after Wittgenstein*, p. 80.

How then do truth, knowledge, and meaningful communication become possible at all? Thomas problematizes the relationship between language and the body in a way that his monastic predecessors would not have thought to do, because for them language was more transparently and uninhibitedly a medium of prayer, praise, and devotion.[62] Their scholarship emerged not from the need to reconcile two potentially conflicting worlds—the world of revelation and the world of reason—but from the contemplative desire to know God above and beyond the transient demands of material life, in a spirituality deeply influenced by Neoplatonism and organically immersed within the natural world.

In his theological reshaping of Aristotle, Thomas introduces into Christian thought a more thorough-going materialism than was the case before (not least because he is reacting to the challenge of Catharism with its condemnation of matter as evil),[63] but he also occupies a pivotal moment when the relationship between nature and grace, body and spirit, perhaps attained its greatest equilibrium in Christian thought, even as it contained the seeds of its own undoing. As Lacan suggests, the elusive relationships of body, desire, and language by way of which Freudian psychoanalysis reveals the 'truth' of the human condition by exposing its abysmal depths, were in Thomas's time more clearly acknowledged and integrated than they would become in the transition to modernity.

This chapter constitutes the preamble to a more sustained discussion of different aspects of Thomas's thought. In order to develop this conversation between Lacan and Thomas, we have to follow Thomas's guidance in asking our questions first of revelation and only derivatively of reason and explanation. This means we have to venture into the most problematic area of language for Thomas—namely, when it seeks to speak meaningfully of the self-revelation of God, beyond what human reason can comprehend. What do we mean by 'God', and what does 'God' mean? It is to these unanswerable questions that I now turn.

---

[62] See Pegis, 'Introduction', in *God and the Order of Creation*.
[63] See Kerr, *Theology after Wittgenstein*, pp. 4–5.

3

Speaking of God in the World

Although many philosophical readings of Thomas Aquinas set aside his stipulation that true knowledge begins in revelation and ends in mystery, rather than beginning in reason and ending in certainty, a Lacanian approach to Thomas gains much by beginning with his problematization of language and knowledge. In other words, if we are better to understand how Jacques Lacan's anthropology is informed by Thomism, we would do well to begin with Thomas's theology rather than his anthropology (although these are always in Thomas two sides of the same coin, for ultimately the human in particular and being in general are not thinkable without God).

In what follows, I consider more closely how Thomas's insistence on the unknowability and transcendence of God, the participation of creation in God, and the capacity of the human soul to know God, pose an almost insurmountable challenge to theological language. I also raise a series of questions, which I address in more detail later, with regard to Thomas's insistence that, while creation participates in God, God does not participate in creation. How far does this prepare the way for the kind of radical dualism inherent in postmodern theories of language? How compatible is this claim with the doctrinal claim that 'the Word was made flesh and dwelt among us' (John 1:14)? Might a more incarnational and creation-centred theology provide a way beyond the present crisis in meaning, not by an overcoming of metaphysics but by a weakening of its hold on the theological imagination? This would entail the opening up of other pathways of meaning—pathways towards the meaning of otherness—by the invocation of the excluded (m)Other of Thomas's theological vision. This is the road less taken by Thomas in the development of his arguments, although it lures him repeatedly and with particular persistence in his discussions of the Trinity. Yet even as we encounter the maternal God in Thomas's contemplation on the ultimate Christian mystery of the Trinity, he also seeks to block entry to this alternative theological cosmology with its linguistic possibilities through an over-reliance on Aristotle and, more especially, on Plato. Heir to a tradition of fear and resistance with regard to sexual embodiment, maternity, and matter which medieval theologians intensified in their borrowing from Greek philosophy, Thomas did not dare to follow where today, his ideas might naturally and reasonably seem to lead.

The fact that Lacan himself seems oblivious to this maternal aspect of Thomas's trinitarian theology is telling, and it is I suspect a symptom of his reliance on secondary sources, particularly the work of Étienne Gilson, for his understanding of Thomas. We must come back to that, but for now suffice it to say that the most interesting aspects of the *Summa theologiae* from a Lacanian feminist perspective, are those which appear to have caused the greatest difficulty to Thomas's liberal twentieth-century interpreters, leading them to downplay, rationalize, or omit altogether the gendered cosmology and maternal Trinity that shape Thomas's understanding of the relationship between God and the world.

LANGUAGE AND THE UNKNOWING OF GOD

Early in the *Summa theologiae*, before saying anything significant about God, Thomas cites Dionysius in arguing that language about God should settle for less rather than more exalted imagery, because that serves as a reminder that 'what God is not is clearer to us than what God is'.[1] So, although Thomas must use conventional theological language to speak about God, he begins by undermining his own theological endeavour by pointing to the inadequacy of the language he is nevertheless obliged to use.

However, he also wants to argue that God is 'supremely knowable' in terms of divine self-knowledge, and the ultimate beatitude of human life is to know God.[2] The desire to know God is aroused by wanting to know the cause of the world, and this awakens a sense of wonder which can only be satisfied through full union with God after death. In this life, the intellect participates in God to the extent that the divine light illuminates the human mind sufficiently for it to have some knowledge of God, even by way of natural reason, because 'the light of natural reason itself is a participation of the divine light'.[3] Thus Thomas affirms what the theologians of the Reformation would later deny— natural human knowledge is already graced, because it is a form of participation in God. The refulgence of the divine within creation awakens desire for God, but beyond the natural powers of the intellect, beyond what any created being can communicate, and beyond any capacity of the senses or the imagination, the divine light suffuses the knowledge of the blessed in Christ with supernatural grace that enables them to recognize the truth and beauty of God within and beyond all created objects. Thus knowledge is transformed into

---

[1] ST I, 1, 9.   [2] ST I, 12, 1.   [3] ST I, 12, 11.

love and a heightened desire for God, which translates into loving activity in the world.

Ultimately, however, the claim to knowledge of God is fraught with ambiguity and paradox:

> Although by the revelation of grace in this life we cannot know of God what God is, and so we are conjoined to Him as though to an unknown, revelation still helps us to know God more fully by showing us more and greater of His works, and insofar as through divine revelation we attribute to God things which could never have been known by natural reason, such as that God is three and one. . . . Faith is a kind of knowledge, in that the intellect is determined by faith to a knowable object. But this comes not from the vision of the believer, but from the vision of the one who is believed. Since faith falls short of seeing, it lacks the rational understanding which belongs to science, because science determines the intellect to another according to the act of seeing in the light of the first principles of understanding.[4]

Knowledge of the truth, then, begins in an act of faith, originating not in any philosophical capacity of the human mind to arrive at knowledge of God, but in the willingness of God to communicate such knowledge to the receptive mind.

This means that all language about the mystery of God, insofar as it seeks coherence and meaning, can only ever point to the absence and unknowability of that of which it speaks. Denys Turner suggests 'that for Thomas, to prove the existence of God is to prove the existence of a mystery, that to show God to exist is to show how, in the end, the human mind loses its grip on the meaning of "exists"'.[5]

This is a vital insight for any reading that seeks resonances and dissonances between the Lacanian real and Thomas's God, and it is what separates my own theological project from that of much liberal theology. It is my contention that the fundamental task of Christian theology is not the systematization of know-ledge about God, nor is it the practical working out of the values and institutions needed to sustain the good life, important though these are. The primary task of theology—like that of great art, music, and literature—is to bring us face-to-face with the dazzling darkness and thunderous silence of the trinitarian God who is incarnate within the visceral and fleshy depths of our own humanity in a way that makes us a mystery unto ourselves, and within the wondrous energies and relationships that bind the cosmos together and makes that too a mystery within which we are mothered and sustained. Only then, when we have been stunned into unknowing by the mystery within which we discover ourselves to be, can we turn again to the world and to our neighbour in need and ask, 'Who art thou?', knowing that we ask this question not only of her but also of ourselves,

---

[4] ST I, 12, 13.
[5] Denys Turner, *Faith, Reason and the Existence of God* (Cambridge: Cambridge University Press, 2004), p. xiv.

and ultimately of the God in whose trinitarian image we are made. It is from this perspective that we must approach the Lacanian real, and ask what—if anything—it might have to do with the God of the Christian faith.

As Erin Labbie points out, the real, like God, requires an act of faith that shapes our understanding of what it means to be human (see Chapter 1). Both entail an acceptance of a dense mystery at the core of human existence which is impenetrable to science and conceptualization, but which leaks an uncanny sense of otherness and insufficiency into all our experiences and ideas. When this is interpreted in terms of the manifestation of the divine within the fabric of creation, Christians call it grace, but Lacan repeatedly hints at a dark grace to be discovered in the psychoanalytic deconstruction of the 'I' of humanism. In the introduction to a volume of essays on Lacan and theology, David Fisher asks, 'Is the space cleared by postmodernism one that allows for a return of grace—or is it a space in which, as the critics of postmodernism sometimes argue, nothing, no one, can live?'[6]

There can be no single answer to this question, for it is very much a matter of hermeneutics: how do we interpret the chasm that postmodernism with its psychoanalytic influences opens up within human consciousness? Once an individual has made a step away from scientific rationalism into an acceptance of this inescapable other, it becomes a question of personal decision and responsibility, because there is no rational or empirical resolution to the question as to whether this is all or nothing, God or the abyss. To interpret it as God, to name it as grace, is to endow it with personal significance that invites a response in the form of worship, communal identity, and ethical practice, so that 'God' is a word that means not just being but more importantly doing, not only in terms of the divine initiative, but also in terms of the human response. In the words of John Caputo, this is 'less a matter of asking how do I apply and translate this authoritative figure of the God of Christianity to the contemporary world' and more a matter of asking what do I love when I love my God?'[7]

To choose the alternative, Lacanian interpretation—which resonates with the spirit of existentialism that prevailed in France at least during the years of his early work—is to make an ethical commitment to love's truth in accept-ance of its ultimate futility and tragedy. As I have suggested, this commitment is shot through with the Catholic visions and values that shaped Lacan's own early life, and it is also burdened with the knowledge that radical evil is no less rational a choice than radical good, as we shall see when we discuss his reading

---

[6] David H. Fisher, 'Introduction: Framing Lacan?', in Edith Wyschogrod, David Crownfield, and Carl A. Raschke (eds), *Lacan and Theological Discourse* (Albany NY: State University of New York Press, 1989), p. 20.

[7] John D. Caputo, 'Spectral Hermeneutics', in John D. Caputo and Gianni Vattimo, *After the Death of God*, ed. Jeffrey W. Robbins (New York: Columbia University Press, 2007), p. 85.

of Kant and de Sade. The individual therefore bears an awesome responsibility for his or her own decision for or against love, bereft of the solace of any life to come, of any future reward or consolation, and beyond all collective responsibility for that decision. Alenka Zupančič considers the radical responsibility and ethical abandonment which confront the modern subject living in full awareness of the implications of the death of God:

> 'Highbrow relativism' (we have too much knowledge and historic experience to take anything as absolute) may well be regrettable, but it is nevertheless real.... We find ourselves in a kind of Hamletian burlesque, saturated with ghosts of ancient authorities and ideals that haunt us in order to say to us: 'We are dead', or 'We are impotent'.[8]

This 'we' might be challenged of course, because Zupančič's perspective is, as she herself acknowledges, that of 'highbrow relativism' and it might have little purchase on the lives of the billions of non-highbrow religious people who still make up the majority of humankind. Yet, as Charles Taylor points out, no modern individual is really free from the kind of responsibility that secularism puts upon us with regard to what we believe and why. Secular humanism thrusts us into a disenchanted world of 'multiple modernities' in which 'Naiveté is now unavailable to anyone, believer or unbeliever alike.'[9] Each of us thus bears ultimate responsibility for what we believe and why, and how that affects the ways in which we live. We begin to see why this is a perspective that introduces a dark instability into the ethical values of liberalism.

To ask if Lacan's real might yet invite translation as Thomas's God is not a question of philosophical debate or popular consensus, but of personal consent or resistance. It involves approaching the question of what it means to exist, not in terms of a propositional truth, but in terms of effects and their possible causes, for Lacan no less than for Thomas. Just as we can, according to Thomas, know that God *is* because we experience the effects of God's being in the being of the world, so according to Lacan we can know that the real *is* because we experience the effects of its being in the being of the subject—and for Lacan, this makes the question of God inescapable.

Yet here is the paradox, for the Lacanian real, like Thomas's God, is beyond all that we can say and yet it is the condition within which we are able to speak at all, and so Lacan no less than Thomas speaks most about that of which he says he cannot speak. The human species is a linguistic animal, and speak we must, but in such a way that we acknowledge that the truth of which we speak is always elsewhere, and our language trails behind it along a cobbled path of broken meanings and haunted desire.

---

[8] Alenka Zupančič, *Ethics of the Real* (London: Verso, 2000) pp. 255–6.
[9] Charles Taylor, *A Secular Age* (Cambridge MA: Harvard University Press, 2007), p. 21. Taylor attributes the phrase 'multiple modernities' to Victor Turner.

However, when reading Thomas no less than when reading postmodern theorists, we need to bear in mind that it is much easier to problematize language in theory than in practice. No matter how many caveats a writer might inscribe within a text about the inadequacy of language, no matter how *avant garde* a writer might be, inherent in the very desire to write or to speak is the desire to communicate meaningfully, and the quest for comprehensibility tends towards an unavoidable literalism in which words must carry more weight than they can bear. One cannot break the spine of meaning in every word without falling into incoherence. So the casual reader of the *Summa theologiae* may think that Thomas's theology is informed by a greater sense of certainty about the knowability of God than Thomas actually allows for (an insight which he himself sometimes overlooks). This continues to provoke numerous theological debates around the extent to which Thomas does or does not distort the mystery of the Christian God by an over-reliance on philosophy[10]—a question to which I shall return.

We might also note an apparent difference between Thomas's intention and that of Lacan. Thomas knows that he must wrest meaning from mystery, sculpting language around the presence of an unknowable Other from whom all meaning flows, and towards which all desire is directed. Notwithstanding its subtlety and complexity, the *Summa theologiae* was written 'for the instruction of beginners',[11] and therefore it must explain as clearly and logically as possible that which resists explanation and logic, while discouraging its more enthusiastic apprentices from claiming too much. Lacan, on the other hand, seeks not to elucidate but to obfuscate, in order to reveal to a culture that is too certain about its knowledge how little it actually knows. Consider, for example, his question:

> What is the upshot of all that these words articulate? Not knowledge, but confusion. Well then, from this very confusion we have to draw some lessons, since it is a question of limits and of leaving the system. Leaving it by virtue of what? – by virtue of a thirst for meaning, as if the system needed it. The system doesn't need it. But we feeble beings . . . we need meaning.[12]

For Lacan as for Thomas then, desire draws us to seek meaning beyond the system of language and the meanings it claims to offer, but while Thomas understands this beyond as a source of meaning that flows from an unsayable plenitude, Lacan understands it as the dissolution of meaning within an unspeakable abyss.

---

[10] Cf. Karen Kilby, 'Aquinas, the Trinity and the Limits of Understanding', *International Journal of Systematic Theology*, 7/4 (2005): pp. 414–27.

[11] ST I, Prologue.

[12] Jacques Lacan, *The Other Side of Psychoanalysis, The Seminar of Jacques Lacan, Book XVII*, ed. Jacques-Alain Miller, trans. Russell Grigg (New York and London: W.W. Norton & Co. Ltd, 2007), p. 15.

SCRIPTURE, THEOLOGY, AND ANALOGY

Thomas makes clear at the beginning of the *Summa theologiae* that only the authors of the canonical scriptures can be considered ultimate authorities with regard to divine revelation.[13] All other authoritative sources, including not only natural philosophers but even the doctors of the Church, may be open to error and subject to correction. Only once scriptural revelation is accepted as the authoritative first principle of all doctrinal and theological debate, can that debate proceed according to the demands of reason. While reason can never bridge the gap between the mind and God, it can play a secondary role in enabling us better to understand the truths communicated by way of divine revelation. These are truths that creation cannot reveal, for they belong not to the works of creation, but to the being of God. They pertain to God 'as far as He is known to Himself alone and revealed to others'.[14]

It was this insight about the vocation of theology to probe the frontiers of possibility in the context of scripture but also in the context of new philosophical and scientific resources that made Thomas such an innovative thinker in his engagement with Aristotle. Today, theologians face very different challenges from those confronting Thomas—in this book, the combined ethical challenges of gender and nature, and the philosophical challenges of postmodernism—but the underlying question does not change: how can Christian theology remain faithful to its own scriptural and doctrinal traditions, while taking seriously the changing perspectives of different historical, scientific, intellectual, and cultural contexts? These invite a theological response that emanates not from a spirit of complacent triumphalism nor from an abandonment of core Christian doctrines through conformity to the latest intellectual fads, but from an intellectually rigorous and ethically committed struggle towards an elusive and mysterious truth which Catholic Christianity nevertheless holds to be opaquely recognizable within the 'books' of both scripture and nature.

This entails acknowledging with Thomas that, as the self-revelation of God, scripture constitutes a concealing as well as a revealing, for it delineates a rupture in the order of knowledge and the opening up of a mystery before which all other forms of knowledge fail. In the very process of the divine self-revelation, God withdraws from language and conceptualization. This means that all language about God, including the language of scripture, is approximate: it uses what is knowable and familiar to us, to express what is beyond comprehension and experience.

Scripture communicates its truths in the veils of metaphor, but this means that 'the manner of its speech transcends every science, because in one and the

---

[13] ST I, 1, 8.   [14] ST I, 1, 6.

same sentence, while it describes a fact, it reveals a mystery'.[15] There is therefore a multi-layered function to scriptural language, which opens itself to ever deeper levels of mystery the more one allows its meanings to unfold. In order to approximate to the abundance of the divine mystery, theological language must resist the temptation to attach itself to its object, but must ceaselessly remain open to new forms of expression if it is to communicate the unknowability of that of which it speaks. So, says Thomas, 'new names had to be found for the God of ancient faith when arguing with heretics. Nor should such novelty be avoided, for it is not profane and it does not disagree with the sense of Scripture'.[16] The objects to which scripture refers metaphorically are themselves signifiers for that which cannot be signified, for they function as metaphors for the being of God.

The universe is thus a complex interweaving of signs within signs, whether these are words or objects, which refer to God but which can in no way make God present to human comprehension. For Thomas as for Lacan, every object is an *objet a*, even the words we use to describe those objects. The more we allow ourselves to reflect on the material objects that present themselves to our senses, the more we focus our desire upon them, the more translucent they become to a mysterious otherness that eludes our comprehension but awakens some deeper intuition of lack (Lacan) or love (Thomas).

We might ask what the limits are, for what is to prevent theological language from spiralling outwards into ever more random meanings, so that everything and nothing becomes sayable of Christianity's God? This is where analogy enters the scene, constituting as it does a way of speaking in which the referential function of language is destabilized through a threefold process of affirmation, negation, and reaffirmation, in which the balance tilts slightly in favour of affirmation, but without ever over-riding the negation. So the approximation between theological language and the being of God is stretched almost but not quite to breaking point.

Because classical Christian theology is predicated upon the ultimate incomprehensibility of God, the language of divine plenitude is often used interchangeably with the language of the abyss, and negative theology weaves its way through the claims of positive theology as a reminder of the unspeakable other whose mystery unravels all naming and knowing. Gregory P. Rocca offers a metaphorical account of what it means for Christians to 'talk about God, that dark blaze and blazing darkness on top of Mount Sinai or at the bottom of the abyss':[17]

---

[15] ST I, 1, 10, quoting Gregory (*Moral. xx*, 1).   [16] ST I, 29, 3.
[17] Gregory P. Rocca OP, 'Aquinas on God-Talk: Hovering over the Abyss', *Theological Studies*, 54 (1993), pp. 641–61, 641.

Picture a deep, narrow abyss cleaving the face of the earth down to its core, where super-hot magma bubbles and percolates, gushing and spurting through the labyrinthine tunnels which are our planet's fiery arteries. Smoke gyres upward in widening spirals. Towering cliffs angle upwards and backwards from the chasm to left and right, so that one standing atop either cliff would be too high up and too far back to view the chasm's nucleus. To behold the depths, one would somehow have to hover below the canyon rim along the rocky wall on either side, without a secure hold and in constant danger of being buffeted by upwelling air currents. Even then, all an observer could see would be a mass of hazy, congealing clouds backlit and limned by a reddish glow – a dark blaze and a blazing darkness.[18]

Those who have seen Terrence Malick's film, *The Tree of Life*, will recognize the similarity between Rocca's metaphorical extravagance and the imagery by way of which Malick's film seeks to express the divine mystery within and beyond creation and human experience.[19] This amounts to a knowingly futile attempt to evoke the sublime—the awe and the terror of the beyond. It suggests why, after the death of God, an abysmal darkness still blazes beneath the crust of human consciousness, and is capable of causing tectonic upheavals and volcanic eruptions on the surface of the mind.

The difference between the theological approach described by Rocca and what Lacan diagnoses as the malaise of modernity is that classical theology knows that it does not know, whereas the language of modern scientific rationalism and its theist derivatives mask but cannot eliminate the absent other in their totalizing claims to knowledge. Philosophical or theological debates about the existence of God, couched in the language of rational propositions and self-evident truths, are endlessly worked over by Anglo-American philosophers of religion and more recently in confrontations between Christian theologians and the so-called 'new atheists',[20] but these debates are already constructed on the foundations of modernity's rationalizing ideology, like a city of skyscrapers built on a fault line.

In the analogical balance between affirmation and negation, Rocca argues that Thomas's positive theology bears a greater weight than his negative theology insofar as, unlike thinkers such as Dionysius, he 'continually asserts that we can make true judgments about God's very nature and being, whether by reason or by faith'.[21] This means that his language is 'a subtle and intricate weaving of negative and positive theology, the latter being the more funda-mental, even though in order to thrive as *theologia* it must first pass through

---

[18] Rocca OP, 'Aquinas on God-Talk', p. 641.
[19] *The Tree of Life*, directed by Terrence Malick (2011).
[20] I discuss this in Tina Beattie, *The New Atheists* (London: Darton, Longman and Todd, 2007; Maryknoll NY: Orbis Books, 2008).
[21] Rocca, 'Aquinas on God-Talk', p. 649.

the corrective lenses of negative theology'.[22] However, Rocca also quotes an extended passage from Thomas's *Summa super libros Sententiarum*, in which 'the continuing negations finally burst the confines of all rational pursuits and lead us into the darkness of ignorance':

> When we proceed into God through the way of negation, first we deny of him all corporeal things; and next, we even deny intellectual things as they are found in creatures, like goodness and wisdom, and then there remains in our understanding only the fact that God exists, and nothing further, so that it suffers a kind of confusion. Lastly, however, we even remove from him his very existence, as it is in creatures, and then our understanding remains in a certain darkness of ignorance according to which, as Dionysius says, we are best united to God in this present state of life; and this is a sort of thick darkness in which God is said to dwell.[23]

This is an excellent example of the analogical nature of Thomas's theological language. The semantic process destabilizes the affirmative claim, acknowledging that between the signifier 'God' and the absent signified there extends an unbridgeable difference—the signified does not exist in any sense that the human mind can grasp. The affirmative claim must therefore be allowed to migrate out of conceptual human knowing into an infinite and unknowable beyond, without altogether losing its purchase, however tenuous and contingent, upon comprehensibility and truth. The latter proviso marks the difference between the positive orientation of Thomas's theology, and the more radical apophaticism of negative theology in which the negation dissolves every claim to truth and meaning predicated upon the knowability of God.

Let's also note that metaphor of 'thick darkness'. Surely that draws its suggestive potency, not from analogies of transcendence, light, and form, but from a visceral 'thinginess' that suggests that God might be discovered in the density of matter which, in philosophical terms, occupies the opposite end of the spectrum of unknowability from the transcendence of form? This is a vital question to which I shall return in some detail later.

If Thomas does allow any literalism in theological language, it is only insofar as certain qualities such as goodness and life itself are attributable to God with a fullness and perfection of meaning that is only ever experienced derivatively and imperfectly in created beings.[24] To call something 'good' is to recognize in it something of the goodness of God, not because God causes its goodness, but because the word 'good' is only fully true when referring to God, and all manifestations of good in the world constitute a participation in the divine goodness. Nevertheless, the abrupt ending of Thomas's theological quest—the claim that everything he had written seemed as straw—reminds

---

[22] Rocca, 'Aquinas on God-Talk', p. 649.

[23] Thomas Aquinas, *Summa super libros Sententiarum* I, 8, 1, 1 ad 4, quoted in Rocca, 'Aquinas on God-Talk', p. 649, pp. 648–9.

[24] Cf. ST I, 13, 3.

us of just how precarious the linguistic endeavour is when theology seeks to navigate a precipitous conceptual path above that blazing abyss, trying to discern the footholds of truth while never losing sight of the 'thick darkness' which constantly threatens to engulf the path we are on.

THE GRAMMAR OF GOD

How is it possible then for the human to speak meaningfully of knowing God? The answer—subtle, complex, and elusive—is that language itself is an analogy for God: 'the Divine Persons are distinct from each other by reason of the procession of the Word from the Speaker, and the procession of Love connecting Both.'[25] As David Burrell suggests, Thomas uses language in order 'to elucidate the parameters of responsible discourse about God'.[26] This entails a dependence on language to say what language cannot say:

> Thomas is concerned to *show* what we cannot use our language to *say*, yet there is no medium of exposition available other than language itself.... He is reminding us of certain grammatical features of our discourse to make us aware of how we might use those features to show what something which transcended that discourse would be like.[27]

Thus in the process of recognizing that there is a superfluity to language which language cannot encompass, Thomas wants to say that that very superfluity makes it possible to speak meaningfully of God. Language has a mysterious capacity to encode within itself a mystery beyond what it can grasp—a mystery that is to do with a desire for love beyond any love we discover within the world—and this is why we discover Thomas's God no less than Lacan's real by focusing on the dynamics of language and desire. Beyond the familiarity of language, there is a linguistic otherness that dispossesses language of its claims to know. In order to consider in more detail what this means for theological language, I want to consider Thomas's discussion of relationships within the Trinity in the *Summa theologiae*.[28]

In questions 2–26 of Part I of the *Summa theologiae*, Thomas discusses God in the context of the divine unity—the God of creation as revealed in the Old

---

[25] ST I, 93, 7.
[26] David B. Burrell, *Aquinas: God and Action* (Chicago IL: University of Scranton Press, 2008), p. 9.
[27] Burrell, *Aquinas: God and Action*, pp. 6–7.
[28] For the treatise on the Holy Trinity, see ST I, 27–43. There is a vast literature on the doctrine of the Trinity from every possible theological angle. The discussion that follows is a brief and therefore necessarily limited reading of a section of the *Summa theologiae* that has in itself been repeatedly commented upon and analysed.

Testament, and as discernible up to a point by natural reason through reflecting on causal relationships within creation.[29] He then circles back on himself in questions 27–43 to revisit the question of God from the perspective of the Trinity—the God of redemption as revealed in the New Testament and affirmed by Christian doctrine. Again, we might note here the chiastic structure of the *Summa theologiae* in its parts as well as in its whole, but we should also note an implicit suggestion that one can only approach the question of the ineffable by a shift in the order of language which also ruptures its claim to comprehension.

We can talk about the one God in metaphors and arguments appropriate to what we understand by unity, but then we must talk again about the three-in-one God in a way that requires the juxtaposition of a different set of metaphors and arguments. It is in this very shift and the conceptual confusion it creates, that we become conscious of the impossibility of what we are trying to understand. At least, that's the suggestion I'd like to pursue for now. Later, I too am going to circle back on myself, to suggest that Thomas's attempt to reconcile the divine unity of the creator God of the Hebrew scriptures with the Aristotelian prime mover and final cause, and then with the trinitarian God of Christian theology, is rather more contradictory and problematic than some of his recent interpreters are willing to acknowledge.

The doctrine of the Trinity, we could say, is discovered neither in the first discussion on the divine unity nor in the discussion that follows on the three persons, but in the gap between the two which logic refuses to bridge. To quote Karen Kilby, in his treatment of the Trinity in the *Summa theologiae*, 'Thomas serenely presents us with something that we can make nothing of, and that he does not expect us to',[30] and he does this by 'simultaneously displaying the grammar, the pattern of speech about the Trinity, and displaying it as beyond our comprehension'.[31] In Kilby's reading, Thomas intentionally introduces a series of 'theological dead-ends'[32] into his argument, to confound our attempt to make sense of what he is saying.

Thomas argues that the human capacity to speak of God as a relational unity of three distinct persons must come from revelation, because it could not be discerned through reflection on creation.[33] This is because the creator God is all three persons of the Trinity, so that creation participates in the trinitarian life of its creator but in such a way that the rational mind cannot distinguish between the persons. So while creation yields up awareness of the existence of God, it cannot possibly offer an insight into the trinitarian life of God, and nor

---

[29] Cf. ST I, 32, 1.
[30] Kilby, 'Aquinas, the Trinity and the Limits of Understanding', p. 418.
[31] Kilby, 'Aquinas, the Trinity and the Limits of Understanding', p. 423.
[32] Kilby, 'Aquinas, the Trinity and the Limits of Understanding', p. 414.
[33] See ST I, 32, 1.

can the created mind comprehend the Trinity. But why then, asks Thomas, do we know about the Trinity at all, albeit in a way that falls short of what counts as knowledge in scientific terms? The answer is first that it enables us to have 'the right idea of creation', but more importantly, that we must know about salvation, and this requires knowing the Incarnate Son being made flesh and the giving of the Holy Spirit.[34]

Thomas opens his exploration of the trinitarian mystery with a delicate gambit, and here we must simply accept the impossible task which he sets himself. In searching for a language within which to express himself, he alights upon language itself as it functions within the human intellect—that aspect of being human that corresponds most closely to the image of God. So, even while he must maintain an absolute distinction between the inner life of God and the natural understanding of the human soul, Thomas must also in a sense make God in the image of the soul, if the human is to speak about God. God is both like and not like us, and therefore even the most subtle linguistic analogy is too fragile to bear any weight. We shall see later that this analogy necessarily tends towards mysticism, for if the God whose essence is hidden from us is in some sense analogous to our way of being in, knowing, and loving the world, then the essence of our own being is also paradoxically more hidden from us, the closer we come to the divine mystery.

Following Augustine, Thomas argues that it is in the soul that the human most approximates to the Trinity, particularly in our intellectual capacity to form concepts and use language through the threefold interactions of intellect, knowledge, and love: 'the image of the Trinity is to be found in the acts of the soul, that is, inasmuch as from the knowledge which we possess, by actual thought we form an internal word; and thence break forth into love.'[35] What does this mean? We must enter the circularity of Thomas's argument, not in order to understand more, but in order to understand more clearly what it is that we cannot understand.

Thomas argues that, while we have no quantitative or qualitative words that meaningfully signify God, we can speak of God in terms of processions and relations of origin.[36] The immediate problem is that procession implies an outward movement from one to another, and the supreme simplicity of God precludes this. When we speak of procession we refer to some movement of or change in a body or bodies in time and space—a procession marches through a street; processed food refers to food that has been through a series of material changes from one condition to another—and this cannot be said of the inner life of God. Nevertheless, Thomas suggests that if we reflect on how the human intellect functions, we realize that understanding is a process internal to the mind, by way of which our intellectual understanding proceeds from our knowledge of

---

[34] ST I, 32, 1.   [35] ST I, 93, 7.   [36] ST I, 27, 1.

an object. We express this knowledge through the spoken word—to conceptualize is to name something in order to speak meaningfully about it—but
because for Thomas knowledge and love go hand in hand, the conception is
'the word of the heart signified by the word of the voice'.[37] In other words,
when we know something truthfully we love and desire it, because it communicates to us something of the divine light, and our speaking about it flows
from the love we feel for it. If the Word of God (Christ) can be spoken about
(but not understood) in terms of the relationship between knowing and
speaking, the Spirit of God can be spoken about (but not understood) in
terms of the relationship between knowing and loving. So Thomas writes:

> The will acts not by taking in a likeness of what it wills, but by inclining towards
> the thing willed itself. What issues in willing therefore is not a likeness but more
> an impulse and urge towards something; and what issues in the way of love in
> God is not a begotten son, but rather a spirit. This word [the Latin for *breath* or
> *wind*] names some urge or impulse of life, such as a lover feels when impelled or
> moved to do something.[38]

Because for Thomas, true knowledge always translates into love—to know
something truly is to love it—God's being is expressed within the unity of
knowledge and love. The knowledge and love of God—the mind and the will
of God—are identical,[39] but they are distinguished in a way analogous to the
human difference between knowing and loving. We know something when
we form a concept that enables us to speak truthfully about it, but we love
something when knowledge and desire experience a mutual transformation in
the context of willing, so that the interiority of the concept becomes the
interiority of the beloved other within ourselves, and desire directs our will
towards that beloved other in our bodily activities.

This metaphor falls short because, even if language proceeds from conceptual
understanding, there still remains a difference between the intellect, the word,
and the object of conception. In order to be human, we must experience the
process of separation and differentiation that language entails which enables
us to give meaning to the world within the spirit/body duality that we are.
We should note the Lacanian echoes here—the human condition entails
separation, and language is only possible because there are gaps between
and among beings. But in God, suggests Thomas, there is no such separation.
By collapsing the linguistic gap, Thomas also creates a density within which
meaning itself collapses. Language in God enacts the being of God and the
doing of God, so that there is no possible distinction between the Word of

---

[37] ST I, 27, 1.

[38] ST I, 27, 4. Timothy McDermott (ed.), *Summa Theologiae: A Concise Translation* (London:
Methuen, 1992), p. 66.

[39] ST I, 27, 3. McDermott (ed.), *Summa Theologiae*, p. 66.

God, the love of God, and the being of God, but as soon as we ourselves use language to attempt to express that, we have attributed difference, distance, and change to God, through the imposition of our time- and space-bound concepts. So, although to speak meaningfully of three persons in God involves speaking of processions, we cannot meaningfully speak of processions within God.

Thomas concludes that, although everything we can say about God falls short, the closest we might come is to talk in terms of relations within God: 'relations exist in God really; . . . in relations alone is found something which is only in the apprehension and not in reality'.[40] While every other relationship implies a separation between one body or concept and another—and therefore a procession from one to another—in God there is no difference between the being of God and relationships within God. The names that pertain to the persons of the Trinity therefore designate, not substantial differences, but differences in their relational positioning by and for one another. Yet whereas in creatures, there is more to us than our relationships so that relational language does not communicate all that we are—it is one among several characteristics of created beings—in God reality is all in all, and this reality is essentially, and without remainder (for what could such remainder possibly be?), relational. The being of God is the knowing of God is the loving of God is the doing of God, and this being love as expressing love as doing love constitutes the inner relational life of the persons of the Trinity. Fergus Kerr, citing Robert W. Jenson's work on Thomas, observes that for Jenson, Thomas's God is 'an event, an exchange, a conversation, finally . . . "a great fugue"'.[41] Although such analogies might go further than Thomas, our greater awareness of 'the importance of language and of music'[42] enables us to use them in a way that Thomas might not have done.

The divine simplicity means that these dynamic relations are all one God, but the language of relationality implied by Father, Son, and Spirit—the naming of the persons of God and the ways in which those names designate the relationships among them—offers some distant possibility of talking about what we cannot comprehend. Nevertheless, this is a venture that must be undertaken with the utmost humility, not in order to prove that we know what we are talking about, but to demonstrate the possibility of believing as we (Christians) do: 'we must not attempt to prove what is of faith, except by authority alone, to those who receive the authority; while as regards others it suffices to prove that what faith teaches is not impossible'.[43]

---

[40] ST I, 28, 1.
[41] Fergus Kerr, *After Aquinas: Versions of Thomism* (Malden MA and Oxford: Blackwell Publishers, 2002), p. 205, citing Robert W. Jenson, *Systematic Theology, Vol. 1, The Triune God* (Oxford: Oxford University Press, 1997).
[42] Kerr, *After Aquinas*, p. 205. [43] ST I, 32, 1.

It is in exploring the generation of love and the formation of relationships within the Trinity that Thomas opens up an altogether different theological vista from that which appears in his patriarchal understanding of the fatherhood of God derived from Aristotelian philosophy, which we shall explore in more detail later. In his maternal relational Trinity we encounter the most fruitful area for taking Thomas's theology beyond the constraints of his own medieval context and possibly his own psychological inhibitions, to a more lavish incarnational vision that remains faithful to all the essentials of his theology while resisting the more repressive and body-denying instincts with it.

THE MATERNAL TRINITY

If we cannot speak about processions in God without risk of distortion, Thomas asks if we might speak of generation in God, analogous to the ways in which living species procreate or things come into existence from non-existence.[44] Is the Word in relation to the Father in some way like/not like the concept in relation to the mind, which is like/not like the child in relation to the mother who conceives it?

Knowledge, for Thomas, entails forming concepts—conceiving words—within ourselves, which we then express in speech. Analogously, a species reproduces itself when a living being gives birth to one of its own kind, so we can say that it conceives within itself its own likeness, which it then externalizes. In the process of intellectual reflection, we internalize the forms of the objects that we experience through our senses, and in the process of speaking we externalize that understanding in our communication with others. If our knowledge were perfect, then there would be no distinction between the activity of knowing, the one who knows, and that which is known. The knower, the concept, and the object would be one perfect unity.

Thomas's analogy here can bear very little weight, for he is clearly straining to find appropriate metaphors, perhaps partly at least in the face of his own resistance to associating God with motherhood. Nevertheless, there is something about the relationship of God to the Word (Christ), which is distantly imaged in maternal analogies. If the use of language to express a concept can be likened to the relationship of a mother conceiving and giving birth to her offspring, this allows Thomas to say that 'We call the emitting of this word in God *begetting* or *birth*. . . . [T]his emitting is in God a begetting and the word emitted is a Son.'[45] This is not a conception in time since the Word is always with the Father, but the relationship between God the Father and God the Son

---

[44] ST I, 27, 2.   [45] ST I, 27, 2. McDermott (ed.), *Summa Theologiae*, p. 65.

is like (and also unlike) the relationship between the mind of the knower, the formation of a concept (a word) and its communication in language, and this in turn is like (but also unlike) the relationship between the mother of a species and the young of the same species which she conceives within herself and to which she gives birth.

Thomas gathers all these trinitarian analogies into a reflection that over-flows all philosophical boundaries to suggest the saturation of language with the divine love of the Trinity. Here we see him venturing into the very being of God, far beyond his own limits with regard to what language can say or humans can comprehend, and therefore we are moving away from Thomas as philosopher towards Thomas as mystical theologian.

Thomas is concerned with justifying why the Holy Spirit is said to proceed from the Father and the Son, rather than just from the Father. He begins by pointing out that 'There is no proper name for the coming forth of a love in God, nor for the relationships and person involved.'[46] So there is an acute sense in this section of Thomas's caution with regard to the language he must nevertheless use to say the unsayable. Bearing this in mind, he seeks to elucidate the question of trinitarian procession in terms of the linguistic relationship between knowledge and love, so that the inner life of the Trinity reveals itself in the form of grammar—the relationships that words have to one another and the meaning they derive from those relationships. In McDermott's lyrical translation,

> to love is to breathe out a love, just as to say is to produce a word, and to bloom is to produce a flower. And as the tree blooms in its flowers, so the Father says himself and his creatures in his Word or Son, and Father and Son love both themselves and us in the Holy Spirit, the love coming forth in them. The Father loves not only the Son but himself and us in the Holy Spirit, because the Holy Spirit comes forth as a love of the primal goodness with which God loves himself and all his creatures.[47]

Within the Trinity then, Thomas describes relationships of perfect mutuality in a continuous and eternal communication of love given and received among the three in a way that extends to the whole of creation. Each generates the other's meaning in terms of non-identical but mutually dependent relation-ships. The Father is only the Father in relation to the Son who is the Word of God in person, and the Spirit who proceeds from the Father and the Son is the love of the one for the other in the person of the third.

---

[46] ST I, 36, 1. McDermott, *Summa Theologiae*, p. 36. See also ST I, 27, 4.
[47] ST I, 37, 2. McDermott, *Summa Theologiae*, p. 75. See also the discussion in SCG IV, 11, in which Thomas adopts maternal language to describe the relationship between God and the Word: 'Therefore, the Word of God is truly begotten by God speaking the Word; and His proceeding can be called "generation" or "birth".' I discuss these themes in more detail later.

Discussing such linguistic analogies, Janet Martin Soskice points out that '"father" is a semantically dependent title—it is because there is a child that someone is called a father. It is, in the *technical* sense, a *relational term*. The advent of the child "gives birth" to the father.'[48] So, suggests Soskice, 'the Father *is* Father in virtue of the Son—because it is the child who "makes" someone a father'.[49] We might in this context consider a similar suggestion in Alice Meynell's poem, 'Maternity':

> One wept whose only child was dead,
> New-born, ten years ago.
> 'Weep not; he is in bliss,' they said.
> She answered, 'Even so,
>
> 'Ten years ago was born in pain
> A child, not now forlorn.
> But oh, ten years ago, in vain,
> A mother, a mother was born.'[50]

Thinking on the very edges of the thinkable, let me suggest that these linguistic, relational analogies have profound resonances with Lacan's understanding of how language functions. Soskice points out that the sense in which relation is used in terms of the Trinity is 'a *formal one*'.[51] It is to do with the semantics of how names derive their meanings in relation to other names. The persons of the Trinity are thus related to one another in the way that signifiers are related to one another in the linguistic order. Language functions—at least according to postmodern theory—not because of any necessary relationship between words and that to which they refer, but because of the dynamic relationality in difference between signifiers in chains of signification. In other words, this too is a question of form—the form that language has, internal to itself, makes it meaningful, rather than its referential capacity. So, in speaking of God, we cannot speak of the Father except insofar as we refer to the Son and the Spirit, nor can we speak of the Son except insofar as we refer to the Father and the Spirit, nor can we speak of the Spirit except insofar as we refer to the Father and the Son. It is relationality, not identity nor referentiality, which allows us to speak of the mystery of the Trinity.

If, as thinkers from Heidegger onwards have argued, we 'inhabit the house of language' to such an extent that 'we don't speak language, language speaks us', then we are very close to being able to say that, in postmodernity, language has taken the place of the Trinity of medieval theology. Beings participate in language, but language does not participate in beings except insofar as it

---

[48] Janet Martin Soskice, 'Trinity and the "Feminine Other"', in *The Kindness of God: Metaphor, Gender, and Religious Language* (Oxford: Oxford University Press, 2007), p. 117.

[49] Soskice, 'Trinity and the "Feminine Other"', p. 117.

[50] Alice Meynell, 'Maternity', in *Collected Poems of Alice Meynell* (New York: Charles Scribner's Sons, 1913), p. 51.

[51] Soskice, 'Trinity and the "Feminine Other"', p. 120

speaks us into being and holds us within the human world, while its original source of authority and meaning eludes us. As Lacan and Thomas insist, we are material beings for whom bodies and/or God/the real provide a mysterious point of resistance to language. There is 'something' outside of language, which frustrates the linguistic desire to say what we mean and mean what we say, and therefore there is more to us than we can say.

Complex questions flow from hypotheses about language and meaning explored in this chapter. In particular, I want to return later to Thomas's insistence that, while creation participates in God, God does not participate in creation. This, I shall suggest later, prepares the way for the more radical forms of dualism that open up beyond Thomas, first in the theologians of the Reformation and then in the philosophers of the Enlightenment, ultimately leading to the denial of all significance to bodiliness and nature in the linguistic theories of postmodernism. We must explore other theological possibilities by re-opening questions about the relationship between form and matter, body and God, male and female, in the construction of meaning, in order to ask if a more thorough-going incarnationalism would entail a more radical deconstruction of the dualities and dualisms that Thomas inherits from Greek philosophy, which might have paved the way for a less conflicted and oppositional intellectual culture than that which modernity inherits from its Greek and medieval forebears.

For now, however, from a Lacanian perspective there is an important point to note with regard to the difference between the grammar of the Trinity and a postmodern approach to language, and that is to do with questions of lack and desire. There is no frustration or thwarting of purpose within Thomas's God. God is a Trinity of inter-personal relationships—an eternal conversation or fugue—within which words express and enact their meanings with a perfect immediacy, sufficiency, and delight of one to another, creating and giving meaning to all that is with a plenitude that never incorporates any createdness or meaning back from that process, but rather expresses and re-gathers all that is within the overflowing abundance of creative love.

Thomas's God neither desires nor needs creation, and if the Trinity is best expressed in relational and maternal analogies, these cannot avoid the lack which thwarts their referential function and makes all such analogies fail before the abysmal plenitude of the divine being. The closest we could possibly come to knowing God would be if object, word, and desire coalesced in such perfect oneness that all desire was silenced in the joy of being with, for, in, and as the other. This, for Lacan, is what we desire beyond all else—the (m)Other in whom self and other enjoy bliss without differentiation or otherness, and it is for Thomas what we long for when we long for union with God—a God who awakens a mysterious sense of maternal relationality beyond the paternal singularity of Thomas's philosophical God, which we must explore in more detail.

In this chapter, I have tried—and necessarily failed—to introduce Thomas's understanding of God in relation to language and in engagement with Lacan. I want to turn now to the question of knowledge, love, and desire, in order to consider another aspect of Thomas's thought which has profound resonances with that of Lacan.

4

Desiring God in the World

The last chapter touched on how the human can know God deductively, by way of revelation, and on the problems this poses for theological language. We have seen that Thomas Aquinas uses human knowing, speaking, and loving as an analogy to speak of the inner life of the Trinity—albeit without taking us any further towards understanding what he is talking about. In this chapter, I focus on the ways in which Thomas understands desire in the context of knowing God and knowing the world.

Thomas addresses questions of human knowing and acting in all three parts of the *Summa theologiae*, in the context of creation (Part I), living in the world (Part II), and the sacramental life (Part III). In what follows I am primarily concerned with ST I 75–89, in which he discusses the human in the context of creation, culminating in the creation of humankind in the Book of Genesis. My main focus in this chapter is Thomas's account of desire, but I situate this in the context of a brief summary of his more general epistemology.

RATIONAL ANIMALS

In following Aristotle rather than Plato, Thomas argues that the soul is the form of the body,[1] so that the human exists in the interdependent duality of body and soul.[2] Thomas would agree with Darwin (and against the Enlightenment concept of the man of reason), that we are an animal species which shares most of its characteristics with other animals. Robert Pasnau argues that, according to Thomas, 'Of the human soul's various capacities, only two—intellect and will—distinguish us as human.'[3] While every living being has a soul (*anima*), the human soul has an intellectual capacity that allows it to go

---

[1] Cf. ST I, 76, 1.   [2] Cf. ST I, 75.

[3] Robert Pasnau, *Thomas Aquinas on Human Nature: A Philosophical Study of* Summa Theologiae *Ia 75–89* (Cambridge: Cambridge University Press, 2002), p. 200.

beyond sensory intuitions and perceptions to conceptual and rational thinking. Thomas calls our species a 'mortal rational animal'.[4]

This means that human knowing has to navigate a complex path between the animality of our species with its senses, needs, and appetites, and the rationality, freedom, and creativity of our intellects with their capacity to evaluate and discriminate, in order to shape the ethos that informs our way of being in the world. This makes the human unique in creation. Unlike angels, humans are embodied souls, as are all other living bodies (in inanimate objects, the soul or form remains entirely disconnected from the body). However, unlike the souls which animate animals and plants, the human soul is subsistent—it is incorruptible and it can survive independently of the body. In all other embodied species, the soul perishes with the body—a suggestion that we must return to later when we consider creation in the context of the environmental crisis.

As a relevant aside, we might note that the doctrine of the resurrection of the body introduces a knotty problem into Thomas's Aristotelianism. Thomas rejected Muslim philosopher Averroes' interpretation of Aristotle which posited a single universal consciousness, insisting instead upon the individuality of the soul.[5] There is much debate about what Aristotle means by the soul, but whether individual or cosmic, in Aristotle's philosophy all parts of the soul except the intellect are dependent on the body and cannot survive without it.[6] Only the intellect—whether universal or individual—is immortal and not subject to corruption. Thomas attempts some accommodation of this idea by specifying that 'this principle by which we primarily understand, whether it be called the intellect or the intellectual soul, is the form of the body'.[7] However, this leaves him with the problem that the human vocation to eternity includes the body, and therefore one cannot reduce the essence of the human to the disembodied intellect. He points out that 'To be united to the body belongs to the soul by reason of itself',[8] and he also insists that 'since the soul is united to the body as its form, it must necessarily be in the whole body, and in each part thereof'.[9] This interdependent duality of body and soul means that, in the interim between death and the resurrection of the body, the soul does not encompass the full human essence, for it has 'a natural inclination to be united to the body'.[10] So Thomas argues that, between death and resurrection, the soul is endowed by God with a natural capacity for knowledge because it is deprived of the senses upon which it depends, although this does not amount to immediate knowledge of God such as the angels have. We

---

[4] Cf. ST I-II, 2, 5.   [5] See ST I, 76.

[6] See Aristotle, 'On the Soul', in Jonathan Barnes (ed.), *The Complete Works of Aristotle: The Revised Oxford Translation, Vol. 1* (Princeton NJ and Chichester UK: Princeton University Press, 1995), pp. 641–92.

[7] ST I, 76, 1.   [8] ST I, 76, 1.   [9] ST I, 76, 8.   [10] ST I, 76, 1.

could say it is a kind of life-support system for the soul until it is reunited with the body.[11]

I mention this here because, like Thomas's reflections on angels, it gives us a sense of the problems he is grappling with in his attempt to synthesize Aristotelian philosophy with Christian doctrine in relation to the spirit/body dilemma. Like his attempt to express the inner life of God, there is a point at which we must accept that we simply do not understand our own nature enough to know what it means to believe in the resurrection of the dead and life everlasting.[12] However, Thomas's struggle to reconcile the ambiguity of the Aristotelian soul with the unity of the individual body/soul of Christian doctrine can be interpreted as a distant precursor to the challenge faced by psychoanalysis in exposing the inner fragmentation of the psyche to the reluctant gaze of the Cartesian self. Like Freud and his successors, Thomas must find a way to account for the plurality of the soul's powers and functions, some of which are mysterious to us, without dissolving human identity. We must bear this caveat in mind when we discuss Aristotle's influence on Thomas.

Like Jacques Lacan, Thomas positions the emergent self at the interface between consciousness and materiality. His Aristotelianism leads him to reject any Platonic separation between forms and material objects—there is no essential soul that exists independently of the body's contingencies and limitations. The soul comes into being as a *tabula rasa*[13] when the matter of the body realizes its human form (not at conception, but when the foetus becomes recognizably human).[14] Moreover, Thomas understands the soul as cumulative in both its development and its operation. The three types of soul—vegetative or nutritive, sensory, and rational—pertain to different species, to different stages of human development, and to different functions of the mature soul.[15] So the vegetative soul is the animating power of plant life, and it is active in the animation of bodily organs in their biological functions such as digestion and, to a certain extent, reproduction. As we shall see, this can be interpreted in terms of the Lacanian real, for it relates to the physical drives and their impact upon the soul. The sensory soul we have in common with other animals that have sense organs and mobility, and it is related to our appetites, desires, and movements associated with our sensory experiences. This would be analogous to the Lacanian imaginary. This is also the earliest form of the human embryo. The rational capacity of the soul is unique to the human, and this is concerned with our capacity for conceptualization and discerning the truth of the world by drawing on our experiences, memories, and desires. In Lacanian terms, this is analogous to the symbolic.

---

[11] See ST I, 89. [12] Cf. Pasnau, *Thomas Aquinas*, p. 152.
[13] Cf. ST I, 79, 2. [14] ST I, 76, 3. See also ST I, 118, 2. [15] Cf. ST I, 76, 1.

All this means that 'The human mind is only potentially a mind'.[16] It has no innate knowledge, for its potential is only realized when the intellect actively engages with our experiences and impressions of the world in order to translate them into concepts that inform our understanding. So, says Thomas, 'the intellect knows itself not by its essence, but by its act'.[17] The mature soul, endowed with reason, intellect, and desire as well as with appetites and sensory perceptions, is continuously filtering its experiences and activities through several levels of consciousness, in order to motivate the body in the world as an expression of the soul's desire.

This involves a dynamic continuum of the different powers within the soul. We absorb impressions of material objects through our senses and these give rise to phantasms within the imagination, during which process the intellect is passive and receptive in relation to the objects of perception. The work of the agent or active intellect entails the abstraction of concepts and the derivation of universal principles from these experiences and phantasms through the use of reason. In the higher states of wisdom associated with revelation rather than reason, the intellect once again becomes passive and receptive in order to understand [*intellegere*], which is, says Thomas, the same as 'reading inwardly' [*intus legere*].[18] Comparing the relationship of reasoning to understanding, he says that 'Reasoning relates to understanding as journeying to rest'.[19] In understanding, the divine light illuminates all that the soul has discovered in a way that reveals the inner truth, beauty, and goodness of the creator within creation.

The pervasive significance of contemplation on the things of God as revealed in the things of the world is fundamental to any appreciation of Thomas's epistemology, and it means recognizing that his philosophy begins and ends in theology, expressed in the loving creativity of God and in the loving response of the creature. As we shall see, in the contemplative life the individual withdraws from the activities of the world in order to remain in this highest state of being at rest in wisdom. However, in the active life, the will, informed by wisdom, transforms knowledge of the truth into intentional activity in the world through disciplining and directing desire towards the goodness of God within the materiality of the world and human relationships. In Aristotelian terms, this is the *askesis* or disciplined practice that constitutes the virtuous life.

So, we inhabit a world of diversity, particularity, and plurality, and from our bodily experiences we are able to arrive at universal truths and concepts by way of an intellectual process of combination, abstraction, imagination, and

---

[16] ST I, 87, 1. Timothy McDermott (ed.), *Summa Theologiae: A Concise Translation* (London: Methuen, 1992), p. 139.

[17] ST I, 87, 1.   [18] ST II-II, 8,1.

[19] ST I, 79, 8. McDermott (ed.), *Summa Theologiae*, p. 123.

categorization. It is the work of reason to sift and process our initial impressions, forming concepts of actual and possible forms of existence through abstraction and the imaginative combination of features and characteristics. For example, I can imagine a unicorn which does not exist because I can combine various features of animals that do exist. (If we bear in mind the colourful imaginative forms of medieval culture with its art and architecture, its glorious illuminations and celestial visions, and its bestiaries, gargoyles, and nightmares of hell, we can see that this process in no way limits the possibilities of the human imagination.) Reason delivers to the graced intellect the formal concepts it needs to understand the truth or the essence of the things of the world in terms of their relatedness to God, whose trinitarian being informs all life forms.[20]

KNOWLEDGE, TRUTH, AND LOVE

Although knowledge, truth, and love are ultimately the same because they issue from the perfect simplicity of doing in being that is God, in the human they are the product of different mental faculties. This is because 'love presupposes knowledge'.[21] In order to attain to the pleasure and enjoyment that we desire we must love God in the things of the world, but in order to love we must know the truth of their being in the world. So the intellect is concerned with what is true, and the will is concerned with what is good. Knowing takes in, and love goes out,[22] so that our knowing of the world directs our way of being in the world. But, argues Thomas, 'the will is bound to follow reason, right or wrong. For reason presents its judgment as true and as issuing from God, the author of all truth.'[23] In other words, we might will what is objectively bad because faulty reasoning or ignorance makes us believe it to be good, but Thomas is ambivalent as to how far we can will what we know to be wrong. We shall come back to this question later.

The soul thus develops through the body's being in the world, and the eternal soul bears the shape and identity of our existential, finite experience of material existence. For Thomas, as for other thinkers of his time, the individual is derivative rather than originary. We become who we are, not by a process of interiority moving outwards as in Descartes' *Meditation*, but through the assimilation of external stimuli, experiences, and relationships into our consciousness by way of exposure, reflection, analysis, and action. Explaining Aristotle's influence on Thomas, Fergus Kerr writes that

---

[20] Cf. ST I, 45.
[22] See ST I, 60, 2.
[21] ST I, II, 3, 4. McDermott (ed.), *Summa Theologiae*, p. 177.
[23] ST I, II, 19, 5. McDermott (ed.), *Summa Theologiae*, p. 197.

> Our sense of the intelligibility of the world is not, for Aristotle or for Thomas, a projection of mind onto nature, as it seems to many philosophers and others nowadays. To the contrary, Aristotle's world is a projection of intelligible, teleologically ordered nature onto the human mind.[24]

We emerge into self-consciousness as we come to know the world, rather than being the centre from which our consciousness of the world emanates. So, argues Thomas, 'the human mind primarily understands not itself but external material things; secondarily its own act of understanding such things; and finally itself, the power of understanding realized in that act'.[25] The intellect realizes its potential gradually as we absorb the world through our senses and seek to understand its meaning, its purpose, and its truth, and in that process to discover the truth of our own being. However, there remains at the heart of this process an impenetrable mystery which is impervious to thought, no matter how much we experience and how much we conceptualize.

This means that Thomas, like Lacan, positions human consciousness in a space of radical ambiguity, despite the different meanings they give to that ambiguity. On the one hand, the 'I' is formed in me by language, culture, and society, and my identity emerges as a filtering of the inchoate drives and appetites of the young human animal through a linguistic grid of meanings and relationships in my material interactions with the world of objects. On the other hand, as a human animal I have a unique capacity for freedom which allows me to act contrary to my animal instincts and my social conditioning, for better or worse.

For Thomas, that freedom comes from belonging to a species that is made in the image of God, called to a unique relationship with God, and therefore responsible for our being in the world in a way that pertains to no other bodily creature. This is not an absolute freedom of the individual such as that posited by modern concepts of autonomy, for it is a freedom rooted in the dependence of our being on the being of God and subject to the creaturely constraints of the human condition. Yet relative to other forms of animal life, it is a freedom that enables us to shape our characters and to accept responsibility for ourselves so that the final arbiter is no human relationship, law, or society, but the dictates of personal conscience before God, informed by revelation and reason, and directed by desire for union with God.[26]

For Lacan, these coordinates no longer shape our modern understanding of freedom, but the result has not been greater freedom but more subtle and pervasive forms of oppression. Desire, evacuated of its divine *telos*, has been colonized by the laws and masked powers of the state and the symbolic order, so that the rediscovery of freedom entails the liberation of desire. We must

---

[24] Fergus Kerr, *Thomas Aquinas: A Very Short Introduction* (Oxford: Oxford University Press, 2009), p. 28.

[25] ST I, 87, 3. McDermott (ed.), *Summa Theologiae*, p. 140.

[26] See ST I, 79, 13; ST I-II, 19, 5.

come back to the questions this raises, but that is the context in which I explore Thomas's understanding of desire in the context of the human condition.

DESIRE IN TRANSLATION

Describing Lacan's relevance for theology, Edith Wyschogrod writes that

> It is . . . to Lacan's break with standard discourse that theologians turn to see what there is in Lacan's treatment of desire, absence, and lack, of the Other and most particularly of the reading of psychological life in terms of its linguistic character, that interests and provokes. No longer can psychoanalysis merely declare God a projection in order reductively to dismiss the necessity of further interpretation. Instead the open-ended inquiry into the unconscious dimensions of the sacred and of the self offers itself as an infinite theological task. The theologian, in this sense like the psychoanalyst, stands before the bubbling up of desire and its transposition into language.[27]

If we are to explore the proximity of Lacan to Thomas in his account of desire, we have to address certain difficulties in translation. Lacanian desire encompasses our relationship to all the animate and inanimate objects among which we find ourselves in the world, so that we need a broad understanding of the role of desire in the formation of the subject. If one turns to translations of and commentaries upon Thomas's writings, one will search in vain for the word 'desire' in most indices. However, for a post-Lacanian reading of Thomas, there is some justification for using the word 'desire' to translate a number of Latin terms such as *'appetitus'* (appetite) and *'voluntas'* (will) which, although not strictly synonymous with the Latin *'desiderium'*, can be included within the more expansive Lacanian sense of desire. There are also parallels between *appetitus* and Lacan's understanding of the drives in his later work, but we shall come back to that.

Although for Thomas the intellect, the will, reason, the appetites, and desire have subtly different roles to play in the acquisition of knowledge and wisdom, in forming the habit of virtue and in the translation of these into action, the human intellect participates in the divine intellect in such a way that knowing and loving become inseparable, because our way of being in and knowing the world is analogous to God's way of being in the Trinity, as we have seen. This means that desire for God suffuses every encounter, experience, and relationship with mystery, so that to approach the human as the *res desiderans* of

---

[27] Edith Wyschogrod, 'Re-Marks', in Edith Wyschogrod, David Crownfield, and Carl A. Raschke (eds), *Lacan and Theological Discourse* (Albany NY: State University of New York Press, 1989), p. x.

Lacanian theory may be closer to Thomist anthropology than the *res cogitans* of Cartesian philosophy, even though ultimately for Thomas desiring and thinking are inseparable in the human.

To illustrate the similarities between Thomas and Lacan in their understanding of desire, we might consider Eleonore Stump's explanation of the difficulties associated with translating the word '*appetitus*':

> The basic sense of the verb '*appeto*' involves the notion of striving after, which also seems to play a part in Aquinas's account of the will. Perhaps the least unsatisfactory one-word counterpart of '*appetitus*' is 'wanting', as long as 'wanting' is not understood as implying the absence of the object of *appetitus*. On this basis we could say that for Aquinas the will is a self-directed intellectual wanting of the good, or a self-directed wanting of what is good, essentially connected with some understanding of goodness in general.[28]

Stump's caveat—that 'wanting' does not imply 'the absence of the object of *appetitus*'—underscores why Lacan's understanding of desire resonates with the sense of *appetitus*, for the difference between Thomas and Lacan revolves not around the meaning or nature of desire, but the ultimate presence or absence of its object.

The Lacanian crisis of desire arises because, contrary to the pre-modern belief in 'goodness in general', modernity's abandonment of the concept of a Sovereign Good means that there is today only a multiplicity of goods with no general agreement as to the nature of the good, and therefore no orchestration of desire around a unifying theme or *telos*. Our 'wanting of the good' has become a utilitarian wanting of goods, fuelled by consumerism and relativism, with no possibility of achieving a consensus about 'the good'.

Stump also suggests that Thomas understands the will as well as the appetites as implying a sense of 'striving after'. To appreciate the significance of this in terms of desire, we need to be aware that our modern understanding of will is dominated by a Kantian approach in which willing has more to do with control and duty abstracted from our pleasures and sensory relationships within the material world, than with materially enacted expressions of desire and happiness. As Brian Davies points out, the concept of the will was more comprehensive for Thomas than for many modern interpreters, because

> For him, human action is a matter of will inasmuch as acting people are doing what they find it desirable to do. But he also thinks that what we find desirable depends on how we view things – that is, that willing and understanding go together.... We think of what we are *attracted* to thinking of, and we are attracted to what we *think* of.... This, of course, means that, for Aquinas, there is no place for the notion of willing as something we have to do *after* we have cleared our minds and decided what it is good for us to do.... For him, our

---

[28] Eleonore Stump, *Aquinas* (London and New York: Routledge, 2003), p. 496, n. 40.

perception and wanting of what is good are of a piece. We naturally want what we take to be good.[29]

Timothy McDermott observes that

the word *will* for Aquinas does not first connote a power to dominate things but a *willingness* to be attracted by them. The fundamental activity of will is not making decisions, choosing between things, but the activity of loving, of consent to their creation.[30]

This suggestion that the will enables us to consent to the creation of others—to make space in order for other beings to be with us rather than over and against us within creation—has vast ramifications from the perspective of Lacanian ethics, and we must consider this later when we discuss the relationship between lack and love.

From these explanations we can see that for Thomas, the will is not about the control of our appetites and desires in the Kantian sense that moral duty entails sacrificing our desire for happiness—or at least, deferring it to some post-mortem horizon. For Thomas, it is not a question of control, but of insight and purpose. In all our various stages of experiencing, reasoning, reflecting, and acting, desire is the animating influence that draws us towards God through our love of the things of this world. While every creature naturally desires the good, rationality enables the human soul to desire in a more perfect way, because like God we are capable of both knowing and loving creation, and therefore our desire exceeds the natural inclination of non-rational species: 'This more perfect inclination is the soul's ability to desire. We are aware of things as perceptible or understandable, but we desire them as congenial or good.'[31] To quote Davies, 'we deliberate in the light of desire'.[32] We must bear in mind that, just as desire has a more extensive function for Thomas than it does in modern usage (apart from Lacanian interpretations), so rationality is a much richer and more inclusive concept for Thomas than what we understand by that word today. It has much more in common with the all-encompassing wisdom of our way of being in the world than with modern rationalism understood as a purely intellectual activity.

For Thomas then, all that exists arouses our desire because in the very fact of being it whispers to us of the beauty and love of the one who holds it in being. As we look beyond the material body to the love of its creator, our desire is intensified so that, knowing God more truthfully, we are motivated to act in the world more lovingly through the influence of our desire. But, because

---

[29] Brian Davies, 'Introduction', in Thomas Aquinas, *On Evil*, trans. Richard Regan (New York: Oxford University Press, 2003), p. 27. See also ST I, II, 19.

[30] McDermott (ed.), *Summa Theologiae*, p. xli.

[31] ST I, 80, 1. McDermott, *Summa Theologiae*, p. 124.

[32] Davies, 'Introduction', in Aquinas, *On Evil*, p. 29.

mind and body are a duality sharing interdependent but different states of existence, the mind cannot act directly on the body. This is why desire is so central for Thomas, because it enables our minds to guide the movement of our bodies in the world, and thus we could say that desire is the energy by way of which the processes of the mind direct the activities of the body. A post-Lacanian reading of Thomas invites the rehabilitation of desire and the restoration of happiness as the *telos* of the good life, beyond Kant but also beyond Lacan himself.

However, the pervasiveness of desire extends far beyond the human, because it is seeded within the very being of matter itself in order to prepare it for the reception of forms. Prime matter is not non-being for Thomas but lack of forms and potentiality for becoming, and this means that it is desirous of the act of being: 'Consequently, to be desirable is not its property, but to desire.'[33] Prime matter—that mysterious substrate out of which God evokes into being all that is—is lack animated by desire. We must explore this in more detail when we come to Thomas's account of creation. However, we should note at this stage that desire is inseparable from the materiality of beings. It is the dynamic energy that makes forms and matter mutually attractive to one another through the conjunction of lack and perfection, potency and act, and it is also the animating capacity of the human to translate intellectual knowledge into material activity. It moves the body to act in accordance with the intellect's understanding of the good, and in so doing it realizes the potential of our freedom to decide. Desire thus mediates between forms and matter, language and the body, connecting the one to the other in order to rend them coherent, purposeful, and unified.

We begin to see why Lacan argues that the elimination of the language of desire evacuates the space of mediation and meaning between the symbolic and the real, so that language no longer connects our consciousness to the material objects to which it refers. Thomas's world, although ordered by reason and governed by the intellect, is one in which imagination and desire play a central role in materializing language—in transforming linguistic concepts into meaningful acts. Modern rationalism seeks to purge the mind of its imaginative and desiring capacities, so that what for Thomas was in some sense horizontal, verbalized, and interdependent in the make-up of the soul, becomes more layered, separated, silenced, and repressed in the modern mind. Lacking the language of desire that flows along the spectrum between forms and matter, the symbolic and the real, we inhabit a ruptured and alienated world of disembodied power vested in linguistic forms on the one hand, and consuming lack associated with formless matter on the other. We must develop these ideas later.

---

[33] ST I, 5, 3.

PLEASURE AND DELIGHT

I want to consider two other expressions used by Thomas—pleasure [*voluptas*] and delight [*delectatio*]—in relation to the Lacanian understanding of desire and enjoyment. Thomas acknowledges that humans are easily satisfied by bodily pleasures or delights, but these are a symptom rather than a cause of happiness.[34] While we desire delight for its own sake, the delight we find in bodily pleasures is not to be confused with the happiness that the soul seeks in its desire for the good, even though our transient experiences of bodily pleasure derive in some sense from the soul's capacity for happiness. So, although experientially, desiring delight is the same as desiring good, because delight 'is nothing other than desire being at rest in the good' [*nihil est aliud quam quietatio appetitus in bono*],[35] formally there is a difference between the two.

Delight, like the good, is desired for its own sake, but the good is the object and therefore the principle which gives form to delight, 'because the reason we desire delight, is that it is being at rest in the good desired'.[36] If we translate this into the language of Lacanian psychoanalysis rather than medieval theology, we might say that enjoyment becomes possible when our desire can settle on an object in and of itself, albeit transiently, rather than continuously seeking the Other beyond in a way that negates the potential of any and every object to provide pleasure. In Lacan's later work, this entails a negotiated settlement between the insatiability of desire and the capacity for fleeting bodily enjoyment associated with the drives. Lacanian *jouissance* or enjoyment suggests a capacity for being at peace or being at rest in the object of desire in a way that brings temporary relief from the restlessness of desire, and this comes close to Thomas's account of delight.

The difference is that the Thomist subject interprets these transient delights in the context of an enduring desire for the eternal and ultimate good that is God, so that every joy participates to some extent in that eternal joy. For the Lacanian subject, the transience of enjoyment must be liberated from its captivity to a deferred plenitude, in order to accept the episodic and ephemeral nature of all pleasure, which will find its ultimate rest not in God but in death. For Thomas, the otherness that pervades all objects of desire is the desire for God. Desire only really becomes an expression of my own good when I understand its relationship to the God who created me and in whom I shall one day discover the fullness of love and knowledge beyond the horizon of death. For Lacan, the otherness that pervades all objects of desire is the horizon of death itself, beyond which there is nothing to speak of.

---

[34] Cf. ST I-II, 2, 6.   [35] ST I-II, 2, 6.   [36] ST I-II, 2, 6.

We begin to see why Lacan is a thorough-going Thomist in his account of desire. For Lacan as for Thomas, desire mediates between the animality of the body and the linguistic and conceptual capacities of the mind. For Lacan as for Thomas, desire is stimulated not by the intrinsic desirability of material objects, but by a mysterious Other that we intuit through and beyond their existence. For Lacan as for Thomas, this Other eludes our grasp and means that no object in and of itself can deliver the happiness it seems to promise. But for Thomas, the being of God provides the sustaining communicative milieu within which desire circulates and within which mind and body share with all other forms of being a common unifying source and origin. For Lacan, desire circulates around a lack without any such communicative link with its objects.

But for Lacan, the Other that we desire is also the desire of the Other. What does 'it' want of me? To paraphrase the car advertising slogan to which I referred earlier, 'God wants you to have it all.'[37] Is this a similarity or a difference between Thomas and Lacan in their understanding of the nature of desire? Let me conclude this chapter by considering that question.

THE DESIRE OF THE OTHER

If, as Lacan suggests, desire is controlled by the desire of the Other, this means that we become compliant or resistant in relation to what we perceive to be some impossible demand being made of us that we can never satisfy. For Lacan, this originates in Christianity's God, but the end of faith in God does not bring liberation, because the imperative of the desire of the Other transfers to the symbolic order and the power of the law. That is the context in which we must approach the question of desire in Thomas's theology.

It is not possible here even to begin to cover the debates that have arisen during the last half century or so considering classical theological arguments about God's omnipotence, impassibility or aseity, simplicity, and self-subsistence, but classical Christian theology has been widely criticized for its insistence that God is self-subsistent, perfect, unchangeable being and is not in any way affected by creation in its suffering and struggles. Many of these debates are couched in the language of philosophical theology,[38] or more recently from the perspectives of

---

[37] See Chapter 1, p. 33, n. 47.
[38] Cf. Jeffrey E. Brower, 'Simplicity and Aseity', in Thomas P. Flint and Michael Cannon Rea (eds), *Handbook of Philosophical Theology* (Oxford and New York: Oxford University Press, 2009), pp. 105–28; Timothy O'Connor, 'Simplicity and Creation', *Faith and Philosophy*, July 1999, pp. 405–12.

various feminist, liberationist, political, and process theologies.[39] Particularly since the genocidal horrors of the twentieth century, including the Holocaust, the classical view of God is seen as being culpably remote from and indifferent to the anguish of the human condition, a criticism that was brilliantly anticipated by the character of Ivan in Dostoyevsky's *Brothers Karamazov*.[40] My concern, however, is not with these theological debates but with the way in which Lacan might help us to understand what is at stake in terms of psychology and ethics if we abandon the idea of the divine simplicity. I must explore this in more detail later, but let me introduce the argument briefly here.[41]

For Thomas, 'a thing is good according to its desirableness'.[42] God therefore is perfectly good because God is the perfection that all things desire. In other words, we do not desire a thing because it is good, but rather it is good because it is desirable, and it is desirable because it has its being in God. In this, Thomas argues that goodness is prior even to being, for all forms of being except God: non-existence is good because it has a potential to be.[43] We must bear in mind that this is the section of the *Summa theologiae* in which Thomas is discussing the divine being, so language cannot be pushed too far before it dissolves into mystery.

However, we can see that, if God is the goodness that all desire, then what could God desire outside of God? There is neither desire nor need in God.[44] God does not desire creation but God loves creation, because creation comes into being as an expression of the divine activity of loving, which is the same as the divine act of being. So 'God is in all things',[45] and, because of the immediacy of God—for God to be is to love is to act—God 'acts immediately in all things. Hence nothing is distant from Him, as if it could be without God himself'.[46] Even demons, says Thomas, have their being in God, although they are 'deformed in their nature'.[47]

---

[39] For a very small selection of some of the most influential of these, see Paul S. Fiddes, *The Creative Suffering of God* (Oxford and New York: Oxford University Press, 2002); Daphne Hampson, *Theology and Feminism* (Oxford UK and Cambridge MA: Blackwell, 1990), pp. 151–2; Elizabeth Johnson, *She Who Is* (New York: Crossroad, 1992); Catherine M. LaCugna, *God for Us: The Trinity and Christian Life* (San Francisco: HarperSanFrancisco, 1993); Jürgen Moltmann, *The Trinity and the Kingdom: The Doctrine of God* (Philadelphia: Fortress Press, 1993); Dorothee Sölle, *Thinking About God: An Introduction to Theology* (London: SCM Press, 1990); Alfred North Whitehead, *Process and Reality: An Essay in Cosmology* (corrected edition) (New York: The Free Press, 1985). See also the discussions in Nancy Frankenberry, 'Feminist Approaches: Philosophy of Religion in Different Voices', in Pamela Sue Anderson and Beverley Clack (eds), *Feminist Philosophy of Religion: Critical Readings* (London and New York: Routledge, 2004), pp. 3–27; Cherith Fee Nordling, *Knowing and Naming the Triune God: A Conversation between Elizabeth A. Johnson and Karl Barth* (New York: Peter Lang Publishing, Inc., 2010), and Janet Martin Soskice and Diana Lipton (eds), *Feminism and Theology* (Oxford: Oxford University Press, 2003).

[40] Fyodor Dostoyevsky, *The Brothers Karamazov*, trans. Richard Pevear and Larissa Volokhonsky (London and New York: Vintage, 1992).

[41] The most relevant section of the *Summa theologiae* in what follows is ST I, 3–10.

[42] ST I, 6, 1.   [43] ST I, 4, 2.   [44] Cf. ST I, 27, 3.
[45] ST I, 8, 1.   [46] ST I, 8, 1.   [47] ST I, 8, 1.

We can see here that, according to Lacan's understanding of desire as lack, and according to Thomas's understanding of desire as the longing for God, there can be no desire in God because there is nothing outside of God that could set in motion the dynamic between love and lack. But this in no way signifies a distance between God and creation in the mind of God—such distance is a consequence of our perception, it is not a distance in God. All that is participates in God, but God does not participate in anything that is, for God is already the perfect fullness of all that is, and the perfection that all seek to enjoy.

At least in theory, Lacan helps us to understand why, far from adding to the oppressiveness of Christianity's God, this lack of desire should liberate human desire. It suggests that God neither needs nor asks anything of us other than to be fully what we are created to be. In the often-quoted words of Irenaeus, writing in the second century, 'The glory of God is a person fully alive'. This is not a desire that must reach across a distance between God and myself, but an invitation to become more fully human by exploring the extent to which my being is already fully within the being of God. I do not have to draw God to myself by arousing God's desire, but rather I have to allow myself to be drawn to God by the arousal of my own desire. If we want to understand what this means in terms of a mystical awakening that goes beyond philosophical analysis, we might consider William Harmless's poetic translation of St Augustine's famous prayer, 'Late have I loved You' from *The Confessions*:

> Late have I loved You,
> beauty so ancient,
> so new,
> late have I loved You.

> And see; You were within, inside me,
> and I was outside,
> and out there I sought You,
> and I – misshapen – chased after
> the beautiful shapes You had made.

> You were with me,
> but I was not with You.
> Beautiful things kept me far off from You –
> things which, if not in You, would not be,
> not be at all.

> You called and shouted out
> and shattered my deafness.
> You flashed, You blazed,
> and my blindness fled.
> You were fragrant, and I drew in my breath
> and panted for You.
> I tasted You, and hunger

and thirst for more.
You touched me,
and I burned for your peace.[48]

God is the peace we burn for, the fragrance we pant for, the source of all our craving, but God is already closer to us than we are to ourselves, and therefore God does not have to reach across any gap nor seek satisfaction for any lack. In Thomas's theology, there is ostensibly no desire of the Other, and therefore no anguished endeavour to establish what the Other desires of me in order that my desire can conform to its commands.

Yet even a cursory glance at the scriptural and theological tradition challenges this account of the divine aseity. The God of the Bible is a God who is intensely caught up in the struggles, desires, and hopes of history, and whose emotional life seems intimately bound up with the people of Israel and the person of Jesus Christ. In Thomas's own theology, as we shall see, the commands and laws of God form a powerful regulatory influence in human affairs, and the threat of punishment and damnation is very real. Not only that, but redemption seems to depend upon an arbitrariness in the divine will that no amount of philosophical justification can explain away, so that the more benign aspects of Thomas's theology seem to be in direct conflict with its more austere, regulative, and punitive aspects.

We shall come back to ask how Lacan can help us to address some of these issues, but I want to turn now from questions of language and desire to questions of the nature of being. As we shall see, a Lacanian approach to questions of God, nature, and gender requires some appreciation of the lingering effects of medieval ontology on the modern and postmodern soul, but this in turn entails an appreciation of the extent to which gendered Greek philosophical concepts of paternal form and maternal matter have left a profound imprint upon western thought, before and beyond its medieval contexts. So I begin the next section with a brief summary of philosophical accounts of being, in order to ask how these influenced not only Thomas's own ideas, but, more significantly, the institutionalization of Aristotle through the emergence of the universities and the hierarchical, gendered ordering of medieval society.

---

[48] Augustine, *Confessions* 10.27.38 (CCL 27:175) in William Harmless, *Augustine in His Own Words* (Washington DC: The Catholic University of America Press, 2010), pp. 33–4.

Part II

Ordering Desire

5

Greek Philosophy, Theology, and Gender

Having set out a comparative reading of Thomas Aquinas and Jacques Lacan in terms of their understanding of language, desire, and God/the real, I now want to probe more deeply into how philosophical influences shape Thomas's theology with regard to questions of gender, nature, form, and matter. These questions are necessary if we are to ask how far Lacan's psychoanalytic project can be read as an account of the postmodern disintegration of the last remnants of Thomist Aristotelianism and its formative influences upon western society.

The Aristotelian hegemony was established through the influence of the medieval universities and popularized through the preaching and teaching of the Catholic Church. Long after this medieval world view had lost its grip on western culture, the Aristotelian ordering of knowledge prevailed and indeed has become globalized through the influence of the western model of the university. The slow decline of this model may have begun with the advent of secular modernity, as attested to by Cardinal Newman's somewhat idealized vision of what the university might be in *The Idea of a University*.[1] However, its decline has accelerated since the 1960s with the rise of post-modernism, postcolonialism, feminism, and a multitude of rights-based and liberationist claims to knowledge. The disintegration of western modernity's rationalizing and universalizing metanarrative through discourses of other-ness and difference, including those of gendered and sexual differences, constitutes an epochal crisis for those generations of men and women made in the image of the dominant model of the human in western society. It is this crisis that Lacan exposes in his ludic appropriation of the voice of the Freudian unconscious.

As I seek to demonstrate in this section of the book, few issues pose as radical a challenge to Thomist philosophy and theology as the dismantling of the gendered cosmology according to which Thomas's universe/university was organized. Lacan takes us to the very heart of the traumatic confusion of

---

[1] See John Henry Newman, *The Idea of a University*, ed. Frank Turner (New Haven CT: Yale University Press, 1996).

identity and otherness that this continues to generate in the western soul. Yet I also want to argue that there are resources within Thomas's writings to construct a different account of the relationship between God and creation, to develop a more fluid epistemology capable of accommodating a postmodern approach to knowledge beyond Aristotelianism without sacrificing the quest for coherence, wisdom, and truth, and to imagine a less totalizing but more hopeful vision of the human species earthed in creation and dreaming of heaven, than that which postmodernism offers. Although postmodern inter-pretations of Thomism proliferate, there is still a repressed otherness in Thomas that awaits an outing.

PHILOSOPHICAL ORIGINS

Western philosophy might be said to originate in a conceptual shift in pre-Socratic Greek thought associated with the idea of *physis*, later translated into Latin as *natura* and subsequently into English as nature. *Physis* in Greek and *natura* in Latin signify origin, generation, or birth, and they refer to the characteristics that any particular being has as its way of existing derived from its source of origins. We have already seen how Thomas uses this as an analogy for relationships within the Trinity.

The question of *physis* had been addressed by pre-Socratic poets and thinkers on the basis of their observation of the world and their beliefs about the gods. However, it was Parmenides (fifth century BC) who raised this question in a way that would have a formative influence on the develop-ment of Greek philosophy and therefore on the history of western thought.[2] Parmenides is known to us through surviving fragments of one philosophical poem, but also because he is the subject of Plato's dialogue, *Parmenides*. Aristotle's philosophy of being in motion is primarily a response to Parmeni-des, so in Thomas's Aristotelian philosophy of being we must also be mindful of its Parmenidean influences, if we are to follow Lacan in our reading of Thomas.

In Parmenides' poem, the philosopher is transported to a vision of the goddess who addresses the nature of being. She does this not from the perspective of

---

[2] See David Gallop, *Parmenides of Elea: Fragments*, trans. David Gallop (Toronto: University of Toronto Press, 1984). The interpretation of Parmenides' account of nature and being continues to generate philosophical debate. Here I offer only a very brief summary of his ideas. For a more extensive analysis see Frederick Copleston, *A History of Philosophy, Vol. 1: Greece and Rome* (London and New York: Continuum, 2003); Patricia Curd, *Elatic Monism and Later Presocratic Thought: The Legacy of Parmenides* (Princeton NJ: Princeton University Press, 1998); Ivor Leclerc, *The Nature of Physical Existence* (London: George Allen & Unwin Ltd, 1972).

empirical observation but from the perspective of rational deduction, and this is what makes Parmenides a pioneer in the development of western philosophy. The goddess argues that something cannot come from nothing, that non-being is unthinkable and unnameable, and that therefore being must be one—eternal, motionless, timeless, and unchanging. Thinking and thought are themselves evidence of being (making Parmenides a distant precursor to Descartes), and because one cannot think the unthinkable, one cannot meaningfully posit a condition of non-being. Birth, growth, and change all imply gaps in being, as beings move from being one thing to becoming another, and there can be no such gaps. Being is therefore necessary, shackled by Fate to be whole and unchanging. All perceptions of time and motion, change and difference, diversity and particularity, are illusions, even though the truth about the singular nature of being is accessible only to very few minds. Plato's philosophy is in large measure influenced by this distinction between truth as that which transcends and is abstracted from the diversity of material beings, and illusion which fails to grasp the immateriality and perfection of the forms. To Parmenides we owe the widely debated principle that 'nature abhors a vacuum'—sometimes rendered in the Latin *horror vacui.*

Lacan suggests that this unacknowledged problem still haunts the postmodern soul. The void at the heart of language—God or the real—is not nothing and neither is it something. It is the question of infinitude that necessarily opens up whenever we approach the question of being articulated by Parmenides, so that the One of being can only be interrogated from the perspective of the Other of an infinite multiplicity: 'Where there is being, there is a requirement of infinitude'.[3] This strange co-dependence of being and infinitude—the One and the many—constitutes a formless turbulence in the Lacanian soul which emerges in the unresolved encounter between the inchoateness of bodily sensations and encounters, and the attempt to integrate these conceptually and linguistically into the singularity of the subject. Ultimately, these are questions to do with the gendering of western knowledge, but before we can ask what this means from the perspective of Lacanian Thomism, we must consider how Plato and Aristotle develop the insights of Parmenides in different ways.

Parmenides is associated with the quest among pre-Socratic philosophers for an understanding of *physis* that would provide a more constant account of reality than the flux and corruptibility of material objects. This would eventually give rise to the idea of forms and prime matter as expressed differently in the writings of Plato and Aristotle, both of whom sought to tackle the question of what must eternally be in order for anything to become. They answer in different ways that, as well as the Idea, the Form, or the Substance, there must

---

[3] Jacques Lacan, *Le Séminaire Livre XX: Encore* (Paris: Éditions du Seuil, 1975), p. 18.

be some formless condition of being within which differentiation and becoming might originate. According to Plato this is the *khora*, a mysterious maternal receptacle referred to in *Timaeus*, which I discuss in Chapter 18. In Aristotle's account it is *hyle*, a word signifying wood, woodiness, or woodlands.[4] Just as wood constitutes the material medium of all woody objects, there is a substrate of matter that connects all material beings, which is never accessible to human observation and thought except as composite objects of form and matter.

We might relate this to the probable discovery in 2012 of the elusive Higgs boson by scientists working at the Hadron Collider in the Cern laboratory in Geneva.[5] This is variously described in populist interpretations as the cosmic 'custard' or 'treacle' that came into being milli-seconds after the Big Bang—a dense field of particles that fills the universe and creates a weight or a drag on other particles and gives them mass. Only light photons are immune to this cosmic weightiness which drags particles into materiality. While nothing in this book is intended to confuse the ultimate mystery of God with the discoveries of science, nor to suggest that there is any incompatibility between this mystery and scientific discovery, descriptions of the Higgs boson make it sound very like philosophical accounts of prime matter. However, as we shall see later, the fact that modern science suggests that the universe had an origin and does not exist eternally, makes scientific theory more consistent with Judaeo-Christian accounts of creation *ex nihilo*, than with Greek philosophical accounts of the eternity of form and matter—an important point to be continued.

BEING AND BECOMING IN PLATO AND ARISTOTLE

The most significant of Aristotle's works for my purposes here are *Physics* and *Metaphysics* (a first-century compilation of selections of his works). In *Physics*, Aristotle sets out to delineate the proper subject of study for natural science by identifying the principle of nature. He argues that nature includes both form

---

[4] See Aristotle, 'Physics', Book IV, 9, in Aristotle, *The Complete Works of Aristotle: The Revised Oxford Translation, Vol. 1*, ed. Jonathan Barnes, trans. R. P. Gaye and R. K. Hardie (Princeton NJ and Chichester UK: Princeton University Press, 1995), pp. 368–9. See also Aristotle, 'Metaphysics', Book VII (Z), in *The Complete Works of Aristotle, Vol. 2*, ed. Jonathan Barnes, trans. W. D. Ross (Princeton NJ and Chichester UK: Princeton University Press, 1995), pp. 368–9, and Aristotle, 'Metaphysics', Book IX, pp. 1651–61. There is debate as to how far Aristotle's later concept of *hyle* corresponds to his understanding of primary substance in the 'Categories'—see Aristotle, 'Categories', in *The Complete Works, Vol. 1*, pp. 3–8. See also the discussion in Dennis F. Polis, 'A New Reading of Aristotle's *Hyle*', *The Modern Schoolman*, LXVIII/3 (1991), pp. 225–44.

[5] See 'Higgs boson-like particle discovery claimed at LHC' at *BBC News Science & Environment* website: <http://www.bbc.co.uk/news/world-18702455> [accessed 6 July 2012].

and matter, because the two are inseparable from the perspective of human knowing. Therefore, natural science is properly concerned with forms and matter, which cohere by way of the principle of motion so that 'Nature is a principle of motion and change'.[6] Importantly for my argument, Thomas agrees with Aristotle that the study of nature is the study of composite entities of forms and matter, and of the ways in which these two interact and change by way of motion.[7] However, Aristotle argues that it is beyond the remit of natural science to study the rational soul or the unmoved mover, because these do not conform to the order of forms and matter in motion of which nature is the principle. In *Metaphysics*, Aristotle introduces theology along with mathematics and natural science as the 'three theoretical philosophies' concerned with the eternal causes of things.[8] Theology is the highest of these, for it is concerned with 'that which can exist apart and is unmovable . . . And if there is such a kind of thing in the world, here must surely be the divine, and this must be the first and most important principle . . . the highest of existing things'.[9] This is 'a mover which moves without being moved, being eternal, substance, and actuality'.[10] This philosophical definition of theology is what Thomas regards as natural theology, which is consistent with but less comprehensive in its understanding of truth than revealed theology.

Aristotle's unmoved mover is a more dynamic concept than Plato's concept of the Good, since it is associated not with the Ideal Existent but with the Existing of Existence or the substance of being.[11] We could say, at the risk of over-simplification, that according to Plato, God made the world because God is good and therefore being is secondary to the Good,[12] whereas for Aristotle (and therefore for Thomas) God moves the world into being because God is, and therefore goodness is secondary to being. The difference is not only one of emphasis, because in Christian theology it unfolds in the form of two quite different accounts of the relationship between created beings and their creator, which has considerable significance for a Lacanian reading of Thomas.

In Platonic accounts of the nature of being, God becomes identified with the One of Form, abstracted from the materiality of the many in a way that divests the latter of any intrinsic significance. However, in Aristotelian/Thomist accounts, all beings participate in the oneness of being that is God—as we saw in

---

[6] Aristotle, 'Physics', Book III, 200b, p. 342.

[7] Thomas Aquinas, *Commentary on Aristotle's Physics*, Book I, Lecture 1 (184a9–b14), trans. Richard J. Blackwell, Richard J. Spath, and W. Edmund Thirlkel (New Haven CT: Yale University Press, 1963), html edition by Joseph Kenny OP at <http://www.dhspriory.org/thomas/Physics.htm> [accessed 6 April 2013].

[8] Aristotle, 'Metaphysics', 1026a, p. 1620; 1064a–b, p. 1681.

[9] Aristotle, 'Metaphysics', 1064a–b, p. 1681.

[10] Aristotle, 'Metaphysics', 1072a, p. 1694.

[11] See Aristotle, 'Metaphysics', Book VII (Z), pp. 1623–44.

[12] Cf. Plato, 'Timaeus', 29e–30c in *Plato: Complete Works*, edited by John M. Cooper, trans. Donald J. Zeyl (Indianapolis IN and Cambridge UK: Hackett Publishing Co., 1997), p. 1236.

Chapter 2. This means that the word 'One' functions in quite different ways in Plato and Aristotle. In Plato, the One is a numerical singularity over and against the many, whereas in Aristotle the One is the plenitude of being within which difference comes to be through lack and partiality. This is a difference that we must consider more closely in a later chapter (see Chapter 14). However, we must also bear in mind that Thomas's theology is a weaving together of at least three major influences, and this accounts for the many inconsistencies and contradictions that my own reading of the *Summa theologiae* seeks to tease out.

First, as we have seen, Thomas privileges the authority of scripture and Christian doctrine as constituting the first principles to which theology is held accountable. Next, he turns to Aristotle in an attempt to marry reason and revelation, philosophy and theology, in what might be described as an unfinished revolution in Christian thought. The third significant influence is Christian Neoplatonism, which pervades Thomas's thought as a result of his engagement with his theological predecessors. This results in considerable ambiguity, which is of fundamental significance in terms of the relationship between the God of Christian theology and the ordering of sexual relationships within Christian thought and culture. If, as Aristotle suggests, forms and matter belong within the order of nature, then the Aristotelian prime mover is a dynamic source of being beyond all forms and matter, from which the concept of the good derives. However, if God becomes equated with the One of Form, then a quite different theological scenario shades into view which is much more susceptible to the Lacanian critique of metaphysics. As we shall see, Thomas has great difficulty in keeping the two apart, so that his theology shifts between the affirmation of God as form, and the denial that God is form. With that in mind, let me return to Aristotle's account of being.

Aristotle argues with Parmenides and against the Pythagoreans and others with regard to the possibility of there being a void—a space of emptiness or source of motion other than or separate from being.[13] His main concern is to demonstrate that, if existence is primarily associated with movement from non-being to being, or from one form of being to another, then no existence could follow from the existence of the absolute void, because it has no capacity for movement or differentiation. The void is different from existence not just rationally but qualitatively, and it has no possibility of becoming anything other than what it is.

Aristotle has a more interactive and ambiguous understanding than Plato of the relationship between the universality, causality, and substance of forms and their particular manifestations, as discussed in *Metaphysics* Book VII. The main debate hinges on the question of the universality as opposed to the particularity of forms in relation to matter, and on the question as to whether

---

[13] Aristotle, 'Physics', Book IV, 8 and 9, pp. 365–9.

there is a universal intellect that persists beyond the particularity of every other form, including the human soul. Aristotle lends himself to either interpretation,[14] and in medieval debate this separated the Averroists—who argue for the universality of the form of the intellect—from Thomas, who argues that the intellect is part of the soul, and therefore particular to each individual.[15] As we have already seen, this was important because of the Christian doctrine of the resurrection of the body and the immortality of the human soul: if I am a hylomorphic creature destined for eternal bodily life, then my soul—including my intellect—must be as particular to me as my body.

A second important distinction between Plato and Aristotle is that Aristotle's prime mover is not a creator or a first cause but a *telos* or final cause. It is 'an end, and that sort of end which is not for the sake of something else, but for whose sake everything else is'.[16] Unlike Thomas's God, it does not create out of nothing, but rather draws beings towards itself through the dynamism of desire, without ever being affected by or involved in the being of the universe. We could say by way of comparison that a magnet attracts magnetic objects but is not attracted to or affected by them. All that exists comes about by a process of movement (*kinesis*) from potentiality (*dynamis*) to actuality (*energeia*), and ultimately to a state of completion wherein it has achieved its intended or perfected state of being (*entelechia*).[17] Thus there is a dynamism and a purpose to being, and this is situated in the interactive co-dependence between forms and matter, by way of which matter has some capacity or desire to become, and forms activate it and realize this potential when it becomes a particular kind of being. These philosophical propositions are all seminal (*sic*) for Thomas's understanding of God and for Lacan's understanding of Thomas. With these preliminary thoughts about incarnation, soul, and body in mind, I want to return to the Aristotelian cosmology that underwrites Thomas's account of being, in order to bring out the gendered aspects of that cosmology and the implications of this gendering for postmodern theology.

GENDERING THE COSMOS

Thomas inherits from Greek philosophy the idea that relationships of matter/ form, potency/actuality, passivity/activity, are all gendered—the former in

---

[14] For a list of sources representing different sides of the debate, see Sheldon M. Cohen, *Aristotle on Nature and Incomplete Substance* (Cambridge and New York: Cambridge University Press, 1996), pp. 157–63.

[15] See Ralph McInerny, *Aquinas Against the Averroists: On There Being Only One Intellect* (West Lafayette IN: Purdue University Press, 1993).

[16] Aristotle, 'Metaphysics', Book II, 994b, p. 1571.

[17] See Aristotle, 'Metaphysics', Book IX, pp. 1651–61.

each pairing is maternal and the latter is paternal. Although there is consider-able semantic slippage between the language of paternity and maternity and maleness and femaleness, the procreative language of parenthood is more appropriate here than female/male or feminine/masculine, because it is in terms of generativity and the origins of being that Aristotle and Thomas understand the relationship between man and woman, and not in terms of essential characteristics of masculinity and femininity.

In the following passage, which comes after a critique of Parmenidean and Platonic accounts of the relationship between matter and privation, Aristotle explains what he understands by persistent matter in relation to non-being:

> For the one which persists is a joint cause, with the form, of what comes to be – a mother, as it were. But the other part of the contrariety may often seem, if you concentrate your attention on it as an evil agent, not to exist at all.
>
> For admitting that there is something divine, good, and desirable, we hold that there are two other principles, the one contrary to it, the other such as of its own nature to desire and yearn for it. But the consequence of their view [i.e. Parmenides and Plato] is that the contrary desires its own extinction. Yet the form cannot desire itself, for it is not defective; nor can the contrary desire it, for contraries are mutually destructive. The truth is that what desires the form is matter (*hyle*), as the female desires the male and the ugly the beautiful – only the ugly or the female not in itself but accidentally.[18]

At first glance, one could say that all feminist critiques of western philosophy and theology can be traced back to ideas such as these—the association of the female with defectiveness, ugliness, and formless matter, and the male with perfection, beauty, and form. As we shall see, through the rise of scholasticism and the dissemination of popular Aristotelianism in medieval preaching and teaching, these ideas would embed themselves in western culture with devas-tating consequences for women. They sowed the seeds of numerous tensions and contradictions in Thomas's theology, and they undermined the potential in his thought for a richer, more incarnational account of the created goodness of both sexes and the dignity and equality of the human before God.

Nevertheless, we should also note that Aristotle paves the way for a less dualistic and more integrated account of material being than that offered by Plato. Over and against the dualistic model of mutually destructive forces (being and non-being, plenitude and the void), Aristotle's cosmos is not a site of conflict but of perpetually dynamic becoming. Evil or the void can be said to exist only insofar as it represents some lack or unrealized potential within the order of being. So, although Aristotle's comparison of *hyle* as female and ugly, to form as male and beautiful might irk his feminist readers, it is perhaps more important to bear in mind that these are accidental and not essential attributes

---

[18] Aristotle, 'Physics', Book I, 192a, p. 328.

of *hyle*. The essential characteristic of *hyle* according to Aristotle, and of matter according to Thomas, is desire—the desire to become something rather than nothing, by way of which matter draws forms to itself. This is a vital point to which we must return.

Neither Aristotle nor Thomas posits a universe in which violence is onto-logical. Theirs is not an order of being that must constantly assert its power over the void and wrest something out of nothing by force. In gendered terms, this ontology of force means that male form wages war on female matter, in order to resist its annihilating horror. This has profound implications from a Lacanian perspective, as we shall see, for modern rationalism ushers in a more conflicted and dualistic attitude that does indeed find violent expression in the politics of sexuality, identity, and otherness. At times, Thomas's theology too is lured towards the more dualistic and conflicted Platonism that such a scenario implies, and we must consider in more depth what this means. Nevertheless, Aristotle's rejection of the essential void would have a formative influence on Thomas, because it rejects the possibility of non-being as an evil or destructive force opposed to the goodness of being. In the ongoing struggle of Christian theology to free itself from the pervasive influences of Manichae-ism in its various historical forms, Aristotle with his Parmenidean influences is a potent resource.

Moreover, while Plato's Craftsman in *The Timaeus* creates the world soul within the pre-existent space of the *khora* in a way that entails a passivity of matter in relation to form, Aristotle's prime mover draws beings to itself through the dynamic encounter between forms and *hyle*, in a way that attri-butes co-causality to the two: 'the one which persists is a joint cause, with the form, of what comes to be—a mother, as it were'. To develop the implications of this, we must privilege one interpretation of Aristotle over another—namely, that which holds that matter too is inseminated with active potential, albeit in a way that is secondary to the inseminating act of form.[19]

The attempt to interpret Christian doctrine from the perspective of Platonic and Aristotelian accounts of being introduces into Thomas's theology a per-sistent tension and an underlying contradiction. On the one hand, he adheres to a fully incarnational, trinitarian, and sacramental account of God as found in Christian doctrine, and on the other hand, he attempts to weld this to the impersonal and disembodied Supreme Being of Aristotelian philosophy. His account of the human is relational, embodied, and constituted by desire, and yet his idea of the contemplative life is solitary, disembodied, and repressive of desire. My task is to unpick this dense interwovenness of theology and philoso-phy, not in order to render Aristotle redundant, but to loosen the weave, to allow it to fray and come undone at the edges, in order to enlarge the space

---

[19] Cf. Polis, 'A New Reading of Aristotle's *Hyle*'.

occupied by mystery but also by bodiliness and desire, by weakening the philosophical structure within which Thomas sometimes too rigidly contains these. With this in mind, I turn now to consider how Aristotelian concepts of gender inform Thomas's account of being.

READING THOMAS THROUGH
THE LENSES OF GENDER

In an influential book published in 1994, Sandra Lipsitz Bem used the term 'the lenses of gender' to appeal for a deeper understanding of how unequal power relationships between men and women are perpetuated in ways that often remain invisible from the perspective of liberal campaigns for sexual equality. She argues that 'hidden assumptions about sex and gender remain embedded in cultural discourses, social institutions, and individual psyches that invisibly and systemically reproduce male power in generation after generation'.[20] I read Thomas through the lenses of gender in order to demonstrate the extent to which many of these ongoing influences can be traced back to the spread of Aristotelianism through the universities and popular medieval culture—a development in which Thomas played a pivotal role.

A casual reading of Thomas might detect relatively little of interest from the perspective of sex and gender. Although he frequently refers to sexual transgressions as examples of sin—sometimes in extreme terms—he regards hatred of God as the most serious sin,[21] closely followed by pride, hatred of neighbour, and envy.[22] Compared to many other Christian thinkers, not least Augustine, Thomas has a positive view of sexual pleasure within marriage, so long as it retains its procreative function.[23] He makes relatively few references to women, some of which affirm the equality and glory of women in the eyes of God, and others of which reflect the sexual prejudices of a man of his time.

Yet these are not casual prejudices, and once one attends to the separation of the sexes that constituted Thomas's social environment, and the differentiation of gendered aspects of being that constitute his epistemology, we see that Thomas's whole intellectual edifice is constructed upon difference understood in gendered terms of perfection and lack. Thomas's reading of Aristotle thus gives intellectual legitimacy to the sexual status quo of the medieval world, in a way that would seal the boundaries of western learning for some seven hundred years, until women began to bring the seepage of bodiliness, desire, and matter into the linguistic domain of the academic world in the late twentieth century.

---

[20] Sandra Lipsitz Bem, *The Lenses of Gender: Transforming the Debate on Sexual Inequality* (New Haven CT: Yale University Press, 1993), p. 2.
[21] ST II-II, 34, 2.   [22] See ST I, 63, 2; ST II-II, 34 and 36.   [23] ST II-II, 153, 2.

Many recent works nostalgic for the Aristotelian ideal remain hermetically sealed against these influences and the questions they raise with regard to the western order of knowledge.[24] Thomas's gendered understanding of the ordering of creation lent philosophical order and divine authority to the sexual hierarchies within which he lived, and blocked from view the sexual anxieties and conflicts that are encoded within his texts.

The most significant difference between Aristotle and Thomas to bear in mind in what follows is the doctrine of creation *ex nihilo*, although I shall address that in more detail later. While Thomas acknowledges that it is philosophically coherent to argue for the eternity of the world, it is an article of the Christian faith that, according to the Book of Genesis, God created the world and it has a beginning.[25] In other words, creation *ex nihilo* is a deductive claim based on revelation rather than an inductive claim based on reason, and we must remember that, in Thomas's thought, this means that it can be reasonably defended as a belief but not rationally demonstrated as a proof. The story of Genesis commits him to defending the doctrine that God creates *ex nihilo*, and therefore forms, matter, time, and space have a beginning in God. Moreover, as I mentioned before, this also commits Thomas to agreeing with Aristotle that the scientific study of nature (*physis*) entails the study of both forms and matter because both are aspects of nature, which means that both are created by God according to the principles that order the cosmos.[26]

Approaching the question of prime matter in his study of Aristotle's *Physics*, Thomas summarizes the latter's argument that there are three principles in every coming to be: the subject, the end or purpose of its existence, and its opposite.[27] With Aristotle, Thomas understands these opposites not as dualistic conflicts, but as related to one another in terms of potency and act. Each term contains its opposite as potential—lack has the potential to become plenitude or perfection, and plenitude has a negative capacity to suffer deprivation and become lack. Thomas reiterates Aristotle's argument that 'the potency of matter is not some property added to its essence. Rather, matter in its very substance is potency for substantial being'.[28] We have already seen that this potency takes the form of desire, and we must not let go of that insight. Forms acquire material existence and also suffer entropy and decay, while matter can pass through numerous forms of existence without thereby losing its continuity. The construction of sexual difference in terms of lack and perfection, and the role of desire in the relationship between forms and matter

---

[24] Cf. Alasdair MacIntyre, *God, Philosophy, Universities: A Selective History of the Catholic Philosophical Tradition* (Lanham MD and Plymouth UK: Sheed & Ward, 2009), which offers a robustly androcentric defence of the Catholic University.

[25] ST I, 46, 2.

[26] Thomas Aquinas, *Commentary on Aristotle's Physics*, Book I, *Lectio 1*, Chapter 1.

[27] Aquinas, *Commentary on Aristotle's Physics*, Book 1, *Lectio 11*, Chapter 6.

[28] Aquinas, *Commentary on Aristotle's Physics*, Book I, *Lectio 15*, Chapter 4, 131.

are, as we shall see, vital for a Lacanian reading of Thomas. Now, I turn to consider how Thomas understands the maternity of matter and the paternity of form, and the implications of this for his understanding of social and sexual relationships.

MATERNAL MATTER AND PATERNAL FORMS

Thomas uncritically reiterates Aristotle's concept of matter as maternal and passive in relation to forms, which are paternal and active. The biological justification for this is based on Aristotle's mistaken beliefs about the process of conception. The semen is the active agent in conception, so that the male body imparts form to the female flesh, which is matter awaiting form. The mother thus contributes nothing active or essential to her offspring, and its soul owes nothing to her. The implications of this are clear when Thomas explains his reasons for rejecting the Immaculate Conception in the third part of the *Summa theologiae*, which is concerned with the incarnation and the sacraments.

The claim that Mary was conceived without original sin was a topic of heated debate in medieval theology, but Thomas's Aristotelian biology leads him to part company from his teacher Albert and reject the Immaculate Conception. His argument brings to light how Aristotelian ideas determine his beliefs both in terms of his ontology and his understanding of the right social ordering of relationships between the sexes, despite the fact that at various points these beliefs contradict his theological understanding of creation and the human made in the image of God.

First, Thomas argues that Christ took flesh, not from Mary's flesh and bones, but from her blood, because her blood was more pure, being only potentially a body.[29] The Virgin's blood here seems to function as prime matter awaiting form.[30] However, while ordinary conception involves the admixture of blood with semen, the absence of semen in the conception of Christ means that his flesh is made of the pure blood of the Virgin.[31] Christ's human flesh is formed of the Virgin's blood and is therefore fully human, but the transmission of original sin is not through matter but through the concupiscence or disordered desire that necessarily infects every sex act as a consequence of Adam's sin, through the active agency of the semen. The virginal conception means that neither concupiscence nor semen was involved in the conception of

---

[29] ST III, 31, 6. See also ST III, 5, 1.

[30] For an exploration of Mary as prime matter, see Sarah Jane Boss, *Mary*, 'New Century Theology' (London and New York: Continuum, 2004), pp. 74–100.

[31] ST III, 31.

Christ, when Mary conceived the Son of God the Father by the power of the Holy Spirit.

Later, Thomas considers the question as to 'Whether the Blessed Virgin cooperated actively in the conception of Christ's body?'[32] Three propositions are put forward in favour of this claim. The first comes from a quotation from Damascene (*De Fide Orth.* iii): 'the Holy Ghost came upon the Virgin, purifying her, and bestowing on her the power to receive and to bring forth the Word of God'. This suggests that the Holy Spirit 'bestowed on her an active power of generation', even though 'she had from nature the passive power of generation, like any other woman'. Second, Aristotle attributes active powers to the vegetative soul (*De Anima* ii). Since the vegetative soul is responsible for the generative power of both man and woman, this entails that 'both in man, and woman, it cooperates actively in the conception of the child'. Third, a child's body is naturally formed from the matter that is supplied by the woman in conception, but given that 'nature is an intrinsic principle of movement . . . it seems that in the very matter supplied by the Blessed Virgin there was an active principle'.

Not so, answers Thomas, reiterating that the active principle in generation is seminal, and quoting Augustine (*Gen. ad lit.* x) in his defence: 'as Augustine says, Christ's body "was taken from the Virgin, only as to corporeal matter, by the Divine power of conception and formation, but not by any human seminal virtue." Therefore the Blessed Virgin did not cooperate actively in the conception of Christ's body'.[33] Although Christ's mother cooperated insofar as she prepared the matter (her own body) for his conception, she exercised no active power in his conception, because she was 'not Christ's Father, but his Mother'.[34]

We must remember here that Thomas wants to say that it is God, not the biological father, who imparts the soul to the foetus when it is sufficiently developed to take human form. So he suggests that the semen prepares the maternal flesh to receive the soul, and in this preparatory formation it transmits the inheritance of original sin. But while only the male body is capable of producing the active seed that inseminates the flesh, the female body also has a passive seed.[35] This relates to the idea that matter is invested with the potency of desire, so it is not entirely without some vestigial active capacity. We must return to this question later, but Thomas seems to be suggesting that, in the absence of semen, Mary herself had to prepare her flesh to receive the form of Christ's humanity from God. The main point to bear in mind here is that it is the father, not the mother, who is the agent responsible for the transmission of original sin, and it is Adam's sin, not Eve's, that infects humankind:

---

[32] ST III, 32, 4.   [33] ST III, 32, 4.   [34] ST III, 32, 4.   [35] ST I, 115, 2.

[I]mmortality and impassibility, in the original state, were a result, not of the condition of matter, but of original justice, whereby the body was subjected to the soul, so long as the soul remained subject to God. Now privation of original justice is original sin. If, therefore, supposing Adam had not sinned, original sin would not have been transmitted to posterity on account of Eve's sin, it is evident that the children would not have been deprived of original justice: and consequently they would not have been liable to suffer and subject to the necessity of dying.[36]

For this reason, argues Thomas, the prevenient purification of the Virgin Mary was to make her worthy to receive God, and not to protect Christ from the transmission of original sin.

A number of questions have now loomed into view—questions that touch on the meaning of salvation, the ontology of woman, and the nature of the incarnation. The privileging of paternal agency and activity over maternal passivity and potentiality with regard to the relationship between form and matter forms a blueprint not only for Thomas's biology, but for his whole understanding of the right ordering of relationships between men and women in the family and in society. As Prudence Allen argues, 'For St Thomas, the concept of woman in relation to man is analogous in some respects to the relation that exists between God and prime matter.'[37] With that in mind, let me turn to the wider question of 'woman' in Thomas's thought, bearing in mind that once again, different interpretations present themselves depending on which aspect of the *Summa theologiae* one privileges.

WOMAN ACCORDING TO THOMAS

Thomas's account of woman in the order of creation refers to three levels of existence, the first two of which he takes from Aristotle. The third level—that which is unique to Christian theology and cannot be ascertained by philosophical reflection alone—is for a later chapter. Here, I focus mainly on what he borrows from Aristotle.

There are scattered references to women throughout Thomas's work, but the most commonly cited reference is in ST I, 92 in which he discusses the creation of woman, beginning with three objections.[38] The first objection is that woman should not have been part of the original perfection of creation, because,

---

[36] ST I-II, 81, 4.

[37] Prudence Allen RSM, *The Concept of Woman: The Aristotelian Revolution 750 B.C.–A.D. 1250* (Grand Rapids MI and Cambridge UK: William B. Eerdmans Publishing Co., 1997), p. 387.

[38] See also Thomas Aquinas, *Commentary on the Sentences*, trans. Joseph Kenny, O.P., Book II, Question 3, 18 at <http://dhspriory.org/thomas/Sentences2.htm> [accessed 22 October 2012].

according to Aristotle, 'the female is a misbegotten male' (*mas occasionatus*) (*De Gener.* ii, 3), and 'nothing misbegotten (*occasionatum*) or defective (*deficiens*) should have been in the first production of things'. The second argues that, since subjection and limitation are a result of sin, and since woman is subject to man and is 'naturally of less strength and dignity than man', she should not have been created before sin. Thomas's interlocutor quotes Gregory: 'Where there is no sin, there is no inequality.' The third objection is that God knew that 'the woman would be an occasion of sin to man', so God should not have made woman. It is worth unpacking Thomas's response to these in some detail, drawing on some of his other writings for elaboration where necessary, and gradually enlarging the focus to tease out some of the contradictions and insights in his account of sexual difference.

Thomas begins by responding that woman was made to be man's helper, specifically with regard to the work of procreation, since a man would have been a more effective helpmate for any other work. Here, he follows Augustine.[39] (Obviously, direct references to the Book of Genesis do not come from Aristotle.) However, Thomas goes on to introduce an Aristotelian perspective, when he argues that different forms of life procreate in different ways, sometimes without sexual differentiation, but among 'perfect animals the active power of generation belongs to the male sex, and the passive power to the female'. Why is sexual difference an aspect of perfection? Thomas explains that it is because, whereas in plants the most noble work of life is generation, in the human (*homo*) it is the work of understanding (*intelligere*). In the *Summa Contra Gentiles*, he describes the intellect as 'the supreme and perfect grade of life . . . for the intellect reflects upon itself and the intellect can understand itself'.[40] Thus the generative function is not continuous in the human, and the carnal unity of the sex act is not an expression of the highest human activity, which is that of the intellect made in the image of the trinitarian God. This is a vital insight. Sexual differentiation has biological, ethical, and social implications for Thomas, but neither man nor woman can be understood solely in terms of sexual identity. Ultimately, the most significant aspect of our humanity is a shared vocation to God. Far from functioning to express this vocation to God—as some modern Catholic accounts seem to suggest—sexual differentiation actually limits the extent to which we are sexual beings, in order to free us for the non-sexual activities associated with prayer, contemplation, and knowledge of God.

This refers to the creation of woman, although this is an exposition of the ideas of Peter Lombard rather than Thomas's own interpretation.

[39] See Augustine, *Ancient Christian Writers: The Literal Meaning of Genesis*, Vol. 2, Book IX (Mahwah NJ: Paulist Press, 1982), p. 75.

[40] SCG IV, 11, 5.

Thomas then goes on to deal with each objection in turn. First, he agrees with Aristotle that 'As regards the individual nature, woman is somewhat deficient and unintended' (*aliquid deficiens et occasionatum*). This is because the active power of the male seed would under the right conditions produce its own likeness in another male, so the production of a female suggests some defect in the seed or in external conditions. This is more clearly spelled out in *Summa Contra Gentiles*. Still following Aristotle, Thomas goes on to argue that, with regard to human nature in general, 'woman is not misbegotten, but is included in nature's intention as directed to the work of generation'. Because for Thomas, God is 'the universal Author of nature', we can therefore conclude that God formed the female as well as the male. In other words, while an individual woman results from a defect in the process of conception and embryonic development, this is not a defect in terms of the order of nature as a whole (Aristotle) or in terms of the divine creation (Thomas).

Michael Nolan points out that Thomas uses the medieval neologism *occasionatus*, which indicates an indirect or unintentional consequence of a cause. So, suggests Nolan, damp wood will produce smoke rather than flames, which would be the natural outcome if the wood were dry. But whether or not this unintentional outcome is good or not depends on what purpose it serves. If one is warming a house then smoke is bad, but if one is curing bacon, smoke is good.[41] So, while at the level of the particular nature of the act of conception, a woman is produced by a defect in the process, at the universal level she is not defective but intended. In *Summa Contra Gentiles* Thomas writes:

> The particular agent tends to the good of the part without qualification, and makes it the best that it can, but the universal agent tends to the good of the whole. As a result, a defect which is in accord with the intention of the universal agent may be apart from the intention of the particular agent. Thus, it is clear that the generation of a female apart from the intention of a particular nature . . . is in accord with the intention of the universal nature, that is, of the power of the universal agent for the generation of inferior beings, that a female be generated; for without a female the generation of a number of animals could not be accomplished.[42]

Woman, then, is a defect at the level of the particular but not at the level of the universal. The suggestion that she exists as an inferior being for the purpose of reproduction may offer scant consolation to a modern feminist, but we must qualify this by the insistence that woman and man are both made in the image of God, and that the vocation to God transcends and relativizes the sexual relationship in terms of what it means to be human.

---

[41] See Michael Nolan, 'The Defective Male: What Aquinas Really Said' <http://www.women priests.org/theology/nolan.asp> [accessed 1 June 2011].
[42] SCG 3, II, 94, 11.

Later, Thomas returns to the question of woman and adds an additional explanation. Repeating his argument that male and female were both intended in creation, he argues that, in a state of original goodness, a female would not have been conceived as a result of any fault in matter, but as a result of external circumstances.[43] As Nolan points out, insofar as woman is produced by a defect, the defect is not in the female body but in the male semen and there could have been no such defective matter in the original goodness of creation. So Thomas puts forward an explanation offered by Aristotle, that 'the northern wind favours the generation of males, and the southern wind that of females' (*De Animal. Histor.* vi, 19), but the birth of a female might also be because 'the body was more subject to the soul' in the state of innocence, 'so that by the mere will of the parent the sex of the offspring might be diversified'. Without original sin then, parents might have sufficient mental control over their own bodies to be able to choose the sex of their children, which adds an interesting twist to the modern idea of sex selection as a mimesis of the return to Eden!

Responding to the second objection in ST I, 92, Thomas distinguishes between the servility associated with sin, in which a superior uses another subject for his own benefit, and the subjection associated with the good ordering of society and the family, in which a man's leadership is for the good of his subjects. This form of subjection belongs within the pre-lapsarian order of creation, and it is for the good of the woman that she is governed by the man: 'For good order would have been wanting in the human family if some were not governed by others wiser than themselves. So by such a kind of subjection woman is naturally subject to man, because in man the discretion of reason predominates.'[44] Later, in considering the effects of original sin, Thomas argues that suffering in childbirth and being subject to her husband's authority are the punishments allocated to the woman, while labouring to produce the necessities of life is the punishment allocated to the man. Without original sin the woman would not have suffered in childbearing but her husband would still have been her 'head' (*caput mulieris*) and her 'governor' (*gubernator*). However, as a result of sin she now has to 'obey her husband's will even against her own'.[45]

Thomas's reply to the third objection is pragmatic: 'If God had deprived the world of all those things which proved an occasion of sin, the universe would have been imperfect.' Individual evil cannot be avoided if that would be destructive of the common good, and God is powerful enough to 'direct any evil to a good end'. This explanation falls somewhat short of what feminism might demand, but it reveals the optimism of Thomas's theology and his faith in the enduring goodness of creation.

Continuing the discussion—and we should note that throughout this section, we can read between the lines if we want to understand the kind of

[43] ST I, 99, 1.   [44] ST I, 92, 1.   [45] ST II-II, 164, 2.

debates that were occurring in medieval culture regarding the role of women—
Thomas considers the objection that the woman should not have been made
from the man's body. He defends the Genesis account, first because 'as God
is the principle of the whole universe, so the first man, in likeness to God, was
the principle of the whole human race'.[46] Moreover, the fact that she is made
from his body predisposes the man to love the woman and to bond with her
for life, in a relationship in which their domestic life can be properly ordered
according to their respective duties, in which 'the man is the head of the
woman' and is her principle. Finally, the relationship between woman and
man is sacramental, since the woman has her origin in the man as the Church
has her origin in Christ. But the woman is created by divine power and not by
natural generation, so Eve is not Adam's daughter. Thomas goes on to explain
why the woman was created from the man's rib:

> First, to signify the social union of man and woman, for the woman should neither
> "use authority over man," and so she was not made from his head; nor was it right for
> her to be subject to man's contempt as his slave, and so she was not made from his feet.
> Secondly, for the sacramental signification; for from the side of Christ sleeping on the
> Cross the Sacraments flowed – namely, blood and water – on which the Church was
> established.[47]

Here, we glimpse the possibility of a different configuration of the significance
of sexual difference, when Thomas's biblical theology is allowed to break free
from its Aristotelian moorings. Nevertheless, this is a signpost towards that road
less travelled. It is impossible to exaggerate the social and ethical implications of
his overall insistence that the creation story in Genesis supports the patriarchal
order of the ancient Greek world, on the basis of the man being the paternal,
formal principle of the woman as God is the paternal formal principle of
creation, and on the basis of the woman being less rational than the man.

The doctrine of the incarnation and the theology of creation had the
potential to overturn the sexual and patriarchal hierarchies of the ancient
world, and we shall see that there are glimmers of an altogether different
reading of Thomas. However, the rise of Aristotelianism and its widespread
dissemination from the universities out into popular culture supported a
robust patriarchal order at the very heart of medieval society, through the
linking of Aristotle's prime mover with the creator Father God of the Christian
tradition. Aristotle's active inseminating principle was never invested with
the characteristics of a human father, and one could argue that the apophaticism of Thomas's theology should have put a check on the extent to which the
fatherhood of God could be invoked in patriarchal terms. However, what
actually happens is that the fatherhood of Christianity's God fuses with the
prime mover of Greek philosophy, and the consequence is a thorough-going

---

[46] ST I, 92, 2.   [47] ST I, 92, 3.

divinization of the patriarchal order at every level of human relationships and extending throughout the order of creation.

We begin to see why Lacan repeatedly has recourse to Thomas in order to trace the origins of the linguistic structure that orders modern society and forms the modern mind around implicitly gendered constructs of body and soul, in relation to the masked function of the phallus in establishing meaning around sexually differentiated concepts of perfection and lack. I have suggested that the ancient copulative encounter between male form and female matter is inscribed onto the sexual body in pervasive and far-reaching ways through the influence of Aristotelianism on medieval knowledge, and I want to ask in Chapter 8 how that relates to the rise of the universities. For now, however, I turn to consider how this Aristotelian ordering of knowledge in terms of paternal act and maternal potency mapped itself onto the social order through Thomas's understanding of natural law, in ways that would leave an indelible imprint on the values and structures of western society.

6

Fatherhood, Law, and Society

In order to explore the social and ethical implications of the previous chapter, we must briefly consider Thomas Aquinas's understanding of law and the ways in which it operates according to faith, knowledge, and ethics. I do not here offer any close analysis of the concept of natural law and the continuing debates it provokes, particularly in feminist discourse,[1] but it will be helpful for what follows to summarize some of the key features of the scholastic understanding of natural law in its wider theological context.

We have seen that law, according to Jacques Lacan, imposes itself with a violent authoritarian power which the modern symbolic order derives from beyond itself, while never acknowledging or identifying the source of that authority. This is because it acquires its power from the lingering vestiges of God in the unconscious, perpetrated by the unresolved traumas and taboos associated with the oedipal process. Thomas has a more benign view of the function of law, for he sees it as the means by which all of creation is harmoniously interrelated and sustained within the love of God. Natural law and the human laws that it informs in a just society are orientated towards human flourishing, in a way that enriches the co-dependent lives of the individual and the community. However, as we shall see, there is considerable tension between Thomas's desire to affirm natural law as a means to human flourishing rooted in reason and nature, and his attempt to tether natural law to a patriarchal order that operates at all levels of being.

If we analyse how Thomas's failure to reconcile Aristotelian concepts of gender with his incarnational theology produces a number of tensions in his thought, then we might go some way towards appreciating how Lacan's Thomist atheism can help us to understand the wounding of the modern

---

[1] For an example of a feminist theological interpretation of natural law, see Cristina L. H. Traina, *Feminist Ethics and Natural Law: The End of the Anathemas* (Washington DC: Georgetown University Press, 1999). For a critique of Traina and a rejection of natural law from a feminist philosophical perspective, see Christine Pierce, *Immovable Laws, Irresistible Rights: Natural Law, Moral Rights, and Feminist Ethics* (Lawrence KA: University Press of Kansas, 2000). See also Tina Beattie, '"Justice enacted not these human laws" (Antigone): Religion, Natural Law and Women's Rights', *Religion and Human Rights*, Vol. 3, No. 3, 2008, pp. 249–67.

soul with its insatiable and violent desires, a wounding that was seeded within modernity's cultural and psychic formations by the troubled marriage between Christian theology and Greek philosophy. A selective reading of Lacan can guide us through the structured and orderly relationships of Thomas's world, to discover therein the seeds of a process of disavowal, repression, and denial that would continue to have a cumulative effect on western consciousness, until Freud discovered this dark inheritance lurking deep within the chasms of the modern mind.

LAW ACCORDING TO THOMAS[2]

The scholastic understanding of natural law is rooted in what Jean Porter describes as three 'traditional loci for moral reflection: nature, reason, and Scripture'.[3] Scripture provides what today we might refer to as the narrative context within which reason operates and nature is interpreted.[4] It reveals the meaning and purpose for which the cosmos was created, and within that narrative framework it allows the Christian to discern the contours of the good life through reasoned reflection on nature, bearing in mind that we are created for eternal happiness with God.

Thomas posits four interconnected levels of law. The eternal law is unknowable to the human, for it is the overarching truth by which God holds the world in being, which is knowable only to God. It is the order upon which all other order depends, and we cannot think outside the laws we think with. Even Richard Dawkins, in a television interview, acknowledges that there is something that science might never be able to know—'where did the laws of physics come from in the first place?'[5] This is no insignificant admission from a theological perspective, although it seems unlikely that Dawkins would allow the word 'mystery' to enter the scene at this point.

Next, there is the divine law that is revealed in scripture but not accessible by reason alone. This relates to the doctrinal content of the Christian faith. We could not know it if it had not been revealed, but it offers a certainty that is

---

[2] The following refers to the discussion in ST I-II, 90–108. For a nuanced contemporary reading of the possibilities inherent in the biblical understanding of natural law, see Eugene F. Rogers Jr, *Thomas Aquinas and Karl Barth* (South Bend IN: University of Notre Dame Press, 1995), pp. 46–70. See also Jean Porter's critique of Rogers in Jean Porter, *Natural and Divine Law: Reclaiming the Tradition for Christian Ethics* (Grand Rapids MI and Cambridge UK: William B. Eerdmans Publishing Co., 1999), pp. 173–5.

[3] Porter, *Natural and Divine Law*, p. 51.

[4] Cf. Pamela M. Hall, *Narrative and the Natural Law: An Interpretation of Thomistic Ethics* (Notre Dame and London: University of Notre Dame Press, 1994).

[5] Richard Dawkins, BBC *Hard Talk* (3/3) at <http://www.youtube.com/watch?v=eOBTtdcII-TU&feature=relmfu> [accessed 8 July 2012].

lacking from rational interpretations of natural law. Third, there is the natural law that is scripted into the order of creation and accessible to the rational creature. Through our experience, observation, and interpretation of the world around us, we are able by way of reason to discern the general contours of a moral and social order that enables us to organize our lives and relationships so as to orientate us towards the good and turn us away from evil. Fourth, there is human law which, in a just society, is informed by natural law so that it reflects the intrinsic coherence and order of creation directed towards the good within the social order.

It is worth noting that the discussion of natural law forms a relatively minor part of the *Summa theologiae* and there is some debate as to how far it can be lifted out of its theological context. Thomas has only one question that deals specifically with natural law,[6] and he situates that question in a wider context that addresses human law, Mosaic law, and the New Law of the Gospel.[7] Western philosophy and legal theory have focused disproportionately on Thomas's account of natural law and have elided its theological context, thereby giving rise to distorted and misleading interpretations.

Nevertheless, even within its theological context, it is clear that Thomas roots natural law within the order of creation and natural reason, and not solely within Christian revelation. It belongs to the capabilities of the human animal so that we can flourish as a natural species, and this makes his account different from that which informs many modern theological and philosophical interpretations. Porter criticizes modern natural law theorists for their conformity to 'the modern view that nature, understood in terms of whatever is pre- or non-rational, stands in contrast to reason'.[8] She argues that this runs counter to the scholastic concept of natural law, of which 'one of its most striking features is its naturalism'.[9] Porter refers to

> the pervasive scholastic sense of the continuity between us, considered precisely as moral agents, and the other animals. This sense of continuity, in turn, presupposes that there is a kind of goodness that is more fundamental than human moral rectitude: namely, the goodness displayed in any life that unfolds in accordance with its intrinsic principles of operation. Furthermore, the goodness is an expression of the still more basic goodness that each creature enjoys simply by virtue of being the creature of a good Creator.[10]

The divine will is for the flourishing of creatures, including the human, within the natural order. Through the virtuous life—that is, a disciplined life in which our appetites, desires, and instincts are harmoniously orchestrated and moderated in accordance with our human nature—we discover a capacity for natural happiness which is a foretaste of the eternal happiness in God for

---

[6] ST I-II, 94.   [7] See ST I-II, 90–108.   [8] Porter, *Natural and Divine Law*, p. 93.
[9] Porter, *Natural and Divine Law*, p. 98.   [10] Porter, *Natural and Divine Law*, p. 83.

which we were created and in which we discover the *telos* of our existence. Although sin has distorted our capacity for virtue and our ability to act in accordance with the guidance of reason, we still retain enough of these faculties as a rational species for us to come to an awareness of the goodness of God in the order of creation, and to live in such a way that we experience and express this goodness in our own lives. To quote Porter again, 'for Thomas, terrestrial happiness is said to consist in the practice of virtue, which does not consist simply in good moral character, but more fundamentally in the full development and exercise—the perfection—of all the capacities of the human agent'.[11]

Our individual capacity for flourishing is inseparable from our social environment, for the human is by nature a social animal. Human laws hold the social order in balance by maintaining justice, punishing wrongdoing, and creating the conditions for individuals to flourish in hierarchically ordered relationships of mutual respect and responsibility. However, Porter argues that scholastics were more aware than many later natural law theorists of the constructed character of social conventions and institutions, which emerge not directly in response to the promptings of nature, but through historical processes of reflection and negotiation. She writes that

> they never lost sight of the fact that social practices and institutions are always more or less conventional, and in some cases contrary to the law of nature, at least seen from some perspectives. In this respect they follow Cicero rather than Aristotle. That is, rather than endorsing Aristotle's view that social conventions stem immediately from natural inclinations, in such a way as to reflect human nature directly, they appropriate Cicero's view that human society reflects a long-standing process of human reflection and invention, in which natural inclinations are given expression through negotiation, legislation, and the emergence of custom.[12]

This allows for considerable variety in political and social institutions and laws. Thomas argues, in agreement with Isidore of Seville, that positive law should be informed by custom so that it reflects a particular society's values and practices.[13] Moreover, because natural law pertains to general principles and not to specific contexts, it accommodates a diversity of interpretations by different societies.[14]

All this means that, at least according to some readings, Thomas and the scholastics open the way to a more pluralist ethos and a more liberal interpretation of the individual in relation to society and the law than Aristotle (or, in a more modern context, Hegel), for whom natural law cedes its authority

---

[11] Jean Porter, *Nature as Reason: A Thomistic Theory of the Natural Law* (Grand Rapids MI and Cambridge UK: William B. Eerdmans Publishing Co., 2005), p. 50.
[12] Porter, *Nature as Reason*, p. 18.
[13] ST I-II, 95, 3.   [14] ST I-II, 95, 2.

once it is inscribed within positive law.[15] Thomas cites Augustine (*De Lib. Arb.* I, 5) in support of his view that an unjust law is not a law, and he goes on to argue that 'every human law has just so much of the nature of law as is derived from the law of nature. But if in any point it deflects from the law of nature, it is no longer a law but a perversion of law'.[16] In theory then, the laws of society are relative to the natural law, and an appeal to an informed conscience should usually take precedence over obedience to the law, even if one is in error.[17]

A final important point from a Lacanian perspective is Thomas's argument that the sovereign who promulgates the positive law is above the coercive power of the law, but is obliged by conscience and by God to obey it freely and to apply it in the interests of the people.[18] So, whatever form of political authority promulgates the law (Thomas thought a form of devolved monarchical power was best, which included aspects of aristocratic and democratic participation within the sovereign power of the ruler),[19] the lawmaker is held accountable before God but not before the law.

The question of the origins, authority, and limits of the law continues to generate much scholarly debate, even or especially after its theological justification has been removed.[20] Without some shared consensus as to the common good rooted in a transcendent notion of justice, the good, or God before which every individual is held accountable, law will always be subject to a certain arbitrariness and randomness which will be experienced as violence by some and security by others, and the power of the state and its leaders will continue to be underwritten by the threat of punishment and violence even in the absence of any divine judgement. We do not have to look far in this post-9/11 world to discover many examples of the tyranny and irrationality of the law as a barely veiled mechanism for reinforcing the power of the state and its ruling elites through the manipulation of fear and the threat of violence.[21] Later, we must return to some of the questions this raises, but now I want to consider how Thomas applies the natural order of the cosmos described in the last chapter, to the social order of human society through its values and institutions.

---

[15] Tony Burns argues that there are two contradictory accounts of natural law in the *Summa theologiae*, including both Stoic and Aristotelian versions. The former supports a more liberal interpretation, while the latter lends itself to more conservative readings. See Tony Burns, 'Aquinas's Two Doctrines of Natural Law', *Political Studies*, Vol. 48: 5 (2000), pp. 929–46.

[16] ST I-II, 95, 2.   [17] ST I-III, 96, 4.   [18] ST I-II, 96, 5.

[19] ST I-II, 95, 4; ST I-II, 105.1.

[20] Cf. the readings in Dennis Michael Patterson (ed.), *Philosophy of Law and Legal Theory: An Anthology* (Blackwell Publishing, 2003). See also Austin Sarat (ed.), *Law, Violence, and the Possibility of Justice* (Princeton NJ: Princeton University Press, 2001).

[21] Cf. Helena Kennedy, *Just Law: The Changing Face of Justice, and Why It Matters to Us All* (London: Vintage, 2005).

THE PATRIARCHAL ORDER

It is clear that Thomas's account of law is patriarchal through and through— promulgated by God the Father as the supreme Law Giver and extending through all the structures of society by way of paternal authority. The trinitarian mystery is simultaneously revealed and concealed within creation as the prime mover of Aristotelian philosophy, so that natural theology orders the world according to Aristotelian principles. The gendering and engendering of created beings emanates from God as the inseminating first principle (an idea that combines Neoplatonism with Aristotelianism), so that God is, analogically but sometimes literally in Thomas's language, form in relation to matter, mind in relation to body, and implicitly paternal and masculine in relation to a maternal and feminine creation. Natural law, revealed within these gendered cosmological dualities, is the pattern for the laws and institutions of society and human relationships, all of which derive their authority from God the Father and follow a paternal logic/*logos*.

The Father God of the Christian faith establishes His laws within the human soul by making it in his image and likeness, so that it recognizes in the paternal ordering of the cosmos an intimation of the divine law revealed in scripture— grace perfects nature. The man made in the image of the Father thus seeks to shape society in his own image, which is also indirectly the image of the Father. Humans flourish best in relationships in which father figures rule society as God rules creation, with a paternal benevolence and order. Although only the sovereign power of a state can make binding laws, an individual father governs his family in a way that authorizes him to 'make certain commands or ordinances, but not such as to have properly the force of law'.[22] Patriarchal society which accords men priority over women in terms of their greater perfection, rationality, and aptitude for leadership is underwritten by Aristotelian biological concepts of reproduction, and these in turn derive their authority from ontological concepts of the dynamism of being and becoming understood in terms of potency and act, lack and perfection, agency and passivity, fatherhood and motherhood. Thus natural law is a vast conceptual construct that extends from the furthest reaches of the cosmic order to the most intimate relationships of human life. From this perspective, the image of God that is unique to the human is the rational intellect which orders the world according to generative principles of paternal act and maternal potency. Women share this image equally with men, but within the order of creation they are not equal, for they occupy the position of matter/mother in relation to form/father.

In modernity, this authorization/authoring of human law through the divine law (revealed in scripture) and the natural law (discerned through

---

[22] ST I-II, 90, 3.

reason) has been eliminated, and law derives its authority from the power of reason alone, vested in the autonomous, self-legislating individual of Kantian rationalism and/or in the power of the state, and severed from its divine and natural referents. Yet according to Lacan, the law retains its invisible power. Thomas's God once informed human conscience through the mediating influence of the university and the Church which interpreted His laws, communicated them in teaching and preaching, wrote them into its codes of canon and secular law, diffused them through all the institutions and hierarchies of the social order, and inscribed them on the human heart in the form of punishment and reward, the threat of hell and the promise of heaven. All this, according to Lacanian linguistics, insinuates itself into consciousness through the structures of language and the masked authority of the symbolic order. In today's rationalized bureaucracies, the divine and the demonic, the love and the terror, the yearning and the abjection, that found expression in the carnivalesque excess of medieval life have been silenced but not eliminated, and in place of the Father God, the phallus now rules unseen over the soul. According to critics such as Luce Irigaray, it has lost none of its power to subordinate and exclude women in the Name of the Father. Institutionalized patriarchy has ceded its authority to linguistic phallocentrism, in such a way that gendered constructs of masculine perfection and feminine lack retain their power to order the individual psyche and the institutions of society.

If we bear in mind Thomas's argument that natural law reflects the customs and values of particular societies, we could argue that his patriarchal interpretation of law is only what one might expect, given that he was a man of his times and his thinking reflects the scientific and social context within which he lived. Yet there is a tension running through Thomas's account of law with its gendered hierarchies, because from a doctrinal perspective he is committed to affirming the full equality of all human beings as created by God and called to eternal glory, in such a way that there will be no inequality in heaven. So, as Kari Elisabeth Børresen points out,

> In the modern Atlantic (Western European and North American) mind, woman's equivalence with man is taken for granted; in Augustine and Thomas the perspective is precisely the reverse: their reasoning begins with the accepted idea that woman is subordinate, and this idea is so deeply rooted that it becomes an integral part of their interpretation of the order of creation. On the other hand, equivalence according to the spirit of the Gospel, belongs to the order of salvation, as the realisation of the quality of divine image borne equally by man and woman. The earthly condition of humanity, furthermore, is determined by the penalty of sin, although elements of the order of creation are preserved. Finally, this condition has the plenitude of the resurrection as its own destiny.[23]

---

[23] Kari Elisabeth Børresen, *Subordination and Equivalence: Nature and Role of Women in Augustine and Thomas Aquinas* (Rowman & Littlefield Publishers, 1995), pp. xvi–xvii.

In Thomas's grappling to reconcile Aristotelian philosophy with Christian theology, he discovers in the former a potent resource for naturalizing and therefore sanctifying that which was regarded as normal in terms of the sexual hierarchies of the medieval status quo. However, in the process he also reinforces those hierarchies and lends them divine legitimacy, even though this entails straining the logic of his theological position almost to breaking point. If we consider how Thomas seeks to account for society in terms of Greek rationality on the one hand and Christian theology on the other, we can I believe gain considerable insight into the formation of the cultural and linguistic constructs that form the heart of Lacan's anti-Thomist analysis of sexuality, identity, and otherness. In order to illustrate this, I am going to refer briefly to three issues in the *Summa theologiae*—filial love, marriage, and leadership.

In what follows, we must bear in mind the point I made earlier, that the arguments which Thomas attributes to his opponents in the *Summa theologiae* can be read as hypothetical propositions, but it is also reasonable to assume that they constitute commonly held opinions and ideas against which Thomas was defending what he saw as correct philosophical and doctrinal principles, even when he does not explicitly say that this is the case. So in debates about family loyalties, maternal and paternal roles, and the place of women in society, he is sometimes pitting himself against more egalitarian alternatives and offering justifications for the ordering of social institutions and relationships according to Aristotelian categories which would retain their regulative and normative status well into modernity. In so doing, he was closing down other interpretative possibilities that were also in play, as the medieval universities took control of the production of knowledge and organized it according to a universal order in which the subordination of mother/matter/female to father/form/male was the principle from which all other social, scientific, and ethical principles flowed.

FATHERS, MOTHERS, AND SONS

The first issue I want to consider is filial love. Thomas considers the argument that a man (*homo*) ought to love his mother more than his father, because he owes his body to his mother but his soul to God and not to his father.[24] Moreover, a mother loves her child and suffers for it more than the father does. Thomas responds that the primary debt of love is not to the mother but to the father. He quotes Jerome's commentary on Ezek. 44:25, which says that '"man ought to love God the Father of all, and then his own father," and

---

[24] ST II-II, 26, 10.

mentions the mother afterwards'. In individual relationships the capacity to love is influenced by the vices and virtues of the persons involved, but in principle:

> the father should be loved more than the mother. For father and mother are loved as principles of our natural origin. Now the father is principle in a more excellent way than the mother, because he is the active principle, while the mother is a passive and material principle. Consequently, strictly speaking, the father is to be loved more. In the begetting of man, the mother supplies the formless matter of the body; and the latter receives its form through the formative power that is in the semen of the father. And though this power cannot create the rational soul, yet it disposes the matter of the body to receive that form.[25]

This is an illuminating example of the phallocentrism that informs the logic of Thomas's natural law theology. The biological facts of reproduction—as understood by Aristotelian science—provide the blueprint for ethical principles. Yet this account, rooted as it is in definitions of fatherhood and motherhood which derive from biological laws of nature as understood by Aristotle, sits uneasily alongside Thomas's more relational and linguistic account of fatherhood in his trinitarian theology.

We have seen that, in his account of relationships within the Trinity, Thomas insists that fatherhood derives its meaning from God's relationship to the Son. This is a non-phallic understanding of fatherhood in relational rather than inseminating terms, and the language is that of conception and birth, not of insemination. There is a hiatus between this account, and the Aristotelian account in which love of God the Father translates into a duty of the child to love the biological father because the inseminating function of the penis belongs within the copulative order of form in relation to matter, which in turn has to do with the fatherhood of God in relation to creation. So from the role of the semen in sexual intercourse flows a whole system of divinely commanded duties and loyalties, beginning with the requirement for the child to abandon its first love for the mother to whom it owes its bodily origins and its earliest experiences of love, and to transfer these onto the father because of a formal phallic principle of generation. As we shall see in the next chapter, Daniel Boyarin refers to the symbolic phallus losing the biological penis.[26] By a theological sleight of hand, Thomas makes the brief experience of sexual ejaculation the cornerstone of the social order, so that the symbolic phallus acquires a mighty power that can scarcely be imagined in relation to the bodily organ that bestows upon it such significance.

---

[25] ST II-II, 26, 10.

[26] Daniel Boyarin, 'On the History of the Early Phallus', in Sharon Farmer and Carol Braun Pasternack (eds), *Gender and Difference in the Middle Ages* (Minneapolis MN: University of Minnesota Press, 2003).

So, whether in Thomist or Lacanian mode, the infant relationship entails a process of denial and paternal intervention into the maternal relationship, subjugating the child's desire for the mother to the religious duty to love God the Father and the ethical duty to love the human father. This results in a linguistic order—in Thomas no less than in his distant postmodern interpreters—in which there is no language for the expression and cultivation of maternal desire, nor for the formation of female subjectivities and genealogies exemplified by the relationship between mothers and daughters and inspired by a maternal divine.[27] This blights not only the maternal relationship but also the relationship between culture and nature with a threatening and consuming otherness, so that the female body and nature come to be seen as a voracious and dangerous force ('formless matter') that must be controlled by the rational masculine subject (the 'formative power') of the linguistic order.

Thomas sets in motion all these forces in his rationale for privileging the father over the mother in terms of the loyalty of the child. The subject of the western social order is formed through the repression of the bodily, desiring relationship to the mother by way of a codified set of principles in which patriarchal social hierarchies are underwritten by the fatherhood of God. From a Lacanian perspective, the symbolic and the real now occupy the position of form and matter, but the former continues to be paternal/male and the latter continues to be maternal/female.

Yet this rationalization and ordering of filial love runs contrary to Thomas's privileging of desire as the dynamic orientation of creation towards God. If the most natural and fundamental experience of desire is that of a child for its mother, one might surely argue that this is the original source of our longing for God and the primal relationship that informs our understanding of divine love, nurture, and compassion?[28] If this were so, a different language would be needed than that of Aristotelian natural theology, and the maternal God of the Christian faith would pose a significant challenge to the patriarchal order of the ancient world. This would be a more coherent development of Thomas's trinitarian theology than his capitulation to the Aristotelian social order, but it is the road not taken by the Christian tradition.

The suppression of infant desire in order to follow the dictates of virtue and reason forms the western soul with its conscious and unconscious dynamics of duty, desire, and transgression, all played out in the Name of the Father and the unconscious yearning for the mother. If a man is to fulfil his vocation to cultivate the life of the intellect as the highest expression of the *imago Dei*, and if he is to privilege his rational soul over the inferiority of his body, then he

---

[27] See Luce Irigaray, *Sexes and Genealogies*, trans. Gillian C. Gill (New York: Columbia University Press, 1993).

[28] I discuss this in relation to the theology of Hans Urs von Balthasar in Tina Beattie, *New Catholic Feminism: Theology and Theory* (London and New York: Routledge, 2006), pp. 249–53.

must resist his desire for his mother in order to love his father more, because it is his father, not his mother, who predisposed him to receive his soul from God. (We must remember that Thomas is writing for his male students—he is not remotely concerned with the mother–daughter relationship.)

HUSBANDS AND WIVES

My next focus is Thomas's understanding of marriage, for if the patriarchal principles of Aristotelian philosophy infect his representation of parenthood with what could be called a matricidal ethos, they also have implications for his representation of a man's love for his wife. Thomas considers the argument that a man should love his wife more than his mother and father,[29] on the basis that Genesis refers to a man leaving his father and mother to join to his wife (Gen. 2:24); St Paul says that men should love their wives as themselves (Eph. 5:33), and Aristotle includes the virtue of friendship among the goods of marriage (*Ethic.* viii, 12). Thomas disagrees. Although a man loves his wife with greater intensity than his parents because of their bodily union, he should love his parents with greater reverence. This is because he should love his neighbours more than his own body, and his parents are his principles and should therefore be loved most of all. When the Apostle (St Paul) refers to a man loving his wife as himself, he does not mean that he should love her equally with himself, 'but that a man's love for himself is the reason for his love of his wife, since she is one with him. . . . [T]he particle "as" denotes not equality of love but the motive of love. For the principal reason why a man loves his wife is her being united to him in the flesh'. It's interesting to note here, as a relevant aside, that Thomas uses the Latin '*homo*' and '*vir*' interchangeably in this discussion, even though the context makes quite clear that he is talking about male in relation to female (husband in relation to wife). This suggests that even when Thomas uses the generic '*homo*', there is not necessarily an intention to distinguish between that which pertains exclusively to the male and that which pertains to men and women alike. Thomas's thought is androcentric through and through, and we can presume the absence of any particular concern with women's ideas, perceptions, and interpretations even when he uses '*homo*' rather than '*vir*'.

The Christian understanding of marriage is promoted as the apotheosis of human relationships in modern Catholic doctrine. Yet if we consider carefully what Thomas is suggesting in this discussion of marriage and friendship in the *Summa theologiae*, we see that in subtle ways, his understanding is a

---

[29] ST II-II, 26, 11.

devaluation rather than an enrichment of the Aristotelian view of marriage. For Aristotle as for Thomas, friendship is one of the most noble and selfless forms of human love, and for Aristotle the virtue of friendship is one of the potential goods of marriage.[30] In *Summa Contra Gentiles*, Thomas places considerable emphasis on the importance of equality and friendship in marriage, as part of his argument against divorce and polygamy,[31] but in the *Summa theologiae* he does not consider marriage in terms of friendship.[32] At the very least, then, we should note an inconsistency in Thomas's view of marriage and in the relationship of equality and/or subordination which a virtuous marriage entails. In the *Summa theologiae*, the invocation of the principles of generativity allows Thomas to devalue the natural loving relationship between husband and wife, to insist that there is a duty of love to the parents which in principle exceeds that of marriage. In the process, he seems to rob the wife of her personality and subjectivity, reducing her to the level of a fleshy union that incorporates her into a man's love of himself. Thomas offers a more thoughtful and rich view of marriage elsewhere in the *Summa theologiae*,[33] but this short discussion of filial responsibility gives some insight into the far-reaching effects that Aristotelianism had on the ordering of even the most intimate relationships in medieval society.

So far then, we have seen that the domestic world of marriage and parenthood is not, in Thomas's view, primarily a space of graced desire in which the natural desire of a child for its mother and a husband and wife for one another becomes a source of revelation and wisdom. Rather than learning from such desires, the virtuous life demands that they are overridden by a rational philosophical principle premised upon an abstract notion of fatherhood and motherhood devoid of the material bonds of emotional life. Of course, Thomas is pragmatic enough to know that such principles cannot always be adhered to in practice, but they are nevertheless the ideals that he promotes. The flourishing and happiness of human relationships become subjugated to duty in the interests of the good ordering of society and the cultivation of the intellect in its longing for God, all organized around phallic principles of origination as paternal insemination. This may be troubling enough, but it

---

[30] Cf. *Nicomachean Ethics* 1162a, 25–7. For a helpful discussion of Aristotle's views of marriage and family life, see Lorraine Smith Pangle, *Aristotle and the Philosophy of Friendship* (Cambridge: Cambridge University Press, 2003), pp. 89–104. For Thomas's view of friendship, see Daniel Schwartz, *Aquinas on Friendship* (Oxford and New York: Oxford University Press, 2007).

[31] SCG III, 2, 123–4.

[32] There is a discussion of marriage in the Supplement to the *Summa theologiae*, compiled after Thomas's death. Here, Thomas makes a brief reference to friendship, but this is not in the context of the bond between husband and wife but in terms of the extension of bonds of friendship between different kinship groups, with reference to the incest taboo. See *Summa theologiae*, Supplement, 49.

[33] See ST II-II, 153, 2.

becomes even more troubling when we consider how Thomas appeals to the belief that women are created to be less rational than men, to justify their subordination in society as well as the family. Interestingly from a Lacanian perspective, Thomas focuses explicitly on the function of language as a graced medium of communication and authority. My third focus, then, is the question of women in relation to knowledge.

WOMEN, LANGUAGE, AND AUTHORITY

Thomas considers the extent to which language can be said to be endowed with gratuitous grace.[34] Earlier, he has distinguished between sanctifying grace, which is given to the individual to unite him or her with God, and gratuitous grace by way of which some lead others to God.[35] Thomas argues that such language must be endowed with gratuitous grace, because it is through teaching and speaking that we make ourselves understood by others, and only by speaking can a person's wisdom and knowledge be communicated to lead others to God. However, Thomas quotes from 1 Cor. 14:34—'Let women keep silence in the churches', and from 1 Tim. 2:12—'I suffer not a woman to teach', to argue that 'the grace of the word is not becoming to women'.[36] Although women might have such grace in the context of private conversations, they must not be allowed to address themselves publicly to the whole Church:

> First and chiefly, on account of the condition attaching to the female sex, whereby woman should be subject to man, as appears from Gen. 3:16. Now teaching and persuading publicly in the church belong not to subjects but to the prelates (although men who are subjects may do these things if they be so commissioned, because their subjection is not a result of their natural sex, as it is with women, but of something supervening by accident). Secondly, lest men's minds be enticed to lust, for it is written (Ecclus. 9:11): 'Her conversation burneth as fire.' Thirdly, because as a rule women are not perfected in wisdom, so as to be fit to be entrusted with public teaching.

Passages such as these are often cited by feminist critics of Thomas, but from a Lacanian perspective such criticisms seldom penetrate deeply enough into the nature of the problem. The whole linguistic distinction between sanctifying and gratuitous grace—the former as fundamental to what it means to be human in relation to God, and the latter as an authoritative medium for public teaching and preaching that is exclusively male—paves the way for the twofold ordering of language that informs Lacanian psychoanalysis. As we

---

[34] ST II-II, 177, 1.   [35] ST II-I, 111, 1.   [36] ST II-II, 177, 2.

shall see, the rise of the universities effects a rupture in the order of discourse. Men of learning would appropriate to themselves the highly specialized and combative dialectics of Latin scholasticism and would claim the authority to teach, preach, and form the social body, while women would lay claim to a vernacular language of theological desire, lavishly expressed in bodily images of erotic and maternal union, which claimed direct and intimate knowledge of God and paved the way for the Lacanian reclamation of this site of linguistic otherness in *Seminar XX* (see Chapter 15).

We should note how Thomas's justification for this linguistic separation is based on the idea of women as naturally subject, women as sexually dangerous, and women as lacking in wisdom. Thomas's words might appear to have lost their purchase on modern understanding (except perhaps in the Roman Catholic Church which still excludes women from ordination and positions of ecclesial authority), but from different perspectives both Lacan and Luce Irigaray would insist that the concepts he invokes have lost none of their power. The social order still functions in terms of gendered hierarchies encoded and perpetuated in the privileging of one form of language over another, with the excluded and silenced other being the bearer of forbidden meanings to do with nature, sexuality, and lack of wisdom or, in modernity's more reductive meanings, rationality and the bodily excess of desire and enjoyment that it refuses to acknowledge.

THE LEGACY OF SCHOLASTICISM

What scholasticism gives with one hand, it takes away with the other. On the one hand, in its account of natural law, personal conscience, eschatological equality, and the common good, it democratizes Aristotle and relativizes the power of the state and the sovereign in far-reaching ways. Porter points out that 'Moral commitments that are so basic to late-twentieth-century Western moral thinking that they now seem self-evident were in fact mediated to modernity through the scholastic concept of the natural law.'[37] She argues that the scholastics' emphasis on rationality and freedom, with its ethical characteristics of non-maleficence and equality, 'leads them to affirm an ideal of equality grounded in shared humanity and moral agency, even though they also qualify this ideal in important (and often regrettable) ways'.[38]

On the other hand, while Thomas and his contemporaries filter Aristotle through the potentially liberating vision of Christian accounts of human equality and freedom informed by Stoic accounts of law and individual

---

[37] Porter, *Natural and Divine Law*, p. 165.   [38] Porter, *Natural and Divine Law*, p. 142.

conscience, they also invest the Father God of Jesus Christ with the attributes and authority of an ancient Greek patriarch, implicitly invested in the inseminating phallus of Neoplatonism with devastating consequences for the sexual ordering of Christian and post-Christian societies. Thomas's attentiveness to linguistic nuance seems to desert him when dealing with the divine fatherhood, so that a dangerous literalism creeps in which infects not only his theology but his cosmology, his anthropology, his ethics, and his politics. There is nothing analogous about the relationship between Thomas's Aristotelian God and the socio-sexual laws of the medieval world. There is no slippage, no freedom, no space for difference. God the Father unambiguously orders the hierarchies and relationships of the cosmos in ways that directly image his paternal authority and his phallic power. This is what feminist theologians refer to when they criticize Christian patriarchy, and various forms of contemporary Thomism still fail to take seriously the well-grounded challenges that feminism poses.

These ideas seeded themselves in the Aristotelian ordering of knowledge in the universities, from where they spread through all levels of social life so that they became the normative and naturalized world view of western culture, until the disruptions of late modernity began to shake their foundations. Today, liberal individualism retains and develops the egalitarian vision of its Christian antecedents, but it also retains the conflicts and contradictions that arise from the uneasy juxtaposition of philosophical reason with Christian revelation, so that (according to Lacan) these exercise an unconscious power over the human soul. Ancient sexual turmoils still seethe beneath the gloss of liberalism, and Lacan insists that we cannot understand and address these unless we understand the theological context within which they were fomented.

There are, however, other ways of reading Thomas and remaining faithful, not to the letter but to the spirit of his theology. This is also true of the natural law tradition. Natural law is, as we have seen, not a fixed set of rules, but a generalized set of principles as to how humans understand themselves in relation to the living world of which we are a part. It is open to different interpretations, and will always be subject to theological and anthropological assumptions about what it means to be human and what kind of God or transcendent vision a culture or individual does or does not believe in. So, for example, Porter writes that

> The difference between Nietzsche's moral vision and Christian morality is not that one is natural and the other is not. Both are visions grounded in natural human inclinations, but each one gives priority to a different set of inclinations and subordinates and directs the others in accordance with those it privileges.[39]

---

[39] Porter, *Natural and Divine Law*, pp. 144–5.

The natural law that prevailed in ancient Greece was a pagan order, under-stood by a culture that had a radically different concept of the human in relation to God than that which was introduced by Christianity, which was different again from the culture of Hebrew monotheism. That both of these visions have been historically incorporated into Christianity is beyond dispute, and there is quite simply no other Christianity than that which has developed within this syncretistic matrix of philosophical and religious narratives. But the very fact that Greek philosophy and the Hebrew scriptures have so profoundly shaped Christianity attests to its fundamental characteristic as a universal and incarnational faith that seeks common ground with its religious and philosophical counterparts. The challenge is—as it always has been—to ask in what ways Christianity is continuous with the story of humankind in its long historical coming to be, and in what ways it interrupts and disrupts this story in a way which effects a break with all that went before and brings about a paradigmatic transformation in the relationship between humankind, God, and the rest of creation. It is far beyond my purposes here to explore how many complex responses have been offered to that question, but natural law has always been the way in which the Catholic tradition has kept its boundar-ies open to historical and cultural diversity, so that there has been a flexibility and plurality within the multiple sub-traditions that make up its complex history. Whether or not medieval society could have been ordered according to a different model of gender, nature, and God is an anachronistic question, but today it is one of the most urgent questions facing not only the Catholic Church, but all humankind.

I am proposing that it would be possible for Catholic theology to provide an effective response to the challenges posed by feminism on the one hand and the environmental crisis on the other, not by breaking with the greatest thinkers of its own tradition, but by bringing them to a greater fullness than they themselves were able to achieve. Among the many Thomisms that have expressed what it means to be Catholic in a changing world that is always expressive of the goodness of God, there are yet more Thomisms to be discovered, including a Lacanian Thomism that can both learn from and respond to Lacan.

However, this entails going further still in my critique of Thomas. In this chapter, I have suggested that there are unresolved tensions in his attempt to reconcile Greek philosophy and Christian theology with regard to the father-hood of God and an Aristotelian account of natural law and the social structures that it informs.

I want to ask later how closer attention to Thomas's maternal Trinity might challenge his interpretation of natural law and the consequences that flow from it. However, in the next chapter, I ask how the tensions we have explored in this chapter are internalized and manifest themselves in Thomas's under-standing of the contemplative life, so that we begin to see how profoundly the

Christian soul—and its Lacanian derivative—is riven through with similar tensions and inconsistencies. Here, we must attend to Platonic as well as Aristotelian influences, which are by no means unique to Thomas, and which have from the beginning influenced the ways in which Christian man has positioned himself before God. In the next chapter then, the *Summa theologiae* provides a window through which it is possible to discern how unresolved anxieties associated with dualistic relationships between form and matter, sexuality and God, wounded the western soul and contributed towards the symptoms that manifest themselves in the Freudian unconscious of the modern psyche.

7

Angels, Demons, and the Man of God

The *Summa theologiae* of Thomas Aquinas is more than a text about the world, for it is also a text that has helped to create a world—not only the world of Roman Catholicism but western culture more generally through the pervasive influence of Aristotelianism on academic and institutional life, at least until late modernity. It belongs within the Aristotelian modelling of the western world, woven together from many who went before Thomas and filtered through the interpretations of many who would come after him, which inscribed itself upon the human heart in the practice of prayer and contemplation, and on the social body through the teaching and preaching of the medieval Church and the universities.

In this chapter, I consider in more depth how the shaping of the contemplative spirit according to Thomas bears the marks of contradiction and conflict that I have identified in his ideas about ethics, law, and sexual difference. In the next chapter, I ask how these ideas were absorbed and disseminated through the rise of the medieval university. In order to maintain a Lacanian perspective, I begin by suggesting ways in which the following can be read as an early precursor to the more dualistic and body-denying philosophies of the Enlightenment, and to the ruptured consciousness of the western soul that is exposed in Freudian psychoanalysis.

DESIRE, IMAGINATION, AND DAMNATION

We have seen that, according to Lacan, the formation of the individual psyche is inseparable from its cultural, political, and religious environments. In secular society, the authority of the Father God of the Christian tradition is re-invested in the symbolic order. Our social encryption comes about by the power of the symbolic to form us in its image and make us subservient to its commands by way of a traumatic process of separation, bodily alienation, and the repression of desire associated with the maternal relationship and with the effects of castration. Fearing separation above all else, the subject finds himself already cut off from that which he desires above all else, although he has no language for either his fear or his desire. They lurk at the outer fringes of his unconscious, blending into a limitless and abysmal otherness that threatens his dissolution—a dissolution that he both seeks and avoids, for it is the meeting point between love and abjection, ecstasy and horror, *eros* and *thanatos*, that in modernity constitutes the Kantian sublime and/or the Lacanian real (see Chapter 10).

In the rationalized cultures of modernity, a powerful linguistic taboo associated with the phallus functions to bar these unresolved desires and fears from the consciousness of the subject. They have become unmentionable, except through the permission to speak accorded by psychoanalysis. However, in the porous culture of pre-modern Christianity, language was a bearer of more diverse and expressive meanings, and there was far greater seepage between the rational and the non-rational. The imagination held the self in being as a fluid conjoining of spirit and flesh, matter and form. The hopes and fears engendered by this found potent expression in the exuberant excesses and devotions of popular religion and in the more constrained but nonetheless expressive contemplative practices, charitable works, and intellectual activities of those in the universities and religious orders.

In such a culture, the stream of desire flows freely between the intellect and the body, and the purification of this stream is the major challenge of the Christian life, at least for the educated and devout. In the virtuous soul, desire is a crystal stream of longing through which the self rises towards God, and the imagination is home to only the most noble and exalted of phantasms. Even these are a distraction, for the ultimate aspiration is union with God, in which every form of human knowledge dissolves within the divine mystery.

However, this level of contemplation is attainable only by the few, and for the vast majority of people, desire is not so much a mountain stream as a muddy bog silted up with the body's cravings and infected with the demonic fantasies of a corrupted imagination. This, for Thomas, is the conflicted milieu within which the human must seek union with God, as a fallen creature with a vocation to transcend the corruption and pollution of sin in order to attain to the beatific vision. Moreover, from a modern perspective it seems that a disturbing arbitrariness attaches to this vocation to God, for Thomas—like all pre-modern theologians—upholds the doctrine of predestination.[1]

This is one of those sections in the *Summa theologiae* where Thomas tries to rationalize a deeply problematic scriptural doctrine by arguing that it violates neither human freedom and contingency, nor divine providence and perfection. It is beyond my purposes here to attempt to unravel the complexity of his argument, except to note that it adds an additional level of anxiety to the

---

[1] See ST I, 23.

already vexed question of what one can or must do to be saved. This anxiety would reach a sublimated crescendo in the Calvinist theologies of the Reformation, but it is not lacking from Thomas's account of sin and grace, damnation and providence.[2] The possibility of squandering one's eternal hope through a life of sin was very real, for while one could do nothing to change the divine will, even the elect who were pre-destined for heaven could forfeit their destiny through mortal sin, while those who were not among the elect might take their place through a life of virtue.[3]

In considering how the soul navigates between the body and God, we must bear in mind that for Thomas, there is always a gendered dimension to its various capacities, even when this is not explicitly spelled out, and regardless of a person's biological sex. When it is in passive, receptive mode the soul is maternal/female in relation to whatever is acting upon it—receiving, conceiving, and being at rest in God—and when it is active it is paternal/male—forming concepts, arousing the will, and generating desire. These are, however, only theoretical distinctions, for in the actual processes by way of which we experience, interpret, reflect upon, and act within the world, they are inseparable. Just as forms and matter are hypotheses that do not exist except insofar as they exist together, so the active and passive capacities of the soul are always conjoined in the one movement by way of which the human continuously experiences the unity of body and soul as the condition of his or her being—except, as we shall see, in the highest states of contemplation or rapture, when the soul is entirely passive and at rest in God. This is the most 'feminized' condition of the soul, although in Thomas this is not spelled out as it is in some of his monastic counterparts, who adopt the language of the *Song of Songs* and use highly eroticized nuptial imagery to speak of the soul as the bride who longs for her bridegroom, Christ. The elimination of this flamboyant language of gendered mystical desire is, from a Lacanian perspective, one of the most enduring impacts of the rise of scholasticism on the making of the western mind, but we must return to that suggestion later.

The conjoining of form and matter suggests the potential for the contemplative life to be portrayed as a harmonious marriage of body and soul, through the orchestration of desire, the overcoming of concupiscence, and the delight of the corporeal self within the being of God. Yet as we shall see, Thomas represents it rather in terms of a sustained struggle of mind over matter, which has far-reaching implications for the Christian and post-Christian understanding of sexuality, nature, and God. Thomas's understanding of contemplation is Platonic rather than Aristotelian, and it is implicitly predicated upon a dualistic

---

[2] I am grateful to Phillip Taliadoros for alerting me to the significance of the theology of predestination in Thomas's theology.

[3] See ST I, 23, 6.

concept of God as form and body as matter, so that the closer one comes to union with God, the more one rises above one's material condition.

But this is not quite as straight as it seems, for as we have seen, the God whom Thomas encounters in contemplation is not paternal but maternal, not One but trinitarian. By the a-logic of Thomas's own mystical theology, contemplation within the Trinity might invite maternal analogies of the infant soul in the womb of God, rather than either the Platonic analogies of mind over matter that he adopts, or the more eroticized nuptial imagery used by some of his monastic counterparts as well as by some of his recent interpreters such as Hans Urs von Balthasar.[4] Thomas's unconscious resistance to such analogical maternal language through the repressive influences of Greek concepts of the One, Form, and First Principle underlies the whole question I am raising in this book.

CONTEMPLATION, EMBODIMENT, AND THE SOUL

While Thomas is traditionally interpreted as embracing Aristotelianism over and against Platonism, recent scholarship has drawn attention to the extent to which Platonism pervades his thought with regard to the relationship between the soul, the body, and God.[5] An acknowledgement of this is vital for any Lacanian feminist enquiry into Thomas's understanding of the relationship between mind and body; the relationship between God, forms, and matter; and the implications of this in terms of postmodern concepts of language, gender, desire, and God.

An Aristotelian account of knowledge allows for no transcendent capacity by way of which the soul (the human form) might escape its material context in order to contemplate God directly, and on one account Thomas agrees with this (see Chapter 2). The mortal human cannot know the essence of God because he or she is essentially embodied. The soul's receptivity to the grace of God illuminates our sensory experiences, and therefore wisdom emerges from within and not over and against the composite interdependence of form and matter that constitutes the human person. Nevertheless, there are two degrees

---

[4] See Tina Beattie, *New Catholic Feminism: Theology and Theory* (London and New York: Routledge, 2006).

[5] See Patrick Quinn, *Aquinas, Platonism, and the Knowledge of God* (Aldershot: Avebury, 1996). See also Quinn, 'St. Thomas Aquinas's Concept of the Human Soul and the Influence of Platonism', in John M. Dillon (ed.), *The Afterlife of the Platonic Soul: Reflections of Platonic Psychology in the Monotheistic Religions* (Leiden: Koninklijke Brill NV, 2009), pp. 179–86. See also Fran O'Rourke, 'Jacques Maritain and the Metaphysics of Plato', in William Sweet (ed.), *Approaches to Metaphysics* (Dordrecht: Kluwer Academic Publishers, 2004), pp. 229–48, for an interesting study of Plato's influence on Thomism in the work of Jacques Maritain.

of spiritual experience in which Thomas minimizes or even negates altogether the soul's dependence on the body for its awareness and perceptions. These are contemplation, and rapture.

Thomas wants to say that, by way of supernatural grace, even in this life the soul can attain to contemplative knowledge of God beyond all conceptualization and language (but not, significantly, beyond the phantasms produced by the imagination), and this entails a capacity to sublimate the sensory influences of the body in order to enter more fully into the mystery of God. Given that the intellect has both a contemplative and an active capacity—directed towards inner reflection on truth and external activity in the world respectively—these can be understood as two alternative forms of human life.[6] Thomas distances himself from Aristotle's threefold understanding of human activity as orientated towards contemplation, active participation in society, and the pursuit of pleasure, since he regards the latter as pertaining to our animality and therefore not as a characteristic that is uniquely human.[7] This subtle devaluing of the desire for pleasure has significant implications for the subsequent development of western values. It finds potent affirmation in the Kantian privileging of duty over desire and in the pall of suspicion that hangs over the pursuit of pleasure in modern ethics, until postmodern consumerism would eventually overwhelm the ethical virtue of moderation and would instead make concupiscence—the cravings and obsessions of disordered desire—the driving force behind the politics of economic growth and the consumption of goods.

In proposing two alternative forms of human life, Thomas privileges the contemplative life as the one that most fully expresses the meaning and vocation of human existence, since the contemplative life approximates most closely to our eternal life with God. Sexual pleasure is included in the proper activities of the active life, even though it allows the body temporarily to exceed the rational control of the mind, providing the sex act itself is directed towards its proper end. This is the good of procreation of the species within the context of marriage, for only monogamous marriage produces the conditions under which a child can be responsibly reared.[8]

However, the contemplative life, shunning all such pleasures, encounters its most sustained struggle in the area of sexuality, for 'venereal pleasures above all debauch a man's mind'.[9] Sexual union is incompatible with the religious life, first because the intense pleasure associated with sexual intercourse fuels inordinate desire (concupiscence), and second because the responsibilities of marriage and family life distract a man from his duty to God. Thomas quotes Augustine: 'I consider that nothing so casts down the manly mind from its

---

[6] For Thomas's discussion of the relative merits of the active and contemplative life, see ST II-II, 179. Thomas uses the generic '*homines*', not '*viri*'.

[7] See ST II-II, 179, 2.   [8] ST II-II, 153, 2 and 154, 2.   [9] ST II-II, 153, 1.

height as the fondling of women, and those bodily contacts which belong to the married state.'[10]

Contemplation constitutes a state of delight and self-sufficiency ordered to the divine rather than the human, and it is enduring because it is concerned with eternal truth. It is the state of the human intellect when it conforms most closely to the inner life of God—at rest in knowing itself. This is a knowing that is mystical rather than conceptual, because it is illuminated by the divine light through and beyond the natural illumination of creation. The contemplative life, although it does not constitute perfect union with God, seeks to cultivate as fully as possible a state of mind that constitutes intimate nearness to God by transcending the fluctuating desires and conflicting impulses of the body. Nevertheless, the active life is a necessary training ground for the contemplative, in teaching us to control our passions and to better understand our reactions and relationships to others.

SOLITUDE, LOVE, AND CONTEMPLATION

While Thomas insists that charity encompasses both love of God and love of neighbour, the contemplative life is better because 'that which pertains more directly to the love of God is generically more meritorious than that which pertains directly to the love of our neighbour for God's sake'.[11] He comes precariously close here to suggesting that love of neighbour is a means to an end and not an end in itself, so that the most perfect love of God would seem to entail liberation from all human relationships and demands. Indeed, Thomas sees the highest form of contemplative religious life as that of the hermit, because 'solitude befits the contemplative who has already attained to perfection'.[12]

So the male contemplative seeks knowledge of God by withdrawing from the world, its affective and sexual relationships, and its neighbourly demands, implying that proximity to one's bodily environment and social milieu militates against drawing closer to God. The human may indeed be a social animal, but the equation of knowledge of God with solitude and abstraction is a rich seedbed for the growth of modern masculine individualism, particularly when, as we shall see in the next chapter, the intellectual community of the university takes this contemplative model as its ideal.

Even so, Thomas's understanding of the contemplative life so far can be accommodated within an Aristotelian account of the body–soul relationship. His insistence that it serves its apprenticeship in the active life and in acquiring

---

[10] ST II-II, 186, 4, quoting Augustine, *Solil.* I, 10.
[11] ST II-II, 182, 2.   [12] ST II-II, 188, 8.

a deeper understanding of God's effects through reflection on created beings, suggests a more organic spirituality than that which results from a Neoplataonic opposition between body and soul, in which knowledge is acquired not through sensory experience but through direct divine illumination. Thomas does not represent the body and its faculties as an enemy from which the soul must struggle to liberate itself. Rather the soul, while retaining its unity with the body, disciplines itself to such an extent that it is unaffected by bodily instincts and relationships when it arrives at the contemplative state. But even in contemplation, the human soul encounters God only in its duality of form and matter, and Thomas stops short of associating the contemplative state with a direct encounter with God. In this life we know the divine truth 'imperfectly, namely, "through a glass" and "in a dark manner"' (1 Cor. 13:12).[13] This mode of contemplation still depends upon the imagination for its forms and phantasms, even though it sees beyond them to the purity of the truth that they manifest.

Thomas also acknowledges that there is an affective dimension to the contemplative life, because it has to do with our desire and love for God and neighbour.[14] It is our will that moves us to contemplation as an expression of our desire for God, so that 'the contemplative life terminates in delight, which is seated in the affective power, the result being that love also becomes more intense'.[15] So, although the solitude of the hermit is the highest aspiration of the contemplative, Thomas reflects the ancient Christian belief that, even or particularly in the eremitic life, the capacity for love is enriched rather than diminished by withdrawal from the world, and this love finds its most perfect expression in the intensity of mystical prayer.

It is also worth noting that, unlike Aristotle, Thomas insists that there is a moral dimension to the contemplative life. Although the moral virtues are not essential to contemplation, they predispose us towards the contemplative life through their refinement of our love of God and neighbour, and our capacity to recognize and appreciate beauty, justice, and holiness.[16] Study can also be an important aid to the contemplative life, protecting from error and helping those in religious orders 'to avoid the lusts of the flesh'.[17] We shall return to that point in the next chapter.

So far, then, contemplation is not so much a rejection of the body by the intellect, as a refinement of the intellect's capacity to subdue and discipline the desires of the body. It entails sublimation rather than repression, insofar as it seeks not the elimination of the body and its desires but their subordination to a higher purpose. The contemplative life, although ideally experienced in

---

[13] ST II-II, 180, 4.   [14] ST II-II, 180, 1.
[15] ST II-II, 180, 1. See also ST II-II, 180, 7.
[16] ST II-II, 180, 2.   [17] ST II-II, 188, 5.

solitude and withdrawal from the world, also intensifies our love for others and for the world seen through the eyes of grace and purified desire.

RAPTURE

However, Thomas suggests that there is a rare degree of contemplative experience that is not dependent upon any sensory perceptions or imaginative capacities. This is

> the bare contemplation of the truth itself, [which] is more effective than that which is conveyed under the similitude of corporeal things, for it approaches nearer to the heavenly vision whereby the truth is seen in God's essence. Hence it follows that the prophecy whereby a supernatural truth is seen by intellectual vision, is more excellent than that in which a supernatural truth is manifested by means of the similitudes of corporeal things in the vision of the imagination.[18]

Thomas refers to this as 'rapture' and, following Augustine, he associates it with Moses and St Paul who both 'saw God's very essence'.[19] The difference between rapture and the beatific vision is that the former is transient whereas the latter is the eternal condition of those in heaven. Rapture is, argues Thomas, natural insofar as it pertains to the truth which the human naturally seeks. However, it is also an involuntary carrying away by God so that the mind withdraws from the senses in a way that 'is not contrary to nature, but above the faculty of nature'.[20] Rapture goes beyond all emotion and affectivity so that it becomes an intellectual state outside of all the senses and the appetites,[21] and it does not beatify the body but only the mind for a limited period.[22]

It is a small step from Thomas's account of rapture to a psychoanalytic account of psychosis. Consider Catherine Clément's lyrical account of depression which she describes as 'the desire for night':

> Depression is that solitary, initiating exercise of the desire for night. It may seem strange to consider depression as an exercise even when it sweeps down on the subject like a vast, uncontrollable shadow. In appearance, it is a collapse; a despondency so radical that doctors speak of a 'depressive *raptus.*' The subject who is prey to a depression has actually been stolen from the world; he is the object of an abduction. We forget that the words 'abduction' (*rapt*) and 'raptus' come from the same root as 'rapture'; we ignore the fact that the depressive is also enraptured.[23]

[18] ST II-II, 174, 2. See also the discussion in ST I, 12.
[19] ST II-II, 174, 4. See also ST II-II 175, 3. See 2 Cor. 12.1–7.
[20] ST II-II, 175, 1.   [21] ST II-II, 175, 2.   [22] ST II-II, 175, 3.
[23] Catherine Clément, *Syncope: The Philosophy of Rapture*, trans. Sally O'Driscoll and Deirdre M. Mahoney (Minneapolis MN: Univeristy of Minnesota Press, 1994), p. 25.

Was Thomas's final breakdown a succumbing to the rapture that he had spent his life so carefully feeling his way around but perhaps also trying to avoid in the ponderous logic of his Aristotelianism? Did Aristotle castrate Thomas, as the cost of his entry into philosophical reason that protected him from the blinding paradoxes of the revelation of God—the trinitarian rapture that might seduce him and hold him captive, as once his own mother had arranged for him to be held captive and seduced? And is this castration the price we must all pay, if we are not to dissolve within that wordless rapture wherein the Thing seizes me, rapes me, violates every taboo, transgresses every law, engulfs me within that time out of time which is, in the words of Julia Kristeva, 'a time of oblivion and thunder, of veiled infinity and the moment when revelation bursts forth'?[24]

When we turn to consider Kantian ethics, we must bear in mind this otherness of God that seizes the knowing subject with such violence, for it can also be interpreted in terms of the Kantian sublime. However, for now I want to focus on Thomas's attempt to explain rapture in terms of the highest intellectual state, in which all bodily constraints are removed.

In his influential studies of Thomas's Platonism, Patrick Quinn argues that Thomas's epistemology is Platonic rather than Aristotelian in his account of rapture. He quotes a passage from *De Veritate* to illustrate this:

> for the understanding to be raised to the vision of the divine essence, one's whole attention must be concentrated on this vision, since this (the vision of God) is the most intensely intelligible object, and the understanding can reach it only by striving for it with total effort. Therefore it is necessary to have complete abstraction from the bodily senses when the mind is raised to the vision of God.[25]

Quinn suggests that 'Aquinas implies that were the senses to be somehow involved, this would result in a form of sensory pollution that would taint the purity of the mental act of seeing God's essence'.[26] He quotes further from the same text:

> Nevertheless, in so far as the purity of intellectual knowledge is not wholly obscured in human understanding, as happens in the senses whose knowledge cannot go beyond material things, it has the power to consider things which are purely immaterial by the very fact that it retains some purity. Therefore, if (the mind) is ever raised beyond its ordinary level of immaterial things, namely, the divine essence, it must be wholly cut off from the sight of material things during that act. Hence, since the sensory powers can only deal with material things, one

---

[24] Julia Kristeva, *Powers of Horror: An Essay on Abjection*, trans. Leon S. Roudiez (New York: Columbia University Press, 1982), p. 9.

[25] Quinn, 'St. Thomas Aquinas's Concept of the Human Soul', p. 179, quoting Thomas Aquinas, *De Veritate*, 13.3.

[26] Quinn, 'St. Thomas Aquinas's Concept of the Human Soul', p. 179.

cannot be raised to the vision of God unless he/she is wholly deprived of the use of the bodily senses.[27]

As Quinn points out, Thomas turns to Platonism to account for 'the metaphysical nature of the mind and . . . his Christian belief that our destiny is to share God's life fully in a wholly spiritual way after death'.[28] However, whereas in Plato's *Phaedo* the liberation of the intelligent psyche from the body allows for reality to be 'seen at its most sublime' so that death can be 'philosophically welcomed as the liberator of our psychic being from its material and physical constraints',[29] Thomas has a more complex understanding of the body–soul relationship. Quinn argues that, although this is primarily Aristotelian, against Aristotle Thomas also argues for 'the substantial independence of the soul'. In other words, Thomas introduces into Aristotle's understanding of the psyche as 'the first principle of life and as the substantial form of a living being', a further attribute of independence of the soul.[30] This means that, in Quinn's reading of Thomas,

> The soul on the one hand . . . is part of the human being as its substantial form which makes each of us to be the kind of composite beings we are. Yet *anima* is also a simple intelligent substance which, though naturally related to its human body and indeed constituting the latter *as* a human body, is nonetheless essentially independent of it because of the soul's intelligent nature. . . . This complexity is formulated by Aquinas in terms of regarding the human being and the human soul itself as having an intermediate state of existence between the physical bodily and temporal world of sensory experience, on the one hand, and the immaterial, eternal and intelligible realm of divine spiritual existence, on the other.[31]

In order to appreciate how Thomas juggles these potentially conflicting philosophical perspectives, we need to consider the influence of Platonism on his understanding of creation. Thomas's account of creation is that of 'the emanation of things from the First Principle . . . the emanation of all being from the universal cause, which is God; and this emanation we designate by the name of creation'.[32] This idea of creation as emanation is not Aristotelian but Neoplatonist, mediated through the work of Dionysius to whom Thomas refers repeatedly. It has a number of implications for an understanding of creation that is Platonic rather than Aristotelian: it presumes a First Principle rather than a Prime Mover, it suggests a cycle of emanation and return through the dispersal and reintegration of beings from and back to God, and it constitutes difference as hierarchy. The more immediately a being emanates

---

[27] Quinn, 'St. Thomas Aquinas's Concept of the Human Soul', p. 180.
[28] Quinn, 'St. Thomas Aquinas's Concept of the Human Soul', p. 181.
[29] Quinn, 'St. Thomas Aquinas's Concept of the Human Soul', p. 181.
[30] Quinn, 'St. Thomas Aquinas's Concept of the Human Soul', p. 181. See ST I, 75.
[31] Quinn, 'St. Thomas Aquinas's Concept of the Human Soul', p. 182.
[32] ST I, 45, 1.

from God, the more perfect it is, and the further it is from the divine emanation, the lower its place in the ranking of being.

Quinn explains how this hierarchical ranking of beings influences Thomas's account of the soul as both the form of the body and as intelligent substance— that is, as having an existence independent of the body. I have already referred to Eleonore Stump's phrase 'metaphysical amphibians' to describe Thomas's anthropology, and it is this amphibious nature that lends to humankind its ambivalent position in the hierarchy of being. Quinn refers to Thomas's 'significant preference for describing our human way of being as being on the boundary of this physical world of time and of the non-physical eternal world to come'.[33] So, according to Quinn,

> in the hierarchy of being . . . the human body as an intelligent body is supreme in the category of bodies whereas the intelligent soul is the lowest of all the intelligent substances precisely because of its natural dependence for knowledge on the bodily senses. . . . The status of the human being for Aquinas thus becomes one in which its intelligent part, the soul, is an intelligent substance which functions at the lowest level of such intelligences because it naturally operates through the body whereas its bodily part constitutes the human being as supreme in the category of bodily substances.[34]

These ideas are also explored in another study of Platonic influences on Thomas by Wayne J. Hankey, who argues that, in the whole of the *Summa theologiae* as well as in some of its particular treatises, Thomas describes 'the Neoplatonic structure of remaining, going out, and return by which all things except the One revert upon their principle'.[35] He quotes an extract from the final Book of the *Summa contra Gentiles*, in which Thomas makes a 'thoroughly Neoplatonic assertion' about the divine unity:

> Because the most perfect unity is found in the highest summit of things, God, and because with each reality so much the more it is one, so much the greater is its power and dignity, it follows that, to the extent that things be further away from the First Principle, so much greater is the diversity and variety found in them. Therefore it is necessary that the process of emanation from God be united within this Principle itself, and be multiplied according to the lowliness of things, where it comes to its end.[36]

As we shall see later, this suggestion that multiplicity denotes distance from God stands in direct contradiction to Thomas's claim elsewhere that the diversity of

---

[33] Quinn, 'St. Thomas Aquinas's Concept of the Human Soul', p. 184.

[34] Quinn, 'St. Thomas Aquinas's Concept of the Human Soul', p. 183.

[35] Wayne J. Hankey, 'Aquinas, Plato, and Neoplatonism', in Brian Davies and Eleonore Stump (eds), *The Oxford Handbook of Aquinas* (Oxford and New York: Oxford University Press, 2012), p. 61.

[36] Hankey, 'Aquinas, Plato, and Neoplatonism', pp. 60–1, quoting Thomas Aquinas, SCG 4, 1, premium.

creation is an expression of the abundance of God, and it opens into a conflicted theological hinterland with regard to the relationship between God and the order of creation. It also undermines his insistence that the unity of God must be understood in terms of the perfect simplicity of the divine being, and not in terms of singularity. In other words, it is a qualitative rather than a quantitative unity. This is of fundamental significance for Lacan's critique of western theology and its philosophical inheritance. (See Chapters 14 and 18.)

In the Neoplatonic hierarchy of being, we discover ourselves to be the highest of the animals and the lowest of the intelligent spirits. To repeat a quote I used earlier, 'We turn out to be a crowd of hobbled angels, each isolated "behind the wall of the body", like a hermit in a moated grange.'[37] Of course, awareness of this ambiguity arrives on the scene of human consciousness long before the encounter between Greek philosophy and Christian theology, for it is arguably of the very essence of all religious awareness. Nevertheless, we see in Thomas that the attempt to think through these hierarchical relationships in philosophical terms leads to a number of inconsistencies and tensions which will one day appear as deep fissures within western consciousness.

The human soul, when understood in terms of subsistent intellect made in the image of God, has a life independent of the body. The closer it becomes to God, the more it transcends its awareness of the body and the materiality of its environment. This state can come about through disciplined attentiveness to the body, its relationships, and demands in order better to understand and control these, but it can also come about through an involuntary state of rapture when God intervenes to lift the soul entirely out of its body so that it no longer depends on any of the body's senses or faculties. Either way, the body is at least to some extent in conflict with the soul with regard to its desire for union with God, and this lends to Thomas's understanding of human nature a perplexing inconsistency. As Quinn argues, Thomas's suggestion that the higher states of contemplation are associated with a state of spiritual purity that risks being polluted by the senses, indicates the extent to which a pervasive Platonic dualism informs his understanding of the relationship between body and soul, even though this is modified and at times even negated by a more Aristotelian perspective.

SEXUAL DUALISM AND THE PHALLIC GOD

If we consider this in terms of the gendered relationship between forms and matter, soul and body, we see that Thomas is consolidating and promoting a form of sexual dualism and perpetuating a masculine desire for a disembodied

---

[37] Fergus Kerr, *Theology after Wittgenstein* (Oxford and New York: Basil Blackwell, 1988), p. 80.

mind that has infected Christian theology from the beginning. This desire is masculine, not because it is particular or essential to the biological male, but because it is the inevitable corollary of a sexual ideology that identifies man with mind and woman with body. This sense of dissociation between feminized body and masculinized mind would be increased rather than diminished in the transition from medieval Christendom to the Enlightenment. It manifests itself in two related propositions that inform Thomas's understanding of contemplation.

First, the closer one comes to knowing the mystery of God, the more one must detach one's mind from one's bodily sensations and desires. This striving for detachment encounters its greatest distraction in the form of sexual anxieties, so that the avoidance of women is an imperative for the man who is called to contemplation, and homosexuality constitutes a deadly threat to his soul—not surprisingly, perhaps, given that the avoidance of men is somewhat more difficult than the avoidance of women for all but the most solitary hermit.[38]

Second, while love of neighbour and friendship are godly dimensions of the active life, love of God alone and solitude are the characteristics of the perfection of religious life. Thomas's *homo religiosus* is a man who must choose between the ordinary relationships, desires, and affections of his social and sexual nature which, although good and given by God, are also distractions from God, and the abandonment of all relationships, desires, and ordinary affections in order for his mind to rise to a state of near-angelic contemplation of the divine mystery. Moreover, in his amphibious state he finds his highest desire calls him to intellectual union with God beyond the animality of his body, so that he knows himself to be 'a little lower than the angels' in the hierarchy of being, but higher than any other creature in the independence of the soul that is uniquely his amidst the materiality and flux of creation.

But to be human is not to be an angelic spirit free from the animality of the body. The body retains its persistent claim upon the intellect, particularly when, as in Thomas's thinking, the senses are the medium whereby the mind attains its knowledge. So the contemplative mind, with its imagination still active to provide the phantasms that it needs to think with even when purged of all bodily senses and concepts, becomes home to demons as well as angels, and the imagination becomes the battlefield wherein the fate of the soul is decided.

We must explore this in more detail, but first let me introduce a Lacanian perspective with regard to Neoplatonism and the power of the phallus. I have suggested that, for Thomas, the passive, contemplative soul is implicitly feminized

---

[38] For Thomas's discussion of the various forms of lust or concupiscence, see ST II-II, 154–5.

in relation to God, but if we push this in terms of Neoplatonic images and associations, a scenario begins to emerge that may have been deeply disturbing to Thomas—so disturbing that perhaps he was unable to think it, unlike his Neoplatonic predecessors who were sometimes explicit in associating the *Logos* of God with the phallus of antiquity.

I referred briefly in the last chapter to Daniel Boyarin's suggestion that, historically, the symbolic phallus became separated from the biological penis. Boyarin suggests that this separation acquires its decisive function within Christian theology by way of Plotinus and Neoplatonism 'The crucial step in the Phallus losing its penis is the third century Neoplatonism of Plotinus.'[39] Boyarin quotes Plotinus:

> Only the form, the idea, the *logos* are fruitful. That is the meaning of the perpetual erection of god the inventor. Matter is only the receptacle and a wet-nurse: it is sterile and receives without giving. The only true principle of generation, includ-ing perceptible things, is in the *logos*. It was for this reason, I think, that the ancient sages, speaking in riddles secretly and in the mystery rites, make the ancient Hermes always have the organ of generation ready for its work, revealing that the intelligible formative principle [*ton noeton logon*] is the generator of the things in the sense-world, but revealing too.[40]

According to Boyarin, this illustrates that

> Lacan's association between the Phallus and the Logos is . . . not an arbitrary, 'wild,' aleatory representation within western culture, but a precise interpretation of its foundations, for there can be little doubt but that Plotinus's Neoplatonism has found its way deeply into those very foundations, primarily by way of the crucial patristic thinkers who were so influenced by him.[41]

In Thomas's theology, the phallus has become veiled by a rational order that perpetuates its organizing power through descending hierarchies of fatherhood rather than phallic logocentrism, organized according to Aristotelian philosophy and underwritten by the fatherhood of God. Yet the language of divine insemin-ation cannot be evacuated of its phallic associations, and by extrapolation of its associations with the role of the penis in reproduction. We have seen in the last chapter that this is the premise upon which Thomas constructs the patriarchal order of human relationships. So the logic of Thomas's thought permits us to ask

---

[39] Daniel Boyarin, 'On the History of the Early Phallus', in Sharon Farmer and Carol Braun Pasternack (eds), *Gender and Difference in the Middle Ages* (Minneapolis MN: University of Minnesota Press, 2003), p. 10. For a discussion of Plotinus's influence on Christian Neoplaton-ism, see Vivien Boland OP, *Ideas in God according to Saint Thomas Aquinas: Sources and Synthesis* (Leiden: E. J. Brill, 1996), pp. 49–92.

[40] Plotinus, *Enneads*, trans. A. H. Armstrong, Loeb Classical Library 287 (Cambridge MA: Harvard University Press, 1987), Vol. 5, quoted in Boyarin, 'On the History of the Early Phallus', p. 10.

[41] Boyarin, 'On the History of the Early Phallus', pp. 10–11.

if, lurking in the unvoiced hinterland of his idea of the mind at rest in contemplation, is an unsettling image—a phantasm perhaps—of the female soul being penetrated by the divine phallus. Such an idea might have conjured up sexual images that Thomas would have found abhorrent. Do we begin to see why he regarded sexuality as the greatest threat to contemplation, and the avoidance of women as a fundamental necessity for the contemplative mind? While other less inhibited mystics were happy to revel in the eroticism of their desire for God, we sense a profound unease in Thomas over any such association. In order to keep the contemplative mind pure and free from sexual images, even as it opens itself to be penetrated and inseminated by God, one must resist the demonic phantasms that haunt the soul and seek to distract its desire from God primarily by way of sexual images and desires.

We begin to understand how the attempt to reconcile Aristotelian philosophy with medieval Catholicism began to produce the complex entanglements of desire, fear, and sexual confusion that Freud would discover within the modern soul—he repeatedly explained medieval beliefs in witchcraft, demon possession, and miracles in terms of hysteria.[42] However, I am not offering this kind of reductive Freudian explanation, for Lacan invites a somewhat different approach. While Freud sought to bring scientific rationalism to bear on the study of the human soul as part of advancing the cause of atheist western civilization, Lacan is more interested in showing that the ruination of the soul is the price that was paid for a civilization that is now itself in ruins. When the poet Rainer Maria Rilke was asked why he stopped psychoanalysis after only a few sessions, he is said to have replied that he was afraid that if he lost his demons, his angels would take flight as well. With Lacan, he might well have learned to live with both as the cost of being human. We therefore need to approach the latent voices of the demonic and angelic—now speaking as the voices of the Lacanian imaginary—as the sources of a serpentine truth nesting within the grids and structures of western rationality. So I want to spend some time considering the implications of that strange fusion between Aristotelian rationality and medieval angelology and demonology, by way of which Thomas paved the way for the coming to be of the Freudian soul.

ANGELS AND DEMONS

The origins of Greek philosophy can be traced back to the struggle to purge the rational mind of its religious influences, by way of which human life was

---

[42] Cf. the discussion in William J. McGrath, 'Freud and the Force of History', in Toby Gelfand and John Kerr (eds), *Freud and the History of Psychoanalysis* (Hillsdale NJ: The Analytic Press, 1992), pp. 79–98.

largely determined by the capricious whims of the gods. A similar endeavour marks both the Reformation and the Enlightenment—as we shall see. However, Thomas's medieval world was in some ways more akin to pagan religious culture than to the more rigorous biblical monotheism of Protestantism or the rationalism of the Enlightenment and its aftermath. For all Thomas's genius in developing a synthesis between Aristotelianism and Christian theology, he was a man of his times who still inhabited the world of magical and demonic powers that Charles Taylor describes in *A Secular Age*.[43] Walter Stephens observes that 'Aquinas is known to Catholic tradition as the *Doctor Angelicus* in homage to his interest in angels, but he could also be called the *Doctor Diabolicus* because he rarely discusses angels in isolation from demons.'[44]

Stephens points out that Aristotle's philosophy posed a particular challenge to medieval theologians when it came to demons, for it was unable to accommodate an account of 'suprahuman beings' within its understanding of the soul.[45] He argues that 'Aquinas provided rigorously argued, protoscientific explanations of demonic corporeality and physiology in Aristotelian terms, with a view to proving that physical interaction between humans and demons was possible.'[46] Paraphrasing Umberto Eco, Stephens suggests that 'where yes and no are opposed, Aquinas's solution was to combine them and create a "nes"'. He continues, 'Without declaring it in so many words, Aquinas argues that angels and devils have bodies that both are and are not real.'[47] Like other men of his time, Stephens points out that Thomas showed a particular concern with incubi and succubi, to such an extent that his 'entire consideration of angelic and demonic corporeality in the *Summa theologiae*' gives 'pride of place to demonic copulation'.[48]

With this in mind, I want to consider Thomas's discussion of demons in the context of Dyan Elliott's study of medieval ideas of pollution, sexuality, and demonology. Elliott focuses mainly on male clerical writings from the twelfth and thirteenth centuries, but she situates these in the context of the ongoing effects of the Gregorian reform, including the ritual purity implied in compulsory priestly celibacy, the distance this created between priests and lay people, and the increase in priestly powers associated with changes in the sacramental understanding of the Eucharist and transubstantiation.

Drawing on Mary Douglas's book *Purity and Danger*, and on psychoanalysis and other theoretical perspectives, Elliott identifies 'psychic processes'[49] which suggest a spreading culture of sexual anxiety and increasing misogyny,

---

[43] Charles Taylor, *A Secular Age* (Cambridge MA: Harvard University Press, 2007).

[44] Walter Stephens, *Demon Lovers: Witchcraft, Sex and the Crisis of Belief* (Chicago: University of Chicago Press, 2002), pp. 66–7.

[45] Stephens, *Demon Lovers*, p. 58.   [46] Stephens, *Demon Lovers*, p. 59.

[47] Stephens, *Demon Lovers*, p. 62.   [48] Stephens, *Demon Lovers*, p. 65.

[49] Dyan Elliott, *Fallen Bodies: Pollution, Sexuality, and Demonology in the Middle Ages* (Philadelphia PA: University of Pennsylvania Press, 1999), p. 8.

particularly among Dominican writers, with a growing tendency to associate women with the demonic. Using Freudian terms, she attributes this to a return of the repressed, insofar as anxieties about pollution and bodily effluvia which seeped into early Christian culture from Judaism and the surrounding cults resurfaced with renewed vigour in the Middle Ages, paradoxically, as a result of the relaxation of taboos and concerns about pollution. Elliott writes that 'The very relaxation of pollution concerns generated considerable anxiety, while theoretically moribund prohibitions continued to enjoy a covert and almost eerie afterlife.'[50] She suggests that these changing attitudes with their dark repressive undertow emerged partly through a shift in emphasis from fears associated with the risk of physical pollution to a 'revived emphasis on intention and conscious culpability as the vector for impurity', and through 'a theological refurbishment of the sacraments [which] made them theoretically impervious to many of the ancient conditions of ritual impurity as well as to the personal sinfulness of the officiating priest'.[51] Within this ostensibly rationalizing framework, Elliott argues that fears of pollution associated with such bodily functions as nocturnal emissions, impregnation, menstruation, and childbirth led to a preoccupation with questions of demonic activity, many of them focused on female sexuality. Under the pressure of needing to remain sexually pure, celibate men experienced their sexual desires and arousals as an 'intimate enemy'[52] to be overcome. So, argues Elliott,

> The distance between the pure ideal and the inevitability of an impure reality – the pure being constantly impugned by transgressions in both deed and thought – was the space within which the symbolic terrain of the demonic world was constituted.... By virtue of original sin, the human body was fallen – rendered irretrievably impure from the outset and thus vulnerable to onslaughts of demons, who were perceived as inherently the enemies of purity.... Humanity's doomed battle against the powers of defilement is exemplified in the predicament of woman, perceived both as self-contaminating (thus in a sense already a casualty of the diabolical war against humankind) and as a source of contagion to others.[53]

Elliott builds her argument through a series of case studies, including a chapter on the theological 'erasure' of the sexual female body as an expression of anxiety about the threat posed to the purity of the priesthood by the sexually active woman in the form of the priest's wife (Chapter 4). Borrowing a concept from Melanie Klein, she suggests in the next chapter that this increase in sexual anxiety results in a process of 'splitting', in which the rise of the cult of the Virgin goes hand in hand with the emergence of demonic representations of women as polluting, sexually voracious witches.

---

[50] Elliott, *Fallen Bodies*, p. 6.
[52] Elliott, *Fallen Bodies*, p. 29.
[51] Elliott, *Fallen Bodies*, p. 6.
[53] Elliott, *Fallen Bodies*, p. 2.

Before I turn to Thomas's treatment of demons and sexuality in the *Summa theologiae*, let me add a number of caveats. First, the phenomena described by Elliott were still in their infancy during Thomas's life. It would be another two centuries before two of his Dominican confreres, Heinrich Kramer and Jacob Sprenger, would write *The Malleus Maleficarum* or *Hammer of the Witches* in 1486, a document which sought to prove the existence of witches and to provide guidance to magistrates on how to identify and prosecute them. As Stephens points out, Thomas 'certainly did not recommend the discovery and prosecution of witches in the way in which these things were practised after his time'.[54]

Second, with regard to his attitudes to women, Thomas's commitment to Aristotelian philosophy makes many of his ideas repugnant from a modern feminist perspective, but there is little sign of real misogyny in his writings. What comes through is a certain indifference tinged (one suspects) with a deep underlying anxiety. He was traumatized by his early encounter with a prostitute who attempted to seduce him at the bidding of his mother and brothers, and his hagiographer reports that after that, he avoided women as a man avoids snakes.[55] However, we should bear in mind that one of Thomas's sisters, Theodora, remained his close companion and loyal supporter until his death. Reports of Thomas's attempts to avoid women are probably exaggerated, although even if they tell us little about Thomas himself, they tell us much about the emergent culture of male scholarly celibate sanctity of which he was a part.

Third, the overall style of Thomas's theology is in keeping with reports of his personality as a socially awkward and modest man (today, one might even ask if descriptions of his behaviour suggest a level of autism), and his commitment to reason manifests itself throughout the *Summa theologiae* in the pedantry of its style and its plodding attentiveness to the detail of arguments. When he discusses questions of lust and the possible influence of demons, he does so without any sense of flamboyance or repugnance, although sometimes one senses that perhaps he finds it slightly unfortunate that he has to address such topics for the benefit of his readers, who are more prey to the seductions of the flesh than he is. As I suggested earlier, we might also speculate that he was aware of the potent phallic symbolism that lurked within Neoplatonic imagery, and was assiduously trying to avoid the implications of that. The guiding hand of Aristotle steers him towards pragmatic common sense and reasoned optimism throughout his work, even though at times this tends towards a more mystical and affective trinitarian theology at one end of the spectrum, and a more disembodied Platonic dualism at the other. So in what follows, I am following Elliott in suggesting how perceptions of the

---

[54] Stephens, *Demon Lovers*, p. 59.
[55] See Anthony Kenny, *Aquinas* (Oxford: Oxford University Press, 1980), p. 2.

activities of demons can be read as symptomatic of changing psychical formations in the increasingly influential community of priestly scholars associated with the medieval universities, without wanting to read too much into them by way of Thomas's personal psychological make-up.

'SEXY DEVILS'[56]

Angels and demons are the same kind of being for Thomas, so that his extensive discussions as to the capacities and functions of angels often include references to demons as well—they are the bad and good sides of the same form of being. Thomas argues that God gives every human being a guardian angel to accompany and assist him or her on the dangerous journey through life, helping us in our struggle to be good and protecting us against the constant assault of demons, until we share the heavenly condition with an angel, or find ourselves punished by demons in hell.[57] He resists the suggestion that demons are naturally evil on the basis of his conviction that existence itself is always a good that tends towards the good. Since demons exist there is a sense in which they participate in God's being, although not in the deformity of their nature which results from sin,[58] and demons are naturally good because they belong within the original goodness of creation.[59] However, like the other angels they are endowed with freedom of will, and their sin comes from turning away from God by choosing to seek their own good apart from the divine will.

As disembodied spirits, demons have no capacity for carnal sins and derive no pleasure from them. Rather, their sins are those of pride in refusing to be subject to God, and envy in relation to the goodness of God and human goodness which serves the glory of God. This envy leads them to use the world and the flesh as weapons by which to tempt and assail humans, even though God 'knows how to make orderly use of evil by ordering it to good'.[60]

Considering how demons attack humans, Thomas argues that they have no access to a person's inner disposition, for that is known by God alone, nor do they have any power to change the will, although they can influence it and incline it to wrong-doing if it is weak.[61] However, in order to interact with human consciousness they have to appear in a form that humans can comprehend—just as scripture has to use analogies drawn from human experience in order to speak of mysteries that are beyond human comprehension. This

---

[56] I have borrowed this phrase from the title of Chapter 3 of Stephens' book, 'Sexy Devils: How They Got Their Bodies', in Stephens, *Demon Lovers*, pp. 58–86.

[57] ST I, 113.   [58] ST I, 8, 1.   [59] ST I, 63.

[60] ST I, 114, 1.   [61] ST I, 114, 2.

means that demons are able to assume what Stephens refers to as 'virtual bodies' for the purposes of engaging in activities with humans.[62] According to Stephens, 'The whole point of angelic corporeality is to *represent* angelic reality in human terms for a human audience. Otherwise, we would have no way of experiencing them and no proof that they are not imaginary.'[63] The demons' ability to induce a person to sin rests upon the extent to which they can successfully use 'the flesh and the world'[64] as sources of temptation, almost it seems through a process of trial and error. With no capacity to judge a person's weaknesses and vulnerabilities by seeing into his or her soul, they must try various forms of bodily temptation to discover what he or she might succumb to. These attacks are sometimes permitted rather than sanctioned by God, but they are also sometimes used by God as forms of punishment, in which case the demons are sent by God. With regard to the question as to whether all sins are due to the devil's temptation, Thomas answers that indirectly they are, insofar as the devil instigated original sin.[65] However, given that original sin can disrupt our reason and disorder our appetites and desires, post-lapsarian sin can come about through a failure of the will and not through direct intervention of the devil.

Thomas also argues that demons can perform miracles, not in the specific sense of intervening within the order of creation from outside as God alone can do, but in the general sense of bringing about real changes in matter. However, this happens not by changing the forms of material beings, for neither angels nor demons have such powers, but by the capacity of demons to 'employ certain seeds that exist in the elements of the world'.[66] We must come back to that point, because the suggestion that there are seeds within matter is an important distinction between Aristotelianism and Platonism in Thomas's thought, suggesting as it does that there is some active potency to matter. We have seen that Thomas is reluctant to pursue this idea, but it will be important when we come to consider more closely the relationship between forms and matter.

Demons also have the power to play tricks on the imagination. Thomas quotes Augustine (*De Cv. Dei* xviii, 18): 'Man's imagination, which whether thinking or dreaming, takes the forms of an innumerable number of things, appears to other men's senses, as it were embodied in the semblance of some animal.'[67] In other words, what we might call a figment of the imagination can also be made to appear to another person in the illusion of a material form, which might be either angelic or demonic.[68] Spiritual beings can thus acquire some objective reality, which Stephens argues would become important for later witchcraft theorists in their pursuit of women accused of having sex with

---

[62] Stephens, *Demon Lovers*, p. 62.   [63] Stephens, *Demon Lovers*, p. 66.
[64] Cf. ST I, 114, 1–2.   [65] ST I, 114, 3.   [66] ST I, 114, 4.
[67] ST I, 114, 4.   [68] See ST I, 51, 3.

the devil. To explore the implications of this, let me turn to Thomas's account of demonic intercourse.

Thomas agrees with Augustine in suggesting that demons might occasionally assume the form of incubi in order to have intercourse with women and conceive offspring. However, while Augustine is prepared to accept that demons can therefore be corporeal, Thomas wants to retain the idea that demons are immaterial beings that only assume the appearance of corporeality. He argues that the impregnating seed comes not from their assumed bodies but from seeds they have taken from men, so that they assume 'first the form of a woman, and afterward of a man', which means that the child conceived is that of a man and not of a demon.[69] Demons then, although sterile, have a dangerous anamorphic capacity, and the idea that they are capable of harvesting semen has implications for all male sexual relationships, including not only heterosexual intercourse but also homosexuality and masturbation, as well as nocturnal emissions.

Thomas argues that demons have 'nocturnal knowledge', because by the darkness of their turning away from worship of God they are separated from the divine illumination.[70] It is in contemplation and during sleep that the imagination is most susceptible to angelic and demonic influences and the production of phantasms, because of the lack of corporeal stimuli and external distractions.[71] As Elliott points out, the problem of nocturnal emissions had considerable power to exercise men's minds and cause them moral anxieties. Thomas carefully considers the different situations in which such phenomena occur, and he concludes that they are only sinful if they are caused by some sexual fantasy whose pleasurable effects linger and arouse the sleeping body. Otherwise, they can be attributed to natural causes, to the fact that the sleeping soul is not under the control of reason and is capable of phantasms that arouse the body, or to the wickedness of the devil. Thomas cites here an example from the *Collationes Patrum* (Coll. Xxii, 6) 'of a man who was ever wont to suffer from nocturnal pollution on festivals, and that the devil brought this about in order to prevent him from receiving Holy Communion'.[72] We see here the association between the Eucharist and ritual purity and the medieval blurring of boundaries between moral intentionality and pollution to which Elliott refers. Although unintentional emissions involve no personal sin from Thomas's perspective, they are still sources of pollution that come between the desire for God and the body's capacity to come into contact with the presence of God in Communion. Body and God are once again in conflict through a natural sexual function, even though there has been no intention to sin.

In much of the foregoing discussion, Thomas is straining to defend a proposition that he is clearly reluctant to discuss at length, for it sits so

---

[69] ST I, 51, 3.
[70] ST I, 64, 1. I am indebted here to the unpublished research of Rebecca de Saintonge.
[71] Cf. ST I, 86, 4.   [72] ST II-II, 154, 5.

uneasily within his Aristotelianism. Given his claim never to have experienced sexual arousal after the encounter with the prostitute, he is addressing issues that clearly troubled the men he was teaching, even if he himself was protected from such disturbances of the flesh.

Yet these are all revealing exchanges if we bear in mind that Thomas was pioneering ideas that would establish themselves as normative in the pre-modern world, and which would impact with catastrophic results upon the bodies of those accused of witchcraft and consorting with the devil, the majority of them women. The association of sex with demonic possession, the idea that men face their most sustained spiritual battle in the area of controlling their sexuality and avoiding women, and the ways in which these ideas shaped the western understanding of the intellectual life as well as the life of contemplation would have far-reaching effects. In order to explore this more, I turn now to the rise of the medieval universities as the medium by way of which Aristotelianism entrenched itself at all levels of western know-ledge, with profound consequences for the participation and representation of women.

8

The Rise of the Universities

Thomas Aquinas's Aristotelian understanding of a gendered cosmic order emanating from the fatherhood of God had a pervasive influence on his understanding of the social order and the contemplative life. A close reading of Thomas's attribution of gender to forms and matter, and the consequences that flow from that in terms of a vast metanarrative which spans every aspect of being, lends potent support to Jacques Lacan's insistence that the repression of this gendering of being in terms of perfection and lack has done nothing to deprive it of its power to order sexual relationships and western concepts of subjectivity, identity, and otherness.

I turn now to consider how the emergence of the medieval university with its Aristotelian influences constitutes a pivotal moment in Lacan's understanding of the development of western culture. If we want to understand the discursive cuts that rupture the western soul there are several places we might start, but the rise of scholasticism is one such place. The new universities soon became the think tanks of the late medieval world. We might even say they were the sperm banks, because from them flowed the ideas that would inseminate the social body with a pervasive Aristotelian influence which would endure long after they ceased to be centres for the production and dissemination of knowledge organized around the unifying and controlling vision of Christian doctrine. Through this influence, philosophical constructs of sexual difference understood in terms of perfection and lack, act and potency, form and matter, became normative and naturalized, until the very attempt to think in gendered terms disappeared behind an impenetrable screen of androcentrism which still prevails today. In its attempt to reanimate questions of gender, sexuality, nature, embodiment, and otherness, feminism shatters the solid bedrock upon which western knowledge had established itself, and it is no wonder that the resulting struggle is epochal in its implications.

THE QUEST FOR ORDER

John O'Malley describes the creation of the university as 'the greatest and most enduring achievement of the Middle Ages ... for which there was no precedent in the history of the West'.[1] Although there are many theories as to why and how these institutions of learning spread across Europe, it seems they were at least partly a response to growing urbanization and to the quest for order and structure at a time when western culture was seeking to extricate itself from the flux and uncertainty of an anarchic past. Even as our world tips towards a future seething with violent and chaotic possibilities that become ever more probable as the crises surrounding us deepen, we should remember that this was in some ways the kind of world from which western Europe was emerging between the eleventh and thirteenth centuries, albeit within a very different technological and cultural context.

John Witte Jr refers to a series of revolutions in the relationship between religion and law in western history, revolutions that were 'products of radical shifts in the dominant metaphors, in the dominant belief-systems of the people',[2] and he includes among these the Papal Revolution of 1075 and its aftermath. Beginning with the Gregorian Reform and extending through to the thirteenth century, this was a period of 'an enormous transformation of Western society', referred to by Harold Berman as 'the "first modern age" of the West'.[3] Here is how Witte summarizes this revolutionary era:

> The West was renewed through the rediscovery and study of the ancient texts of Roman law, Greek philosophy, and patristic theology. The first modern Western universities were established in Bologna, Rome, and Paris with their core faculties of theology, law, and medicine. A number of towns were transformed into city-states. Trade and commerce boomed. A new dialogue was opened with the sophisticated cultures of Judaism and Islam. Great advances were made in the natural sciences, in mechanics, in literature, and in art, music, and architecture.[4]

An appreciation of how the universities were positioned in relation to this era of transformation is crucial for a Thomist reading of Lacan, and also for any attempt to think through Lacan's Thomism from the perspective of gender and postmodernity.

---

[1] John O'Malley, 'Were Medieval Universities Catholic Universities?', *American Magazine*, 14 May 2012, <http://www.americamagazine.org/content/article.cfm?article_id=13417> [accessed 25 July 2012].
[2] John Witte Jr, *God's Joust, God's Justice: Law and Religion in the Western Tradition* (Grand Rapids MI: William B. Eerdmans Publishing Co., 2006), p. 7.
[3] Witte Jr, *God's Joust, God's Justice*, p. 12, referring to Harold J. Berman, *Law and Revolution: The Formation of the Western Legal Tradition* (Cambridge MA: Harvard University Press, 1983).
[4] Witte Jr, *God's Joust, God's Justice*, p. 12.

In the opening chapter of a four-volume study titled *A History of the University in Europe*, Walter Rüegg points out that the rise of the universities was accompanied by widespread debate and conflict about the ordering and categorization of knowledge.[5] These arguments spilled over into all ranks of society in a thirst for knowledge that served different purposes among different classes. For ecclesiastical authorities and intellectuals the universities were a means to greater power and social advancement, while for peasants they might provide the scientific means to alleviate the struggle for existence. In particular, the popes recognized that the universities might provide the intellectual order and justification needed to undergird the doctrines of the Church in a time of competing and divergent beliefs and 'expanding heresies', while also serving to 'strengthen the central papal powers against the aspirations of the earthly powers'.[6]

What emerged in this process was an ethos which

> alongside *amor sciendi*—intellectual integrity, broad learning, and conceptual clarity—... sought to sustain virtues like humility, love of one's neighbour, piety, fatherly solicitude towards students, loyalty and collegial solidarity towards the university, and deference towards the ecclesiastical and earthly incumbents of high university offices.[7]

In other words, this aspired to be a community of celibate male scholars bound together by the paternalistic benevolence of their masters, who knew their place within a cosmic hierarchy ordered by God the Father and presided over by an eternal law which extended from the most basic elements of the universe through the social and scientific order to the heights of heaven.

Rüegg asks why ultimately the medieval university settled on four faculties—the *artes*, medicine, law, and theology—while leaving out the technological sciences and the applied natural sciences. He responds by referring to 'the significance of the *amor sciendi*', which meant that

> The social value of academic education for the professions... could only be realized by the university because the learning and teaching of the rational pursuit of truth were the substance for which institutional regulations and collegially ordered courses of study provided the context. The heart of the university is the ill-famed ivory tower; its manifest function is to provide for the Aristotelian *bios theoretikos*, intellectual training for its own sake.[8]

We begin to see that the contemplative ideal spills over into the idea of the university, which creates a sense of separation between the male scholarly

---

[5] See Walter Rüegg, 'Chapter 1: Themes' in Hilde de Ridder-Symoens (ed.), *A History of the University in Europe, Volume 1: Universities in the Middle Ages* (Cambridge and New York: Cambridge University Press, 2003).

[6] Rüegg, 'Themes', p. 16.

[7] Rüegg, 'Themes', p. 32.

[8] Rüegg, 'Themes', pp. 22–3.

community with its abstract intellectual pursuits and the social body with its needs and demands. This relationship is clear in a quotation from P. Classen, in a passage in which Rüegg is considering the interaction and mutual influence between the medieval university and its social context: 'Without the intellectual stimulus of the rationally controlled search for knowledge, there could be no university. "But the spirit alone cannot create its body".'[9] The community of scholars thus imitates the contemplative life, so that the university has the same relationship to the social body as the contemplative soul has to the individual body—a relationship of dependence and denial.

This is apparent when Rüegg considers why Thomas unsuccessfully resisted the inclusion of medicine among the natural sciences. Rüegg points out that, in his commentary on Boethius, *De Trinitate*, Thomas rejects the argument that the study of medicine includes a speculative dimension which would merit it a place in the natural rather than the mechanical sciences—in modern terms, we would refer to philosophy or theory and the physical sciences. Thomas argues that medicine, like all the mechanical sciences, is 'aimed not at knowledge but at a practical use and should therefore be considered as activities which belonged to the unfree part of the human being, i.e. to his body. They should be regarded not as free arts but as servile arts, as *artes serviles*'.[10]

Academic discourse, then, as we understand it today, begins to emerge when scholasticism defines its relationship to the social and individual body in terms of the relationship between body and soul, matter and mind, female and male. The intellect must free itself from the domination of the body, the university must free itself from the control of both politics and church (while remaining faithful to the doctrines of the Church), and man must free himself from the demands and seductions of woman, if the collective scholarly mind is to transcend its material circumstances and attain to that contemplative state of wisdom which constitutes the most truthful way of knowing and ordering the world.

TEXTS AND MASTERS

This gradual process of detachment from the wisdom inherent in matter and the body meant that the analysis and interpretation of texts became the organizing framework within which truth was discovered, knowledge was

---

[9] Rüegg, 'Themes', p. 11, quoting P. Classen, *Studium und Gesellschaft im Mittel-alter*, ed. J. Fried (Stuttgart, 1983), (note 4), p. 25.
[10] Rüegg, 'Themes', p. 27, referring to Thomas Aquinas, *Commentarii in Boethii De Trinitate*, Quaest. II, Art I, English translation by A. Maurer, *St. Thomas Aquinas, The Division and Methods of the Sciences* (Toronto, 1953; 4th edn 1986), pp. 19–22.

constructed, and authority was conferred. François Regnault describes this in terms of the complex interdependencies in the hierarchies of the medieval university. The masters themselves did not speak as solitary authoritative voices but from the midst of discursive communities constituted by scripture and the writings of others—in other words, they were subservient to the texts with which they conversed and debated.[11] Their role, argues Regnault, was to be confused neither with the teaching of the Church nor with the edict of the emperor or king, even though they formed an integral part of the composition of the Catholic Church as a whole. Until Descartes changed the coordinates of knowledge with his privileging of reflection on present experience over the texts of the past, the authority of the medieval *Summa* prevailed:

> As for the *Summa*, it contains that which it is necessary to know, less for faith than for examination. The book of Catholic truth by which to oppose infidels and heretics becomes the *Summa* of theses written by a master among masters and for future masters, those 'who were destined to fill the place of our masters', according to the witticism of Descartes. And the success of aligning the greatest masters who are multiplying themselves within the University with the Fathers and the Doctors, opens up an indefinite task of condemnation and canonization.[12]

Truth, heresy, and holiness become questions of textual authority, and those who study and interpret such texts derive their mastery from service to these texts. Thus academic texts acquire a commanding presence in western society as the established canon of western learning—and the long historical process by way of which truth will gradually migrate from the world to words, from speech to writing, from the expressive flux of the body's desires and responses within the materiality of the universe to the rationalized discourse of the university, begins with the ordering of knowledge in the medieval study and writing of texts.

For Thomas, this acquisition of knowledge theoretically remains inseparable from prayer on the one hand and sensory experience on the other, for the intellect cannot know itself except in the lacuna between material nature and God, mediated by desire and illuminated by grace. Yet although Thomas produced poetry, sermons, and biblical commentaries as well as academic texts—some would argue that his biblical commentaries should be made to bear a greater weight than his philosophical discourses[13]—his enduring influence is vested in his works of philosophical theology.

---

[11] See François Regnault, *Dieu est Inconscient: Études Lacaniennes autour de Saint Thomas d'Aquin* (Paris: Navarin, 1985), p. 25.

[12] Regnault, *Dieu est Inconscient*, pp. 26–7.

[13] Cf. the collection of essays in Thomas Gerard Weinandy, Daniel A. Keating, and John Yocum (eds), *Aquinas on Scripture: An Introduction to His Biblical Commentaries* (London and New York: T & T Clark International, 2005).

In Thomas's world, knowledge was organized into disciplines and ordered according to rational principles which emanated from the being of God and orchestrated the cosmos in descending ranks of spiritual and corporeal, animate and inanimate beings, all interconnected through their participation in the Trinity and their hierarchical place in the order of being. It was the task of the scholar to probe as far as he could the meaning of these orderly relationships, processions, causes, and effects of being through his engagement with the texts of his pagan and Christian predecessors. Only the male mind was capable of undertaking this task, since it was concerned with form and not matter, and only like can understand like.

At least until the nineteenth century, the idea of a university was formulated and perpetuated by men made in the image of these medieval masters, labouring under the illusion that, as far as the quest for knowledge and truth is concerned, they function best as disembodied minds. Thomas and his contemporaries might have been appalled by the withering of wisdom which accompanied the rise of modern scientific rationalism, and yet with hindsight they themselves bear no small responsibility for the ways in which western knowledge evolved. Hovering in the background of modernity's destructive dualisms is the contemplative man seeking to transcend his bodily sensations, sexual desires, and imaginative phantasms in order to attain to pure knowledge of God, as we saw in the last chapter. It is a small step from this theological desire to the hubristic ambition to displace God and make the rational scientific mind the sole authoritative source of truth.

Not only did medieval scholasticism transform the order of knowledge, it also introduced a specialized form of language that excluded those who were not versed in its conventions and usages. To quote O'Malley again:

> Intellectual problem solving was perhaps nowhere more evident than in the Arts and theology faculties because of their appropriation of dialectics (disputation or debate) as central to their method. Logical, left-brain, agonistic, analytic, restless and relenting questioning was the method's hallmark, in which the resolution of every question led only to further questions.[14]

However rooted Thomas remained in the material practices of communal worship, preaching, and service to the poor, he was a major influence in the crafting of a linguistic style that would seek the greatest possible abstraction of ideas and arguments from their corporeal and affective contexts. To quote G. K. Chesterton (who was rather less restrained in style),

---

[14] O'Malley, 'Were Medieval Universities Catholic Universities?' See also Walter J. Ong SJ, *Fighting for Life: Contest, Sexuality, and Consciousness* (Ithaca NY: Cornell University Press, 1981), and the discussion of Ong in Tina Beattie, *New Catholic Feminism: Theology and Theory* (London and New York: Routledge, 2006), pp. 229–34.

[Thomas] had, so to speak, the imagination without the imagery.... [H]is style, unlike that of St. Augustine and many Catholic Doctors, is always a penny plain rather than twopence coloured. It is often difficult to understand, simply because the subjects are so difficult that hardly any mind, except one like his own, can fully understand them. But he never darkens it by using words without knowledge, or even more legitimately, by using words belonging only to imagination or intuition. So far as his method is concerned, he is perhaps the one real Rationalist among all the children of men.[15]

This rationalism that delegates imagination or intuition to an inferior and indeed dubious role in the construction of knowledge—that 'only' is telling—needs to be qualified if we remember how much emphasis Thomas places on the role of the imagination in the acquisition of knowledge. Nevertheless, as we shall see in the next chapter, when modernity eliminated both God and the body as sources of knowledge, it brought to completion this gradual abstraction and rationalization of knowledge that Thomas mastered so consummately. Only the individual rational mind, trapped in the myth of its own disembodiment, would remain as a reliable source of truth, and scientific rationalism would become the only valid way of knowing the world.

A deadly rupture comes about in the making of the western mind when men begin to create institutions of learning predicated upon and committed to perpetuating the fantasy that the intellectual pursuit of truth is best served by eliminating the body as far as possible from consciousness. This process of abstraction produces the body as the dangerous and irrational female other that will eventually become the Lacanian imaginary, vaporized matter nesting as a brooding and deadly presence within the symbolic order that inherits the mantle of form. The components of modernity were fabricated in the production houses of the medieval university, and they would finally burst through the constraints of theology in the Enlightenment as modern man found his metier.

Let me turn now to ask how Lacan can help us to analyse the ways in which the understanding of the body/soul relationship in the context of the formation of the university has left an indelible imprint upon the gendered constructs of western epistemology. Unless we appreciate how these constructs inseminate and perpetuate themselves in the ordering of knowledge and its academic transmission, we postmoderns are doomed to intensify rather than deconstruct the dualisms that set mind and language over and against body and nature.

---

[15] G. K. Chesterton, *St. Thomas Aquinas* (Teddington: The Echo Library, 2007), p. 74.

THE BEGINNING OF 'DISCOURSE'

In *Seminar XVII, The Other Side of Psychoanalysis*, a number of tectonic shifts appear in the structure of Lacan's thought—in his interpretation of the Oedipus complex, and in his understanding of the coordinates of sexuality and language. Here, Lacan begins to question Freud's theory of the Oedipus complex, which he modifies by representing it in terms of discursive structures in which the master of knowledge takes the place of the oedipal father. Thus the Freudian structure of Lacanian linguistics is replaced by a more complex topology of the linguistic subject in terms of discourses of mastery, otherness, knowledge, and the unknown/unknowable. Let me unpack this, because it is of some significance for understanding how the gendered ordering of medieval knowledge retains an enduring influence over the coordinates of reason and madness, mastery and hysteria, rationalism and romanticism, which psychoanalysis locates within the order of western discourse, but which also then inscribes psychoanalytic theory into its own discourse of academic mastery and otherness. Lacan revisits these questions in *Seminar XX*, so in what follows I am weaving together perspectives from both seminars.

In *Seminar XVII*, Lacan sets out four related forms of discourse—that of the University, that of the Master, that of the Hysteric, and that of the Analyst.[16] He tracks the shifting discursive positions of the subject (S) through four degrees of rotation in relation to the Master or Master Signifier (S_1) which lays claim to truth, the chain of signifiers or objects over which the Master claims his authority (S_2), the divided subject ($\bar{S}$) who falls beneath the chain of signification, and the absent object of desire and source of *jouissance*, the *a* or *objet a*.

These relationships of mastery and subordination are less convoluted than they appear if we bear in mind the hierarchical ordering of authoritative/authorial knowledge in the medieval university as the blueprint for the validation of knowledge in the western intellectual system. God is the master/master signifier—the single authoritative source of truth from which all true knowledge flows, and yet which remains inaccessible to the one who seeks to know. The discourse of the university subordinates itself to God, but its understanding of the divine is mediated through the texts within which language about God is analysed and rationalized. The texts themselves therefore occupy a position of mastery in relation to the scholars who study them. However, as a scholar becomes a master, he begins to occupy the subject position that marks the authoritative position of the mastery of truth, in such a way that the subject begins to colonize the claim to truth invested in the

---

[16]   Relevant to the discussion here is the essay by Thomas Lynch, 'Making the Quarter Turn', in Clayton Crockett, Creston Davis, and Marcus Pound (eds), *Theology After Lacan* (Eugene OR: Wipf and Stock, forthcoming).

master signifier. In theological terms, we could say that the language of the theological master claims authority from God. In Lacanian terms, the masculine subject lays claim to the phallus.

However, as we have seen in our reading of Thomas so far, the divided bodily self, torn between demons and angels, riven by conflicting desires, haunted by erotic fantasies and forbidden longings, is always present and cannot be eliminated in the quest for mastery. Indeed, the master has to be constantly on his guard lest the demons exploit his sexual weakness and lure him towards sin and damnation through his fleshy desire. Contemplation and study require a sustained struggle against sexual temptation. Thomas attempts to sift his awareness of this flamboyant religious and bodily excess through the constraining logic of the philosophical dialectic, but at least he acknowledges the claim it makes upon the knowing self so that it still finds linguistic expression—albeit sublimated and rationalized. Only with the advent of the more thorough-going rationalism of scientific modernity will it be eliminated altogether from the scene of representation. We shall see in the next three chapters how heroically the modern subject has had to pit himself against such forces of matter and desire in order to persuade himself that they have no claim upon him. The modern master and the divided subject are anticipated in the emergent order of medieval scholasticism, but in medieval texts we can still see the scaffolding of desire before the linguistic structure has covered it over and denied its presence.

In the rationalized discourses of modernity, these visceral elements of desire and otherness that populate the imagination with phantasms of demonic lust and angelic grace are banished from symbolization. They thus fall beneath the bar—in Lacanian terms, the phallic prohibition—that constructs the rational subject of the symbolic order by refusing access to the forbidden other of corporeality and desire. In medieval discourse, this linguistic otherness would become the voice of the mystic and the female saint, as male scholars claimed mastery of theology and therefore, in some sense, of God, and female mystics eluded this mediating and controlling influence by claiming a knowledge that came directly from God. This, as we shall see later, is vital in terms of Lacan's discussion of female mysticism in *Seminar XX* (see Chapters 14 and 15). In modern psychoanalytic discourse, this voice of female otherness becomes the voice of the hysteric, speaking through the linguistic order in the visceral immediacy of an unformed language that emerges from the body and is redolent with the forbidden fantasies, longings, terrors, and joys of the bodily self.

But the order of discourse undergoes another twist, when the analyst claims mastery over the voice of the analysand, writing it down and offering it up for theorization and rationalization by the masters of the modern university. In the modern academy, theory takes the place of theology, and the analyst takes the place of the theologian as the one whose knowledge is parasitic upon the feminized body of the other—his own banished body, but also the mystic/ hysteric whose language of desire he colonizes, translates, and offers up for scrutiny, eviscerated of the immediacy of desire that emanates from the site of the woman who speaks. This process of the master/analyst appropriating the voice of the hysteric/analysand is first discussed in *Seminar XVII*, but Lacan returns to it to explore its implications with regard to the sexual relationship in more detail in *Seminar XX* where, as we shall see, he situates it in the context of a wide-ranging and highly allusive discussion of the question of being.

We have seen that Thomas's epistemology acknowledges the essential role of the body and the senses in the acquisition of knowledge, even as he seeks to transcend the soul's dependence on the body in the pursuit of a more pure and absolute wisdom informed by Platonism rather than Aristotelianism. Platonism would finally triumph over Aristotelianism in the emergence of scientific modernity, so that the dependence of the mind on the body would be denied altogether. Yet still the bodily senses and desires retain a threatening otherness, reminding the rational subject that beyond what he knows and controls there is a less controllable and more powerful knowledge that eludes his grasp and threatens to overthrow him.

This is why, in *Seminar XVII*, Lacan begins to refer to 'discourse', as the organizing structure by way of which language stabilizes the modern subject in society, by eliminating the non-discursive bodily excess that threatens his mastery. But in this process of elimination, the subject of discourse produces his other, which for Lacan means that the rationalized discourse of the university produces the hysteric, the discourse of the psychoanalytic master (Freud, but also Lacan himself) produces the analysand, and beyond these, all discourse produces the Other as that from which it derives its authority on condition that it remains outside the linguistic frame (God, the phallus). Dominant discourses invert themselves in the discourse of the other, upon which they are parasitic through the process of sublimation and appropriation: 'the intervention of the signifier makes the Other emerge as a field'.[17]

To appreciate the contemporary relevance of this, we have to bear in mind that theory has supplanted theology in the modern university, and the language of psychoanalysis has been incorporated into the theoretical regimes of the postmodern academy. However, Lacan suggests that this has done nothing to change the coordinates of knowledge. Psychoanalytic theory (i.e. the appropriation of psychoanalysis by academics) simply provides one more veil behind which to hide, functioning as yet another set of signifiers to substitute for the absent object of desire. Here, I think we have to see Lacan shifting adroitly between the position of the master and that of the hysteric/slave—as the master

---

[17] Jacques Lacan, *The Other Side of Psychoanalysis: The Seminar of Jacques Lacan, Book XVII*, ed. Jacques-Alain Miller, trans. Russell Grigg (New York and London: W. W. Norton & Co. Ltd, 2007), p. 15.

who lays claim to knowledge, and as the mimetic voice of otherness where true knowledge is to be found and the fiction of the master is exposed.

So, as master, the analyst offers the discourse of psychoanalysis for theoretical appropriation, but in such a way that he takes control of the voice of the analysand and masks her absence. He borrows her voice, he even sometimes speaks as 'her' to challenge the mastery of his academic audiences by playing the hysteric among them, but in the process he simply exercises yet another form of mastery. So Lacan asks, 'What does the analyst institute?', and he provides a response of sorts:

> If we characterize a discourse by focusing on what is dominant in it, then the analyst's discourse exists, and this is not to be confused with the psychoanalyzing discourse, with the discourse effectively engaged in in the analytic experience. What the analyst establishes as analytic experience can be put simply – it's the hysterization of discourse. In other words, it is the structural introduction, under artificial conditions, of the hysteric's discourse.[18]

Psychoanalytic theory thus becomes yet another locus for the university's discourse of mastery and the mastery of discourse, allowing the hysteric to speak only by filtering her voice through that of the master who controls, interprets, and mimics her language. In this scenario, the master/academic is necessarily masculine and the other/body is necessarily feminine, because the structure of language bears within itself those ancient copulations of being with their erotic configurations of desire and otherness, form and matter.

GENDER, POWER, AND KNOWLEDGE

Lacan's analysis of discourse is gendered through and through, creating a complex interweaving of discursive positions which deconstruct the subject even as they masquerade as the conditions of identity and otherness through which he comes to know himself. Jeanne Schroeder offers a helpful summing up of this complex Lacanian scenario. She refers to 'the "sexual impasse"' as 'a single paradox that underlies every aspect of Lacan's theory'. However, this cannot be applied in any straightforward way to either anatomy or 'gender', because

> The terms masculine–feminine do not refer to persons either biologically or socially identified as male or female. Rather they refer to incompatible ways of confronting alienation and contradiction. The 'masculine' attitude is denial. It attempts to resolve contradiction in order to create a complete and closed social universe. The feminine attitude is acceptance of contradiction's inevitability.[19]

---

[18] Lacan, *The Other Side of Psychoanalysis*, p. 33.
[19] Jeanne Lorraine Schroeder, *The Four Lacanian Discourses, or, Turning Law Inside-Out* (Abingdon UK and New York: Birkbeck Law Press, Routledge-Cavendish, 2008), p. 1.

This means that discursive relationships need to be understood, not in terms of the power of gender, but in terms of the gendering of power:

> From the perspective of the sexual impasse, the master's and university's discourses are structurally discourses of *power* and, therefore, masculine. The analyst and hysteric are structurally discourses of *critique* and, therefore, feminine. The masculine does not merely fail to hear, it affirmatively refuses to acknowledge the feminine. Indeed, the masculine side of personality creates itself through *repression* of the feminine.[20]

In all the discourses of postmodern theory, the language of otherness and alterity mask the homogenizing power of the scholar. They constitute the appropriation and rationalization of otherness, its taming and domestication in terms of the organizing grids and disciplines of the university, predicated upon those ancient relationships between paternal forms and maternal matter. Matter is passive, inert, lack in relation to the form which must give it shape, interpret it, make it meaningful and identifiable as something rather than nothing. The body/matter/woman have no concepts, no language, no meaning, except when mind/form/man renders them comprehensible.

Today, the university is no longer an exclusively male scholarly community, but it remains masculine through and through. Indeed, the secular academy is arguably more masculine than its medieval predecessors, for its boundaries of desire and otherness are vigorously policed by a post-Kantian secular ideology that closes off the horizons of transcendence, divinity, and desire. The intellectual life of the scholarly community is divorced from any shared ethical, social, or religious practice, while the parodies and mimeses of postmodernism have severed the body of discourse from the bodies it incorporates into its language by way of the appropriation of voices of otherness and difference. Postmodern pretensions to knowledge thus result in the stultifying banality of sameness, which masks a profound intolerance of those who dare to object or to dissent. What scholars have in common today is not a shared vision of the good life, far less a shared aspiration to discover the wisdom and truth of the universe as created and sustained by God. What binds us today is that we are servile slaves of a bureaucratic tyranny in thrall to market forces and utilitarian imperatives. The voice of truth, meaning, and wisdom has faded to a distant echo, while the marketing and consumption of research has turned scholarship into yet another commodity.

There is no point in seeking escape from this regime by turning to the various forms of machismo Christian theology which appeal for a return to Aristotelian Thomism in the university and more widely in western culture and values, for this world view remains trapped within the narrow androcentrism and gender-blindness of the system upon which it feeds. The masters of

---

[20] Schroeder, *The Four Lacanian Discourses, or, Turning Law Inside-Out*, pp. 1–2.

theology generally remain as hostile as they always have been to the bodily murmurings of otherness and desire that seep into language like the ooze of a woman's blood or the muffled cries of her coming—her coming into being that is always in the present tense, never finished, never over, never written, never fully known, for, according to Lacan at least, she is the (be)coming of God.

How did this banishment and silencing occur, and how can we understand not only its history but its implications for the wisdom of the future? I want to conclude this chapter by turning to Prudence Allen's evaluation of the impact of the rise of Aristotelianism on the place of women in western culture.

WOMAN AND THE END OF WISDOM

Allen argues that, until the emergence of the medieval universities, gender was a pervasive aspect of all philosophical reflection to such an extent that 'nearly every single philosopher over the first two thousand years of western philosophy thought about the identity of woman in relation to man', meaning that 'the concept of woman has been a fundamental area of philosophical research since the sixth century BC'.[21] Allen groups these diverse theories into three broad categories which she identifies as sex unity, sex polarity, and sex complementarity. The first privileges equality over difference, the second privileges difference over equality (one sex, usually male, is regarded as superior to the other), and the third affirms equality in difference.[22] I have elsewhere been critical of this idea of complementarity, for Allen interprets it in a way which serves to underwrite the deeply problematic sexual essentialisms of contemporary Catholic doctrine.[23] A Lacanian approach entails recognizing that the idea of complementarity perpetuates the fantasy of sexual union in a way which undermines our human capacity to love in relationships that are necessarily less than all we desire. For Lacan, female *jouissance* is not complementary but supplementary to the masculine subject[24]—a question to which we shall return. However, bearing in mind this caveat, I shall use the term 'complementarity' as Allen uses it in the following discussion.

---

[21] Prudence Allen RSM, *The Concept of Woman: The Aristotelian Revolution 750 B.C.–A.D. 1250* (Grand Rapids MI and Cambridge UK: William B. Eerdmans Publishing Co., 1997) p. 1.

[22] See Allen, *The Concept of Woman*, p. 3.

[23] See Beattie, *New Catholic Feminism*, p. 25. My criticism refers to one of Allen's later essays: 'Can Feminism Be a Humanism?', in Michele M. Schumacher (ed.), *Women in Christ: Toward a New Feminism* (Grand Rapids MI and Cambridge UK: William B. Eerdmans Publishing Co., 2004), pp. 251–84.

[24] See Jacques Lacan, *Le Séminaire Livre XX: Encore* (Paris: Éditions du Seuil, 1975), p. 94.

Allen suggests that Platonic influences in Christianity sometimes accommodated the model of sex unity and produced a theological tendency towards sexual egalitarianism, because of the devaluing of the significance of the body in Platonism. Plato's dualistic distinction between form and matter, which posits the soul as 'an independent sexless entity', leads to a philosophical position in which 'women and men are fundamentally the same'—what she calls 'the sex-unity thesis'.[25] Allen rejects this model of equality, opting instead for a complementary theory of equality in difference, because she sees in Plato and in all subsequent attempts to formulate a 'sex unity' theory—including contemporary liberal feminism—'a devaluation of the materiality of human existence and, in particular of male and female bodies'.[26]

Allen argues that the sex polarity thesis—in which sexual difference is understood hierarchically in terms of the superiority of men and the masculine over women and the feminine—has prevailed in western society since the triumph of Aristotelianism in the medieval universities. However, she also produces significant evidence that, for five centuries prior to the rise of the universities, Christian thought reflected the endeavours and influence of women as well as men who worked together in monastic communities of prayer, learning, and preaching. She traces 'the slow but steady development of a philosophical foundation for sex complementarity'[27] in the writings of women and men such as Hilda of Witby (614–680), Roswitha of Gandersheim (*c.*935–1002), St Anselm (1033–1109), Heloise (1101–1164), Hildegard of Bingen (1098–1179), and Herrad of Landesberg (1130–1195). This was an era when

> For the first time in history, significant numbers of women and men together studied and discussed philosophy within the context of double monasteries.... [O]ne central factor in the preparation for a philosophy of sex complementarity is the actual experience of women and men jointly participating in the practice of philosophy.[28]

It is beyond my purposes here to summarize Allen's tracking of complex changes in western thought in different contexts relating to the influence of Aristotle, so let me focus on her representation of Thomas and his aftermath. Allen describes Thomas as 'the most influential philosopher in the Christian west. He taught at the University of Paris in the faculties of arts and theology, he taught at the University of Naples, and his several hundred books became the source of nearly all western Christian thought for centuries'. She quotes from an account of how, after defending Thomas's views against the Bishop of Paris in 1277, Thomas's teacher Albert the Great re-read all his student's works:

---

[25] Allen, *The Concept of Woman*, p. 81.   [26] Allen, *The Concept of Woman*, p. 81.
[27] Allen, *The Concept of Woman*, p. 408.   [28] Allen, *The Concept of Woman*, p. 408.

At a solemn convocation convened by him, he put forward an exceedingly great and glorious commendation, concluding with the assertion that the latter's writings had put an end to the labours of all other men till the end of time, and that henceforth they would labour in vain.[29]

As Allen observes, 'With this pronouncement, the stage was set for St. Thomas's thought to dominate the Christian world.'[30] In 1879 Pope Leo XIII insisted that all theology was to be based on Thomas's writings.

Whereas from 800–1200 Christian learning had taken place primarily in the mixed communities of Benedictine monasteries, providing education and participation in philosophical reflection for women as well as for men, the exclusion of women from the universities was accompanied by a widespread ideological shift which would shape western culture for centuries to come:

> The University of Paris, founded in the early thirteenth century, excluded women from its ranks of students and masters until 1868. This resulted in women being isolated from the centre of all significant philosophical activity. In addition, the new trend to founding religious orders with a specific separation of women and men meant that even within the monastic setting, women became limited in their access to information and teachers of the highest rank in philosophy. Consequently, the side-effect of the institutionalization of Aristotelian sex polarity was the exclusion of women from the philosophic endeavour. Aristotle had argued that women could not be wise in the same way as men; European society became structured in such a way that this theory inevitably became true.[31]

Allen refers to the disputed claim that Hildegard of Bingen travelled to Paris in 1174 with copies of her *Scivias, Liber Divinorum Operum*, and *Liber Vitae Meritorum*, in an attempt to persuade the Bishop of Paris that her texts should be included in the theological curriculum as the centres of learning shifted from the Benedictine monasteries to the schools. She writes: 'The process is described as having taken three months for one single master of theology, who gave the works back and simply affirmed them as "divinely inspired." The works, however, were not integrated into the curriculum.'[32]

These last words fall like a curtain across western history, closing off the possibility of an entirely different culture, predicated upon a different configuration of knowledge, a different understanding of gender and sexuality, a different linguistic and social order, and a different approach to the relationship between God, nature, man, and woman. There is no knowing what

---

[29] Allen, *The Concept of Woman*, p. 407, quoting James A. Weisheipl, 'Thomas D'aquino and Albert His Teacher', *The Gilson Lectures on Thomas Aquinas* (Toronto: Pontifical Institute of Mediaeval Studies, 2008), pp. 1–18, 20–1.

[30] Allen, *The Concept of Woman*, p. 407.

[31] Allen, *The Concept of Woman*, p. 415.

[32] Allen, *The Concept of Woman*, p. 315. On 7 October 2012, Hildegard of Bingen was declared a Doctor of the Church by Pope Benedict XVI, 833 years after her death.

western culture might have become if the writings of women like Hildegard and Heloise had been incorporated into the medieval university and had played a formative role in the development of modern knowledge. It would have made the rise of the universities a more integrated and organic process than it actually was—not a struggle for mastery of mind over matter, soul over body, and male over female, but a quest that might have followed the call of desire along the complex pathways of love and abjection, knowing and being, thinking and feeling, which Thomas believed were the persistent promptings of the love of God in the human heart. In other words, this is the path of wisdom, and it was left abandoned and forsaken by those who sought to travel the straight highways of the mind that would ultimately lead to knowledge of everything but what matters most in human becoming. Only women and other vagrants were left to travel the overgrown paths of wisdom.

In synthesizing Aristotelian philosophy with Christian theology in the context of the medieval university, Thomas helped to establish an ancient cosmology as a dominant sexual ideology that would determine the ordering of western knowledge for centuries to come. The ontological identification of man with the perfection of form and God, and of woman with the evil of matter and lack was institutionalized and reinforced at every level of society and human relationships, so that the hypothetical lack of matter in relation to form was given potent linguistic and social expression through the exclusion of women from all positions of authority, intellectual formation, public representation, and social influence. That this was never realized as fully in practice as it was in theory goes without saying, but the hierarchical organization of medieval life according to the gendered hypotheses of Greek ontology has shaped western culture by way of a double splitting in the order of language and the order of society.

With regard to language, the rise of scholasticism brought with it the rational organization of knowledge according to a dialectical style that made it impenetrable to all but those schooled in its methods. The masters of the university put themselves at the service of God through the texts they studied, but in so doing they claimed their own form of divinely sanctioned mastery that defined the parameters of knowledge and excluded all voices of otherness and difference, especially those of women.

Mirroring and reinforcing this linguistic split was the social division of the sexes, so that the idea that women were lacking in reason and needed men to give form and order to their lives was reinforced by the growing gap between men in positions of authority and all the rest, including almost all women. Not all men were masters, but all the masters were men. Not all those subordinated were women, but all women were subordinated. Thomas maps the dualities of forms and matter onto the human body in a way that denies the social and sexual significance of the body/soul unity of the human being. In the ordering of the family, society, and knowledge itself, a woman has to act 'as if' she is matter in relation to form and a man has to act 'as if' he is form in relation to matter, even though both are equally constituted by soul and body, intellect and appetites. In order to sustain this illusion of a gendered ontology, she has to minimize her intellectual and rational faculties, and he has to minimize his bodily and emotional faculties. She must act 'as if' she is naturally subservient, and he must act 'as if' he is naturally dominant. The relationship between the sexes becomes an elaborate mimesis of a philosophical hypothesis, gradually embedding and embodying itself within the social and psychological dynamics of western culture until it begins to seem 'natural' and 'normal' to behave in this way.

The idea that in one generation all these lingering effects of an enduring ideology can be overturned without reopening deep questions about God and gender in relation to language, meaning, and truth is, as Lacan recognizes, naïve and doomed to failure. We need far more than either liberal feminism or the rights-based rhetoric of modern secularism if we are to understand the crisis confronting us. We also need a more penetrating and radical analysis than any offered by postmodern theologies.

The failure of liberal feminism to understand the depths of the human soul is attested to by the increasingly violent and misogynistic backlash against women, the rise of new forms of sexual exploitation and abuse, and the increasing commodification and manipulation of the female body to suit the idealized fantasies of a consumerist culture. The effects of human trafficking, migration, economic injustice, and various forms of religious and ethnic extremism inflict torture and death on female bodies in ways that match or even surpass the worst excesses of medieval misogyny. Authors Nicholas D. Kristof and Sheryl Wudunn refer to 'the brutality inflicted routinely on women and girls in much of the world, a malignancy that is slowly gaining recognition as one of the paramount human rights problems of this century'.[33] E. L. James has made publishing history since her *Fifty Shades* trilogy out-stripped all previous records for paperback sales.[34] These books tell of a young virgin, Anastasia Steele, who becomes obsessively attached to sado-masochist Christian Grey, and agrees to be his willing sex slave. Within months of their phenomenal success, scholars and journalists began attempting to analyse and explain why an ostensibly liberated generation of women have flocked to read these books, but at the very least their popularity suggests that desire and the fantasies on which it feeds are a more complex and at times dark and violent

---

[33] Nicholas D. Kristof and Sheryl Wudunn, *Half the Sky: How to Change the World* (London: Virago, 2010), p. xiii.

[34] See Zoe Williams, 'Why women love Fifty Shades of Grey', *The Guardian*, Friday, 6 July 2012, at <http://www.guardian.co.uk/books/2012/jul/06/why-women-love-fifty-shades-grey?news-feed=true> [accessed 9 July 2012]. The trilogy consists of E. L. James, *Fifty Shades of Grey* (London: Arrow Books, 2012), *Fifty Shades Darker* (London: Arrow Books, 2012), and *Fifty Shades Freed* (London: Arrow Books, 2012).

aspect of human sexuality—women's as well as men's—than liberal feminism has been willing to acknowledge. It is with these questions in mind that I turn now to consider the transition from the ancient to the modern world by way of the various religious and epistemological upheavals of the Reformation and the Kantian Enlightenment.

Part III

Conquering Desire

9

The Making of Modernity

Crucial to Jacques Lacan's project—and indeed to the project of this book—is a recognition of the extent to which a primordial sexual mythology shapes the human soul in all its religious and philosophical ruminations.[1] In western culture, this constitutes the pre-modern division of the cosmos into forms as paternal and matter as maternal, the scientific repression of this mythology in the Enlightenment and its aftermath, and its re-emergence in the form of the Freudian unconscious.

Lacan interprets the Judaeo-Christian tradition as the 'true religion',[2] because the doctrine of creation *ex nihilo* eliminates the sexual mythologies of creation found in other religions, and posits instead a primordial lack within all that is (see Chapters 13 and 16). The sexual mythologies of Greek epistemology made something of a comeback in medieval Aristotelianism, and they were not entirely eradicated from Christian thought until the Reformation banished natural law and philosophical theology and focused on scripture alone as the sole source of truthful knowledge. Protestantism thus ushers in a different order of knowledge, but it also prepares the way for the return of the repressed when scientific rationalism refigures once again the relationship between mind and body, reason and nature, with a more violent dualism than had been the case before. This in turn produces as its other modern romanticism, with its myths and yearnings for sexual fulfilment, its exaltation and terror of nature, and its reweaving of the veils of fantasy around the illusion of wholeness. From a Lacanian perspective, this means that pre-modern constructs of form and matter split along the lines of rationalism and romanticism in modernity. Their mythological power of copulation and generativity is repressed through the elimination of desire but persists nevertheless, not as two different orders of knowledge connected to one another by

---

[1] For more on the sexualization of knowledge, see George Joseph Seidel, *Knowledge as Sexual Metaphor* (Cranbury NJ, London, Mississauga, Ontario: Associated University Presses Inc., 2000).

[2] See Jacques Lacan, *Le Séminaire Livre XX: Encore* (Paris: Éditions du Seuil, 1975), p. 137. See also Alexandre Leupin, *Lacan Today: Psychoanalysis, Science, Religion* (New York: Other Press, 2004), p. 106.

the filaments of desire, but as the logic of the same and its excluded other, sundered by the banishment of desire from the scene of representation.

As Carolyn Merchant argues, nature was not just mechanized but bifurcated with the rise of science. On the one hand, it came to be viewed as inert matter to be explored and exploited by men of science, but on the other hand, it was invested with dangerous sexual qualities that constantly threatened to rise up and destroy the man of reason and the progress he was making towards mastery of the world. Anxieties about order and control led to a relentless drive to penetrate the secrets of nature as one might penetrate the female body. Merchant sees a powerful connection between this rage for order, the rise of the witch hunts, and the widespread misogyny of early modern culture. She writes:

> Symbolically associated with unruly nature was the dark side of woman. Although the Renaissance Platonic lover had embodied her with true beauty and the good, and the Virgin Mary had been worshipped as mother of the Savior, women were also seen as closer to nature than men, subordinate in the social hierarchy to the men of their class, and imbued with a far greater sexual passion. The upheavals of the Reformation and the witch trials of the sixteenth century heightened these perceptions. Like wild chaotic nature, women needed to be subdued and kept in their place.[3]

We must return to these claims in more detail, but it is important to bear in mind that the ordering of knowledge in the medieval university was predicated upon the sexual mythologies of Aristotelian philosophy, and here is where Lacan sees the foundations being laid for the modern discursive order with its rationalized symbolic and its romanticized other.

In order to appreciate how the Lacanian soul continues to be played upon by the distant hopes and hauntings of Thomism, we need to fill in the gap between Thomas Aquinas's world view and our own with some very broad brushstrokes by way of which Lacan superimposes the modern psychoanalytic subject on the medieval soul. The big picture always obscures too much detail and too many contradictions and paradoxes to be anything other than a sketch, and even then one might question the accuracy of Lacan's sketch. Nevertheless, I think it will be helpful to offer a sketch of the sketch here, in order to see how—according to Lacan—certain dominant values and ideas emerged in western society through a series of paradigmatic shifts. These set boundaries around the 'porous self' of the medieval world and ushered in the 'buffered self' of modernity (to use Charles Taylor's phrases),[4] creating a deep

---

[3] Carolyn Merchant, *The Death of Nature: Women, Ecology and the Scientific Revolution* (San Francisco: Harper & Row, 1990), p. 132.

[4] See Charles Taylor, *A Secular Age* (Cambridge MA: Harvard University Press, 2007).

sense of alienation and anxiety in the subject it produced. Here is how Alexandre Leupin summarizes this process:

> In the last analysis, the universe of modern science is an impoverished context, radically hostile to the subject of desire; in this universe, there is no sexual rapport, no soul, no totality or wholeness, no serenity, no wisdom, no interiority to console us and compensate for our narcissistic wounds.[5]

Against this background, I trace the shift to modernity by focusing on several seminal thinkers that Lacan associates with the transition from the cosmological, theological, and sexually differentiated person of Thomas's anthropology to the alienated, atheological, and non-sexed subject of modernity: Martin Luther (1483–1546), Johannes Kepler (1571–1630), Galileo Galilei (1564–1642), René Descartes (1596–1650), and, in the following two chapters, Immanuel Kant (1724–1804). Hegel is another important figure in Lacan's understanding of identity, otherness, and desire, but he is less significant than Kant with regard to Lacan's understanding of paradigmatic philosophical influences that contributed to the making of modernity.

LUTHER AND THE DISGRACING OF NATURE

In his book, *The Master and his Emissary*, Iain McGilchrist describes the Reformation as 'the first great expression of the search for certainty in modern times'.[6] He quotes Schleiermacher's observation that 'the Reformation and the Enlightenment have this in common, that "everything mysterious and marvellous is proscribed. Imagination is not to be filled with [what are now thought of as] airy images"'.[7] We should remember how important the imagination and its 'airy images' (phantasms) were for Thomas's account of human understanding.

From a Lacanian perspective, the Reformation brings a decisive end to the lingering medieval apprehension of the synchronicity between beauty and goodness, ethics and desire, and ushers in a more dualistic, alienated, and divided relationship between God, the human, and creation. Luther was responsible for awakening a sense of radical human exile in relation to the world, as a consequence of sin. His florid language of the diabolical in anal

---

[5] Leupin, *Lacan Today*, p. 102.

[6] Iain McGilchrist, *The Master and His Emissary: The Divided Brain and the Making of the Western World* (New Haven CT: Yale University Press, 2010), p. 315.

[7] McGilchrist, *The Master and His Emissary*, quoting F. Schleiermacher, *On Religion: Speeches to Its Cultured Despisers*, trans. J. Oman (London: Kegan Paul, Trench, Trubner & Co., 1893), p. 126.

images of excrement marks a turning point in western consciousness,[8] initiating the traumatization and alienation of the modern subject which Freud will eventually uncover. Luther writes of 'God's eternal hatred of men, not simply of their failures and the works of their free will, but a hatred that existed even before the world was created'.[9] In uniting the symbolic with the diabolical, in dismissing the value of all good works, and in placing all natural human existence in the grip of the satanic, Luther situates *das Ding*, evil, at the heart of human consciousness,[10] in a way that anticipates Kant and Freud. Slavoj Žižek explains the role this plays in the making of the modern subject:

> One could say that Martin Luther was the first great antihumanist: modern subjectivity is announced not in the Renaissance humanist celebration of man as the 'crown of creation' . . . but, rather, in Luther's famous statement that man is the excrement that fell out of God's anus. Modern subjectivity has nothing to do with the notion of man as the highest creature in the 'Great Chain of Being', as the final point of the evolution of the universe: modern subjectivity emerges when the subject perceives himself as 'out of joint', as *excluded* from the 'order of things', from the positive order of entities. For that reason, the ontic equivalent of the modern subject is inherently *excremental*: there is no subjectivity proper without the notion that at a different level, from another perspective, I am a piece of shit.[11]

In order to appreciate the significance of this, we need to hold in tension two different effects of Luther's theology. On the one hand, one can argue that, in his condemnation of what he experienced as the tyranny and corruption of late medieval Catholicism, Luther struck a blow for human freedom, wrenching divine revelation away from ecclesiastical control and situating it within the reach of anyone able to read the Bible for themselves. This is the beginning of the age of the autonomous individual who stands in radical solitude before the judgement of God, although it would be many generations before ordinary Christians had the literacy needed to avail themselves of this new individualism.

Second, and just as importantly, in his dismissing of the value of all human works through his ringing proclamation of salvation by faith alone, Luther brought to an end what some might see as the decadence of late medieval

---

[8] Lacan's passing allusions to Luther may not stand up to sustained theological scrutiny, but for a well-reviewed scholarly study which lends some support to his hypothesis, see Heiko A. Oberman, *Luther: Man between God and the Devil*, trans. Eileen Walliser-Schwarzbart (New Haven: Yale University Press, 2006).

[9] Jacques Lacan, *The Ethics of Psychoanalysis 1959–1960: The Seminar of Jacques Lacan, Book VII*, trans. Dennis Porter (London and New York: Routledge, 1999) p. 97.

[10] Cf. Lacan, *The Ethics of Psychoanalysis 1959–1960*, pp. 96–7. Lacan refers to Luther's *De Servo Arbitro*. For a more careful theological analysis of this work, see Dietmar Wyrwa, 'Augustine and Luther on Evil', in Henning Graf Reventlow and Yair Hoffman (eds), (London and New York: T & T Clark, 2004), pp. 124–46.

[11] Slavoj Žižek, *The Ticklish Subject: The Absent Centre of Political Ontology* (London and New York: Verso, 2000), p. 157.

Catholicism, mired as it was not only in the corruption of its leaders but also in the magic, fear, and superstition of popular religion. Taylor writes that, 'in propounding salvation by faith, Luther was touching on *the* neuralgic issue of his day, the central concern and fear, which dominated so much lay piety, and drove the whole indulgences racket, the issue of judgment, damnation, salvation'.[12]

Taylor describes the Reformation as 'an engine of disenchantment' because it brought about 'the abolition of the enchanted cosmos, and the eventual creation of a humanist alternative to faith'.[13] It had popular appeal because it spoke to

> strong urges for religious renewal, on at least . . . three axes . . . : the turn to a more inward and intense personal devotion, a greater uneasiness at 'sacramental' and church-controlled magic, and then latterly the new inspiring idea of salvation by faith, which erupted into a world riven with anxiety about judgment and a sense of unworthiness.[14]

Taylor comes close to a Lacanian interpretation of Luther's influence when he focuses on 'a reversal of the field of fear'[15] as one of the key features of the Reformation, so let's spend a little time analysing what he means by this.

Taylor points out that Judaism and Christianity both entailed a break with the pagan world of magic and supernatural divinized powers, but this was not a clean break until Luther disempowered all those other powers and made God alone the only source of power. He writes:

> God's power conquers the pagan enchanted world. And this can proceed either through a good, God-willed enchantment; or else by annihilating all enchantment, and in the end emptying the world of it. But to flip from one of these tracks to another requires a reversal of the field of fear. Beforehand, what you fear most is this magic power; the bad kind, of course, that of demons, but you also have a healthy fear of the good kind, and keep a safe distance from it. The flip comes when you take all that fear and transpose it into a fear of God, sole rightful object of fear, confident that it can arm you against all magic. . . . So what is needed is a kind of reversed field, where precisely what you most feared before is that the facing of which, we should say: the facing down of which, now fills you with courage and energy. The reversed field draws on the power of God in a new register.[16]

This facing down of fear entails draining away the power of the most 'magical' of all material practices and objects—the sacraments. It is this bleeding dry of the sacramental imagination that does more than anything else to herald the emergence of a symbolic order in which matter mutates from graced organic

[12] Taylor, *A Secular Age*, p. 75.   [13] Taylor, *A Secular Age*, p. 77.
[14] Taylor, *A Secular Age*, p. 75–6.   [15] Taylor, *A Secular Age*, p. 73.
[16] Taylor, *A Secular Age*, p. 74.

life to meaningless and inaccessible otherness which, as we shall see, would fill the Lutheran Kant with awe and horror.

Taylor argues that the stripping away of sacramental power broadens the scope of the sacred, so that the saved can find God's sanctifying grace in all the aspects of ordinary life. However, it also constitutes a narrowing of the channels of sanctification because it withdraws everything from the external world and relocates it within the transformation of the inner self. Most importantly of all however, this disenchantment of the world prepares the way for the rise of modern humanism by releasing new energy into society, removing the constraints on human endeavour so that 'we can rationalise the world, expel the mystery from it (because it is all now concentrated in the will of God). A great energy is released to re-order affairs in secular time'.[17]

But we can see that with this freedom comes a more radical responsibility than any that has gone before, for the soul stands bereft of its natural desires and consolations, bereft of its sense of belonging within the being of God and the being of the world in a divinely ordered cosmos, bereft of any possibility of goodness, truth, or knowledge except that which comes from the unmerited gift of grace predicated upon the disgracing and condemnation of the world through original sin. The human stands alone, helpless and disgraced before God—more specifically, before the cross of Christ—and from that space of abandonment and torment he or she is confronted with a radical decision for or against Christ. No longer does God's grace shimmer within the materiality of the world, awakening desire, kindling fear, and speaking through the senses to draw the human closer to the divine along the phantasmic furrows of the imagination with their angelic and demonic presences.

The horizons of Thomas's lucent and optimistic cosmology had been darkened long before Luther arrived on the scene, not least by the Black Death and its social consequences and, as Taylor suggests, by a growing sense of disillusionment with the clergy and the abuses of the sacraments. However, it was Luther who finally extinguished the light that had irradiated Thomas's universe and effected a far-reaching transformation in western consciousness.

Once God withdraws from nature and matter, becoming the judge over and against whom each and every human life is measured and found wanting, by whom all natural moral worth is condemned, the human ceases to be a natural animal. The desire to please God, to satisfy God's desire, can no longer be expressed in terms of the pleasure and goodness to be discovered in the context of an orderly and reliable natural order. Rather, it must position itself before an arbitrary and incomprehensible will that must be obeyed without reason or justification, and which pits itself against nature, including human

---

[17] Taylor, *A Secular Age*, p. 80.

nature. Stripped of grace, nature would eventually become the inert and mechanized matter of Newtonian science, to be ordered, dominated, and exploited by the rational human will. This is, as we shall see later, only half the story, because nature also becomes associated with dangerous female sexual powers that the man of reason must subdue and conquer,[18] but let's leave that discussion aside for now. Luther paves the way for the triumph of scientific materialism over theological and philosophical naturalism. In the process of these theological and spiritual transformations, the idea of God migrates into the hidden depths of the soul, where it splits into the apparently conflicted but paradoxically co-dependent oedipal father figures of the tyrannical real and the authoritarian symbolic.

THE JANUS-FACED GOD

The Reformation heralds the beginning of a split between the God of the philosophers and the God of the theologians that will come about with the Enlightenment. Pascal famously—and perhaps futilely—protested against this attempt to privilege the impersonal and rational God of the philosophers over the personal God of the Christian faith: 'Fire. God of Abraham, God of Isaac, God of Jacob, not of philosophers and scholars.'[19] While Christianity's personal God has survived the transition to modernity and is indeed worshipped, loved, feared, and fought over by record numbers today, the God of the philosophers also enjoyed a brief flourishing, before a more hardened version of scientific atheism squeezed him out of the scene altogether—we might say knocked him out, if we bear in mind Lacan's idea of the unconscious God of scientific modernity. Of course, the God of the philosophers survives in the backwaters of Anglo-American philosophy of religion, but as Heidegger rightfully observed,

> Man can neither pray nor sacrifice to this god. Before the *causa sui*, man can neither fall to his knees in awe nor can he play music and dance before this god. The god-less thinking which must abandon the god of philosophy, god as *causa sui*, is thus perhaps closer to the divine God.[20]

---

[18] Cf. Merchant, *The Death of Nature*.

[19] Blaise Pascal, 'The Memorial', in *Pensées and Other Writings*, trans. Honor Levi (New York: Oxford University Press, 1995), p. 178. See also the discussion in François Regnault, *Dieu est Inconscient: Études Lacaniennes autour de Saint Thomas d'Aquin* (Paris: Navarin, 1985), pp. 31–47.

[20] Martin Heidegger, 'The Onto-theo-logical Constitution of Metaphysics', in *Identity and Difference*, trans. Joan Sambaugh (San Francisco: Harper & Row, 1974), p. 72.

In post-Heideggerian Catholic theology, much debate surrounds the question as to whether or not Thomas himself is guilty of 'ontotheology', and I shall deal with this question in more detail later in order to suggest that, while Thomas lends himself to such a reading if one focuses primarily on his Aristotelianism, he also lends himself to a quite different reading if one focuses mainly on his biblical and doctrinal insights. For now, suffice it to say that this tension (and possibly contradiction) in Thomas's theology certainly prepares the way for the more radical splitting apart of the Christian God in the Reformation and modernity. From a Lacanian perspective, this splitting lends to the Freudian oedipal process a potent explanatory function for the structuring of the modern psyche.

Post-Reformation Christianity configures its relationships in the Name of the Father, but that name masks an unspeakable and dreadful secret as to the real nature of the God it serves. Žižek refers to 'the well-known Pascalian distinction between the God of Philosophers (God *qua* the universal structure of *logos*, identified with the rational structure of the universe) and the God of Theologists [*sic*] (the God of love and hate, the inscrutable "dark God" of capricious "irrational" Predestination)'.[21] The transition from the pervasive awareness of sacramental and magical presences in the medieval cosmos to the more austere and punitive God of post-Reformation Christianity infected both Catholicism and Protestantism in different ways, and recent scholarship suggests that medieval Christianity was on the whole less authoritarian and controlling than its modern counterparts. Although I have suggested that the medieval universities were part of a widespread quest for order which entailed the control of women/matter by men/form, the witch hunts were fuelled not by medieval misogyny but by the early modern quest for order.[22] The end of the Middle Ages and the rise of early modernity saw the spread of more authoritarian and punitive attitudes across religion, philosophy, and society,[23] which had a particular impact upon coeval changes in the representation of nature and gender.[24]

---

[21] Žižek, *The Ticklish Subject*, pp. 317–18.

[22] See Merchant, *The Death of Nature*, pp. 132–43.

[23] Cf. Eamon Duffy, *The Stripping of the Altars: Traditional Religion in England c.1400–c.1580* (New Haven CT: Yale University Press, 2005); Stephen Toulmin, *Cosmopolis: The Hidden Agenda of Modernity* (Chicago: The University of Chicago Press, 1992).

[24] In addition to sources already cited, see Sarah Jane Boss, *Empress and Handmaid: On Nature and Gender in the Cult of the Virgin Mary* (London and New York: Cassell, 2000); Allison P. Coudert, *Religion, Magic and Science in Early Modern Europe and America* (Santa Barbara CA: ABC-CLIO, LLLC, 2011); Jean Bethke Elshtain, *Public Man, Private Woman: Women in Social and Political Thought* (Princeton NJ: Princeton University Press, 1993); Sandra G. Harding, *The Science Question in Feminism* (Ithaca NY: Cornell University Press, 1986); Genevieve Lloyd, *The Man Of Reason: 'Male' and 'Female' in Western Philosophy* (London and New York: Routledge, 1993); Lynn Hankinson Nelson and Jack Nelson (eds), *Feminism, Science, and the Philosophy of Science* (Dordrecht, The Netherlands: Kluwer Academic Publishers, 1997); Merry E. Wiesner, *Women and Gender in Early Modern Europe* (Cambridge: Cambridge University Press, 2000).

This is the context in which we must situate Lacan's psychoanalytic evaluation of the lingering effects of religious and scientific divisions on the modern psyche. The conflicted and violent tensions to which the modern subject is prey can be attributed to the unconscious influences of oedipal father figures associated with the real and the symbolic. The former is an anarchic force beyond the limits of the law and its oedipal prohibitions, associated with the violent enjoyment of the father of the primal horde. The pre-oedipal father, like the phallic mother, occupies the molten core where language melts into impenetrable otherness. He is associated with a state of raw and unrestrained bestiality without limits or boundaries, inaccessible to consciousness but exerting a subliminal force that lures the subject towards visceral and violent fantasies while at the same time threatening him with annihilation. This is the (always already dead) Other that pre-exists the formation of culture and language, but which must have been present to perform the castrating cut that delivers the self into society by denying it access to the mother. He is the Sadean bedrock of the psyche and, as we shall see, according to Lacan his influence renders untenable Kant's faith in the power of reason to order the moral law according to the good.

The father of the symbolic takes up the prohibitive power of the father of the real, and enshrines it in the rationalized laws, taboos, and bureaucracies of the modern social order. In Lacanian terms, he is the (non-existent) bearer of the phallus—the only one so endowed—and he derives his power from the (always already enacted) threat of castration. He symbolizes the structure of the symbolic which imposes its commands and desires in the form of laws that must be obeyed on pain of an unvoiced but ever-present threat, invested in the father of the real. Thus the symbolic order is experienced as the big Other which bears down upon the subject with its commands and prohibitions, and the phallus takes the place of God as the master signifier that acts as a lawgiver outside the law—an unconscious source of paternal authority before which the secular subject remains compliant. In the words of Žižek, the father of the real denotes

> the subject's 'impossible' relationship to an Otherness which is not yet the symbolic big Other but the Other *qua* the Real Thing.... [T]his Thing is ... *Father himself*, namely, the obscene Father-*jouissance* prior to his murder and subsequent elevation into the agency of symbolic authority (Name-of-the-Father).[25]

The symbolic father acts in the name of an unnameable and tyrannical force which never reveals itself within the symbolic, but which is the precondition for its existence.

---

[25] Žižek, *The Ticklish Subject*, p. 314.

The transition from the medieval to the modern and then to the postmodern can thus be read in terms of the transition from pre-modern Catholicism to Protestantism to Enlightenment theism and to post-Enlightenment atheism, in a way that allows us to track the changing functions of the oedipal gods of Lacanian psychoanalysis. The tyrannical and irrational aspect of God is not lacking from medieval theology, particularly with regard to the doctrine of predestination which is resistant to any attempt to render reasonable and accountable Christian beliefs about salvation and damnation. Nevertheless, the elimination of imagination and desire in the Reformation's quest for theological certainty paradoxically fuelled ever greater uncertainty as to the goodness and compassion of God. Robbed of the mediating presences of the angels, demons, phantasms, and desires by way of which medieval Christians navigated between the materiality of God's creation and the immateriality of the human soul, the early modern soul found itself torn apart between the competing and unmediated demands of God and the devil. As we shall see when we turn to Kant, this would infect the modern rational mind with a pervasive sense of an evil presence that had to be eliminated in order for the good to prevail, and this constitutes the apotheosis of Lacan's father of the real.

THE DEVIL AND ALL HIS WORKS

Taylor argues that, in the process of the transition from the medieval to the modern, and along with the Protestant liberation of the human from enchantment and magic, comes a drive to establish order in a world bereft of divine grace and infected with evil in all its aspects. Initially, this takes the form of a more rather than less intense struggle against the demonic. While all the intrinsic goodness that suffuses the things of creation is withdrawn and focused within God alone, all the demonic and dark magical powers within creation become focused on 'one enemy, THE devil, Satan'.[26] Gradually, rationalization and the quest for order overlay the violence provoked by this fear of the demonic, but they never quite disappear. Rather, they remain latent and ready to be aroused by any outside force which is perceived to threaten the order that has been so carefully established, first in the name of God and later in the name of reason. So, argues Taylor,

> Just because we fight evil forces through social order, or see this as our protection against these, there can be a certain kind of tremendous fear when what we identify as crucial to this social order is being undermined.... We can argue that this kind of fear survives into the secular age. A modern society can be deeply

---

[26] Taylor, *A Secular Age*, p. 88.

shaken when it learns that some of its young people have taken up terrorism, just because this undercuts the very bulwark of what they understand as order, which is the security of the person.[27]

The cauldron of superstition and magic that seethed within the medieval imagination and suffused the natural world with mysterious potencies for good or evil was driven deep underground but not eradicated by the Reformation, the Enlightenment, and the advent of modern scientific rationalism. It retains its subliminal power to disrupt and disorder human relationships at the individual and social level, so that the greater the drive for order, the more furiously we must resist its dark intimations, projecting them onto all those others that we perceive to be forces of darkness, superstition, violence, and irrationality corroding the goodness of the world we believe ourselves to have created. Modernity's others—the sexual, racial, economic, and cultural others of the modern, autonomous, rational, heterosexual white man—inhabit the psychic space once inhabited by demons. In the words of Julia Kristeva, we have become 'strangers to ourselves', and the war that the alienated subject wages within his own soul lays the foundations for the spiralling violence of the modern political order.[28]

McGilchrist summarizes what he describes as 'common elements' in the Reformation, despite its diverse forms of expression in different cultures and contexts. These common elements include shifts in culture which invite Lacanian interpretations, such as

the preference for what is clear and certain over what is ambiguous or undecided; the preference for what is single, fixed, static and systematised, over what is multiple, fluid, moving and contingent; the emphasis on the word over the image, on literal meaning in language over metaphorical meaning, and the tendency for language to refer to other written texts or explicit meanings, rather than, through the cracks in language, if one can put it that way, to something Other beyond . . . In essence the cardinal tenet of Christianity—the Word is made Flesh—becomes reversed, and the Flesh is made Word.[29]

The Reformation and its aftermath affected every aspect of western life—Catholic and Protestant alike. Joseph Koerner, in his influential study of the art of the Reformation,[30] describes the loss of ambiguity and paradox that came about with the destruction of the imaginative, sacramental, and visually expressive faith of the Middle Ages, in favour of a more absolute and rigid distinction between truth and falsehood, good and evil. This was accompanied

[27] Taylor, *A Secular Age*, pp. 88–9.
[28] See Julia Kristeva, *Strangers to Ourselves*, trans. Leon S. Roudiez (Hemel Hempstead: Harvester, 1991).
[29] McGilchrist, *The Master and His Emissary*, p. 323.
[30] Joseph Leo Koerner, *The Reformation of the Image* (Chicago: University of Chicago Press, 2008). See also the discussion in McGilchrist, *The Master and His Emissary*, pp. 314–23.

by the 'triumph of the verbal over the visual'[31] and the written word over the material object. The image, the statue, or the Eucharistic elements that were pregnant with the presence of God were destroyed, desecrated, and reviled, with the emergence of a religious and visual culture in which presence yielded to representation—a change in vision which, argues Koerner, is clearly visible in art inspired by the Lutheran Reformation, in which 'words acquired the status of things by their aggressive material inscription'.[32]

In the non-literate cultures of the medieval world, art had the power to connect people with the incarnate Christ through emotion and affectivity, weaving the body of the Christian into the visual and performative narrative of the incarnate and redeeming God played out upon the finite worldly stage of created time, space, and matter. The Reformation inserted the worshipper into a radically altered and more abstract environment, where the written and preached word erased the tactile and visual sacramental presence of God within the fabric of the world.

As is clear in the foregoing, there is an ongoing project of revisionism associated with writing the history of the Reformation. To suggest a cross-over between this and Lacanian psychoanalysis, and to introduce into it a gendered perspective that is almost entirely lacking from the accounts cited here, is to contribute to this project but also to destabilize it—to push it further from the confidence it derives from the very modernity that it calls into question, by reminding it of the excluded otherness of both gender and psychoanalysis in its evaluations. Anglo-American scholarship is more securely rooted in a modernist approach to knowledge than its continental counterparts, as I hope my staging of a Lacanian encounter between the two makes clear. While the more accessible histories to which I am referring here help to elucidate and to substantiate some of Lacan's more obscure psychoanalytic theories, Lacan can help to introduce a new appreciation of the topology of the modern soul and its sexual and spiritual hauntings into these historical studies.

GALILEO AND THE DESEXUALIZATION
OF THE COSMOS

Luther is, for Lacan, one of the founding fathers of modernity, and another is Galileo, to whom he attributes the beginning of a science which seeks 'symbolic mastery'[33] over a material world regulated by laws of order but devoid of

---

[31] Koerner, *The Reformation of the Image*, p. 46.
[32] Koerner, *The Reformation of the Image*, p. 283.
[33] Lacan, *The Ethics of Psychoanalysis*, p. 122.

any purpose beyond its factual, observable existence. However, prior even to Galileo, we must consider how Lacan interprets Kepler's discovery of the laws of interplanetary motion as a metaphor for the divided self of the Cartesian *cogito*.

In presenting the discovery of psychoanalysis as a Copernican revolution in the understanding of the soul, Freud could still posit a centre to the self—albeit a radically altered one—along the lines of the Copernican model. However, Lacan uses the ellipsis instead of the circle, to represent the way in which the linguistic self is pulled in different directions by two centres of gravity. Shoshana Felman picks out one quotation in which she thinks that Lacan, knowingly or not, touches on a fundamental Freudian insight:

> The linguistically suggestive use of Copernicus' name has more hidden resources that touch specifically on what has just slipped from my pen as the relation to the true, namely, the emergence of the ellipse as being not unworthy of the locus from which the so-called higher truths take their name. The revolution is no less important for concerning only the 'celestial revolutions'.[34]

Felman writes that Lacan

> brings out the originality of Freud's Copernican revolution by radicalizing the ambiguity between the two centers. In so doing he pursues Freud's discovery, curiously enough, in the same way that Kepler, Copernicus' disciple, discovered in his turn, on the basis of his predecessor's investigations, that the revolving movement of the planets is in fact not *circular* but *elliptical*, that is, revolving not around one but around two so-called foci.[35]

She points to the double meanings—the 'two discrete semantic centers'—of the words *ellipse* and *revolution*. The ellipse designates the non-circular movement of the planets around two spatial centres, and the ellipsis as a figure of speech refers to that which is left out of the chain of signifiers. Similarly, an elliptical revolution denotes both subversion and return, suggesting the capacity of the signifier to subvert its own claim to singularity of meaning by repetitively returning to a site of difference.

Language then—the vehicle of desire—circulates elliptically around the divided self in two senses. The gravitational pull of two different centres distorts its circularity, its singularity, while the denial of this duality results in an ellipsis of meaning.

Jacques-Alain Miller points out that the elliptical movement of the planets displaced an ancient cosmology predicated upon the perfection and beauty of the heavenly bodies, which required that planetary revolutions be perfect and

[34] Shoshana Felman, *Jacques Lacan and the Adventure of Insight: Psychoanalysis in Contemporary Culture* (Cambridge MA: Harvard University Press, 1987), p. 66, quoting Jacques Lacan, *Écrits*, trans. Bruce Fink (New York and London: W.W. Norton, 2006), p. 647.
[35] Felman, *Jacques Lacan and the Adventure of Insight*, p. 647.

therefore circular. The challenge—tackled by Newton—of mapping the entire creation according to numerical calculations, entailed 'the disappearance of all the imaginary values attributed to the movements of the stars. It required, according to Lacan's expression, the extermination of all imaginary symbolism from heaven'.[36] Thus we could quote Miller as summing up the crisis that Lacan sets before us—a crisis in and of the imaginary—born of the fact that 'Science assumes the disjunction of the symbolic and the imaginary, of the signifier and the image.'[37]

The cosmological changes which originated with Kepler reach their apotheosis in Galileo. Lacan's attempt to link the emergence of psychoanalysis with Galileo's mathematic scientific theory is primarily informed by the ideas of philosopher Alexander Koyré.[38] In what follows I allow myself to be guided by various interpretations that are relevant for my own argument, without exploring the wider context of Lacan's reading of the history of science.

References to Galileo are scattered throughout Lacan's work, but perhaps a significant key to understanding the link between the science of Galileo and his own psychoanalytic theory is Koyré's claim that 'it is thought, pure unadulterated thought, not experiences or sense perception, as until then, that gives the basis for the "new science" of Galileo Galilei'.[39] Lacan claims that 'the psychoanalyst's *eppur si muove!* has the same impact as Galileo's, which is not that of a fact-based experiment but of an *experimentum mentis*'.[40] Modern science was 'born with Galileo', says Lacan:

> The increasing power of symbolic mastery has not stopped enlarging its field of operation since Galileo, has not stopped consuming around it any reference that would limit its scope to intuited data; by allowing free rein to the play of signifiers, it has given rise to a science whose laws develop in the direction of an increasing coherent whole, but without anything being less motivated than what exists at any given point.[41]

With Galileo, the natural world of organic, dynamically inter-related objects communicating by way of desire and teleologically orientated towards God

---

[36] Jacques-Alain Miller, 'Elements of Epistemology', in Jason Glynos and Yannis Stavrakakis, *Lacan and Science* (London: H. Karnac (Books) Ltd, 2002), pp. 147–66, 153.

[37] Miller, 'Elements of Epistemology', pp. 147–66, 153.

[38] For more on this, see Teresa Brennan, *History after Lacan* (London and New York: Routledge, 1993), pp. 68–9; Dany Nobus, 'A matter of cause: reflections on Lacan's "Science and truth"', in Glynos and Stavrakakis (eds), *Lacan and Science*, pp. 89–118; Russell Grigg, *Lacan, Language and Philosophy* (Albany NY: State University of New York Press, 2008), Chapter 10: 'Descartes and the Subject of Science'.

[39] Alexandre Koyré, 'Galileo and the Scientific Revolution of the Seventeenth Century', *The Philosophical Review*, Vol. 52, No. 4 (July 1943), pp. 333–48, p. 346, quoted in Brennan, *History after Lacan*, p. 69.

[40] Lacan, *Écrits*, p. 215. Galileo is reputed to have said 'And yet it moves' after the Church authorities made him recant his theory that the Earth moves around the Sun.

[41] Lacan, *The Ethics of Psychoanalysis*, p. 122.

fractures into the atomistic and disconnected facts and objects of mathematical science. To understand the significance of this, we might consider Galileo's much-quoted claim that the book of nature is written in mathematical symbols:

> Philosophy is written in this grand book—I mean the universe—which stands continually open to our gaze, but it cannot be understood unless one first learns to comprehend the language and interpret the characters in which it is written. It is written in the language of mathematics, and its characters are triangles, circles, and other geometrical figures, without which it is humanly impossible to understand a single word of it; without these, one is wandering about in a dark labyrinth.[42]

We have seen that for Thomas, the language of scripture is open to complex interpretations as its meanings are filtered through different levels of human reasoning and wisdom. The natural world, on the other hand, communicates itself with a vivid immediacy to the bodily senses and, even though nature too has to be interpreted in the context of scripture for its deeper truths to be discerned, the arousal of the body by the materiality of the world constitutes the beginning of all knowledge and the primordial medium of communication between the soul and God. The language of nature translates into the language of human communication, so that there are deep and meaningful resonances between the words we use and the objects to which they refer—which are, for Thomas, always objects of desire. Galileo, however, introduces a deep mistrust into the reliability of the human senses and perceptions to discern the truth of nature. The telescope gave access to factual knowledge about the cosmos that contradicted sensory perception, such as giving evidence of the mobility of the earth and the movement of the planets around the sun.

Galileo thus overturns a truth to which Christianity had adhered at least since the time of Augustine, who exhorted his audience: 'It is the divine page that you must listen to; it is the book of the universe that you must observe. The pages of scripture can only be read by those who know how to read and write, while everyone, even the illiterate, can read the book of the universe'.[43] Not so, argues Galileo. Although not referring directly to this passage from

---

[42] Galileo Galilei, *Il Saggiatore*, 1623 (Milano: Fetrinelli, 1965), p. 38, quoted in Peter Machamer, 'Galileo's Machines, his Mathematics, and his Experiments', in Peter K. Machamer (ed.), *The Cambridge Companion to Galileo* (Cambridge and New York: Cambridge University Press, 1998), pp. 53–79, 64–5. See the discussion of this passage in James MacLachlan, 'Drake Against the Philosophers', in Trevor H. Levere and William R. Shea (eds), *Nature, Experiment, and the Sciences: Essays on Galileo and the History of Science*, Essays in Honour of Stillman Drake (Dordrecht: Kluwer Academic Publishers, 1990), pp. 123–46. See also Carla Rita Palmerino, 'The Mathematical Characters of Galileo's Book of Nature', in Klaas van Berkel and Arjo Vanderjagt (eds), *The Book of Nature in Early Modern and Modern History* (Leuven: Peeters, 2006): pp. 27–44.
[43] Augustine, *Enarrationes in Psalmos*, XLV, 7 (PL 36,518).

Augustine, Galileo insists that nature—feminized and secretive but also obedient to absolute laws—is decipherable only by philosophers familiar with the laws of mathematics, whereas scripture is written in language accessible to the common people.[44]

Most interesting from a Thomist perspective is Lacan's claim, again informed by Koyré, that Galileo's mathematical cosmology overcomes the medieval imaginary through the substitution of a Platonic model of knowledge in place of the earlier Aristotelian model. To tease out the implications of this for our modern understanding of nature and gender, I want to turn to Dušan Bjelić's book, *Galileo's Pendulum: Science, Sexuality, and the Body-Instrument Link*.[45]

Bjelić points out that Galileo 'admired Copernican science as "a rape upon the senses"',[46] although Koyré, in what Bjelić sees as a double move of Neoplatonism, elides this metaphorical sexuality in his reading of Galileo. Bjelić quotes a passage from Koyré which, setting aside any attempt to analyse how accurately this describes Galileo, gives a clear insight into how Lacan understands Galileo as a key figure in the transition from the medieval to the modern. Bjelić quotes Koyré's claim that 'Good physics is done a priori', and he continues with a lengthier quotation:

> Fundamental laws of motion (and of rest), laws that determine the spatio-temporal behavior of material bodies, are laws of a mathematical nature. Of the same nature as those which govern relations and laws of figures and of numbers. We find and discover them not in Nature, but in ourselves, in our mind, in our memory, as Plato long ago has taught us.
>
> And it is *therefore* that, as Galileo proclaims it to the greatest dismay of the Aristotelians, we are able to give to propositions which describe the 'symptoms' of motion strictly and purely mathematical proofs, to develop the language of natural science, to question Nature by mathematically conducted experiments, and to read the great book of Nature which is 'written in geometrical characters'.[47]

Bjelić describes Galileo as cutting 'the old bellycord between the body and knowledge'.[48] He also contrasts the relationship between knowledge and pleasure (*askēsis*) in terms of the Aristotelian association between rational truth and sensory pleasure, and the Platonic and Neoplatonic dissociation of the pleasure that comes through truth from the erroneous pleasure of sensation: 'While Aristotelian *askēsis* cultivates the bodily senses as a vehicle to truth, Platonic *askēsis* cultivates its *negation* as a vehicle for truth.'[49] Galileo's

---

[44] See Palmerino, 'The Mathematical Character of Galileo's Book of Nature', pp. 28–9.

[45] Dušan I. Bjelić, *Galileo's Pendulum: Science, Sexuality, and the Body-Instrument Link* (Albany NY: State University of New York Press, 2003).

[46] Bjelić, *Galileo's Pendulum*, p. 38.   [47] Bjelić, *Galileo's Pendulum*, p. 39.

[48] Bjelić, *Galileo's Pendulum*, p. 39.   [49] Bjelić, *Galileo's Pendulum*, p. 42.

science, suggests Bjelić, 'does not represent only the change of a dominant metaphysical system . . . but also a history of the "body and pleasure"'.[50]

This may make too clear a distinction between modernity and pre-modernity, because we have seen that Neoplatonism had already weakened the association between rational truth and sensory pleasure in Thomas's understanding of the contemplative life. Moreover, the university was modelled on the contemplative life insofar as it constituted a withdrawal of the male mind into a linguistic and textual world away from the sensory and erotic relationships of the social milieu on the one hand, and the sacramentality of the natural world on the other. Thomas did his best to strip theological language of any expressive or emotional content, paring it down to the most rigorous forms of philosophical argument. The makings of modernity were present long before Galileo. Nevertheless, with Galileo and the rise of modern science, language increasingly lost its expressive potency to communicate truth metaphorically and analogically by way of bodily sensations and experiences, filtered through the refining lens of scripture, tradition, and the accumulated wisdom of the past. The sense of a continuity of being that linked the human person, other living beings, and the material world to one another in God, yielded to a more dualistic and Platonic order. This was the birth of the modern subject.

THE CARTESIAN SUBJECT

For Lacan, the birth of modern science and the birth of the modern subject go hand in hand. Indeed, to quote Russell Grigg, 'The emergence of scientific knowledge required . . . the emergence of the Cartesian subject'.[51] If we bear in mind the foregoing discussion of Galileo—the stripping bare of scientific language of any metaphorical or poetic content, and the subjection of nature to necessity by mathematical laws imposed by the rational mind—we see that this requires a transformation in the understanding of how and what the human mind is capable of knowing.

Taylor attributes to Descartes what he describes as 'The transition . . . which takes us from an ethic grounded on an order which is at work in reality, to an ethic which sees order as imposed by will.'[52] Taylor continues:

> It no longer makes sense to speak of the things of nature as expressing or realizing a form. No causal explanation of them in these terms can be made intelligible any

---

[50] Bjelić, *Galileo's Pendulum*, p. 42.
[51] Grigg, *Lacan, Language and Philosophy*, p. 136.
[52] Taylor, *A Secular Age*, pp. 130–1.

more. Forms and their expression belong exclusively in the domain of minds. Matter is to be explained as mechanism.[53]

There is of course always a risk of projecting back onto Descartes the perceptions of later Cartesian subjectivity in a way that elides the more nuanced and affective aspects of Descartes' thought. As Taylor points out, Descartes did not seek to destroy the passions but 'to bring them under the instrumental control of reason'.[54] He regarded wonder as 'the first of all the passions',[55] and his understanding of the human is more affective than many critics of Cartesian dualism acknowledge. Nevertheless, Taylor points out that Descartes accords ethical pride of place to the virtue of generosity, in a way which emphasizes the essential interiority and self-referentiality of the modern subject:

> The key motivation here is the demands laid on me by my own status as rational being, and the satisfaction is that of having lived up to the dignity of this station. What moves us now is no longer a sense of being in tune with nature, our own and/or that in the cosmos. It is something more like the sense of our own intrinsic worth; something clearly self-referential.[56]

Let's bear these comments in mind as we return to *Seminar XVII*, where Lacan discusses the impact of Descartes on the making of modernity.

In the medieval university, the Aristotelian master subjected himself to the authority of the texts he studied, extracting their knowledge (*episteme*) which established his mastery over the students he taught. However, Descartes— along with Galileo—casts a thick pall of scepticism over these claims to truth invested in authoritative texts. He too seeks a certainty that cannot be gleaned from textual knowledge alone, and decides that only in the rational thinking subject is it possible to ground enduring and stable truth. Descartes can therefore be seen to have brought about a 'renunciation' of the knowledge acquired by the medieval master:

> It was only when, by a movement of renunciation of this wrongly acquired knowledge, so to speak, someone, for the first time as such, extracted the function of the subject from the strict relationship between S_1 and S_2—I named Descartes, whose work I believe I am able to spell out, not without agreement with at least a significant number of those who have discussed it—that science was born.[57]

We must remember that Lacan uses the symbols S_1 and S_2 to denote the shifting position of the subject in relation to the authority of the master or master signifier,

---

[53] Taylor, *A Secular Age*, p. 131.   [54] Taylor, *A Secular Age*, p. 131.

[55] René Descartes, *The Passions of the Soul*, 373, 53, in *The Philosophical Writings of Descartes*, Vol. 1, trans. John Cottingham, Robert Stoothoff, and Dugald Murdoch (Cambridge: Cambridge University Press, 1985), p. 350.

[56] Taylor, *A Secular Age*, p. 134.

[57] Jacques Lacan, *The Other Side of Psychoanalysis: The Seminar of Jacques Lacan, Book XVII*, ed. Jacques-Alain Miller, trans. Russell Grigg (New York and London: W. W. Norton & Co. Ltd, 2007), p. 23.

and the authority of the set of signifiers or texts through which that authority is mediated and exercised. In Lacan's account, modern science emerges when the subject claims autonomy from all such external authorities and establishes his own mind as the sole source of certainty about the world.

In seeking a firm foundation for knowledge, Descartes must arrive there by a route of radical scepticism. Here is a widely quoted passage from the *Second Meditation*, in which he reflects on the possibility of a supremely powerful deceiver who calls into question all claims to knowledge, leaving only the certainty of one's own existence:

> I have persuaded myself that there is absolutely nothing in the world: no sky, no earth, no minds, no bodies. Is it then the case that I too do not exist? . . . [T]here is some deceiver or other who is supremely powerful and supremely sly and who is always deliberately deceiving me. Then too there is no doubt that I exist, if he is deceiving me. And let him do his best at deception, he will never bring it about that I am nothing so long as I shall think that I am something. Thus, after everything has been most carefully weighed, it must finally be established that this pronouncement 'I am, I exist' is necessarily true *every time I utter it or conceive it in my mind*. [my emphasis][58]

Lacan positions the Cartesian 'I' in the context of the modern anxiety created by Aristotle's dynamic account of being in motion which, in the absence of God, fails to provide any fixed point at which the subject might stabilize his existence. Language, for Lacan, is the medium by way of which this dynamic being-ness of being weaves us into its stream, and the attempt by the modern non-theistic subject to establish a firm foothold within this flux and mutability of linguistic being is doomed to failure. In the Cartesian '*cogito ergo sum*', the permanent and stable 'I' that Descartes seeks to identify exists only within the time of the utterance itself. It is 'necessarily true *every time I utter it or conceive it in my mind*'. Only through endless repetition of the claim to exist can the 'I' secure itself against the pervasive scepticism that Descartes seeks to overcome, and thus the 'I' is double: it is the evanescent, elusive self whose existence is open to radical doubt, and it is the 'I' of the subject of enunciation, who knows that he exists so long as he keeps saying that he exists. To quote Lacan:

> When Descartes introduces the concept of a certainty that holds entirely in the *I think* of cogitation, marked by this point of non-exit that exists between the annihilation of knowledge and scepticism, which are not the same thing—one might say that his mistake is to believe that this is knowledge, to say that he knows something of this certainty, and not to make of the *I think* a mere point of fading.[59]

---

[58] René Descartes, *Meditations on First Philosophy*, 'Meditation Two: Concerning the Nature of the Human Mind: That It Is Better Known Than the Body', 3rd edn, trans. Donald A. Cress (Indianapolis IN: Hackett Publishing Co., 1993), p. 18.

[59] Jacques Lacan, *The Four Fundamental Concepts of Psychoanalysis: The Seminar of Jacques Lacan, Book XI*, trans. Alan Sheridan (New York: W.W. Norton, 1981), p. 224.

Why is this Cartesian self the subject of science? Grigg argues it is because science requires both the rational, disembodied subject and the removal of that subject from the horizon of scientific study:

> the subject in question, the subject of science, is not *only* the subject that makes science possible but *also* the subject that science excludes—to use Lacan's term, the subject that science 'sutures'. This combination of what makes science possible and of what science excludes is what is distinctive about the Lacanian subject of science. This is why *science* cannot articulate this subject.[60]

The subject of psychoanalysis is the scientific subject because, in its focus on the unconscious, psychoanalysis is concerned with the divided self that science unsuccessfully attempts to 'suture'.[61] The scientifically knowing 'I' who seeks objective knowledge of the world hides even from himself the elusive quarry— the disappearing self—at the heart of his quest.

Lacan exposes the inescapable uncertainty at the heart of the Cartesian project by removing God as the guarantor of knowledge. He points out that, 'In order to assure himself that he is not confronted by a deceiving God, [Descartes] has to pass through the medium of a God—indeed, in his register, it is a question not so much of a perfect as of any infinite being.'[62] Lacan asks if this means that Descartes 'remain[s] caught, as everyone up to him did, on the need to guarantee all scientific research on the fact that actual science exists somewhere, in an existing being, called God?—that is to say, on the fact that God is supposed to know'.[63] In resisting this theological move, Lacan presents Freudian psychoanalysis as a subversion of the Cartesian subject, so that doubt becomes the consequence and not—as Descartes suggests—the starting point of the desire for certainty.

In his appeal to God, Lacan points out that Descartes brings about a split between knowledge and truth which becomes a hallmark of the modern scientific subject. Even when secularism banishes God, there remains some masked faith in a source of truth—science itself by some accounts—against which the human quest for knowledge through the pursuit of doubt can be secured. One need only read Richard Dawkins' *The God Delusion* or the many blogs and subsidiary works it has spawned, to see how confidently the scientific subject attributes to science itself an ultimate, God-like certainty about the world. Thus the enigmatic aporia between the mystery of God and human knowledge is collapsed, and a fantasy of wholeness comes to occupy the space of the Other. But of all the sources I have surveyed in this chapter, only Lacan and those who read him acknowledge that that Other is a sexualized

---

[60] Grigg, *Lacan, Language and Philosophy*, p. 145.
[61] Grigg, *Lacan, Language and Philosophy*, p. 147.
[62] Lacan, *The Four Fundamental Concepts of Psychoanalysis*, pp. 224–5.
[63] Lacan, *The Four Fundamental Concepts of Psychoanalysis*, p. 336. See also the discussion in Miller, 'Elements of Epistemology'.

Other, variously fantasized as Woman and God, against which the subject who knows establishes himself as normative, universal, rational, and whole—not in any way limited or marked by the body and its cultural and sexual inscriptions.

THE TRIUMPH OF SCIENCE

Modern scientific man emerges with Cartesian scepticism banished, nature conquered, and knowledge secured by way of a progressive ideology that thrusts him into the future and renders him contemptuous of all the fragile murmurings of faith and fear that wove his ancestral souls into a cosmic mystery. For anybody seeking to understand the paradigmatic shifts in knowledge that separate the pre-modern and the postmodern from the modern, particularly as far as language and meaning are concerned, it is worth reading Benjamin Jowett's commentary on Plato's *Timaeus*, written in 1892. This is a paradigmatic example of the modern subject's approach to knowledge. It is against this subject that Lacan pits himself in his psychoanalytic deconstruction of all that passes for truth and certainty.

Jowett begins by pointing out that 'Among all the writings of Plato the *Timaeus* is the most obscure and repulsive to the modern reader'. The ancient physical philosopher is, says Jowett,

> hanging between matter and mind; he is under the dominion at the same time both of sense and of abstractions...His mind lingers around the forms of mythology, which he uses as symbols or translates into figures of speech. He has no implements of observation, such as the telescope or the microscope; the great science of chemistry is a blank to him. It is only by an effort that the modern thinker can breathe the atmosphere of the ancient philosopher, or understand how, under such unequal conditions, he seems in many instances, by a sort of inspiration, to have anticipated the truth.

Jowett is willing to persevere in the face of these ancient confusions to discern the contours of truth, but first he finds it necessary to clear away the theological obscurantism of Jewish and Christian Neoplatonists. He observes that

> There is no danger of the modern commentators on the *Timaeus* falling into the absurdities of the Neo-Platonists....We know that mysticism is not criticism.... They are the feeble expression of an age which has lost the power not only of creating great works, but of understanding them. They are the spurious birth of a marriage between philosophy and tradition, between Hellas and the East... Whereas the so-called mysticism of Plato is purely Greek, arising out of his imperfect knowledge and high aspirations, and is the growth of an age in which philosophy is not wholly separated from poetry and mythology.

Later, Jowett identifies one of the key differences separating ancient philosophers from their modern scientific counterparts:

> Language . . . exercised a spell over the beginnings of physical philosophy, leading to error and sometimes to truth; for many thoughts were suggested by the double meanings of words [here he lists several Greek terms], and the accidental distinctions of words sometimes led the ancient philosopher to make corresponding differences in things [again, he gives several examples]. The modern philosopher has always been taught the lesson which he still imperfectly learns, that he must disengage himself from the influence of words. . . . [U]pon the whole, the ancients, though not entirely dominated by them, were much more subject to the influence of words than the moderns.[64]

Here is the ultimate illusion of the scientific mind that claims to have transcended even language itself, in order to gain secure knowledge of the world through telescopes, microscopes, and chemistry. Jowett's contempt for medieval thought masks a virulent anti-Catholicism typical of his time and culture, but the views he embraces were gestated in the medieval Catholic university, when philosophical rationalism gradually began to ease theological wisdom from her throne. Defying everything that Thomas would have privileged as truth and knowledge, Jowett observes that

> We know that 'being' is only the verb of existence, the copula, the most general symbol of relation, the first and most meagre of abstractions; but to some of the ancient philosophers this little word appeared to attain divine proportions, and to comprehend all truth. Being or essence, and similar words, represented to them a supreme or divine being, in which they thought that they found the containing and continuing principle of the universe. In a few years the human mind was peopled with abstractions; a new world was called into existence to give law and order to the old. But between them there was still a gulf, and no one could pass from the one to the other.[65]

Scientific modernity bridges that gulf, collapses the ancient cosmologies, neuters them, and flattens them out. Being loses its mystery and its mysticism, first in various forms of philosophical rationalism, and then in various forms of scientific materialism—epitomized by the transition from Hegel to Marx. The mind begins to map its journey through time from savagery to civilization, from superstition to knowledge, from faith to reason, and man turns his back on the wisdom of the past, its texts and scriptures, its longings and terrors, as he embarks on his linear journey of progress towards knowledge of everything along the highway of science. But Lacan twists the linearity of this myth of progress and loops it into the tangled knot of the post-humanist psyche,

---

[64] Benjamin Jowett, 'Commentary', in Plato, *Gorgias and Timaeus*, ed. Paul Negri (Dover Thrift Editions; Mineola NY: Dover Publications, Inc., 2003), pp. 143–4.

[65] Jowett, 'Commentary', pp. 144–5.

joining its ends and exposing the gulf that still remains, not now in terms of the ancient cosmology of being organized around forms and matter, the celestial spheres and the earth within, but in terms of the linguistic gap that remains at the core of things when every attempt at plugging the void with calculations, experiments, and scientific certainties has collapsed.

Yet if psychoanalysis seeks to discover the wounded self that the scientific gaze elides, this is an asymmetrical relationship. Psychoanalysis can see through the pretensions of science, but modern science is predicated upon the denial of the unknown and/or absent Other within and beyond the material world. This is why Lacan, unlike Freud, does not believe that psychoanalysis can establish itself as a science unless there is a paradigmatic shift in the self-understanding of the scientific enterprise. In this as in much else, Lacan is much closer to theology than science, for theology too cannot find a voice within the paradigms established by modern science. Like psychoanalysis, it constitutes the voice of the excluded and negated other that is banished by the linguistic pretensions of the symbolic order. But, like the psychoanalytic theorist, in bringing the language of God into the academy with its philosophical and theoretical codes of practice, the theologian also domesticates the other, appropriates it, and exerts his mastery over it. God, like the analysand, is elsewhere, offering a truth that is accessible only to the one who learns to listen attentively in silence to a mystery that is being revealed on the body's threshold into the world. But that is to anticipate.

The foregoing constitutes vast brushstrokes across the canvas of the modern world, which necessarily obliterates the detail, plurality, and ambiguity of the lives and differences of the people who make up that world. Yet this is what western knowledge has been since the rise of the medieval universities: a quest for the universal capable of accommodating and categorizing the particular by eliding its messy materiality, and a quest to establish the sovereignty of order, law, and reason over the inchoate plurality of human lives and relationships. This is what is now disintegrating in the trend we refer to as 'postmodernism', although even in the undoing of all universals we are unable to resist inventing yet another '-ism' that claims another universal truth, namely, 'there is no universal truth'. The western mind is trapped in its conceit of universalism, as it wends its way from Christian revelation through the age of science and reason to the age of universal human rights and beyond, to the post-human world that now looms before us. The 'I' now finds himself standing abandoned and alone on a rocky outcrop, surveying the 'naked shingles' of the world and seeking mastery over his domain, even as the tides of an avenging nature rise ever higher around him.

We can understand the story of modernity as the story of the banishment of the Thomist imaginary, that imagined and imagining dimension of desire that constituted the loom on which the human self was woven, a loom that connected heaven and earth, body and soul, self and other in the dynamism of love and hate, good and evil, all contained within the eternal being and doing of love that is God. With the Reformation, the scaffolding of reason is kicked out from under the biblical claims of faith, and with the Enlightenment this process is reversed. Reason provides the only reliable scaffolding for the construction of knowledge, faith is banished to the margins where it is believed it will eventually wither and die, and God begins to fade to a faint watermark beneath the scripting of modernity. As a consequence of these revolutionary epochs in western thought—the Reformation and the Enlightenment—desire has lost its mediating potency to unite forms and matter, language and objects, thought and activity, through the transformation of knowledge and reason into wisdom and love. 'What will survive of us is love', says the poet,[66] but what happens to the human when all that survives of us is reason?

Our intellectual and theological history leaves a spoor within the soul, accumulating layers of conscious and unconscious ways of knowing as the relationship between language, soul, and body shifts and shifts again. Nothing is lost, nothing is truly forgotten. We retain deep within us a silent longing for a different way of being associated with the maternal, with desire, with the erotic copulations of an ancient and abandoned mythology that still haunts us with its seductive promises of more than we see, more than we know, more than we are. Whatever theoretical explanations we might offer, some profound crisis has now become impossible to ignore as the edifice of modernity cracks, and we feel the ooze of some remembered substance cloying at our souls:

> Surely some revelation is at hand;
> Surely the Second Coming is at hand.

And yet . . .

> The darkness drops again; but now I know
> That twenty centuries of stony sleep
> Were vexed to nightmare by a rocking cradle,
> And what rough beast, its hour come round at last,
> Slouches towards Bethlehem to be born?[67]

---

[66] W. H. Auden, 'An Arundel Tomb'.

[67] William Butler Yeats, 'The Second Coming', in *The Collected Poems, 1889–1939*, Internet Archive at <http://www.archive.org/details/WBYeats-CollectedPoems1889-1939> [accessed 24 January 2013].

10

Kant, Ethics, and Otherness

For much of western history, the wound of separation within language has been made bearable by a religious tradition that has veiled it in the language of theology and celebrated our capacity to encounter the uncanny Other within through contemplative silence, communal acts of worship and mercy, and meditation on the natural world. Even if Kant gave the most influential philosophical articulation to the triumph of reason over faith, he remained firmly rooted in a theistic world view that only made sense if there was a God. His denial of human knowledge of God did not preclude the possibility of sensing an awesome and mysterious other within and beyond the phenomenal self, for the one who contemplated 'the starry heavens above and the moral law within'.[1] But today, philosophy's transcendent self and its divine Other have dissolved, so that in the silence behind the divided mask of the modern self we encounter only emptiness. William Desmond writes,

> Kant is filled with wonder about the starry skies, but the day will come when admiration will congeal into horror at the emptiness of those cold spaces, and men will feel less jubilance than bewilderment at our freakish place in the immensity of the nothing.[2]

Jacques Lacan's central concern is to unmask that horror and enable us to accept 'our freakish place in the immensity of the nothing', for 'even if one once located them there, there is no point now in seeking the phallus or the anal ring in the starry sky; they have been definitely expelled'.[3] We no longer live in that time when 'a world soul existed, and thought could comfort itself with the idea that there was a deep connection between our images and the world that surrounds

[1] Immanuel Kant, *Critique of Practical Reason, and Other Works on the Theory of Ethics*, trans. Thomas Kingsmill Abbott (Forgotten Books, 2008), p. 138, available at <http://www.forgottenbooks.org/info/Critique_of_Practical_Reason_and_Other_Works_on_the_Theory_of_Ethics_1000308607.php> [accessed 26 July 2012].

[2] William Desmond, *Hegel's God: A Counterfeit Double?* (Aldershot and Burlington: Ashgate Press, 2003), p. 21.

[3] Jacques Lacan, *The Ethics of Psychoanalysis 1959–1960: The Seminar of Jacques Lacan, Book VII*, trans. Dennis Porter (London and New York: Routledge, 1999), p. 92.

us'.[4] Lacan seeks to reconcile the modern soul to the emptiness of the cosmos and to Christianity's dead God by exposing the lack at the heart of desire, and by making possible an ephemeral joy within rather than beyond the horizons of death and nothingness. This means accepting that, beyond the rationalizations and calculations of science, 'the Freudian project has caused the whole world to reenter us, has definitely put it back in its place, that is to say, in our body, and nowhere else'.[5]

In this chapter and the next, I explore the ethical implications of this by making a detour through Kant, viewing his philosophy through the lens of its Lacanian interpreters, in order to pay particular attention to what is repressed, denied, and feared in Kant's construction of the moral law and its autonomous rational subject. As we shall see, in the empty formalism of the Kantian moral law, Lacan sees a monstrous other emerge by way of which the tyranny of the real begins to manifest a visceral Sadean influence within the unconscious of the Kantian subject and the citizen of the modern state. I should make clear that what follows is a view of Kant as seen through a Lacanian lens, and it makes no claim to approach Kant's work independently of that rather idiosyncratic perspective.

FORM AND MATTER—THE GREAT DIVORCE

In *The Critique of Pure Reason*, Kant acknowledges, in keeping with his philosophical predecessors, that all morality hinges upon the quest for happiness. He identifies three questions that are central to his philosophical endeavour:

1. What can I know?
2. What ought I to do?
3. What may I hope?[6]

In response to the third question, he argues that morality derives its meaning and purpose from 'the postulate of a supreme *original* good',[7] which vindicates human hope in a '*corpus mysticum*'[8] of perfectly rational beings acting under the rulership of a supremely rational and good being. The transcendent self that inhabits this kingdom of ends is beyond all natural constraints of time and space, constituting a postulate stripped of any attributes or characteristics

---

[4] Lacan, *The Ethics of Psychoanalysis 1959–1960*, p. 92.
[5] Lacan, *The Ethics of Psychoanalysis 1959–1960*, p. 92.
[6] Kant, *Immanuel Kant's Critique of Pure Reason*, trans. Norman Kemp Smith (London and Basingstoke: The Macmillan Press Ltd, 1983), p. 635.
[7] Kant, *Immanuel Kant's Critique of Pure Reason*, p. 639.
[8] Kant, *Immanuel Kant's Critique of Pure Reason*, p. 637.

other than the unknowable and inherently Christian theological concepts of freedom and immortality of the soul. This is the hypothetical subject in whom law and ethics are invested with their ultimate significance. Beyond the horizons of what can be known or experienced by any finite human, we are morally bound to treat each person as an end, as one who belongs within the kingdom of ends that constitutes the ultimate community of rational, autonomous beings.[9]

The longing for happiness can only be fulfilled in the future '*kingdom of grace*' within which this person ideally exists.[10] In the '*kingdom of nature*'[11] our capacity for happiness is thwarted by the weaknesses and limitations of human behaviour in which our freedom and satisfaction are constrained by the unreasonable demands and actions of others. The command to follow the moral law therefore involves a denial of the desire for immediate gratification in the interests of being morally worthy of ultimate happiness. Thus duty overrides happiness, and desire functions not as a guide and incentive but as an obstacle to the moral life.

The transcendental self—which is a less absolute and abstract hypothesis than the transcendent—has as its other the transcendental object, constituting a hypothetically stable and inert matter upon which the mind can impose its rational order, beyond the flux and unknowability of nature and material objects. The positing of this self as an organizing and ordering mind set over and against the phenomenal world constitutes what Kant described as a Copernican turn in philosophy, although we have seen that such revolutions had been set in motion well before his time. They can all be understood in the context of the modern quest to secure the 'I' against a disorientating and alienating otherness that lacks the stability required to establish a sense of independent and autonomous identity.

Kant's Copernican turn marks the final break in metaphysics and ethics between the pre-modern and the modern. In the words of Christine Battersby, according to Kant, 'It is man's transcendental ego—not matter or God—that constitutes the creative centre of the knowable (phenomenal) world.'[12] Kant was heir to a Lutheran tradition which, as we have seen, had already banished the sexual mythology of being that had shaped the world view of his Catholic medieval predecessors. In seeking to extricate the rational form of the self from the medieval soul and to make it the focal point of human knowing, he brought to completion the philosophical shift from an Aristotelian to a Platonic world view which had always held a certain attraction for the Christian spirit. The

---

[9] These ideas are first explored in Immanuel Kant, *The Metaphysics of Morals*, trans. and ed. Mary Gregor (Cambridge and London: Cambridge University Press, 1996), Section II, 14, p. 191.
[10] Kant, *Critique of Pure Reason*, p. 637.
[11] Kant, *Critique of Pure Reason*, p. 640.
[12] Christine Battersby, *The Phenomenal Woman: Feminist Metaphysics and the Patterns of Identity* (Cambridge: Polity Press, 1998), p. 62.

Platonic mind with its conceptual apparatus already in place imposes its meaning on inert and lifeless matter, and neither God nor desire activates the relationship between them. In this great divorce, Thomas Aquinas's fertile marriage between grace and nature, revelation and reason, forms and matter, becomes a hostile and sterile battle of mind over matter, an expression not of desire for the material other and its divine creator with all the erotic energy which that implies, but of rational power over the mute and impenetrable otherness of material objects.

It would be hard to over-estimate the anthropological and epistemological difference that this creates between Thomist and Kantian conceptions of the self, nature, and God. An abyss has opened up between grace and nature and between humanity and God that no human mind can bridge, and desire has become the enemy of the good. On the far side of the phenomenal world there endures a kingdom of grace that retains all the qualities of its Christian antecedents and would seem to be a psychological requirement as well as a rational necessity as an incentive to morality, but this kingdom of grace no longer bleeds its goodness into the matter of the world.

THE DIVIDED WILL

For the self-denial of happiness in the interests of duty to be rationally defensible, a God is necessary: 'God and a future life are two postulates which, according to the principles of pure reason, are inseparable from the obligation which that same reason imposes upon us.'[13] The possibility of moral responsibility rests upon the positing of an unknowable but necessary noumenal realm constituted by the transcendent *a prioris* of 'the freedom of the will, the immortality of the soul, and the existence of God',[14] which are not themselves subject to the scrutiny of reason. If so-called free will (*Wilkür*) is determined by nature, then our decisions and actions can have no moral value or responsibility. Only if our will is ultimately free of all determining influences, can we be accountable in deciding to pursue the universal reason of the moral life over the self-seeking animality of the sensual life. Iain McGilchrist refers to 'Kant's derivation of God from the existence of moral values, rather than moral values from the existence of a God'.[15] This ushers in a very different understanding of both God and the moral life than that which informed Thomas's world view, for it makes morality the measure of God

[13] Kant, *Critique of Pure Reason*, p. 639.
[14] Kant, *Critique of Pure Reason*, p. 631.
[15] Iain McGilchrist, *The Master and His Emissary: The Divided Brain and the Making of the Western World* (New Haven CT: Yale University Press, 2010), p. 86.

and allows for no recognition of divine goodness beyond the narrow sphere of what counts as moral in human terms. It also breaks what for Thomas was the fundamental connection between the pursuit of the good life understood in terms of human flourishing and the desire for happiness, and the cultivation of the good life understood in terms of acquiring the habits of virtue.

However, Kant's defence of the ultimate authority and universality of reason is undermined by a problematic arbitrariness which he acknowledges is difficult if not impossible to reconcile. The Kantian will is heterogenous—divided between sensuality and self-love (*das Wohl*) and moral duty (*das Gute*). Only by overcoming the desires and intuitions associated with self-love does one become a moral agent, and freedom entails the choice between good and evil rooted in rationality and sensuality respectively. To indulge one's sensual desires is to choose to subordinate good to evil—it is to make happiness the criterion for the pursuit of virtue. Conversely, to follow the universality of the moral law abstracted from personal inclination is to choose good over evil, or to make the pursuit of virtue the criterion for happiness. Without such universality and the duties associated with it, the selfish pursuit of happiness would lead to moral anarchy, with each individual free to use others for his or her own ends, and with no objective moral consensus. However, the fact that these are freely chosen options is fundamental to Kant's account of the moral law, and this is where, as we shall see, Lacan exposes its fatal weakness.

Ultimately, because reason is divided within itself, the rationality of choosing good over evil, duty over happiness, rests on a precarious hypothesis. In his *Critique of Pure Reason*, Kant identifies a series of antinomies embedded within the functioning of reason, of which two (the mathematical antinomies concerned with the existence of the universe in time and space, and the composite or simple nature of substances), can be coherently tackled if one accepts his insistence that we have no truthful knowledge of things in themselves. However, the second antinomies are more challenging, for Kant admits that they are capable of being rationally defended in a way that leads to an irreconcilable contradiction between conflicting claims. These are the conflict between freedom and determination, and between the necessity or non-necessity of a transcendent intelligent being (God). Kant resolves these by arguing that freedom and God belong to the noumenal realm whose necessity we can postulate yet which remains empty of content, for that which is the condition upon which all knowledge and conceptualization is possible cannot be known or conceptualized. The contradictory argument—that there is no ultimate freedom of will and no transcendent being—acquires its rational coherence from the phenomenal perspective of finite human experience and concepts, for we have neither any empirical experience nor any intelligent concept of pure reason and its infinite and transcendent correlatives of freedom and God.

The postulate of a Sovereign Good is a necessary hypothesis, but it cannot in itself be the measure of a moral act because we do not know what the good in itself is. We can only function morally within the confines of practical reason, which respects the limits of what can be known in this mortal life. Pure reason functions only in the negative—it is a restraint and a limit which acts as a safeguard against the hubris of metaphysics when it forgets its exclusive task of positing *that* (not *what*) freedom, the immortality of the soul, and God are: 'The greatest and perhaps the sole use of all philosophy of pure reason is . . . only negative; since it serves not as an organon for the extension but as a discipline for the limitation of pure reason, and, instead of discovering truth, has only the modest merit of guarding against error.'[16] We saw in the chapter on contemplation how, for Thomas, the purified intellect comes to rest in the bliss of the divine mystery (see Chapter 7). For Kant, it functions instead as a barrier beyond which thought must not seek to venture.

Respecting this limit, the morality of an act must be judged, not according to some standard of the good but according to the rationality of the maxim that the self-legislating subject chooses to follow, purged of all desire and self-gratification. A maxim that ensures conformity to the moral law is one that can be universalized according to the categorical imperative: 'act only on that maxim through which you can at the same time will that it should become a universal law'.[17] But here we encounter a problem with Kant's reasoning. To act is to give material expression to one's will, and how is that possible for the mind that has disowned any causal or necessary connection with the body?

THE ETHICAL MIRACLE OF BODILY ACTS

Kant is the gatekeeper whose philosophical prohibition denies us access to materiality and to God, in the name of a practical reason that must be held accountable before the court of empiricism and the moral law, and is allowed no escape through the doorways of metaphysics, theology, or desire. We have no access to the *Ding an Sich* (the thing in itself), whose objective existence is secured against a metaphysical horizon in such a way that it is closed off to human knowledge. In place of the sensually awakened desire for the goodness of God that informs Aristotelian theological accounts of morality and goodness, Kant evacuates morality of its pathological and theological content and renders it purely formal.

---

[16] Kant, *Critique of Pure Reason*, p. 629.
[17] Cf. Kant, *Groundwork of the Metaphysics of Morals*, trans. and ed. Mary Gregor (Cambridge and London: Cambridge University Press, 1998).

However, from a Lacanian Thomist perspective, this creates an insurmountable problem if we attempt to understand how pure form moves the body to act. We have seen that, for Thomas, desire mediates between the intellect and the body. Desire moves us to act in accordance with our will, and it occupies a fluid space between the animal appetites of the body and the willed intentions of the intellect. This is an implicitly erotic relationship, constituting as it does the arousal of desire in matter through the beauty of the form, and the fertile coupling between them. So, according to Thomas, in order for us to direct our activities and act purposefully and knowledgeably in the world, the intellect must arouse our desire for the good: 'the only way my mind acts on my body is by arousing its desire [*appetitum*], and that presupposes understanding'.[18]

In removing the medium of desire, Kant divorces the body from the mind in a way that leaves no satisfactory account of how the body gives material expression to the will. In her Lacanian reading of Kant, Alenka Zupančič points out that his attempt to evacuate the form of an ethical action of all its material content entails that conformity to duty is 'the only "content" or "motive" of that action'.[19] This means that the form functions as a drive so that it takes the place of matter, if by matter we are referring to the physical pleasures, appetites, and satisfactions of the subject as motivating drives for action. Zupančič uses the term 'ethical transubstantiation' to describe this conversion of 'a mere form into a materially efficacious drive'. The transformation of form into causal drive cannot be reduced to a process of purification, because it is an ethical 'miracle'.[20] Deprived of the mobility of desire, form impacts upon matter with an inexplicable force, in order to direct the body according to the will. So whereas for Thomas the will cannot move the body except by way of desire—and thus will becomes an expression of love for the object that is willed and therefore desired—for Kant there is a dangerous chasm between the power of the will and the resistance of the body.

If we want to understand the difference between these two accounts of will, we might turn to a passage in which Simone Weil is comparing the attitudes required for study and prayer. She writes,

Will power, the kind that, if need be, makes us set our teeth and endure suffering, is the weapon of the apprentice engaged in manual work. But contrary to the usual belief, it has practically no place in study. The intelligence can only be led by desire. For there to be desire, there must be pleasure and joy in the work. The intelligence only grows and bears fruit in joy. . . . It is the part played by joy in our studies that makes of them a preparation for spiritual life, for desire directed towards God is the only power capable of raising the soul. Or rather, it is God

---

[18] ST I, 76.1. (McDermott, p. 113).
[19] Alenka Zupančič, *Ethics of the Real* (London: Verso, 2000), p. 14.
[20] Zupančič, *Ethics of the Real*, p. 15.

alone who comes down and possesses the soul, but desire alone draws God down.[21]

This is a beautiful reclamation of a Thomist vision conceived in the midst of war and darkness. However, from a Kantian perspective it offends at a number of levels, not only in its affirmation of the motivating power of desire and joy, but also in its suggestion that God possesses the soul. Few ideas could be more in violation of the autonomy of the Kantian self. The Kantian will does indeed involve setting one's teeth and enduring a struggle in order to act morally.

If we are to understand what Zupančič means in associating the Kantian form with the drive, we must remember that, in Lacanian terms, the drive is a more primordial force than desire, for its aim is not the substitutionary *object a* but the unattainable object of the real—the thing in itself. While desire tends towards the symbolic end of the spectrum of the imaginary—always seeking but never finding its object beyond the veils of language and symbolization—the drive seeks entry into the real. It has no object, but seeks rather the impossible satisfaction that might come from the total elimination of the gap between the conscious self and its material others. The drive derives its pleasure not from any goal or object but from the bodily sensation towards which it is directed. So, for example, I might be driven to guzzle a large bar of cheap chocolate, but the drive associated with that gluttonous pleasure would be different from, say, the more codified and culturally conditioned pleasure that might make me want to nibble delicately on a particular kind of hand-made, gourmet chocolate.

The drive entails risk as well as gratification, for while desire shifts restlessly from object to object in its quest for satisfaction, the drive has no object other than the sensation itself, and so it propels us to seek greater and greater intensification of such sensations as a way of pushing the self towards con-summation, consumption, and fusion with the real. Long after my hunger has been sated and my sense of taste has been dulled, I am compelled to keep eating chocolate by some insatiable need that has no object and no end other than itself. When these drives are associated with sexuality and the pleasures that we demand from the bodies of others, they become invested with a sadistic capacity for violence and torture—a subject to which I shall return in the next chapter.

In suggesting that the form becomes the drive in Kant, Zupančič is arguing that, in its pursuit of the absolute form of the ethical act purged of any material content, Kantian morality drives the subject relentlessly towards an absolute beyond any possible satisfaction or gratification of its goal, for the Sovereign Good towards which it is directed cannot be known or possessed. This means

---

[21] Simone Weil, 'Reflections on the Right Use of School Studies with a View to the Love of God', in *Waiting on God*, trans. Emma Craufurd (Fontana Books, 1950), pp. 66–76, 71.

that it can only be a negation, and that negation is arrived at through a radical process of self-erasure—a purgation of the will that entails the most far-reaching and all-embracing destruction of the phenomenal self. Kant writes,

> If a man is to become not merely *legally*, but *morally*, a good man . . . this cannot be brought about through gradual *reformation* so long as the basis of the maxims remains impure, but must be effected through a *revolution* in the man's disposition. . . . He can become a new man only by a kind of rebirth, as it were [through] a new creation.[22]

This 'new creation' is the moral subject, emptied of all the particularities that might pollute the universality of the moral law. That law has no exceptions, no casuistry, no content or contexts. It is an absolute autonomy by way of which I as law giver must eliminate the desiring, pleasure-seeking, corporeal self that hinders my compliance with my own maxim. However, this has all the deadly force of the drive, because in order to eliminate the body one must go to the furthest extremes and beyond, to purge the mind of its darkest and most terrible depths. This purifying drive brings about a confrontation with a mysterious evil presence within the human heart. In *Metaphysics of Morals*, Kant writes:

> Moral cognition of oneself, which seeks to penetrate into the depths (the abyss) of one's heart which are quite difficult to fathom, is the beginning of all human wisdom. For in the case of a human being, the ultimate wisdom, which consists in the harmony of a being's will with its final end, requires him first to remove the obstacle within (an evil will actually present in him) and then to develop the original predisposition to a good will within him, which can never be lost. (Only the descent into the hell of self-cognition can pave the way to godliness.)[23]

This brooding apprehension of the demonic other within would be driven deep underground when post-Kantian modernity purged Kant himself of his lingering theological and mystical influences and arrived straight at the fully formed subject of modern scientific individualism, but it surfaces again in all its turbulent otherness before the clinical gaze of Freudian psychoanalysis.

Kant's creation of the new self *ex nihilo* produces the dangerous excess that psychoanalysis uncovers, for it drives the subject towards a receding horizon of the elimination of his own being as the condition of freedom. Ultimately, all that remains is some resistant residue or, as Zupančič expresses it, a '"leftover" element that can serve as the basis for the constitution of the ethical subject'.[24]

---

[22] Kant, *Religion within the Limits of Reason Alone*, trans. Theodore M. Greene and Hoyt H. Hudson (New York: Harper Torchbooks, 1960), pp. 42–3, quoted in Zupančič, *Ethics of the Real*, p. 11.

[23] Kant, *The Metaphysics of Morals*, Section II, 14, p. 191.

[24] Zupančič, *Ethics of the Real*, p. 33.

This 'leftover' is the ineradicable persistence of that which resists the negation. It is the stubborn barrier that the rationally purified subject encounters at the frontiers of the infinite, which throws him back into the finite bodily world within which he must act. But in order to establish where that barrier is—in order to ensure that the negation is as radical as it is possible to be—one must transgress. How do I glimpse the impossible, unless I attempt to breach the prohibition? So, in order to arrive at the horizon of the unknowable good before which the morally good act is positioned, the subject must go to the very limits of the known, where the boundaries of the finite blur and the mind encounters a dangerous otherness beyond its knowledge or control. Kant's attempt to purify reason of its emotional and bodily influences and its metaphysical content creates a sense of a mystifying and mystical hinterland that he famously describes as follows:

> We have now not merely explored the territory of pure understanding and carefully surveyed every part of it, but have also measured its extent, and assigned to everything in it its rightful place. This domain is an island, enclosed by nature itself within unalterable limits. It is the land of truth—enchanting name!—surrounded by a wide and stormy ocean, the native home of illusion, where many a fog bank and many a swiftly melting iceberg give the deceptive appearance of farther shores, deluding the adventurous seafarer ever anew with empty hopes, and engaging him in enterprises which he can never abandon and yet is unable to carry to completion.[25]

At the frontiers of rationality, the subject encounters an unknown that is both God and nature—the apotheosis of perfect form without matter, and the abyss of infinite matter without form. The modern rational subject finds himself trapped within that ancient dualism, only now there is no copulation, no fertile exchange between mind and matter, body and soul. He must establish his own mind as absolute form, and therefore his body itself becomes the source of the infinite and terrifying otherness that he seeks to transcend.

Zupančič points out that, in seeking to establish 'An island of truth in wide and agitated ocean of illusion', the Kantian subject occupies a precarious position in relation to nature: 'Once we have covered and measured the land which bears the enchanting name of truth, this land loses its charm for adventurous spirits, and they take off to seek adventure elsewhere. But they do not know that they are headed only towards their own ruin.'[26] This is the difference between the beautiful and the sublime, which is

> the difference between a natural world in which everything seems to be in its perfect place, where harmony reigns, and a chaotic Nature, full of sudden and

---

[25] Kant, *Critique of Pure Reason* (London: Macmillan, 1929), p. 257, quoted in Zupančič, *Ethics of the Real*, p. 67.
[26] Zupančič, *Ethics of the Real*, p. 67.

unexpected 'eruptions'—between a Nature which makes us feel safe and comfortable (the beautiful) and a Nature which leads us 'beyond the pleasure principle', toying with us as the wind toys with a grain of sand (the sublime).[27]

THE MATERNAL SUBLIME

In her study of the phenomenal significance of the maternal body for questions of subjectivity and embodiment, Battersby draws attention to the fact that the Kantian sublime is invested with maternal characteristics. She quotes Kant's *Critique of Judgment*, in which he writes: 'Perhaps nothing more sublime has ever been said, or a thought ever been expressed more sublimely, than in that inscription above the temple of *Isis* (Mother Nature): "I am all that is, that was, and that will be, and no mortal has lifted my veil".'[28] We might contrast Kant's lingering apprehension of the veiled mystery of nature with the more robust stripping away of all the veils which is the quest of modern scientific rationalism. Consider, for example, Richard Dawkins' adoption of the *burqa* as a metaphor for furthering the aims of science. After observing that 'One of the unhappiest spectacles to be seen on our streets today is the image of a woman swathed in shapeless black from head to toe, peering out at the world through a tiny slit', he continues:

> The one-inch window of visible light is derisorily tiny compared with the miles and miles of black cloth representing the invisible part of the spectrum, from radio waves at the hem of the skirt to gamma rays at the top of the head. What science does for us is to widen the window. It opens up so wide that the imprisoning black garment drops away almost completely, exposing our senses to airy and exhilarating freedom.[29]

The veiled Muslim woman is an affront to the western scientific mind. She is a sign of the potent resistance that the impenetrable body—a body that is both sexual and religious—poses to his insatiable and penetrative rationalism. She must be stripped and exposed to the all-seeing, all-knowing gaze of the man of science, in order to take away his uneasy awareness that his senses are not free, and to feed his desire to conquer nature in all its aspects. Such scientific fantasies are not innocent, for they have a dangerous power to become tomorrow's political tyrannies—see, for example, the legislation that now forbids women from wearing the *burqa* in public places in France.

---

[27] Zupančič, *Ethics of the Real*, pp. 67–8.
[28] Kant, *Critique of Judgment*, trans. Werner S. Pluhar (Hackett, 1987), #59, p. 185 fn. 51, quoted in Battersby, *The Phenomenal Woman*, p. 93.
[29] Richard Dawkins, *The God Delusion* (London: Bantam Press, 2006), p. 362.

According to Battersby, Kant represents 'nature' as

> an infinite and ever-receding horizon that entices the gaze. It is a feminized
> nature that is the elusive 'object' that acts as the counterpart to the 'I'. 'Mother'
> nature is magnificent and infinite. However, she is also presented by Kant as
> horrid, in so far as he registers the hypothesis of a 'primal mother' of self-forming
> matter that is not created by the 'I'.[30]

The Kantian subject is irresistibly drawn beyond the boundaries of his carefully constructed rational, masculine self to the turbulent dissolution of the
forces of nature beyond his control, where an uncanny and potent maternal
otherness threatens to overwhelm him. This is where the Lacanian imaginary
emerges as the repressed desire of the modern subject, a banished desire that
circulates between the closed horizons of the body and God in a restless
attempt to resist the gravitational tug of the maternal spoor that has been
excreted by the purified mind.

In attending to the maternal associations of this desire and its unconscious
manifestations, Lacan's later work sets off along a different path from that
followed by Freud, for Freud too was more trapped than he acknowledged in
the Kantian impasse. In striving to present himself as the modern man of science,
reason, and progress, Freud found himself confronted by an unthinkable maternal otherness when he contemplated the struggle of reason against nature, mind
against matter. In *The Future of an Illusion*, he explains the first step in religion in
terms of 'the humanization of nature',[31] by way of which the power of the oedipal
father gods is enlisted as protection against the annihilating powers of nature and,
implicitly at least, the pre-oedipal mother. Freud writes of the state of nature that

> Nature would not demand any restrictions of instinct from us, she would let us do
> as we liked; but she has her own particularly effective method of restricting us.
> She destroys us coldly, cruelly, relentlessly, as it seems to us, and possibly through
> the very things that occasioned our satisfaction. It was precisely because of these
> dangers with which nature threatens us that we came together and created
> civilization, which is also, among other things, intended to make our communal
> life possible. For the principal task of civilization, its actual raison d'être, is to
> defend us against nature.[32]

For Freud, the process of humanization is associated with the emergence
of the oedipal father gods. The pre-oedipal mother, like nature, is inhuman
and, as we shall see, this maternal inhumanity continues to position woman
as the not-all, the non-subject who remains ambiguously and dangerously

[30] Battersby, *The Phenomenal Woman*, p. 79.
[31] Sigmund Freud, 'The Future of an Illusion', in SE Vol. 21 (London: Hogarth Press, 1927),
pp. 3–58.
[32] Sigmund Freud, 'Beyond the Pleasure Principle', in SE Vol. 18 (London: Hogarth Press,
1920), pp. 7–66, 15.

unformed, defective, a male *manqué*. It is the civilization of men banded together in a war against maternal nature that, in Lacanian terms, constitutes the making of the modern symbolic order with its seething disruptions of identity and otherness. For another example of this conflation of nature and maternality with the forces of death and destruction, consider the following quotation from Sam Keen's Foreword to Ernest Becker's highly praised book, *The Denial of Death*. Keen writes: 'To say the least, Becker's account of nature has little in common with Walt Disney. Mother Nature is a brutal bitch, red in tooth and claw, who destroys what she creates.'[33]

In the medieval world view represented by Thomas, nature certainly manifests destructive as well as creative tendencies, but this has no moral significance. It is part of the unfathomable wonder of God's creation, and not susceptible to the moral judgements of human calculations and values. If this natural order is implicitly invested with maternal characteristics on account of philosophical concepts of the relationship between forms and matter, it is an impersonal maternal aspect of being which is ontologically free from the kind of moral judgements that are particular to the rational human animal. In the transition to modernity, the ontological maternality of nature in all its majesty and mystery becomes personalized, sexualized, feminized, and moralized. 'She' is 'a brutal bitch', cold, cruel, relentless, and bent on the destruction of all that men have achieved. This leads to Luce Irigaray's charge of matricide rather than patricide as the founding event of western culture. I shall return to that, but I want to focus on Thomas for a little longer.

According to one reading, Thomas's understanding of the mutual fecundity of forms and matter avoids the kind of violent dualisms that modernity invests in the split between reason and nature, masculine mind and feminine body/maternal nature. As we saw in the last chapter, through the changes wrought by the Reformation and the Enlightenment, the demonic powers that haunted the medieval soul gradually migrated from the spirit world to nature itself, and the graced conjoining of forms and matter became instead a violent conflict between the two—a conflict that is well illustrated by the foregoing quotations from Kant and Freud. Yet we have also seen that Platonism intrudes upon Thomas's Christian Aristotelianism, so that he is at times more modern than medieval in his representation of the intellect's struggle to be free of the body.

More importantly for my purposes here, however, is the way in which Thomas's maternal Trinity appears and disappears within his theology, as a mystery that undoes the claims to knowledge secured in the One of Greek philosophy, and as an enigma that cannot be contained or expressed in the rational order of his Aristotelianism. Thomas's maternal Trinity is, to repeat Battersby's expression, 'an infinite and ever-receding horizon that entices the gaze'. Like his ancient and modern counterparts, Thomas is unable to think through or express the relationship to the mother, even though it haunts his dreams, desires, and prayers in the inter-personal fecundity of the Trinity. The breach between the integrated and porous self of medieval theology and the buffered and atomized individual of post-Enlightenment philosophy is not absolute. In both cases, the male mind projects itself onto the Other as the One, the Father, the law giver, the form, and in both cases an elusive maternal otherness confuses the logic of form with a gloopy and unformed fleshiness that awakens phantasms in the imagination and renders futile the struggle for order, knowledge, and control.

IMAGINATION AND DESIRE

In approaching Kant from a Lacanian Thomist perspective, we need to bear in mind the subtle but profound difference that separates Thomas's understanding of the phantasms from that of Kant, and the ways in which this refigures the role of the imagination and desire in the making of the modern subject. We have seen that the imagination plays a key role in Thomas's account of knowledge and desire. Through the formation of phantasms, the imagination acts as a medium of desire within which knowledge is transferred from the receptivity of the senses to the activity of the intellect and back again, so that our capacity for willed activity is a function of our desire for the divine good that we perceive within and beyond created objects by way of the phantasms to which they give rise. The phantasms are impregnated with the real, because matter is not entirely passive. It is potent and fertile, and so the concepts we form bear a real relationship to the objects that they communicate.

Kant too attributes activity to the impetus of a representation (*Vorstellung*), which informs the will by arousing sentiments of pleasure or displeasure. However, whereas in medieval Aristotelianism this is part of the natural process by way of which humans come to know the good and to act well in the world, in Kantian ethics it is part of the lingering residue of corporeality and desire that must be evacuated of content, if the moral freedom of the self is to be asserted. Kant drains the material world of any capacity to communicate a truth beyond itself, and this endows the phantasm with a haunting sense of the void out of which it emerges. This initiates a process that Freud will bring to completion in his reinterpretation of *das Ding* as the horror that the pleasure principle seeks to avoid and the death drive lures us towards. By evacuating the phantasm of the communicative function and the meaningful content that it has in Thomist epistemology, Kant removes its capacity to lubricate and mediate the relationship between self and other, mind and body in terms of desire, love, and knowledge.

This is why Lacan traces the roots of psychoanalysis back to Kant's *Critique of Practical Reason*, because, according to Slavoj Žižek, 'Kant was the first to outline the dimension of what Freud later designated as "beyond the pleasure principle".'[34] *Das Ding* is, says Lacan, 'the beyond-of-the-signified'.[35] It is an originary and foundational absence, 'something that presents and isolates itself as the strange feature around which the whole movement of the *Vorstellung* turns'.[36] Freud unmasks the aporia with which the theory of representation has grappled in western philosophy since the time of Aristotle, revealing its phantasmagorical quality that philosophers have failed to fully confront:

> [Freud] assigned to [the *Vorstellung*] in an extreme form the character philosophers themselves have been unable to reduce it to, namely, that of an empty body, a ghost, a pale incubus of the relation to the world, an enfeebled *jouissance*, which through the age-old interrogations of the philosophers makes it the essential feature. And by isolating it in this function, Freud removes it from its tradition.[37]

Let's remember the change in the order of visualization that I mentioned in the last chapter, which Joseph Koerner and McGilchrist interpret as a shift from the image as presentation to the image as representation. In modernity, matter can no longer be the bearer of the real presence of God, not only in the Eucharist but in all the sacramental objects of liturgy and popular devotion, and in the sacramental capacity of nature to reveal the grace of its creator. Deprived of grace, shadowy, ghostly, and dangerous, the phantasms lurk within the imagination as the enemy of reason, even as they become the source of creativity and fantasy upon which romanticism will construct its dreams, fictions, and nightmares. Above and beyond all this, there is nothing to speak of and nothing to know—there is only the Thing.

As the absent condition upon which the good and the bad depend, 'the Thing is not nothing, but literally is not. It is characterized by its absence, its strangeness. . . . There is not a good and a bad object; there is good and bad, and then there is the Thing'.[38] So, whereas for Thomas desire is awakened by the trace or grace of God latent within the object that presents itself as a phantasm to the intellect, for Kant that trace must be eliminated along with desire, so that the phantasm appears to consciousness as empty of all possible meaning and yet retaining within itself the horror of a consuming absence.

One can discern the contours of a lingering Christian mysticism in Kant, not only in his representation of the maternal sublime but in his idea that the

---

[34] Slavoj Žižek, *For They Know Not What They Do: Enjoyment as a Political Factor* (London and New York: Verso, 2008), 2nd edn, p. 229.
[35] Lacan, *The Ethics of Psychoanalysis*, p. 54.
[36] Lacan, *The Ethics of Psychoanalysis*, p. 57.
[37] Lacan, *The Ethics of Psychoanalysis*, p. 61.
[38] Lacan, *The Ethics of Psychoanalysis*, p. 63.

freedom of the self entails the undoing of the self through the purgation of all its desires and sensual appetites. However, for the mystic, the purpose of this relentless disciplining of desire and the body's appetites is in service to the ultimate desire for the good that is God, and this purified desire enables us to know and love the material objects that we encounter as phantasms because they are an evocation of God. For Kant, this desire for God is a dangerous pathway to illusion and futility. It too must be purged, in order to evacuate the will of everything except the empty formalism of the moral law that makes it possible to do one's duty according to one's freely chosen maxims, with no trace of desire or pleasure to pollute the freedom of the act.

Yet the practicality of Kantian reason—the need to transform the pure will into material activity—allows for a return of the repressed. Desire cannot be banished entirely, if the subject is not to be reduced to a state of helpless impotence in relation to his bodily capacity for action. In his later work, Kant arrives at a position where he cautiously introduces an acknowledgement that desire might have some role to play in the moral life:

> For from [the fact] that a being has reason it by no means follows that this reason, by the mere representing of the fitness of its maxims to be laid down as universal laws, is thereby rendered capable of determining *Wilkür* unconditionally, so as to be 'practical' of itself. The most rational mortal being in the world might still stand in need of certain incentives, originating in objects of desire, to determine his *Wilkür*.[39]

Here, we can read Kant as conceding ground to his Aristotelian predecessors. Will as power over the self yields, however grudgingly and minimally, to the motivation of desire in the translation of universal maxims into practical moral activity. There is, as Battersby points out, a lingering hylomorphism in Kant's philosophy insofar as the transcendental self impresses form on matter 'in a top-down way'.[40] Unlike the Cartesian subject, the Kantian self is not a thinking thing. It is a self that asserts itself over and against the uncanny otherness of matter. The will is responsive to desire, and desire moves the self to act in one way rather than another. But this makes clear the futility of the quest for the formal purity of the moral act, for all human activity is unavoidably tainted by the pollution of pleasure and desire which arouse the body to act. In its relentless pursuit of moral perfection, Kantian ethics drives the subject beyond all the contexts and constraints of the desiring, imagining, and bodily constituted self, in order to eliminate the resistance that prevents the freely chosen formal act from achieving its enactment in the body, but desire creeps back and the quest for the perfectly dutiful moral act is thwarted and frustrated at every turn by the animality of the self. This is why Lacan relates the

---

[39] Kant, *Religion within the Limits of Reason Alone*, p. 21.
[40] Battersby, *The Phenomenal Woman*, p. 73.

making of the Kantian subject to the trauma of castration and the oedipal process.

Kant's banishment of the transcendent object (the Good) from the form of the moral law and his eradication of its pathological content (desire) becomes, for Lacan, an act of 'symbolic castration', which Žižek describes as 'the renunciation of the incestuous object, of the Mother as Supreme Good—it is by way of this "wiping out" of the incestuous *content* that the paternal law emerges as its *formal* metaphoric substitute'.[41] Freud erases the noumenal perspective of Kant's Sovereign Good and relocates it within the soul, as the forbidden object of desire. In so doing, he shows us 'that there is no Sovereign Good—that the Sovereign Good, which is *das Ding*, which is the mother, is also the object of incest, is a forbidden good, and that there is no other good. Such is the foundation of the moral law as turned on its head by Freud'.[42]

The Kantian will produces the castrated subject, for it reinforces the taboo that renders nature/the mother untouchable, unknowable, and unnameable. Although modernity banishes the sexual mythologies of the ancient world, it cannot erase the forbidden desire that proliferates before the prohibition of the object of desire. The infantile relationship with the maternal body oozes into the masculine mind in a way that pervades all nature with the same cloying presence, no matter how strenuously he tries to purify his thoughts and raise his mind to the realm of pure form without the taint of matter.

We might recall here Thomas's account of rapture—a state that constitutes the ultimate liberation of the intellect from the body, and yet which also opens into the maternal mystery of the Trinity. The attempt to empty the mind creates awareness of a mysterious other, for Kant no less than for Thomas, and in both cases this other is redolent with intimations of the mother.

Kant's world is continuous as well as discontinuous with Thomas's world, for both are formed within the same intellectual tradition, consolidated and disseminated by the universities, in which Platonic dualism would ultimately prove a more alluring prospect to the masculine mind than a more integral Aristotelianism. Yet both are also formed within a religious tradition which teaches the resurrection of the body, and this is the question to which I turn now.

RESURRECTION AND IMMORTALITY

We have seen that, for Thomas, the body–soul unity of the human is an enduring reality, beginning in time but extending beyond death to eternity.

---

[41] Žižek, *For They Know Not What They Do*, p. 230.
[42] Lacan, *The Ethics of Psychoanalysis*, p. 70.

God creates the soul out of nothing and (in)fuses the developing body with it so that the two remain united for the rest of eternity, except for the period between death and the resurrection of the body. This doctrine modifies Platonic influences on classical theology and secures for the body a necessary role in all accounts of what it means to be human. With Enlightenment philosophy, Plato comes into his own and the theological rupture between nature and grace which can be traced back to Luther becomes a philosophical rupture between mind and body, rationality and materiality, which defines the Kantian subject. The Kantian mind does not regard the body as its co-existent for all eternity, for better or worse. Rather, like the Platonic form, the Kantian mind is pitted in a futile struggle to be free of the body, and there is in Kant no room for a doctrine of the resurrection of the body. Nevertheless, the immortality of the individual soul is an indispensable doctrine for Kant.

In order to justify the heroic and futile struggle to achieve the perfect moral act, Kant posits the immortality of the soul as a necessary hypothesis. Only if a person can look forward to some future happiness is he or she rationally justified in the sacrifice of happiness in this life that morality requires. Zupančič points out that this extends the pursuit of the good beyond death, but she argues that this exposes Kant's idea of pure practical reason as 'fantasy'.[43] The immortality of the soul entails an infinite progress towards moral perfection:

> Complete fitness of the will to do the moral law is holiness, which is perfection of which no rational being in the world of sense is at any time capable. But since it is required as practically necessary, it can be found only in an endless progress to that complete fitness.... This infinite progress is possible, however, only under the presupposition of an infinitely enduring existence and personality of the same rational being; this is called the immortality of the soul. Thus the highest good is practically possible only on the supposition of the immortality of the soul, and the latter, as inseparably bound to the moral law, is a postulate of pure practical reason.[44]

However, as Zupančič argues, if the soul is immortal then, upon death, it is 'no longer a denizen of the world of space and time; and if the soul is no longer subject to temporal conditions, how are we to understand "continuous and unending progress"?' She goes on to offer a vital insight:

> We might also ask why the soul, delivered of all 'bodily chains', would need such progress, for in this case holiness could be accomplished instantly. And if not—if the presupposition of the eternity of the soul included continuous change (for the better)—then we would be dealing not with an eternal but with a temporal mode of existence. The notion of change makes sense only within time.... These questions

---

[43] Zupančič, *Ethics of the Real*, pp. 79ff.
[44] Kant, *Critique of Practical Reason* (New York: Macmillan, 1993 [1956]), p. 126, quoted in Zupančič, *Ethics of the Real*, p. 79.

lead us to the inevitable conclusion: *What Kant really needs to postulate is not the immortality of the soul but the immortality of the body.*[45]

This would, argues Zupančič, be 'an immortal, indestructible, *sublime* body . . . a body that exists and changes through time, yet approaches its end, its death, in an endless asymptotic movement'.[46]

This suggests that Kant's philosophical project founders on its Christian foundations. The immortality of the individual soul is, as we have seen, a necessary corollary to the doctrine of the resurrection of the body, and it is the premise upon which Thomas bases his opposition to Averroist interpretations of Aristotle. It would be unthinkable from the dualistic perspective of Kantian philosophy to grant matter a stake in the immortality of the self, given that his whole understanding of the perfection of the self is premised upon the absolute transcendence of the mind. Yet it would be equally unthinkable to pursue a monist option in which the individual soul would melt and dissolve within the oneness of being, for then Kantian ethics really would lose its purchase upon the individual's stake in eternity. So Kant's transcendental self must, like Shakespeare's Hamlet, long to 'shuffle off his mortal coil', rid himself of the encumbrance of the body that fragments and warps his sense of self, and set his sights on the transcendent person whose reward in heaven may be rather more a matter of the body than Kant can bring himself to acknowledge.

Yet here too Thomas is not entirely free of complicity in the making of modernity, for a key question arises with regard to the relationship between God, form, and matter (see Part V). Thomas denies any analogical likeness between God and prime matter, and in his absolute refusal to contemplate the possibility that matter might be an appropriate analogy for God, he leaves matter in a state of perplexing ambiguity, occupying a limbo in which there is a beginning but no end. Not only that, but the same is true of the human body. To be human is to be an indestructible body, emerging into being from nothingness—*ex nihilo*—but enduring forever in a state of joy or horror, glory or torture, heaven or hell. We are 'immortal, indestructible, *sublime*' bodies, forever moving in a vertiginous fall towards the curve of the infinite. We must come back to the questions this poses to theology in postmodernity, but I turn now to ask what this means in terms of the Sadean other of Kantian ethics, when evil rather than good provides the content for the empty formalism of the moral law.

---

[45] Zupančič, *Ethics of the Real*, p. 80.   [46] Zupančič, *Ethics of the Real*, p. 80.

11

The Sadean Violence of the Kantian Other

Philosopher John Gray has written repeatedly about modernity in terms of failed utopian ideologies that translate into violent and sometimes genocidal tyrannies. Gray confronts the liberal humanist belief in progress with the murderous catastrophes that have followed in the wake of modern revolutions, and he attributes these to the same apocalyptic impulse that has driven historical outbursts of Christian violence, but that now clothes itself in scientific rather than religious justification. His critique of the relationship between Christianity and post-Christian states of violence is not, he insists, to deny the evidence of extreme forms of violence and mass killings in non-western societies. Rather, 'Where the West is distinctive is in using force and terror to alter history and perfect humanity.'[1] However, whereas Christian apocalypticism recognized that ultimately, the perfect world towards which it aspired, free from all conflict and violence, could only come about through the divine will at the end of history, its secular derivations seek to achieve this through human endeavour alone. So, argues Gray,

> Modern politics has been driven by the belief that humanity can be delivered from immemorial evils by the power of knowledge. In its most radical forms this belief underpinned the experiments in revolutionary utopianism that defined the last two centuries. . . . Today as in the twentieth century the dangers of utopianism are denied. Now as then it is believed that there is nothing to stop humans remaking themselves, and the world in which they live, as they please. This fantasy lies behind many aspects of contemporary culture, and in these circumstances it is *dystopian* thinking we most need.[2]

Gray directs his readers towards various works of fiction such as Huxley's *Brave New World* or Orwell's *1984*, but Lacan also provides a dystopian corrective to modern political utopianism and its justifications in secular scientific rationalism.

---

[1] John Gray, *Black Mass: Apocalyptic Religion and the Death of Utopia* (London and New York: Penguin Books, 2008), p. 35.
[2] Gray, *Black Mass*, p. 19.

Lacan and his interpreters ask what conditions make possible the savagery that is the other face of scientific modernity, and they trace an answer of sorts back to the empty formalism of Kantian ethics. In exploring how they analyse this most perplexing and impossible of questions—there is no satisfactory answer to the question of evil—I am once again seeking continuities and discontinuities between Thomas and Lacan, and within Thomas's own theology. How did the rise of Aristotelian scholasticism as represented by Thomas prepare the way for modernity, and how did the Enlightenment and its scientific aftermath distort or interrupt the continuity of the classical theological tradition? I want to return to Lacan's idea of the unconscious God of the postmodern condition, in order to consider more closely how Lacan understands the lingering effects of modernity's not-quite-dead God on desire, prohibition, and transgression. In the next chapter, I pose similar questions to Thomas. Only by going all the way with Lacan into the very heart of modernity's darkness and its theological antecedents can we hope to begin again, in order to trace the contours of redemption through and beyond Thomas, through and beyond Lacan, to a postmodern future in which hope might yet materialize among us.

ATHEISM BEYOND SCIENCE

Lacan argues that 'the problem of evil . . . is radically altered by the absence of God',[3] and this is above all a crisis in the meaning and function of desire in the post-Kantian subject.

Without any divine creator or Sovereign Good, the origins of desire must be located in a primal lack emanating from the needs of the human organism as other than the linguistic subject. This lack is associated with the onset of language—i.e. the codified laws and prohibitions that sever the subject from the fantasized plenitude of the phallic mother by whom every need is anticipated and met, and in whose body there is no self and other, no gap, no wound of separation. Only a mother of the impossible—an impossible mother—loves with perfect, unconditional love. Thus it is not that the law castrates us, but that our capacity to enter into society and live by its rules awakens us to the fact that we lack something vital in the order of happiness, and this becomes the fantasy of the (non-existent) m(O)ther. The animal instincts of the castrated creature become underwritten by a need so vast that they cry out beyond the satisfaction of every need and every demand, driving the self onwards through the body, on and on beyond every pleasure to the furthest

---

[3] Jacques Lacan, *The Ethics of Psychoanalysis 1959–1960: The Seminar of Jacques Lacan Book VII*, trans. Dennis Porter (London and New York: Routledge, 1999) p. 185.

212 Theology after Postmodernity

extremes of pain and torment, always seeking that which eludes it: the perfect union that is the *telos* and termination of desire.

This is the abysmal truth of the human condition, for there arises within us a demand that is unique to an animal with consciousness and language, which is aware that it is other than the 'I' that it declares itself to be. The demand for unconditional love sets the human apart as a species whose hunger cannot be satisfied through the meeting of its physical needs, and this constitutes the peculiar tragedy of the human condition so that, in the words of Malcolm Bowie, Lacanian desire is 'a place of permanent catastrophe':[4]

> the paradox and the perversity to be found in any recourse to persons is that the other to whom the appeal is addressed is never in a position to answer it unconditionally. He too is divided and haunted, and his *yes*, however loudly it is proclaimed, can only ever be a *maybe*, or a *to some extent*, in disguise.
>
> Desire has its origin in this non-adequation between need and the demand for love, and in the equally grave discrepancy between the demand itself and the addressee's ability to deliver.[5]

Let's bear in mind that Thomas would say that desire has its origin in the asymmetry between the fullness of being that is God, and the sense of lack and separation that is the condition for our own coming into being as other than God. From this perspective, desire is not a tragedy but a magnetic attraction that orients human life towards its end understood not as termination but as fulfilment of its purpose. The tragedy arises when that source of desire is negated and only the wound of lack and separation remains, but Lacan would not countenance the restoration of any theological alternative to this tragedy. We must learn to see it for what it is and bear it as best we can.

Because desire is generated by this insatiable demand, rooted in the fantasized union of the maternal relationship and projected in various ways onto God, it can never achieve its object—there is no such object. So if scientific rationalism is to validate its faith in its ability to achieve human well-being by extending its knowledge of the empirical reality of a godless material world, it must suture the wound and prohibit the copula of desire that arches across the yawning gap between the soul and the real. It must in itself become another fantasy of plenitude, promising its disciples that it is pushing further and further against the frontiers of knowledge, eliminating bit by bit the ignorance that masquerades as mystery.

For Lacan, this plenitudinal scientific fantasy must be displaced by an acceptance of the void with which atheism confronts the modern subject. If atheism is to be real, then it must confront the impossibility of the real. Slavov Žižek describes it as follows:

---

[4] Malcolm Bowie, *Lacan* (London: Harper Collins, 1991), p. 138.
[5] Bowie, *Lacan*, p. 136.

Perhaps the ultimate difference between idealism and materialism is the difference between these two forms of the Real: religion is the Real as the impossible Thing beyond phenomena, the Thing which 'shines through' phenomena in sublime experiences; atheism is the Real as the grimace of reality—as just the Gap, the inconsistency, of reality. . . . Atheism is *not* the position of believing only in positive (ontologically fully constituted, sutured, closed) reality; the most succinct definition of atheism is precisely 'religion without religion'—the assertion of the *void* of the Real deprived of any positive content, prior to any content; the assertion that any content is a semblance which fills the void.[6]

From this perspective, the transition from medieval theology through Enlightenment theism to modern atheism brings the human subject into direct confrontation with and avoidance of the abysmal character of his desire. Confronted with the real, the modern 'I' swerves and takes a detour around the desire of and for the other, treading a narrow and tightly woven linguistic path around the void. In terms of Gray's analysis, religion cedes its eschatological hope to secular politics, and revolutionary violence, wars on terror, and bombs dropped in the name of democracy and human rights become the means to an end that never arrives, the endless pursuit of a perfect world that is worth the cost of a hundred, a thousand, a hundred thousand, a million, six million lives and more.

The question of God is inseparable from the question of death. Lacan belongs among continental atheists who, influenced by Nietzsche, Marx, and Heidegger as well as by Freud, and traumatized by the violence of modernity, have reflected at length on the question of the death of God and its significance for human attitudes towards death and dying. However, Anglo-American scientific atheists allow no such dilemmas to obscure their horizons. As Charles Taylor observes, 'Modern humanism tends to develop a notion of human flourishing which has no place for death. Death is simply the negation, the ultimate negation, of flourishing'.[7]

Lacanian psychoanalysis lays bare the cost of this avoidance of the real and its relationship to death, with its inescapably violent undertow and its restless claims upon the soul. Lacan seeks to loosen the weave of language so that desire can flow and imagination can once again speak between the symbolic and the real, yet without recreating the consolation or motivation of religious faith that was prohibited by Kant. The Thing that psychoanalysis discovers is not to be worshipped but neither is it to be conquered by science. When psychoanalysis exposes the effects on the western soul of the Lutheran disgracing of the

---

[6] Slavoj Žižek, *For They Know Not What They Do: Enjoyment as a Political Factor*, 2nd edn (London and New York: Verso, 2008), p. xxix.

[7] Charles Taylor, *A Secular Age* (Cambridge MA: Harvard University Press, 2007), p. 320. See also Ernest Becker, *The Denial of Death* (London: Souvenir Press, 2011), for a psychoanalytic critique of modern attitudes to death.

world and the Kantian banishment of God that followed, it reveals that before which the human must endure with neither gods nor science to save us now. That is why Lacan insists upon recognizing 'the filiation or cultural paternity that exists between Freud and a new direction of thought—one that is apparent at the break which occurred toward the beginning of the sixteenth century, but whose repercussions are felt up to the end of the seventeenth century'.[8] If the fluidity of desire is to elude both the tyranny of the law and the terror of the real, it can only do so by addressing the split that Luther and Kant between them introduced into the modern soul. This necessarily entails the re-opening of the medieval imagination with its angelic and demonic phantasms, clothed now in the language of the psychoanalytic imaginary, hysteria, and desire, and stripped of its eschatological end.

Lacanian psychoanalysis claims to bring the postmodern subject face-to-face with the truth that philosophy, theology, and science cannot acknowledge. It offers no cure to the tragi-comedy of the human condition. We must learn to enjoy the torment of our enjoyment, which alights upon us in rapturous epiphanies of delight only to evaporate again into the endless hauntings of desire. Yet this is a hazardous path that weighs upon the individual as an almost unbearable weight, for we must recognize that modernity has thrust us into a space of metaphysical abandonment and radical responsibility, with no guidance from any divine or moral law.

Each individual must navigate a narrow path through the stirrings of ateleological desire, towards some purposeless but meaningful truth that emerges from the confrontation with the infinity of emptiness that the self contains. This entails a certain joyous vivacity in the face of futility—the link between Søren Kierkegaard and Lacan is clear[9]—as the only meaningful and ethical alternative to the relentless drive towards the all-sufficient plenitude that lures the psyche from the far side of annihilation. A consumerist ethos anaesthetizes desire and makes it compliant with the authority vested in the symbolic. The 'happy' citizen of the modern state, blunting her desire with retail therapy, turns a blind eye to the violence that is done in her name and the imprisoning force of a bureaucracy that closes in around her with ever-increasing vigilance and surveillance.

In the words of Alenka Zupančič, the metonymic movement of desire with its continuous evasion of satisfaction 'proves to be not an infinite pursuit of some ideal that transcends us, but a flight from the infinite that pursues us in this world'.[10] So, argues Zupančič, 'The ethics of desire *is* the ethics of fantasy',

---

[8] Lacan, *The Ethics of Psychoanalysis*, p. 97.
[9] See Marcus Pound, *Theology, Psychoanalysis and Trauma* (London: SCM Press, 2007).
[10] Alenka Zupančič, *Ethics of the Real* (London: Verso, 2000), p. 54.

and in that it is the preserve of those who are ready to die or to kill to realize their fantasies:

> Those who practise such an ethics today are called terrorists, fanatics, fundamentalists, madmen. . . . We are (post)modern, we know a great deal, we know that all these people are dying and killing for something which does not exist. Of course, we all have our fantasies and our desires, but we are very careful not to realize them—we prefer to die, rather than to realize our desire.[11]

Modernity's hedonistic culture emerges with the decline of Kantian ethics. Western liberal consumerism and its libertarian precursors invert the traditional relationship between law and desire, without resolving the conflict and interdependence between them. Guilt is no longer generated by the conflict between a disciplined society ordered by God and the unruly desires and appetites of the inner self with its temptations and sins, but by a permissive society that demands our happiness in denial of our inner inhibitions and anxieties. We begin to feel guilty because of our lack of well-being, our failure to meet the demands of a consumer society that commands our pleasure.

Religion becomes caught up in this culture of consumption, for that too must satisfy its followers with the offer of phallic wholeness. Whether it is the increasingly confident and extremist assertions of traditional religions about the truth of their particular version of God and the moral values enforced in His name (this God is always a He with a capital 'H'), or the passive aggressive resistance of various forms of New Age spirituality, the people who have it all and know it all are ferocious enemies of those who refuse to comply with the myth by acknowledging the inescapability of lack and unknowing.

As Žižek argues,

> Traditionally, psychoanalysis was expected to allow the patient to overcome the obstacles which prevented him/her the access to normal sexual satisfaction: if you are not able to 'get it,' go to the analyst who will enable you to get rid of your inhibitions. Today, however, we are bombarded from all sides by different versions of the injunction 'Enjoy!', from direct enjoyment in sexual performance to enjoyment in professional achievement or in spiritual awakening. *Jouissance* today effectively functions as a strange ethical duty: individuals feel guilty not for violating moral inhibitions by way of engaging in illicit pleasures, but for not being able to enjoy. In this situation, psychoanalysis is the only discourse in which *you are allowed not to enjoy*—not prohibited to enjoy, just relieved of the pressure to do so.[12]

The postmodern self toys with desire, but in the process she becomes the plaything of ideological forces that manipulate her desire by exploiting the

---

[11] Zupančič, *Ethics of the Real*, p. 54.
[12] Slavoj Žižek, *How to Read Lacan* (London: Granta Books, 2006), p. 104.

wilful ignorance that lies at the heart of any attempt to experience desire in terms of happiness and gratification. If desire is for a good beyond any goods that the world can deliver, then for the post-religious subject no less than for the religious subject, the aim of desire is some elusive quarry through and beyond death. The difference is that, while the religious subject, including the Kantian subject, interprets this pursuit in terms of God, the Sovereign Good, and personal immortality, the post-Kantian atheist knows that there is no Sovereign Good, no God, and no immortality. To fail to confront this futility of desire in all its starkness is to collude in its continuous trivialization and deflection by the proliferation of choices and goods in place of earlier concepts of freedom and the Good. The inverse of this consuming cycle of distraction and frustration is the spiralling violence of desire as it seeks its object beyond every prohibition and law that stands in its way.

In the concluding section of *Seminar XI, The Four Fundamental Concepts of Psychoanalysis*, Lacan makes an oblique reference to 'the dark God' under whose 'monstrous spell' the lure of sacrifice retains its grip on human desire, manifest in the Holocaust.[13] There is, he suggests, 'an averting of the eyes' from that mystery through which 'the offering to obscure gods of an object of sacrifice' still plays out as a way of trying to discern the desire of the Other that constitutes our desire. Lacan cites Spinoza's idea of the *Amor intellectualis Dei*, which 'produces a serene, exceptional detachment from human desire' such that it 'may be confused with a transcendent love'.[14] This is a position that Lacan declares is 'not tenable for us', for experience shows Kant to be more true. Kant's moral law is 'simply desire in its pure state, that very desire that culminates in the sacrifice, strictly speaking, of everything that is the object of love in one's human tenderness—I would say, not only in the rejection of the pathological object, but also in its sacrifice and murder'.[15] The ethical demand for sacrifice emanates from the desire of the Other, the desire to satisfy the Other, and it continues to function as a veiled religious dynamic that manifests itself in modernity's violence. Kant's pure form of the ethical act, behind which is the all-seeing eye of the unseen and unknowable God, makes the attempt to desire what God desires—the attempt to discern the desire of the Other—an impossible demand. This, in Lacanian terms, is the dark underside of Kantian ethics that psychoanalysis unveils, and we need to explore it more fully by turning first to questions of transgression and desire, and then to the Freudian death drive.

---

[13] Jacques Lacan, *The Four Fundamental Concepts of Psychoanalysis: The Seminar of Jacques Lacan, Book XI*, trans. Alan Sheridan (New York: W. W. Norton, 1981), p. 275.

[14] Lacan, *The Four Fundamental Concepts of Psychoanalysis*, p. 275.

[15] Lacan, *The Four Fundamental Concepts of Psychoanalysis*, pp. 275–6.

LAW, TRANSGRESSION, AND DESIRE

Twisting Ivan's claim in Dostoyevsky's *The Brothers Karamazov* that without God everything is permissible, Lacan suggests that 'God is dead, so nothing is permissible.'[16] In oedipal terms, the murder of the primal father is intended to remove the source of prohibition against the satisfaction of desire, but the guilt it engenders reinforces the prohibition in such a way that 'everything that is transferred from *jouissance* to prohibition gives rise to the increasing strengthening of prohibition. Whoever attempts to submit to the moral law sees the demands of his superego grow increasingly meticulous and increasingly cruel'.[17] The superego—the modern citizen or, in Lacanian terms, the obedient subject of the symbolic order—constitutes the interiorization of the old external laws of the Judaeo-Christian socio-religious order, so that the conflict between prohibition and desire migrates inwards without losing any of its dialectical force. The prohibitive voice of conscience sustains and feeds the drive through the guilty pleasure of transgression, so that the greater the power of the prohibition, the more powerful the desire to transgress becomes.

Lacan explores the relationship between law and transgression with reference to St Paul's reflection on the relationship between sin and the law in Romans 7:

> What then should we say? That the law is sin? By no means! Yet, if it had not been for the law, I would not have known sin. I would not have known what it is to covet if the law had not said, 'You shall not covet.' But sin, seizing an opportunity in the commandment, produced in me all kinds of covetousness. Apart from the law sin lies dead. I was once alive apart from the law, but when the commandment came, sin revived and I died, and the very commandment that promised life proved to be death to me. (Romans 7:7–11)

Addressing a Catholic audience during the year when he was delivering *Seminar VII*, Lacan declared himself unable to accept that anybody, 'believing or unbelieving, would not be compelled to respond to a text such as this whose message is based on a mechanism which is absolutely alive, meaningful and palpable for a psychoanalyst'.[18]

Psychoanalysis affirms the significance of guilt—its 'omnipresence'[19]—with regard to the function of desire, so that hedonistic attempts to liberate eroticism and sexuality from prohibition and guilt are doomed to failure because desire is

---

[16] Jacques Lacan, *Le Triomphe De La Religion Précédé De Discours Aux Catholiques* (Paris: Éditions du Seuil, 2005), p. 36.

[17] Lacan, *The Ethics of Psychoanalysis*, p. 176.

[18] Lacan, *Le Triomphe De La Religion*, pp. 29–30. Lacan makes oblique reference to this in *The Ethics of Psychoanalysis*, p. 171, where he contrasts an audience of believers with an audience of psychoanalysts.

[19] Lacan, *The Ethics of Psychoanalysis*, p. 3.

produced by the law, and the sense of the Other as Judge persists even after the death of God, owing to the function of the symbolic order in its repression of desire.[20] Desire is awakened only when its object—the pre-oedipal mother—is prohibited, and therefore prohibition stimulates and sustains desire. This is what Saint Paul recognizes: 'Transgression in the direction of *jouissance* only takes place if it is supported by the oppositional principle, by the forms of the Law.'[21] *Jouissance*, therefore, far from being destroyed by the law, derives its satisfaction from transgression of the law. Thus, in the act of risk-taking defiance, the law plays 'the role of a means, of a path cleared that leads straight to the risk'.[22]

In the early Lacan, *jouissance* is always abysmal, endowed with a deadly impetus that propels it towards annihilation through ever-greater transgression. However, Lacan later modified his understanding of *jouissance* and the drives associated with it—which, as we shall see, is of fundamental significance for his changing representation of the mother, desire, femininity, and embodiment. He came to suggest that the *jouissance* attainable through the drives could be liberated from the deadly dynamics of prohibition and transgression, by teasing it away from the insatiability of desire. While desire is incapable of satisfaction, the drive allows for transient enjoyment—*jouissance*—associated not with attachment to the object but with a response to the body's appetites and instincts. Desire has the absent other as its object, but the drive seeks enjoyment unrelated to the object so that the copula of desire is briefly eliminated through a sensory experience of pleasure or torment intense enough to fill the gap. The 'cure' that Lacanian psychoanalysis offers is the freedom to experience this episodic *jouissance* without attaching to it a greater weight of permanence or plenitude than it can bear. It is not an epiphany of some future joy or some deferred plenitude—it is all the joy we'll ever have and all the plenitude we'll ever know. To quote Zupančič, 'the aim of the late Lacan is surely not to affirm the place of enjoyment as "full". Instead he tries to find a conceptualization (of the status) of enjoyment which would simultaneously embrace these two features: that *jouissance* does not exist, and that it is found everywhere'.[23] Liberated from the pursuit of some satisfaction beyond itself, the corporeal self discovers a fragile capacity for delight in the here and now. However, when the infinite enters the scene, when *jouissance* is pursued or banished as a means to an end rather than as an end in itself, it becomes invested with a deadly impetus which propels it beyond all the boundaries and prohibitions it encounters. We might evoke William Blake to express what this means:

---

[20] Cf. Lacan, *Le Triomphe De La Religion*, pp. 3–4.
[21] Lacan, *The Ethics of Psychoanalysis*, p. 177.
[22] Lacan, *The Ethics of Psychoanalysis*, p. 195.
[23] Zupančič, *Ethics of the Real*, p. 242.

> He who binds to himself a joy
> Does the winged life destroy;
> But he who kisses the joy as it flies
> Lives in eternity's sun rise.

Is an ethics possible at all from such a perspective? Yes, answers Lacan, but only on condition that we come to terms with the insatiability of desire and the transience of *jouissance*, so that the former does not blight every experience of the latter with its drive towards all. To appreciate the nature of this ethical challenge, we need to consider how, according to Lacan, Freud's discovery of the death drive brings into view the horror that Kant introduced into modern consciousness with his divided will.

THE FREUDIAN DEATH DRIVE

The death drive constitutes a relatively late development in Freud's thinking. He first explores it in *Beyond the Pleasure Principle*,[24] where he explains why he has had to modify his understanding of the drives associated with *eros*—the sexual impulses whose orientation is towards life and the survival of the species—by recognizing that there is a conflicting drive at work in the psyche, which he calls the death drive (he never refers to it as *thanatos*, although subsequent literature uses that term). It is a drive that Freud explains in terms of Darwin's theory of evolution, for it aims not just at the death of the individual but at the destruction of the very possibility of life. It is an inexplicable urge to return to a primordial condition of stasis and non-being associated with the pre-organic stage of evolution, and it seduces the unconscious with the lure of annihilation.

Lacan argues that Freud confronts us with an unbearable truth about the human condition, for beyond the pleasure principle, his discovery of the death drive unveils the negated heart of darkness in the modern soul. Quoting Freud, Lacan observes that

> Those who like fairy stories turn a deaf ear to talk of man's innate tendencies to 'evil, aggression, destruction, and thus also to cruelty.... Man tries to satisfy his need for aggression at the expense of his neighbour, to exploit his work without compensation, to use him sexually without his consent, to appropriate his goods, to humiliate him, to inflict suffering on him, to torture and kill him.'[25]

Freud's discovery of the death drive leads to Lacan's early suggestion—which, as I suggested above, he later modified—that '*jouissance* is evil. Freud leads us

---

[24] Sigmund Freud, 'Beyond the Pleasure Principle', in SE Vol. 18, pp. 1–64.
[25] Lacan, *The Ethics of Psychoanalysis*, p. 185, quoting Freud, SE Vol. 21 (1930), p. iii.

by the hand to this point: it is suffering because it involves suffering for my neighbour'.[26] This evil emerges from the site of modernity's God whom we know to be dead, but 'God himself doesn't know that'. As a result of this limbo existence, '*jouissance* still remains forbidden as it was before, before we knew that God was dead'.[27]

The death drive has devastating implications for an ethical system based on the biblical commandment to 'love your neighbour as yourself'. Lacan refers to Freud's horror being aroused, 'the horror of the civilized man he essentially was. It derives from the evil in which he doesn't hesitate to locate man's deepest heart'.[28] Freud recognized—even if he did not fully explore its implications—the 'harmful, malignant *jouissance*'[29] that his discovery of the death drive entailed. According to Lacan, 'at the heart of everything Freud taught, one finds the following: the energy of the so-called superego derives from the aggression that the subject turns back upon himself'.[30] This means that a man's neighbour is not primordially an object of love but a lightning rod for aggression, arousing violence towards the other by awakening the punitive aggressivity that haunts his own consciousness, which gives the Law its prohibitive power over him, and upon which his desire feeds.

This scenario contradicts the enduring tendency by liberal humanists to equate pleasure with goodness for, as we saw earlier, pleasure is fuelled not by obedience but by transgression. Moreover, there is a transgressive point at which all limits have been crossed, including the limit that serves to delineate the emptiness and evil of my own self from the emptiness and evil of my neighbour's self:

> My neighbour possesses all the evil Freud speaks about, but it is no different from the evil I retreat from in myself. To love him, to love him as myself, is necessarily to move toward some cruelty. His or mine?, you will object. But haven't I just explained to you that nothing indicates that they are distinct? It seems rather that they are the same, on condition that those limits which oblige me to posit myself opposite the other as my fellow man are crossed.[31]

Lacan suggests that Freud's repressed horror at the idea of unconditional love for the neighbour arises from his awareness of the evocation of 'that fundamental evil which dwells within this neighbour. But if that is the case, then it also dwells within me. And what is more of a neighbour to me than this heart within which is that of my *jouissance* and which I don't dare go near?'[32] This,

[26] Lacan, *The Ethics of Psychoanalysis*, p. 184.
[27] Lacan, *The Ethics of Psychoanalysis*, p. 184.
[28] Lacan, *The Ethics of Psychoanalysis*, p. 194.
[29] Lacan, *The Ethics of Psychoanalysis*, p. 187.
[30] Lacan, *The Ethics of Psychoanalysis*, p. 194.
[31] Lacan, *The Ethics of Psychoanalysis*, p. 198.
[32] Lacan, *The Ethics of Psychoanalysis*, p. 186.

as we shall see, is the challenge that the Marquis de Sade poses to Kantian ethics. The command of neighbourly love entails the transgression of the boundaries of separation between self and other. In Kantian form, it entails the total destruction of the self in order to be free to perform my duty towards my neighbour, but if I love my neighbour as myself, must I not also destroy her so that she too can be free of her desire in order to attain to the formal perfection of the law? We begin to see why Lacanian ethics offers a critique of modern totalitarian and fascist ideologies, executed by those who carry out their commands to serve a greater good by torturing, imprisoning, and killing their fellow citizens, for the greater good of their nation, race, creed, or religion.

For Lacan as for Freud, the Kantian attempt to eradicate all self-interest and desire from the relationship between the autonomous moral subject and his other removes the very condition upon which peaceful co-existence is possible, for only through a recognition of mutual selfishness is it possible to transcend the impetus towards destruction. The ego, under the influence of the pleasure principle, seeks contentment in equilibrium. Thus a society of equally selfish pleasure-seeking individuals has some chance of maintaining social bonds through self-interest constrained by recognition of the self-interest of others, based on the more or less fair distribution of moral and material goods. But once these constraints are removed—once the necessary boundaries between self and other are dissolved through the imperative to love unconditionally, without limits—we must transgress the pleasure-seeking impulses that keep the death drive at bay.

So, claims Lacan,

> at the heart of everything Freud taught, one finds the following: the energy of the so-called superego derives from the aggression that the subject turns back upon himself. . . . I retreat from loving my neighbor as myself because there is something on the horizon there that is engaged in some form of intolerable cruelty. In that sense, to love one's neighbor may be the cruellest of voices.[33]

This predicament emerges from the 'I', the law giver, the superego, the father of the real, which in Kantian ethics must eliminate the bodily desiring self in order to assert its will. But the law emerges from a void because the law giver is dead and has always been dead as the condition upon which the law came to be. The law emanates from the murdered, castrating Father whose death enforces the prohibition, who has always been dead as the ground upon which the prohibition acquires its force through the operation of transgression and guilt. The 'I' who forbids my desire is an empty voice that comes from nowhere. It is the voice of the Other that echoes within me, in the name of a paradoxical desire that desires the elimination of my desire, but only by my desire can

---

[33] Lacan, *The Ethics of Psychoanalysis*, p. 194.

I hope to understand what it desires of me. It does not exist, but the more I tell myself that it does not exist—the more I push my desire to discover what is really there or what is not really there at all—the more all-consuming and real its commanding absence becomes. To quote Lacan:

> On the horizon, beyond the pleasure principle, there rises up the *Gut, das Ding*, thus introducing at the level of the unconscious something that ought to oblige us to ask once again the Kantian question of the *causa noumenon*. *Das Ding* presents itself at the level of unconscious experience as that which already makes the law. . . . It is a capricious and arbitrary law, the law of the oracle, the law of signs in which the subject receives no guarantee from anywhere, the law in relation to which he has no *Sicherung*, to use another Kantian term.[34]

This brings us to the dark heart of *Seminar VII*, in which Lacan posits Sade as the logical corollary to Kant, in order to unmask the impossibility of an ethics predicated upon the rational primacy of the good. Sadean and Kantian ethics are equally rational, and no appeal to reason alone can help us to resolve the predicament that Kant himself acknowledges (but shies away from) in his moral antinomies. And if such a claim strikes us as a flight of Lacanian fantasy, we need only look back over the moral vacuum at the heart of modern history, in order to confront the challenge that Freud poses to us.

KANT AND SADE

Kant's ethical imperative depends upon a benign and life-preserving normativity as the source of human motivation, even though it can offer no persuasive rational account as to why this is so. As we have seen, he struggles to account for what he sees as a persistent evil presence alongside the good within the human heart.

Freud exposes what Kant himself was unable to follow through to its logical consequence—namely, that there is no rational reason for privileging good over evil, and the maxim of Kant's moral law can as easily be used to justify radical evil as moral good. In stripping away any grounds for choosing between them except for the empty formalism of the universal maxim, Kant fails to recognize that, in the conflicting rationalities of the antinomies, the evil will is no less rational a choice than the good will. To quote Zupančič,

> The fundamental paradox of ethics lies in the fact that in order to found an ethics, we already have to presuppose a certain ethics (a certain option of the good). The whole project of Kant's ethics is an attempt to avoid this paradox: he tries to show that the moral law is founded only in itself, and the good is good only 'after' the

---

[34] Lacan, *The Ethics of Psychoanalysis*, p. 73.

moral law. This insistence, however, has a price.... We test our maxims against something which is 'external' to the moral law, and determines the horizon of that which is generally acceptable and what is not.[35]

As Zupančič and other Lacanian critics of Kant point out, this emphasis on obedience to the rational formalism of the law before and beyond the good opens up the whole question of how modern totalitarian and fascist political ideologies acquire their power over people's minds, for one can substitute Führer, God, or any other external law giver beyond the law as a moral authority that must be obeyed, providing his exemption from the law is in itself constituted according to the law, for example, in the form of a democrat-ically elected leader (as Hitler was), or a divinely appointed king. Kant's attempt to reinscribe morality within the limits of reason alone paradoxically makes the human prey to greater rather than lesser tyranny, for rationality is not per se inherently good—the fully rational self can pursue the greatest evil just as rationally as he or she can pursue the greatest good.

One does not, according to Kant, obey the king because he is good—one obeys him because he is the king. This is why, in a footnote in *Metaphysics of Morals*, Kant gives an extravagant account of the horror associated with the formal execution of a monarch under the law, which he compares to 'what theologians call the sin that cannot be forgiven either in this world or the next'.[36] This constitutes for Kant an act of collective suicide by the people that is the most extreme violation of the categorical imperative. Why? For Kant, the king symbolically represents the laws that constitute the people. To murder the king is to destroy his personal body, but it does not destroy the body of the law that he symbolizes. However, his formal execution uses the law to destroy the giver of the law, and thus it destroys the very foundation upon which the law exists and by which it creates the people. But what if that is the purpose towards which the ethical act is directed?[37]

Kant's moral will is, as we have seen, premised upon the radical destruction and renewal of the self before the law, but Kant smuggles into the ruthless logic of this demand a persistent and unchallenged assumption that people will choose good over evil, life over death, law over transgression. By his own rules, this is an unwarranted assumption. The good will of Kantian ethics asserts itself with the hidden authority of the good that Kant seeks to deny. Only if the

---

[35] Lacan, *The Ethics of Psychoanalysis*, p. 94.

[36] Immanuel Kant, *The Metaphysics of Morals*, ed. and trans. Mary Gregor (Cambridge: Cambridge University Press, 1996), p. 97, explanatory footnote.

[37] I am reluctant to further complicate this argument by introducing yet more scholarly sources. However, it would be interesting to pursue these suggestions further in engagement with Louis E. Wolcher's sombre and challenging study, *Law's Task: The Tragic Circle of Law, Justice and Human Suffering* (Aldershot UK and Burlington VT: Ashgate Publishing, 2008), which in turn invites engagement with Giorgio Agamben, *Homo Sacer: Sovereign Power and Bare Life*, trans. Daniel Heller-Roazen (Stanford CA: Stanford University Press, 1998, first published 1995).

a priori can indeed seep across the boundary of materiality and knowability in order to become a motivating factor in the moral life can one account for the imperative that the formal maxim must seek good and avoid evil. If, as Kant insists, the good is not the motive but the consequence of the formality of the act, then what would happen if the evil will were allowed to prevail over the good?

One might rationally take as one's law giver, not the good will but the evil will, and one might seek to destroy the law itself, in order to achieve the true creation *ex nihilo* that Kant himself stops short of pursuing. If one must go all the way in order to inaugurate the moral self, if one must purge the evil that lurks in the pollution of desire, matter, and the body, and if there is no good except that which is produced by the emptiness of the form that remains after this purgation is complete, then the ethical act might well be pursued through following the dictate of the evil will. This is what Kant cannot fully confront, and it is what enigmatically appears when psychoanalysis permits the haunted soul to speak beyond the controlling voice of the superego. This is why Lacan posits Sade as the logical alternative to Kant. Sade's philosophy explores the consequences of asserting a savage and destructive nature as the driving force behind human relationships, and therefore it constitutes the logical corollary to Kant's ethics—the privileging of one side of the antinomies over the other.

For Lacan, at least during the intermediary stage of his thought when he delivered *Seminar VII*, desire is associated with the pleasure principle, and *jouissance* is associated with the death drive. They operate in conflict with one another. While desire is stimulated and sustained by its transgressive relation to the law, *jouissance* seeks to overthrow the law through its anarchic, nihilistic compulsion towards non-being, a 'second death' which involves not only the death of the organism but the death of the very systems and structures by which organic life is made possible. As I mentioned before, this relates to Freud's attempt to account for the death drive in terms of a reversal of the process of evolution as described by Darwin. In Lacanian terms, this refers not only to the biological order of life but to the symbolic order of language and law that sustains the subject. Lacan traces this drive towards annihilation in terms of Kant's idea of the ethical self as a creation *ex nihilo*. It is

> a will to create from zero, a will to begin again. . . . [A]s soon as we have to deal with anything in the world appearing in the form of the signifying chain, there is somewhere – though certainly outside of the natural world – which is the beyond of that chain, the *ex nihilo* on which it is founded and is articulated as such.[38]

We shall see later that Lacan sees the doctrine of creation *ex nihilo* as the founding truth of the human condition, at least as that condition has been produced and perpetuated in western culture with its biblical influences.

---

[38] Lacan, *The Ethics of Psychoanalysis*, p. 212.

Kant's ethical formula claims that there is a necessary act of destructive creativity that requires the elimination of the phenomenal self, associated with the evil of animality, the body, and desire, so that all that remains is the law itself, but such elimination is impossible. The moral law therefore produces some stubborn remnant, so that a surplus enjoyment is generated by the very endeavour to eliminate the pathological content of the law. The more the moral subject strives to free himself from enjoyment, the more a vicious other enjoys the futility of his endeavour. The formalism of the categorical imperative assumes, in the words of Žižek, 'the tone of cruel, obscene "neutrality"'.[39] Yet what is to stop one making the opposite choice—to eliminate the law through subservience to a destructive and violent nature, until one even eliminates the laws by which nature itself exists? Lacan suggests that

> Sade's thought goes as far as forging the strangely extravagant notion that through crime man is given the power to liberate nature from its own laws. For its own laws are chains. What one has to sweep aside in order to force nature to start again from zero, so to speak, is the reproduction of forms against which nature's both harmonious and contradictory possibilities are stifled in an impasse of conflicting forces.[40]

Again, we should note here the difference that Lacan is implicitly positing between the sexual cosmology of pre-modern philosophy and theology, in which the reproduction of forms is a fertile copulation with matter according to the laws of nature, and the Kantian moral law which seeks the elision of the copula of desire and sets up the will/the form in deadly opposition to nature/matter.

Yet Kant's revulsion at the thought of regicide is rooted in his belief that it is contrary to nature, and is therefore inexplicable. It defies 'lawgiving reason' which is, according to Kant, 'in accordance with the mechanism of nature'. He declares that 'it is impossible for a human being to commit a crime of this kind, a formally evil (wholly pointless) crime'.[41] However, the motivation of Kantian ethics is not the pursuit of good over evil, but the formality of the act that is empty of content. It is this which determines the good, rather than being determined by it. If, as Kant acknowledges, the moral antinomies cannot be resolved by an appeal to reason alone, then his argument against regicide fails. The regicidal act, the 'most extreme evil',[42] just goes one step further than Kant can bring himself to go in the quest to create anew *ex nihilo*. It seeks the destruction of the laws of nature upon which Kant's objection rests, but Kant

---

[39] Žižek, *For They Know Not What They Do*, p. 232.
[40] Lacan, *The Ethics of Psychoanalysis*, p. 260.
[41] Kant, *The Metaphysics of Morals*, p. 97.
[42] Kant, *The Metaphysics of Morals*, p. 97.

has already insisted that the ostensible goodness of nature must be destroyed if the form of the law is to prevail.

Kantian ethics must overcome the abysmal threat that rises up from beyond the boundaries of reason, beyond all language, form, and knowledge, where the laws of God and the laws of nature are locked in an interminable conflict between good and evil. Paradoxically, then, one's choice of the good can only have as its underlying motivation a fear of nature, an acceptance of the prohibition which says that one must remain on the near-side of what can be rationally known and empirically verified if one is not to be lured towards that dangerous dissolution on the far side of knowledge. But what if one chooses Kantian nature rather than God, evil rather than good, as the absent law giver? The one seeks to fulfil the law by going as far as it is possible to go within the limits of reason, knowing that its ultimate end is the noumenal beyond of God, freedom, and the immortality of the soul. But one might rationally choose a different end—a freedom that comes not through God and immortality but through the elimination of every possibility of being or becoming, to arrive back at a state of primal, unformed, unevolved, undifferentiated, infinite matter.

This is where Sade's 'second death' enters the scene, a death that must go beyond any individual death to destroy the very conditions of being. The violent rapist God of the Freudian unconscious—the father of the real—is seen to underscore the authority of the law invested in the symbolic, acting through and beyond the symbolic to assert a visceral destruction of every law as the ultimate authority achieved through the ultimate annihilation. It is this annihilating force that Sade exposes in his fantasies of torture and dismemberment. The Sadean torturer is the mirror image of the Kantian subject. Sade's work

> achieves an absolute of the unbearable in what can be expressed in words relative to the transgression of all human limits. . . . It is nothing else but the response of a being, whether reader or writer, at the approach to a center of incandescence or an absolute zero that is physically unbearable.[43]

Sade's heroes imagine a second death—'death insofar as it is regarded as the point at which the very cycles of the transformations of nature are annihilated'.[44] This is not, we must remember, biological death. It is Sade's anticipation of the Nietzschean death of God as the death of language, meaning, grammar, law, and the subject. Lacan quotes Sade:

> Nature wants atrocities and magnitude in crimes; the more our destructions are of this type, the more they will be agreeable to it. To be of even greater service to

---

[43] Lacan, *The Ethics of Psychoanalysis*, pp. 200–1.
[44] Lacan, *The Ethics of Psychoanalysis*, p. 248.

nature, one should seek to prevent the regeneration of the body that we bury. Murder only takes the first life of the individual whom we strike down; we should also seek to take his second life, if we are to be even more useful to nature. For nature wants annihilation; it is beyond our capacity to achieve the scale of destruction it desires.[45]

We should note carefully what is being proposed here. Sade is not advocating the lawless (i.e. formless) pursuit of anarchic pleasure as an end in itself. Rather, he is seeking to make the law serve a different master, to obey the law of nature rather than the Kantian moral law. As Žižek points out, destruction of the Kantian moral law has as its motive the inauguration of an entirely different order of law and moral authority. Sade, like Kant, upholds the empty formalism of the law but he makes it subject to a different order of reason, a different law giver outside the law. So, says Žižek,

> the Sadeian ghost denies chance, rejects the unforeseen, and is boringly static.... The pervert wants to eliminate the unexpected event that shakes a previous assumption; his desire to break the law conceals the pervert's deepest wish: to substitute himself for it. Sadeian society is a codified one, with guidelines and rules but devoid of eroticism, if by eroticism we mean allusive, ambiguous, suggestive language that is home to the unexpected.[46]

Lurking within every attempt to maintain order through violence, Lacan suggests there is a Sadean drive directed towards the total annihilation of all that is unpredictable, erotic, spontaneous, charged with that *jouissance* which is the very energy and desire of matter itself by way of which life is created and regenerated. We shall return to that.

Obedience to the repressive command of modernity's psychic father god (the superego) produces the Kantian subject ruled over by the insatiable demands of duty. Defiance produces the Sadean law giver seeking to eliminate the insatiable demands of *jouissance* rooted in the persistent remnant of the bodily drives. In relation to the Thing, 'morality becomes, on the one hand, a pure and simple application of the universal maxim and, on the other, a pure and simple object'.[47] Note again the dissolution of the boundary between absolute transcendence and absolute immanence—the transcendent, unbounded, and disembodied universality to which Kantian ethics is tethered is ultimately inseparable from the visceral, consuming boundlessness of bodily and personal dismemberment enacted in Sadean fantasies of annihilation. To seek form without matter (Kant) or matter without form (Sade) become goals that are indistinguishable from one another, because both entail the most absolute

---

[45] Lacan, *The Ethics of Psychoanalysis*, p. 211, quoting from Sade, 'System of Pope Pius VI', from Volume IV of *The Story of Juliette*.

[46] Slavoj Žižek, *The Silent Partners* (London and New York: Verso, 2006), pp. 83–4.

[47] Lacan, *The Ethics of Psychoanalysis*, p. 70.

possible transgression of the conjunction between forms and matter that being entails. In Kant, form sets out to annihilate matter. In Sade, matter sets out to annihilate form. We are back with a conflict more extreme and deadly than any Platonic dualism, and this is the conflict that underwrites the ethos of liberal modernity.

VIOLENCE AND POLITICS

This is why Lacanian ethics translates into a critique of politics. At the furthest extreme, an annihilating will drives the subject so that the father of the symbolic becomes a tyrant whose means and ends are indistinguishable from those of the father of the real. Torture and annihilation can be ends in themselves if the object of moral choice is the evil will, but they can also be the means to an end in the service of the purifying destructiveness commanded by the good will. In the name of a greater duty, the 'good' citizen renounces his personal inclinations, endures a heroic sacrifice, and embarks upon a process of elimination. He must become an agent of purification, a servant of the annihilating master whose will he serves, in a way that seeks to eradicate all the lingering traces of desire and suffering in the body, and it matters not whose body it is. Every body that pollutes or infects the purity of the ideal embodied in the law giver outside the law must be eliminated, but the law giver recedes further and further behind the law, so that there is an infinite regression in the quest for the ideal, the real, the thing in itself.

Perhaps no figure symbolizes the Sadean other of Kantian ethics more fully than the suicide bomber. Only he (and sometimes she) really loves—loves in the real—his or her God, neighbour, and self with the annihilating purity that Kant demands. But we might ask, can we really tell the difference between this 'terrorist' and the soldier whose killing and dying is commanded and legitimated by the state? The former exceeds all the normal social limits in a destruction that overthrows the law, and the latter exceeds all the normal social limits in a destruction that defends the law. For the mother of the dismembered and mutilated child, for the orphaned family, the vulnerability of the body knows no such distinctions.

The monstrous modern citizen lurking beneath the veneer of the ethical ideal can be described in Hegelian as well as Kantian terms, for Lacan sees in the logic of the Hegelian dialectic the same drive towards a universal absolute that must constantly assert itself against otherness. Hegel pours contempt on Kant's idea of cosmopolitanism as potentially offering an end to war and an era of perpetual peace based on a new international order,[48] since war for

---

[48] See Immanuel Kant, *Perpetual Peace*, trans. Mary Campbell Smith (New York: Cosimo Inc., 2005).

Hegel is the highest expression of Spirit in human affairs. War asserts the universal power of the state over the threat posed to the community by individual relationships and associations, so that 'government has from time to time to shake them to their core by war':

> By this means the government upsets their established order, and violates their right to independence, while the individuals who, absorbed in their own way of life, break loose from the whole and strive after the inviolable independence and security of the person, are made to feel in the task laid on them their lord and master, death.[49]

Describing the role of the military (which he refers to as 'the class of universality'[50]), Hegel writes:

> The content of bravery as a sentiment is found in the true absolute final end, the sovereignty of the state. Bravery realizes this end, and in so doing gives up personal reality.... An utter obedience or complete abnegation of one's own opinion and reasonings, even an absence of one's own spirit, is coupled with the most intense and comprehensive direct presence of the spirit and of resolution. The most hostile and hence most personal attitude toward individuals is allied with perfect indifference, or even, it may be, a kindly feeling towards them as individuals.[51]

This chillingly anticipates twentieth-century fascism and totalitarianism. It is informed by the same ethos that informs Kant's ethical act—a transcending of every personal desire and affection in order to obey some abstract and universal principle, to such an extent that one can feel kindness towards those one annihilates—as Freud points out, the death drive can be an expression of neighbourly love. If I as an individual must sacrifice all in the pursuit of the universal, then it is for your own good that you should be made to serve this greater good by joining me in my sacrifice. Death is 'the lord and master' of the modern state, and all the liberalizing and egalitarian gloss of consumerism and human rights cannot, according to Lacan, completely eliminate that lurking awareness deep within the soul. Against the hubristic optimism of scientific modernity, Lacan posits the triumph, not of the evil will but of the formality of the law in which good and evil alike are subordinated to the demands of rationalism. The modern bureaucratic state eliminates from consideration every human desire, every particularity, every appeal to mercy and gentleness, every exception, by the exceptionless law that derives from the absent

---

[49] G. W. F. Hegel, *Phenomenology of Spirit*, trans. A. V. Miller (Oxford, New York, Toronto, Melbourne: Oxford University Press, 1977), #453.

[50] G. W. F. Hegel, *Philosophy of Right*, trans. S. W. Dyde (Mineola NY: Dover Publications, Inc., 2005), #327, Addition.

[51] Hegel, *Philosophy of Right*, #328.

Other—the unconscious God of the Judaeo-Christian tradition, who slumbers deep in human consciousness.

I turn now to Thomas to consider how he approaches questions of love of neighbour, prohibition, and transgression, in order once again to tease out the ways in which Lacanian psychoanalysis shines a dark light on Thomas's theology, as part of my enterprise to seek a less violent, more healing Thomism for our times.

12

Love, Law, and Transgression

For theological optimists, there is a reading of Thomas Aquinas that would situate him at a great distance from the dark underside of the Reformation, the Enlightenment, and the scientific revolution. Nature and the body are, for Kant as for Luther, the filth that is excreted from the graced Word (Luther) or banished from the rational mind (Kant). For Thomas, the goodness that we recognize and desire in nature is not opposed to but revealing of God. Grace perfects nature, it does not destroy it. Goodness is a more all-embracing concept than morality. It is a pervasive capacity for happiness that unites soul and body, self and neighbour in flourishing relationships of mutual care and well-being in a graced creation.

All this can be argued and supported through a selective reading of Thomas, and it is a legacy that asks to be rediscovered and lived anew. Yet simply to reclaim this and elide the rest by way of a modernizing gloss is to fail to acknowledge the extent to which the theological tradition, including Thomism, is implicated in the crises and catastrophes of modernity. It is also to fail to take seriously enough how a warped form of Thomism fuels the sexual essentialisms and violent impulses of a certain kind of postmodern Catholic theology under the pervasive influence of Hans Urs von Balthasar.[1]

Before we can allow Thomas to speak back to Lacan, we must allow Lacan to challenge Thomas. If postmodern theology is not simply to perpetuate the old theological dualisms and the violent conflicts that these produce in the individual and society, then it must allow psychoanalytic wisdom to permeate its readings of its own tradition. In what follows, I consider Thomas's account of love of neighbour, then I turn to his reading of Romans 7 in the light of Lacan's interpretation, and finally I consider themes of evil, violence, justice, and heresy.

---

[1] See Tina Beattie, *New Catholic Feminism: Theology and Theory* (London and New York: Routledge, 2006).

LOVE OF NEIGHBOUR

Thomas addresses the question of neighbourly love by responding to arguments that differentiate between love of God and love of neighbour, and which claim that the former takes precedence over the latter.[2] Thomas replies that 'the aspect under which our neighbour is to be loved, is God, since what we ought to love in our neighbour is that he may be in God. Hence it is clear that it is specifically the same act whereby we love God, and whereby we love our neighbour'. He goes on to argue that we owe to ourselves the same love that we owe to our neighbour, because 'the love with which a man loves himself is the form and root of friendship', because we ourselves belong among the things of God which are to be loved, and because we should desire for ourselves what we desire for others, namely, 'the good things which pertain to the perfection of reason'.[3] From this perspective, love of self and love of neighbour go hand in hand, and Thomas insists that this includes the body. So, whereas for Kant the perfection of reason and the demands of the moral law must go as far as possible towards eliminating the effects of the body, matter, and corporeal pleasures, for Thomas these embrace the body and its capacity for pleasure. He argues that,

> Although our bodies are unable to enjoy God by knowing and loving Him . . .
> from the enjoyment in the soul there overflows a certain happiness into the
> body. . . . Hence, since the body has, in a fashion, a share of happiness, it can be
> loved with the love of charity.

I owe a kindness to myself and my neighbour and this includes the care of my own body and hers, because my body is not other than myself, and my capacity for sensual pleasure is evidence of the goodness of God.

It would be difficult to be less Kantian than this, for Kant's thought is implicitly if not explicitly predicated upon a Lutheran theology of grace which is altogether different from that of Thomas. Kantian ethics with their Lutheran hinterland offer a Hobbesian view of nature as the enemy of the good. A society motivated by natural self-interest would be a degenerate and anarchic society in which human greed and aggression would triumph over duty and responsibility. We begin to see why, from such a perspective, love of neighbour mutates into deadly aggressiveness masked by unflinching moral rigour.

Thomas sees that our attitude towards ourselves is inseparable from our attitude towards our neighbour, for we are united by the desire we share. My desire is my neighbour's desire, and I desire for her what I desire for myself. Lacan explores the implications of this, if my desire is for the elimination of all my bodily capacity for delight and the pushing beyond every material

---

[2] See ST II-II, 25.   [3] ST II-II, 25, 4.

influence in the name of an absolute purity of form that alone can be called good. What I desire for myself I must desire for my neighbour, for I must love her as I love myself. Sado-masochism becomes the ethical imperative that underwrites the Kantian moral code.

There is a certain kind of Thomism that would stop there—and most do. Postmodern Thomism is asserted as the redeeming other of the violence of modernity,[4] and a pervasive nostalgia for a lost age infects the theological imagination—sometimes expressed in shockingly violent rhetoric for all its assertions of ontological peace. However, Lacan invites us to go beyond this complacency to probe some of the darker tensions and dualisms in Thomas's theology.

Consider, for example, Thomas's response to the proposition that love of neighbour is more meritorious than love of God. He rejects this suggestion, arguing that 'the love of one's neighbour is not meritorious, except by reason of his being loved for God's sake. Therefore the love of God is more meritorious than the love of our neighbour'.[5] This relativizing of love of neighbour by love of God relates to the idea I explored earlier, that the solitary life of contemplation (avoidance of one's neighbours) is a higher form of life than the active life of service to neighbour. At least implicitly, Thomas suggests that personal communion with one's neighbours can become an obstacle to the desire for union with God which is the highest object of contemplation. Love of God—the solitary yearning of a man for God which seeks transcendence, disembodiment, and the closing down of the imagination with its phantasms and hauntings of desire—matters more than love of neighbour in all the messy animality, sexuality, and desire of the body that she represents. I must love my neighbour whom I can see, but I must do so for the sake of God, and I must love more the God whom I cannot see. We have seen how, in Thomas's understanding of family relationships, the natural inclination of desire must yield to the duty to obey God in the patriarchal ordering of love.

It is not a giant leap but a series of gradual, barely perceptible steps from this theology to a form of modern idealism in which loyalty to an idea, a cause, a state, or a system transcends the delicate corporeal bonds of human love and vulnerability. Hegel is the master who delivers us into this world of abstraction—a world that manifests itself equally in the form of ruthless individualism or in the form of tyrannical collectivism—but Thomas and his contemporaries pave the way. As soon as these ideas implant themselves within the heart, mind, and soul of the modern man of reason gestating in the medieval university, the die is set. Christianity—a religion that uniquely

---

[4] Cf. John Milbank and Catherine Pickstock, *Truth in Aquinas* (London and New York: Routledge, 2001). See also the critique of Milbank and Pickstock in Paul DeHart, *Aquinas and Radical Orthodoxy: A Critical Inquiry* (London and New York: Routledge, 2012).

[5] ST II-II, 27, 8.

embodies God in the form of the vulnerable, the marginalized, the newborn child born from the maternal flesh, the religiously persecuted and politically tortured other, and says that here and nowhere else is God to be discovered—has never been able to resist the temptation to insist that, nevertheless, there is a God over and beyond the human condition, an unknowable but commanding God who must be obeyed at all costs, and who sometimes demands the sacrifice of human lives as the cost of pleasing him.

If in one sense Thomas can be read as an antidote to post-Kantian modernity, in another sense he can be read as its precursor, by way of the continuation of a dark connecting thread that runs through the western tradition from Athens to Jerusalem to Rome to the modern nation state. So let me probe further into Thomas's account of the body, sin, and evil, beginning with his reading of Romans 7.

LAW AND TRANSGRESSION

In his *Commentary on Romans*,[6] Thomas focuses on the nature of covetousness, distinguishing between natural law, which is knowable by reason, the Old Law, which is revealed in the Old Testament, and the New Law, which is revealed in the New Testament. He considers the argument that, if the Old Law teaches sin, then the lawgiver also sins by decreeing the law,[7] but he differentiates between the natural law and the divine law. While natural law enables us to distinguish between good and evil, divine law teaches us 'that human sins displease God, since he forbids them and commands that they be punished'.[8] The law does not cause sin but rather sin takes advantage of the opportunity provided by the law. Although human law does not forbid covetousness, divine law forbids it because the very act of coveting gives pleasure which induces the desire to sin, and this inclination to sin persists as a consequence of the effects of original sin even after the coming of grace.[9]

Conscious as we are of the destructive impact of our modern consumerist cultures, both on the environment and on the lives of the poor whose resources we plunder and whose labour we exploit, we can recognize much wisdom in Thomas's critique of covetousness. We know its destructive impact

---

[6] Thomas Aquinas, 'Lectures on the Letter to the Romans' (Ave Maria University Aquinas Center). I have used the translation by Fr Fabian Larcher, edited by Jeremy Holmes, and made available online by the Aquinas Center for Theological Renewal at Ave Maria University: <http://nvjournal.net/index.php?option=com_content&view=article&id=53&Itemid=62> [accessed 27 July 2012].
[7] Aquinas, 'Lectures on the Letter to the Romans', n. 533.
[8] Aquinas, 'Lectures on the Letter to the Romans', n. 536.
[9] Aquinas, 'Lectures on the Letter to the Romans', n. 542.

very well through the addictions and obsessions of modernity. We are counting the environmental and economic cost of neo-liberalism with its insane policies of economic growth without end, and we experience the personal effects of consumption without moderation or reason on our health and well-being. We know how deadly covetousness becomes when it embeds itself as the driving force of our political and social ethos—and 'economic growth' is in itself a form of covetousness, given that our voracious economies are already too vast for the planet to sustain.

Yet, paradoxically, it is societies shaped by Christianity—Protestant Christianity in particular—that have shaken off the constraints that the sin of covetousness imposes upon human behaviour, in order to pursue neo-liberal goals of the unlimited generation of wealth and consumption of goods, heavily defended by militarism and protectionist economic policies. We might remember Max Weber's theory that capitalism arose in the first place because of a Protestant combination of hard work, frugality, and the anxieties generated by the theology of predestination.[10] Covetousness—a sin which only Christians recognize and know to be wrong, because we know this not by way of reason but by revelation (according to Thomas)—breeds the transgressive drive towards consumption, so that consumerism can be seen as a vast act of Christian transgression.

According to Thomas's account, covetousness creates a transgressive intensification of pleasure in and of itself, even before it translates into desire for any particular object. It is an undefined bodily wanting, stimulating a sense of arousal that attaches itself to different objects of desire, generating an excess that leads to all forms of gluttony, lust, and avarice, driving the self towards destruction and damnation. The very nature of covetousness entails, for Thomas, lack as well as desire—the lack associated with the absence of original justice that would moderate and regulate desire, and the lack of any object that would be sufficient to satisfy the covetous nature of unbridled desire, because its ultimate object is the good that is God. Desire succumbs to evil when it loses sight of that good and gives itself over to the immediacy of sensual pleasures until it becomes enslaved by them and loses its intrinsic freedom—a freedom that is from and for God alone. Little wonder perhaps that the politics of consumption requires as its counterpart the constant threat of scarcity, for covetousness is inseparable from a sense of lack.

William Cavanaugh suggests that the consumerism of modern secular society can be interpreted as just that—an insatiable quest for a lost transcendence, fuelled by lack. He writes that

---

[10] Max Weber, *The Protestant Ethic and the Spirit of Capitalism*, trans. Talcott Parsons (Mineola NY: Dover Publications Inc., 2003).

Consumerism represents a constant dissatisfaction with particular material things themselves, a restlessness that constantly seeks to move beyond what is at hand. Although the consumer spirit delights in material things and sees them as good, the thing itself is never enough. Things and brands must be invested with mythologies, with spiritual aspirations; things come to represent freedom, status, and love. Above all, they represent the aspiration to escape time and death by constantly seeking renewal in created things. Each new movement of desire promises the opportunity to start over.[11]

That mythological and spiritual investment in material things is evident throughout the world of advertising, but it is exemplified by that BMW advertisement that I referred to earlier, which tells us that joy wants us to have it all (see p. 33).

Yet Cavanaugh is too quick to offer a theological solution to this problem, by reminding his readers of the alternative vision offered by the Christian faith. I am suggesting that, before we can discover a solution in Christian theology, we must probe far more deeply into the ways in which the dominant theological tradition has been a major part of the problem. Let's not forget that the redemptive readings I seek and discover in Thomas are not the readings one can find in traditional or new forms of Thomism, particularly with regard to the maternal Trinity and the glimmers of a different way of configuring materiality, difference, and desire—topics I discuss in more detail later.

So let me return to that suggestion that it is divine law rather than natural law that produces the sense of sin associated with covetousness. This could be interpreted as deeply Lacanian. There is some abstract law, unknowable from the perspective of reason alone, which prohibits bodily pleasure. Of course, in Thomas this prohibition is relative rather than absolute, for all pleasures are good when moderated by reason. Even so, there is a surplus to pleasure that is displeasing to the God of the Bible. As we shall see later, this idea that God sets his face against our natural appetites and desires, particularly those associated with sexuality, is of profound significance for a Lacanian interpretation of the Hebrew scriptures. Following Thomas's interpretation, we could say that the divine law legislates against something that reason, operating in accordance with natural law, does not recognize as wrong. There are laws given by a divine law giver that seem arbitrary from the perspective of reason, and which apply only to those who are chosen by God or who acknowledge the truth of revelation. These regulate bodily appetites that are sinful, not because of some rational explanation as to why they are wrong but because they violate the divine law and make us liable to punishment if we transgress. They do not apply to humans in natural societies, but only to those governed by the doctrines of the Christian faith.

---

[11] William T. Cavanaugh, *Being Consumed: Economics and Christian Desire* (Grand Rapids MI and Cambridge UK: William B. Eerdmans Publishing Co., 2008), p. 48.

In the *Summa theologiae*, Thomas describes this in terms of divine law governing the interiority of human acts, whereas natural law and human law are focused more on external acts and the common good.[12] We should keep a Lacanian perspective in focus, bearing in mind that the Lacanian symbolic is an exterior influence that operates on the subject through language and the social order, whereas the imaginary and the real are interior functions of the human psyche. Thomas takes the cultic prohibitions and taboos that set the Hebrews apart from their pagan neighbours and internalizes them, so that the individual Christian soul absorbs all the ritual codes of purity and pollution which order Jewish society, in a way that inevitably produces a tension between the law and conscience. The natural law regulates society and laws according to a rational and coherent order, but the Christian soul is privy to a higher, revealed order of knowledge that refines the natural order through a stricter regime of control, discipline, and virtue regarding the bodily appetites and instincts. When we add to this the demonic and angelic influences that Thomas introduces into Aristotelian philosophy, we begin to see how the western soul becomes a battle ground of competing and divided forces: on the one hand, a rational order inherited from the ancient Greeks and transmitted to modernity through Thomas and later through Kant, and on the other hand, a mysterious source of good and evil beyond what can rationally be known, which commands greater authority than the laws accessible by reason alone. It was this that introduced such a dark and perplexing undercurrent to Kant's account of the human heart with its contradictory masters of the good and evil will. Christianity subordinates the law and makes love the highest commandment, but the shadow side of that is the opening up of an infinite and impossible yearning deep within the fibres of our bodily being—to love and be loved with an absolute, unconditional love, and to crucify the body in the name of that love.

This process of separation and the internalization of laws to do with purity, pollution, and sexuality is crucial for a Lacanian reading of how the Christian understanding of sin and grace shapes the western soul. The introduction of purity codes as a mark of separation in the Hebrew scriptures is primarily associated with those practices and bodily conditions and secretions associated with birth, death, and the maternal body—which constitutes the symbolic separation of the chosen people from the surrounding pagan maternal cults.[13] Thus the sense of holiness—of being called and set apart by God—is inseparable from a sense of loss and pollution associated with the maternal body that sets in motion the interdependent dynamics of guilt and grace in the soul. Thomas's Trinity invites a re-opening of the imaginary space between body and soul wherein a maternal divine might come to dwell, but his Aristotelian/

---

[12] ST I-II, 91, 4.
[13] For more on this, see Beattie, *New Catholic Feminism*, pp. 212–15.

Platonic God—the One—repeatedly bars access to that relational, incarnate Other. We shall return to this.

Thomas inherits and perpetuates a dualistic order that anticipates Kantian ethics, but he blurs the boundaries of reason and introduces a turbulent otherness into the Aristotelian order, by appealing to themes of revelation, love and judgement, grace and sin, which elude the gaze of the rational mind. As we have seen, even when Kant seeks to purge western thought of its theological subservience, he too remains mesmerized and horrified by the tug of sublime and evil forces that appear to have nothing to do with the rational ordering of human life. The reification of evil in post-Reformation western thought introduces a more virulent dualism than what went before, but Thomas's blurring of evil as ontological lack and moral transgression still has a visceral power over the soul.

EVIL, LACK, AND THE DEMONIC

Evil is always negation for Thomas, insofar as it does not exist in and of itself. It is only ever the lack of some good, and even at its most demonic it remains within the bare givenness of being. It is at the furthest extreme of what can be said to exist within the goodness of God.

Thomas argues that, 'In the demons there is their nature which is from God and also the deformity of sin which is not from Him; therefore, it is not to be absolutely conceded that God is in the demons, except with the addition, "inasmuch as they are beings".'[14] The demons are being at the most primordial unformed level of raw existence—goodness stripped of every characteristic of the good except some vestigial remnant of being that holds them in existence.

Yet here we find ourselves confronted with the unthinkable, just as we do when we contemplate the mystery of God, for at this extreme minimum of being what is there to distinguish the demonic from prime matter? Both seem to constitute raw being with nothing else to be said except that it is, so is there a difference? Let me suggest that the difference according to Thomas, elusive and mysterious though it is, is that prime matter is ontological material evil and the demonic is moral spiritual evil.[15] We should remember that, according to Thomas, original sin is a corruption of form, not of matter. It is communicated by way of the father, not the mother, and the actual sins to which it gives rise are associated with the intentionality of the will, not with the

---

[14] ST I, 8, 1.

[15] This representation of lack as ontological evil finds potent expression in Hegel's philosophy. Cf. Daniel Berthold-Bond, *Hegel's Theory of Madness* (New York: State University of New York Press, 1995), Chapter 7, 'Madness and Tragedy'.

acts of the body that result. Prime matter is evil insofar as it is being in the most radical material condition of lack, but it is endowed with the potency of desire that orientates it towards God and the good. It has all the ontological potential to become, and it belongs within the creation that God declares 'very good' in the Book of Genesis, even though it lacks all intelligence and form. The demonic is evil insofar as it is intelligent immaterial being in which all potency and possibility have been eliminated by pride and the wilful turning away from God. The demons are damned and they have no hope of redemption, because they chose to rebel against God with the fullness of the angelic intellect that they possess. These dark spirits that wage war upon human desire are indestructible and irredeemable, and their action is motivated not by desire but by envy. They seek to divert the human from God and to inflict upon his body and soul the eternal torment which they themselves are condemned to endure. Yet these are all areas on the very edges of cognition, according to Thomas. We cannot possibly know God, nor can we know form or matter except in their complex states of being. We can experience the effects of angelic and demonic spirits, for they are messengers who mediate between heaven and hell—they are the creatures of the Thomist imagination or the Lacanian imaginary—but they derive their uncanny power to bless and to curse our lives from the extremes of being to which we have no access. This inevitably means that the attribution of evil to both matter and demonic spiritual beings invites a blurring of the boundary between the two. While that boundary could perhaps be more or less defended in the context of a material world that retains the original grace of creation, we have seen that the denial of created grace to the material world resulted in the fusion of these two categories of evil, so that the demonic and matter both became moral enemies of the human soul.

It is not hard to see why Lacan associates the topology of the Freudian soul with the transition from medieval Thomism through Luther to Kant. Protestantism evacuates nature of its spiritual and magical powers, but these become reinvested in a single, transcendent, and terrifying source of all evil—the devil—who is nowhere and everywhere within the material world. When the Lutheran Kant seeks an escape from the grip of this theological tyranny with its manifestations of violence and mental enslavement in the social, religious, and political order, he finds it impossible to destroy the evil within. When the metaphysical speculations of theology disappear behind the barriers of Kantian practical reason, evil and matter fuse and become the absolute other of God and the good, no longer having any connection to mind and form, but unconquerable and terrifying to the rational mind that tries to control and subdue them. The near-absolute lack that constitutes evil/prime matter in Thomas's Aristotelianism becomes the absolute lack of intrinsic meaning and signification accorded to matter in Kantian formalism, and this evaporation of the material world into the rational mind with its a priori rationalism and empirical constraints is the linguistic matrix within which Lacanian psychoanalysis rediscovers the divine, the demons, the mother, and the matter that continue to haunt the post-Christian soul.

The power of evil becomes even more mystifying and dangerous for the soul if we remember that, for Thomas, moral evil and guilt enter the scene when rational beings—angels or humans—rebel against God and wilfully choose evil over good. Yet this cannot be a choice for evil, because there is nothing in evil capable of arousing desire or attracting the rational soul. One cannot desire evil, argues Thomas, because one cannot desire non-being:

> Non-being is desirable, not of itself, but only relatively – i.e. inasmuch as the removal of an evil, which can only be removed by non-being, is desirable. Now the removal of an evil cannot be desirable, except so far as this evil deprives a thing of some being. Therefore being is desirable of itself, and non-being only relatively, inasmuch as one seeks some mode of being of which one cannot bear to be deprived; thus even non-being can be spoken of as relatively good.[16]

So moral evil is always a choice for some good as a result of a will that is distorted, ignorant, or confused about its object, whether it is a good that is sought through the acquisition of something desirable, or through the elimination of something that detracts from the capacity for happiness. The degree of guilt depends on the intentionality and awareness that the good which is sought distracts and diverts the soul from God. However, the human can also be deceived by demonic influences, and so there is a brooding anxiety—again, focused with particular intensity on the area of sexuality—as to when something good may in fact be evil in disguise. The beautiful woman may be an anamorphic incuba, a sexual fantasy dreamed up in order to harvest a sleeping man's sperm, or even a phantasm capable of objectifying its appearance so that to all intents and purposes it seems real. The other lurking behind the human face may not be God—it might be a demon, and the human form might only be a projection of one's own imagination intent on luring one away from God. In Lacanian terms, the human before me might be nothing other than the demonic other I discover within myself so that I am no longer certain of the boundary between us. And if that other is female, the confusion of matter, mother, evil, and sex forms a potent brew of lust within the soul that must be resisted on pain of eternal damnation.

When Thomas's God migrates inwards to become the product of the human soul in Lacanian psychoanalysis, he retains all the attributes of being with which Thomas knowingly and unknowingly endowed him—sublime mystery, creator *ex nihilo*, repressed mother, punishing judge, and sexually demonic other. The benign father God of the imaginary is also a God who imposes his law on the human with the ferocious and demonic violence of the

---

[16] ST I, 5, 2.

father of the real. Moreover, the demons have some participation in God insofar as they exist, and this opens up a conflicted and dark horizon at the furthest reaches of being and the nature of evil.

THE SECOND DEATH AND THE HELL OF BEING

When the medieval continuum of being that flows along the spectrum of the imagination between the senses and the intellect fractures into the good and evil will of Kantian ethics, the persistent being of evil feeds the drive that seeks to push being further and further to the very limits of its endurance, insatiably seeking an impossible return to non-being, in order to create *ex nihilo*. This is the death drive that Lacan associates with Kant. In Kant there is still some Sovereign Good that rationalizes this destructive battle against evil, but with the advent of a more nihilistic world view predicated upon the death of God, nihilism is faced with the horror of some infinite expanse of the futility of being without end—some evil Thing that cannot be destroyed. This is the Sadean core which, according to Lacan, underlies the formation of the Christian soul, for according to Thomas, there is no possible escape from being to nothingness. God creates *ex nihilo*, so that creation has a beginning but it has no end. Not only that, but every bodily individual is destined for an eternity of redemption or damnation. Having been created out of nothing, I am condemned to exist, come what may. For Lacan, atheism must embark on an epochal and traumatic journey into the depths of the soul if it is to remove this taproot from the western understanding of what it means to be human.

Consider, for example, Thomas's insistence that the body as well as the soul will experience the torments of the damned. In the Supplement to the *Summa theologiae*,[17] compiled after Thomas's death from his early writings, the question of the corporeality of the damned is considered, including the question of whether or not the bodies as well as the souls of the damned are incorruptible. Thomas quotes from the Book of the Apocalypse: 'In those days men shall seek death, and shall not find it, and they shall desire to die, and death shall fly from them.' (Apoc. 9:6.)[18] He affirms that 'The damned will be punished with an everlasting punishment both in soul and body', and he quotes from the Gospel of Matthew: 'These shall go into everlasting punishment.' (Mat. 25:46.) He goes on to explain that 'even as the body co-operates with the soul in merit, so does it co-operate in sin'.[19] Matter, although free from original sin, cannot escape the influences of the soul for good or for ill. The description in this section of the supplement portrays a terrifying account

---

[17] ST, Supplement, 86.   [18] ST, Supplement, 86, 2.   [19] ST, Supplement, 86, 3.

of the eternal and inescapable torment of the body in hell, so that we begin to see a distant intimation of why only a second death can put an end to suffering—but in Christianity, there is no final death. When the Book of Revelation refers to the second death, it refers not to annihilation but to damnation: 'But the cowardly, unbelieving, abominable, murderers, sexually immoral, sorcerers, idolaters, and all liars shall have their part in the lake which burns with fire and brimstone, which is the second death.' (Rev. 21:8.)

It is not difficult to see how medieval Christianity sets in motion the fantasies of annihilation that torment the modern soul, for deep down there is still the dread that we are condemned to the torments of hell without end. According to Thomas, even suicide offers no escape from the infinite trajectory of being that arouses our desire for the good, for suicide is not, argues Thomas, a wish to do evil to oneself but results from a mistaken understanding of the good: 'No man wills and works evil to himself, except he apprehend it under the aspect of the good. For even they who kill themselves, apprehend death itself as a good, considered as putting an end to some unhappiness or pain.'[20]

Death cannot put an end to being, so whatever he does, the nihilist cannot eliminate himself. However, there is a terrible catch here, because suicide is unforgivable. Thomas discusses suicide in the context of the lawful killing of sinners. Just as an infectious body part can be removed for the good of the whole, so a human being can be lawfully put to death when he or she is 'dangerous and infectious to the community'.[21] Let's note in passing this idea of the individual who threatens society as an infection. In late modernity, genocidal politics would feed on the notion of the racial other as a dangerous pollutant or disease threatening the racially pure body.

To sin is to depart from the order of reason so that one becomes like an animal, and Thomas argues on the basis that humans can kill 'dumb animals, in so far as they are naturally directed to man's use, as the imperfect is directed to the perfect'.[22] So when a person's behaviour goes against reason to such an extent that he or she becomes a threat to the community, it is as legitimate to kill that person as it is to kill a beast, so long as this is carried out by those with the authority to do so.[23] Unlike the killing of animals, the killing of other humans must always be done with the authority of those entrusted with the common good, and in such cases it is not the one who carries out the execution but the sovereign or judge on whose authority it is done who is responsible for the act. This abdication of personal responsibility by those who kill under orders from higher authorities reaches its nadir in the militarized bureaucracies of the modern state.

---

[20] ST I-II, 29, 4.   [21] ST II-II, 64, 2.   [22] ST I-II, 64, 2.   [23] ST II-II, 64, 3.

However, 'suicide is always a mortal sin', because it violates natural law and the love one owes to oneself, it injures the community to which one belongs, and it sins against God because life is God's gift and only God can take one's life away. The argument about legitimate authority cannot apply here because 'no man is judge of himself', so even if he is guilty of a sin which merits death he must submit to the judgement of the authorities.[24] This points to the difference between Thomas's idea of the limits of human self-government and the far more radical concept of autonomy that informs modern campaigns for voluntary euthanasia and the right to die.

If we remember that the fear of hell was a pervasive feature of medieval Christianity, we see how an enduring dread seeds itself in the human soul. Having been created out of nothing, the individual is condemned to live forever, no matter what he or she does or how fervently he or she desires not to exist, and the possibility of eternal torment may be a more vivid reality to the guilty soul than the distant hope of heaven. In Kant, this terror is internalized in the form of the evil will, which retains the animality that Thomas attributes to the irrational human and which leads him to argue that such a human can be killed as one would kill any other beast. Sade asks what happens if a man unleashes the beast and allows it to pursue its bestial appetite to the very limits of being where nothing persists except that which ultimately cannot be eliminated—being itself.

The compulsive futility of the Sadean drive towards annihilation has its origins in the Christian belief that the body as well as the soul—whether in heaven or hell—is individual, indestructible, and eternal. Modern theism eliminates the resurrection of the body, just as it eliminates the Trinity from Christian consciousness, but in so doing it does not really eliminate them at all. It drives them inwards where they brood, until the Catholic Lacan seeks to winkle them out of hiding in a way that calls into question all that modern man believes himself to be and to know.

Kant calls for the creation of the autonomous 'I' *ex nihilo*, through the destruction of the evil will that motivates the desiring self, but Kant must thus leave in place a disavowed remnant that Sade sets out to destroy. According to Lacan, this Sadean phantasm must be traced back to the lingering influence of Christianity—its 'skeleton'[25]—which situates the post-Christian subject in a permanent condition of suffering between creation *ex nihilo* and the crucifixion. The Sadean imagination recognizes suffering as 'a stasis which affirms that that which is cannot return to the void from which it emerged'.[26] This is 'the limit that Christianity has erected in the place of all the other gods, a limit

---

[24] ST II-II, 64, 5.

[25] Jacques Lacan, *The Ethics of Psychoanalysis 1959–1960: The Seminar of Jacques Lacan Book VII*, trans. Dennis Porter (London and New York: Routledge, 1999), p. 260.

[26] Lacan, *The Ethics of Psychoanalysis*, p. 261.

that takes the form of the exemplary image which attracts to itself all the threads of our desire, the image of the crucifixion'.[27] This image holds Christian desire transfixed, and in its equation of suffering with holiness it unleashes a crucifying zeal upon the world as Christian missionaries go in pursuit of their dead gods.[28] If I interpret Lacan correctly—at least in one possible interpretation—the Christian doctrine of creation *ex nihilo* positions the western subject in being against a void that Greek philosophy strenuously sought to avoid with its theory of the eternal existence of matter and form, while blocking the horizon at the other end of existence with the dead God on the cross. Behind us yawns the void, and ahead of us hangs the body of the tortured and dead Christ—beyond which is the unthinkable, the unknowable. My desire must pass through that body—through the body of the one whose death bears the torture of my guilt—in order to be redeemed. But if one is dead, how can one ever know that one has 'realized one's desire', if not from the perspective of a Last Judgment?[29]

The modern subject, vulnerable and abandoned in the short space of transgression and guilt that accompanies him from birth to death, hates the God who created him out of nothing and condemns him to suffer in perpetuity. He hates the creator 'who made him such a weak and inadequate creature'.[30] Again, there is a Lutheran resonance to this Lacanian claim—the filthy human creature who is despised by God and who secretly despises God in return.

The imaginary father, the benevolent and tender God who sent angels to console and strengthen the medieval soul, whose presence was woven into the material fabric of medieval life in the devotions and sacraments of the maternal church (topics barely touched upon by Lacan himself), has been crucified by the superego, the father of the symbolic scavenging on the tyranny of the father of the real with his punitive and insatiable demands. This means that 'the function of the superego in the end, from its final point of view, is hatred for God, the reproach that God has handled things so badly'.[31] God has been inscribed into the narrow spectrum of human moral reasoning, so that humankind stands judge and jury over God because of his moral culpability.

Psychoanalysis provides a tortuous path through this guilt, desire, and transgression, exposes the emptiness at its heart, and seeks to liberate the desiring self from the power that has, since the time of Aristotle, exercised itself through the control of desire. So, says Lacan,

---

[27] Lacan, *The Ethics of Psychoanalysis*, pp. 261–2.
[28] Lacan, *The Ethics of Psychoanalysis*, p. 262.
[29] See Lacan, *The Ethics of Psychoanalysis*, p. 294.
[30] Lacan, *The Ethics of Psychoanalysis*, p. 309.
[31] Lacan, *The Ethics of Psychoanalysis*, p. 308.

Aristotle's morality is wholly founded on an order that is no doubt a tidied-up, ideal order. But it is nevertheless one that corresponds to the politics of his time, to the organization of the city. His morality is the morality of the master, created for the virtues of the master and linked to the order of powers.[32]

We have seen that Thomas's God too is a God of order who operates in all the ways Lacan describes. Although a fragile alternative of natality, maternality, vulnerability, bodiliness, suffering, and desire presents itself in the incarnate God of Jesus Christ and the mystery of the Trinity, this never interrupts the logic of Thomas's social Aristotelianism. Christianity ushers in a radical eschatological vision of incarnate human equality in the order of redemption which might have rearranged Aristotle's social and sexual hierarchies around entirely different configurations, but such a move does not happen. With this in mind, let me conclude this chapter with one more troubling aspect of the quest for order and the killing that it justifies—Thomas's treatment of heresy.

HERESY, PUNISHMENT, AND THE LEGITIMACY OF KILLING

There is one notorious passage in Thomas's *Summa theologiae*, which is repeatedly seized upon by critics. That is his discussion of the treatment of heretics, where he argues that, if a heretic refuses to repent even after repeated warnings, he or she should be put to death both on account of his or her sin and for the greater good of the Church:

> With regard to heretics, two points must be observed: one on their own side; the other, on the side of the Church. On their own side there is the sin, whereby they deserve not only to be separated from the Church by excommunication, but also to be severed from the world by death.... On the part of the Church, however, there is mercy which looks to the conversion of the wanderer, wherefore she condemns not at once, but 'after the first and second admonition,' as the Apostle directs: after that, if he is yet stubborn, the Church no longer hoping for his conversion, looks to the salvation of others, by excommunicating him and separating him from the Church, and furthermore delivers him to the secular tribunal to be exterminated thereby from the world by death.[33]

Heresy is both a sin and a crime. It requires a double exclusion—exclusion from the Church through excommunication legitimated by the religious authorities, and exclusion from the world by death legitimated by the secular authorities. It is also a very particular form of wrong-doing, applicable only to those Christians who knowingly violate the doctrinal truths of the Catholic

---

[32] Lacan, *The Ethics of Psychoanalysis 1959–1960*, p. 315.   [33] ST II-II, 3.

faith. Thomas was opposed to forced conversions, and his judgement on heretics did not apply to Jews or Muslims who had to be tolerated unless they posed a direct threat to the Church. Once again, we see that Christians are subject to a particularly rigorous and punitive form of law that does not apply to those outside the sphere of grace that constitutes the blessed. Throughout Thomas's thought, then, we see that sin and grace are inseparable, for together they constitute the warp and weft of the Christian soul. Paradoxically, it is the graced soul, loved and redeemed by Christ, who also experiences the most profound sense of guilt and threat of punishment.

Michael Novak makes the additional point that, in the legal code promulgated by Frederik II at Melfi in 1231, heresy is presented as treason:

> Those who deny the articles of the Catholic faith implicitly deny the claims of rulers to derive their authority from God. They are enemies not merely of God and of the souls of individuals, but of the social fabric. Their questioning of religious truth involves a questioning of the monarch's command over the law; as enemies of the law, they are its legitimate targets, and the position of primacy accorded to legislation against heretics is thus entirely proper.[34]

It is interesting to link this with Kant's horror of regicide, and his argument that to murder the king is to kill the man, but to execute the king is to use the law to destroy the law. This suggests how profoundly the idea of a law giver outside the law who authorizes all human laws through divinely appointed leaders has an enduring hold on western thought. Long after the idea of religious heresy has been banished by rational liberalism, the implicit threat of punishment to those who commit the heresy of treason exerts its subtle power over the mind. Now, the nation state takes the place of God, but it retains all the mystical and authoritative powers that God once had. In Britain today, one risks prosecution under law for mistreating an animal or for using sexist, homophobic, or racist language in public, there are vigorous campaigns to outlaw bullying and all forms of corporal punishment, yet when soldiers go out to kill in the name of Queen and Country, taking part in wars in which hundreds of thousands of people are killed, maimed, and left homeless and impoverished, they are proclaimed heroes. It is hard to exaggerate the gap between bourgeois liberal values of tolerance and non-violence, and the savagery that these same liberals endorse in the name of defending and promoting their own liberal ideals. Thomas too was willing to endorse killing in the name of a higher cause, before which human lives could be sacrificed, but before we condemn him, we should surely interrogate the brutality we

---

[34] Michael Novak, 'Aquinas and the Heretics', *First Things* 58 (December 1995), pp. 33–8, available online at <http://www.firstthings.com/article/2008/09/003-aquinas-and-the-heretics–17> [accessed 27 July 2012].

ourselves tolerate in the name of that abstract and Godlike entity, the nation state.

In Thomas's discussion of the treatment of heretics, the earlier discussion about Kant and Sade begins to merge with the darker aspects of Thomas's theology. Love of neighbour is not absolute: there is a point when the good of the community and divine authority comes first, not only with regard to criminality but also with regard to heresy. An abstract form—the grammar of faith which *in*forms the collective body of the faithful—is of greater significance than the individual mortal body of the one who refuses to *con*form. The law enforcers—secular and ecclesiastical—enact the will of the law giver outside the law and inflict the punishments he decrees for those who violate truths that come from outside the realm of human knowledge. In order to maintain the purity of faith—in order not to allow the corruption of heresy to spread—Thomas almost reiterates the law that crucified Christ: 'It is better for you that one man die for the people than that the whole nation perish.' (John 11:50.) This is the beginning of all ideology—when human beings can legitimately be killed, not because they pose a physical threat to others but because they dissent from the ideas and beliefs that sustain the written and unwritten laws of the community, state, party, religion, or race, which derive their authoritative status from some unaccountable source which is not open to scrutiny, reason, or debate. Form is more noble than matter, and when matter threatens the form that constitutes law and order, state and Church, politics and society, the form must assert itself with absolute force.

Thomas lived at a time when heretics and their opponents were engaged in mutual practices of torture and barbarism. Novak makes the point that 'When the term "heretic" was used, it was not for Thomas Aquinas or his contemporaries an abstraction.'[35] The Dominican Order that Thomas had struggled so zealously to join had been established for the purpose of refuting heresies, and a troubling scenario begins to form if we reflect on why he is so insistent on the goodness of creation and the body, while so much in his theology also seems to tug against that insight.

The most popular and threatening heresy in Thomas's time was that of the Cathars.[36] Catharism was not a single creed or ideology but a diffuse form of Manichaeism which spread through southern France. The Cathars believed that matter was evil, the sacraments were wicked, and only the spirit was saved. The Cathars were dualists, but they were also pacifists. Although by no means egalitarian, they may have afforded women a greater degree of freedom to own property and exercise leadership roles than the Catholic Church, and it seems likely that some of them were relatively relaxed regarding rules

[35] Novak, 'Aquinas and the Heretics', pp. 33–8.
[36] See Michael D. Costen, *The Cathars and the Albigensian Crusade* (Manchester and New York: Manchester University Press, 1997).

concerning sexuality and marriage, at least compared with the increasing control that the Church sought to exercise in these areas. These were all beliefs that militated against Thomas's social conservatism and, as Novak suggests, Thomas probably saw a close connection between heresy, anarchy, and violence. Yet during the Albigensian crusades between 1209 and 1255, somewhere between two hundred thousand and one million Cathars were tortured and killed, making it one of the greatest slaughters in Europe's bloody history. One struggles in vain for any sense of outrage or hesitation in Thomas with regard to these atrocities when he rationalizes his views on the punishment of heretics.

Iris Murdoch suggested that 'It is always a significant question to ask of any philosopher; "what are they afraid of?"'[37] This might be an impossible question to ask of Thomas across such historical distance, but I want tentatively to suggest that Thomas was afraid of disorder, perhaps with some justification. Those who live in the midst of violence well understand St Augustine's widely quoted insight that 'The peace of all things is the tranquillity of order.' What is less widely quoted is what follows: 'Order is the distribution which allots things equal and unequal, each to its own place.'[38] Thomas's hierarchical ordering of society was a defence against what he perceived to be the greatest threats to the order that form must impose on matter if we are to resist the threat of chaos—the threat that female sexuality poses to the individual male soul, and the threat that heresy poses to the soul of the Church. Aristotle's philosophy provided him with a golden opportunity to build up a substantial theology of resistance to the dualism of the Cathars, while also justifying the rigorous ordering of society according to patriarchal hierarchies that would keep women firmly under the control of men and deny them access to positions of authority, leadership, and learning. All he had to do was to show that this was really what Christianity had been about, from the beginning.

We might also remember the rise of the beguines, a movement largely led by women, which spread through northern Europe during the twelfth and thirteenth centuries. As part of their mission to counter heresy, the Dominicans exercised a widespread ministry of preaching and teaching to women, and many of the best-known beguines and women mystics had Dominican spiritual advisors and confessors.[39] Not all heretics were women, but all women were viewed as particularly vulnerable to heresy because of their diminished rational faculties and their emotional susceptibility. In the centuries following

---

[37] Iris Murdoch, *The Sovereignty of Good* (Boston: Ark, 1985), p. 72.
[38] Augustine, *The City of God*, trans. Marcus Dods (2009), Book XIX, Chapter 13, p. 515, eBook published by Digireads.com at <http://www.digireads.com/> [accessed 30 July 2012].
[39] Cf. Walter Simons, *Cities of Ladies: Beguine Communities in the Medieval Low Countries, 1200–1565* (Philadelphia PA: University of Pennsylvania Press, 2001), pp. 113–15.

Thomas, women heretics and witches would become victims of the first but not the last great act of human incineration in European history.

No matter how many allowances one makes with regard to differences of time and context, culture and values, there is a chilling ruthlessness to Thomas's views on heretics. The law must obey the law giver, and if necessary it must put to death anyone who transgresses the law which comes from a source beyond the law, beyond reason, beyond nature—a law that must be obeyed under pain of eternal damnation. But is this truly the life of grace that is promised by Christ? No, answers Thomas, and this brings me to the final point—the persistent distinction in Catholic theology between the higher and more perfect order of faith represented by the religious and contemplative life, and the lower order of faith applicable to the ordinary laity.

According to Thomas, clerics are not permitted to kill, first because in their ministry they represent the Passion of the crucified Christ who did not retaliate against his persecutors, and second because they are 'entrusted with the ministry of the New Law, wherein no punishment of death or of bodily maiming is appointed'.[40] This is clear evidence of the double standards that prevailed in differentiating between priests and laity in the medieval church, but it also suggests the extent to which Thomas insulates ordinary Christian life and society from the graced transformation that the incarnation effects. It is priests who are custodians of the new life in Christ, while the rest of society more or less conforms to the old pagan order described by Aristotle.

There are different possible readings of Thomas than those which he and his followers promote, one of which might have set western knowledge and faith along an incarnational and sacramental path of seeking the good within the being of the world. That is the road less travelled, an obscure and uncharted road that has been travelled along by heretics, women, and all who have eluded the sometimes deadly control of the masters of theology, politics, and science. It is also a road strewn with the corpses of those who were hunted down, tortured, burned, and murdered by those in thrall to the ideas of the masters, who have travelled along the highway of knowledge that leads from Thomas through Luther and Kant to the dazzle and darkness of modernity. In the final part of this book, I want to consider what might happen if we allow a different reading of Thomas to emerge. First, however, I turn to an aspect of Lacan's Thomism which is the heart of the problem that this book seeks to address—the question of woman as lack.

---

[40] ST II-II, 64, 4.

Part IV

Sexing Desire

13

Sexual Mythologies and the Making of Modernity

The philosophical understanding of being in terms of a copulative relationship between paternal form and maternal matter has exerted a pervasive influence over western thought, through all the changing permutations and combinations of theology, philosophy, science, and linguistics. Long after this cosmology has ceased to offer a credible explanation as to how material beings are formed and reproduced its lingering legacy has encoded itself within language in such a way that it continues to organize human relationships and sexual identities in terms of wholeness and lack, activity and passivity, with the phallus now taking the place of God as the One against which being is secured and from which meaning is derived. This, at least, is the world according to Lacan, whose denial of the sexual relationship is targeted at the enduring grip of this copulative fantasy on western sexual constructs.

Before we can consider more redemptive readings of Thomas Aquinas and the theological tradition, we must go further still into the heart of darkness that Jacques Lacan exposes—and, in his early work, perpetuates—in his analysis of the female body in relation to the western symbolic order. If Lacan is to help theology to move towards the reintegration of Thomism as a response to the challenges posed by postmodernity, then it is necessary to subject Thomas's Aristotelianism to a radically deconstructive reading informed by the insights of Lacanian psychoanalysis, without capitulating to the nihilism that entails in some readings of Lacan.

Two of Lacan's seminars focus on questions of Aristotelianism and sexual difference in a way that makes them particularly relevant to this chapter and the next: his 1959–60 *Seminar VII*, translated as *The Ethics of Psychoanalysis*[1], and his 1972–3 *Seminar XX* published in English as *On Feminine Sexuality:*

---

[1] Jacques Lacan, *The Ethics of Psychoanalysis 1959–1960: The Seminar of Jacques Lacan, Book VII*, trans. Dennis Porter (London and New York: Routledge, 1999).

The Limits of Love and Knowledge, also known as *Encore*.[2] The timing of these seminars is crucial for teasing out shifts in Lacan's theory, which could be interpreted as a response of sorts to the epochal changes that occurred during the 1960s with regard to the position of women in western society.

Seminar VII was delivered at the height of the Cold War and before the emergence of the women's liberation movement in the early 1960s—although Simone de Beauvoir's book, *The Second Sex*, was published in 1949.[3] As Bruce Holsinger suggests, whatever its historical credentials, *Seminar VII* can be read as offering an insight into prevailing attitudes in the early 1960s.[4] It is apocalyptic in tone, delivered in the shadow of the Second World War and the Holocaust at a time when the threat of nuclear annihilation seemed imminent. Lacan's brooding on the Sadean impetus to pursue a destruction so total that it brings to an end the very possibility of life is motivated by these and other catastrophic ethical failures of late modernity. Today, the environmental crisis adds a new sense of urgency to such insights.

In the twelve years or so between *Seminar VII* and *Seminar XX*, not just western society but indeed the global order underwent a series of revolutions by way of the liberation movements of the 1960s. The end of colonialism, the dismantling of racist ideologies, the emergence of demands for sexual and social equality across previously impenetrable boundaries and taboos, the political confrontation between East and West, the anarchic upheavals of the 1968 student movement—all of these made the 1960s a decade of turbulent and radical change, and this needs to be borne in mind when comparing these two seminars that were delivered at either end of this era. Although Lacan rarely engages directly with his feminist critics—least of all his psychoanalytic *doppelganger* Luce Irigaray—it is possible to read *Seminar XX* in terms of a revision of his earlier representation of femininity and desire, prompted at least to some extent by the changing role of women and the challenges posed to his work by feminism. In fact, one can go further than this and suggest that, in *Seminar VII*, Lacan aligns himself with the male position even as he problematizes that position. From where he stands, the female body is mute and devouring flesh scantily clad in the linguistic veils of seductive femininity. In *Seminar XX*, he shifts his position to speak from the site of woman in order to ask what woman knows and how she knows, and this has a prismatic effect on the themes explored in *Seminar VII*—refracting them and regrouping them through different configurations of language, embodiment, desire, and love.

So in using *Seminar VII* and *Seminar XX* to mark a turning point in this book—from nihilism to a fragile and ephemeral hope—I am tracking changes

---

[2] Jacques Lacan, *On Feminine Sexuality—the Limits of Love and Knowledge: The Seminar of Jacques Lacan, Book XX, Encore, 1972–1973*, ed. Jacques-Alain Miller, trans. Bruce Fink (New York and London: W. W. Norton & Company, 1999).

[3] Simone de Beauvoir, *The Second Sex* (Harmondsworth: Penguin Books, 1986).

[4] See Bruce Holsinger, *The Premodern Condition: Medievalism and the Making of Theory* (Chicago and London: University of Chicago Press, 2005), pp. 61–2.

in Lacan's representation of the real, *jouissance*, and God in order to ask if these reflect cultural—and potentially theological—shifts in the position of women: from silence to speech and from invisibility to presence within the institutions of global culture (for such changes are not confined to the western democracies), even if this remains a movement that is contested, partial, and multivalent. By comparing these two seminars, I want to demonstrate a key argument in this book—namely, that ideas of God, woman, and nature are inextricably interwoven in the formation of western consciousness, so that a shift in the understanding of any one has implications for the other two.

SEXY BODIES—SCIENCE, ROMANCE, AND PORNOGRAPHY

With the scientific revolution, nature came to be seen as inert matter to be understood on the basis of mathematical calculation and economic utility—an epistemological shift that coincided with the rise of capitalism and the spread of Europe's imperial conquests. At the same time, the founding fathers of modern rationalism could not shake off the lingering philosophical apprehension of matter as a dangerous and chaotic force, endowed with potent female sexual characteristics, which had to be tamed and controlled by the rational male mind. This gave rise to various forms of romanticism in art, literature, and spirituality, as a way of expressing those non-rational aspects of desire and terror, sex and death, which found no place within the rationalizing discourses of science. So, writes Carolyn Merchant,

> The image of nature that became important in the early modern period was that of a disorderly and chaotic realm to be subdued and controlled.... The images of both nature and woman were two-sided. The virgin nymph offered peace and serenity, the earth mother nurture and fertility, but nature also brought plagues, famines, and tempests. Similarly, woman was both virgin and witch: the Renaissance courtly lover placed her on a pedestal; the inquisitor burned her at the stake. The witch, symbol of the violence of nature, raised storms, caused illness, destroyed crops, obstructed generation, and killed infants. Disorderly woman, like chaotic nature, needed to be controlled.[5]

These conceptual changes with regard to nature and woman are also associated with the rise of pornography from the seventeenth century, and this too invites reflection from a Lacanian perspective. In an essay in a collection titled *The Invention of Pornography*, Margaret Jacob argues that 'The conceptual

---

[5] Carolyn Merchant, *The Death of Nature: Women, Ecology and the Scientific Revolution* (San Francisco: Harper & Row, 1990), p. 127.

ability to mechanize and atomize physical nature emerged roughly between
the 1650s and the 1690s within a single Northern and Western European
generation, the same generation that also invented a new materialist and
pornographic discourse.'[6] Jacob argues that the scientific revolution and
the individualism to which it gave rise created new urban societies free from
traditional social hierarchies, in which the rise of pornography was the
corollary to what she describes as the 'heresy' of 'metaphysical materialism'
that the new science legitimated—not necessarily intentionally.[7] While most
men of science adhered to a theological perspective, seeking to retain some
sense of divine agency that would restrain the rise of materialism, what the
scientific revolution actually did was to collapse the Aristotelian relationship
between matter and form, and therefore to gradually eliminate the sense of a
transcendent divine who orders and regulates the cosmos through erotic
energies of copulation and regeneration. As I have already suggested, the
Reformation began to clear a path towards this epistemological revolution,
with its theology of a radically fallen humanity and a totally disgraced nature.

Jacob interprets the rise of pornography as an inverse version of Aristotelianism, in which matter itself gains the upper hand, and the properties with
which matter had been invested by ancient philosophy became the impetus for
a new celebration of the sexual power of matter, often philosophized and
interpreted by the fictitious female protagonists of anonymous pornographic
literature written by men. So argues Jacob, 'Metaphysical materialism was
seized upon by pornographers eager to describe, eroticize and, not least, to
preach the ethics of the libertine driven by desire, by the relentless motion
inherent in matter.'[8] Positioned on the side of matter, the narrative voice of the
pornographic woman speaks out of an unbounded voluptuousness of sexual
self-expressiveness, constituting the voice of material desire unleashed from
the forms that have controlled and dominated it for much of western intellectual history. She gives voice to the insatiable sexual drive of matter for the
benefit of the men who write about her and those who enact their fantasies
upon her—not necessarily against her will.

Ostensibly stripped of its metaphysical moorings, sexual matter seduces and
ravages form by its ceaseless, dynamic, craving for the pumping and thrusting
of procreative being, modelled on the mechanics of nature itself, and appropriating rather than discarding the ancient Aristotelian copulative energies,
now drained of their cosmic significance and condensed into the atomized

---

[6] Margaret C. Jacob, 'The Materialist World of Pornography', in Lynn Hunt (ed.), *The Invention of Pornography: Obscenity and the Origins of Modernity, 1500–1800* (New York: Zone Books, 1993), p. 158.

[7] Jacob, 'The Materialist World of Pornography', p. 159.

[8] Jacob, 'The Materialist World of Pornography', p. 160.

space of the private sexual encounter. Paradoxically, this gives at least the semblance of a greater level of sexual equality:

> Whether they are masturbating or observed while having sex, whether alone or in a crowd, the atomized bodies in the new pornography are totally privatized. In the process, they become roughly, perhaps inadvertently, equalized; they are as similar, as equal and metaphysically ungendered as the atoms and planets. They occupy a place conceptually analogous to the space and time of mechanical philosophers: an abstraction divorced from the everyday space in which are seen only the appearances or qualities of bodies clothed and decorated, disguised by color and texture, bodies visible to the public eye, encoded with the actual or imagined symbols of status, power and sexuality.[9]

Here again, presentation has yielded to representation. The soul has vanished, and the human body becomes a mirage against the empty horizons of the void. Woman as matter has lost her soul, as surely as man as form has lost his body.

In another essay in the same volume, Kathryn Norberg points out that the Marquis de Sade's fiction shows little concern with sexual difference or gender.[10] Rather, its pornographic focus is on the master–slave relationship and on relationships of domination and self-gratification at the expense of the other. This is a radical deviation from Thomas's theology, but if that is stripped of its moorings in divine grace and in the Christian story of incarnation and redemption, then all that remains are raw relationships of violent copulation in which form and matter wage war on one another. Christianity needs to go much further in its revision of Greek philosophy than Thomas was willing to go, if it is to find a way beyond these violent origins and sadistic endings. As it is, it has provided a potent vehicle for their perpetuation through its lingering influences on western intellectual and psychic formation. Fast forward to E. L. James's record-breaking *Fifty Shades of Grey* trilogy, with its sado-masochistic relationship between the dominant male (whose name, Christian, may be intentionally ironic, although I doubt it), and his submissive sex slave Anastasia (they are coupled as dom and sub), which has been swept off the bookshelves by avid female readers. The vast and complex darkness of human sexuality sinks like sludge beneath the rhetoric of so much liberal feminism.

With the early modern invention of pornography, the worst nightmares of Thomas and his scholastic contemporaries were, it seems, being realized. Jacob includes a frontispiece to a 1748 work titled *Thérèse Philosophe*, depicting a full-frontal female nude with the text: 'Sensual pleasure and philosophy make the sensible man happy. He embraces pleasure by taste and he loves philosophy with his reason'.[11] It would be hard to articulate a more anti-Thomist ethos

---

[9] Jacob, 'The Materialist World of Pornography', p. 182.
[10] Kathryn Norberg, 'The Libertine Whore', pp. 225–52.
[11] Jacob, 'The Materialist World of Pornography', p. 184.

than that, not only in its celebration of sexual pleasure unrelated to procreation and marriage, but in its implied dualism of mind and body, philosophy and pleasure, which for Thomas are always moving towards the same goal of delight and wisdom in knowledge of God. Jacob argues that materialism rendered the clergy powerless objects of derision, for it 'removed the dominance of spirit and made matter and spirit essentially one, thus leaving the clergy useless as arbitrators of a separate spiritual realm'.[12] I think a more subtle evaluation would be needed to reflect the spirit of Thomism. Certainly, Thomas promoted in sometimes highly dualistic ways the dominance of spirit over matter, but in the end he did more than any other theologian in the Catholic tradition to affirm the essential inseparability of matter and spirit. If this aspect of his thought had been more vigorously embraced and promoted, and its more divisive and dualistic philosophical claims had been recognized as an aberration from the doctrinal positions he sought to promote, his influence in shaping the culture of medieval Catholicism and its subsequent corruption and decline might have been very different.

Jacob and other contributors to *The Invention of Pornography* suggest that the relationship of actual women's experiences and desires to the sexual adventures of their mimetic pornographic counterparts was complex and multifaceted. We might ask how much these various modern and postmodern pornographic fantasies were or are informed by or contribute to women's capacity for sexual enjoyment. In an article in *The Guardian* blog, sex therapist Pamela Stephenson Connolly says that she found the *Fifty Shades of Grey* trilogy 'boring, repetitive, and [it] leads women to aspire to undesirable—and frankly unattainable—goals, such as simultaneous orgasm, which occurs between the protagonists most of the time'.[13] In June 2012, *The Observer* magazine carried a story by Eva Wiseman which asked, 'Why do we hate the way we look?'[14] Citing an increasing amount of research that attests to the destructive impact on female health and well-being of the pressure to look sexy at all times, Wiseman asks if anxieties about body image are 'slowly killing women', because 'to be feminine, today, means to hate your body'.[15]

Women have always inhabited complex intersecting narratives of loss and gain, empowerment and victimization, largely determined by factors other than sex alone. Yet it remains as true now as it ever has been, that the institutions of politics, economics, war, and religion, are subservient to male power and driven by male interests, in a way that leaves women at best complicit and at

---

[12] Jacob, 'The Materialist World of Pornography', p. 162.

[13] Pamela Stephenson Connolly, '*Fifty Shades of Grey* is bad for bondage', *The Guardian: Shortcuts Blog—A Sideways Look at the News* at <http://www.guardian.co.uk/theguardian/shortcuts/2012/jul/08/fifty-shades-grey-bad-bondage> [accessed 13 July 2012].

[14] Eva Wiseman, 'The Body Image Report: Uncomfortable in our Skin', *The Observer Magazine*, 10 June 2012, pp. 14–23.

[15] Wiseman, 'The Body Image Report', p. 23.

worst victimized. So it was—and still is—with the rise of pornography and the modern commodification of nature and the female body.

Thomas Laqueur, in his book *Making Sex*, points out that, in the late Enlightenment, scientists dispensed with the idea that the female orgasm was necessary for conception, ushering in a new belief in the essential sexual passivity of women:

> The ancient wisdom that 'apart from pleasure nothing of mortal kind could come into existence' was uprooted. Previously a sign of the generative process, deeply embedded in the bodies of men and women, a feeling whose existence was no more open to debate than was the warm, pleasurable glow that usually accompanies a good meal, orgasm was relegated to the realm of mere sensation, to the periphery of human physiology – accidental, expendable, a contingent bonus of the reproductive act.[16]

Laqueur observes that, although in principle this change in perception applied to both sexes,

> no one writing on such matters ever so much as entertained the idea that male passions and pleasures in general did not exist or that orgasm did not accompany ejaculation during coition. Not so for women. The newly 'discovered' contingency of delight opened up the possibility of female passivity and 'passionlessness.' The purported independence of generation from pleasure created the space in which women's sexual nature could be redefined, debated, denied, or qualified. And so it was of course. Endlessly.[17]

With the scientific revolution, 'woman' emerges from behind the screens of medieval Aristotelianism, but her body has meaning only for those who inscribe their fantasies and their ambitions upon it. Her joy, her soul, even her orgasms, count for nothing except in terms of their utility for men, as sources of scientific investigation or sexual self-pleasuring. When feminism conspires with neo-liberalism to give women back their bodies, it can only do so as the tortured, surgically manipulated, self-hating bodies of sex slaves, masochists, and mutants. The Catholic response to this is simply its mirror image—Aristotelianism dressed up in modern romantic garb, with the female body as ontological mother/matter always open to impregnation, or as virginal fantasy of man's desire for Christ.[18]

This is the background against which we must approach Lacan's linguistic analysis of sexual difference and the role of female sexuality in the making of

---

[16] Thomas Laqueur, *Making Sex: Body and Gender from the Greeks to Freud* (Cambridge CA: Harvard University Press, 1990), p. 3. The quotation comes from Philo, *Legum allegoriae*, 2.7, cited in Peter Brown, 'Sexuality and Society in the Fifth Century A.D.: Augustine and Julian of Eclanum,' *Tria corda: Scritti in onore di Arnaldo Momigliano*, ed. E. Gabba (Como: New Press, 1983), p. 56.

[17] Laqueur, *Making Sex*, p. 3.

[18] See Tina Beattie, *New Catholic Feminism: Theology and Theory* (London and New York: Routledge, 2006).

the Freudian mind. Only by acknowledging the crisis in which we find ourselves regarding the place of the female body in modern society, might we discern the truth behind Lacan's florid explorations of the female body as lack and horror in *Seminar VII*.

SEXUAL DIFFERENCE AS WHOLENESS AND LACK

Lacanian psychoanalysis approaches the question of sexual difference and language from the perspective of Thomist Aristotelianism. The construction of sexual difference focuses on concepts of plenitude and lack organized around the unattainable fullness of being that is God (Thomas) or the phallus (Lacan). In both cases, sexual difference is not established in terms of the biological sex organs nor in terms of any secondary sexual characteristics. One becomes male or female according to where one stands with regard to a copula in the order of being between form and matter (Thomas) or the symbolic and the real (Lacan). Desire arcs across this copula (that is why we copulate), and sustains beings in being, with sexual difference understood in terms of the relative perfection or relative lack of one and the same species of being.

But the perfection of the man is illusory, for he does not possess the fullness of being associated with God (Thomas) or the phallus (Lacan). This situates man in a precarious and unstable position as far as sexual identity is concerned. Sexual difference is a charade whose coordinates and performances have over millennia been determined by the demands that masculinity puts upon the male and by the positioning of the woman as the sexual, material other to his abstract form, in order to maintain his illusion that, relative to her at least, he has what it takes to be. With the rise of modernity this has generated an intense anxiety and frustration focused on the sexual relationship and its inadequacies: 'What constitutes the basis of life, in effect, is that for everything having to do with the relations between men and women, what is called collectivity, it's not working out (*ça ne va pas*).'[19]

The ordering of language around the phallus/God as a marker of sexual difference sets up a profound asymmetry in the order of desire. For woman, says Lacan, 'A man is nothing but a signifier'.[20] He occupies the position of the system, the linguistic form that she needs in order to become something/someone rather than nothing/no one. But she awakens in him a more consuming and insatiable desire because she is 'not-whole—there is always something in her that escapes discourse'.[21] Her relationship to the signifier

---

[19] Lacan, *On Feminine Sexuality*, p. 32.
[20] Lacan, *On Feminine Sexuality*, p. 33.
[21] Lacan, *On Feminine Sexuality*, p. 33.

is incomplete; she is not fully formed as far as language is concerned. As a result, she arouses his desire for something beyond herself, some forbidden Thing that eludes language—God, the phallic mother, the Other—evoking within him the unsettling awareness that he too lacks something in the order of being and meaning. He is castrated.

Here is how Juliet Mitchell summarizes all this in relation to the Freudian castration complex:

> Freud always insisted that it was the presence or absence of the phallus and *nothing else* that marked the distinction between the sexes.... The castration complex ends the boy's Oedipus complex (his love for his mother) and inaugurates for the girl the one that is specifically hers: she will transfer her object love to her father who seems to have the phallus and identify with her mother who, to the girl's fury, has not. Henceforth the girl will desire to have the phallus and the boy will struggle to represent it. For this reason, for both sexes, this is the insoluble desire of their lives and, for Freud, because its entire point is precisely to be insoluble, it is the bedrock beneath which psychoanalysis cannot reach. Psychoanalysis cannot give the human subject that which it is its fate, as the condition of its subjecthood, to do without:
>
>> At no other point in one's analytic work does one suffer more from an oppressive feeling that all one's repeated efforts have been in vain, and from a suspicion that one has been 'preaching to the winds', than when one is trying to persuade a woman to abandon her wish for a penis on the ground of its being unrealizable.[22]

By the time of *Seminar XX*, Lacan has called into question this entire Freudian scenario in ways that have far-reaching implications for a Lacanian reading of Thomas and the meaning of being, but in order to appreciate the significance of that we have to recognize the extent to which Lacan's representation of the female body as lack in *Seminar VII* is underwritten by Thomas's Aristotelian ontology.

Seminar VII is peppered with gnomic and often provocative allusions to the (non) signification of 'woman' and the lack that she represents in relation to the masculine subject. *Jouissance* has not yet become an expressive language of corporeal desire with the potential to disrupt the homogeneity of the masculine subject of the symbolic order. Rather, it is the hard core of mute resistance that the speaking subject encounters as the beyond of language and the law. With the modern scientific and philosophical elimination of desire and the juxtaposition of form over and against matter, mind over and against body, and reason over and against nature, the medieval copula of potentially fertile encounter between the two yields to a more dualistic and violent struggle.

This is the scenario that Lacan confronts in *Seminar VII*, when the body, nature, and God have been banished behind the screens of signification by the Kantian prohibition, to dissolve in a viscous and threatening intra-linguistic otherness that lures the subject towards his undoing by way of *jouissance* or the death drive. In *Seminar VII*, these congeal in the female sex. Feminized *jouissance* is associated with the real as the annihilating other of the masculine subject, and the female body is a deadly source of putrefaction and obscenity masked by the language of feminine beauty and erotic desire.

Lacan seeks to subvert and unsettle the modern man of reason through the invocation of this deadly otherness, but he does not change the coordinates by way of which the real, the imaginary, and the symbolic relate to one another in the construction of subjectivity and otherness. The encounter with the sexual female body is one in which the masculine subject confronts the voracious emptiness at the limits of his own subjectivity, breaching the veils of romantic illusion to penetrate the horror of nothing beyond. Her body becomes the container of emptiness, masquerading in the linguistic veils of beauty and romance as the object of desire, but ultimately constituting the Freudian 'horror of nothing to see'. Within 'her' sex, 'he' encounters not the fulfilment of the self in the sexual other that he craves, but the threat of the annihilation of the self in the formless other that he dreads. We need to remember the Kantian hinterland to these theories, with Kant's simultaneous attempt to transgress and avoid the boundary that marks the limit of reason, beyond which is a horrifying force of nature, the realm of Sadean destruction.

THE ROMANCE AND HORROR OF
THE COURTLY LOVER

Lacan explores these ideas in the context of the medieval courtly love tradition, although it is beyond my purposes here to ask how effectively he interprets these texts in terms of their medieval contexts.[23] However, if we read trouba-dour poetry as the beginning of secular romanticism—a tradition that has a complex relationship to the theological and devotional context of late medieval Catholicism, particularly in terms of its overlap with Marian devotion[24]— then we can see courtly love as a step along the way with regard to the shifts in the western understanding of sexuality that mark the gradual separation of the modern from the pre-modern.

---

[23] Cf. Irving Singer, *The Nature of Love: Courtly and Romantic* (Chicago: University of Chicago Press, 2009).

[24] Cf. Gary Waller, *The Virgin Mary in Late Medieval and Early Modern English Literature and Popular Culture* (Cambridge and New York: Cambridge University Press, 2011).

The elegant rhetoric of medieval courtly love constructs an illusory woman whose idealized femininity masks the dread of the sexual encounter. Veiled in the language of desire, the female body conceals its abysmal lack from the masculine subject who, thinking he is all, longs for her to be all—he wants to be all and to have all. But in *Seminar VII*, there is nothing between the romance and the horror. The woman unmasked is the real. She neither speaks nor signifies. Mute and exposed, the fantasy of her consuming wholeness becomes the horror of her consuming hole. For Lacan, all sexual romance is predicated upon this linguistic veiling of the 'nothing to see', the formless void of prime matter or, even more horrifying for the masculine subject of Judaeo-Christian monotheism, the void of creation *ex nihilo*. By its avoidance of the actual female body and its idealized language of femininity, romanticism affords a florid escape from the reality of sex and its opening into the void.

The inaccessibility of the woman is a condition of romantic love, so that she functions as the screen against which desire can weave its fantasies of sexual fulfilment without the inevitable disappointment that would accompany the act of consummation. Thus the feminine hints at a totality of pleasure, union, and bliss, only on condition that it remains unattainable. The feminine other functions as the ultimate object of desire of the masculine subject, and yet her simulated otherness is his most perilous and threatening encounter with the other behind the mask, the consuming void in which lurks decomposition, the visceral horror of the stripped and speechless flesh which, being speechless and meaningless, is inseparable from *das Ding*, the real.

For this reason, the female sex organs constitute a source of horrified fascination to the male gaze, because all the intensity of desire and difference is focused on the lack/the formlessness that he sees there. In linguistic terms, this means that the naming of the female genitalia functions as a metaphor for the lack they both create and conceal, having 'the form of an opening and an emptiness' which acknowledges that 'there is a gap in the text, a leap beyond the supposed reference'.[25] So the lack that the man associates with the female sex organs becomes caught up in the lack within language and therefore within the subject of language, the masculine 'I'.

Lacan illustrates this idea by citing (with great relish) a troubadour poem in which a Lady commands her knight to 'put his mouth to her trumpet'[26] as proof of his love. The poet, Arnaud Daniel, responds to the suggestion with pornographic horror:

> For so as to 'put his mouth to her trumpet,' he would need the kind of beak that could pick grain out of a pipe. And even then he might come out blind, as the smoke from those folds is so strong.

[25] Lacan, *The Ethics of Psychoanalysis*, p. 169.
[26] Lacan, *The Ethics of Psychoanalysis*, p. 162.

He would need a beak and a long, sharp one, for the trumpet is rough, ugly and hairy, and it is never dry, and the swamp within is deep. That's why the pitch ferments upwards as it continually escapes, continually overflows.[27]

In *Seminar VII*, the sexual encounter is the site of a subjective confrontation with the beyond of the death drive, the Thing.[28] The close proximity between the Thing and the object of desire means that beauty functions as the 'envelope' for truth,[29] dazzling the subject and acting as a barrier which holds him back 'in front of the unspeakable field of radical desire that is the field of absolute destruction, of destruction beyond putrefaction'.[30] Lacan describes this in terms of the Kantian sublime, and he illustrates it with reference to Sophocles' Antigone, whose entry into the tomb constitutes a moment of stark encounter with the frontier beyond which gapes the impossibility of the real, leaving the audience dumbstruck. At this point of entry into the beyond of all symbolization, we must remember that Kant melts into Sade, for the sublime is ultimately indistinguishable from the horror that confronts the subject as reason is consumed within the void of matter. All of this can be traced back to that unhappy fusion of Aristotelian ontology with Christian ideas of sin, transgression, covetousness, and desire which I explored in the last chapter.

SURPLUS *JOUISSANCE* AS THE FOMES OF SIN

Thomas's account of sexual difference is about a difference in degrees of being rather than in kinds of being. However, we have seen that this introduces a problematic ambivalence into Thomas's understanding of the female sex, because as mother woman is matter/lack in relation to form, but as sexual other she is the greatest threat man faces in terms of his vocation to God. If the invention of modern pornography constitutes a sustained fantasy about the female body as sexual matter to be enjoyed, penetrated, dominated, or destroyed, that fantasy feeds upon an earlier theological horror of lust, sin, and depravity.

In the *Summa theologiae*, Thomas argues that, as a result of original sin, human sensuality eludes the control of reason and this violates the natural condition of the human in a state of original justice, when sensual pleasures would have been regulated by reason. Now, our bodily appetites are bestial and

---

[27] Lacan, *The Ethics of Psychoanalysis*, p. 162. For a full version of the original poem with an English translation, see Arnaut Daniel and Paul Blackburn, 'Sirventes', *Boundary 2*, Vol. 8, No. 3 (Spring, 1980), pp. 147–50.

[28] Cf. Lacan, *The Ethics of Psychoanalysis*, p. 214.

[29] Cf. Lacan, *The Ethics of Psychoanalysis*, pp. 216–17.

[30] Lacan, *The Ethics of Psychoanalysis*, p. 217.

reason struggles to assert its control. He refers to the 'fomes of sin', by which he means the 'incentive to evil' which persists even in a state of grace and makes us susceptible to excessive sensuality. This is the transgressive impulse that divine law seeks to restrain.[31] The natural animality of the body becomes bestial through the infection of sin, and the soul/form must therefore set itself up in opposition to body/matter with regard to the appetites.

However, whereas in Kant the evil will associated with this bestial materiality is entirely opposed to the good will associated with God and the noumenal and must be destroyed, for Thomas it still remains within the goodness of being and it is of God rather than opposed to God. Ultimately, it is good because it exists, and therefore it has some participation, however minimal, in the being and willing of God. So Thomas argues that disordered desire is part of the law, because it is God's punishment for original sin. In the *Commentary on Romans* he writes, 'in this sense the very disobedience of the lower powers constitutes the inclination to sin and is called a law, inasmuch as it was introduced by the law of divine justice'.[32] Punishment is a consequence of justice, originating within the law and intended to correct the wrongdoer. It is therefore a manifestation of grace—the original grace of creation and the revealed grace of God's justice.

We begin to see how Thomas's interpretation of Romans 7 produces a conflict with regard to sensuality and excessive desire. The God who orders the cosmos and sanctifies desire has a punitive aspect that manifests itself through the condemnation of desire in relation to the body's capacity for pleasure, beyond any rational explanation as to why this is so. The condemnation of covetousness or concupiscence is an arbitrary command, given by revelation rather than reason, and issuing from a God who seems to be, in Lacanian terms, ferociously ignorant of the nature of human sexuality in particular—for as we have seen, Thomas regards sexual desire as the greatest threat to the contemplative or scholarly man of God. While the Aristotelian God of natural theology orders the world according to a rational and benevolent paternalism encoded in law and mediated through the material world, the Father God of the Christian faith offers an impossible union to the man who can successfully overcome his material desires, appetites, and natural relationships, while threatening punishment and hell to those who succumb to them. It is through the arousal of sexual desire that the demons are most able to lure men away from God. The uncontrollability of the male erection is a divine punishment for transgression, an inescapable reminder to the man of God of his own sinfulness and weakness to temptation.

In order to see the existential impact of these theological ideas on the formation of male Catholic spirituality, we might turn to hagiographical

---

[31] ST I-II, 91, 6.

[32] Thomas Aquinas, 'Lectures on the Letter to the Romans' (Ave Maria University Aquinas Center). I have used the translation by Fr Fabian Larcher, edited by Jeremy Holmes, and made available online by the Aquinas Center for Theological Renewal at Ave Maria University: <http://nvjournal.net/index.php?option=com_content&view=article&id=53&Itemid=62> [accessed 27 July 2012]. n. 587.

accounts of how Thomas was said to have been delivered from the torment of sexual arousal by a miraculous girdle given to him by angels. However embellished it might have become in the telling, the way this story is told reveals much about the kind of attitude towards male sexuality for which Thomas has been held up as an exemplary role model. I refer here to a flamboyant devotional account of Thomas's life written by an anonymous Dominican in the early twentieth century.[33] The author tells of the desperate attempts by Thomas's brothers and mother to dissuade him of his decision to join the Dominicans, culminating in their failed attempt to defeat him by 'dragging him into the nets of the flesh'. The author continues:

> They found a poor young creature, who had lost woman's most precious ornament, but who was outwardly very beautiful, and shut her up alone with Thomas in his prison. The contest was short; he saw the poor creature enter, understood the meaning of her detestable arts, felt the stimulus of the flesh arise in him by permission of God to make his victory all the more glorious, raised his heart to God for a brief moment, then, snatching a burning brand out of the fire, chased the temptress from his presence. Then with the brand he made a cross upon the wall of his chamber, and falling upon his knees before it, poured out his soul to God, who had given him the victory, and renewed the vow of chastity he had made in the depths of his heart, when he had received the holy habit of religion.
>
> But while he prayed a sweet ecstatic sleep fell upon him, like that of Adam in Paradise, and two angels came to him and girded his waist with a cord, saying: 'We come to thee from God to give thee the grace of everlasting virginity;' and from that time he never felt the slightest temptation against purity; a grace not accorded even to St. Paul, who thus complains: 'There was given me a sting of my flesh, an angel of Satan to buffet me.' (2 Cor. 12, 7.)
>
> When the angels girded the holy youth he felt the pain so keenly that he cried out aloud, and his guards entered to see what was the matter; but he said nothing, and kept this wonderful grace a secret until nearly the end of his life, when he revealed it to Father Reginald, his confessor.

Written several centuries after the time of Thomas, this extraordinary account attests to the enduring power of the idea that the sexual female body is an agent of Satan, and the 'outward beauty' of the female form masks a demonic presence at work in the 'detestable arts' of the seductress. There is more than a hint here of that ancient fear of the female incuba that haunted the phantasms and dreams of the medieval man of God.

---

[33] A Father of the Order of Friar Preachers, 'The Life of the Angelic Doctor, St. Thomas Aquinas' (New York: P. J. Kenedy and Sons, 1881), available online at *The Internet Archive*: <http://www.archive.org/stream/lifeofangelicdoc00cavauoft/lifeofangelicdoc00cavauoft_djvu.txt)> [accessed 27 July 2012].

The author goes on to describe the history of the miraculous cord, which was worn by Thomas until his death and remained in the custody of the Dominicans. He records that

> Many miracles were worked by it, and in the sixteenth century a custom arose to make cords like it, which were blessed by touching the original, and these also were the means of countless graces to those who, tempted by the domestic enemy, used them as a pious preservation against sin.

There is a disturbing violence in the idea of Thomas chasing 'a poor young creature' from his room with a burning brand. One rather wishes that the hagiographical imagination had portrayed him as reaching out to the 'poor young creature' rather as Christ reached out to prostitutes and the woman caught in adultery.

This disputed story appears in a compilation prepared by William of Tocco in 1323 for Thomas's canonization.[34] In an alternative version, a rather different picture emerges of both Thomas and the woman. She is more clearly portrayed as having the upper hand, and it is the saint who comes across as a poor young creature, in a state of panic brought on by sexual arousal. She is not a victim deprived of 'woman's most precious ornament' (in an account that today cannot help but evoke images of child sexual abuse and rape), but 'a very attractive girl decked out like a prostitute' who 'tempted him to sin, using all the devices at her disposal'.[35] The author goes on to say that

> The fighter [Thomas] had taken God's wisdom as his spouse and beloved, and he was not overcome by her appearance. Yet when he began to feel fleshly desire rise within him, which he always had kept under rational control (this exception was allowed by consent of divine providence, so that he might rise to a more glorious triumph from this test), he snatched a burning stick from the fireplace and indignantly chased the girl out of his room.
>
> Internally raging, he strode to a corner of the room, made the sign of the cross on the wall with the point of the burning stick and, prostrating himself tearfully on the floor, prayerfully begged God for the girdle of perpetual virginity to keep himself immaculate in temptation.[36]

This portrayal of Thomas in a state of despair over a perfectly natural bodily function, and the use of this as an example to future generations of men who would seek to emulate him, raises disturbing questions about the spiritual and psychological formation of celibate men in the Catholic tradition. William of

---

[34] See William of Tocco in Kenelm Foster (ed.), *The Life of St Thomas Aquinas: Biographical Documents* (London and Baltimore, 1959).

[35] See Vernon Joseph Bourke, *Aquinas' Search for Wisdom* (Milwaukee: Bruce Publishing Co., 1965), p. 37.

[36] Bourke, *Aquinas' Search for Wisdom*, p. 37.

Tocco tells of how 'from that time onwards it was his custom always to avoid the sight and company of women—except in case of necessity or utility—as a man avoids snakes'.[37] As Richard Akeroyd observes, 'Such a defensive, fearful attitude hardly corresponds with the gift of the belt of chastity, granted out of divine liberality, which was supposedly impregnable in any temptation.'[38]

In fact, Thomas is reported to have remained on good terms with his family and was particularly close to his sisters, and it seems likely that these accounts of his avoidance of women tell us more about his hagiographers than about Thomas himself. Nevertheless, they also constitute a potent mythology by way of which the Catholic Church has used the lives of the saints to perpetuate highly distorted and dysfunctional models of Christian sanctity predicated upon an unhealthy preoccupation with the avoidance or control of sex. The sex abuse crisis is the culmination of a long history during which spirituality has been in bondage to a pathologically dysfunctional attitude to sex, particularly with regard to male celibacy, spirituality, and communion with God.

Sexuality—for the modern Catholic hierarchy as much as for medieval theologians—is primarily functional. Although Catholic teaching today is more affirmative of the positive aspects of sexual love in marriage than it has been in the past, it remains committed to the belief that any intention to thwart the procreative purpose of the sex act renders it evil.[39] For Thomas, the pleasure that derives from sex in marriage is only justified if it serves its primary function of procreation. In Lacanian terms, there is no surplus *jouissance* in Thomas, at least as far as sex is concerned. Intentionally unproductive sex is a deadly sin contrary to nature, for procreative sex belongs within the fundamental order of being. Procreation, we could say, mops up the excess sexual energy generated by *jouissance*. To unleash that energy within matter for no generative purpose is to threaten the form—it is to drag the man of God into hell.

In the uncoupling of erotic desire from procreation and marriage, courtly love celebrates a sexual fantasy that must avoid seeing what Thomas saw long before Freud came on the scene—the horror of nothing to see that is prime matter/female flesh/the female sex, when it is removed from its essentially copulative function. Only when draped in the Platonic veils of the ideal woman can the knight's lady meet his fantasies of sexual bliss. Any encounter with the material obscenity that she represents—the voracious lack of her unproductive sex—evokes not romance and attraction but horror and revulsion. For the knight no less than for Thomas himself, the plunging into the

---

[37] Quoted in Anthony Kenny, *Aquinas* (Oxford: Oxford University Press, 1980), p. 2.

[38] Richard H. Akeroyd, *Reason and Revelation From Paul to Pascal* (Macon GA: Mercer University Press, 1991), p. 29.

[39] See Pope Paul VI, *Humanae Vitae*, 'Encyclical Letter on the Regulation of Birth', 25 July 1968, at <http://www.vatican.va/holy_father/paul_vi/encyclicals/documents/hf_p-vi_enc_250 71968_humanae-vitae_en.html> [accessed 8 December 2012].

female body in pursuit of pleasure surplus to reproductive need rather than for the ordained purposes of marriage and procreation is a plunging into hell.

MODERN BODIES

To turn to Lacan to grapple with problems such as these is to resist liberal responses which trivialize or underestimate the potency of human sexuality and desire to create harm as well as good. It is to acknowledge that there is a dark undercurrent of lack and need woven into every sexual relationship which can and often does mutate into violence towards the sexual other. Half a century of sexual liberation has not brought with it an increasingly well-adjusted and balanced population of adults enjoying responsible and consensual sex. To acknowledge that the Catholic Church has profound problems in its attitude to sex which have ancient historical origins is not to concede that secular liberalism has the answers. The questions we face are, as Lacan reminds us, more deeply rooted than that. Indeed, they go to the very core of the western understanding of what it means to be.

The rise of pornography, the simultaneous eroticization and mechanization of nature, and the emergence of modern secular and religious romanticism with its feminine and masculine stereotypes are all related. While these can be interpreted in terms of philosophical and scientific changes in western modernity and the changing sexual politics that reflect these, they have their roots in more ancient sexual mythologies that were inscribed on the body politic and its human sexual couplings by the masters of the medieval universities. Despite undergoing repeated historical transformations, the philosophical relationship between maternal matter and paternal form understood in terms of the copulative regeneration of being has underwritten the values and sexual mores of western culture in subtle but pervasive ways, and the same is true today.

Modernity has stripped human sexuality of its essentially procreative function, and we no longer experience nature as an eroticized swarm of couplings and (be)comings. We have become more sterile in our relationships with one another and with the natural environment, but we have also become frozen within the coordinates of form and matter to which the ancients assigned us in the gendering of the universe. Liberal feminism opens up spaces for women within the dominant form of the socio-political order, but on condition that we leave our bodies behind. The fashion and cosmetic industries, the regimes of fitness, dieting, and plastic surgery, the insatiable modern preoccupation with appearance, all attest to the triumph of form over matter. The ultimate achievement of the pornographic asceticism of modern sex must surely be anal bleaching, described by *Cosmopolitan* magazine as 'some sort of torture technique'.[40] This is the triumph of the visual fantasy over the body's truth. The modern symbolic order cannot accommodate the messy, smelly, fatty, leaky, bloody, sweaty, menstruating, birthing, shitting, dying stuff of which we are made, and its intrusive power now extends into the most intimate aspects of human sexuality, procreation, and the female body. Meanwhile, the Internet swarms with teenage vaginas and anuses for sale, and the desperate young girls behind the advertisements vanish into an undifferentiated sea of trafficked flesh that constitutes the hidden face of modern neo-liberalism and its 'freedoms'.

These social changes are accompanied by yet another shift in our intellectual constructs, as the scientific collapse of the copulative relationship between form and matter results in a profound sense of disjunction between the conscious mind and its material others. Now, the postmodern theorist views all matter through a linguistic haze of obscurity and doubt, wondering if there is anything at all out there beyond the ribbons of language that spiral out into emptiness. The question of the body acquires a new urgency and intensity through its theorization and representation, but in the process the body itself becomes ever more elusive, ever more disturbing, ever more enigmatic and disruptive, ever more tortured, abused, exploited, and commodified.

To learn from and go beyond Lacan, Thomism needs to re-examine its relationship to Aristotelianism at the most fundamental level of being and becoming. Male and female are both alike an irreducible complexity of consciousness and materiality, body and soul, which intersect, conjugate, and inform one another at every moment of our existence through the mysterious copulations of desire, materiality, and knowledge. The attempt to divide up the world between feminine females and masculine males according to the rigid grids of procreative heterosexual norms becomes ever more zealous the more these norms disintegrate. At the very heart of the panic over sex that has made the Catholic Church a vociferous ally of conservative politics and a powerful political force to be reckoned with is the ancient belief that the female body is matter in relation to form, that the relationship between the sexes belongs within the order of being that connects all beings to the divine being, and that the disruption of the reproductive relationship between male form and female matter threatens the cosmos with some nameless but terrifying chaos. When this disruption emanates from matter itself—the female body claiming the right to control her own reproductive capacities—a voracious horror looms in the mind of the man of God.

Lacan and the Catholic hierarchy agree on one thing: the heterosexual relationship is the bedrock upon which the western social order has been established, and the disordering of that relationship signifies the breakdown of

---

[40] Zoe Ruderman, 'The Scary New Butt Beauty Trend', *Cosmopolitan* website: <http://www.cosmopolitan.com/advice/health/anal-bleaching-trend> [accessed 30 July 2012].

society as we know it. From the perspective of modern Catholic doctrine, this order is inscribed into creation itself by the creator so that the modern nuclear family appears to be the blueprint for creation from the beginning, with little attempt to analyse the extent to which it is also freighted with the violent economic and sexual ideologies of modernity. The resistance of the contemporary Catholic hierarchy with regard to other possible configurations of just and ethical sexual relationships, including same-sex marriage, leads to a serious ethical failure to confront the injustices inherent within culturally sanctioned heterosexual norms, so that one could be forgiven for thinking that a Hollywood romance shows us the world as God always intended it to be. The content might vary but the form remains the same, and who worries that this heaven is defended by military and economic regimes that wreak havoc on all who dare to threaten it? Who worries that out of sight and out of mind bodies are imprisoned, tortured, bombed, exiled, exploited, and killed in order to protect the social environment needed to sustain this fantasy? Who worries that those who feel trapped within it are increasingly miserable, alienated, and violent, and that women are battling against their own bodies in order to conform to the myth? Who worries that these nuclear families are destroying the planet with their voracious appetites? None of this is to deny the fragile beauty and grace of married love, nor the importance of loving and stable sexual relationships for the raising of children, but those most vociferous in their defence of marriage so often seem to have little insight into the complex realities of married life, including its sometimes agonizing and irredeemable failures.

One way or another, modernity wages war upon the body, and I have argued that the roots of this war can be traced back to the rise of the universities and the ordering of society around Aristotelian categories of form and matter, male and female. My question is how Lacan can help us to read Thomas anew, in order to go beyond the violent conflicts and impasses of the situation in which we find ourselves, towards a new vision in which sexuality finds a less consuming, more 'natural' place in our understanding of who we are in the goodness of creation. So let me turn now to *Seminar XX* with these questions in mind.

14

Being Beyond Philosophy

I suggested in the last chapter that *Seminar XX* can be read as a feminized reinterpretation of *Seminar VII*. Here, Lacan takes us to the edge of a new way of speaking of the relationship between desire, embodiment, and God, associated with the language of the medieval mystic and the modern hysteric. 'Woman' shifts and some murmured intimation of bodily joy and suffering emerges from the shadows and silence to which Lacan consigned her in *Seminar VII*. The not-all begins to speak, and a different voice begins to be heard.[1]

The idea that the constructed space of femininity in western culture generates a feminized voice that is different from the masculinized voice of the normative subject is by no means unique to Lacan. Luce Irigaray has taken up that suggestion and used it to criticize Lacan throughout her work, by a mimetic and subversive appropriation of the voice that he assigns to the female body. From a different cultural perspective, Carol Gilligan's influential book, *In a Different Voice*, has informed a generation of Anglo-American scholarship.[2] As I have suggested earlier, the difference between English-speaking and continental theorists may on the face of it be more apparent than real, but I am not convinced. It seems to me that Lacan takes us further in his analysis than any equivalent line of enquiry among English-speaking theologians and theorists—feminist or not—and that is why I focus here on his edging towards a reconstructed feminized voice in *Seminar XX*. Although this provides a less than satisfactory response to the questions that women ask of western ideas and institutions today, it raises questions that enable me to return to Thomas's understanding of the relationship between forms and matter in terms of the doctrine of creation *ex nihilo* which are theologically radical, transformative, and I believe necessary if there is to be a viable postmodern

---

[1] Amy Hollywood offers a complex and multifaceted reading of *Seminar XX* which, although I do not directly cite it here, has influenced my own reading. See Amy Hollywood, *Sensible Ecstasy: Mysticism, Sexual Difference, and the Demands of History* (Chicago and London: The University of Chicago Press, 2002), pp. 149–70.

[2] See Carol Gilligan, *In a Different Voice: Psychological Theory and Women's Development* (Cambridge MA: Harvard University Press, 1982).

Thomism. The fact that in *Seminar XX* Lacan positions his analysis of feminized *jouissance* in the context of Aristotelian concepts of being, informed by Étienne Gilson's Thomism, makes this all the more relevant for informing a feminist reading of Thomas.

In approaching *Seminar XX* from a Thomist perspective, I am distilling down and necessarily over-simplifying a much more complex and abstruse lecture series which ranges over a rugged terrain of psychoanalytic, mathematical, philosophical, and theological questions. My intention is to draw out from this seminar the questions that I think are vital to a reading of Thomas for our times, and to allow Lacan to shed light on why these questions matter and on how to make them matter. In *Seminar XX*, Lacan has stopped battling against the ferocious God of his Catholic faith who, in *Seminar VII*, lurked within the *jouissance* of the real that Lacan contemplated with such horror. In *Seminar XX*, Lacan lets *jouissance* be, and in so doing he cannot help but let God be, and woman become.[3]

LACAN, RELIGION, AND BEING

In an address to a Catholic audience during the year when he delivered *Seminar VII*, Lacan refers to the 'criss-crossing' of the two principles of desire and interdiction which constitute the discursive positioning of the human subject before the ontological '*trompe-l'oeil*' of Being.[4] In *Seminar XX*, he revisits this '*trompe-l'oeil*' in order to examine its linguistic effects more closely, and in particular to explore the relationship between religion, desire, sexuality, and the real.

François Regnault contrasts Lacan's understanding of religion with that of Freud in *Moses and Monotheism*.[5] Freud represents Christianity as a late form of Judaism or, in the case of Catholicism, a relapse into paganism, with its Virgin Mother and female saints. According to Regnault, Freud's doctrine 'combines the grandeur of science with the universality of Judaism' so that

---

[3] I refer to the French text of *Seminar XX* in what follows, because some of the Thomist and Aristotelian nuances are lost in English translations: Jacques Lacan, *Le Séminaire Livre XX: Encore* (Paris: Éditions du Seuil, 1975). I include page numbers for Bruce Fink's English translation in brackets: Lacan, *On Feminine Sexuality—the Limits of Love and Knowledge: The Seminar of Jacques Lacan, Book XX, Encore, 1972–1973*, ed. Jacques-Alain Miller, trans. Bruce Fink (New York and London: W. W. Norton & Company, 1999). Cormac Gallagher's alternative English translation is available at the *Lacan in Ireland* website: <http://www.lacaninireland.com/web/wp-content/uploads/2010/06/Book-20-Encore.pdf> [accessed 28 July 2012]. I have consulted both Fink and Gallagher in translating the dense obscurities of the French text.

[4] Jacques Lacan, *Le Triomphe de la Religion précédé de Discours aux Catholiques* (Paris: Éditions du Seuil, 2005), p. 32.

[5] See Sigmund Freud, 'Moses and Monotheism', in SE 23 (1939), pp. 1–138.

Freud's 'religion' is 'scientific atheism and theoretical Judaism. Jew with the Christians, but scientist against the Jews'.[6] However, 'The perspective of Lacan is altogether different.'[7]

Lacan seeks to explain religion, as Freud does, in psychoanalytic terms, but he is more theologically literate than Freud, and more attentive to the ways in which different religious cultures produce different psychic structures. He also suggests that the idea of God is an effect of the unconscious that may be impossible to eradicate. Regnault explains that, according to Lacan,

> one cannot arrive at atheism without doubt either by affirming it or by willing it. What one desires of it, how one arrives at it, requires a more difficult path which penetrates into the structure, form and content of the question of God, although atheism is hardly anything other than an empty form.[8]

Reading this, I was reminded of a series of articles I wrote for a newspaper blog on Thomas Aquinas which, like all such blogs, provided fodder for an interminable joust between Christian and atheist dogmatists.[9] A repeated claim of several atheist contributors was that atheism is not any form of belief, it is simply a lack of belief in all and any gods. An empty form, indeed—or one that deceives itself as to its lack, for few 'lacks' assert themselves with such vehement conviction. Lacan exposes the extent to which such atheist certainties are always shot through with unexamined religious assumptions.

In *Seminar XX*, Lacan suggests that religion is a symptom of a relationship to the real that eludes the control of the symbolic, which opens up a linguistic space of desire and otherness that is vital to being human. We could describe it as a necessary fantasy—a desiring relationship to an unspeakable mystery purged of its theological content. He applies this to the particular insight that Christianity brings to the human condition by exposing the mythical nature of Greek philosophical accounts of being as a copulative relationship between paternal form and maternal matter, thereby revealing the lack that constitutes the subject and the impossibility of the sexual relationship:

> Let us only consider the terms of active and passive, for example, which dominate all that has been cogitated about the relationship between form and matter, so fundamental a relationship, to which each step of Plato refers, then of Aristotle, concerning the nature of things. It is visible, palpable, that these utterances

---

[6] François Regnault, *Dieu est Inconscient: Études Lacaniennes autour de Saint Thomas d'Aquin* (Paris: Navarin, 1985), p. 53.

[7] Regnault, *Dieu est Inconscient*, p. 53.

[8] Regnault, *Dieu est Inconscient*, p. 54.

[9] See Tina Beattie, 'How To Believe—Thomas Aquinas', *The Guardian—Comment is Free* at <http://www.guardian.co.uk/commentisfree/belief/2012/jan/30/thomas-aquinas-modernity> [accessed 13 July 2012].

support only a fantasy by way of which they have tried to make up for that which can in no way express itself, to know the sexual relationship.[10]

This makes Christianity 'the true religion',[11] and it means that Christianity's God must be rediscovered as the Other of the philosophical One which is inscribed within the sexual fantasy. But because this God is not the masculine One of the symbolic, it must be discovered through attentiveness to the language of the feminized other—woman as hysteric or mystic who speaks within the context of the body prior to the abstraction and writing down of what she says within the grammatical order of language. Before we can ask what this means, we have to situate our discussion in the context of Lacan's analysis of the question of being.

BEING AND GOD

Lacan addresses the question of being from the perspective of the copulative function of the verb 'to be'. Ontology, he says, 'is what highlighted in language the use of the copula, isolating it as a signifier.[12] He asks what it means to believe and to know with regard to the question of being—'*ce qu'il en est de l'être*'[13]—in the context of the idea of the One that has shaped western philosophy since the time of Parmenides, whether it is the Platonic form, the Aristotelian unmoved mover, or the Hegelian absolute. This leads him to return to a theme he first addressed in *Seminar XIX* the year before—the claim that 'There is something of the One' (*Y a d'l'Un*).[14] Bruce Fink's translation— 'There's such a thing as One'[15]—elides the Thomist allusion in Lacan's enigmatic French phrase, but his translator's footnote explains that Lacan's emphasis is not 'on the "thing" or on quantity. "The One happens," we might even say.... Lacan is *not* saying "there's some One" (in the sense of some quantity of One) since he is talking about *the One of "pure difference"*.' (My italics.)[16] Let's try to tease this out because, as we shall see later, it is a defining moment in which Lacan gleans a crucial insight from Thomas, by way of Gilson, about the difference between a Platonic and a Thomist approach to the question of being.

In Lacan's reading of Plato, knowledge of the form constitutes the totality of all that there is to know. The a priori One of form sets itself over and against the diversity of matter and the flux of desire. The masculine subject made in the image of this One also sets himself over and against the materiality of the

---

[10] Lacan, *Seminar XX*, p. 104 (p. 82).   [11] Lacan, *Seminar XX*, p. 137 (p. 107).
[12] Lacan, *Seminar XX*, p. 43 (p. 31).   [13] Lacan, *Seminar XX*, p. 11 (p. 3).
[14] Lacan, *Seminar XX*, p. 13 (p. 5).   [15] Lacan, *On Feminine Sexuality*, p. 5.
[16] Lacan, *On Feminine Sexuality*, p. 5, n. 19.

body, nature, and desire because of their resistance to the singularity of form—
to the disembodied 'I' that he is trying to convince himself that he is, without
remainder or excess. By exploring the conditions that make it possible for a
woman to speak from a site of linguistic and bodily otherness from which the
subject is barred, Lacan begins to distinguish between God as the One of
philosophy and God as the Other of Christian faith, and this leads him to play
with the possibilities inherent in Thomism.

Resisting the Platonic concept of the singularity of the form and the totality
of knowledge that this implies, Lacan posits an alternative interpretation of the
One—*Y'a d'l'Un*—'The One happens'. We could give the French a more literal
translation by reading it as 'There is of the One'. In both cases, we are very
close to Thomas. Let's remember two vital points here. First, for Thomas the
being of God is inseparable from the activity of God, so that God's being is
essentially active, expressive, and communicative. Lacan gleans this insight
from his familiarity with the writings of Gilson, and it leads him to reflect
upon the implications of Thomas's argument that God's existence or being
(*ente*) is the same as God's essence (*esse*).[17] Second, for Thomas the divine
unity is not quantitative but qualitative—it refers not to the numerical singularity of God's being but to its perfect simplicity without division, lack,
complexity, or limit. God's being is the 'I am' of Exodus, so that the name of
God is the act of being—being is God's (n)am(e).

Let me quote Gilson at some length, in order to situate the discussion of
Lacan's understanding of God in *Seminar XX* in its Thomist context. Gilson
argues that, in Thomas's mind, 'the notion of being underwent a remarkable
transformation', away from the idea of 'entity' (*essentia*) to the idea of being as
'the act pointed out by the verb "to be"'. Gilson continues:

> [I]n the doctrine of Thomas Aquinas, being has received the fullness of its
> existential meaning. . . . [B]ecause it is to act, 'to be' is something fixed and at
> rest in being: *esse est aliquid fixum et quietum in ente*. In short, this act is the very
> core of all that is, inasmuch precisely as what is, is a being.
>
> As Thomas Aquinas understands him, God is the being whose whole nature it
> is to be such an existential act. This is the reason why his most proper name is, HE
> IS. After saying this, any addition would be a subtraction. To say that God 'is this,'
> or that he 'is that,' would be to restrict his being to the essences of what 'this' and
> 'that' are. God 'is,' absolutely.[18]

---

[17] These terms refer to a widely debated text that I do not engage with, although it would be
relevant for a more extensive discussion of Thomas's understanding of being. See Thomas
Aquinas, *De Ente et Essentia*, translated as *Aquinas on Being and Essence*, adapted and html-
edited by Joseph Kenny OP (1965) at <http://dhspriory.org/thomas/DeEnte&Essentia.htm>
[accessed 6 April 2013].

[18] Étienne Gilson, *History of Christian Philosophy in the Middle Ages* (London: Sheed and
Ward, 1955), pp. 368–9, quoting SCG I, 20, 4.

That phrase, '*esse est aliquid fixum et quietum in ente*', may lose some of its dynamic implications in the translation of *fixum* as fixed. It might be better to say established, rooted, or grounded, to communicate the sense that the infinite act of God's being (*esse*) is the condition within which every finite being exists. If we add a biblical gloss to this, we can say that God is the being within which we ourselves 'live and move and have our being'. (Acts 17:28.) It is the 'still, small voice' of being—or, in a more literal translation, 'a sound of soft stillness' (1 Kings 19:12)—that we discover beyond the earthquake, wind, and fire of the existential dread of being. From a feminist perspective, we can also insist that the 'is-ness' of God is not a 'He', but that's another point to which we must return.

Gilson provides the context in which to situate Lacan's exploration of the question of being in *Seminar XX*. If God is not the singular entity of the philosophical form, if God is being beyond all differentiation and beyond every predicate of existence—God is 'pure difference'—then God is, as we have already seen, beyond language. Pure, undifferentiated difference cannot be divided up and categorized in terms of linguistic concepts. It can only be posited as a difference so extreme that we have no way of conceptualizing or naming what it might be, beyond that it is as the very condition of being.

This is an entirely different way of speaking of difference than Derridean *différance*.[19] *Différance* always risks falling into the trap of a God of the gaps— God becomes associated with the slippage in meaning, the aporia that makes meaning elusive and language paradoxical. Lacan, with Thomas, is speaking of a difference within being that is beyond but also contains and makes possible every difference, every *différance*. If it is *différance*, it is not it. If it is something or anything at all, it is not it. If it is nothing, it is not it. It is. *Qui est*. The verb of God's being is not a copula but an active, generative matrix within which the copula of being comes to be through the creation *ex nihilo* of forms, matter, desire, copulation, and the procreation of living beings. All desire is in and for God, but God does not desire, for there is already an eternal relational perfection within God. There is no lack in God's being—in the trinitarian relationship that is God—and so there is no possibility of defining God without introducing a limit into that plenitude of being. What we can know of God through reason, we can know only through the quiddity or 'whatness' of material beings,[20] and through the intuition that there is a nameless, unknowable Other that lures us through and beyond all particularities and differences to an ineffable depth of what we might call absolute and ever-present 'is-ness'. This mystery—conceptually indistinguishable from the Lacanian real—is altogether different from the philosophical One in whose

---

[19] Cf. John D. Caputo, 'God Is Not *différance*', in *The Prayers and Tears of Jacques Derrida: Religion Without Religion* (Bloomington IN: Indiana, 1997), pp. 1–19.

[20] See Gilson, *History of Christian Philosophy*, p. 369.

image the Cartesian subject is formed—the One that is, Lacan tells his audience, 'a kind of mirage of the One one believes oneself to be'.[21]

This mirage calls to mind feminist philosopher Grace Jantzen's pithy critique of Richard Swinburne's thought-experiment, in which he invites his reader to imagine God in terms of his own subjectivity:

> Imagine yourself, for example, gradually ceasing to be affected by alcohol or drugs, your thinking being equally coherent however men mess about with your brain. Imagine too that you cease to feel any pains, aches, thrills, although you remain aware of what is going on in what has been called your body. You gradually find yourself aware of what is going on in bodies other than your own and other material objects at any place in space... You also come to see things from any point of view which you choose, possibly simultaneously, possibly not. You remain able to talk and wave your hands about, but find yourself able to move directly anything which you choose, including the hands of other people... You also find yourself able to utter words which can be heard anywhere... Surely anyone can thus conceive of himself becoming an omnipotent spirit. So it seems logically possible that there be such a being.[22]

As Jantzen remarks, this thought-experiment suggests that 'anyone who can imagine "himself" as an infinitely extended (and disembodied) version of an Oxford professor is an analogue of the divine'.[23] (The mind boggles at the confusion that might be caused by everybody being able to wave everybody else's hands about as well as their own—metaphysically speaking of course—but let's not be too nit-picking. Maybe heaven is an assemblage of disembodied Oxford professors doing an eternal Mexican wave with one another's hands.) Jantzen argues that Swinburne's view of God reveals 'the untroubled notion of the rational subject, human and divine; and an implicit investment in the symbolic of death, since it is only when the rational human subject is released from its troublesome body that it will truly be godlike'.[24] We should bear in mind Thomas's idea of contemplation as a striving towards God that transcends the body, for those more radically orthodox among us who may be tempted to deny that such examples of modern philosophical theism have their roots in classical Christian theology. This must, however, always be qualified by the fact that, unlike modern philosophical theism, medieval theology insisted upon the resurrection of the body as the only possible condition for the eternal life of the human individual.

[21] Lacan, *Encore*, p. 61 (p. 47).
[22] Richard Swinburne, *The Coherence of Theism* (Oxford: Clarendon Press, 1977), pp. 104–5, quoted in Grace M. Jantzen, *Becoming Divine: Towards a Feminist Philosophy of Religion* (Manchester: Manchester University Press, 1998), p. 28. I have slightly extended the quotation from Jantzen's edited version.
[23] Jantzen, *Becoming Divine*, p. 28.   [24] Jantzen, *Becoming Divine*, pp. 28–9.

The God of the philosophers is the God of the symbolic—a rational proposition purged of the contaminating otherness of the personal, the historical, and the real (flesh, matter, nature, particularity, desire). This One understood as the totality of being achieved by way of the infinite extension of the singularity of being, is symptomatic of the modern philosophical, scientific, or bureaucratic quest for the accumulation of facts, statistics, and proofs. It secures being against a fixed horizon of incremental facts which will eventually add up to all there is to know about everything. Remember that quotation from Richard Dawkins about scientific knowledge—'we may eventually discover that there are no limits'.[25] This produces the fantasy of the One as the sum total of all others. Not only does this result in an idea of God as that infinitely extended professor referred to by Jantzen, it also allows for the deification of any totality, any totalitarian system—the One of the state, the race, the party, the cause, the revolution, the church, the *ummah*, outside of which no other counts, no other is saved, no other must be allowed to exist to call into question the totality of the One that has been achieved by the addition of everything that counts within it.

It is over and against this model of the quantitative One that Lacan—with Thomas as his guide—posits the qualitative 'One of "pure difference"'. God's being is not like an infinitely extended, unified, or perfected version of the human subject—a Feuerbachian projection of man. The One of pure difference is altogether Other than the One of philosophical reason. As the man of reason begins his postmodern disintegration, an overgrown path opens up through psychoanalytic discourse that leads back to the future in the company of this elusive and awesome Other—an Other which, insofar as it is other than the philosophical One, must have something to do with the other sex. Before we consider that, let me say something about Lacan's understanding of the symptom, and how this relates to his revision of the idea of the symbolic and God in *Seminar XX*.

THE OTHER OF THE ONE

Referring to Descartes's *cogito ergo sum*, Lacan explains why psychoanalysis offers a way of reclaiming what has been sacrificed in the construction of the modern subject:

> First, one can say that we have noticeably modified the thinking subject. Since this *I think*, which by supposing itself establishes existence, we have had to take a step, which is that of the unconscious. . . . This formula [the unconscious is structured

---

[25] Richard Dawkins, *The God Delusion* (London: Bantam Press, 2006), p. 374.

like a language] totally changes the function of the subject as existing. The subject
is not he who thinks. The subject is properly the one that we urge, not, as we tell
him in order to charm him, to say it all–one cannot say it all–but to talk nonsense.
All is there [*tout est là*].[26]

It is in talking nonsense that the unconscious reveals itself as the other of the
masculine subject, and therefore this is necessarily a feminized language. It
marks the position of woman as one (not the One, but a series of ones, an
infinite series of exceptions) as the multitude of bodies excluded by the
singular 'I' of the symbolic—'it is another thing altogether than the One of
universal fusion'[27]—whatever the biological sex of the speaking body.

Here, Lacan is at his most provocative from the perspective of his feminist
interlocutors, because he situates this question of subjectivity and otherness in
terms of the philosophical distinction between form and matter, perfection
and lack. A woman lacks the definite article, because her otherness derives
from the fact that she is on the side of the not-all, as the excluded other of the
universal One of the form: 'The Woman can only be written with a line through
The. There is no Woman with the definite article designating the universal.
There is no Woman because . . . of her essence, she is not all.'[28] Yet all is there, in
the nonsense spoken by a woman, because she speaks as/to/of the Other of the
One. So, to the acknowledged consternation of his audiences—those who
belong within the 'pure philosophical tradition'[29]—Lacan reintroduces the
question of God into the relationship between man and woman, 'this God of
whom I said that he has dominated every philosophical debate about love'.[30]
This is, Lacan claims, a way of 'exorcising' the 'good Old God' by way of
showing in what sense this God exists.[31]

By displacing the One of the subject with the Other as divine object of desire
of and for woman, Lacan exposes the masculine subject of the symbolic as a
symptom of the desire for an Other beyond. The enigmatic space—occupied
by woman—where unformed speech emerges on the borders of the real
becomes the site of a different understanding of God. To attend to this
Other, it must be differentiated from 'the idea of a God that is not that of
the Christian faith, but that of Aristotle—the unmoved mover, the supreme
sphere'.[32] Over and against this concept of God, Lacan posits the Other of
woman's desire:

> The whole foundation of the idea of the Good in Aristotle's ethics is that there is a
> being such that all other beings with less being than him can have no other aim

---

[26] Lacan, *Encore*, p. 31 (pp. 21–2).   [27] Lacan, *Encore*, pp. 18–19 (p. 10).
[28] Lacan, *Encore*, p. 93 (pp. 72–3).   [29] Lacan, *Encore*, p. 88 (p. 68).
[30] Lacan, *Encore*, p. 88 (p. 68).   [31] Lacan, *Encore*, p. 89 (p. 68).
[32] Lacan, *Encore*, p. 104 (p. 82).

than to be the most being they can be . . . [I]t is in the opaque place of the jouissance of the Other, this Other as being which might be the woman, if she existed, that the Supreme being, manifestly mythical in Aristotle, is situated, the unmoved sphere from which there proceed all movements whatever they may be. . . .

It is insofar as her jouissance is radically Other that woman has more of a relationship to God than all that could have been said in ancient speculation following the pathway of that which manifestly articulates itself only as the good of the man.[33]

This is a complex claim, but if I interpret him correctly I think Lacan is suggesting that to know the truth of the human condition one has to let go of the pretensions to be spirit/form by taking up the position of body/matter. The soul (*l'âme*) is the focus of Lacan's attention in *Seminar XX*—the soul of Aristotelian philosophy and modern romanticism that appropriates the body of woman as its other, and the soul of female mysticism and hysteria that speaks from the site of the body as other. Woman, who is free from inscription in the phallic pretension to be the One, expresses the desire of material being as otherness in a more truthful way than the man, who labours under the illusion that he can become (like) God. We must come back to that.

In using the non-subjectivity of woman to challenge the godlike singularity and autonomy of the masculine subject, Lacan introduces God rather than man as the Other of woman's desire, thereby bringing about an act of philosophical *coitus interruptus* with regard to the engendering of being. In the process, he radically revises his understanding of the nature of the symptom and the power of the symbolic.

In his earlier work, the symptom was for Lacan interpreted in terms of neurosis and obsession in relation to the symbolic. It signified a failure in the analysand/hysteric to accommodate her desire to the structure of the symbolic at a point of mute resistance or non-compliance rooted in repetition of the lack and mourning associated with the Oedipus complex, and therefore it was an exception to the rule of the symbolic. It was a bodily excess that overflowed the boundaries of the symbolic subject and offered a perverse otherness of suffering and pleasure, parasitic upon and produced by the symbolic and orientated towards the *objet a*, the lack produced by the prohibitive power vested in the symbolic.

In such a system, the symbolic retains its mastery. We have seen in Chapter 8 that, in the structure of the four discourses that Lacan introduced in *Seminar XVII*, a new topology replaces the old Lacanian linguistic structure, but the voice of the hysteric remains barred by the normativity of the subject

---

[33] Lacan, *Encore*, pp. 104–5 (pp. 82–3).

of the symbolic. 'She' knows the master better than he knows himself, but her wisdom is conditional upon everything remaining in place. As soon as she seeks to rise above the bar—to achieve mastery—she loses her claim to truth. The hysteric knows the master/analyst only insofar as she does not seek to take his place, because she retains her subversive position only on condition that she remains in the position of the excluded other—the exception that constitutes her as his symptom, the symptom of his lack.

In *Seminar XX*, Lacan introduces a different understanding of the symptom in relation to the symbolic, for now the symbolic itself becomes a symptom, and therefore there are only symptoms, only exceptions. The symbolic is a symptom of the lack of the subject, a perverse desire for authority and singularity that emerges as the abstract structure and rationality of the One from the site of a more truthful, elusive, and material other. The Big Other— God or the symbolic order—is a symptom among symptoms, not a cause of those symptoms. Lacan thus uncouples the irreducible diversity of beings from any reference to a sexual order of being—linguistic, theological, or philosophical—that problematizes lack in relation to ontological perfection or to the accomplishment of masculine subjectivity in terms of the symbolic. The affirmation of such an order functions as a benchmark against which to pathologize the symptoms of those who fail to conform to its demands (i.e. to satisfy the desire of the Other), but it is in itself a symptom of the futile and frustrated desire to find an explanatory cause or a totalizing perspective from which to diagnose the human condition as less than it could or should be, from the perspective of the masculine One. But, declares Lacan, 'there is no Other of the Other'.[34] Insofar as she expresses desire for the absolute Other—that radical otherness in which all that can be known of the nature of being is dispossessed and unknown (Thomas's God, after a fashion)—woman's *jouissance* exposes the fantasy of the sexual relationship. The Other she longs for is not the sexual other, and the being to which she has access is other than the forms of being that multiply through copulation.

Over and against the idealization of woman as the other of man—the Woman who plays the phallus in order to collude with him in his desire to have the phallus so that with her in his possession he is all (that he dreams of) being—Lacan offers us the uncoupled, lacking, and irreducible singularity of each and every castrated being. I would suggest this could just as meaningfully be written as 'created beings'. However, here we have to navigate a difficult path between two Thomisms, which I am exploring here more explicitly than Lacan does—although it is everywhere implicit in *Seminar XX*.

---

[34] Lacan, *Encore*, p. 102 (p. 81).

THOMAS BETWEEN ARISTOTLE AND LACAN

I have suggested that Lacan uses a Thomist account of being (which he learns primarily from Gilson) to challenge philosophical concepts of the One. In that sense, Thomas's God can be interpreted as the Other to which Lacan refers. But Thomas also introduces a Greek philosophical account of copulative being into Christian theology, and therefore Christianity creates a deep ambivalence within western consciousness, which according to Lacan relates to the contradiction between Jewish and Greek philosophical relationships to the divine.[35]

According to the Hebrew scriptures, the dividing line between God and human knowledge is absolute. To be chosen by God is to be set apart by a command and a call that is absolutely unknowable and unnameable from the human perspective. One can betray and disobey the source of this command, but one cannot hate God because hatred emerges through resentment of being, and Yahweh God does not exist in the way that other beings exist—in such a way that a lesser being might hate the greater being that is God.

Thomas confuses this absolute otherness of God with an Aristotelian account of being, thereby shaping Christian consciousness around a sense of lack in relation to the perfection of being, which becomes caught up in the relationship between form and matter, paternal and maternal, male and female. Lacan reminds his audience of Freud's concern about the command to love one's neighbour as oneself, which generates a sense of hatred towards the other. This is because of the envy and disappointment associated with the perception that (a) the other has more of being than I do, and (b) the other fails to satisfy the hunger for more of being that I experience in terms of castration/lack. So, says Lacan, 'we are so suffocated that nobody realizes that a hatred, a solid hatred, addresses itself to being, to the same being of someone who is inevitably not God'.[36] Lacan refers to a passage in St Augustine's *Confessions*, in which he reflects on the jealousy and fury he witnessed in a baby as it watched another baby at the breast, despite the fact that it already had been nursed and had its hunger satisfied.[37] The baby wanted more of the mother than the satisfaction of its hunger, and it hated the other baby for appearing to have more. Theologians who are quick to dismiss Lacan ignore the ways in which so many of his insights relate back to such ideas gleaned from Christian texts.

Lacan relates this sense of castration and lack to the confusion of woman as sexual other with woman as mother. As mother, she does not have an

---

[35] The most relevant section of *Encore* for what follows is pp. 126–8 (pp. 98–100).

[36] Lacan, *Encore*, p. 127 (p. 99).

[37] Augustine, *Confessions*, trans. Henry Chadwick (Oxford and New York: Oxford University Press, 2008), I. vii (11). See Lacan pp. 127–8 (p. 100). The next section in the *Confessions* in which Augustine reflects on an infant's acquisition of language is also relevant here.

unconscious—she is the man's unconscious, and he looks to her for the plenitude he lacks. However, as woman she lacks what he has—the godlike perfection of form—and so he wants her to love him as (a) God. All this belongs within the masculine unconscious, with its insatiable hunger for the fullness of being that he seeks in the maternal relationship, or the reassurance that he seeks in the sexual relationship. But a woman harbours fewer illusions about the perfectibility of her own being. She knows she is not-all—she is body/nature, and the Other for which she longs is not the man but that Other on the far side of language that enables her to enjoy and to suffer as the bodily being that she is. Her plenitude, the nature of her being, is not form but matter, not knowledge but desire. So she does not know what she wants, she wants without knowing it. That is why Freud was so perplexed by what a woman wants, and let me suggest it is why, in a quotation I used in the last chapter, Juliet Mitchell is wrong to say that the answer to Freud's question is that 'she simply *wants*'.[38] Lacan suggests that what woman wants is God, although few secular feminists would tolerate such a suggestion. However, this is altogether Other than the God that man wants/wants to be as the One. And it is because he confuses her with this m(O)ther, that every sexual relationship is blighted with failure. All this needs greater reflection in terms of Thomas's attempt to reconcile the Exodus account of God with that of Aristotle's account of being, and I shall return to that later. However, let me here indicate a path along which we can follow Thomas, in order to see better how Christianity might relearn its own wisdom from Lacan.

We have seen that for Thomas, each human soul is created by God to be one for all eternity with the body. There is no universal intellect into which all individual minds dissolve after death, no Hegelian absolute that seeks the overcoming of difference, no Platonic fusion of the two into One. There is only an eternal active simplicity of being that sustains within itself all the goodness and diversity of created beings, but lack is the condition of this diversity. What we lack of God's perfection is the condition of our freedom to be other than God. It is lack, not plenitude, that allows us to be individuals—one human plus one human never makes One, it always makes two, ad infinitum. The One of God is absolutely other than the sum total of any and every one we can think of. We shall analyse these claims in more detail in Chapter 18.

We begin to see why it is woman, positioned on the side of lack, who can reawaken man to the lack that is the condition of his own being—a lack that is qualitative and not quantitative in relation to God, and that is the condition of creation's desire for God. By following her through the earthquake, wind, and fire of her desire, he too might discover a space of rest and delight within the

---

[38] Juliet Mitchell, 'Introduction—I', in Juliet Mitchell and Jacqueline Rose (eds), *Feminine Sexuality: Jacques Lacan and the École Freudienne* (Basingstoke and London: Macmillan Press, 1982), p. 24.

quietude of being that is God—attentive to that 'sound of soft stillness' that emanates from the real when we create a silence attentive and deep enough for it to be heard. This is the silence of contemplation wherein one responds to the love of God or, in Lacanian terms, it is the silence that the analyst creates in an act of love for the analysand, in order for her voice to be heard. As the medieval mystic finds a space to speak within the silence of God's love, so the modern hysteric finds a space to speak within the silence of the analyst's love. As God withdraws from the fullness of being in order to let us become—a becoming that is necessarily less than the all that God is—so the analyst must withdraw from the position of mastery and ultimately from the transference that makes the analysand want him to make her complete, in order that she can live within the less than all that is love. I want to consider more closely the implications of this for desire, sexuality, and God.

We have seen that modernity constitutes the philosophical erasure of copulative accounts of being and its substitution by the singularity of the One. This in turn gives rise to various forms of both romanticism and pornography, as sexually defined subjects seek fulfilment by conforming to or violating the positions to which they have been assigned in terms of form/ matter, soul/body. But Lacan points us towards a rediscovered Thomism— beyond what Lacan himself offers—which might liberate embodied and sexual humans from these destructive options, played out in modern Catholic sexual essentialism on the one hand, and the radical postmodern overturning of all ontologies and sexual identities on the other.

SEXUAL FANTASIES AND ROMANTIC MYTHS

In classical Christian theology—exemplified here by Thomas—the human desire for God relativizes or seeks avoidance of the sexual relationship. For Thomas, humans are sexually differentiated not in order to draw us towards a consummate sexual unity of being beyond lack but, on the contrary, because procreation is not the highest *telos* of the human species (Chapter 5). What we lack is not the sexual other but God. For women as well as men, the avoidance of the sexual relationship offers a higher form of life associated with contemplation in anticipation of perfect union with God. Humans were not created simply to be part of a natural order of copulation between forms and matter in the perpetuation of the species—good though this is—and Thomas can see absolutely no other purpose or justification for sexual intercourse.

However, as this transcendent aspect of desire fades from western consciousness, the sexual relationship becomes the focus of all the sense of lack and frustration that is part of the human condition, and romance takes the place of prayer and contemplation in fuelling the fantasy of union and plenitude. The sexual other takes the place of God as the fantasy of the perfect One that the sexual encounter might bring into being. Medieval courtly love and modern romanticism hide from the subject that his perfectly fulfilled self which he seeks through the sexual other does not exist, by perpetually deferring the moment of consummation—'by feigning that it is we who pose an obstacle to it'.[39]

Perhaps one of the most sumptuous cinematic renditions of such romanticism is Martin Scorsese's 1993 film of Edith Wharton's book, *The Age of Innocence*, set amidst the stifling social conventions of New York high society in the late nineteenth century. Newland Archer (Daniel Day-Lewis) likes to think of himself as a non-conformist, and he is irresistibly drawn to the more radically non-conformist Countess Ellen Olenska (Michelle Pfeiffer), cousin of his future wife May Welland (Winona Ryder). Ellen becomes a cause of gossip and scandal when she returns to New York from Europe after the breakdown of her marriage. As Newland's desire for Ellen deepens, the music provides a rich tapestry of longing against which the gaze of the camera lingers and fills the screen with voluptuously seductive images, from the oysters at a lavish dinner party to the labial red satin gown worn by Ellen. In the end, however, Newland opts for the status quo, and he spends his life trapped in the tedium of marriage to the homely and unimaginative May, loving Ellen and longing for her from afar, with their few encounters haunted by unconsummated embraces and a thwarted intensity of erotic desire. In the closing scene of the film, the elderly Newland, widowed and with nothing to prevent him from renewing his relationship with Ellen, walks away rather than meet her again. The romance of the film—its *jouissance*—is unbearably heightened by this unconsummated desire. The last thing we want is for Newland to go upstairs to Ellen's flat and have sex with her—that would give us what we say we want by way of a happy ending, but it would spoil the yearning of the romance.

The film is a good representation of the romanticized opposition between the maternal woman who represents morality and the social order (the good woman), and the seductress who violates the laws of propriety and decency (the bad woman). The wife and mother is sexually available and therefore undesirable, playing out her destiny in marriage and motherhood while laying a subtle claim to her husband's loyalty through the dynamics of the social order. The other, who is sexually unavailable because of that same social order, constantly reminds the man that the woman he has is not the woman he wants. The object of desire is always elsewhere, always positioned behind the bar of prohibition. The alternative to romance—the pornography that overrides the unattainability of the object and breaches every taboo in its attempts to possess and to satiate—only intensifies the lack. Pornography, as

---

[39] Lacan, *Encore*, p. 89 (p. 69).

reviewers of the *Fifty Shades* trilogy keep reminding us, is boring. We—the reader/audience—want Scorsese to persuade us that the relationship between Newland and Ellen had the potential to be the perfect sexual relationship, but deep down we know that only by not calling our bluff, can it continue to deceive us into believing that such a relationship might have been possible. The elusive glance between frustrated lovers will always be more sexually compelling than the pornographic copulation between those who only seem to be getting what they want. Modern Hollywood with its explicit sexual couplings has never risen to the erotic heights of films such as *Casablanca*, with the ambiguity of the relationship and the undecidability of the outcome proving to be the most potent cinematic aphrodisiac.[40]

To quote Slavoj Žižek, 'sexual difference does not designate any biological opposition grounded in "real" properties but a purely symbolic opposition to which nothing corresponds in the designated objects—nothing but the Real of some undefined x that cannot ever be captured by the image of the signified'.[41] This is the Aristotelian mythology of the copulation of forms and matter as the consummation of being, but it cannot be reconciled with the Christian doctrine of creation *ex nihilo*, whatever Thomas believed to the contrary. Creation *ex nihilo* removes the ontological necessity of the sexual relationship. The act of creation *ex nihilo* is repeated when God becomes incarnate from the body of a virgin.[42] The doctrine finds expression in the idea that the Christian person ideally should forego sex if she wants intimacy with God, for the ontological necessity of copulation and the perpetuation of the cycle of sex and death as the only condition or being has been done away with. Eventually, as this doctrine mutates and morphs into modern nihilism, the western subject discovers that he exists within an unfathomable void in which neither God nor woman can satisfy his desire. The doctrine of creation *ex nihilo* deprives the maternal/paternal coordinates of sexual being of their eternal sufficiency and gouges a deep well of loneliness in the western soul, so that sexual relationships continue to be organized around desire for an impossible unity that blights the bodily capacity to enjoy the other as less than all. According to Lacan, if we are to escape the dynamics of this endless and violent repetition of desire and frustration, we need to be divested of our investment in the One as the unattainable perfection of being which leaves us locked in battle with the lack that we discover within our own being.

---

[40] Cf. Slavov Žižek, *How To Read Lacan* (London: Granta Books, 2006), pp. 81–2.

[41] Žižek, 'The Real of Sexual Difference', in Suzanne Barnard and Bruce Fink (eds), *Reading Seminar XX: Lacan's Major Work on Love, Knowledge, and Feminine Sexuality* (Albany NY: State University of New York Press, 2002), pp. 57–76, 63.

[42] See 'The Symbolic Significance of the Virgin Birth', in Tina Beattie, *God's Mother, Eve's Advocate: A Marian Narrative of Women's Salvation* (London and New York: Continuum, 2002), pp. 115–40.

We must come back to the questions this raises, but by this shift in perspective Lacan seeks to challenge the masculine subject and the One that he represents by repositioning knowledge within the imaginary that emerges from the particularity of the body, rather than within the universality of the symbolic. Instead of the masculine symbolic positioning the feminine body on the side of lack, Lacan asks what would happen if he recognized in her the abjected knowledge that comes from his own negated relationship to the body, in a way that might enable both to acknowledge and live with the condition of castration that sets in motion the desire for the Other as a fantasy of the impossible. So let's follow Lacan as he leads us towards love by following the voice that speaks from the body of (a) woman. What are the theological implications of following Lacan down this dark linguistic path which is haunted by the cries of *jouissance*?

15

She Who Speaks

In this chapter, I consider questions of bodiliness and desire from a Lacanian perspective, but still keeping in view the various ways in which this invites comparison with Thomas's theology. Only by opening the theological imagination to possibilities beyond what it currently imagines, is it possible to revisit some of the most fundamental questions of Christian doctrine as understood by Thomas, in order to make these liveable and lovable again in the context of our times.

Let me quote one of my students, Mary Witts, who is doing doctoral research into the dramatic performance of the Bible in non-literate African communities. Although her work did not initially have a gendered focus, she has come to realize that the question of gender is central to what she is trying to do, because of the different ways in which women and men relate to the biblical text. Here, she is describing what she observed during her fieldwork on the Sudanese/ Ethiopian border:

> In church on Sundays, the Mothers' Union choir sing, but it is always men who read and expound the Scriptures. It can be no other way, for the majority of women cannot read. The text remains locked in a meaningless code of black squiggles. It is the 'word of the Lord', but also a metaphorical silence, one that waits to be broken through interpretation.[1]

During her stay, the leader of the Mothers' Union visited her to ask if she would work with women's groups to facilitate their own dramatic performances of the text. By working only with male community leaders and participants, she was helping to elide the meanings that women might offer but could not express.

This vignette is a potent example of Christianity's global perpetuation of a gendered structuring of society and language through its hierarchical ordering of the sexes with regard to preaching and teaching, its adherence to the authority of the biblical text, and its privileging of the written word over oral traditions. But that is only half the story, because beyond writing—that

---

[1] Mary Witts, draft chapter of doctoral thesis, University of Roehampton, 2012.

'meaningless code of black squiggles'—the word of the Lord sings through women's bodies, possibly subverting but never entirely escaping the control of the authorized version. These singing voices are 'a sound of soft stillness' that can be heard when the men fall silent with their preaching and expounding, a sound that asks to be performed, to be enacted in a way that is not controlled by the authoritative interpretation of the written word. To explore the significance of this for theological language, we need to look more closely at how Lacan represents speech as a corporeal language that expresses the particularity of desire, over and against the disembodied universality of the written word.

THE BODY'S TRUTH

The rise of the universities constitutes the beginning of the age of writing—a theme that has attracted widespread attention from postmodern theorists. Today, we live in an era that has been described as the end of the book, when the written text is displaced from its hegemonic place in the ordering of western knowledge, and new technologies and forms of communication are opening up which fracture the universality of the Aristotelian system of knowledge. If, in Thomas's time, knowledge began its migration from monastic communities of prayer, agriculture, and good works into the libraries and laboratories of the academy, today knowledge is once again migrating to new and as yet unpredictable locations—more virtual and disembodied even than the university environment, but more democratic, participatory, disordered, and contested too. Thomas and Lacan are the book-ends that mark the era of writing—at least, according to Lacan—so that Lacan can be positioned as a liminal figure at the end of modern humanism, who mirrors Thomas's positioning as an equally liminal figure at its beginning.

Erin Labbie suggests that Lacan's seminars are modelled on the *Summa theologiae* in style as well as content.[2] We need to bear in mind that much of Thomas's work was dictated to scribes, so that he occupies the overlapping boundary between speech and writing. In a similar way, Lacan's seminars were recorded and written down by others, and he displays a highly ambivalent attitude towards this process of transcription. In revisiting the question of writing from the perspective of the four discourses that Lacan introduced in *Seminar XVII*, *Seminar XX* maps out the problematic relationship between the master/analyst and the mystic/hysteric understood in Aristotelian terms of the body/soul relationship, which can also be analogously understood as the relationship between the spoken and written word.

---

[2] Erin Felicia Labbie, *Lacan's Medievalism* (Minnesota: University of Minnesota Press, 2006).

Referring to Aristotle's *De Anima*, Lacan points out that, 'If there is something that grounds being, it is assuredly the body.'[3] But according to Lacan, Aristotle fails to link this to 'his affirmation . . . that man thinks *with*—instrument—his soul'. This means, says Lacan, that 'man thinks with Aristotle's thought. In that sense, thought is naturally on the winning side'.[4] Through the influence of Aristotle (although more significantly through Platonic influences), the mind has displaced the body as a source of knowledge, so that man/form/mind is 'on the winning side' over woman/matter/body. But this is an illusion, because in saying that the man thinks with his soul, Aristotle denies that the source of thought is the body. So, says Lacan, 'He animates nothing, he (mis)takes the other for his soul' [*il prend l'autre pour son âme*].[5]

Lacan seeks to expose this inverted order of truth that constitutes intellectual mastery in the western ordering of knowledge, by bringing into view the excluded other of the body. Language (*le langage*) constitutes the conceptualized and rationalized sphere of the symbolic, but this conceals the body's mother tongue (*la langue*), that constitutes the voice of the unconscious with its visceral and unformed expressions of lack and longing, horror and ecstasy, love and loss. There is therefore an inversion in the order of reality, when western philosophy privileges soul over body and mind over matter, for in fact, without the medium of the body, the soul would know nothing. As Thomas himself acknowledges, 'The proper act is produced in its proper potentiality. Therefore since the soul is the proper act of the body, the soul was produced in the body.'[6]

This is why it is essential to recognize that Lacan is both deconstructing the Aristotelian/Thomist order of knowledge, while also appropriating it as offering a more truthful account of reality than Platonic and later Cartesian and Kantian accounts of the subject. With Thomas/Aristotle, he is insisting that the soul is empty of content except insofar as this is provided by the experiencing body. Against Thomas/Aristotle, he is refusing to ontologize reproductive/sexual difference as fundamental to the order of being. In this, I am going to argue later that Lacan is more Christian than Thomas.

For Lacan, the priority that Aristotle (and therefore Thomas) accords to the body and the senses with regard to the accumulation of knowledge means that, contrary to what they argue, it is the body and not the soul that is the privileged bearer of truth. In the insistence that the soul must have mastery over the body, Lacan suggests a double mastery comes about: the dependence

---

[3] Jacques Lacan, *Le Séminaire Livre XX: Encore* (Paris: Éditions du Seuil, 1975), p. 140. Lacan, *On Feminine Sexuality—the Limits of Love and Knowledge: The Seminar of Jacques Lacan, Book XX, Encore, 1972-1973*, ed. Jacques-Alain Miller, trans. Bruce Fink (New York and London: W. W. Norton & Company, 1999), p. 110.

[4] Lacan, *Le Séminaire Livre XX*, p. 141 (p. 111).

[5] Lacan, *Le Séminaire Livre XX*, p. 104 (p. 82).   [6] ST I, 90, 4.

of the soul on the body is overridden by the illusion that the soul is the source of truth, and Aristotle's knowledge becomes the master discourse in western culture. Referring to Aristotle's *De Anima*, Lacan says that 'The soul—you have to read Aristotle—is obviously what the dominant thinking (*la pensée du manche*) culminated in.'[7]

Over and against this inversion of the source of truth, Lacan asks what kind of truth the body reveals. There are, he says, 'miracles of the body'.[8] As an example, he refers to the lachrymal gland which must produce tears in order for the eye to function, but which also expresses emotion and grief from which the subject shies away.

This expressive capacity of the body is lyrically explored in Peter Carey's book, *The Chemistry of Tears*, where he describes how even the chemical composition of tears marks this difference between functionality and expressiveness:

> He told me that tears produced by emotions are chemically different from those we need for lubrication. So my shameful little tissues, he said, now contained a hormone involved in the feeling of sexual gratification, another hormone that reduced stress; and finally a very powerful natural painkiller.
>   'What is that one called?' I asked.
>   'Leucine encephalin,' he smiled. I wrote it down.[9]

This is an exquisite cameo to illustrate what Lacan means. Tears have a subtlety of language all of their own. They know a truth about the self which the 'I' who claims to know does not know. When the subject enters the scene, the immediacy of the body's language yields to naming and writing, and thereby it loses its eloquent capacity to express a truth beyond what we think we know.

Lacan expresses this in terms of the difference between the enunciated and the enunciation, which can be explained in terms of the Cartesian *cogito*—'I think therefore I am'. The 'I am' (the enunciation) is not the same 'I' that thinks (the enunciated). The 'I am' is simply whatever it is that the animated matter of my being does as it lives—weeping, laughing, gasping, exclaiming, groaning, gesturing, communicating in all those spontaneous ways that express something of myself which 'I' might disown or rationalize upon reflection. It is an endless, unformed stream of expressiveness—akin to prime matter—that flows through and beyond my bodily self and connects me to everything else. The 'I' who thinks is empty of content, for it is a grammatical form—a concept—that enables me to abstract myself from my body in order to enunciate myself as a continuous, cognitive, and communicative

---

[7] Lacan, *Le Séminaire Livre XX: Encore*, p. 139 (p. 109).
[8] Lacan, *Le Séminaire Livre XX: Encore*, p. 139 (p. 109).
[9] Peter Carey, *The Chemistry of Tears* (London: Faber and Faber, 2012), p. 265.

individual who knows and acts. But really, the 'I am' who reacts spontaneously and enunciates in the present tense, as a body that speaks without thinking, knows what it is to be more truly and more really than the 'I' who is the subject of the sentences within which I am enunciated in order to assert my identity as the owner and master of my acts.

The Cartesian *cogito* can be seen as an inversion of the medieval construction of the self, which would be better expressed as 'I am therefore I think'. It is psychoanalysis that now reclaims this lost order of corporeal knowledge, which Lacan describes as 'the very backbone of my teaching':

> I speak with my body and I do so without knowledge. So I always say more than I know of it.
>
> That is where I arrive at the meaning of the word 'subject' in analytic discourse. What speaks without knowledge makes me 'I,' subject of the verb. That is not enough to make me be. That has nothing to do with what I am forced to put in being – enough knowledge for it to hold up, but not one drop more.
>
> That is what used to be called form. According to Plato, the form is the knowledge that fills being. The form doesn't know any more about it than it says. It is real in the sense that it holds being in its glass, but full to the brim. It is the knowledge of being. The discourse of being presumes that being is, and that is what holds it.
>
> There is some relationship of being that cannot be known.[10]

Lacan also expresses this in terms of the preposition 'of' or 'to' (*à*) as signifying a subtle but important distinction between one way of thinking and another. 'I think of you. That does not mean I think you.'[11] In the same way, 'I love to you' might better express the indirect nature of love for the other than 'I love you'.[12]

The task of psychoanalysis is to reconnect the thinking self with the wisdom of the body that *jouissance* makes possible, and this entails rehabilitating the space of imagination and desire that was repressed in the making of the modern mind. However, let me tease out what is implied but not fully explored in *Seminar XX*, by suggesting that this means reclaiming a Thomism that is less Aristotelian and more Christian in its ways of knowing and being.

REALITY, THE REAL, AND THE TRUE

Reality is for Lacan more true than the truth—more real than the real—because it is the way in which humans really experience the world through

---

[10] Lacan, *Encore*, pp. 150–1 (p. 119).   [11] Lacan, *Encore*, p. 133 (p. 104).

[12] Lacan, *Encore*, p. 133 (p. 104). Luce Irigaray appropriated this expression as the title of her book *i love to you: Sketch of a Possible Felicity in History*, trans. Alison Martin (New York and London: Routledge, 1996).

the conjoined relationships of the symbolic, the real, and the imaginary. Lacan depicts this in terms of the Borromean knot, which involves knotting three loops together in such a way that to cut any one leads to the uncoupling of all three—an analogy that he enigmatically suggests can be likened to the Trinity. In Thomas's approach to knowledge, if we take the threefold interlocking of the Lacanian symbolic, the imaginary, and the real as analogous to the relationship between the intellect, the imagination, and the body, we could say that, for both, knowledge necessarily includes a dimension of fantasy or imagination that creates a link between body and mind by way of desire, or, in Lacanian terms, that creates a link between the real and the symbolic. We cannot ever know the Thing in itself, the real, matter, the form, and/or God, because consciousness and matter encounter one another in the context of the impossible. Anything we can possibly say about the real or God we say as a result of the imaginative and imagined relationship we have to material objects. So, says Lacan, 'everything we are allowed to approach of reality remains rooted in fantasy'.[13]

For Thomas, the imagination is populated by phantasms by way of which the phenomena encountered by the senses translate into knowable and name-able mental objects. Lacan makes the point that, even at the most rudimentary level, this is still a question of the relationship of language to the body. There is no prediscursive reality, for the phantasm is other than the object that it represents. It occupies an intermediate space between the bodily drives and senses, and the linguistic concepts and narratives by way of which we impose meaning, continuity, and truth on our experiences:

> How is one to return, if not on the basis of a peculiar discourse, to a prediscursive reality? That is where the dream is – the dream, founder of every idea of knowledge. But there too is what must be considered as mythical. There's not any prediscursive reality. Every reality is founded and defines itself by a discourse.[14]

No matter what we say or claim to experience of the real, we are using language to say it. In Lacanian psychoanalysis, the phonemes and particles of speech are analogous to the swarm of impressions that flood our senses before we begin to make sense of the world. These are the fragments of language that billow on the currents of desire which continuously emerge from the immediacy of the body's response to the material world. In *Seminar XX*, these become for Lacan the expressions of *jouissance* associated with the drives—bodily expressions of joy and anguish that are always excessive to the meaning we give to them, so that they express a desire for something beyond anything that can be said or anything that the subject can contain within the enclosed boundaries of the fantasized completeness of the body. Insofar as the concepts we form—the linguistic signifiers we use to denote

[13] Lacan, *Encore*, p. 121 (p. 95).   [14] Lacan, *Encore*, p. 43 (p. 32).

the universal and the true—refer to these unformed particles of speech, we can say that the relationship between the language of the symbolic and the language of the imaginary is that of the signifier to the signified. The closest we can get to a prediscursive reality is through attentiveness to the immediacy of speech that emanates from the body before it is encrypted in writing, for writing always elides the body. This is a 'peculiar discourse', because it is a return to a fantasy or a myth of the lost origins of the self in the body.

Again, in order not to lose sight of the Thomist perspective, we must remember that the medieval person is altogether other than the Cartesian 'I' of modernity. For Descartes, the 'I' is what remains when everything else is eliminated, whereas for Thomas (and for Lacan), the self is an elusive, relational fluidity of being that emerges from and overflows the porous boundaries between the bodily self and the material world. Evacuate these, and there is no 'I' that remains—the human soul cannot exist except as a body in relation to other bodies.

This brings me to another vital insight that Thomas might bring to Lacan, even if Lacan himself does not explicitly refer to it. There is a fundamental difference between Aristotle and Thomas when it comes to the role of the imagination. For Aristotle, the soul is not essentially indivisible, because at least in some readings of Aristotle, the intellect can survive death whereas the other aspects of the soul are as mortal as the body. However, Thomas's belief in the immortality of the conjoined body and soul means that the whole of the soul is present throughout the whole of the body. This means that the imagination as well as the intellect has eternal and not just temporal significance, because it is the medium of communication between the body and the intellect, and for all eternity the body will remain the intellect's source of knowledge. (We have seen that, in the temporary separation of the two after death, God keeps the soul alive by providing knowledge that the body would normally supply.) To be human, for Thomas, is to be a material, sensory, imaginative, intellectual being with a beginning but no ending. We are neither rational minds nor animal bodies, but creatures of desire whose being is woven together out of form and matter on the copulative loom of the imagination. Remove this loom and we fall apart. We cease to be human persons in the fullest sense of the word. Without the mediating function of the language of the imaginary we lack some vital characteristic that enables us to be real—that is, in Lacanian terms, to recognize that what we call reality is an imaginative transformation of the impossible real into something we can understand and render meaningful.

That is why the Lacanian imaginary is the missing coordinate in the construction of the modern self, in whom the interlocking trinitarian structure of the soul has been replaced by dualistic oppositions. The healing of the human requires the recovery of the missing link of the soul, and this is to be discovered in the language of the imagination—the language of the phantasmic—that constitutes the desiring immediacy of our being in the world. But this is altogether different from any form of phallic romanticism—be it courtly love, the modern love story, or the varieties of pantheism and spirituality that constitute New Age religions and philosophies. To seek escape from the insatiability of desire in the abstract One of the form/the symbolic/the scientific, or in the undifferentiated oneness of matter/the real/the romantic, is to remain trapped in the phallic myth of totality which always generates violence against the unconquerable other—be it the other of matter or the other of form. As we saw in comparing Kant and Sade, in any Platonic ordering of knowledge, either form/rationality must set itself against matter/nature, or matter/nature must set itself against form/rationality. If we are to love without conquest, violence, or consumption, we must accept that there is no plenitude, for to be human is to lack, to desire, and to imagine as well as to know—that is what human reality is. That is what it really means to be human.

This is why, in the end, Lacan has to revert to the question of God, and he discovers a way of framing that question by referring to medieval Christianity's refiguration of the ancient relationship between form and matter within the copula of desire. In *Seminar XX*, Lacan approaches the question of God from the perspective of a psychoanalytic Thomism that has been freed from its metaphysical, androcentric, and Aristotelian constraints. This involves a paradoxical subversion and restoration of Thomism to the order of knowledge. Why does this entail the feminization of knowledge? Let me keep the focus on Thomas, although Lacan's critique is clearly intended as a more general critique of the western philosophical tradition, particularly in its modern scientific and rationalist versions.

THE ETERNAL BODY

Although Thomas—like Aristotle—inverts the relationship between the soul and the body in the way that Lacan suggests, Thomas is not ultimately a philosopher content to think within the limits of reason alone. If he were, he could fix his sights on the form or the One as his *telos* and his God, so that freedom from the body would be the goal of his existence. We have seen that Thomas is by no means immune from the seductions of philosophy in this respect. But ultimately, Thomas is a Christian theologian, and there is a surplus to his desiring and knowing that cannot be captured or contained by the philosophical One, because it is the desire of and for the incarnate Other. At the heart of Thomas's understanding of the nature of being there is an enigma and a mystery that is nonsense from the perspective of reason, and no matter how hard he tries to make sense of it, there is a bone in the spirit, a core of resistance that will not let him be, for the *telos* of his being is a *telos* of the body, a *telos* of God incarnate that emanates from the trinitarian love that creates him out of nothing and holds him as an eternal body within the being of God. Nothing in the philosophical order of being can answer to the love and longing that this arouses not only in his soul but, much more importantly from a Lacanian perspective, in his body—a body that is hers from the perspective of reason but God's from the perspective of faith. Why?—because while Aristotelian philosophy feminizes the body as the maternal other of paternal form, Christian theology divinizes it as God incarnate. No wonder Thomas's Aristotelian God gets so messily caught up in the maternal Trinity—but we'll come back to that.

No matter how far Thomas's soul is seduced along the pathway of philosophical knowledge that leads up and away from the body to the One God, ultimately he knows that God is Other than that One. The doctrine of the resurrection of the body arouses in the Christian soul an insatiable bodily desire for God that nothing we can conceive of or conceive by can satisfy. Before the intellect knows itself to be, the body's desire for God is aroused. Before the ordering of knowledge and the disciplining and naming of desire, the animal body wants God in everything it sees, touches, tastes, hears, and smells—and, Lacan would add, in everything it fucks.

Over and against the dualism that pits the One of philosophical form against the many of material beings, Thomas's trinitarian order of being triangulates desire by making God the absolute Other of all desire. This desire is not a phallic trajectory from the many to the one, neither is it a romantic desire for the sexual other. Rather, it is a threefold relationship of being within which all beings exist. Lacan insists that only a rediscovery of this triangular or trinitarian relationship—which he constitutes as the intertwined knot of the symbolic, the imaginary, and the real—can restore to us a reality in which it might be possible to love.

This is why, in privileging the imaginary over the symbolic as a source of truth, Lacan offers us an inverse but truer Thomism. Thomas remains captive to philosophy in elevating form over matter, intellect over body, and man over woman, so that the radical implications of the Christian doctrines of creation *ex nihilo*, the creation of the human (male and female) in the image of God, the Trinity, the incarnation, and the resurrection of the body are never fully developed by scholastic theology in a way that would displace the intellectual and social hegemony of Aristotelianism and Platonism. When Luther does indeed banish philosophical knowledge as truth, he does so from the perspective of the truth revealed in the biblical text alone—*sola Scriptura*—in a way that renders the body inert or evil in relation to truth. The graced body of medieval Catholicism dissolves into the Word, and this paves the way for the Enlightenment with its contempt for matter and its absolutization of form. Had Luther exalted Christ as God incarnate, flesh of Mary, over the decadent power of the late medieval church, rather than Christ as crucified Word of God, the story might have been altogether different.

Nevertheless, in spite of all this, Christianity has brought about a transformation in the order of knowledge at the level of the body in relation to God, and the symptoms and effects of this cannot be eradicated, however strenuous the endeavours of modernity to banish them. One has to return to the body as the site of a disavowed knowledge that is necessarily Christian, because it was Christianity that aroused in the body a *jouissance* that has nothing to do with sex, a *jouissance* of and for God that is surplus to every functional requirement of copulation and reproduction, that will always render the sexual relationship somewhat redundant from the perspective of the body's desire. If the body exists eternally in God, it has no need to copulate or to reproduce itself. That is no longer the purpose of existence. Nor must the soul seek escape from the prison of the body in order to attain to the Form or the One of the divine intellect, for its body is created for the endless *jouissance* that is generated by the imagined bliss of heaven or the torments of hell.

This is why Lacan claims that Christianity is 'the true religion'—true insofar as it is the only religion that can help to explain the topology of the soul that psychoanalysis uncovers, and the relationship of this to the question of being which belongs within the matrix of the culture that Christianity helped to create. Through the doctrine of the incarnation and resurrection, Christianity places the emphasis not on Christ's soul but on his body. It offers a noncopulative expression of bodily *jouissance*, rejecting the sexual couplings of pagan religions and putting in their place the oral incorporation offered by the Eucharist:

> Christ, even resurrected, is valued for his body, and his body is the means by which communion in his presence is incorporation – oral drive – of which the wife of Christ, the Church as it's called, contents itself very well, having nothing to expect from copulation.[15]

In removing copulation from the order of being, Christianity unveils the falsehood of Greek ontology and modern romanticism, and it expresses the truth of human reality by exposing the hole that constitutes the Other in/of being. But this is an 'obscenity'[16] so that Christians, like psychoanalysts, 'are disgusted by what has been revealed to them'.[17] This is the only explanation as to why 'the philosophy of Aristotle was reinjected by Saint Thomas into what one could call Christian consciousness, if that meant anything'. Lacan says he rolls about laughing when he reads Saint Thomas, because 'it's awfully well put

---

[15]	Lacan, *Encore*, p. 144 (p. 113).		[16]	Lacan, *Encore*, p. 144 (p. 113).
[17]	Lacan, *Encore*, p. 145 (p. 114).

together'.[18] By introducing the logic of philosophy with its ordered relation-ships of form and matter into Christian theology, Thomas allows Christians to hide from themselves the obscenity of their faith behind a philosophical mask. It is in the scientific stripping away of this philosophical mythology that Christianity once more confronts the subject with the hole in the order of being—a hole that is quickly covered over by science itself, lest its Sadean fantasies consume the masculine mind.

Christian revelation is mad from the perspective of reason—an outrage from the perspective of the philosophy of being. From the very beginning, this mewling, puking, newborn God in a manger and this bleeding, shitting, dying God on a cross has been 'foolishness to the Greeks' (1 Cor. 1:23). Philosophical reason refuses to let the 'I' rest within the being of hysterical/mystical otherness that allows the mystery of God to speak through the body, and we have seen how carefully Thomas arranges things to avoid the linguistic breaking open of form that incarnation might require. If Thomas's God is to regain consciousness, we must reanimate the effluvia of language that he so meticulously sought to eliminate in the writing of his theology, for only then might we discover God in/as the body of the Other whose body we desire to become.

THE EMPTINESS OF LOVE

Christianity seeks refuge in the myths of philosophy and romance to hide from itself what it knows to be true—that there is no sexual relationship. Yet it also embodies the truth within its forgotten relationship to the body and God as the Other of the philosophical One, and (according to Lacan) it is the task of psychoanalysis to rediscover that truth and relocate it where it belongs—within the human soul. This means recognizing that 'What makes up for the sexual relationship is, quite precisely, love.'[19]

To understand what Lacan means by this, we might return to his discussion of the transference in *Seminar XI*. Here, he suggests that the analyst must accompany the analysand through and beyond the transference which pro-jects onto the other the narcissistic demand of and for an all-sustaining love, to a renunciation of the object. Only by accepting lack through a recognition of the limits of desire and its capacity for gratification does love become possible: 'Love . . . can be posited only in that beyond, where, at first, it renounces its object.'[20] This entails acceptance of the necessary act of separation, acceptance

---

[18] Lacan, *Encore*, p. 145 (p. 114). '*Parce que c'est rudement bien foutu.*' One might suggest a more Lacanian innuendo by translating this as 'it's fuckingly well put together'.

[19] Lacan, *Encore*, p. 59 (p. 45).

[20] Jacques Lacan, *The Four Fundamental Concepts of Psychoanalysis: The Seminar of Jacques Lacan, Book XI*, trans. Alan Sheridan (New York and London, 1981), p. 276.

of lack as the condition by way of which love might mediate between desire and the drive:

> [A]ny shelter in which may be established a viable, temperate relation of one sex to the other necessitates the intervention...of that medium known as the paternal metaphor. The analyst's desire is not a pure desire. It is a desire to obtain absolute difference, a desire which intervenes when, confronted with the primary signifier, the subject is, for the first time, in a position to subject himself to it. There only may the signification of a limitless love emerge, because it is outside the limits of the law, where alone it may live.[21]

In *Seminar XX*, Lacan recognizes that this description of love is too conformist. It conforms the desire of the hysteric to the symbolic order. The 'paternal metaphor' remains in place, and the analysand is reconciled to the lack that it represents. It retains its universality, and makes of her the symptom as the excluded other. In *Seminar XX*, a more radical possibility emerges when Lacan makes the symbolic itself a symptom, for this drains it of its overarching power—its formative power over desire. Now, the mystic/hysteric is interpreted in the context of an Other that violates the phallic prohibition, not in terms of a transgressive and ultimately futile desire for the all to which the phallus forbids access, but in terms of a *jouissance* that delights in the impossibility of the Other, that makes absolute lack the site of an ecstasy of joy and suffering that knows neither prohibition nor expectation. Lacan refers to Kierkegaard who, beyond reason and resignation, cuts himself off from love in the paradoxical conviction that only thereby will he gain access to it.[22] In Marcus Pound's interpretation, 'Kierkegaard's God is not invoked as a neurotic defence against difference, but is instead the very principle *of* difference.... [T]he embrace of law need not be construed as a resignation to lack, but the very opposite: we are entertained by the plenitude of God's difference.'[23]

Lacan relates this to what he sees as the orgasmic quality of female mysticism, in which the experience of joy is not conditional upon knowledge of its object but, on the contrary, derives its intensity from the impossibility of knowing its object.[24] Nineteenth-century attempts to interpret this in terms of sexuality miss the point (and so does Lacan, when he interprets Bernini's statue of St Teresa of Ávila in terms of sexual orgasm).[25] The mystic's delight flows from the radical otherness and difference of God, not from any projection into that relationship of sexual difference and desire. I shall return to this in more detail in the last chapter, when I discuss Catherine of Siena.

[21] Lacan, *The Four Fundamental Concepts of Psychoanalysis*, p. 276.
[22] Cf. Lacan, *Encore*, p. 98 (p. 77).
[23] Marcus Pound, *Theology, Psychoanalysis and Trauma* (London: SCM Press, 2007), p. 85.
[24] Cf. Lacan, *Encore*, pp. 97–8.
[25] Lacan, *Encore*, p. 97 (p. 76). See also Irigaray's ironic riposte in *This Sex Which Is Not One*, trans. Catherine Porter with Carolyn Burke (Ithaca NY: Cornell University Press, 1985), p. 91.

The difference constituted by Christianity's God as Other is altogether other than the difference between form and matter that constitutes the philosophical account of being. It is a difference so radical that it is, we could say, full to the brim of the joy of being empty, for it is only in the utter abandonment of knowledge that the body is capable of experiencing the Other. Yet because this is obscene from the point of reason and romance, Christianity too falls prey to the romantic fiction of philosophy and the sexual relationship. It reintroduces God as 'the third party in this business of human love',[26] and by way of what Lacan refers to as Saint Thomas's 'physical theory of love', it adopts the Aristotelian idea that the Supreme Good—God's *jouissance*—is somehow related to the human good:

> The first being we have a sense of is clearly our being, and everything that is for the good of our being must, by dint of this very fact, be the Supreme Being's jouissance, that is, God's. To put it plainly, by loving God, we love ourselves, and by first loving ourselves – 'well-ordered charity,' as it is put – we pay the appropriate homage to God.[27]

This, suggests Lacan, constitutes a confusion between love and knowledge. The love of God becomes confused with philosophical accounts of knowledge, in a way that inevitably diminishes its radical otherness and domesticates it within the copulative relationships of form and matter, male and female.

This philosophical shift that confuses the absolute alterity of God with the continuum of philosophical being also interrupts Christianity's ties to the God of the Jewish tradition. To rediscover the Other of God—the Other of mystical/hysterical *jouissance*—the God of Exodus must be posited as a contradiction or an exception to the Aristotelian concept of being, not as the greatest and most sublime expression of that being. Lacan suggests that, if this can be approached from an Aristotelian perspective, it might be by way of Aristotle's obscure concept of *enstasis*—the obstacle or exception by way of which the universality of the symbolic is shown to be false.[28] There is an exception that uses language to say that it cannot be spoken of, and this exposes the failure of language to encompass the totality of being. To explore this further, let me turn to an essay in which Slavov Žižek discusses *Seminar XX*.

Žižek suggests that, in opening up questions of otherness and desire from the perspective of woman, Lacan's interpretation of the Christian God might be interpreted as 'the very passage from Judaism to Christianity' which 'ultimately obeys the matrix of the passage from the "masculine" to the

---

[26] Lacan, *Encore*, p. 90 (p. 70).   [27] Lacan, *Encore*, p. 91 (pp. 70–1).
[28] See Lacan, *Encore*, pp. 89–92 (pp. 68–71). See also Gilbert D. Chaitin, *Rhetoric and Culture in Lacan* (Cambridge, New York, and Melbourne: Cambridge University Press, 1996), pp. 144–6.

"feminine" formulas of sexuation'.[29] Žižek refers to Lacan's engagement with the Pauline dialectic of transgression and the Law in *Seminar VII*, and he suggests that *Seminar XX* can be read in the context of Saint Paul's passage on love in 1 Corinthians 13. According to Žižek, this constitutes the feminized corollary to the dialectic between law and transgression—a dialectic which is 'clearly "masculine" or phallic: it involves the tension between the All (the universal Law) and its constitutive exception. Love, on the other hand, is "feminine": it involves the paradoxes of the non-All.'[30] Here is the famous passage from Corinthians to which Žižek refers, as quoted by him:

> If I speak in the tongues of mortals and of angels, but do not have love, I am a noisy gong or a clanging cymbal. And if I have prophetic powers, and understand all mysteries and all knowledge, and if I have all faith, so as to remove mountains, but do not have love, I am nothing. If I give away all my possessions, and if I hand over my body so that I may boast [alternative translation: 'may be burned'], but do not have love, I gain nothing. . . .
>
> Love never ends. But as for prophecies, they will come to an end; as for tongues, they will cease; as for knowledge, it will come to an end. For we know only in part, and we prophesy only in part; but when the complete comes, the partial will come to an end. . . . For now we see in a mirror, dimly, but then we will see face to face. Now I know only in part; then I will know fully, even as I have been fully known. And now faith, hope, and love abide, these three; and the greatest of these is love.

Love here is paradoxically the only eternally enduring condition of the fullness of knowing, but it is also a condition of the partiality of knowledge. The limitation of knowledge is the necessary condition within which we experience the abiding reality of love. As not-all, we discover what love is, for it shows us that even the totality of knowledge is nothing compared to what truly is. Between love and knowledge there is an unbridgeable gap. The order of knowledge—the complete knowledge of everything that adds up to One that is the quest of philosophy and science—is altogether different from the fullness of being known and being loved within which I become not One but an ecstatic Nothing. To quote Žižek again,

> the point of the claim that even if I were to possess all knowledge, without love, I would be nothing, is not simply that *with* love, I am 'something.' For in love, *I also am a nothing*, but as it were a Nothing humbly aware of itself, a Nothing paradoxically made rich through the very awareness of its lack. Only a lacking, vulnerable being is capable of love: the ultimate mystery of love is therefore that incompleteness is in a way higher than completion.[31]

[29] Slavoj Žižek, 'The Real of Sexual Difference', in Suzanne Barnard and Bruce Fink (eds), *Reading Seminar XX: Lacan's Major Work on Love, Knowledge, and Feminine Sexuality* (Albany NY: State University of New York Press, 2002), pp. 57–76, 59.

[30] Žižek, 'The Real of Sexual Difference', p. 61.

[31] Žižek, 'The Real of Sexual Difference', p. 61.

I am going to return to this rich insight about the nature of love later, but first I want to return to Thomas's *Summa theologiae*, to ask what becomes of Thomas's theology if we take seriously Lacan's suggestion that Aristotelian philosophy obscures and diminishes the radical otherness of the God of the Hebrew and Christian traditions. So I turn now to arguably the most important section of Thomas's theology—his interpretation of Exodus 3 upon which hinges his whole attempt to show the coherence between Aristotle's God and the God of biblical revelation. He fails, but a greater love emerges from his failure—for that too is the paradox of the Christian faith.

Part V

Embodying Desire

16

In the Beginning

It is time to go back to the beginning—a beginning in which the word 'time' means nothing, for time has not begun. The idea of the beginning—creation *ex nihilo*—is, according to Lacan, a doctrine that marks out the western religious subject from all other subjects, for it inflicts upon western religious consciousness the unique and irreparable wound of monotheism, from the beginning. This constitutes the primordial 'lack' that Lacan identifies with the influence of the Jewish and Christian scriptures upon western consciousness.

I have shown the extent to which Thomas Aquinas's attempt to portray God the Father in terms of the Greek philosophical One produced a sexualized social order that mimicked that of ancient Greek society as prescribed by Aristotle, eliminating the alternative possibilities inherent in the Christian understanding of the trinitarian God and the incarnation. Now, guided by Lacan, I begin to offer a different reading of Thomas by attending to some of the neglected and undeveloped aspects of his thought—those which have never found a space of resonance and significance within the dominant theological tradition. By invoking this alternative to mainstream readings of Thomas—which are in themselves manifold and not always consistent[1]—I hope to show that the traditional Catholic understanding of God is potentially enriched and deepened, maybe even redeemed and rescued, by the insights offered by psychoanalysis, and that this has far-reaching implications for what it means to be human made in the image of God.

My task in these final chapters is twofold. First, I seek to show how Lacan can offer a different reading of Thomas, if we take seriously some of the psychoanalytic insights he brings to questions about the nature of being, sexual difference, and God in western consciousness. Second, I seek to go beyond Lacanian psychoanalysis to recover an incarnational Thomism capable of encompassing the natural order in all its aspects within a sacramental understanding of the trinitarian presence of God in creation. This cannot be and nor does it pretend to be a return to a prediscursive reality—in that Lacan is right.

[1] See Fergus Kerr, *After Aquinas: Versions of Thomism* (Malden MA and Oxford: Blackwell Publishers, 2002).

However, theology can seek to inhabit a different language and a different world of meaning from the rationalized and systematized debates that were established by the medieval university, which still retain a potent grip on the discipline. The contextual, feminist, and liberationist theologies that flourished in the 1970s and 1980s challenged but failed to disrupt the hegemony of a particular theological style and system—a particular style of being a theologian perhaps—and some of the postmodern theologies that have followed are, I shall suggest in the next chapter, still deeply inscribed with the dualisms and powers that Thomas invested in the academic theological tradition. The final chapters will suggest how a different theological style might replenish the desiccated senses and resources of Christian theology, while suggesting that, if our theologies do not result in bodily performances of neighbourly love, they are indeed as straw. With that aim in mind, let me begin with the question of creation. I am returning here to *Seminar VII*, where Lacan first approaches Thomist–Aristotelian questions of being.[2]

CREATION *EX NIHILO*

At the core of the biblical account of creation, Lacan identifies three forms of lack that in his interpretation make western monotheism unique among religions in its historical impact upon the formation of the soul. First, there is the primal lack—God creates *ex nihilo*. Second, there is the absence of God from creation. Third, there is the lack constituted by God's Sabbath rest, and by the commandment that humans too must rest on the Sabbath. All of these have traumatic implications for those who discover themselves to be within the fissure between God and the world, chosen uniquely for a relationship with the absent and unknowable God in whose image they are made, alienated from the materiality of their desire by way of a set of linguistic commands that override their primal animality and set them apart from their pagan neighbours, and commanded to love God above all else and their neighbour as themselves.

Jewish monotheism and its Christian refigurations open up in the western imaginary a possibility that was unthinkable, even for a mind as great as Aristotle's, by rejecting the idea that matter is eternal, and by asserting that something is made from nothing—*ex nihilo*.[3] Like the potter who creates a vase in order to enclose emptiness (Lacan finds the biblical metaphor of the potter particularly apt), God shapes creation around nothing, the divine

---

[2] See Jacques Lacan, *The Ethics of Psychoanalysis 1959–1960: The Seminar of Jacques Lacan, Book VII*, trans. Dennis Porter (London and New York: Routledge, 1999).
[3] Lacan, *The Ethics of Psychoanalysis 1959–1960*, p. 121.

emptiness, the real, the Other beyond all otherness. Lacan refers to Heidegger, who 'situates the vase as the center of the essence of earth and sky'.[4] Like the vase (and, for the early Lacan, like the female sex organs), matter and the temporal order contain and conceal an abysmal emptiness, for a creation that emerges out of nothing retains that nothingness within itself, and is subject to fundamental contingency and existential facticity.[5] That is why the quasi-paganism of medieval Catholicism constitutes an aberration in the unfolding story of monotheism, which rediscovers itself in the moral rigour of Protestantism, in the rational theism of the Enlightenment, and in the scientific revolution.

The second lack is related to this first lack. God creates and then withdraws from creation, and this withdrawal is marked by the seventh day—the day of divine and human rest. But how are we to interpret this rest? Lacan refers to it only in passing, as a day which, 'in a land of masters', leaves 'the common man . . . no happy medium between the labor of love and the most stultifying boredom—that suspension, that emptiness, clearly introduces into human life the sign of a gap, a beyond relative to every law of utility'.[6] This theory might lead to the suggestion that the elimination of the Sabbath through the normalization of commercial activities on Sundays as well as on every other day of the week constitutes far more than a response to the demands of consumerism. This commodification of time is a symbolic necessity for a culture in flight from God, for only when Mammon becomes Lord of the Sabbath is it possible to evade the mystery of the being of God that manifests itself when our own way of being as ceaselessly, frenetically doing is arrested and held captive before the tedium of the infinite.

The monotheistic subject takes shape in the gap created by the Sabbath, in which the human images God by obeying the commandment that he or she observes the lack within creation by ceasing all creative activity—an anticipation, suggests Lacan, of Luther's tormenting insight that 'no merit should be attributed to any work'.[7] Kenneth Reinhard and Julia Lupton argue that, in Lacan's interpretation

> The subject of religion . . . only emerges in the decompletion of the symbolic universe, through the positive addition to the cosmos of an instance of negation, of suspended activity. In this moment of arrest, the subject comes forward as the bearer of the lack that has engendered him, in relation to an as yet unrealized positivity beyond or left over by lack, as its remainder or "rest".[8]

---

[4] Lacan, *The Ethics of Psychoanalysis*, p. 120. Fergus Kerr has pointed out to me that Heidegger's reference is actually to a jug.

[5] Lacan, *The Ethics of Psychoanalysis*, p. 122.

[6] Lacan, *The Ethics of Psychoanalysis*, p. 81.

[7] Lacan, *The Ethics of Psychoanalysis*, p. 122.

[8] Kenneth Reinhard and Julia Reinhard Lupton, 'The Subject of Religion: Lacan and the Ten Commandments', *Diacritics*, Vol. 33, No. 2 (2003), pp. 71–97, 83.

This monotheistic 'lack' is allied to the naming of God as 'I am that I am' (Exodus 3:14). Thomas's influence—mediated by way of Étienne Gilson—is clear in Lacan's reading of Exodus 3, so that Lacan is far closer to Thomas than to later philosophical concepts of God's existence in his understanding of the 'I am who I am' of scripture. In Lacanian terms, the self-referential circularity of God's name as the giver of the Decalogue constitutes the master signifier that withdraws itself from the sphere of all signification, while commanding absolute fidelity: 'Thou shalt have no other gods before me.' (Exodus 20:3.) Thus the Tetragrammaton [YHVW] establishes itself as the primary signifier within monotheism on what Reinhard and Lupton describe as 'the negated ground' of Judaism.[9] Referring to the prohibition in Judaism against speaking this divine name, Reinhard and Lupton explain that

> The Tetragrammaton points towards both meaning and being, yet it is reducible to neither sphere: its letters suggest the verb of being, and thus promise a semantic content that would wed it to ontology, yet the conventions surrounding its articulation sustain the Name as a talismanic set of letters that cannot be translated into any definitive etymology of pragmatics.[10]

This Name is linked to a radical lack of signification—the master signifier that lacks a signified, so that every other signifier is called into question by the pervasive influence of this lack. Referring to the third commandment ,'You shall not take the name of the Lord your God [*shem YHVH Elohechah*] in vain' [Ex. 20:7], Reinhard and Lupton say that it

> is designed precisely to sequester the Name in its status as a primary signifier, to maintain the force of its primal repression: to keep it sacred, but also to *keep it away*, to prevent its annihilative power from bleeding into the language of the everyday. This Name is the gnomic signifier that mutely supports the discourse of the Other as its anchoring point, imposing its imperious commands on a subject defined by the rule of language and the prohibition of *jouissance*. This *jouissance*, however, does not disappear completely, but rather takes up residence in the *Ding*like gravity of the Name itself: the law not only cuts off enjoyment, but also preserves its pain.[11]

We should note that this Lacanian account of the God who is deciphered within the unspeakable Name approximates very closely to the pure act of Thomas's theology—present everywhere in creation, resisting every attempt at articulation or definition, but arousing an intense *jouissance* in the desiring self. We shall come back to that.

The divine law giver of the Hebrew religion forbids all images, naming, and forms of representation. Thus the God revealed in the Hebrew Bible is a God

---

[9] Reinhard and Lupton, 'The Subject of Religion', p. 76.
[10] Reinhard and Lupton, 'The Subject of Religion', p. 77.
[11] Reinhard and Lupton, 'The Subject of Religion', p. 77.

who legislates from outside the religious imaginary, inaugurating a new form of religious consciousness based on law, prohibition, and exclusivity. This one God who is beyond all human knowing and naming is also above all other gods, an exclusive God who must be worshipped exclusively by his chosen people. Thus western religious consciousness comes into being through a process of separation, prohibition, and command, but also through a paradoxical ambiguity that haunts the God of the Hebrew scriptures, which (I have suggested) re-emerges in the Lutheran struggle between God and the devil, and which Freud sought to explain in *Moses and Monotheism*. In a different article to the one cited earlier, Reinhard and Lupton suggest that it is in the fourth commandment that we begin to see what is really at stake in the Lacanian understanding of the real:

> Thou shalt not make unto thee any graven image, or any likeness of any thing that is in heaven above, or that is in the earth beneath, or that is in the water under the earth: Thou shalt not bow down thyself to them, nor serve them: for I the Lord thy God am a jealous God, visiting the iniquity of the fathers upon the children unto the third and fourth generation of them that hate me; And shewing mercy unto thousands of them that love me, and keep my commandments. (Exodus 20:4)[12]

This cluster of divine commandments and prohibitions is, for Lacan, the uniqueness of monotheism and constitutes its formative influence on the western soul. The God of the fourth commandment is, according to Lacan, a God of 'ferocious ignorance': 'when he announces himself . . . he is ferociously ignorant of everything that exists of certain religious practices that were rife at the time, and that are founded on a certain type of knowledge—sexual knowledge'.[13] The Yahweh God, the 'I am who I am' who cannot be named or described, is nevertheless a God of love, hatred, and ignorance. In the forbidding of idolatry this God cuts a community off from its polytheistic neighbours with their cultic and sexual *jouissance*, and binds them to a law encoded in language by an extra-linguistic and non-representable Other, whose image is not to be sought or replicated in any created object or sexual relationship. But this Other is also jealous and punitive, so the lack is associated with a terrifying prohibitive force. To quote Reinhard and Lupton again,

> The master inaugurated by Judaism repudiates pagan pan-sexualism, knows nothing about sex, yet continues to embody a disturbingly violent element of jouissance,

---

[12] Quoted in Kenneth Reinhard and Julia Reinhard Lupton, 'Revelation: Lacan and the Ten Commandments' (2000) at <http://www.jcrt.org/archives/02.1/reinhard_lupton.shtml> [accessed 30 July 2012].

[13] Jacques Lacan, *The Other Side of Psychoanalysis: The Seminar of Jacques Lacan, Book XVII*, ed. Jacques-Alain Miller, trans. Russell Grigg (New York and London: W. W. Norton & Co. Ltd, 2007), p. 136.

precisely through the ferocity of that ignorance. That is, the ignorance at stake is not a passive or neutral lack of knowledge, but a passionate and active not-wanting-to-know, characterized by the violent emotion that the King James translators will call 'jealousy.'[14]

This jealous God constitutes a subterranean breeding ground for the unrepresentable ambiguities and terrors of the real that will continue to haunt the western subject long after his religious history has ostensibly faded into the background of everyday life and been overlaid by a veneer of secularism that does nothing to eradicate the taproot of monotheism from his soul. This is Lacan's unconscious God, and it exerts a tyrannical power over western modernity. We might recall here Thomas's understanding of the sin of covetousness or concupiscence, which is given by way of revelation so that it emerges as a set of divine laws and commands from beyond the sphere of reason, and which is primarily directed against the sexual appetites and desires.

In post-Christian society, the law no longer derives its power from the fear of God and the duty to placate him, but from the fear that continues to haunt the soul even after the death of God, and the desire that continues to proliferate from the site of the non-existent Other which underwrites the symbolic order and commands obedience. To quote Reinhard, 'For Lacan, Freud's myth of the primal horde expresses the ethical paradox that constitutes modernity: even though we no longer believe in the living authority of a moral code that derives from the now debunked religious law, we still obey it.'[15]

In introducing Thomas into this discussion, I shift from Reinhard and Lupton's rabbinic reading of Lacan to introduce a different perspective—namely, that of modern and medieval Catholicism. However, first I want to introduce an important caveat. It is beyond the scope of this book to offer any in-depth account of the complexity and variety of Jewish monotheism at the time of Christ. Lacan's account of monotheism may be a little more theologically informed than that of Freud, but it is also filtered through his own sometimes unchallenged Catholic assumptions about the nature of Judaism.

In the ancient world no less than in the modern world, the everyday practices and beliefs of ordinary people were not determined by the theological ruminations, exegetical debates, and ethical prescriptions of scholars, rabbis, and priests. There is growing evidence that the monotheism of the Hebrew people was not monolithic, nor even always monotheistic. The emergence of monotheism was a gradual process that constituted the formation of a collective identity on the basis of theology rather than nationhood, and it had

---

[14] Reinhard and Lupton, 'The Subject of Religion', p. 81.
[15] Kenneth Reinhard, 'Toward a Political Theology of the Neighbor', in Slavoj Žižek, Eric L. Santer, and Kenneth Reinhard, *The Neighbour: Three Inquiries in Political Theology* (Chicago IL and London: University of Chicago Press, 2005), pp. 11–75.

porous boundaries in relation to the cults and beliefs of its polytheistic neighbours. We must therefore be wary of explanations and accounts that muster this religious plurality into too neat a theory about the history of ideas.[16] However, I outline these Lacanian theories here because, whatever their accuracy in terms of the history of religions, I believe that they do have a certain explanatory weight in terms of Catholic Thomism and its historical and cultural influences.

THOMAS AND THE GOD OF EXODUS

Thomas seeks to demonstrate that Aristotle's philosophical God, understood in terms of prime mover and final cause, fits like a hand into the Christian theological glove. Gilson points to the crucial importance of Exodus 3 in enabling Thomas to reconcile philosophical metaphysics with scriptural revelation, so that the 'pure act-of-being which St Thomas the philosopher met at the end of metaphysics, St Thomas the theologian had met too in Holy Scripture'.[17] This, argues Gilson, constitutes the genius of Thomas's thought. In recognizing that '*He Who Is* in *Exodus* means the *Act-of-Being*', Thomas brings to light not only the compatibility between philosophical reason and scriptural revelation, but also the balanced unity of his own thought. Gilson refers to 'this sublime truth—*hanc sublime veritatem*—whose light illumines the whole of Thomism'.[18]

In this chapter, I return to my argument that—contrary to what Gilson suggests—Thomas's Aristotelian account of the oneness of God the Father does not mesh seamlessly with his understanding of the nature of being, nor with his maternal analogies of trinitarian relations. There is a (m)Otherness to Thomas's God that will not let him go—a mystical beyond which unravels and renders inconsistent the carefully rationalized dialectic of the *Summa theologiae*. What are the implications of this for Thomas's reading of Exodus 3, in which he ostensibly achieves the perfect synthesis of reason and revelation, reconciling the God of Greek philosophy with the God of scripture? In asking this, I seek to unearth the maternal Other from Thomas's theology and to ask what kind of challenge 'she' might pose to postmodern accounts of Exodus 3.

---

[16] There are numerous studies on this. Cf. Karen Armstrong, *A History of God* (London: Vintage, 1999); Bernhard Lang, *The Hebrew God: Portrait of an Ancient Deity* (Yale University Press, 2002); Mark S. Smith, *The Origins of Biblical Monotheism: Israel's Polytheistic Background and the Ugaritic Texts* (Oxford and New York: Oxford University Press, 2001).

[17] Étienne Gilson, *The Christian Philosophy of St. Thomas Aquinas* (London: Victor Gollancz Ltd, 1961), p. 93.

[18] Gilson, *The Christian Philosophy of St. Thomas Aquinas*, p. 95.

Thomas discusses the Tetragrammaton in Question 13 of Part I of the *Summa theologiae*—that is, in the context of his discussion of the divine unity, before he turns to the question of the Trinity. I quote the Latin here, because the translation of '*qui est*' as 'He Who Is' deprives the Latin of its semantic freedom to signify the simple act of being prior to the attribution of any other quality, predicate, or concept, including that of gender. The word 'he' says much, much more than Thomas says and it blocks the very point he is trying to make about the divine being—at least, from a theological perspective informed by the questions that feminism poses to the Christian understanding of God.

Thomas offers three reasons as to why '*hoc nomen qui est . . . est maxime proprium nomen Dei*'.[19] First, it signifies existence itself and not any kind of form: '*Non enim significat formam aliquam, sed ipsum esse.*' Second, by virtue of its indeterminacy it is universal in its application. Thomas quotes John Damascene (*De Fide Orth.* i): '*principalius omnibus quae de Deo dicuntur nominibus, est qui est, totum enim in seipso comprehendens, habet ipsum esse velut quoddam pelagus substantiae infinitum et indeterminatum*'.[20] Third, '*Significat enim esse in praesenti, et hoc maxime proprie de Deo dicitur, cuius esse non novit praeteritum vel futurum*'.[21] Thomas goes on to argue that the Tetragrammaton is most properly applied to God: '*Et adhuc magis proprium nomen est tetragrammaton, quod est impositum ad significandam ipsam Dei substantiam incommunicabilem, et, ut sic liceat loqui, singularem.*'[22]

Let's begin to unpack this by noting the hesitant way in which Thomas affirms the singularity of God. *Qui est* points to the singular substance of God, 'if one may so speak'. Why the hesitation? This is an important question for Thomas, because he wants to distinguish his understanding of the oneness of God from that of Avicenna and others who would argue that reality adds something to being. For Thomas, such an assertion would violate the absolute simplicity of God, and therefore oneness must be understood as something other than a mathematical principle by way of which something is added to something else.[23]

Over and against a mathematical definition of singularity, Thomas posits the concept of one as synonymous with being, by way of which nothing is added to being. This leads him to reject a dualistic interpretation of the one as opposed to the many, in favour of a less polarized duality in which the

---

[19] ST I, 13, 11. 'This name *who is* is the most appropriate name of God'.

[20] '*Qui est* is the principal of all names applied to God; for comprehending all in itself, it contains being itself as an infinite and indeterminate sea of substance.'

[21] 'It signifies being in the present; and this above all properly applies to God, whose being knows neither past nor future.' Thomas cites Augustine (*De Trin. v*).

[22] 'And the Tetragrammaton is an even more appropriate name, because it is imposed to signify the incommunicable and, if one may so speak, singular substance itself of God.'

[23] ST I, 11, 2.

multitude, being divided, lacks the undivided fullness of the oneness of being. In other words, for anything to become other than God, there must be some limit and boundary to its being by way of which it exists as different from other beings and as distinct from the fullness of God's being. Otherwise, there would be no created beings at all—the divine plenitude would be all in all.

In this account, Thomas's God is not the philosophical One of ancient philosophy and modern theism. The lack within being is not deprivation but the condition of coming to be, not an imperfection but a letting be, an opening up of difference within the divine being that allows others to be. Reinhold and Lupton cite rabbinic sources which argue that

> God created rest on the seventh day, bringing his work to completion through this final act – not only ceasing to act, but actively making rest [cf. Genesis Rabbah X]. God completes the world by subtracting something from it, namely his own activity. The seventh day punctuates the unfolding of time, operating as a grammatical period, a full stop that cuts short the profusion of creation and retroactively instills it with lack and hence with the possibility of symbolic significance. The sublime emptiness of the seventh day marks the close of the process of creation *ex nihilo* that began with God's first utterance, an act, the Kabbalah argues, that required God to diminish himself, to decomplete his own fullness in order to make room for the world.[24]

The possibility of language emerges when God withdraws from creation and allows lack to enter being. This is not the fantasized lack and prohibition associated with the Oedipus complex, but the primordial condition for conscious, creative, and free creatures to inhabit a world in which we share in the creativity of God by being able to name and understand the nature of the objects around us, and by having a certain freedom in relation to them. The lack that we perceive in and beyond being is not the lack of any individual creature in terms of its relationship to its particular mode of being—Thomas is clear that every species has the potential for its own perfection. The lack is what we experience of the being of God as the radical Other of the created order, not what we lack in terms of our own way of being. We become more like God, not by rejecting aspects of our own being nor by seeking to add incrementally to the quantity of being we have, but by living to the utmost the divine mystery that we are by virtue of our own unique, particular, and eternal way of being within God. The perfectability of being is a capacity of every created being, not by becoming more than it is, but by becoming fully what it is called to be within God.

---

[24] Reinhard and Lupton, 'The Subject of Religion', p. 83, citing Arthur A. Cohen and Paul Mendes-Flohr (eds), *Contemporary Jewish Religious Thought* (New York: Macmillan, 1972), p. 965.

THE EMANATION OF BEING

Let me turn now to Thomas's Neoplatonic account of creation in terms of emanation, in which he describes creation as 'the emanation of all being from the universal cause, which is God'.[25] Understood in terms of hierarchy, this can imply a progressive diminishing of the fullness of being along a spectrum that extends further and further away from God. Certainly, we have seen that Thomas tends to such an hierarchical account of being, among species and in the social order. But there is another interpretation, far more consistent with the account of creation as freedom and letting be that I am describing here, which sees difference not in terms of hierarchy but in terms of the goodness of diversity as a revelation of the abundance of God's being. Consider this:

> For God brought things into being in order that His goodness might be communicated to creatures, and be represented by them; and because His goodness could not be adequately represented by one creature alone, He produced many and diverse creatures, that what was wanting to one in the representation of the divine goodness might be supplied by another. For goodness, which in God is simple and uniform, in creatures is manifold and divided and hence the whole universe together participates in the divine goodness more perfectly, and represents it better than any single creature whatever.[26]

In this reading, the idea of creation as hierarchical emanation from the divine being yields to a more horizontal celebration of diversity as a good in itself, a diversity in which God is revealed and worshipped. Our capacity to understand something of the being of God is enriched by our ability to see something unique of God in every species and individual that we encounter. Not only does Thomas argue that 'God is in all things',[27] he also argues that 'as the soul is whole in every part of the body, so is God whole in all things and in each one'.[28] This is an astonishing insight that opens into a mystical sense of being beyond all human comprehension. God is one—indivisible and simple—so that wherever life is, there God is, shining within a finite body as a particular aspect of the perfection of the divine being which that creature and no other is capable of communicating. When we read that in Christ, 'all the fullness of the Deity lives in bodily form' (Col. 2:9), we are saying something that is true of every living being, but that finds its most perfect and unhindered revelation in the one whose body is utterly translucent and integrated with his divine soul.

Far from the many being opposed to the one as in more dualistic cosmologies or in Hegelian ontologies, for Thomas the multitude is expressive of and harmonious with the oneness of God. Once again, Thomas's God emerges as the Other of the philosophical One. This insight is not always sustained, for we

---

[25] ST I, 45, 2.   [26] ST I, 47, 1.   [27] ST I, 8, 1.   [28] ST I, 8, 2.

have seen that Thomas is too often lured by a more dualistic form of Platonism that strives to transcend material objects and the phantasms they inspire in order to achieve union with God, so that the unity of God seems to be asserted over and against the diversity of the world. Nevertheless, in terms of Thomas's trinitarian theology, his doctrine of creation *ex nihilo*, and his understanding of the participatory nature of beings within God's being, there is greater integrity and coherence to his theological vision if we set aside its Platonic tendencies and focus on his more holistic understanding of creation. God's being unfurls, spreads out, opens up, and creates a space of welcome for otherness in order to manifest the abundance of the divine goodness of being.

This affirmation of diversity as evidence of the manifold goodness of God has vast ethical as well as environmental implications. Today, social cohesion is everywhere under threat from various forms of religious, nationalist, and ethnic extremism that construe difference only in terms of threat and never in terms of harmonious diversity, and environmental diversity is being destroyed with apocalyptic implications for the human species. Rather than a perception of lack in the other, Thomas invites faith in the goodness of God manifest everywhere in creation by virtue of its many different creatures and forms of life. What I perceive in the other as a reflection of my own desire therefore becomes an epiphany of the plenitude of divine being rather than a terrifying glimpse into the abyss. The ethical challenge posed by Freud—the hatred of neighbour that results from a sense of personal lack—would invite a different interpretation altogether. In loving the other as myself, I love her because she is different from me and I am different from her. The lack that allows us to be in God is a unique revelation of God within being, and it is an aspect of revelation that is destroyed every time human individuality is erased by a system, every time humans are killed for failing to be the same as the rest, every time a dominant group erases its others by way of political, linguistic, or cultural hegemony, every time a human being is deprived of the economic and environmental means to flourish as the uniquely gifted being that he or she is, every time a species is wiped out by the omnipotent urge of humans to control, to master, and to destroy.

In January 1918, Max Plowman wrote a letter which he read at his court martial. Plowman writes,

> I am resigning my commission because, while I cannot comprehend a transcendent God, I believe that God is incarnate in every human being, & that so long as life persists in the human body, soul & body are one & inseparable, God being the life of both. From which it follows that killing men is killing God. I believe that when it is realised that the body is the outward manifestation of God & that divinity and humanity are synonymous, man will hold in the utmost abhorrence the terrible sacrilege of war or capital punishment.[29]

---

[29] Max Plowman, 'Reasons for Resigning', in *Bridge into the Future: Letters of Max Plowman* (London: Andrew Dakers, 1944), p. 772.

Thomas might not be willing to go this far, although we have seen that he does interpret the Gospel as entailing a pacifist and non-violent ethos on the part of clerics who are 'entrusted with the ministry of the New Law, wherein no punishment of death or of bodily maiming is appointed'.[30] Today, when many Christians would reject this ethical distinction between the priesthood and the laity, we might ask if a postmodern Thomism would make radical demands in terms of politics, violence, and the social order.

But this brings me to a question around which everything in this book implicitly revolves, and that is the question of God in relation to form. In the last chapter, I explored why, from a Lacanian perspective, the identification of God with the One of philosophical form has devastating implications for the bodily self-expressiveness and inchoateness of human life, including sexual expressiveness. When theology attempts to conform God to form, a multitude of repressive, anti-body, dualistic hierarchies flows from the logic of that. As Plowman suggests, when belief in a transcendent God collapses and divinity and humanity become integrated, violence becomes far less possible to justify. So is Thomas's God form? This is perhaps the most tantalizing and elusive of all questions that one can pose to Thomas's theology, but upon it hinges the whole attempt to understand if and in what way the Christian understanding of God corresponds to the Aristotelian final cause or the Platonic form.

DEFORMING GOD

In insisting that God is the sole agent of creation, Thomas implicitly suggests a move beyond the idea of God as form, to God as the creator of all forms and all matter. God is the one, perfect, uncreated image, and 'the plurality of ideas corresponds in the divine mind to the plurality of things'.[31] If the diversity of created beings expresses something of the goodness of God through the doing as being of the creative mind of God, it surely follows that God cannot be one form among or over and beyond others, for that would relativize the difference between God and creation, would it not? Let's return to Thomas's account of Exodus 3, by considering forms and matter in relation to God.

Thomas interprets *qui est* as signifying not any kind of form but being itself—*ipsum esse*. This suggests that God cannot be identified with form, but here we encounter a persistent ambiguity and occasional contradiction in the *Summa theologiae*. Rather than affirming that God is neither form nor matter, Thomas seems to conclude elsewhere that God is form: 'whatever is primarily and essentially an agent must be primarily and essentially form. Now God is

---

[30] ST II-II, 64, 4.   [31] ST II-II, 64, 4.

the first agent, since He is the first efficient cause. He is therefore of His essence a form; and not composed of matter and form'.[32] This would suggest that God is form, and the act of creation involves prime matter but not form, so that an eternity of form would be posited over and against the creation of matter *ex nihilo*. But Thomas does not want to allow this either, for he argues that 'Creation does not mean the building up of a composite thing from pre-existing principles; but it means that the "composite" is created so that it is brought into being at the same time with all its principles.'[33] He goes on to reject the suggestion that 'the thing supposed in natural generation is matter. Therefore matter, and not the composite, is, properly speaking, that which is created'. To this he responds, 'This reason does not prove that matter alone is created, but that matter does not exist except by creation; for creation is the production of the whole being, and not only matter.'[34]

If God creates *ex nihilo*, then God creates forms along with matter. As Gilson argues, neither forms nor matter actually exist for Thomas except insofar as they exist in composite beings—they are propositions that function to explain the otherwise inexplicable continuity of beings and the diversity of individuals and species that emerge as different forms from within the flux of matter.[35] So, says Thomas, 'being (*esse*) is that which makes every form or nature actual',[36] and later he says that 'nothing has actuality except so far as it exists. Hence being itself (*ipsum esse*) is that which actuates all things, even their forms'.[37] Forms in and of themselves have no greater actuality than matter. If this is so, the gendered cosmology that sustains Thomas's onto-logical, ethical, and social hierarchies begins to disintegrate. Creation is not the divine, paternal insemination of matter. It is the evoking into being of forms and matter simultaneously as the condition for material beings to become. The philosophical hypothesis of a copulative relationship between the two may function well as an elegant explanation that arouses in us an implicit eroticism in relation to the world, but Christianity reminds us that it is a fantasy. All that exists other than God exists by grace of the active being of God, and God is being before and beyond all forms and matter.

Again, perhaps we can note the moments of hesitation in Thomas, as a key to probing more deeply into the negated and repressed aspects of his theological insight. In affirming the divine simplicity, Thomas writes, 'And so, since God is absolute form (*ipsa forma*), or rather (*vel*) absolute being (*ipsum esse*), He can be in no way composite.'[38] That '*vel*' is telling. Why does the language of divine form seduce Thomas so repeatedly, when it is so potentially misleading in terms of the doctrine of creation *ex nihilo*, the self-revelation of God in Exodus, the relational fluidity of the Trinity, and the affirmation of God as life, being, and

---

[32] ST I, 3, 2.   [33] ST I, 45, 4.   [34] ST I, 45, 4.
[35] See Gilson, *The Christian Philosophy of St. Thomas Aquinas*, pp. 31–4.
[36] ST I, 3, 4.   [37] ST I, 4, 1.   [38] ST I, 3, 7.

source of all that is? Why does Thomas allow these moments of hesitation to interrupt his line of thought—'if one may so speak', 'or rather'? These are symptoms of Thomas's awareness that all is not quite as he is saying it is, that he must be very careful to qualify what he is claiming lest he diminish the mystery of which he speaks, and yet there is a constant tug towards Aristotle that would permit him to say too much. Deep down, Thomas knows that the God of whom he speaks is the (m)Other of the One of Greek philosophy.

Perhaps not surprisingly, Thomas's interpreters are cautious and not very clear when discussing how he understands form in relation to God. In an e-mail exchange when I pressed Fergus Kerr on this question, he advised, 'If you have to bring in the language of matter and form then God has to be described as an odd kind of form', and then he added, 'But he [Thomas] doesn't really like that, it tempts you to ask "form of what?"'[39] Eleonore Stump briefly attempts to explain the tension in Thomas's account of the divine form by suggesting that, in his view, the divine form is unlike any other form because it is self-subsistent and independent of matter. However, she rather hastily dismisses the question—'focusing on God as form is almost entirely more trouble than help in understanding Aquinas's notion of subsistent form'[40]—and she moves on to the angel as a simple, subsistent form which is like God.[41]

Yet for anybody seeking to read Thomas with a consciousness awakened by both feminist and psychoanalytic insights, this is a fundamental question because it is the key to the whole gendered ordering of Thomas's theology, and it provides the basis upon which the more virulent sexual ontologies of post-Vatican II theology have been constructed. So, setting aside the obvious discomfort of his more liberal interpreters, we must probe away at this question of form and matter if a postmodern Thomism is to shape itself in response to the challenges posed to the Catholic theological tradition today, not least of which are those to do with the theological and sacramental representation of gender, matter, and the body. Of all the explanations offered, perhaps the most helpful is that offered by Gilson—again, bearing in mind he is the primary route into Thomism for Lacan. Here is how Gilson explains it.

Gilson argues that 'form is a nobler element of substance than is matter',[42] but that Thomas went beyond the 'metaphysical heights' achieved by Plato and Aristotle, by recognizing that,

> Since neither matter nor form can exist apart, it is not difficult to see that the existence of their composite is possible. But it is not so easy to see how their union can engender actual existence. How is existence to arise from what does not exist?

---

[39] Personal e-mail from Fergus Kerr, 3rd March 2012.
[40] Eleonore Stump, *Aquinas* (Arguments of the Philosophers Series; London and New York: Routledge, 2003), p. 198.
[41] Stump is referring to the discussion about angels in ST I, 54–60.
[42] Gilson, *The Christian Philosophy of St. Thomas Aquinas*, p. 32.

> It is therefore necessary to have existence come first as the ultimate term to which the analysis of the real can attain. When it is thus related to existence, form ceases to appear as the ultimate determination of the real.[43]

By now, it should be very clear why the Lacanian real bears the closest possible resemblance to Thomas's God, but also why God and prime matter inevitably become confused. God is beyond form and matter is below form, but both are ultimately formless, and that means that the human mind cannot think them except as an infinite other beyond what we know. But because man is culturally conditioned to think of himself as closer to God and therefore as nobler than woman, he begins to equate himself with form, which in turn he equates with God, while woman is the 'below' of matter in relation to both.

MATTER AND GOD

If Thomas is ambivalent about form, he is adamant about matter in relation to God: there is no matter in God. In Question 3 of Part I of the *Summa*, he defends the idea of the absolute simplicity of God by addressing various questions regarding form and matter, essence and existence in relation to God. In Articles 1 and 2, he refutes the suggestion that God is a body, or that God is composed of form and matter. The human is made in the image of God not in terms of the body but in terms of the incorporeal faculties of intelligence and reason. Thomas is emphatic that there is no mingling or union between God and anything else that would make of God a composite being. God is not the world-soul, nor is God the formal principle of all things—as suggested by the Almaricians. David of Dinant's teaching that God is primary matter is 'most absurd'.[44] In seeking to distinguish between God and primary matter, Thomas appeals to Aristotle's distinction in *Metaphysics*: '"things which are diverse are absolutely distinct, but things which are different differ by something." Therefore, strictly speaking, primary matter and God do not differ, but are by their very being, diverse. Hence it does not follow they are the same'.[45]

Hold on a minute. Surely, prime matter—created by God out of nothing—is not 'absolutely distinct' from God, for it participates in God as does all being, and God's being is the condition of its existence? Is Thomas suggesting that the being of prime matter is fundamentally and ontologically different from the being of God and, if so, has he not subtly reinscribed the eternity of matter within Christian theology in a way that does away with creation *ex nihilo* and contradicts some of his most central arguments about the nature of

---

[43] Gilson, *The Christian Philosophy of St. Thomas Aquinas*, p. 33.
[44] ST I, 3, 8.   [45] ST I, 3, 8.

creation in relation to God? This is not consistent with the more general direction of Thomas's argument. Prime matter is not 'absolutely distinct' from God. Along with forms, it is created by and participates within the being of God. At the very least, if it is 'most absurd' to equate God with prime matter, it is surely no less absurd to equate God with form? But more important still, if there is no matter in God, then Thomas becomes a docetist. In order to show why, let me turn to his discussion of the incarnation and resurrection of Christ.

In Part III of the *Summa theologiae*, Thomas addresses the question of the incarnation and resurrection. He defends the two natures in the one person of Christ in terms of the perfection of each nature, which would be compromised if Christ were human and divine in one nature:

> The Divine Nature is incorporeal nor after the manner of form and matter, for the Divine Nature cannot be the form of anything, especially of anything corporeal, since it would follow that the species resulting therefrom would be communicable to several, and thus there would be several Christs.[46]

He goes on to quote John Damascene (*De Fide Orth.* Iii, 6, 11):

> the Divine Nature is said to be incarnate because It is united to flesh personally, and not that it is changed into flesh. So likewise the flesh is said to be deified, as he also says (*De Fide Orth.* 15, 17), not by change but by union with the Word, its natural properties still remaining, and hence it may be considered as deified, inasmuch as it becomes the flesh of the Word of God, but not that it becomes God.[47]

The incarnation is a union of two natures in the one person of Christ, but it is, insists Thomas, a real union of body and soul:

> It belongs essentially to the human species that the soul be united to the body, for the form does not constitute the species, except inasmuch as it becomes the act of matter, and this is the terminus of generation through which nature intends the species. Hence it must be said that in Christ the soul was united to the body; and the contrary is heretical, since it destroys the truth of Christ's humanity.[48]

This union of the human and divine natures in Christ means that, in the divine becoming human, human nature is in turn divinized in the incarnation.[49] In a sermon on the Feast of *Corpus Christi*, Thomas preached that 'The only-begotten Son of God, wanting to make us sharers in his divine nature, assumed

---

[46] ST III, 2, 1.   [47] ST III, 2, 1.   [48] ST III, 2, 5.
[49] The question of *theosis* or deification in western theology in general and in the works of Thomas Aquinas in particular has been widely debated. Cf. A. N. Williams, *The Ground of Union: Deification in Aquinas and Palamas* (Oxford and New York: Oxford University Press, 1999).

our nature, so that he, made man, might make men gods'.[50] In the *Summa theologiae* he affirms that, in Christ, one can say 'God is human' (*Deus est homo*),[51] and one can also say that 'the human is God' (*homo est Deus*).[52] Thomas clearly intends this to include the deification of the full human nature (body and soul) when baptized and redeemed in Christ, even though he tends to refer to the deiform human primarily in terms of the intellect,[53] so that the deification of the human body in the incarnate body of Christ becomes highly elusive and difficult to pin down. Nevertheless, the foregoing quotations show that it is the direction in which Thomas's thought wants to go.

Thomas is neither a dualist nor a monist. The particularity of the individual unity of the human body and soul never dissolves into the universality of a divine intellect, and the bodily human nature of Christ is distinct from his eternal divine nature—otherwise, he would not be an individual human nature. Christ's experiences of being born, suffering, and dying can be predicated of his human but not of his divine nature.[54] Nevertheless, 'in Christ each nature is united to the other in person; and by reason of this union the Divine Nature is said to be incarnate and the human nature deified'.[55]

Later, in the discussion of Christ's resurrection,[56] Thomas similarly insists that Christ is really risen corporeally in his glorified flesh, so that he is risen in the same uncorrupted flesh and blood that he assumed on his conception: 'All the blood which flowed from Christ's body, belonging as it does to the integrity of human nature, rose again with His body'.[57] Moreover, the Son who is consubstantial with the Father and sits at the right hand of the Father in glory is not only the divine nature but the full person who is the conjoined human and divine natures. Quoting Damascene (*De Fide Orth.* iv), Thomas says that 'the son of God existing before ages, as God and consubstantial with the Father, sits in His conglorifed flesh; for, under one adoration the one hypostasis, together with his flesh, is adored by every creature'.[58] In the person of Christ, there is matter in God—there is no other possible conclusion in the context of Thomas's theological orthodoxy. To say otherwise is to make the docetist claim that Christ only appeared to be a human body—he was an avatar of the divine, not God incarnate.

In the e-mail exchange cited earlier, Kerr suggests that Thomas's resistance to the idea of there being matter in God arises from his wanting to defend the immutability and simplicity of God against any attribution of complexity, change, or development to God, such as that found in various forms of process

---

[50] St Thomas Aquinas, *Opusc.* 57, 1–4, quoted in *Catechism of the Catholic Church* (Libreria Editrice Vaticana 2003), Part One, Section Two, Chapter Two, #460 at <http://www.vatican.va/archive/ccc_css/archive/catechism/p122a3p1.htm> [accessed 4 August 2012].

[51] ST III, 16, 1. [52] ST III, 16, 2. [53] Cf. ST I, 12, 5–6.
[54] See ST III, 16, 5. [55] ST III, 16, 5. [56] See ST III, 54.
[57] ST III, 54, 3. [58] ST III, 5, 8, 3.

theology today, for example. This is why he repeatedly insists that creation participates in God but God does not participate in creation. Yet it is perhaps possible to offer a way through this dilemma. If neither forms nor matter exist except insofar as God creates a world of existent and composite beings out of nothing—beings which Thomas suggests have always existed in the mind of God—we could say that forms and matter exist eternally as absolute potency within the being of God, and creation begins when God withdraws or introduces the necessary gap/lack within which the two are drawn together through their desire to return to God. If we retain Thomas's gendered analogies, we could then say that all philosophical language of form and matter, paternal and maternal, is a groping towards some mystery about the being of God revealed within the order of creation. From the dualistic perspective of Greek philosophy, paternal form is active and masculine in relation to maternal matter which is passive and feminine, and the relationship between them is hierarchical. However, the mystery of the incarnation calls for a reconciling gesture in which all the ancient antagonisms that emerge in Genesis 3 are healed—the conflict between the sexes, the exile from the Garden of Eden (the beginning of alienation but also, as Lacan suggests, the necessary condition for the emergence of linguistic consciousness), the battle of humankind against the forces of nature (reproduction and marital domination for her, physical labour and hardship for him), and the sense of alienation that severs the intimate communion between God and humankind that existed within the original harmony of creation.

This reconciling move would mean affirming, not that God is paternal form in relation to maternal matter, but that form and matter, motherhood and fatherhood, are equally in God and expressive of God, while both are analogical and therefore cannot be used in any literal or direct way, except insofar as they refer to the essentially relational nature of all being, including God's being. The language of motherhood and fatherhood can evoke this relational meaning, but only if it remains free from the relationships of copulation and necessity that define Greek concepts of being. The relational Trinity is deconstructive of all social and sexual ideologies, transfiguring our most intimate and complex bodily relationships within a love beyond violence, offering forgiveness for the inevitability of failure, and providing a sacramental vision that weaves our individual stories into the new creation that is becoming in God.

CREATION IN GOD

There is an aspect of the creation stories that Lacanian accounts fail to acknowledge, and it unsettles the attempt to provide a psychoanalytic account of the void in human consciousness as a symptom of Hebrew monotheism. In the beginning of the human story, God is not absent: 'Then the man and his wife heard the sound of the Lord God as he was walking in the garden in the cool of the day, and they hid from the Lord among the trees of the garden' (Gen. 3:8). If God is present in the garden of creation, there is no need for naming and representation because there is no perception of absence. It is human shame—the effects of sin—that creates a sense of separation between the human and the divine, after which the human interprets the divine absence in terms of punishment, law, and prohibition. Yet God continues to provide for the human creatures even as they are cast out of Eden, and the promise of healing and reconciliation occurs within that space of human rebellion and distress, when God predicts enmity between the offspring of the serpent and the offspring of the woman (Gen. 3:15). In Christian terms, this is the *protevangelium*, the first good news of the coming of Christ.

God has never been absent from creation, for all the fullness of the divine life is present and active throughout the cosmos and always has been. What has been damaged—or, in some Protestant theologies, destroyed—is the human capacity to recognize God within the glory and harmony of creation.

Christian revelation is a radical act of deconstruction of the idea of God as the transcendent, metaphysical One in whose name every form of violence can be justified if it presents itself as defending that idea. However, this cannot be achieved simply by abandoning metaphysics and transcendence in favour of being as immanence, for we have seen that this too generates a violent capacity for destruction. Whenever reason and nature, spirit and body, God and creation, law and desire, are set up in opposition to one another, violence is generated. A fragile peace becomes possible only when we learn to live within the space of vulnerability, lack, and finitude that constitutes the human condition, uniquely created to inhabit that paradoxical space of being between the material and the spiritual, and to recognize that what we experience as unspeakable lack is the unsayable plenitude of the fullness of God creating space in which we can be fully what we are.

The task of theology is to take all philosophical propositions and to go beyond their rationalizing dualisms, bearing in mind that the knowledge of good and evil upon which all such dualisms rest is fallen and corrupted knowledge. It is a necessary way of knowing for creatures alienated from God and creation if we are to navigate a path of flourishing amidst the seductions of violence that surround us, but it is not in and of itself a path to God. Scriptural revelation dazzles philosophical reason, unveils a deeper truth about the order of things, and calls for a radical transformation of the way in which we interpret the world.

This is why Lacan's scrambling of truth, his opening up of labyrinthine tunnels of desire and lack through language and meaning, can serve as a potent corrective to the complacent assertions of theological language. The task of theology is that of asking what language we must use if we are to speak of a reconciled creation in which all dualisms and antagonisms are overcome in the trinitarian life of God, including those most fundamental antagonisms between form and matter, mind and body, male and female, which manifest themselves across the spectrum of human existence in different religious and secular cultures, languages and epistemologies. In modern western culture, we must add the conflict between nature and reason to that set of dualisms—a conflict that is unique to cultures shaped by Christianity, which now globalizes its dominating and destructive power through its secular, neo-liberal abrogation. Does Thomas provide us with the resources for such a task? Yes, he does, if we allow his reading of Exodus 3 to be the pivotal point upon which his theology rests and through which it must be interpreted.

We are nearing the end of this theological beginning, but I want to consider an example from postmodern theology as to why even the most postmodern of theologies are still in thrall to those philosophical couplings and the fears they engender. In the next chapter, I consider a debate between Richard Kearney and John Caputo regarding Thomas's interpretation of Exodus 3. This allows me to bring out the latent significance of Thomas's maternal Trinity and his incarnate God for postmodern theology, in a way that is both more Thomist and more postmodern than these two most postmodern of postmodern theologians.

17

Theology Beyond Postmodernism

As the ancient order of philosophical knowledge dissolves within the flux and scepticism of the postmodern condition, theology too has become cut adrift from its moorings and must seek new forms of expression and justification if it is to speak of God meaningfully in the postmodern academy. Throughout this book, I have been prising the core insights of Christian doctrine away from the rationalizing grids of Thomas Aquinas's Aristotelianism, not in order to eliminate philosophy from theology, but in order to relativize it and persuade it to relinquish its totalizing grip on the theological imagination. This has meant revisiting the primal philosophical relationship between form and matter, allowing Lacan to reopen profound and elusive questions about the relationship of matter and the body to form and language, and about the ways in which God plays upon our minds and bodies in different registers, as the One and the Other.

The fertile space of theological creativity may depend upon keeping open the tension between these polarities, so long as we remember that they are polarities of desire, not of opposition, and that they are within the divine being. I am not suggesting that the theological solution to the challenge of postmodernity is to dissolve the unity and eternal being of God in favour of some more provisional and emergent process, as process theology seeks to do, for example. Rather, I seek to redress the balance, recognizing that theology, including Thomas's theology, has been profoundly unbalanced in privileging form over matter, the one over the many, so that the Trinity and the incarnate God have continuously been erased and overwritten by the drive towards the One of metaphysics and ontotheology. There is a trinitarian response to this challenge that remains faithful to all the enduring insights of Christian doctrine, while creating an opening—not within God (we do not in any sense control, affect, or alter God)—but within the ways in which those of us within the Catholic theological tradition think and speak of God and—more importantly—materialize God among us. This means recognizing that there are already openings in God—the openings created by the wounds of Christ—that enable us to enter into the being of God in bodies that are deified in the maternal flesh of Christ and Mary.

It is beyond the scope of this book to explore the many shifting horizons and changing perspectives of postmodern theology, so I am going to focus on a debate published in the journal of *Modern Theology*, in the form of an essay by Richard Kearney and responses by John Caputo and John P. Manoussakis on the question of Exodus 3.[1] This opens the way for me to ask what potential there is for developing a maternal theology of matter out of neglected aspects of Thomas's thought, not as an alternative to the Father God of the Christian tradition, but as a way of deconstructing the totalizing and violent power that has been associated with that tradition, in favour of more fluid and open-ended possibilities of meaning. Far from dissolving any ethical perspective (as Kearney fears Lacan does), I suggest that a Lacanian Thomism can open the way to a more not less radical Christian fidelity to the God of creation and incarnation, by allowing a reconfigured Thomism to lead theology through and beyond Lacan.

CONVERSATIONS IN THE *KHORA*

Slavoj Žižek observes that 'In *Seminar XX*, Lacan massively rehabilitates the religious problematic (Woman as one of the names of God, etc.).'[2] Nevertheless, Žižek is adamant that the Lacanian enterprise is 'totally incompatible' with 'the so-called "post-secular" turn of deconstruction, which finds its ultimate expression in a certain kind of Derridean appropriation of Levinas'. Žižek argues that:

> This post-secular thought fully concedes that modernist critique undermined the foundations of onto-theology, the notion of God as the supreme Entity, and so on. Its point is that the ultimate outcome of this deconstructive gesture is to clear the slate for a new, undeconstructable form of spirituality, for the relationship to an unconditional Otherness that precedes ontology. What if the fundamental experience of the human subject is not self-presence, of the force of dialectical mediation–appropriation of all Otherness, but of a primordial passivity, sentiency, of responding, of being infinitely indebted to and responsible for the call of an Otherness that never acquires positive features but always remains withdrawn, the trace of its own absence?[3]

---

[1] See Richard Kearney, 'God Who May Be: A Phenomenological Study'; John D. Caputo, 'Richard Kearney's Enthusiasm: A Philosophical Exploration on the God Who May Be'; John P. Manoussakis, 'From Exodus to Eschaton: On the God Who May Be', in *Modern Theology*, 18:1 (January 2002), pp. 75–107.

[2] Slavoj Žižek, 'The Real of Sexual Difference', in Suzanne Barnard and Bruce Fink (eds), *Reading Seminar XX: Lacan's Major Work on Love, Knowledge, and Feminine Sexuality* (Albany NY: State University of New York Press, 2002), pp. 57–76, 65.

[3] Žižek, 'The Real of Sexual Difference', p. 65.

Over and against all such deconstructive strategies, Žižek argues that, in order to appreciate Lacan's negotiation of the passage 'from the Law to Love, in short, from Judaism to Christianity', it is necessary to acknowledge that

> For Lacan, the ultimate horizon of ethics is *not* the infinite debt toward an abyssal Otherness. The act is for him strictly correlative to the suspension of the 'big Other,' not only in the sense of the symbolic network that forms the 'substance' of the subject's existence but also in the sense of the absent originator of the ethical Call . . . The (ethical) act proper is *neither* a response to the compassionate plea of my neighborly semblable (the stuff of sentimental humanism) *nor* a response to the unfathomable Other's call.[4]

According to Žižek's interpretation then, a certain kind of postmodern theology cannot appeal to Lacan for vindication. Let's bear that in mind in what follows, for I want to suggest that postmodern theology remains insufficiently unsettled by its theoretical conversation partners, so that it is sometimes too assertive in its knowledge, or perhaps too timid in its sense of adventure. Too often, the God of patriarchal power and privilege hovers in the background to police its boundaries and underwrite its claims. I am moving towards the suggestion that we need to unearth the maternal Other of Thomas's neglected Trinity not instead of but within the '*qui est*' of the eternal being of Thomas's God, beyond all Aristotelian projections and rationalizations. By entering into the conversation in *Modern Theology* between Kearney, Caputo, and Manoussakis about possible interpretations of Exodus 3, I seek a postmodern retrieval of Thomas that renders Kearney's approach problematic and invites him to explore more open horizons of theological possibility.[5] In what follows, the discussion of Lacan's account of being in *Seminar XX* needs to be borne in mind. I refer to *khora* here, but I explore its Platonic/Thomist significance in more detail later.

There is a passage in Caputo's conversation with Gianni Vattimo, published as *After the Death of God*, which explains how he seeks to radicalize theology by locating it within the context of the Derridean *khora*:

> Is not a radical theology less a matter of asking how do I apply and translate this authoritative figure of the God of Christianity to the contemporary world and more a matter of asking what do I love when I love my God?—where the name of God is the name of the event that is transpiring in the name of God?

[4] Žižek, 'The Real of Sexual Difference', pp. 68–9.

[5] I am grateful to Richard Kearney for reading this chapter and drawing my attention to his later work, in which he addresses some of the criticisms I make here. This opens the way to an ongoing dialogue in which some—although not all—of my reservations expressed here might be addressed. Cf. Richard Kearney, 'Diacritical Hermeneutics', in Maria Luísa Portocarrero, Luís António Umbelino, and Andrzej Wierciński (eds), *Hermeneutic Rationality—La rationalité herméneutique* (Berlin: Lit Verlag Dr w. Hopf, 2012), pp. 176–92. See also Kearney, *Re-imagining the Sacred: the Anatheist Debate* (New York: Columbia University Press, forthcoming).

Is not a radical hermeneutics a voice of one crying in the desert, praying and weeping in the desert?

Is not a radically weak theology a theology of the desert?[6]

The desert evokes Plato's *khora* as a locus for theological reflection, exemplified for Caputo by the radicalization of Derrida's concept of *différance*.[7] Kearney is critical of this adoption of a conceptual space of such radical formlessness and ambiguity, for he sees it as bringing with it the threat of monstrous violence and the dissolution of all ethical constraints.

RICHARD KEARNEY'S POSSIBLE GOD

Kearney's theological project could be summarized as a semi-deconstructive linguistic dance on the marshy edge of the *khora*, where he remains tenuously attached to the dry land of reason by the slender phenomenological threads of narrative meaning and the hermeneutical imagination.[8] His fear is that if one lets go altogether of this mooring in the solid reality of history and human experience, contextualized and narrated in imaginative tellings and retellings, one drifts too far into the mire of history's horrors and the disorientating lure of the human capacity for violence, in such a way that one loses the critical perspective provided by ethical judgement and decision-making. Lieven Boeve describes Kearney's quest for a new theological language about God as 'a poetics of the possible God', as 'an alternative to the powerful omnipotent God "who is", conceived as a self-sufficient being and as a self-causing cause'.[9] Boeve suggests

---

[6] John D. Caputo and Gianni Vattimo, *After the Death of God* (New York: Columbia University Press, 2007), p. 85.

[7] For a more detailed account of how Caputo understands Derrida's *khora* in terms of the desert as the locus for negative theology, see John Caputo, *The Prayers and Tears of Jacques Derrida: Religion without Religion* (Bloomington IN: Indiana University Press, 1997). For a good critical summary of the debate between Caputo and Kearney regarding the theological significance of Plato's *khora*, see John Rundell, 'Imaginings, Narratives, and Otherness: On Diacritical Hermeneutics', in Peter Gratton and John Panteleimon Manoussakis (eds), *Traversing the Imaginary: Richard Kearney and the Postmodern Challenge* (Northwestern University Press, 2007), pp. 103–16.

[8] Kearney is a prolific writer, but the trilogy *Philosophy at the Limit* would be his most significant work here. See Richard Kearney, *The Wake of Imagination* (London: Century Hutchinson; New York: Routledge, 1988); *Poetics of Imagining: Modern to Post-modern* (New York: Fordham University Press, 1998), and *Strangers, Gods, and Monsters: Interpreting Otherness* (London and New York: Routledge, 2003). See also the exposition of Kearney's work in Lieven Boeve, 'Richard Kearney's Messianism: Between the Narrative Theology of Hermeneutics and the Negative Theology of Deconstructionism', in Lieven Boeve and Christophe Brabant (eds), *Between Philosophy and Theology: Contemporary Interpretations of Christianity* (Farnham Surrey and Burlington VT: Ashgate Publishing, 2010), pp. 7–17.

[9] Boeve, 'Richard Kearney's Messianism', p. 8, quoting from Kearney, 'Poetics of a Possible God', in Lieven Boeve, Joeri Schrijvers, Wessel Stoker, and Hendrik M. Vroom. (eds), *Faith in the*

that 'in this poetics, Kearney strives at "possibilizing" this revelation of the God who in turn "possibilizes" us to bring about the Kingdom of peace and justice, thereby actualizing God's *posse*'.[10]

Kearney is shocked by what he sees as the failure of postmodern theorists to confront the reality of suffering and the concrete ethical claims that it makes upon us. His protest is summarized in an objection to Jean-François Lyotard's suggestion that there is room for confusion between the 'abyssal evil' towards which the Kantian sublime lures us, and the God of the Hebrew scriptures: 'If the divine becomes sublime to the point of becoming sadism, it has, in my view, ceased to be divine.'[11] Maybe, but a great many sadistic things have been done in the name of the God of the Hebrew scriptures, and that is Lacan's point. It is not enough simply to protest, or to say that we need to change the way we speak about God. The roots of violence are deep in the human soul where modernity's unconscious God still slumbers, and that's where we must look if we are to understand how Christian theology and practice have gone so catastrophically astray. To explore and analyse is not to condone and justify. Lacan explores and analyses the source of violence in the real and its associations with the God of the Hebrew scriptures and Christian tradition. Far from condoning violence, his whole project emerges as an attempt to understand and resist the horrors of twentieth-century violence.

Nevertheless, Lacan—mediated primarily by way of Slavoj Žižek—is a key target for Kearney. He complains about the confusion of the demonic and the divine in Žižek, suggesting that 'Lacan, Žižek's mentor, was . . . obsessed with the relation between Kant and de Sade'.[12] I have analysed in some detail what this 'obsession' amounted to, so I shall not return to that here. Kearney summarizes his concern by suggesting that the eruption of monsters and aliens in popular culture is a symptom of what happens when 'the representational and interpretative space of the subject is exploded by the eruption of the death drive'.[13] He finds this 'deeply puzzling', and asks:

> As soon as the human subject dissolves into the void of the Monstrous Real are we not condemned to the indifferentiation of pure drive? Do we not thus regress to the mute traumatism of *tohu bohu*: the condition of the Real before the ethical God spoke the symbolic Word and the world divided into good and evil?[14]

It is interesting that Kearney interprets the primal condition of creation (*tohu-bohu*) in terms of 'mute traumatism' associated with the real, and the symbolic

---

Enlightenment? The Critique of the Enlightenment Revisited (Amsterdam and New York: Editions Rodopi B. V., 2006), pp. 305–23.

[10] Boeve, 'Richard Kearney's Messianism', p. 8.

[11] Kearney, *Strangers, Gods, and Monsters*, p. 95.

[12] Kearney, *Strangers, Gods, and Monsters*, p. 96.

[13] Kearney, *Strangers, Gods, and Monsters*, p. 98.

[14] Kearney, *Strangers, Gods, and Monsters*, p. 98.

Word with its attendant dualism as an ethical good. In the Book of Genesis, creation *ex nihilo* denotes not 'mute traumatism' but the endless love of God evoking creation into being. The knowledge of good and evil is not a division that belongs within the original goodness of creation. It is an aspect of the curse visited upon humanity for the sin and hubris to which our species fell prey. The knowledge of good and evil results from the deadly human craving for godlike omniscience. If that is so, then surely the task of Christian theology is to ask in what ways the doctrine of the incarnation heals that wound and restores creation to a state of goodness that is ultimately beyond good and evil, and more like its original condition of goodness in God? We must come back to that.

It is a mistake to rely on Žižek as a reliable reader of Lacan, if only because Žižek is a flamboyant atheist narcissist who makes a cult out of misanthropy, and Lacan was a flamboyant Catholic narcissist who made a cult out of the quest for truth and love—as I hope I have demonstrated. Lacan is not, as Kearney suggests, abandoning ethics to the real. On the contrary, he is trying to draw attention to the violence that modernity trails in its wake precisely because of the oppositions that Kant did more than anyone else to establish between form and matter, the symbolic and the real, through the repression of desire and the imagination that allow for a space of fluidity between the two. That is why, as Žižek points out, Lacan's project has to be distinguished from that of Derrida. The Lacanian real is not Derridean *différance*. If anything, it is the imaginary that could be said to constitute the sphere of *différance* or the *khora* in Lacan, which provides a buffer against the violent and consuming power of the real understood as the death drive.

Before I take up again with Kearney's account of the ethical God encountered by Moses, I want to refer briefly to his critique of the *khora* in a book chapter titled 'God or *Khora*?' Kearney objects that

> while we might be tempted to think that the Platonic metaphors of matrix, mother and nurse in the *Timaeus* imply a certain act of nurturing beneficence, Caputo and Derrida are adamant that this is no normal mother. We are not dealing here with a recognizable family resemblance. *Khora* is altogether too indeterminate to engender anything.[15]

(As a mother of four adult children, I'm glad Kearney knows what a 'normal mother' is, for I'm not sure I do.) He goes on to quote Caputo: 'What is the wholly other...God or *khora*? Do we have to choose?' Of course we do, suggests Kearney, because 'we *do* whenever we opt to believe in God or not to believe'.[16]

---

[15] Kearney, *Strangers, Gods, and Monsters* p. 200.
[16] Kearney, *Strangers, Gods, and Monsters*, p. 201.

Kearney's main objection to the *khora* seems to be that it neither cares for us nor demands that we care for or worship it. It is outside all ethical and personal relationships. Elsewhere, he expresses a similar objection to Lacan's idea of the phallus.[17] He summarizes his doubts in an interview with Derrida, describing his idea of 'the God-who-may-be' as being located

> somewhere between the God of messianism and being on the one hand and *khora* on the other. The God-who-may-be hovers between these two. It is not identical with *khora*. . . . For me, it is a hermeneutic problem: how do you imagine, speak, name, narrate, and identify a God without falling back into metaphysics and onto-theology–and yet without saying 'God is *khora*'.[18]

I hope the foregoing provides some flavour of Kearney's persistent concerns with theological postmodernism, as a background against which I now turn to focus on the debate in *Modern Theology*, beginning with Kearney's critique of Thomas.

ONTOTHEOLOGY AND THE GOD OF EXODUS

Kearney quotes Étienne Gilson's claim that 'Exodus lays down the principle from which Christian philosophy will be suspended . . . There is but one God and this God is Being, that is the corner-stone of all Christian philosophy.'[19] In Kearney's critique, Thomas's conflation of the Yahweh of the Hebrew scriptures with the supreme Being of Greek philosophy opens the door to 'onto-theology' by allowing the God of Exodus to 'secure ontological tenure in the God of metaphysics'.[20]

Over and against this God of ontotheology, Kearney appeals to an eschato-logical counter-tradition in which Exodus 3:14 'falls within the framework of a solicitation, that is, assumes the task of summoning us towards an eschato-logical horizon'.[21] The Hebrew formula *"ehyeh 'aser 'ehyeh'* effects a dynamic transfiguration of the God of metaphysics. Its relational and narrative significance evokes a response—'Here I am'. These linguistic characteristics of the Hebrew are lost in translation, for a 'Hellenistic ontology'[22] is implied in the Greek *ego eimi ho on/I am the one who is*. The transfiguring moment of

---

[17] See Kearney, *The God Who May Be: A Hermeneutics of Religion* (Bloomington IN: Indiana University Press, 2001), p. 14.

[18] Richard Kearney and Jacques Derrida in conversation, in 'Terror and Religion', in Gratton and Manoussakis (eds), *Traversing the Imaginary*, pp. 18–28, 26.

[19] Kearney, 'God Who May Be', p. 77, quoting Étienne Gilson, *The Spirit of Medieval Philosophy* (Paris: Vrin), p. 51.

[20] Kearney, 'God Who May Be', p. 77.

[21] Kearney, 'God Who May Be', p. 78.   [22] Kearney, 'God Who May Be', p. 79.

self-revelation in Exodus 3, which is God's response to Moses's desire to know the divine name, constitutes, in Kearney's interpretation,

> a radical challenge to the One who has revealed himself as the God of his ancestors to proclaim a new program of action by *becoming different* from what he used to be and has been until now. The fact that Moses returns to Egypt and delivers a message of emancipation to his people signals the inauguration of an utterly novel mode of divine relation. The One who was experienced by them as the God of their *Fathers*, now discloses himself as the God of their *sons and daughters*.[23]

Kearney is on the same ground as Lacan here—and I have suggested that Thomas too can be brought into this framework. I wonder if Kearney might recognize something of his different God in Lacan's Other of the One? This Other evokes a response from the body, calling up a visceral desire and breaking open the singularity of the One to accommodate all the diversity and wonder of creation. Paradoxically though, we should recognize that whereas the Catholic Kearney dismisses Thomas as a resource within which to discover such otherness, the atheist Lacan finds Thomism a rich resource, albeit one that must be purged of its contaminating Aristotelianism in order to let being be.

According to Kearney, the God whose signature is "*ehyeh 'aser 'ehyeh*" is 'the God of the possible, a God who refuses to impose on us or abandon us, traversing the present moment while opening onto an ever-coming future'.[24] This leads Kearney to a Levinasian interpretation of the 'inextricable communion between God and humans' constituting 'a commitment to a shared history of "becoming"', so that

> God may henceforth be recognized as someone who *becomes with us*, someone as dependent on us as we are on Him.... God is what he *will* be when he becomes his Kingdom and his Kingdom comes on earth.... God is in the process of establishing his lordship on earth and the '*ehey 'aser 'ehyeh* may be rendered accordingly as 'I will be what I will be; I will become what I will become'.[25]

To recognize this is to shift from a Greek emphasis on the centrality of being to a Hebrew emphasis on the importance of becoming, being able. Appealing to the counter-tradition discovered in theologians such as Meister Eckhart and Nicholas of Cusa, but also discernible in more modern interpreters such as Schelling and Heidegger, Kearney argues that 'the metaphysics of exodus (being-word-abyss) becomes an exodus of metaphysics'.[26] This calls for 'a new hermeneutic of God as May-Be...*a poetics of the possible*', informed by

---

[23] Kearney, 'God Who May Be', pp. 79–80.   [24] Kearney, 'God Who May Be', p. 75.
[25] Kearney, 'God Who May Be', p. 81.   [26] Kearney, 'God Who May Be', p. 84.

Cusanus's redefinition of God 'neither as *esse*, nor as *nihil*, but as *possest* . . . (absolute possibility which includes all that is actual)'.[27]

Before I comment on this, let me refer to Manoussakis's response to Kearney in the same issue of *Modern Theology*. Manoussakis too seeks to distance the personal, trinitarian God of the Christian faith from the philosophical One of Greek philosophy. According to Manoussakis, 'the Aristotelian God enthrones Himself in the summit of onto-theological assertions'.[28] In Manoussakis's reading, Kearney's possible God inverts the Aristotelian order in which actuality has priority over potency, in order to posit a Heidegerrian understanding of God who, 'instead of being the absolute being and the *causa sui* of His being is rather *in need* of being'.[29] This, suggests Manoussakis, is 'the most crucial and perhaps the most revolutionary moment in the thought of Kearney: *synergy*',[30] for it brings with it 'an ethical imperative for humanity: to help God *be* God'.[31] The consequence of this is indeed radical, for, says Manoussakis,

> The God who may be, but is not yet, not already, the insufficient and inadequate God who always lacks and depends on His other, *this* God cannot be accused of theodicy. Such a God, neither omnipotent nor omniscient, fails every time that one of us falls short in her or his life, in her or his dreams. He fails, in each moment of my despair, in my distress and in my solitude. He fails, as my witness of suffering and misery takes away from Him the chance to be. He fails with me; my failure doesn't miss Him and He can't escape my agony. There and in each of these moments, God fails to be God.[32]

At this point, a number of problems loom into view from a Lacanian perspective. First, we should note how Kearney leaves unchallenged some deeply problematic androcentric concepts. In a review of Kearney's book, *The God Who May Be*, Frances Gray points to 'his persistent and problematic use' of the pronoun 'He' for God which, she suggests, highlights 'Kearney's sex/gender blind spot.' She asks, 'What about a God Who May Be makes God a "He"? Is it that Kearney is unable to dissociate himself from the Hebrew Yahweh God, unable to disrupt the masculine paternal bias of the Christian tradition?'[33] Manoussakis too seems not to notice that his account of a failed God might call into question that masculine pronoun with its capital letter.

[27] Kearney, 'God Who May Be', p. 84, citing Nicholas of Cusa, 'Dialogus de Possest', in *A Concise Introduction to the Philosophy of Nicholas of Cusa* (Minneapolis MN: University of Minnesota Press, 1980), pp. 120–69.

[28] Manoussakis, 'From Exodus to Eschaton', p. 96.

[29] Manoussakis, 'From Exodus to Eschaton', p. 98.

[30] Manoussakis, 'From Exodus to Eschaton', p. 103.

[31] Manoussakis, 'From Exodus to Eschaton', p. 103.

[32] Manoussakis, 'From Exodus to Eschaton', p. 105.

[33] Frances Gray, 'Review of Richard Kearney, *The God Who May Be: A Hermeneutics of Religion* (Indiana University Press, 2001)', *Notre Dame Philosophical Reviews*—an electronic

Perhaps the main weakness with Kearney's critique of Thomas is a lack of sufficient familiarity with the complexities, nuances, and at times contradictions in Thomas's theology. The ontotheological tradition certainly finds some support in a selective reading of Thomas—as I have demonstrated—but an alternative tradition which is far less vulnerable to Kearney's critique finds equal support. It depends on how one reads Thomas and which form of Thomism one subscribes to. I dare to suggest it depends on what one desires of Thomas's God. As Boeve suggests, Kearney 'is not theologian enough to hermeneutically engage the Christian tradition from within, in its complexity as well as in its integrity, operating within it and in relation to its hermeneutical communities'.[34]

From a Lacanian perspective, the God who 'fails to be God', this 'coming God who may-be', should send us running to Thomas for refuge, for He may yet become the Big Other to end all others. Under the guise of an ethical and dependent God, is this not Lacan's God of 'ferocious ignorance'? This is the ethical God of the modern symbolic order no less than of its Christian and Kantian antecedents, who demands of his subjects a devouring fidelity and a duty which drives us to the point of moral exhaustion, for the more we seek to satisfy him, the more exquisitely nuanced, particular, and impossible his demand becomes and the more he recedes, for in truth we can never, ever achieve the becoming of God by our human endeavours. We end up chasing our own tails round and round the abyss.

Kearney's dependent, ethical God asks everything of us in obedience to his lordship and in the pursuit of his Kingdom—and we should note the political and ethical implications of these androcentric nouns which trail in their wake Christianity's long history of imperialism, conquest, and violence. If the familiar and well-worn words of lordship and Kingdom are to be revitalized for Christianity beyond the violence that they have legitimated, then they need to undergo the most radical possible deconstruction and transformation, and it is not at all clear that Kearney acknowledges this.

Kearney's God remains the King and Lord of punitive commandments, for he is never satisfied. In Kearney's words, this is 'a God who puns and tautologizes, flares up and withdraws, promising always to return, to become again, to come to be what he is *not yet* for us'.[35] But what does this Other want—this teasing, elusive God who desires my desire, who needs me in order to become, who tortures me with his games of absence and presence, who lures me

---

journal published by University of Notre Dame (3rd March 2002), at <http://www.ndpr.nd.edu/news/23362-the-god-who-may-be-a-hermeneutics-of-religion/> [accessed 31 July 2012]. Again, this criticism would be less applicable to Kearney's later work, in which he is more attentive to questions of gender in language.

[34] Boeve, 'Richard Kearney's Messianism', p. 17.
[35] Kearney, 'God Who May Be', p. 84.

through and beyond being, through and beyond metaphysics, into an exhausting and all-consuming infinity of doing—demanding my doing as the condition for his being? What must I do to bring this God into being, to secure his future, without being wholly consumed by his insatiable appetite to become more and more, to become infinite, to become God? This is the vindictive God of an insatiable moral appetite who drives the frenetic and futile endeavours of postmodernity's endless protests and campaigns, even as the monstrous powers of greed and death feed on these activist illusions of doing something.

This God who withholds his presence and commands that we keep his word and struggle for justice is ultimately indistinguishable from the God who vanishes behind the screens of the Lacanian symbolic orders and demands our obedience all the same. If every time I am confronted with the yearning and lack of the human condition not only in myself but in the neighbour I must love, if my every demand for unconditional love falls on deaf ears, meets only an echo of the same demand echoing from within the suffering emptiness of the other, and if all this opens my soul to the futility of God's failure, do I not begin to breed a deadly hatred for this vortex between self and neighbour in which even God fails to become? This is the hatred of being to which Lacan refers—the human hatred of God for getting it so badly wrong. It is surely the last word in nihilism, for it is the voracious real that lurks within the hubristic morality of a bourgeois social order that equates its own good causes with the very possibility of God's existence. Can Thomas's God save us from this ambiguous and pathetic God who opens up within the abyss of postmodernity, even though Kearney's refiguration of God is premised upon a rejection of this same abysmal quality that he discerns at the heart of postmodernism? Let me consider John Caputo's response to Kearney's article with this in mind.

JOHN CAPUTO'S GOD OF THE IMPOSSIBLE

Caputo offers a Derridean response to Kearney, developing Kearney's suggestion that there is 'a point of contact between his own conception of a "poetics of the possible", which turns on a post-metaphysical eschatological concept of possibility, and Derrida's notion of "*the* impossible"'.[36] The God of the impossible revealed in scripture 'eclipses subjectivity' so that we are 'driven to a point described by Derrida as *sans voir, sans avoir, sans savoir*, where faith must make up for our lack of *voir*, hope must compensate for our lack of *avoir*, and

---

[36] Caputo, 'Richard Kearney's Enthusiasm', p. 90.

charity supplement our lack of *savoir*.[37] This Derridean account recognizes the impossible as 'something that propels us into the most radical of all possibilities, the possibility of *the* impossible, which is a matter of *faith*'.[38] Whereas for Derrida this '"perhaps" of the impossible is a condition of experience in general', Caputo fully agrees with Kearney that 'it is also a condition of religious experience in particular, which also implies that experience in general, experience in its sharpest sense, has a certain religious quality'.[39]

Caputo goes on to discuss what he describes as Kearney's 'constant and legitimate concern about nihilism, about falling into what some might call the "abyss", or being overwhelmed by what Levinas calls the *il y a*, or being left stranded in what Derrida calls the desert of the *khora*'. This language is perhaps more revealing than it intends, particularly when Caputo adds that 'Richard does not want to be consumed by these monsters.'[40]

Here we are then, back with the monstrous other—the *khora*, prime matter, the consuming void which, as we have seen, is always implicitly feminized as the opposite of the masculine God and evokes horror in the mind of the masculine subject in whose image God is (being) made, no matter how postmodern he might claim to be. It is one thing to toy with letting go of the God of metaphysics—the God of form, singularity, and abstraction, the God of ontotheology, but it is quite another to turn from this letting go to welcoming and letting be the (m)Other wherein there might yet be—as Catherine Mowry LaCugna suggests—a different 'God for us'.[41]

Caputo refers to the various 'limit-states' that are suggested by the abyss, *il y a* and *khora*, but he suggests that for Kearney these tend to represent 'the most extreme states of madness, misery, terror, torture, depression and desolation, the nightmare of a prisoner trapped in the ground or a child crushed by rubble'.[42] Over and against this, Caputo posits 'the mystical abyss which for Meister Eckhart is a font not of terror but of love', and between the two he invokes Derridean *différance*, 'the quasi-transcendental which sees to it that a meaning is a temporary unity that is forged from the flux of signifiers or traces and that lasts just as long as the purpose it serves and the contexts in which it can function endure'.[43]

---

[37] Caputo, 'Richard Kearney's Enthusiasm', p. 90.
[38] Caputo, 'Richard Kearney's Enthusiasm', p. 90.
[39] Caputo, 'Richard Kearney's Enthusiasm', p. 90.
[40] Caputo, 'Richard Kearney's Enthusiasm', p. 91.
[41] Catherine Mowry LaCugna, *God for Us: The Trinity and Christian Life* (San Francisco: HarperSanFrancisco, 1993).
[42] Caputo, 'Richard Kearney's Enthusiasm', p. 91.
[43] Caputo, 'Richard Kearney's Enthusiasm', p. 91.

Caputo then goes on to explore this in terms of *khora* which Derrida says, 'is a surname for *différance*'.[44] Plato's *khora*, suggests Caputo,

> constitutes a kind of counter-part to the *agathon*, a counter-image not beyond *ousia* but below it, a structure that falls below the level of sense and sensibility, of meaning and being, rather than exceeding them.... Whatever we say or pray, think or believe, dream or desire, is inscribed in the shifting sands of *différance*, that is, inscribed in *khora*.[45]

Caputo points out that, while theoretically the *agathon* and the *khora* mirror one another, they also blur together, because 'neither belongs to the medium sized phenomena of daily life, neither has the determinacy, the form, the structure of a definite thing or being'.[46] Caputo refers to Thomas's critique of David of Dinant's argument that equated God with prime matter:

> While Thomas was right to say that we can keep these concepts apart, I would say that David had hit upon a phenomenological point, that our *experiences* of the two are not necessarily so widely divided, for in both cases we experience a certain confusion (Levinas), a kind of bedazzlement (Marion), or what Derrida and I with him would call an 'undecidability', which I think can only be resolved by faith...[47]

These are vital insights in terms of my reading of Thomas in the last chapter, for we have seen that Thomas experiences the same mystical 'bedazzlement' when he shifts from the singularity of God in terms of Aristotelian theology, to the relationality of God in the Christian Trinity. Again, let's bear in mind that, from a Lacanian perspective, Caputo is right to point out that form and matter/the symbolic and the real, overflow the structures and boundaries of experience, so that it is more difficult to separate them phenomenologically than conceptually. This is why, for Lacan, the rational God of the symbolic is parasitic upon the tyrannical God of the real, for the former feeds upon the dread generated by the latter in order to underwrite his power.

In approaching 'the God who comes after metaphysics', Caputo argues that

> we enter a region where we do not know whether it is "God or *khora*"... the sphere, the desert sphere, in which any genuine decision or movement of faith is to be made, where God and *khora* bleed into each other and create an element of ambiguity and undecidability *within which the movement of faith is made*. Without *khora*, we would be programmed to God, divine automatons hard wired to the divine being, devoid of freedom, responsibility, judgment, and faith.... Without *khora*, the situation which evokes the impossible, which demands the impossible of us, which elicits faith, hope and charity would not

---

[44] Caputo, 'Richard Kearney's Enthusiasm', p. 91.
[45] Caputo, 'Richard Kearney's Enthusiasm', p. 92.
[46] Caputo, 'Richard Kearney's Enthusiasm', p. 92.
[47] Caputo, 'Richard Kearney's Enthusiasm', p. 92.

obtain. *Khora* is the *felix culpa* of a phenomenology of the impossible, the happy fault of a poetics of the possible, the heartless heart of an ethical and religious eschatology. *Khora* is the devil that justice demands we give his due.[48]

Here, we see the ancient dualism reaffirmed in postmodern guise, so that in this migration of theological discourse from pre-modern theology (Thomas) to postmodern theology (Kearney and Caputo) through various configurations and refigurations of the relationship between form and matter, spirit and body, God and nature, we might ask if anything has really changed. Caputo might challenge Kearney with regard to the latter's fear of the annihilating violence of the *khora*, but he still posits the *khora* as the opposite of God—even if these opposites bleed into one another. The *khora* is heartless, demonic, the other of God which must be overcome if the ethical is to prevail. It is the site of a freedom attained through resistance and struggle against its enigmatic seductiveness. Not only does God ooze into *khora* around the edges of being, but so does the devil. '*Khora* is the devil that justice demands we give his due.' Continuously then, plenitude and emptiness, love and horror, swirl within the *khora*, the imaginary, the imagination—call it what we will—and even if it is seldom acknowledged today by theologians, Lacan shows us that all such language retains a persistent dualism in which form is associated with God, paternity, and perfection, and matter with evil, maternity, and lack.

For Caputo, the theologian must accept that the *khora* is the Levinisian ghost of *il y a* which 'disturbs our days and haunts our nights', and which 'makes ethics possible—by confronting it with something to be overcome— and impossible, by delimiting ethics as the ever haunting possibility of the anonymous that never goes away, that refused to be banished, that returns night after night'.[49]

She—*khora*, matter, mother, the nameless other—haunts the man of God. Implicitly, Caputo sympathizes with Thomas's endeavour to 'drive out' matter from God, even if this is, in Caputo's interpretation, an impossible task. For Caputo, the unceasing battle to overcome the *khora* with its intimations of violence and death is the task of Christian ethics in its striving towards the impossible God.

The *khora* is not, as Kearney reminds us, a 'normal mother'. So what kind of mother is she? Can one only be a mother when one's being is inscribed within the order of the symbolic—an order which is, Lacan reminds us, conditional upon the destruction of the maternal relationship and the body upon which it feeds? Like Thomas's demonic phantasms, *khora* is a demon mother who plagues a man's sleep with seductive distractions. She is the anamorphic incubus that emerges when his reason no longer stands guard over his desires,

---

[48] Caputo, 'Richard Kearney's Enthusiasm', p. 93.
[49] Caputo, 'Richard Kearney's Enthusiasm', pp. 93–4.

and the demonic other of God comes swirling out of the abyss as the necessary alternative which assures him of his precarious freedom before God: 'Without *khora* there is no *faith*, because then God would have plainly and unambiguously revealed Godself, without any possible confusion.'[50] Implicit in this is the same suggestion that we find in Thomas's Neoplatonism—the desire for God entails resistance to matter. The man of God is free to the extent that he can resist the demonic lure of bodily desire that arises from the miasma of his own animality and threatens his faith in God. The mother—the relational, trinitarian Other of the One God—suffocates within this forbidden *khora*.

The *khora* and God dissolve into one another at the edges of perception and consciousness, just as the Lacanian real becomes indistinguishable from the symbolic as language loops itself around the void that it contains. Men's dreams are never free from nightmares, and those who seek God must continuously struggle against all those ancient seductions and enemies— demons, body, matter, *khora*, mother.

Kearney runs away from this maternal *khora* by seeking to make God anew, Caputo turns to confront her as the other of God who must be overcome by the struggle for justice, but what if they ran towards her instead, and recognized in her warm and viscous depths the body of the God they seek? If we are to escape the hauntings of Sadean violence, then we must sanctify matter and make it the field of our own desire for God, not over and against but awakened, nurtured, and sustained within the divine being. Otherwise, there will always lurk within the theological enterprise a declaration of war on the body, which might have morphed into a multitude of feminist, liberal, liberationist, contextual, and postmodern forms of rhetoric, and yet which will still need to impose its universal vision of how things should be on all the reluctant and protesting particularity/heresy/orthodoxy of the bodies that stand in its way. People will continue to slaughter one another in the name of their ideals, their ideas, their gods, just as Kearney fears—and those gods are always just and good, for nobody desires evil. As Thomas reminds us, every desire is capable of deceiving itself as to its intentions.

We need an altogether different theological idiom, a more radical humility, if we are to let God be God in order that we might become the bodily humans beloved of God that we desire to be. This cannot and should not seek to be an overcoming of the necessary *lacuna* between body and consciousness, creation and God, within which the human condition belongs. To welcome whatever we mean by *khora*, *hyle*, or matter is not to surrender to a kind of New Age romanticism or a neo-pagan fantasy, for Lacan warns us that that does indeed risk ever greater violence as we seek to overcome the lack that positions us within the world. It means accepting that lack with all its unfulfilled yearning

---

[50] Caputo, 'Richard Kearney's Enthusiasm', p. 94.

and the sense of loss that it generates, and asking how an ethos might emerge that can accommodate more of the fragility, desire, and sexuality of human becoming than the Christian theological tradition has been able to. It also means remaining continuously vigilant with regard to all political, economic, and religious systems that would deprive humans of the means to flourish by exploiting them, oppressing them, waging war on them, or destroying the diverse environments upon which different cultures and communities depend, and the vestiges of unspoilt wilderness that survive and which remind us of how insignificant we are as a species within the majesty, mystery, and terror of creation.

With these questions in mind, I want to ask if it is possible to retrieve a Thomism for our times, by returning to the question of matter and Thomas's maternal Trinity. There is indeed an ontotheology in Thomas, a lure of the philosophical One that holds him too tightly in its grip. But there is another Thomas, and that other Thomas can draw us towards another God if we are attentive to the desire that wells up within the abyss and draws creation to God. So let me return to Thomas's understanding of prime matter with that question of desire in mind, focusing on a short and underdeveloped discussion in the *Summa theologiae* which is of central significance from a Lacanian perspective, and for the whole argument of this book.

18

The Maternal Trinity

Just as Aristotle provided Thomas with a new way of reading Christian theology, I am suggesting that Lacan provides us with a new way of reading Thomas, in order to offer a theological response to some of the most urgent and troubling issues facing us in what can sometimes seem like apocalyptic times. This is a contingent and provisional reading, for times change and Christian theologians must always be prepared to ask anew what the love of God means as different questions and cultures emerge in the gradual unfolding of creation in time and space.

However, I am also suggesting that there are aspects of Thomas's Aristotelianism that are fundamentally incompatible with Christian revelation, which run counter to his naturalist account of reason and the role of desire in relation to the natural law and human flourishing. This sets up a number of tensions in his theology, most of them surrounding the relationship between the God of Greek philosophy and the Trinity of Christian revelation. I have explored the implications of this in terms of Lacan's account of the phallic, abstract One and the maternal, bodily Other.

This tension makes Thomas vulnerable to the charge of ontotheology, because it is certainly possible to read him in the way that Richard Kearney does. In recent decades, under the influence of Heidegger and twentieth-century existentialism, different forms of Thomism have emerged that seek to rescue his account of being from the clutches of ontotheology. Both these approaches—the rejection of Thomas on account of his ontotheology, and the reclamation of Thomas by various different approaches to existential questions—can be substantiated by selective readings of his work.

However, even among Thomas's most postmodern and existentialist interpreters, there remains an obtuse resistance to addressing the question of his maternal Trinity in a way that would take seriously the radical implications this has for the rest of his theology, including his understanding of natural law, ethics, and sexual and social relationships. From a Lacanian perspective, I am suggesting that there are resources within Thomas's own theology which have the potential to inform a future Thomism that remains faithful to the spirit of Catholic tradition and to its core doctrinal principles, while making it responsive to the challenges of postmodernity with its changing configurations of gender, nature, and language. The language most pregnant with potency for this task is to be found in Thomas's allusive attempts to articulate something of the maternal mystery of the Trinity, not least because this language is repeatedly barred by the God of Greek philosophy, so that the Trinity disappears behind the One of Plato or the Supreme Being of Aristotle.

In teasing out some of the potential in Thomas's trinitarian language, I begin by returning briefly to the challenge that confronts theologians when speaking of the ultimate mystery of God. I then offer a critical appraisal of Gilles Emery's discussion of Thomas's maternal language in his book, *The Trinitarian Theology of St Thomas Aquinas*, in which he argues that Thomas's maternal Trinity can be shown to be perfectly compatible with his Aristotelian understanding of the unity of God the Father, so that one can properly speak of Thomas's 'authentic Trinitarian monotheism'.[1] Finally, I suggest alternative ways of approaching the question of maternal language in Thomas's account of the Trinity, rendering his Aristotelianism more problematic than Emery acknowledges, but also I hope opening the way to future readings of Thomas that might require a radical reassessment of his Aristotelianism and its social and ethical implications.

SPEAKING OF MYSTERY

The Trinity belongs within the mystical dimension of Thomas's faith, far beyond the probing enquiries of philosophical reason. We have seen that time and again the structure of his analysis falters and fails when he attempts to express what this means. As Karen Kilby reminds us, 'Thomas serenely presents us with something that we can make nothing of, and that he does not expect us to',[2] and he does this by 'simultaneously displaying the grammar, the pattern of speech about the Trinity, and displaying it as beyond our comprehension'.[3] The Trinity is a fleeting epiphany of a dimension of being beyond the grasp of language, too elusive and mysterious to capture and pin down within the grids of grammar and meaning, yet present as a trace of God throughout creation. Kearney gestures towards this possibility in his lyrical description of a perichoretic trinitarian dance around the *khora* of the Virgin Mary's womb, but these ideas remain relatively allusive in his work in terms of

---

[1] Gilles Emery OP, *The Trinitarian Theology of Saint Thomas Aquinas*, trans. Francesca Aran Murphy (Oxford and New York: Oxford University Press, 2007), p. 128.
[2] Karen Kilby, 'Aquinas, the Trinity and the Limits of Understanding', *International Journal of Systematic Theology*, Vol. 7, No. 4 (2005), pp. 414–27, 418.
[3] Kilby, 'Aquinas, the Trinity and the Limits of Understanding', p. 423. See Chapter 3.

not yet offering a close engagement with theological sources that would incorporate them more fully into a theological, sacramental, and liturgical narrative.[4]

There is risk as well as wonder if we seek to ask what this mystical trinitarian insight means, for language that attempts to express this maternal mystery too easily shades back into the old familiar sexual stereotypes, so that the maternal face of God becomes the shadowy feminized other of God the Father. In a culture that views otherness as a threat or a challenge to be conquered and brought into the economy of the same, this maternal other melts into the Lacanian real or the Platonic *khora*, which we have seen sometimes presents itself to the philosophical imagination as an unthinkable horror or a demonic enemy. God as mother becomes indecipherable from prime matter which is believed to be the opposite of God, and therefore the maternal in God opens into an unspeakable abyss that blurs and melts into the fleshy otherness of matter, nature, and woman. These associations pollute the singularity and disembodiment of philosophy's God with a slimy, sticky ooze that has no place in the absolute purity of the One. The ethically commanding God becomes the postmodern theologian's refuge from the suffocating embrace of this material God.

An alternative is the tendency to celebrate the 'feminine' face of God, in such a way that romantic sexual stereotypes are reanimated through the projection into the Trinity of masculine normativity and feminine otherness, for example in using feminized language to speak of the Holy Spirit, or attributing femininity to the human nature of Christ as opposed to the masculinity of his divine nature.[5] Lacan shows why all such attempts to create an ontology or a theology out of sexual difference fail, because by its very nature the sexual encounter entails a bodily immediacy that cannot be inscribed, abstracted, or theorized within structured metanarratives.

Sex is a bodily reality of the here and now, and any attempt to extend this into our relationships with one another *qua* sexual identities and complementarities cannot help but encrypt those relationships in frustration, failure, and the blighting of love. Of course, the sexual encounter has consequences. It weaves us into relationships, it gives bodily expression to a complex range of feelings that arise and endure far beyond the act itself and, for a woman, it

---

[4] Cf. Richard Kearney, 'Diacritical Hermeneutics', in Maria Luísa Portocarrero, Luis António Umbelino, and Andrzej Wierciński (eds), *Hermeneutic Rationality—La rationalité herméneutique* (Berlin: Lit Verlag Dr W. Hopf, 2012), pp. 176–92.

[5] Cf. Leonardo Boff OFM, *The Maternal Face of God: The Feminine and Its Religious Expressions*, trans. Robert R. Barr and John Diercksmeier (London: Collins, 1989). See also the critiques of this approach in Sarah Coakley, '"Femininity" and the Holy Spirit?', in Monica Furlong (ed.), *Mirror to the Church: Reflections on Sexism* (London: SPCK, 1988), pp. 124–35. There is a searching and insightful critique of these issues in Gavin D'Costa, *Sexing the Trinity: Gender, Culture and the Divine* (London: SCM Press, 2000).

remains bound up with questions of procreation and motherhood. But contrary to the romantic myths of a certain kind of Catholicism and a certain kind of secular culture,[6] we are not 'Woman' and 'Man' in every relationship and interaction, except insofar as society imposes such roles upon us. Thomas and Lacan both remind us that who we are cannot be defined by nor restricted to the relationship between the sexes. We have seen that Thomas attributes sexual differentiation to the fact that the ultimate vocation of every human is not sexual copulation in the order of being, but eternal bodily life with God—an insight that he woefully failed to apply to his politics and ethics, in which 'woman' is positioned by her sex in everything she does or, more accurately, in everything she is barred from doing.

So let me turn to Emery's attempt to show the compatibility between Thomas's maternal Trinity and his Father God, in a way that apparently makes not a jot of difference to anything.

THE FATHERLY MOTHER

Emery urges his readers to pay the same meticulous attention to language that Thomas himself did, reminding us that Thomas appropriates Jerome's 'ancient warning' that 'careless words are a slippery slope to heresy'.[7] But one can also reveal vast and problematic assumptions in texts by focusing on highly significant words that are used as if they lack significance so that they are carelessly applied, insufficiently analysed, or picked up and then dropped. In Thomas, as in some of his later interpreters (including Emery), there is no attempt to explore the textures of meaning and possibility within the language of motherhood and to ask how this might deconstruct the language of fatherhood when applied to God.

In analysing Thomas's account of the Trinity, Emery argues that 'the unswerving direction of Thomas' argument is already clearly in view: the name Father must take priority over every other aspect'.[8] But then he continues by suggesting that

> Divine paternity includes the features which belong to mothers, in creatures: conception, childbirth, caring for the child. In accordance with Scripture, maternal traits are ascribed to the Father: the Word is born 'from his womb' (*ex utero*), and he remains 'in the heart of the Father' (*in sinu Patris*). And it is 'for a mother to conceive and give birth'. In line with Scripture, St Thomas accepts maternal

---

[6] Cf. David Matzko McCarthy, *Sex and Love in the Home: A Theology of the Household* (Eugene OR: Wipf Stock Publishers, 2011).
[7] Emery, *The Trinitarian Theology of Saint Thomas Aquinas*, p. 134.
[8] Emery, *The Trinitarian Theology of Saint Thomas Aquinas*, p. 155.

expressions like this, but, nevertheless, keeps the name *Father* for God. The 'things which belong distinctly to the father or to the mother in fleshy generation, in the generation of the Word are all attributed to the Father by sacred Scripture; for the Father is said not only "to give life to the Son", but also "to conceive" and to "bring forth"'. Likewise, he uses the maternal image of childbirth to describe creation. And he also uses the image of the wise-woman to describe the providential activity of God, who does not just create the world, but cares for his creatures by leading them where they will flourish. These maternal features are integrated into the description of the name *Father*.[9]

I wonder if Emery believes that this will console mothers as to their sacramental significance within the life of God? Or might he be persuaded to recognize that this is a devastating indictment of Christian theology for those informed not only by the insights of feminism but, more importantly for my purposes here, by those of Lacanian psychoanalysis? The human longing for maternal love, revealed as much in Thomas's theology as in Lacanian psychoanalysis, finds no expression in a religion that always and everywhere can only speak in terms of God the Father, by men unable to recognize the patriarchal ideology that they are promoting. The same is true if we turn to a later section in which Emery deals with the fatherhood of God. Emery writes:

> From one perspective, human fatherhood is a participation in the paternity of the Father. And although St Thomas does not put it in these words (he is in this respect a child of his times, and depends on antiquated ideas which are now outdated), the same participation primarily effects human maternity, since 'Scripture attributes to the Father, in the generation of the Son, all of that which, in the physical generation of children, belongs to the father and the mother.' This applies to parental paternity and maternity, and also extends, by analogy, to spiritual paternity and maternity: 'someone who leads someone else to an act of life, such as acting well, knowledge, willing, loving, deserves to be called "father"'. In all of the areas of what we today describe as the progress of human dignity, or concern for life, St Thomas invites us to find a participation in the Father's paternity.[10]

Theological arguments such as these provide an excellent illustration as to why feminist theologians might throw up their hands in despair at the obtuse obstinacy of the dominant theological tradition with regard to its ideological commitment to the fatherhood of God. As Janet Martin Soskice points out:

> Feminist criticisms of classical formulations of the doctrine [of the Trinity] vary from simple rejection of what sounds like a three-men club, to more nuanced critiques of the way in which, despite best efforts, the Father always seems to be

[9] Emery, *The Trinitarian Theology of Saint Thomas Aquinas*, p. 156.
[10] Emery, *The Trinitarian Theology of Saint Thomas Aquinas*, p. 162. The quotations are from Thomas Aquinas, SCG IV, 11, and *In Eph.* 3.15.

accorded a status superior to the other two Persons, with the Holy Spirit as a distinct third. The Trinity appears still hierarchical, still male – maleness, indeed, seems enshrined in God's eternity.[11]

Let's consider the passage from the *Summa Contra Gentiles* to which Emery is referring. Here, Thomas argues that 'the fleshy generation of animals is perfected by an active power and by a passive power; and it is from the active power that one is named "father," and from the passive power that one is named "mother"'.[12] This makes clear that sexual difference is quantitative, not qualitative. The female is not a genuine other but the 'other of the same' (to quote Luce Irigaray),[13] the negative against which the man represents himself as positive, the passive against which the man represents himself as active, the lack against which man represents himself as perfection. The naming of a woman as mother and a man as father derives not from any fundamental difference between the two nor from any human relationship of love, commitment, and fidelity to one another and the child they bear. It derives only from their biological functions as active and passive in the act of conception and gestation, which in turn derives from the copulative ontology of the pagan cosmos.

The above quotation comes from a chapter in which Thomas discusses the relation of God the Father to the Son, and this is a clear example of where he struggles to reconcile the relational significance of the divine fatherhood in trinitarian theology, with its inseminating significance in Greek philosophy. Thomas argues that, whereas in animal procreation different roles pertain to the active power of the father and the passive power of the mother—the former gives 'the nature and species to the offspring', while the latter conceives and brings forth 'as patient and recipient'—in God this conceiving and bringing forth are, Thomas insists, active and therefore paternal:

> in the generation of the Word of God the notion of mother does not enter, but only that of father. Hence the things which belong distinctly to the father or to the mother in fleshly generation, in the generation of the Word are all attributed to the Father by sacred Scripture; for the Father is said not only 'to give life to the Son' (cf. John 5:26), but also 'to conceive' and to 'bring forth.'[14]

The father has more of what it takes to be than the mother—he is more of a mother than she can ever hope to be. This is what Mary Daly calls the 'sacred House of Mirrors', presided over by 'anointed Male Mothers, who naturally

---

[11] Janet Martin Soskice, 'Trinity and the "Feminine Other"', in *The Kindness of God: Metaphor, Gender, and Religious Language* (Oxford and New York: Oxford University Press, 2007), pp. 100–24, 111.

[12] SCG IV, 11, 19.

[13] Cf. Luce Irigaray, *Speculum of the Other Woman* (Ithaca NY: Cornell University Press, 1985), pp. 243–364.

[14] SCG, IV, 11, 19.

are called Fathers', and who take from mothers all the natural functions of birthing and nurturing and transform these into sacraments that only male priests—'revered models of spiritual transsexualism'—can administer.[15] Even if we make allowance for Thomas on the basis of his times and culture, what excuse can we make for the failure of theologians like Emery to offer even a passing engagement with feminist theologians and theorists who have something to say about motherhood and God?

It is impossible to exaggerate the effects of this erasure of the maternal from God in terms of the shaping of western culture, values, and institutions, and in the subsequent exclusion of the female body and nature as the abjected matter/mother that has no place in the divine being. As Soskice suggests, in such theological accounts, 'The only true parent is the father, source of seed which it is the female task to nurture.'[16]

There needs to be some way beyond the language of substitution, in which the divine fatherhood incorporates but also elides the significance of the maternal body, or that of opposition in which God the Mother simply displaces God the Father. If we are faithful to Thomas's own understanding of the analogical nature of theological language, then we need to guard against literalism by refusing to make God either Mother or Father, while recognizing that the closest we can come to speaking of God might be in the language of parenthood. We cannot speak at all except in the language that we receive from the world that we inhabit. But we inhabit a world in which mothers, not fathers, remain for most of us the earliest and most formative influences on our lives, for good or for ill. The fact that we exist at all is evidence that somewhere a woman has offered us the hospitality and nourishment of her own body for the period of our gestation, even if we know nothing more about her than that. Even at that by no means insignificant level of human becoming, we surely recognize something of God? But let's begin, not with motherhood but with fatherhood. To say that God is not only a father is not to say that God is not even a father. God is, as Thomas repeatedly reminds us, a father by way of his relationship to Jesus Christ. The question is, how does this understanding of fatherhood relate to philosophical accounts of being which inscribe all that is within copulative sexual encounters between paternal form and maternal matter? The answer is, it doesn't.

FATHERHOOD BEYOND COPULATION

Soskice makes the point that, notwithstanding occasional references to God as 'nursing mother or nesting eagle', biblical images of God are 'overwhelmingly

---

[15] Mary Daly, *Beyond God the Father: Towards a Philosophy of Women's Liberation* (London: The Women's Press, 1986), pp. 195–6.
[16] Soskice, 'Trinity and the "Feminine Other"', p. 110.

styled as masculine', and from a feminist perspective this is exacerbated by Jesus's exclusive use of the title 'Father' in prayer.[17] For some Christian feminists this biblical precedent might preclude calling God 'Mother', although one might ask how this linguistic essentialism fits with Thomas's understanding of analogy, and with his suggestion that 'Men have to find new words to express their old faith because they have to reply to new heresies.'[18] Might it be that the patriarchal order of the ancient world is in itself heretical from the perspective of the Christian understanding of the relationship between God the Father and God the Son, so that we require new words today to challenge the domination of androcentric and patriarchal language with their implicitly—and sometimes explicitly—violent overtones?

At the very least there is a strong case for arguing that, in Thomas's attribution of maternal characteristics to the paternal relationship, the fatherhood of God in relation to Jesus Christ should deconstruct rather than essentialize the patriarchal order of the ancient world. This would entail taking with the utmost seriousness Paul Ricoeur's argument that the death of Christ brings about the death of the phantasm of the murdered oedipal father as a figure of sexual regeneration, and replaces it with the symbol of the father reinscribed within a linguistic relationship of invocation and evocation.[19] In seeking to demonstrate this, Ricoeur urges philosophers to avoid theology in favour of biblical exegesis, in order to have access to a greater immediacy and contextuality of discursive forms than that which theology is willing to entertain.

Following this method, Ricoeur argues that the Old Testament is highly reticent in its attribution of fatherhood to God. This, suggests Ricoeur, constitutes the loss of the idolatrous father figure of oedipal religion in order to prepare the way for the return of the father in a different form. The Yahweh of the Hebrew scriptures does not occupy the position of father. When the divine fatherhood reappears in the New Testament, it has been entirely transformed by the relationship of Christ to the paternal figure. This is no longer expressed in terms of the murdered father but in the self-identification of the suffering Son with the father, in a way which ushers in a new relationship of intimacy and prophecy predicated on Jesus's addressing of God in the intimate use of the word '*Abba*'.[20] According to Ricoeur, the death of Christ effects a transformation in the paternal relationship:

---

[17] Soskice, 'Calling God "Father"', in *The Kindness of God*, pp. 66–83, 70.

[18] ST I, 29, 3. Thomas Aquinas, *Summa Theologiae: A Concise Translation*, ed. Timothy McDermott (London: Metheun, 1992), p. 69.

[19] See Paul Ricoeur, 'Fatherhood: From Phantasm to Symbol', trans. Robert Sweeney, in *The Conflict of Interpretations* (Evanston IL: Northwestern University Press, 1974), pp. 468–97.

[20] Ricoeur, 'Fatherhood: From Phantasm to Symbol', p. 489.

The Just One is killed, certainly, and thereby the aggressive impulse against the father is satisfied by means of the offspring of the archaic paternal image; but at the same time, and this is the essential point, the meaning of the death is reversed: by becoming 'dead for another,' the death of the Just One achieves the metamorphosis of the paternal image in the direction of a figure of kindness and compassion. The death of Christ stands at the end of this development... Here is completed the conversion of death as murder into death as offering.[21]

By the death of Christ and his identification with the father, Ricoeur suggests that this death of the father 'belongs to the nonneurotic outcomes of the Oedipus complex; this is the counterpart of the mutual recognition between father and son in which the Oedipus complex may be resolved happily'.[22]

Soskice sees a possible way forward in Ricoeur's subversion of the oedipal understanding of divine fatherhood. She suggests that 'while the paternal imagery remains in place in the historic literature at least, it may be seen as a figure not "well known" and "invariable" but, as Ricoeur suggests, as an incomplete figure that traverses a number of semantic levels'.[23]

What better way to subvert the grip of the oedipal father on Christian desire than to liberate the language of motherly kindness and compassion which pervades Thomas's trinitarian theology? God the Father of Jesus Christ is like a mother, and therefore totally unlike the oedipal patriarchs that prevail in Aristotle's philosophical cosmology no less than in the religious cosmologies that Aristotle inherited. To say this is not to suggest that we can simply reverse the patriarchal order—substituting God the Mother for God the Father. Rather, concepts of both motherhood and fatherhood, as these have been inherited, sexualized, and essentialized in terms of Greek philosophy, lose their power over the theological imagination when they are brought into a mutually deconstructive and illuminating relationship with one another. This would make clear what Soskice suggests, that 'The doctrine of the Trinity... tells us nothing about sexual difference. But it does let us glimpse what it is, most truly, to be: "to-be" most fully is "to-be-related" in difference.'[24]

Emery suggests that the privileging of the language of fatherhood is scriptural, but a more radical trinitarianism would show the biblical God of the Hebrew people and Father of Jesus Christ to be deconstructive of the God of patriarchal Aristotelianism, as Ricoeur suggests. The God of the Old and New Testaments does not reinforce oedipal relationships but overturns them, ushering in the possibility of an entirely different symbolic order. However, as we have seen repeatedly in this book, patriarchy is reinforced and lent potent justification by the fusing together of Christian revelation and Aristotelian

---

[21] Ricoeur, 'Fatherhood: From Phantasm to Symbol', pp. 492–3.
[22] Ricoeur, 'Fatherhood: From Phantasm to Symbol', pp. 491–2.
[23] Soskice, 'Calling God "Father"', p. 81.
[24] Soskice, 'Trinity and the "Feminine Other"', p. 124.

philosophy around an essentially pagan concept of fatherhood. After the so-called death of God and the rise of scientific rationalism, the phallus takes the place of God the Father in securing meaning by barring access to the maternal body, and nothing substantially changes in the order of being.

The way through and beyond this *impasse* is not through any liberal gloss that would call God 'she' as well as 'he', Mother as well as Father, for Lacan shows us that such language is deeply rooted in the most primordial thought structures that have shaped western consciousness. If the transformation of Christian theological language is to be more than the capitulation to a feminist ideology instead of the age-old patriarchal ideology that still holds sway, then we need to find new ways of speaking about what it means to be a desiring body in a creation that yearns for its creator, which is graced in all its aspects by the maternal love of God that birthed it into being. This means finally letting go of that pagan cosmology with its copulative ontology and its eternal dualisms, to ask what it means to allow the relational, maternal God who creates *ex nihilo* to transform our way of being in the world. At the deepest and most real level of being, a trinitarian mystery enfolds us within a maternal relationship of love continuously conceiving, birthing, and communicating itself within the being of God. Whatever we can say of this being of all being and doing of all doing, it is beyond everything and anything that we can say. We approach it always from within the finitude of the mortal body and therefore we never enter fully into its mystery, but the closer we come to it, the more the self dissolves into the unsayable abyss that constitutes our own being within the being of God.

This apophaticism that draws language towards silence and dissolves all our concepts within the darkness of unknowing translates in modernity into the Lacanian real. Stripped of the contemplative silence within which such otherness is discovered and acknowledged, we inhabit the clamour of a different linguistic order—rationalized, empirical, factual—which seeks to fill up the empty spaces, but cannot plumb the depths where God once formed the absent centre of the soul. The well of silence does not quench the thirst of the postmodern soul. It rises up, dark and toxic, threatening to flood the self with its uncanny and unbearable otherness. And because the Catholic theological tradition has never been able to fully embrace the motherhood of God, particularly in post-Reformation Catholicism, pushing it to the margins or trying to contain and control it by projecting it onto the passive, docile, and obedient *persona* of the Virgin, it has played no small part in the development of this culture of despair. Yet as Soskice suggests, 'We may now stand at a moment of evangelical opportunity in the West, a time in which Christians not only need to hear a fully relational account of the Trinitarian life of God, but may also be receptive to it.'[25] This

---

[25] Soskice, 'Trinity and the "Feminine Other"', p. 119.

entails the monumental task of prising the language of trinitarian theology away from its patriarchal moorings, in order to open it up to the m(O)therness that is latent within it. Thomas might seem an unlikely source for such a task, but let's delve a little deeper.

THE OCEANIC BEING OF GOD

I want to return to Thomas's account of Exodus 3, in the context of his reference to John Damascene's oceanic metaphor for the being of God. The name '*qui est*' is the most appropriate name for God because 'comprehending all in itself, it contains being itself as an infinite and indeterminate sea of substance'.[26]

In seeking to express the inexpressible enigma of '*qui est*', Thomas's language drifts from the philosophical rigour of his Aristotelianism to a more impressionistic and mystical idiom. Thomas's God becomes the oceanic womb of being, 'an infinite and indeterminate sea of substance' in whom there is an eternal present with neither past nor future. The affirmation of the singularity of God's being is preceded by a hesitation—'if one may so speak'— as if Thomas knows that he has waded into a more fluid and boundless possibility of being than that which can be expressed within the singularity of Aristotle's God. The God of Exodus 3 bears some resemblance to Plato's *khora* in the account that Thomas borrows from John Damascene, and this in turn gestures towards the maternal being of the Trinity who has yet to make an appearance in the ordering of Thomas's ideas in the *Summa theologiae*.

Plato's *khora* is subtly other than the *chaos* of pre-Socratic thought. It emerges in the context of a poetic and opaque description of the threefold structure of the cosmos in the *Timaeus*, in which perceptible nature, defined as transient entities that are modelled on the forms, is positioned between two unchanging dimensions: the eternal reality of the forms, which constitutes the domain of true understanding and is accessible only to the gods and to a very few wise people, and the timeless space of the *khora*, which is knowable only by way of an intuitive apprehension of something beyond conceptualization or perception, but which constitutes the necessary condition for the existence of natural and sensory phenomena:

> [W]e must agree that that which keeps its own form unchangingly, which has not been brought into being and is not destroyed, which neither receives into itself anything else from anywhere else, nor itself enters into anything else anywhere, is one thing. It is invisible – it cannot be perceived by the senses at all – and it is the

---

[26] ST I, 13, 11, quoting John Damascene (*De Fide Orth.* i).

role of understanding to study it. The second thing is that which shares the other's name and resembles it. This thing can be perceived by the senses, and it has been begotten. It is constantly borne along, now coming to be in a certain place and then perishing out of it. It is apprehended by opinion, which involves sense perception. And the third type is space, which exists always and cannot be destroyed. It provides a fixed state for all things that come to be. It is itself apprehended by a kind of bastard reasoning that does not involve sense perception, and it is hardly even an object of conviction. We look at it as in a dream when we say that everything that exists must of necessity be somewhere, in some place and occupying some space, and that that which doesn't exist somewhere, whether on earth or in heaven, doesn't exist at all.[27]

Plato attributes maternal and paternal characteristics to his threefold dimension of being:

> we need to keep in mind three types of things: that which comes to be, that in which it comes to be, and that after which the thing coming to be is modelled, and which is the source of its coming to be. It is in fact appropriate to compare the receiving thing to a mother, the source to a father, and the nature between them to their offspring.[28]

Reflection on the *khora* is 'bastard reasoning' because it is fatherless, being neither conceptual nor sensory and associated with the maternal receptacle prior to its insemination and formation into perceptible entities.

Thomas's God is not the *khora*, but the idea of the *khora* provides a potent storehouse of analogies that might enable us to elaborate on his oceanic imagery, while deconstructing the language of form that creeps again and again into his theology in a way that distorts his most fundamental doctrinal insights about the nature of being.

I have shown that Thomas is far more willing to use the language of form as an appropriate analogy for speaking of God than the language of matter, and yet he cannot escape the pervasive influence of material/maternal analogies when he tries to speak of the divine mystery beyond the logic of Aristotelian philosophy. A postmodern Thomism, responsive to the challenge of feminism, needs to make visible this neglected and repressed dimension of Thomas's theological language, in order to bring to the surface a less contradicted, less sexually antagonistic vision of the divine being. Thomas's God is a greater, more all-encompassing, and more personal mystery than Plato's form or Aristotle's prime mover. Only by expanding the analogical framework to include all that is, whatever we call it—form, matter, *khora*, *hyle*—can we begin to break the ideological constraints that for nearly two millennia have

---

[27] Plato, 'Timeaus', in Plato, *Complete Works*, ed. John M. Cooper (Indianapolis IN and Cambridge UK: Hackett Publishing Co.), 52a–b, pp. 1254–5.

[28] Plato, 'Timeaus', 50d, p. 1253.

tethered God the Father of Jesus Christ with violent force to the formal principles of Greek philosophy, with disastrous consequences for gendered and sexual relationships, and for the understanding of nature within the Christian tradition.

If the *khora* is one potential resource for this transformation of theology, then we need to remember that, as Kearney points out, this is in no sense 'a normal mother'—heaven forbid. No mother can or should seek such totality in the life of her child, and no human can ever overcome that primordial cut that births us into the world and makes space for us to be as other than the mother who bore us. But there is a love that emerges within that space of separation, a love beyond all that we can possibly experience, give, or expect as the mortal, finite beings that we are. If we attend carefully enough to what Thomas is telling us, we discover that, in spite of himself, he invites us to recognize that this love is the unsayable plenitude of the maternal Trinity.

Christianity is not monotheistic and neither is it polytheistic. Its God is beyond form and matter, and forms and matter are reconciled with one another beyond the primal cut of philosophical castration through their union within the being of God in the fully human and fully divine natures of Christ. This introduces a radical instability into all attempts to rationalize theological language in philosophical terms. The mystery of the Trinity is a reconciliation between the one and the many, form and matter, creator and creation. The relational unity of God in the Trinity, creation *ex nihilo*, and the incarnation and resurrection, form the parameters within which we can speak of God as mother and father, form and matter, providing we always bear in mind that our language is analogical, poetic, mystical, expressive of a desire for that which the world cannot give in any of its relationships or objects, and yet within which God is present in all its relationships and objects.

MYSTICISM OF THE BODY

This calls for a mystical theology of the body. In Lacanian terms, it means that the desiring and suffering body must replace the phallus as the umbilical cord that connects meaning to truth, not now as the bar that prohibits desire, but as the narrow path that leads through and beyond the incarnate and crucified body of Christ to the delight of being in God. This is what makes meaning true—the love of God materialized in Christ and revealed through the body of the human other and in the wonder of the universe that was created in and through him. Meaning does not float free in the relativistic drift of the postmodern abyss, nor does it transcend all the diversity and desire of bodily beings to become codified in the abstraction of the *diktats* issued by the state, the law, or the magisterium. The body matters, and only by insisting upon that can we discover the meaning that emerges from the site of truth. Instead of the phallic bar against desire, the bar that silences the mother tongue of the body's ecstasy and sorrow, the desiring, ecstatic, and suffering body is an opening into God and the goodness of God's creation. For Thomas, it is the only opening that there possibly can be into God, for we are essentially embodied beings. The body is the threshold between our own souls and the rest of creation, and God passes backwards and forwards across that threshold by way of imagination and desire.

If the body is God's way of entry into the human soul, then anything that hurts that body or causes it to suffer as an act of violence, exploitation, or in the name of some abstract cause is a violation of the being of God. Thus the prohibition against harm becomes the restraint—the taboo—that the body imposes upon form, upon abstraction, upon any idea or ideal, however good it might seem, which would regard the sacrifice of a single human body as a price worth paying for its achievement. That, surely, is the silent protest of Christ on the cross—the protest of the incarnate being of God against every religious and secular authority which declares that 'it is better for you that one man die for the people than that the whole nation perish' (John 11:50). When 'the people' or 'the whole nation' deems that a victim must die for the good of the concept (these are after all only concepts—'the economy', 'the market', 'the nation', 'the people', 'the enemy', 'the law', 'the form'), then the God who is incarnate in the eternal and elemental particularity of the person is crucified anew.

All this means that we have more to fear from the form than the body. Even Thomas acknowledges that matter remains sinless in relation to form, and it is the will, not the body, that constitutes the source of sin—although the body can be dragged into the torments of hell along with the soul. Lacan is right. The truth is not in the form which is corrupted by every kind of theological distortion and hubris and prey to every passing ideology. The truth is to be discovered in the body's innocence and grace, in the body's desire and suffering, in the eloquence of the body that speaks its own language and reveals its own meaning—not just the individual human body, but the wondrous body of nature within which we ourselves belong and upon which we depend.

REDEEMING MATTER

For Thomas, the word 'nature' encompasses all that is not God but is also of God, for it is God's creation. Unlike other creation myths, the Book of Genesis does not begin with an act of ontological violence and separation. God does not impose forms upon eternal *chaos*, nor is there any conflict between forms and matter, because the cosmos coheres by way of love and desire, not by way of conflict and force. God evokes being out of nothing, and creation is desire's response to that evocation. So what is there, in the beginning?

> At the start Elohim created the skies and the earth
> – the earth was tohu-bohu
> darkness on the face of the deep
> and the breath of Elohim
> hovering on the face of the waters – (Genesis 1:1–2)[29]

What is this mysterious darkness of the deep—this '*tohu-bohu*' by way of which the Hebrew poetry of Genesis denotes the origins of creation? The word *Elohim* is plural, although it can also have a singular meaning, and it is used elsewhere to refer to goddesses as well as to gods.[30] The words *tohu-bohu* are translated in the King James Version as 'without form, and void'. The imagery is mystical, perplexing as to the nature of God and the nature of origins, evoking in the human hearer some primal rhythm that is dark and deep, oceanic and formless, profoundly elusive as to its meanings. What is there in the beginning, in that primal void at the very edges of language and being before they dissolve into silence and emptiness? Let me suggest that Thomas invites us to interpret it as desire: creation originates in desire for God. As spaces for otherness open up within the being of God, as the plenitude of the perfection of being recedes to create potency and becoming, the first response that emerges within the lack of being is the desire to become.

Thomas considers an argument that 'goodness implies desirability. Now primary matter does not imply desirability, but rather that which desires. Therefore primary matter does not contain the formality of goodness. Therefore not every being is good.'[31] Here is Thomas's response:

> As primary matter has only potential being, so it is only potentially good. Although, according to the Platonists, primary matter may be said to be a non-being on account of the privation attaching to it, nevertheless, it does participate to a certain extent in goodness, viz. by its relation to, or aptitude for, goodness. Consequently, to be desirable is not its property, but to desire.[32]

I believe this short passage is the key to unlocking the heart of Lacan's Thomism, for it suggests that the primordial other that God brings into being in the act of creation is desire itself, and desire is active, not passive. Thomas seems to be suggesting that prime matter is unformed desire—it is

---

[29] This translation is from Mary Phil Korsak, *At the Start ... Genesis Made New: A Translation of the Hebrew Text* (Louvain: European Series, Louvain Cahiers, No. 124, 1992). The comments that follow are from Korsak's explanation of her approach to biblical translation in a workshop on her website: <http://www.maryphilkorsak.com/1workshop.html> [accessed 20 July 2012].

[30] 1 Kings 11:5: 'For Solomon went after Ashtoreth the goddess [*Elohim*] of the Zidonians'; 1 Kings 11:33, 'Because that they have forsaken me, and have worshipped Ashtoreth the goddess [*Elohim*] of the Zidonians'.

[31] ST I, 5, 3.   [32] ST I, 5, 3.

matter desiring forms. But do we need to edge a little further away from dualism towards an even more elusive possibility? If prime matter is desire, and if all beings desire God's being, then we are still too likely to equate desirous maternal matter with a desirable paternal God as form. There will always be an inherent opposition to matter lurking in such dualisms, for formless matter will continue to be endowed with a voracious appetite which threatens to consume the form that is God and the man made in His image. Pushed to its extreme, the copulation between gendered desirous matter and divine form implied in Thomas's cosmology mutates into an incarnational theology of divine violence as forceful penetration into the sexualized female body of the cosmos or, in ecclesiological terms, the body of the Church, as I have argued elsewhere in an analysis of the theology of Hans Urs von Balthasar.[33]

But we have seen that, for Thomas, desire for God is the movement of mutual attraction that connects forms with matter, concepts with objects, language with bodies, which mobilizes the body to act in the world by materializing the will. Desire is the current that flows through all the filaments of creation and draws all beings towards the being of God. The other of God might then be desire itself, the trace/grace of the divine being that lingers when God creates space for otherness to become. Within this space, desire evokes into being both forms and matter simultaneously as the coming into being of the things of the world, all of which come to be through their desire for God, as the density of the divine being opens itself to allow otherness to become and thus gives birth to creation *ex nihilo*. Although Thomas does not explore the implications of claiming that 'to desire' is the property of prime matter, in making such a claim he acknowledges that even at its most elemental level, being is suffused with the active love of God in such a way that it is always drawn towards God through desire. In other words, before forms or matter come to be, desire is, and it is graced through and through with the being of God. Desire is the wisdom of God transformed into the space of the coming into being of otherness and difference that constitutes creation.

The arousal of desire by the withdrawal of divine plenitude is the primordial creative act by way of which difference comes to be within the being of God. Without such desire, creation would dissipate into an infinitely expanding universe tending towards nothing, beyond all relationality that holds things in being. But if desire loses its equilibrium in the other direction and becomes too voracious or intense, the spaces that allow for difference between beings begin to collapse into a black hole, so that self and other become locked in a violent struggle for fusion and sameness, or the individual lapses into

---

[33] Tina Beattie, *New Catholic Feminism: Theology and Theory* (London and New York: Routledge, 2006).

psychosis. This is what Kearney sees as the threat of the postmodern abyss, with its intimations of madness, torture, and claustrophobic imprisonment (see Chapter 17).

We live in strange and disordered times, but this is no time to tear up the holy books and let go of the wisdom of the ancients. Rather, we must ask what we have missed, what we have to read again, and read differently, to unearth the God of the possible—the God whose coming now rests not in the making of forms but in the gracing of matter. If Thomas is to be a resource for this, I am appealing for a different reading of Thomas, against himself and also against his critics. So let me move on, to seek out more of the wisdom of Thomas beyond Aristotle.

THE WISDOM OF DESIRE

In the Book of Proverbs, wisdom is a mysterious feminized presence who is birthed by God before the beginning of the world:

> The Lord possessed me at the beginning of His way,
> Before His works of old.
> I have been established from everlasting,
> From the beginning, before there was ever an earth.
> When *there were* no depths I was brought forth,
> When *there were* no fountains abounding with water.
> Before the mountains were settled,
> Before the hills, I was brought forth;
> While as yet He had not made the earth or the fields,
> Or the primal dust of the world. (Prov. 8:22–6)[34]

Thomas quotes the Book of Wisdom in the context of his most lavish expression of a maternal trinitarian theology, which is to be found in the Introduction to his *Commentary on Boethius's Trinity*.[35] He opens with a quotation: 'I will seek her out from the beginning of her birth, and bring the knowledge of her to light' (Wis. 6:24). He goes on to contrast that which can be known through the natural light of reason, and that which can be discovered only through the wisdom of revelation. Then he specifies that

---

[34] *The New King James Version*, Thomas Nelson, Inc., 1982.

[35] See Thomas Aquinas, *On Boethius on the Trinity—Questions 1–4*, trans. Rose E. Brennan S. H. N. (Herder, 1946). Sanctum Thomae de Aquino, *Super Boetium De Trinitate*, Textum a Bruno Decker Lugduni Batauorum 1959 editum ac automato translatum a Robert Busa SJ in taenias magneticas denuo recognovit Enrique Alarcón atque instruxit. In what follows, I refer to the parallel Latin/English texts available at the Logic Museum website: <http://www.logicmuseum.com/authors/aquinas/superboethiumq1.htm> [accessed 21 July 2012].

The matter of this work is the Trinity of Persons in the one, divine essence, that Trinity which has its source in the primal nativity in which divine wisdom is eternally generated by the Father: 'The depths were not as yet, and I was already conceived' (Prov. 8:24), and 'This day have I begotten you' (Ps. 2:7).

This nativity is the beginning of every other nativity, as it is the only one involving perfect participation in the nature of the generator: but all others are imperfect according as the one generated receives either a part of the substance of the generator, or only a similitude: from this it follows that from the aforesaid nativity, every other is derived by a kind of imitation; and thus: 'Of whom all paternity in heaven and in earth is named' (Eph. 3:15); and on this account the Son is called the first-born of every creature (Col. 1:15) so that the origin of nativity and its imitation might be designated, but not according to the same meaning of generation; and therefore it is aptly said: 'I will seek her out from the beginning of her birth.' 'The Lord possessed me in the beginning of his ways' (Prov. 8:22); for not only of creatures is the aforesaid nativity the beginning, but even of the Holy Spirit, who proceeds from the Generator and the Generated.

This is an extraordinary passage, so rich with possibilities that we could rewrite the whole *Summa theologiae* from this perspective, and it might look completely different. We have already seen how, when Thomas risks going beyond analogy to say what is real within the Trinity, he tentatively explores the language of relationality expressed in maternal metaphors of conception and birth (see Chapter 3). Here, we see an earlier exploration of the same themes.

The Trinity, in this account, is an eternal process of giving birth, with feminized Wisdom as the second person of the Trinity. The Holy Spirit also has its eternal origins within this birthing, proceeding from the relationship between the generator and the generated. We should note the absence here of any language of conception or insemination. In creation and in the new creation by way of the Virgin Birth, God creates *ex nihilo*, not through phallic insemination but through the spontaneous fecundity of maternal being. There has in the Catholic tradition been a rich intermingling of both Mary and Christ with the figure of Wisdom, in prismatic exchanges of symbolic meanings that cannot be reduced to rational alternatives between one or the other. The mystery that is revealed between the two is the mystery of a God whose wisdom is revealed in the maternal wonder of the Trinity and the materiality of created desire for God—sublimely expressed in Mary's cry of *jouissance*, when through the Virgin's voice creation opens itself to welcome its creator into the matter of the world.[36]

When Thomas speaks of a birthing of the Son as feminized Wisdom by the Father, and a procession of the Holy Spirit from this primordial and eternal

---

[36] Cf. Tina Beattie, *God's Mother, Eve's Advocate: A Marian Narrative of Women's Salvation* (London and New York: Continuum, 2002).

birth, he is implicitly deconstructing the Aristotelian categories of inseminating form and maternal matter which elsewhere he applies with such rigour to the relationship between fatherhood and motherhood. God the Father is like a mother, and Christ the Son is feminized wisdom, in such a way that Thomas simultaneously deprives the paternal function of its inseminating biological analogy, strips the masculinity of Christ of any essential significance, and divinizes the maternal function by using it as an analogy for God.

To conclude this exploration of how Thomas's trinitarian mysticism deconstructs the patriarchal hierarchies of Aristotelian natural law, I want to turn to a highly significant passage in which Thomas discusses Mary's conception of Christ in trinitarian terms. This enables me to suggest the potential of trinitarian language to elude the control of phallocentrism, and to offer a different theological model of conception and embodiment than that which dominates the theological understanding of fatherhood construed in terms of copulation and insemination.

CONCEIVING CHRIST

Thomas argues that 'The whole Trinity effected the conception of Christ's body',[37] but this is attributed to the Holy Spirit because it was through 'the exceeding love of God' that Christ took to himself the Virgin's flesh, and because the Son of God assumed human nature not because of its merits but because of grace. Elaborating on this, Thomas explains that, while the whole Trinity was involved in the conception of Christ, the role of each person in the Trinity differs in relation to the other. So God is Father because of his authority in sending the Son, he is Son because he is the one sent to assume a body, and he is Holy Spirit because he forms the body of the Son. Thus the Son is consubstantial with the Spirit by reason of his divine personhood, but he is formed by the Spirit by reason of his human body. Thomas goes on to consider why the Holy Spirit is not then the Father of the Son. He responds that, while in human generation a man is called son because he bears the likeness of his father, and he is a son of God because he bears an imperfect likeness to God, being created in the image of God, Christ is the Son of the Father in a perfect and eternal relationship. So, although the Holy Spirit was the active principle in Christ's human conception, he is not the Father of Christ in terms of the eternal generative relationship by which the Son is of one being with the Father.

---

[37] ST III, 32, 1.

This discussion is dense and allusive, perhaps because Thomas's trinitarianism introduces a mystical unknowability into his Aristotelian notions of insemination, generativity, and formation. The fecundity of the Trinity scrambles the tidy logic of Thomas's Aristotelianism and invites a paradigmatic shift in our understanding of nature, God, and gender, but Thomas fails to follow through on this to ask what its implications might be for the Christian understanding of motherhood and the role of women in Church and society. Whatever else we can say, it is clear that the direct line of logic by which he underwrites the primacy of the human father and social and domestic patriarchal hierarchies of love and obedience through an appeal to the paternal generativity of the Aristotelian prime mover and the primacy of form over matter, begins to shift and come apart when he has to introduce a trinitarian perspective into the argument. God is not the Father of Jesus Christ because he is an inseminating first principle, but because of the nature of the relationship between them. The Holy Spirit gives form to the body of Christ, but that role does not involve fatherhood. The Virgin remains silent and excluded, and yet she speaks as the matter/mother of creation that actively responds to God with a desire so intense that it materializes itself as the very being of God. The procreative biology of the male body has nothing to do with any of this. Any attempt to link biological insemination with God in order to legitimate the patriarchal social order finds itself on shaky ground from the perspective of trinitarian and incarnational theology.

Beyond these theological and theoretical endeavours, just by immersing oneself within the pages of scripture, one discovers a nature that flourishes and seethes, that sings and shouts and cries out again and again and again, bearing witness to God against the deaf obstinacy of human ignorance. In the beginning, we discover God within the garden of creation, and human defiance of God results in alienation from nature, including human nature with its sexual cadences of love and desire. God offers Job no explanation for his suffering, but directs his attention instead to the majesty and mystery of creation. Nature spurns the well-intentioned theodicies and moralizing platitudes of Job's friends, rising up in Job's imagination as the only reliable witness to and mouthpiece of God. The psalmist sings of a day when the beasts and the trees and the mountains and the rivers will cry out with joy to God and live in the peace of a healed creation. Jesus draws our attention to the lilies of the field, to the mother hen who broods over her chicks. The seas and the trees obey his command. And Jesus brings God into the visceral, bloody, fleshy depths of matter itself, in order to heal the wound that divided matter from God, which castrated creation by the power of the phallic God—the serpent who divides us between good and evil, and makes sure that we will always have good cause to kill one another in the name of God.

How can theology discover a mother tongue that might yet speak into human becoming the maternal trinitarian being of God, a God whose maternal cries struggle to be heard above the militant violence of the men who prophesy in his name?

> The Lord shall go forth like a mighty man;
> He shall stir up *His* zeal like a man of war.
> He shall cry out, yes, shout aloud;
> He shall prevail against His enemies.

> 'I have held My peace a long time,
> I have been still and restrained Myself.
> *Now* I will cry like a woman in labor,
> I will pant and gasp at once.' (Isa. 42:13–14)[38]

What might language look like, if the body became its medium rather than the phallus being its prohibition? In asking this question, I conclude this book with a different voice, with the voice of a woman who might be read as the Other of Thomas—the body wherein Thomas's theology came to dwell, and birthed a different vision of the same God. In Catherine of Siena, the Thomist body speaks.

---

[38] *The New King James Version*, Thomas Nelson, Inc., 1982.

19

Catherine of Siena: Writing the Body of God

In *Seminar XX* Jacques Lacan calls attention to the language of medieval female mysticism as an expression of *jouissance* capable of expressing something of the Other of the One God of philosophy and ontotheology. This is a voice that Lacan claims cannot be written, for like the voice of the analysand, it is essentially embodied and ephemeral. It is a mother tongue that constitutes the body's wisdom, desire, and response to suffering and joy before and beyond its inscription and abstraction within the grammatical structures and intellectual concepts of the linguistic order. This would render impossible any attempt to inscribe an incarnate faith within theology, without thereby surrendering its claim to truth.

In this chapter, I turn to Catherine of Siena to offer a different interpretation of the significance of mystical theology from that offered by Lacan. I choose Catherine because, as a Dominican, her theology is deeply influenced by Thomas, and yet her *Dialogue* offers an altogether different theological style from that of the *Summa theologiae*.[1] It affords an opportunity to ask what form Thomas's theology might take, if instead of seeking to transcend the body in its intellectual quest, it took the body as its primary locus of revelation and meaning.

Bodies ooze, bleed, burn, weep, and suppurate in the pages of Catherine's *Dialogue*. Their linguistic presence makes all the more noticeable the absence of bodies from Thomas's *Summa theologiae*. If, as Lacan suggests, the Aristotelian privileging of the soul over the body and form over matter inverts the relationship between the two, what happens if we seek an incarnational theology that makes the mystical body of the incarnate Christ the only true medium by way of which God can be known and spoken about within the confines of human understanding? Beyond the dualistic separation of form and matter, this is a positioning of all Christian theology within the organic, sacramental body of the incarnate God.

---

[1] See Catherine of Siena, *The Dialogue*, trans. Suzanne Noffke OP (New York and Mahwah: Paulist Press, 1980).

For much of the *Summa theologiae*, Thomas's God is presented in the language of philosophical reason that tames the mystical wilderness and contains it within the rationalized structures of Aristotelian philosophy. To read Catherine is to confront a radical otherness in terms of theological style, although I shall argue that, contrary to what Lacan suggests, this is as carefully crafted and theologically orthodox as Thomas's theology. Yet in theology, language matters, for style and substance are one and the same thing. If grammar is an analogy for God, then the language in which we communicate about God is of fundamental importance. That is why feminism constitutes such a potent challenge to the theological traditions and practices of the Church.

Language ensouls us, for it enables us to develop a sense of a coherent and unified self out of the swirling cosmos within which we discover ourselves to be. At every step of human development, from the ensoulment of the foetus to separation from the mother through the acquisition of language and the gradual formation of a sense of personal identity, the soul is dependent upon the body to provide what it needs in order to become, but it in turn offers back to the body the narratives and meanings it needs to materialize its freedom and desire, its love or its hatred for those around it. If our bodies give form to our souls, our souls in turn give form to our bodies. We need to twist Thomas's Aristotelian and gendered hierarchies of being into the incessant dynamism of mind and matter shimmering together as the wondrous body of God that constitutes creation beyond all the copulations and ontologies of the ancient world, and to discover ourselves within that as the infinitely complex creatures that we are, yearning and crying out for the living God who is nowhere and everywhere around us.

Christian language about God means nothing unless it materializes God within the habits and customs of human life, and therefore there is never a theological style that does not produce a corresponding substance in the form of deified bodies shaped within its linguistic parameters. Language matters, and Catherine shows us a different way of configuring the relationship between the substance of a life, the style of a theology, and the divine mystery that suffuses both with grace.

CATHERINE OF SIENA IN CONTEXT

Catherine was born into a large Sienese family in 1347. In her lifetime Siena was stricken by plague and riven with political conflict. She became a Mantellata—a lay Dominican—in 1364 and, after a life of intense activity of caring for the poor, preaching, and involvement in the complex papal politics of her time, she died a slow and agonizing death brought on by self-starvation and exhaustion in Rome in 1380, a month after her thirty-third birthday.[2] Politician, spiritual leader, tireless servant of the poor, and uninhibited lover and bride of the incarnate Christ, she was, in the words of Suzanne Noffke, 'a mystic activist'.[3] She offers a model of Christian spirituality that turns Thomas inside out, and it is here that I believe she can serve as a guide to a postmodern Thomism through and beyond Thomas, without denying that she is a deeply challenging character with regard to our modern concepts of the flourishing Christian life.

As a young adult, Catherine spent several years in solitude and contemplation, shutting herself away in a small room in the family home, avoiding all human company as far as possible, and waging war on her body with violent practices of self-flagellation and starvation. This was perhaps a mimesis of the eremitical ideal that was promoted by Thomas and his contemporaries, although as in everything she did, Catherine took it to an extreme that might have shocked the more pragmatic Thomas. Much has been written about Catherine's asceticism, and feminist critics have used her as an example of the effects of Christian misogyny and sexual repression on women's lives.[4] As I have already suggested, these are important challenges with regard to the place of the female body in the Christian tradition, but secular culture has, if anything, proved a more virulent enemy. Women today no longer believe in God, but eating disorders proliferate. My purpose here, however, is not to study Catherine's life but her theological style, bearing in mind my caveat that ultimately, in Christian theology, the two are not so easy to keep separate.

Like most people of her time, Catherine was illiterate, at least in her early adult life. As a young woman she learned to read after a fashion, and later in life she claimed that she had been miraculously taught to write in her sleep by God, who was accompanied by the evangelist John and Thomas Aquinas. Like Thomas, Catherine would have produced her theology and letters mainly by dictation to scribes. She subtly made the point that Thomas's study gave him no great theological advantage over her. She said that God had told her to 'Consider the glorious Thomas. With his mind's eye he contemplated my Truth ever so tenderly and there gained light beyond the natural and knowledge infused by grace. Thus he learned more through prayer than through

---

[2] For a scholarly account of Catherine's life, see Suzanne Noffke, *Catherine of Siena: Vision of a Distant Eye* (Collegeville MN: Liturgical Press, Michael Glazier, 1996). For a more popular account, see Don Brophy, *Catherine of Siena: A Passionate Life* (London: Darton, Longman and Todd, 2011).

[3] Suzanne Noffke OP, 'Introduction', in Catherine of Siena, *The Dialogue*, p. 9.

[4] Cf. Grace Jantzen, *Power, Gender and Christian Mysticism* (Cambridge: Cambridge University Press, 1995), pp. 216–23. See also Rudolph M. Bell, *Holy Anorexia* (Chicago and London: University of Chicago Press, 1987), pp. 22–53; Caroline Walker Bynum, *Holy Feast and Holy Fast: The Religious Significance of Food to Medieval Women* (Berkeley CA: University of California, 1987).

human study'.[5] It is prayer, not a university education nor an ability to understand Greek philosophy, that communicates true knowledge of God—a claim that Thomas himself would have endorsed.

Living a century after Thomas, Catherine belonged among the lay women's movements that were widespread across Europe during the late Middle Ages—the beguines in the north, and various groups known as *pinzochere* (penitent women) in Italy.[6] Dominicans and Franciscans provided spiritual direction to these women, acting as their spiritual guides and confessors, and providing such theological education as they needed to guard against heresy and protect their virtue. Always at risk of being accused of heresy, some of these women such as Marguerite Porete were burned at the stake, although recent scholarship is providing evidence of the extent to which their vernacular theologies are often profoundly orthodox, subtle, and worthy of a place alongside their better-known male counterparts within the theological tradition.[7] They are indeed a different theological voice, and one that has been ignored, condemned, or devalued because of the enduring effects of the medieval decision that there was no place for women in the institutions of learning, teaching, and preaching. We have only fragments of this lost vernacular tradition that found a fragile space of survival in forgotten libraries or convent archives, or because the texts had been widely enough distributed to remain in circulation beyond the deaths of their authors, sometimes anonymously.

However, it is also worth noting that the Catholic Church has done more than any other religious tradition to preserve at least some memory of its women saints and mystics through their lives and writings, albeit only those who were approved and validated by the male hierarchy. In the last half century, four women have been made Doctors of the Church—Teresa of Ávila, Catherine of Siena, Thérèse de Lisieux, and, in 2012, Hildegard of Bingen. If we remember the failed attempt to have her writings included in the curriculum of the University of Paris (see Chapter 8), we might mark this as a symbolic moment of epochal change in the intellectual style and traditions of Catholic theology, albeit one that is being birthed with great pain in conflicting interpretations of the Second Vatican Council and its ramifications.

Catherine's lifelong spiritual advisor, confessor, and friend was the Dominican Raymond of Capua, who became Master of the Dominicans soon after

---

[5] Catherine of Siena, *The Dialogue*, p. 339.
[6] See Brophy, *Catherine of Siena*, pp. 32–3.
[7] Cf. Eliana Corbari, *Vernacular Theology: Dominican Sermons and Audience in Late Medieval Italy* (Berlin and Boston MA: Walter de Gruyter GmbH & Co. KG, forthcoming); Bernard McGinn, *Meister Eckhart and the Beguine Mystics* (New York: Continuum, 1994); Bernard McGinn, *The Varieties of Vernacular Mysticism: 1350–1550* (New York: Crossroad Publishing Company, 2013).

her death and wrote the most famous account of her life.[8] Her own work survives in the form of *The Dialogue* and a vast number of letters[9] addressed to the full range of Italian society, from friends and family to popes and nobility. Her theology offers a Thomism that is filtered through the imaginative bodily encounter between Catherine's soul and God within the mystical body of Christ and the Church, in a way that transfigures Thomas's Aristotelianism and gives a vivid sense of what, in Lacanian terms, the Other of Thomas's One God might be, if his lavish maternal trinitarianism were given a greater space of linguistic freedom and creativity.

It is against this brief background that I consider more closely how Catherine might be interpreted in a way that illuminates or calls into question some of the ideas that I have explored in staging this encounter between Lacan and Thomas. I begin with a short critical survey that helps me to position Catherine in relation to Lacan's theory of mysticism.

WRITING THE MYSTICAL BODY

Luce Irigaray is highly critical of Lacan's reading of female mysticism in *Seminar XX*, accusing him of appropriating women's voices—as she claims men always have done—rather than allowing those voices to be heard in their own right.[10] She reminds us that it might be more difficult than it seems for men to avoid inscribing women's experience into their projected interpretations of female desire, so that what we are encountering is not the self-representation of the woman who speaks, but her incorporation into an economy of desire interpreted in terms of men's experience of sexuality, God, and otherness with regard to fear and desire, castration and lack. In her complex historiography of medieval mysticism and French critical theory, Amy Hollywood makes a similar point. She argues that both medieval hagiographers and modern interpreters filter the voices of female mystics through their own grids of meaning, authenticating them, pathologizing them, or demonizing them in ways that meet their own desire for affirmation or express their own anxieties, depriving women of the authority to authenticate and represent themselves.[11]

---

[8] Raymond of Capua, *The Life of Catherine of Siena*, ed. and trans. Conleth Kearns OP (Dublin and Wilmington: Dominican Publications and Michael Glazier, Inc., 1980).

[9] Catherine of Siena, *The Letters of St Catherine of Siena*, Vols I–IV, trans. Suzanne Noffke (Tempe: Medieval and Renaissance Texts and Studies, 2000, 2001, 2007, 2008). I refer here to the edited collection of letters in Catherine of Siena, *I, Catherine: Selected Writings of Catherine of Siena*, ed. and trans. Kenelm Foster OP and Mary John Ronayne OP (London: Collins, 1980).

[10] See Luce Irigaray, 'Così Fan Tutti', in *This Sex Which Is Not One*, trans. Catherine Porter with Carolyn Burke (Ithaca NY: Cornell University Press, 1985), pp. 86–105.

[11] See Amy Hollywood, *Sensible Ecstasy: Mysticism, Sexual Difference, and the Demands of History* (Chicago and London: The University of Chicago Press, 2002).

In her comparison between Raymond of Capua's *Life of Catherine of Siena* and the saint's own writings, Karen Scott points out how Raymond tends to exaggerate the bodily and paranormal experiences of Catherine's life and to downplay both her intense activity and the theological rigour of her writing. He likes to portray her as 'dead', so that she appears to be the passive vehicle for supernatural manifestations by way of which God sought to save souls through her prayer and preaching. Scott suggests that, 'Raymond's "Catherine" tells us much about the history of how live saints were perceived and dead saints were revered . . . [I]n his desire to foster her canonization, he downplayed or omitted information that would have made her appear too strong a woman to be considered a saint.'[12] By contrast, Scott points out that, rather than emphasizing the more spectacular aspects of her mystical experiences and spiritual insights, 'Catherine sought an ever deeper rooting of Christian doctrine within her soul—memory, intellect, and will—through an exchange of words with God. Her mysticism is expressed in speech about divine love, not in visions or silence, and it is unusually sober and theological in nature.'[13]

Every written source comes to us through layers of interpretation that can appropriate or distort the original voice, and this is why Lacan insists that every act of writing violates the body's mother tongue. There is, as Lacan reminds us, no prediscursive reality, and there is no immediacy of access to any encrypted life. There are, however, ways of reading texts so that they become part of the performative materiality of individual lives and communities, and that is how Catholics have always read their theological and devotional texts. The problem with such readings of the texts of women mystics is that they risk rekindling masochistic desires associated with the relationship between the female body and God, as this has been inscribed, communicated, and practised according to the projection of men's fears and desires onto the bodies of women, and women's internalization of these, through much of Christian history.

SEXING THE MYSTICAL BODY

Another question that arises is that of how much significance should be accorded to sexual difference. That Thomas and Catherine write very differently is not in doubt, and neither is the fact that much of that difference in

---

[12] Karen Scott, 'Mystical Death, Bodily Death: Catherine of Siena and Raymond of Capua on the Mystic's Encounter with God', in Catherine M. Mooney (ed.), *Gendered Voices: Medieval Saints and Their Interpreters* (Philadelphia PA: University of Pennsylvania Press, 1999), pp. 136–67, 143.
[13] Scott, 'Mystical Death, Bodily Death', p. 138.

style reflects the gendered differences between the lives of medieval male scholars and women. As a woman, Catherine could not possibly have written in the style of Thomas, for she had no access to the conventions and rules of Latin scholasticism. Gendered difference was institutionalized and codified at every level of late medieval life. Women had to speak from within the worlds to which they were assigned, and to claim such authority as they could through direct authorization by God—which, in Catherine's case, includes 'authoring' God's voice within her own texts.

Yet a more complex question arises if we ask how far the obvious difference in style represents *sexual* difference, rather than the gendered cultural contexts within which people lived and wrote. In other words, is it best to read Catherine as a woman who constitutes a sexual other in relation to Thomas, or is it best to read her as a *human* other who expresses something of the bodily and emotional excess that was sacrificed in the making of Thomas's intellectual world with its abstract ideals and sexual separatism? Not all of those excluded from that elite body of scholars were women but all women were excluded, and therefore the construction of sexual difference cannot help but reflect the differences in opportunity, learning, language, and lifestyle that marked out the medieval scholar from his sexual other, which made of woman a sex primarily defined in terms of negation, lack, and exclusion.

For us today, when the intellectual and social barriers between the sexes are shifting, this is a vital question which goes to the heart of the ongoing struggle to understand how sexual difference does or should shape not only our human identities and relationships but our theological language. Let me turn briefly to Irigaray to ask what it might mean to endorse the language of female mystics in terms of sexual difference.

In a chapter titled 'La Mysterique' in *Speculum of the Other Woman*, Irigaray revisits the site of female mysticism to discern a different possibility—a possibility of difference.[14] The excess of mystical language, its capacity to flood the boundaries of unilinear rationality with a liquid outpouring of desire, its willingness to give voice to the body's extremes of suffering and delight, its endeavour to forge language in the silent extremities of the soul where human consciousness washes up against God and the abyss, might be the speculum, the curved mirror that makes visible the female sex. The speculum warps the Platonic mirrors of western reason and lures 'him' with 'her' into a different way of speaking, but this also threatens 'her' being in the satisfaction of 'his' desire. The woman mystic speaks from the linguistic void where the body's obscene silence and God's unspeakable absence melt and fuse in the Lacanian real. She lays claim to the abyss which she represents, embraces his language of horror

---

[14] See Irigaray, *Speculum of the Other Woman*, trans. Gillian C. Gill (Ithaca NY: Cornell University Press, 1985), pp. 191–202.

and filth, and pushing beyond that arrives at a possible space of her own linguistic coming into being, but she also risks a more radical emptiness and loss. The speculum of female mysticism is a burning glass which sets words on fire, and that fire might be the forge wherein the female subject is formed, or the furnace wherein she is consumed: 'A burning glass is the soul who in her cave joins with the source of light to set everything ablaze that approaches her hearth. Leaving only ashes there, only a hole: fathomless in her incendiary blaze.'[15]

I have engaged with Irigaray extensively in earlier work, but I have increasingly come to see her representation of sexual difference as problematic, for all the reasons I have explored in this book. Her work is a highly subtle, intellectually astute, and ironic deconstruction of the philosophical tradition with its economy of the same and its elision of the sexualized other. Her response is to animate the language of sexual otherness by way of a mimetic parody of femininity, in order to explore the linguistic possibilities of a culture of difference around the copula of divinized desire. Purged of its colonization by the masculine One of the philosophical and theological tradition, this space of the 'sensible transcendental' would open into a fluidity of desire, a third way of being between two which invites the possibility of encounter and differentiation, intimacy and separation, between two sexes without fusion or confusion, rather than the ordering of sexual relationships around perfection and lack, potency and act. The language of fecundity, desire, and the maternal body becomes pregnant with its own symbolic meanings and possibilities, muffling the matricidal and sacrificial discourses of ancient philosophy and modern psychoanalysis, and ushering in a more life-giving culture of embodiment, fecundity, and harmony with nature.

But is this not a return of the same old romanticism—a hunger for the phallic 'all' that the world cannot give, and a refusal of the lack, finitude, and suffering that are an inescapable aspect of what it means to be human? To suggest this is not to deny that there is an urgent need for western culture in general and Christianity in particular to rediscover their lost connections to birth, fecundity, sexuality, and incarnation, and in my earlier work I have explored ways in which that might be expressed through the Marian tradition and the maternal church. Ultimately, however, this must be less than all, if it is to permit us to be human at all. Irigaray reanimates the ancient pagan copula that makes of creation a field of erotic energies flowing towards one another in an incessant dynamism of sexual (be)comings, but in the process Christianity itself becomes caught up in a sexual romance between the incarnate bride/mother and the incarnate lover/son, echoing the erotic fecundity of Christian

---

[15] Irigaray, *Speculum of the Other Woman*, p. 197.

mysticism but purged of its bloody and obscene otherness.[16] It is a Christianity of the imaginary without the haunting absence of the real which Lacan insists has carved an abysmal emptiness in the Christian soul. Paradoxically, this means that Irigaray is all soul and no body—her words are the language of feminized genius, but in the end they lack the stuff that would make them matter.

Hollywood argues that Irigaray fetishizes sexual difference, in such a way that 'she both acknowledges and disavows the fears and desires evoked by human finitude, limitation, and loss—the mortality of the human body'.[17] In Freudian terms, such fetishization fulfils an ambiguous function as 'a substitute for that which is not there' or 'for anxieties generated by what is there'.[18] So Irigaray 'fetishizes sexual difference in response to the absence of women's authority and freedom. At the same time, sexual difference becomes the means through which the losses women (and others) will continue to sustain, even if all women and men were to attain meaningful autonomy, can be evaded.'[19] The fetish thus has a dual function. It becomes the desirable other that will compensate for the sense of lack, and it offers a way of denying that which we fear or resist. Hollywood writes that

> Even in a world in which gender binaries (and other oppressive modes of differentiation) have been overcome or radically transformed, we will still experience bodily limitation and pain; and no matter how long life might extend, we will most certainly die (and no doubt, the experiences of pain and death will continue to be sexualized in various and complex ways). Subjects are always constituted in ambivalent recognition and disavowal of this fragility. Irigaray offers a particularly stark example of how the late twentieth-century return to the body tends to disavow this constitutive fragility through its utopian political projects.[20]

I have already referred to the dangers of modern utopianism and modernity's denial of death (see Chapter 11). Hollywood suggests that attentiveness to the sense of trauma, lack, and anguish that pervades the writings of women mystics can help us to navigate a complex path of joy and suffering through the reality of what it means to be embodied subjects, neither free from nor defined by the effects of sexual difference in biology and culture, but seeking a deeper understanding of the significance of suffering as well as joy, loss as well as desire, for embodied *human* subjectivity rather than *sexual* subjectivity.

---

[16] For the best example of this in Irigaray's writings, see Luce Irigaray, 'the crucified one – epistle to the last christians', in *Marine Lover of Friedrich Nietzsche*, trans. Gillian C. Gill (New York: Columbia University Press, 1991), pp. 164–90.
[17] Hollywood, *Sensible Ecstasy*, p. 235.   [18] Hollywood, *Sensible Ecstasy*, p. 267.
[19] Hollywood, *Sensible Ecstasy*, p. 267.   [20] Hollywood, *Sensible Ecstasy*, p. 272.

Avoidable suffering is not to be welcomed, tolerated, or cultivated, and Hollywood cautions against any acceptance of suffering that would soften the demands of justice. Nevertheless, unavoidable suffering and death itself are part of what it means to be human, and the language of medieval female mysticism can help us towards a deeper understanding of what that means and how to incorporate it into our social rituals and ways of speaking.

DIVINE AND HUMAN BODIES

Although Thomas's ontology is implicitly gendered and his anthropology means that the human is essentially embodied, we never get a sense in the *Summa theologiae* that Thomas or his interlocutors speak from the site of the male body, or indeed any body at all. That they speak as men, to men, and for men is taken for granted, but insofar as 'man' in this intellectual context represents form, the linguistic form itself must be abstracted from the bodies about which it speaks. There is no sense in which the dialectical style of the *Summa theologiae* requires a range of voices that might suggest different bodily positions in relation to one another, for it is the arguments, not the speakers that count. With occasional lapses, it is this abstraction that Thomas strives towards in his theological style—although less so in his biblical commentaries and sermons.

For Catherine, the style is determined by the character who speaks—whether that is God, the soul, or the narrator. While the dialectical style requires an either/or approach, the dialogical style offers both/and, with a much greater sense of plurivocity, fluidity, and subtlety with regard to possible identities, meanings, and subject positions. As Mikhail Bakhtin argues, dialogue deconstructs the unitary self and makes it a relational event, produced within a plurality of voices emanating from differently positioned individual and collective bodies moving in relation to one another in time and space.[21] The 'I' must author itself within these intersecting encounters, for it never has objective access to itself. In Michael Holquist's summary, 'In order to forge a self, I must do so from *outside*. In other words, *I author myself*.'[22] Catherine authors herself as a voice that speaks from within a constantly shifting encounter that entwines body, soul, God, and neighbour in a ceaseless dynamism of love and suffering, hope and anguish. There is no hint of the ontotheology that creeps again and again into Thomas's philosophical theology.

---

[21] For a helpful summary of Bakhtin's ideas, see Michael Holquist, *Dialogism* (London and New York: Routledge, 2002), 2nd edn.

[22] Holquist, *Dialogism*, p. 28.

Catherine knows what she lacks, and she knows that Thomas lacks it too. If we follow Lacan in *Seminar XX*, we might say that her voice is supplementary, not complementary, to that of Thomas. In the division of medieval theology between Latin scholasticism and women's vernacular theologies, women gathered together the bodily and affective metaphors, images, and experiences which constituted the excess or effluvia of scholasticism. From these colourful linguistic scraps impregnated with the flesh and blood of their own bodily lives, they wove together a rich theological tapestry of incarnation, suffering, and Eucharistic devotion, suffused by a visceral intensity of desire.[23]

But Catherine writes not as woman but as human—she repeatedly refers to God addressing her as 'my reasoning creature' (*La mia creatura che à in sé ragione*), which Noffke points out is 'one of Catherine's favourite expressions for the human person'.[24] And, while her God is thoroughly incarnate, the mystical body of Christ transcends gendered definitions. Through the voluptuous enfleshment of theological language, Catherine helps us to see what is lacking in theologies that shun the body in favour of the rationalized discourses of philosophy and systematic theology, or that divide it in terms of ontologies of sexual difference which always leave one sex somewhat empty from the perspective of the other. For Catherine, plenitude and emptiness refer to the relationship between the human and divine, not between man and woman.

But this is not, as Lacan would claim, a stream of consciousness expressing a bodily *jouissance* that she knows nothing about. Catherine is more aware and in control of what she is doing than Lacan would give her credit for in his equation of mysticism with hysteria. The *Dialogue* is a carefully crafted work of theology which knowingly plays with the paradoxes inherent in the language of knowing and not knowing, of being and not being, of speaking as body and speaking as soul, using a variety of narrative voices to express the multiplicity of the self. What might appear as a spontaneous expression of Lacanian *jouissance* is in fact a subtle and painstaking intellectual creation—a literary mimesis of different aspects of Christian experience that is intended to be written, studied, and passed on to educate others. Catherine's texts are not an exercise in female mysticism (she would have had no idea what that term meant), but a contribution to Christian theology. She seeks to take her place alongside Thomas, not as his inferior nor as his feminized mystical other, but as a critic and theologian who—perhaps unintentionally—reveals to us what is too often rendered invisible in his theological style, namely, the incarnate God and the body of the human person made in the image of God.

---

[23] Cf. Caroline Walker Bynum, *Fragmentation and Redemption: On Gender and the Human Body in Medieval Religion* (New York: Zone Books, 1991).
[24] Catherine of Siena, *The Dialogue*, p. 26, n. 3.

That which Thomas conceals in the crafting of his theology, Catherine reveals in the crafting of hers, but this does not make one rational and the other irrational, or one intellectual and the other emotional, or one masculine and the other feminine. Certainly, Catherine's style is more intuitive and free-flowing than that of Thomas, but to say that it is therefore less rational, less intellectual, or more feminine is to impose upon it the very sexual hierarchies and grids of meaning that reinscribe it within the order dictated by Thomas and his contemporaries. As Jane Tylus points out in her study of Catherine's literary style, there is a tendency among scholars of female mystics 'to equate the immediacy associated with femininity and orality with a lack of reflectiveness and agency',[25] but this finds little support in Catherine's actual writings.

Although Tylus makes no reference to Lacan, her study makes clear that Catherine was well aware of how different linguistic styles associated with the spoken and written word function to express different relationships with regard to bodiliness and the symbolic, and she was able to use these with considerable literary nuance. Tylus points out that most of the time Catherine distinguishes between the words *Verbo* and *parola* to communicate subtle differences in meaning. *Parola* refers to the spoken word, which is a more humble term than the incarnate Word (*Verbo*). Generally, Catherine uses *Verbo* in connection with 'adjectives such as *incarnato, vestito, inestato, amoroso*, and *dolce*', in order to communicate a sense of the Word becoming 'grafted onto humanity and made a part of it: "clothed," "enfleshed," at times given to us as food'.[26] Tylus quotes one of Catherine's prayers in which she refers to 'Mary's conception and a birth in which she gave us the 'Word [*Verbo*] through her hands'. ('*Dato è a noi el Verbo etterno per la mani di Maria*').[27]

Elsewhere, however, 'the humbler *parola* becomes either by accident or through design the "*Parola incarnata*"'. Tylus quotes from one of Catherine's letters in which 'she mentions a God who throws the seed of his word into Mary's "field" as he burned with the fire of divine charity ("*gittando el seme de la parola sua nel campo di Maria*"), enabling Mary to "give us the flower of sweet Jesus"'.[28]

'Catherine', then, is a complex literary creation whose author (the woman Catherine of Siena) authorizes herself as the narrator of a life ('I, Catherine'). This narrator is differentiated from the soul whom Catherine refers to always in the third person, and who is addressed by God in a dialogical encounter that is played out within the risen body of Christ. Catherine as author orchestrates

---

[25] Jane Tylus, *Reclaiming Catherine of Siena: Literacy, Literature, and the Signs of Others* (Chicago and London: University of Chicago Press, 2009), p. 21.

[26] Tylus, *Reclaiming Catherine of Siena*, p. 180.

[27] Tylus, *Reclaiming Catherine of Siena*, quoting Catherine of Siena, *Orazioni*, prayer 16, p. 29. It is interesting to note the priestly suggestion here—for it is the priest who gives the body of Christ through his hands.

[28] Tylus, *Reclaiming Catherine of Siena*, p. 181.

all these voices, and is fully aware of their different registers, meanings, and communicative capacities.

Lacan wonders how the academic or psychoanalytic master (who might of course be female) can translate *la parole* into discourse without severing it from the body that produced it, thereby abstracting it and 'mastering' its meaning. But Lacan is a romantic who cannot bring himself to let go of the body of woman as his fantasized other, variously projecting onto her the states of his own troubled soul—from the death drive of *Seminar VII* to the mystical *jouissance* of *Seminar XX*. He needs the lack that she is, maybe he even needs her to be the life support system for his unconscious God. Lacan is barred from speaking about God except through the projected voice of the hysteric and/or mystic, but that bar is kept in place by Lacan's own tormented atheism. If he is to speak of the love of God, he can only do so as a voice that comes from outside of himself, so that he ventriloquizes his own Catholic faith.

Catherine has no such problem. Every subject position from which a voice might speak is available for her to appropriate—God (who is not a forbidding phallus but the crucified body of Christ which opens a fleshy passage between heaven and earth); the subject ('I', Catherine—the words with which she begins many of her letters); the non-subject/not-all ('she who is not',[29] the soul that is lack, emptiness, ecstasy, and longing before God); and the real (the blood and fire of the mystical body of Christ which, like the burning bush of Moses, sets the soul ablaze in a non-consuming fire of rapture).[30] For Lacan, the crucified body of Christ blocks the horizons of eternity with endless Sadean torment. For Catherine, that same body opens to embrace the soul and transport it to heaven. Yet this does not simply make Catherine a proto-Irigarayan, for there are dark and violent aspects to her theology which today might be interpreted in terms of the Freudian death drive.

To give one example of this, Catherine writes of souls that long for death. God tells her that, 'With perfect contempt they have done battle with their bodies. Therefore, they have lost that natural tenderness which binds soul and body, having dealt the decisive blow to natural love with contempt for bodily life and love for me.'[31] This hostility towards the body manifests itself in different ways throughout the *Dialogue*, so that a critical reader might see it as a constant lament against the body and its limitations, but Catherine's style eludes any such reductiveness. It cannot be moralized and ordered to suit modern theological desires for everything to have a moral place and everything to be in its moral place, even when such morality is presented as transgressive of the moral norms of heterosexual conservatism. Queer and feminist theologies are often highly domesticated and moralizing

[29] Cf. Catherine of Siena, *The Dialogue*, p. 273.
[30] Catherine of Siena, *The Dialogue*, p. 273.
[31] Catherine of Siena, *The Dialogue*, p. 154.

affairs which also tend towards the utopian glossing of pain, suffering, and violence and their associations with sexuality and desire. Catherine scrambles our theological boundaries in the same way that Lacan does—opening up fields of language and desire that, for the most part, we prefer to ignore.

For medieval women such as Catherine, the body occupied a dominant place amidst the lavish incarnational devotions of popular religion.[32] Everyday life entailed close proximity to other bodies, embroiled in the messy fecundity of sexuality and desire, the inescapable realities of pain, hunger, poverty, disease, and death, the constant trauma of war and violence, the dangers of childbirth, the demands of motherhood, the reek and stench of city life, the struggle to create a life in which anything other than the care and disciplining of bodies could claim one's attention. Catherine served God amidst the poor and sick of plague-ravaged Siena, where she was in constant contact with the most abject of suffering. She lived in an era of widespread clerical abuse and debauchery— there are not a few resonances with the sex abuse scandal that has swept through the Catholic Church in our own times—and she was vehement in her condemnation of what she saw as lust and sexual wantonness, including homosexuality. She was an enthusiastic supporter of the crusades and saw it as a great honour for somebody to be killed in the field of battle for Christ. In other words, she was a woman of her time, and this meant that bodies intruded upon her consciousness with a persistent, demanding clamour for attention in ways that we may experience far less acutely in our disembodied cultures where we are often insulated from the effects of hunger, disease, over-crowding, and death. The bodies that populate the pages of Catherine's *Dialogue* are sometimes abjected, reviled, and despised, but they also have far more of the real about them than the sanitized and anodyne celebrations of embodiment that feature in some modern theologies.

To say that Catherine internalized the stereotypes of her culture's attitudes towards the female body is only half the story, for in complex and ambivalent ways she subverted and transformed these as well. We have seen how, in *Seminar VII*, Lacan associates female *jouissance* with the real of the body, and therefore with death, corruption, and lack. I have also argued that, in Thomas's theology, the difference between maternal matter and demonic sexuality gets blurred because both are associated with lack, so that the female body shifts dangerously between prime matter as potency awaiting form, and as sexual temptress sent by the demons to seduce the man of God. Catherine neither resists nor ignores such associations, but appropriates them and uses them to affirm her own theological authority.

---

[32] Cf. Caroline Walker Bynum, *Wonderful Blood: Theology and Practice in Late Medieval Northern Germany and Beyond* (Philadelphia: University of Pennsylvania Press, 2007); Bynum, *Christian Materiality: An Essay on Religion in Late Medieval Europe* (New York: Zone Books, 2011).

In a section towards the end of the *Dialogue*, the narrator tells us that the soul gives thanks to God for what she has tasted and seen of the divine mystery:

> Thanks, thanks be to you, eternal Father, that you have not despised me, your handiwork, nor turned your face from me, nor made light of these desires of mine. You, Light, have disregarded my darksomeness; you, Life, have not considered that I am death; nor you, Doctor, considered these grave weaknesses of mine. You, eternal Purity, have disregarded my wretched filthiness; you who are infinite have overlooked the fact that I am finite, and you, Wisdom, the fact that I am foolishness.[33]

Catherine transforms the language of filth, foolishness, and death associated with her sex, to make it the language of the soul's intimacy with God. She goes on to describe the soul gazing into the ocean of the Trinity until it becomes a mirror of which she says, 'holding it in the hand of love, it shows me myself, as your creation, in you, and you in me through the union you have brought about of the Godhead with our humanity'.[34] The Trinity becomes the speculum wherein the implicitly sexual stereotypes of society and theology are refracted and the beauty of the creature shines forth, but there is little in Catherine's *Dialogue* to suggest that gender is a significant feature of either the human creature or the risen Christ. While she uses gendered metaphors of erotic and maternal love, the lavish excess of her language scrambles the dividing boundaries between male and female, mother and lover, Christ's body and ours. This allows her simultaneously to rupture and repair Thomas's epistemological frontiers, by way of an elaborate literary conceit which involves a play of voices, the bodies they inhabit, and the movements between them.

LANGUAGE BEYOND CASTRATION

For Thomas as for Lacan, the unknowable is also the unsayable, and the abyss that is God (Thomas) or the real (Lacan) is sealed off from consciousness by this linguistic barrier. So, for Thomas, because the human cannot escape the body to achieve union with God in this life, we can neither understand nor say anything directly about God. Theological language and knowledge run into the buffers of the body. Yet we have also seen how Thomas portrays the man of God as striving to minimize the effects of the body and the imagination with its bodily phantasms, in order to attain to a state of contemplative nearness to

---

[33] Catherine of Siena, *The Dialogue*, p. 364.
[34] Catherine of Siena, *The Dialogue*, p. 366.

God which requires the purification of the intellect from the taint of the body. This is the closest a human can come to God, except in a state of rapture. The highest level of prayer is mind to mind, not body to body. What might prayer be like if, instead of seeking to transcend matter, it plunged into the fleshy heart of divinized matter that constitutes the body of Christ? Catherine gives us an answer of sorts.

Catherine agrees that only in a state of rapture can the soul experience union with God, but for Catherine it is not the disembodied intellect that experiences this rapture but the soul as a metaphorical body rendered translucent by grace, which constitutes the sublime other of the mortal flesh. While Thomas's theology tells us much about the body, desire, nature, and God, Catherine invites us to immerse ourselves within a visceral poetic space of the imagination wherein we are impregnated with love and drenched in blood through our incorporation into the body of Christ. This is because Catherine's God is body, for the body of Christ gives human form to God. She thus maintains the separation between the conceptual, mortal self and God, and yet she allows the imaginary body to migrate across that aporia by way of a daring appropriation of corporeal metaphors to express the union of the soul with the body of Christ which she, Catherine, knows nothing about. Here is an example of her ecstatic apophaticism, in which she describes an exchange between the embodied Catherine and the sublime soul:

> And what shall I say? I will stutter, 'A-a,' because there is nothing else I know how to say. Finite language cannot express the emotion of the soul who longs for you infinitely. I think I could echo Paul's words: The tongue cannot speak nor the ear hear nor the eye see nor the heart imagine what I have seen! What have you seen? 'I have seen the hidden things of God!' And I – what do I say? I have nothing to add from these clumsy emotions. I say only, my soul, that you have tasted and seen the abyss of supreme eternal providence.[35]

Noffke points out that this is the only time in the *Dialogue* where Catherine uses Latin. The words 'I have seen the hidden things of God' are expressed as '*Vidi arcana Dei!*' There is a clear allusion here to the enigmatic account of St Paul's rapture in 2 Corinthians 12:1–4, but this singular use of Latin suggests something of Catherine's literary skill. If the soul must speak of things which it is forbidden to speak of—in the biblical text, 'unspeakable words, which it is not lawful for a human to utter'—then perhaps the shift to Latin communicates something of the enigma of breaching that prohibition, while saying nothing that the mind can grasp. We should note the audacity though, of Catherine's willingness to breach the frontiers of Thomas's apophaticism to penetrate beyond the linguistic bar of prohibition, yet without offering anything by way of knowledge of God that could be incorporated into language

---

[35] Catherine of Siena, *The Dialogue*, pp. 325–6.

except the ecstatic utterances of the soul. This is an expression of *jouissance*, but Catherine is quite capable of the theological encryption of her own *jouissance*, by situating theological language within that river of desire that flows between earth and heaven, body and soul, through the blood and fire of Christ's mystical body.

There is in the *Dialogue* a *jouissance* of unknowing, as Lacan suggests, but the 'she' who does not know is the narrator, not the author. Catherine shows how it is quite possible to achieve an objective distance from the immediacy of the body's joy and anguish, without thereby surrendering authority/authorship with regard to authenticating her own experience. Catherine, like former American Secretary of Defense, Donald Rumsfeld, knows that there are things that we know that we know and there are known unknowns and there are unknown unknowns[36]—but some of the known unknowns become known from the perspective of the mystical body, while remaining unknown from the perspective of the mortal body.

In Catherine's famous analogy of the bridge, the soul ascends from earth to heaven in penitence and tears by way of Christ's crucified body, climbing up from his pierced feet into his heart and finally into his mouth.[37] God tells Catherine,

> When my Son was lifted up on the wood of the most holy cross he did not cut off his divinity from the lowly heart of your humanity. So though he was raised so high he was not raised off the earth. In fact, his divinity is kneaded into the clay of your humanity like one bread.[38]

This is not essentially different from Thomas's theology of deification in relation to the incarnation, but the imagery evokes a more potent sense of what such a theological claim might mean in terms of the essentially embodied human person.

From a feminist perspective, the idea of Catherine's soul becoming fully incorporated into the mystical body of Christ invites criticism if we interpret it as meaning that the female self is negated in the masculinity of Christ. So, when Catherine says of herself, 'I am she who is not',[39] and of Christ that 'he makes of her another himself',[40] we could say that this constitutes an Irigarayan erasure of the female sex in the privileging of the male Christ. But Catherine's favoured metaphor of incorporation—the soul entering into the body of Christ—is uterine, not phallic. The risen body of Christ transcends gender

---

[36] Cf. 'DoD News Briefing—Secretary Rumsfeld and Gen. Myers', U.S. Department of Defense News Transcript, 12 February 2002, at <http://www.defense.gov/transcripts/transcript. aspx?transcriptid=2636> [accessed 5 August 2012]. Rumsfeld's words have been widely quoted.

[37] Catherine of Siena, *The Dialogue*, pp. 64–160.

[38] Catherine of Siena, *The Dialogue*, p. 65.

[39] Catherine of Siena, *The Dialogue*, p. 273.

[40] Catherine of Siena, *The Dialogue*, p. 25.

in its accommodating openness to the human soul. If anything, it is a maternal rather than a male body, but even that is too reductive. It is every possible body described in every possible metaphor, including that of the besotted courtly lover who pursues the elusive object of desire.

Here, in a section just before the apophatic utterances I quoted above, the narrator begins by introducing the soul, who was

> as if drunk with love of true holy poverty ... filled to bursting in the supreme eternal magnificence and so transformed in the abyss of his supreme and immeasurable providence that though she was in the vessel of her body it seemed as if the fire of charity within her had taken over and rapt her outside her body.[41]

The narrator then addresses God, referring to her soul in the third person:

> O eternal Father! O fiery abyss of charity! O eternal beauty, O eternal wisdom, O eternal goodness, O eternal mercy! O hope and refuge of sinners! O immeasurable generosity? O eternal, infinite Good! O mad lover! And you have need of your creature? It seems so to me, for you act as if you could not live without her, in spite of the fact that you are Life itself, and everything has life from you and nothing can have life without you. Why then are you so mad? Because you have fallen in love with what you have made! You are pleased and delighted over her within yourself, as if you were drunk with desire for her salvation. She runs away from you and you go looking for her. She strays and you draw close to her: You clothed yourself in our humanity, and nearer than that you could not have come.[42]

Catherine plays here with the language of courtly love. God is the lover who pursues the reluctant soul, as the knight pursues his unattainable lady. The language of divine desire is most certainly evident, but I am not sure that this is the desire of the Other that Lacan cautions against. Catherine writes with the confidence of one who knows she is loved by God. Although later in life she would plunge once again into the anguish of doubt and self-punishment, the voice here is of one who knows that God asks nothing of her except to receive the love that has already been offered unconditionally in Christ. We might better understand this lavish unconditionality if we consider her account of damnation, and what she regards as the final unforgivable sin.

Like Thomas, Catherine had a vivid awareness of the threat of hell and the presence of demons. God complains to her vociferously and at length about the wickedness of the greedy, the selfish, the proud, the sexually immoral (including priests), so that a casual reading might suggest that this is very much Lacan's God of 'ferocious ignorance'. Yet in a more radical way than

---

[41] Catherine of Siena, *The Dialogue*, p. 325.
[42] Catherine of Siena, *The Dialogue*, p. 325.

Thomas, Catherine always emphasizes that the compassion, mercy, and love of the Trinity expressed in the incarnate Christ are the motivation behind every act of divine judgement, so that there is an unceasing reaching out of love and mercy across the abyss created by sin and rebellion, through the mystical body of Christ. There is no theology of predestination in Catherine, but rather God holds open the offer of salvation to every human life until its very last moment. It is those who in the end refuse this offer who condemn themselves, for God tells Catherine: 'at the very end they had judged their own wretchedness to be greater than my mercy. This is that sin which is never forgiven, now or ever: the refusal, the scorning, of my mercy'.[43] This soteriology anticipates Luther, for it places radical responsibility upon the human capacity to accept the mercy of God, and it makes that mercy absolutely unconditional but not enforced. God's offer of mercy is never withdrawn and there is nothing we can or must do to earn it except receive it, but the human can at the moment of death make a decision to refuse it, and that seals his or her fate for all eternity. Although she plays with the metaphors of divine desire, there is ultimately no desire or need in Catherine's God, only an infinite offer of love that the finite human is free to accept or reject. God needs and asks nothing of us except to know that we are loved. Like the Christ in Francis Thompson's poem, *Hound of Heaven*, Catherine's God pursues her with an infinite love 'down the nights and down the days, . . . down the arches of the years . . . down the labyrinthine ways of my own mind'.

Yet, so far, we might still be in an elaborate Irigarayan fantasy. Catherine becomes the ultimate postmodern theologian, washing away the dry philosophical structures that form the logic of Thomas's theology in a rising linguistic tide of body and blood, sweeping him out to sea and immersing him within the oceanic mystery of the Trinity. There is no end to the number of books we might write—or indeed that have been written—that revel in this creative linguistic freedom to imagine God as the Other of theology's One. But if we are to follow Catherine, we must recognize that God withdraws from all such endeavours, for the incarnate God is not to be found in language, however flamboyant. The incarnate God is only to be discovered, touched, and loved in the bodies of others who, crying out for the touch of the risen Christ, cry out for us to become that touch, that caress, that kiss, that embrace, that feeding and consoling hand of God. Catherine shows us what is lacking from postmodernism—not the naïve and futile attempt to make the body present in language, but the deliberate transformation of language into material acts that incarnate Christ in the world, and thereby reconnect the broken links between language and matter.

---

[43] Catherine of Siena, *The Dialogue*, p. 79.

GOD THE NEIGHBOUR

The glorious body to which Catherine has access in contemplation must continuously animate the physical body in its service to others, until gradually the two become synchronized in a perfect harmony of praise. God tells Catherine of a move 'from the knowledge of me to the knowledge of oneself, from love of me to love of one's neighbors'.[44] While Thomas too insists upon the centrality of love of self and love of neighbour, which includes love of one's own body and of the bodies of others, we have seen that he also imposes a hierarchy upon this order of love, so that ultimately there could be some conflict between love of neighbour and love of God: 'the love of one's neighbour is not meritorious, except by reason of his being loved for God's sake. Therefore the love of God is more meritorious than the love of our neighbour'.[45] This hierarchy enables Thomas to suggest that it is possible to love God more by detaching oneself altogether from the company of others and, as far as possible, one's intellect from one's body. Contrary to the overall spirit of his theology, Thomas is drawn to a disembodied encounter with a disembodied God, and this enables him to imagine that there is some possibility of distinguishing between love of God and love of neighbour in order to seek God beyond the bodies that we are and the bodies that surround us.

Catherine collapses this hierarchy, because she insists that there is no possibility of loving and serving God except by way of the neighbour and through the involvement of the body. There is a thorough-going materialism to Catherine's understanding of the good life. God tells her that 'Every action, whether good or evil, is done by means of the body',[46] and this is why the body shares in the eternal joy or torment of the soul. God tells her that 'love of me and love of neighbour are one and the same thing: Since love of neighbour has its source in me, the more the soul loves me, the more she loves her neighbors'.[47] She repeatedly insists that there is no good or evil except as this is done through our neighbour, for God tells her that 'every sin committed against me is done by means of your neighbors'.[48]

But Catherine goes further, repudiating those who privilege their spiritual needs and obligations before the needs of their neighbours. God complains vociferously to her about those who ignore their neighbours' needs in order to pray, for in such an attachment to prayer there is a subtle form of selfishness:

> [T]hey are deceived by their own spiritual pleasure, and they offend me more by not coming to the help of their neighbors' need than if they had abandoned all their consolations. For I have ordained every exercise of vocal and mental prayer to bring souls to perfect love for me and their neighbors, and to keep them in this

---

[44] Catherine of Siena, *The Dialogue*, p. 11.   [45] ST II, II, 27, 8.

[46] Catherine of Siena, *The Dialogue*, p. 86.   [47] Catherine of Siena, *The Dialogue*, p. 86.

[48] Catherine of Siena, *The Dialogue*, p. 35.

love. So they offend me more by abandoning charity for their neighbour for a particular exercise or for spiritual quiet than if they had abandoned the exercise for their neighbour.[49]

If we consider carefully what Catherine is saying here, we begin to see once again the depths of her psychological insight, for her ethos of neighbourly love anticipates and addresses Freud's great fear of the latent masochistic and sadistic tendencies in the commandment to love the neighbour as the self. That is why any attempt to separate Catherine's social ethos from her spiritual life fails, because for her the two continuously animate and inspire one another.

There is no lack in Catherine's soul, if by that we mean the echoing emptiness of the modern soul against the empty horizons of the infinite. Catherine's life is not that of the solitary, castrated individual lost within an unspeakable abyss and reaching out to the other with an insatiable desire to love and be loved. For Catherine, neighbourly love comes from the unsayable plenitude of the incarnate love of Christ which overflows all the finite boundaries of her mortal, bodily self, which she can speak of only in terms of her own emptiness. To repeat a quote I used earlier from Slavoj Žižek, referring to 1 Corinthians 13:

> For in love, *I also am a nothing*, but as it were a Nothing humbly aware of itself, a Nothing paradoxically made rich through the very awareness of its lack. Only a lacking, vulnerable being is capable of love: the ultimate mystery of love is therefore that incompleteness is in a way higher than completion.[50]

This ability to experience the rich joy of being nothing is the condition that makes it possible to love the neighbour without violence. Catherine recognizes that neighbourly love can mask the most cruel and vindictive of feelings if it arises from an unsatisfied hunger for God. God complains to her of those who serve others begrudgingly, resenting the fact that responding to the needs of the neighbour deprives them of the spiritual consolation of being with God in prayer and contemplation. God tells her that 'those who are willing to lose their own consolation for their neighbors' welfare receive and gain me and their neighbors, if they help and serve them lovingly'.[51] Then the divine voice continues:

> But those who do not act this way are always in pain. For sometimes they simply must help, if not for love then of necessity, whether it is a spiritual or bodily ailment their neighbour has. But though they help, their help is painful. Weary in spirit and goaded by conscience, they become insupportable to themselves and others. And if you ask them, 'Why do you feel this pain?' they would answer,

---

[49] Catherine of Siena, *The Dialogue*, p. 131.
[50] Catherine of Siena, *The Dialogue*, p. 131.
[51] Catherine of Siena, *The Dialogue*, p. 131.

'Because I seem to have lost my spiritual peace and quiet. I have abandoned many things I was in the habit of doing, and I believe I have offended God by this.'

It would be difficult to find a more perfect example of what Lacan sees as the Sadean destructiveness of any ethical system that interprets the neighbour's need in terms of divine lack and disapproval. Catherine's God turns this system around, for 'the offense lies not in being without spiritual consolation, nor in abandoning an exercise of prayer in favour of their neighbor's need, but rather in being found without charity for their neighbour, whom they ought to love and serve for love of me'.[52]

Just as the soul in rapture experiences union with Christ, so the body in its mundane activities expresses the overflowing abundance of that union—which can only be experienced as emptiness—as love of neighbour. All Catherine's theology begins and ends in the body not just of the other but, paradoxically, as the other, for her bodily self is the neighbour of her soul. God tells her, 'I would have you know that every virtue of yours and every vice is put into action by means of your neighbors. If you hate me, you harm your neighbors and yourself as well (for you are your chief neighbour)'.[53]

Catherine offers us a Thomism that is organic, fluid, corporeal, and material, so that the Other of Thomas's One God comes vividly to life in the mystical body of Christ and the material body of the neighbour in need. In many ways, this could be described as a Lacanian Thomism, for like Lacan she gives expression to all that is lacking, repressed, denied, and forbidden in Thomas's theology. However, she also shows what is lacking in Lacan's psychoanalysis—the body of God, and the body of the neighbour in need, including one's own body. Unless language extends along the full spectrum of the imaginary to encompass both these extremes and to translate them into the materiality of our fleshy relationships with one another, it will remain trapped in the nihilism of a Lacanian system that knows nothing and lacks all. There is no possibility of separating spirituality and materiality, prayer and ethics, body and God, in Catherine's theology. In her transgressive scrambling of all the boundaries of language, knowing, and being, Catherine throws open the doors of heaven and hell and confronts us with the most radical possible mercy that opens into the mystical body of Christ at one end and the hell of eternal alienation at the other. There is no predestination, no arbitrariness, no condemnation. In the end there is only the mercy of God, and hell is the pride of the soul who would rather cling fast to the existential misery of solipsistic being, than abandon herself in rapture and ecstasy to the all in all of the body of God.

---

[52] Catherine of Siena, *The Dialogue*, pp. 131–2.
[53] Catherine of Siena, *The Dialogue*, p. 34.

'WE SHALL SOON BE AT THE WEDDING'

These two aspects of Catherine's theology—the rapture of the soul and the materiality of incarnate love—come together beautifully in her famous letter written in 1375 to Raymond of Capua, in which she describes the time she spent with a condemned man, Niccolò di Toldo, before and during his execution. She begins by wishing for Raymond that he might be 'plunged and drowned' in the sweet blood of Christ, his soul locked 'into the open side of the Son of God' where 'the sweet bride reclines on the bed of blood and fire, and the secret of the heart of God's Son is laid bare'.[54] Even across this vast distance of time, the letter retains an astonishing intimacy and immediacy.

The language is shot through with eroticism, but there is no sense that Catherine feels inhibited or anxious about this. It is a reminder that, paradoxically, men like Thomas were more enslaved by sexual anxieties than the women they sought to control and avoid. One cannot imagine Thomas or any of his male counterparts being free to write about such a tactile and intimate encounter with a woman under similar circumstances. (Imagine, for example, if instead of chasing that female seductress from his room with a burning brand and collapsing in tears of fear and fury, Thomas had been able to reach out to her in the way that Catherine reaches out to a fellow human being in the following description.)

For Catherine, the condemned man's evident desire for her is really an expression of his desire for God: 'God, in his boundless and burning goodness, deceived him, as it were, by instilling into him such love and affection for *me* (in God) that he did not know how to be without *Him*'.[55]

She describes the man's fear and anxiety:

> He kept saying: 'Stay with me and don't leave me; then I shall be all right and die happy' – and all the time he leaned his head on my breast. I was aware of sudden joy, of the odour of his blood in some way mingled with that of my own, which I hope to shed for sweet Jesus my bridegroom. As my own yearning increased and I sensed his fear, I said to him: 'Courage, dearest brother. We shall soon be at the wedding.'[56]

Catherine describes how, waiting for him before the execution, 'I lay down and placed my own head on the block. So I begged, indeed I forced Mary to get me the grace I wanted, which was that I might give him light and peace of heart at the moment of death, and then see him going to God.' [57] She goes on to tell of holding his severed head in her hands, and of how she had a vision of him

---

[54] Catherine of Siena, 'Letter 9 (Dupré XXXI; Tommaseo 273; Gigli 97) to *Fra Raimondo of Capua, OP*, in *I, Catherine*', pp. 71–2.

[55] Catherine of Siena, 'Letter 9', p. 73.

[56] Catherine of Siena, 'Letter 9', p. 73.   [57] Catherine of Siena, 'Letter 9', p. 73.

being received into the open side of Christ after death. Here is how she describes her vision:

> How indescribably moving it was to see God's goodness; to see the gentleness and love with which he waited to welcome that soul – with the eyes of his mercy fixed on it – as it left the body and was plunged into his open side, bathed in its own blood that now possessed merit through the blood of God's Son.... Then the hands of the Holy Spirit sealed him into that open side. But he did such a lovely thing – one last gesture that would melt a thousand hearts ... He looked back, like a bride who pauses on the bridegroom's threshold to look back and bow her thanks to her escort.
>
> When he had gone, my own soul was serenely at peace, and so impregnated with the scent of blood that I could not bear to remove the blood itself that had splashed onto me. Alas, poor me, I can say no more.[58]

---

[58] Catherine of Siena, 'Letter 9', pp. 74–5.

20

The Risen and Remembered Self

Texts and contexts. Bodies and voices. Knowing and desiring. Who knows and what do we know? Who desires, and what do we desire? Questions both pre-modern and postmodern congeal the illusory transparencies and truths of modernity. As the postmodern takes leave of the modern, it seeks to bridge the gap, to take hold of the slippery, elusive bodies that speak from a site of medieval difference. But the bodies and voices are gone and only the skins of writing remain, like the self-portrait of Michelangelo as the flayed skin of St Bartholomew in the Sistine Chapel. This is a taunting absence that lures the postmodern subject across modernity's closed horizons towards an unspeakable abyss or an unsayable plenitude, with no way of telling the difference between them.

I want to conclude this book with the enigma of the resurrected body and its sexual inscriptions. Thomas insists that we cannot arrive at the revealed doctrines of the Christian faith by way of reason alone. We can only offer retrospective reasons as to why we might accept them as true, but even then these will not persuade those who are not already persuaded.

Many of these doctrines constitute the introduction of a paradox into an ordinary human event, so that its meaning is broken open to suggest a mystery within. Birth, food, and death are the most universal of all human experiences, and Christianity's God comes to us clothed in these experiences. Every human life begins in a maternal body and is birthed into vulnerability and dependence, as Jesus was. Not only that, but his birth was an identification with the most abject and marginalized of peoples. We do not need to look far today to find children born into intolerable conditions because of the demands of bureaucracy, politics, and imperial power. Mary gave birth among the animals because every space of human habitation refused her shelter. Every human life ends in death, as Jesus's did. Not only that, but his death too was an identification with the abject and the marginalized. The tortured body on the cross is replicated in the ongoing horrors that human beings inflict upon one another in the name of their laws, their gods, their ideals, and their beliefs. But Christianity points to the vulnerability of the newborn and exiled child and the corpse of the crucified criminal, and calls these 'God'. It book-ends this story with the miracle of the virgin birth and the miracle of the resurrection, which frame the all-too-common life of Jesus of Nazareth—born in poverty and tortured and killed as a criminal and a blasphemer—within the divine mystery in order to say that here and nowhere else is God fully revealed to humankind, beyond all rational understanding or explanation. Then it takes the most ordinary elements of human sustenance and communal participation—water, bread, and wine—and it says that through baptism and the Eucharist, the life of the incarnate God communicates itself anew to every life and incarnates itself anew in every body that is open to receive it.

I have discussed the virgin birth at length elsewhere,[1] but here I focus on the resurrected body and its relationship to personal identity, including the role that sexuality might play in the formation of that identity.[2] This concluding chapter does not seek to present itself as an academic argument, but as an act of imaginative contemplation about what the resurrection of the body might mean and what difference it might make to the here and now of human life.

RESURRECTION, HOPE, AND IMAGINATION

To speak of the resurrection of the body is to speak of an enigma which can only be an exercise in imaginative hope. In the Gospel accounts, there are no witnesses to the moment when the crucified corpse of Jesus is reanimated and becomes the risen Christ. Significantly, the first witnesses to encounter the risen Christ are women, and that too is a theme that I have explored elsewhere.[3] Here, I ask what that resurrection and the promise which it embodies might mean for a Christian today. I ask this in the context of hope, and I position that hope before the options which open up before us in the encounter between Thomas Aquinas and Jacques Lacan. This means rejecting all modern theological and philosophical attempts to minimize or eliminate the body from questions of personhood, meaning, and identity. It means saying with Thomas that, if I exist in eternity I can only do so as the body–soul unity that is me. If this proposition is too incredible—if I am not persuaded by the

---

[1] Cf. Tina Beattie, 'The Symbolic Significance of the Virgin Birth', in *God's Mother, Eve's Advocate: A Marian Narrative of Women's Salvation* (London and New York: Continuum, 2002), pp. 115–40.

[2] Cf. Beattie, 'Sexuality and the Resurrection of the Body: Reflections in a Hall of Mirrors', in Gavin D'Costa (ed.), *Resurrection Reconsidered* (Oxford: Oneworld Publications, 1996), pp. 135–49; Beattie, '"The Touch that Goes Beyond Touching": a reflection on the touching of Mary of Magdala in Theology and Art', in Reimund Bieringer, Barbara Baert, and Karlijn Demasure (eds), *Noli me tangere: New Interdisciplinary Perspectives*, Bibliotheca Ephemeridum Theologicarum Lovaniensium (Leuven, Paris and Dudley MA: Peeters, forthcoming).

[3] Beattie, '"The Touch that Goes Beyond Touching"'.

claims of Christian revelation—then Lacan offers a way to live and love within the abysmal condition of finitude that seals off the horizons of hope and allows me to plunge into the ephemeral joys and sorrows that open up within me as ateleological desire carves its grooves within my soul, and insatiable need animates my bodily drives. What might it mean if, at this point of decision, I go with Thomas rather than Lacan? What if I place my hope in the abyss as the source of a plenitudinal grace and not as the void of consuming absence?

Hope is not optimism. Optimism is a deferral of the present in anticipation of a better future. It is a failure to enter fully into life as it is—to inhabit the here and now with all its vast opportunities and challenges—in favour of planning for or dreaming of a brighter tomorrow that never arrives. Kantian ethics is an ethics of optimism but not of hope. It enables us to endure the bitter demands of the moral law in which no glimmer of bodily delight or personal gratification must cloud the ethical act, in the optimistic belief that one day, God will vindicate this grim struggle against nature and desire with the reward of eternal (disembodied) life. Hope is not like that. Hope is what opens us to the grace of God within creation, and allows us to respond through our own capacity to love and be loved, to suffer for and with others, to delight others and to be delighted by them within the being of God. Hope allows our lives to be shaped by a promise that is incarnate in all the awe and wonder of the material world, if only we know how to look. This way of looking is what Maggie Ross refers to as 'beholding':

> through beholding we are transfigured in every sense: nothing is wasted, nothing is left behind; through our wounds we are healed; our perspective – the way we 'figure things out' – is changed. In the resurrection, the wounds of Christ do not disappear; they are glorified. Only the devil appearing as Christ has no wounds, being too vain to bear them.... [I]n our core silence, through our beholding, we realise our shared nature with God; we participate in the divine outpouring upon the world: incarnation, transfiguration and resurrection become conflated into a single movement of love.[4]

The artist Edward Robinson differentiates between fantasy and imagination.[5] While acknowledging that both have a role to play and that it is wrong to attempt to impose too categorical a difference between them, he associates fantasy with a lack of freedom and a quest for escapism that feeds a sense of self-indulgence and egocentrism. Creative imagination, on the other hand, connects us with the mystery of being. It is not a quest to escape reality but a quest to express and inhabit the mystery within all reality. It is closely associated with faith, so long as faith remains open to the possibilities of the

---

[4] Maggie Ross, *Writing the Icon of the Heart: In Silence Beholding* (Abingdon: The Bible Reading Fellowship, 2011), p. 14.
[5] See Edward Robinson, *The Language of Mystery* (London: SCM Press, 1987).

imagination rather than closing them down. For Robinson, imagination and tradition go hand in hand. The imagination keeps tradition alive and open to change, and tradition keeps imagination from straying too far from its roots within the continuity and meaning of shared historical existence.

I want to suggest that, according to this way of thinking, optimism would belong in the realm of fantasy and escapism, and hope would belong within the realm of creative imagination and mystery. Sometimes we need to be optimistic, but at best optimism offers us some transient relief from a transient difficulty. When optimism becomes a way of avoiding the profound and inescapable demands of love, life, and suffering, it is an enslaving fantasy that saps our freedom and creativity. The modern myth of progress is the ultimate optimistic fantasy, and I have suggested that it opens into every kind of terror and despair. Only hope can hold open the possibility of a future beyond violence, and it is always of the here and now. It embodies within the present the sense that we are part of some eternal mystery beyond our comprehension, and that this is a mystery of redeeming love that holds us eternally within the being of God, along with everything else that comes to be in God. So this chapter is an imaginative and personal reflection on the meaning of hope, in the context of the doctrine of the resurrected body and its sexual and maternal inscriptions.

RESURRECTION AND THE SEXUAL BODY

Catherine of Siena offers a language that incarnates Thomas's theology in the mystical body of Christ and in the body of the neighbour in need, but she belongs within a long tradition that has always been better at dealing with the suffering body than the sexual body. While she provides a potent reminder that theology is never Christian unless its God is materialized in all the particularities of neighbourly love, she is less helpful with regard to some of the most significant questions that Christianity asks of itself today: what does it mean to be a sexual body, and where does that body find a space of flourishing and love within the body of Christ?

Let me consider that question with reference to Mark Jordan's meditation on the significance of the sexuality of the body of Christ.[6] Jordan points out that 'Much Christian theology claims to be about a divine incarnation. It is also, and perhaps more emphatically, a speech for managing that incarnation by controlling its awkward implications.'[7] Jordan discusses the erotic potential of the body of Christ, not because it is beautiful but because even in the

---

[6] Mark D. Jordan, 'God's Body', in Gerard Loughlin (ed.), *Queer Theology: Rethinking the Western Body* (Malden MA and Oxford UK: Blackwell Publishing, 2007), pp. 281–92.

[7] Jordan, 'God's Body', in Gerard Loughlin (ed.), *Queer Theology*, p. 283.

extreme disfiguration and ugliness of the cross, it reveals 'the unspeakable beauty of God'.[8] He concludes with a reflection on the resurrected body:

> We get our bodies back again and stay with them for eternity. We get them back as the best human bodies there are, which means, as bodies with genitals.... Meditating on our multiple shames before a sexed savior may help us a little out of shame, into salvation which is wholeness. Meditating on Jesus' beauty even when crucified may help us a little towards a less fetishistic notion of beauty and its *eros*. Certainly meditating on how we speak of our desire for Jesus will show us something about how to talk of his desires for us. Truth telling about *eros* comes before – and remains with – truth telling about *agape*.[9]

Jordan writes as a gay Catholic man, and his theology is bodily marked by that reality. Like all gay men in religious traditions, he has had to reclaim the beauty and goodness of his body and its desire—to reclaim it and love it—in the face of Christianity's scorn and condemnation. Yet this may be a somewhat different task for a woman. The long history of lack and horror, death and corruption, with which the female body has been branded by Christianity and its secular derivatives, is altogether different from the history of the phallus, which has of course always been rather less or other than the bodily organ to which it refers—but even so . . .

The phallus occupies a place of honour in the making of the western mind. It may be that this sets up potent anxieties in men with regard to body image and genital endowment—'size matters!'—but one can imagine a man dreaming of a heavenly body in which his genitalia are not lacking but, on the contrary, spectacularly risen in glory. I suspect that many women would find it difficult to imagine their resurrected bodies as having a glorious vagina. I have already referred to the extent to which modernity imposes self-mutilating demands upon the female body—including genital plastic surgery—which would have horrified our medieval forebears. They mortified their bodies because of a profound belief in the eternal significance of those bodies as created and redeemed or condemned by God. Today's self-mutilating girls and women are motivated only by the consuming and consumerist male gaze and the demands it makes upon them to become other than the bodies that they are. In the medieval imagination, the soul loved the body even if it disciplined it in sometimes violent and punitive ways. In the modern consumerist fantasy, the soul destroys the body in its quest for the perfection of form that has no place for the body's wounded and vulnerable humanity.

We do not shrug off two millennia of cultural conditioning in the space of a generation. I wonder how many Christian women would find themselves able to enter into the kind of reflection on the genitalia of the resurrected body that Jordan invites? I suspect that many might hope that this 'horror of nothing to

---

[8] Jordan, 'God's Body', in Loughlin (ed.), *Queer Theology*, p. 288.
[9] Jordan, 'God's Body', in Loughlin (ed.), *Queer Theology*, p. 290.

see' will be eternally covered over and forgotten about, along with all the demands it has made upon them by way of blood, birth, and sex, which is not to deny that these demands can also be experienced as gift and joy. There are ancient statues of fertility goddesses which give pride of place to the female genitalia, but Christianity has well and truly erased those images from our imaginations. Eve Ensler's ground-breaking play, *The Vagina Monologues*,[10] runs and runs because for the first time it gives women a language in which to speak about our vaginas across the full spectrum of meaning, from the horror of rape and the trauma of childbirth to the multiple orgasms and tender caresses of sexual love. It achieves the opposite of the bleak pornographic fantasies of E. L. James's *Fifty Shades* trilogy.

Nevertheless, a question remains as to how women might engage with Jordan's invitation to imagine the resurrected body with its genitals as part of its glory. Thomas affirms, along with St Augustine, that the female body will be female in the resurrection, existing not for any procreative or sexual purpose but for the glory and praise of God. We have seen several times in this book that the idea of the erect phallus giving glory to God is almost as old as the idea of God, but what of the fleshy folds and hidden depths of the female genitalia? One could offer an Irigarayan reflection on the trinitarian morphology of the two lips—and I have engaged with her elsewhere on these terms[11]—but I want to try a different approach here.

To say, as Thomas does, that men will be resurrected as men and women as women opens into much larger questions about bodies and sexual identities. In modern western society, the sex organs play a defining role in inserting us into culture as male or female—as Lacan suggests—but we are also increasingly aware that our sexual bodies escape the grids of language when it comes to desire. We are, as Freud pointed out, polymorphously perverse, and we remain so despite society's best attempts to contain and control us, to divide us and rule us, by governing our sexuality. Even if it is no longer true that this is an exclusively heterosexist enterprise (except in the struggles and influences of political and religious conservatism), it is still true, as Michel Foucault has argued, that the discursive positioning of the sexual body in modern society has become a powerful but hidden mechanism of social control.[12] What would it mean to imagine the risen body in all its polymorphous perversity, a body that has shrugged off the time- and space-bound constraints of the dualistic social order and knows itself only as the surplus *jouissance* of God? Isn't it a

[10] Eve Ensler, *The Vagina Monologues* (London: Virago, 2001).

[11] See Tina Beattie, *God's Mother, Eve's Advocate: A Marian Narrative of Women's Salvation* (London and New York: Continuum, 2002), pp. 155–8. See also the reflection in Beattie, 'Sexuality and the Resurrection of the Body: Reflections in a Hall of Mirrors', in Gavin D'Costa (ed.), *Resurrection Reconsidered* (Oxford: Oneworld Publications, 1996).

[12] Cf. Michel Foucault, *The History of Sexuality: An Introduction*, trans. Robert Hurley (New York: Vintage Books, 1990).

polymorphously perverse Christ who pursues Catherine as her 'mad lover' through the fleshy tunnels of her own desire, until she surrenders and mingles the blood of her being with his in the rapture of emptiness? I want to suggest that these are questions, not of sexuality but of memory and imagination, and I am going to return to Thomas to explore the possible implications of this.

IMAGINATIVE SEXUAL REMEMBERING

For Thomas, there are two different functions to memory.[13] There are the ephemeral memories associated with our ordinary sensations and appetites, and these have no eternal significance. However, there is an aspect of memory that belongs within the eternity of the soul, for it is our remembered lives, our remembered identities, our ways of understanding who we are. If I am me for all eternity, then that 'me' has to have content that makes me me and not anybody else, and in terms of Thomas's Aristotelianism this cannot be anything other than the sum total of my experiences woven into the narrative of my bodily life.

Our medieval ancestors were preoccupied with questions of risen bodies, because they imagined us rising more or less in the condition we died in, except more perfect and glorious. So how could dismembered or burned bodies be reassembled in heaven? What about bodies that had been eaten by cannibals?[14] Today, we might be less florid and less literal in the questions we ask. Quantum physics has blurred the distinction between matter and consciousness, and we can perhaps imagine rather more ephemeral and amazing ways of being bodies even than those lurid phantasms of medieval fear and desire.[15] Perhaps there is some eternal quantum self that is already me in some parallel universe. Perhaps the quarks and atoms of my materiality regroup after death in wondrous ways that are beyond my wildest imaginings, so that to speak of any bodily organs is entirely to miss the point.

But if I do not remember who I am, there will be no point at all. Speaking personally, my sense of myself as sexual and maternal is not incidental but essential to the life I live, the experiences I have, the insights I acquire, the relationships I form, and the memories I retain with all their freighting of joy

---

[13] For Thomas's account of memory see ST I, 79, 6. See also ST I, 89 for his account of knowledge that remains when the soul is separated from the body.

[14] See Caroline Walker Bynum, *The Resurrection of the Body in Western Christianity, 200–1336* (New York: Columbia University Press, 1995).

[15] I have not attempted to introduce the new physics into my analysis of Thomas, for this would have been a different project altogether. For an interesting experiment in doing this, see James Arraj, *The Mystery of Matter: Nonlocality, Morphic Resonance, Synchronicity and the Philosophy of Nature of Thomas Aquinas* (Midland OR: Inner Growth Books, 1996).

and sorrow, regret and hope, love and loss. To say this is not to say that my human identity is reducible only to the sexual and maternal aspects of my being, but any human identity can only be said to exist at all insofar as it is made up of all the fibres of imagination, memory, and reflection by way of which we weave ourselves into the world through our sensory experiences and bodily actions. In the context of my particular life, marriage and motherhood are integral to that process. In another life I might have chosen different forms of sexual self-expressiveness, different ways of living, different people to love, but I have only one life and it is this one.

I have been married for nearly forty years, and that has involved a sense of being a woman in relation to a man. Contrary to the sexual romances of some of my Catholic contemporaries, I do not experience this as a continuously procreative love fest of sexual complementarity. The older one gets the more a kind of being together beyond sex becomes part of the equation. Sex becomes less important than it once was, and other, quieter ways of loving begin to appear. The markers of sexual difference become less sharp than they once were, and a blurry old friendship begins to fill that ancient ache of loss and yearning that no sexual relationship can ever satisfy, which creates so much heartache and frustration in the process of falling in love, maturing, learning, and remaining together. Growing older together does not necessarily mean the cessation of sex—for some it does, for others it does not. For some it allows for a rich discovery of sexual pleasure beyond the urgency of youth and the demands of procreation, for others genital activity fades into different forms of loving companionship, and for still others sexuality yields reluctantly to the processes of ageing, illness, and dying. This is a much more complex and diverse scenario than is suggested by popular culture's preoccupation with sexual performance at every age and stage of life, which is yet another way of ensuring that we are constantly compliant with and enslaved by society's consumerist view of sex. Growing older together can mean that sex becomes less a question of sexual performance and hunger for that which the other never will be able to give, and more a question of some deeper and more expressive way of being bodies together.

Such questions of sexuality, love, difference, and identity remain significant whether one is male or female, gay or straight, celibate or sexually active, transgendered or bisexual, or however one slips between and among all these labels to discover a *jouissance* of the body's unforgettable and unforgetting being. There is much more to being than sex, and Christian being is never satisfied with sex alone, because our longing is for God before and beyond any sexual relationship. Nevertheless, there is something about our sexual self-awareness, our desires, and the ways in which we experience and express these, which forms the most hidden dimensions of the self, where the body knows more than we do. Our bodies remember sex in ways that create grooves and furrows in our souls. Our sexual loves and losses, ecstasies and agonies, however ephemeral, whether or not they are genitally expressed, are rarely trivial. They create memories which migrate across that porous boundary between what we do and who we are, and they shape our souls around an absence that echoes with the tears and fears, the joys and sorrows, the woundings and healings, of those experiences of delight and despair that are particular to our ways of loving, and sometimes of hating, as sexual beings.

If we take our bodies with the seriousness they demand, then we must recognize that sex can make us or break us in complex relationships of love and violence, fidelity and betrayal, dignity and humiliation. To imagine ourselves rising again as sexual beings might involve imagining ourselves with resurrected sex organs, but I don't think that's the point. What matters is that we rise with the memories that have become part of us, bodily memories of touch and smell, of intimacy and orgasm, of grief and wounding, of fecund delights and abortive frustrations. These enable us to learn about God's great and complex gift of erotic, material desire which is creation's desire for God beyond all conjugations of forms and matter—the *jouissance* of a primordial wisdom that is surplus to any procreative function. That is what Lacan tries to tell us about the uniqueness and challenge of Christian revelation. Creation does not need to be eternally copulating, for it flows out of nothing from the eternally fertile love of the Trinity, who generates it and keeps it in being beyond every necessity. Yet as creatures whose being emerges from the primacy of desire and whose lives are powerfully shaped by *eros*, sexuality is part of what it means to be a human person.

IMAGINATIVE MATERNAL REMEMBERING

To remember the maternal body as an act of imaginative resurrection entails a subtle shift in experience and meaning, for maternal relationships are not the same as sexual relationships. However we interpret the incest taboo, we know that there is a vital distinction between the body of a mother and the body of a sexual other, and we breach that at our psychological and ethical peril. Although the maternal relationship emerges from the most intimate possible physical bond with another human being, it is one that must remain free from the *eros* of sexual desire. This is not to deny the immense tactile significance of motherhood and its inexpressible *jouissance*, but the maternal body is a body for others, a body that gives of its flesh and blood, its milk and its tears, so that others might be. A good mother must strive not to make her children the focus of her desire and need, just as God does not make us the focus of divine desire and need. There is a plenitude of love that gives all and asks nothing in return, and that is the condition of our human freedom to give and receive love. This is the way in which God mothers us, but good mothering also entails withdrawal and separation. That too is part of our coming to be, for a mother who consumes and suffocates her children's lives with narcissistic dependency and sufficiency is a distortion of the maternal love of God. However we ourselves might have experienced the maternal relationship—either as mothers or as offspring—we have some idea of what a good mother might be. In fact, the less we ourselves have experienced that maternal ideal, the more profoundly we are likely to hunger for it. Only when we recognize that this yearning for maternal love flows from a source of grace beyond anything and everything any human mother can give, are we able to accept the lack that is the shadow side of freedom, and to abandon ourselves in emptiness to the endless fecundity of trinitarian, maternal love.[16]

In terms of personal identity and resurrection, I find it impossible to think of my risen self being me, without the experience of mothering which has played such a vital role in making me who I am today. For that reason I do not want to discover that I am an eighteen-year-old virgin in heaven. I want to imagine that the body which will one day be reunited with my soul for all eternity will be this body, with all the scarred and sagging evidence of its maternal history enfleshed within its memories. Whether or not that body has a uterus, vagina, and breasts really does not matter, but it must remember that once it grew and grew to make space for other beings to come into being. It must remember that it fed children from its own substance, that it watched them grow and let them go in an anguished ecstasy of love and loss and guilt and joy. We mothers are not gods, but by our bodily way of being in relation to other bodies whose lives we gestate and nurture, we can reveal to others something of God that no other body can reveal. If we do not understand what it means to mother, we cannot understand who God is.

Of course I am not saying that people who have not experienced motherhood cannot know God, and I am most certainly not wanting to romanticize motherhood nor to deny the damage that even the best mothers do to their children as part of the messy process of being ordinary human beings in a wounded and suffering world. I am saying that, of all the myriad human and non-human bodies through which God reveals unique aspects of the divine being, the language of the Trinity draws its analogies from the relational paradox of the maternal body and asks us to recognize that this is what it means to be made in the image of God.[17]

The risen body is re-membered, and its members are its memories. Psychoanalysis tells us that there are memories beyond what we know, that there is

---

[16] I explore these themes further in Beattie, *New Catholic Feminism*, pp. 246–68.

[17] To develop this idea further would invite close theological engagement with feminist theorists working in the area of maternal identities and ethics, such as the work of Christine Battersby which I have referred to several times. See Christine Battersby, *The Phenomenal Woman: Feminist Metaphysics and the Patterns of Identity* (Cambridge: Polity Press, 1998).

wisdom in the body's remembering, responding, and anticipating that we know nothing about. In our laughter and tears, in our arousals and orgasms, in our sufferings and agonies, in our moving, living, breathing, pulsing, joyful, tormented, shitting, fucking, lactating, menstruating, birthing, ageing, withering, dying bodies, there is wisdom beyond the knowledge of good and evil, wisdom beyond what we know, the wisdom of matter, a maternal wisdom, the wisdom of God.

THE OTHER SIDE OF SILENCE

In remembering what we have been as a way of creatively imagining what we might become, we need to go beyond Thomas's anthropocentrism to a more organic understanding of redemption. Brian Davies points out that 'We might like to meet our goldfish in heaven. But beatified goldfish seem not to be included in Aquinas's reckoning.'[18] We might be more or less indifferent to the fate of individual members of other species (although maybe not in the case of beloved pets), but it is difficult to imagine a heaven in which humans would remain the beings that we are, without our relationship to the rest of creation. Thomas's theology tells us that our relationships with other forms of life and the beauty of God's creation are no less part of who we are than the humans we have known, for they constitute our sensual awakening to the mystery and goodness of God. The *Letter to the Romans* tells us that 'the whole of creation has been groaning as in the pains of childbirth right up to the present time'. (Rom. 8: 22.) God is giving birth to creation, and creation is God's body—it is the surplus *jouissance*, the wisdom that remains when God withdraws in order for beings to become. God's *jouissance* is pure delight in being, beyond every need and demand and desire, and it encompasses everything that is.

Time and time again, the God of the Bible speaks through nature to confound human logic and to open the imagination to the mystery of the divine presence within creation. The God of the Bible is not a philosopher but a creative genius—a sublime artist in the process of creating. The Books of Job and Isaiah, the parables of Jesus, the story of Genesis, the psalms, all are redolent with images of a natural world that knows and praises God better than humans do. Would heaven be heaven without birds and trees, without butterflies and spiders, without mountains and rivers, without elephants, cats, dogs, hedgehogs, and even pet goldfish? Without the cedars of Lebanon and the lilies of the field and Leviathan and the stormy ocean and the starry sky and the wolf that lies down with the lamb? Whatever forms these created

---

[18] Brian Davies, *The Thought of Thomas Aquinas* (Oxford and New York: Oxford University Press, 1993), p. 169. Davies refers to ST I, 23, 1.

beings take in glory, they are created to give eternal praise to God. It is time for another Copernican revolution, a decentring, an embrace of a postmodern dissolution in which the human returns to its proper orbit with other living bodies around the mystery of being, discovering that the centre of gravity of divine love is everywhere and nowhere, incarnate in the polymorphous perversity of the body of the risen Christ who is also everywhere and nowhere.

Creation confronts us with the mystery of God, beyond all the neo-pagan romances of nature mysticism and New Age spiritualities. When God speaks to Job out of the whirlwind, God confronts a man broken by unbearable anguish. It is only in the context of the enormity, majesty, and mystery of a world that seethes and thunders around him that Job learns how very small he is, how very insignificant within the mystery of creation. The Christian belief that the human is at the centre of creation and the purpose for which it exists has made us the most dangerous and destructive of species. Creation is not made for humankind but for God alone. We have a place within it—a unique and privileged place—but Thomas reminds us that what we perceive as natural evil is an expression of the abundance of the eternal creative act of the divine being, beyond anything we humans can comprehend.

God's being opens wide and creates a space in which others might come to be. The ocean of being withdraws to allow us to become. We hear its 'melancholy, long, withdrawing roar', bringing 'the eternal note of sadness in', and we are afraid because we are stranded and alone on the 'naked shingles of the world'.[19] But hush. Listen. Wait for the roar to subside and you will discover that there is not the smallest gap, not the slightest crack, not the most distant glimmer of emptiness. In the words of Annie Dillard, 'It is a fault of infinity to be too small to find. It is a fault of eternity to be crowded out by time. . . . Where, then, is the gap through which eternity streams? The idea of eternity is that it bears time in its side like a hole.'[20]

It is not the abyss but the plenitude of being that terrifies us. It is not that there is nothing but that there is everything, around us and within us, swirling and screeching, swarming and howling, whispering and shouting, singing and dancing, pulsing and throbbing, dazzling and sparkling. Touch, taste, see, hear, feel, smell, breathe. There is no emptiness anywhere, there is nothing but being, nothing, nothing, nothing but being. It surges and swirls and sweeps around us and within us. It is the wisdom of God, at play within the body of the world from before the beginning of time. In the words of George Eliot, 'If we had a keen vision of all that is ordinary in human life, it

---

[19] Mathew Arnold, *Dover Beach*.
[20] Annie Dillard, 'The Book of Luke', in *The Annie Dillard Reader* (New York: HarperPerennial, 1994), pp. 263–77, 265.

would be like hearing the grass grow or the squirrel's heart beat, and we should die of that roar which is the other side of silence.'[21]

So, to complete this imaginative foray into resurrected worlds and resurrected bodies, let's leave Thomas Aquinas where we might yet imagine encountering him—where he desired himself to be. Is this a solipsistic corner of heaven where, alone with his books and his God, he has at last transcended every bodily desire and every haunting phantasm, so that he sits in disembodied solitude with the divine mind? That's where we have observed him along the way, but that is not the Thomas we have come to know as we have journeyed with him through the elusive labyrinths of language and silence, of thought and prayer. We have discovered instead a Thomas who is divided—as we all are, a Thomas who is too heavily inscribed within the culture that created him—as we all are, a Thomas whose laborious endeavours of the mind were in the end, as straw—as all our intellectual endeavours are.

Mary Clark gives a moving account of Thomas's last days:

> On December 6, 1273, Thomas Aquinas put down his pen and declared: 'I cannot; such things have been revealed to me that all that I have written seems to me as so much straw.' Summoned to Lyons by Gregory X to attend the Church Council that aimed at reunion with the Greek Church Aquinas in weakened health took to the road but fell ill on the way. Taken from his sister's house to the Cistercian monastery of Fossanuova, he died listening to the Canticle of Canticles. As he received the last rites he prayed: 'I receive Thee, ransom of my soul. For love of Thee have I studied and kept vigil, toiled, preached, and taught . . . ' The year was 1274.[22]

Thomas, who believed that sex was a deadly distraction to the man of contemplation and scholarship, and who regarded his sexual impotence as a gift from God, died listening to that great erotic hymn to sexual love that has perplexed all those biblical scholars who have been unable to reconcile God and sexuality. This is the Thomas we can playfully imagine in heaven—a gigantic and glorious soul in a gigantic and glorious body, marvelling in the mystical *eros* that bedazzled him at the end of his life, surrounded by the monks he loved, his sisters, the women he knew, the poor whom he had dedicated his life to serving, in spite of Aristotle.

And what of Jacques Lacan, who died saying 'I am stubborn . . . I am disappearing'?[23] Lacan knows better than most that nobody and nothing disappears. Everything is to be continued. That was his Catholic dread, and his *jouissance*.

---

[21] George Eliot, *Middlemarch* (London: Penguin Books, 1994), p. 194.

[22] Mary Clark, 'Introduction', in *An Aquinas Reader: Selections from the Writings of Thomas Aquinas* (New York: Fordham University Press, 2003), revised edition, p. 12.

[23] Élisabeth Roudinesco, *Jacques Lacan and Co: A History of Psychoanalysis in France, 1925–1985* (Chicago: University of Chicago Press, 1990), p. 679.

Bibliography

Biblical quotations are from *The New King James Version*, Thomas Nelson, Inc., 1982.

Agamben, Giorgio (1998) *Homo Sacer: Sovereign Power and Bare Life*, trans. Daniel Heller-Roazen (Stanford CA: Stanford University Press), first published 1995.

Akeroyd, Richard H. (1991) *Reason and Revelation From Paul to Pascal* (Macon GA: Mercer University Press).

Allen, Prudence RSM (1997) *The Concept of Woman: The Aristotelian Revolution 750 B.C.–A.D. 1250* (Grand Rapids MI and Cambridge UK: William B. Eerdmans Publishing Co.).

Allen, Prudence RSM (2004) 'Can Feminism Be a Humanism?' in Michele M. Schumacher (ed.), *Women in Christ: Toward a New Feminism* (Grand Rapids MI and Cambridge UK: William B. Eerdmans Publishing Co.).

Aquinas, Thomas (1946) *On Boethius on the Trinity—Questions 1–4*, trans. Rose E. Brennan S. H. N. (Herder).

Aquinas, Thomas (1947) *The Summa Theologica*, trans. the Fathers of the English Dominican Province (Benziger Bros.), at http://dhspriory.org/thomas/summa/index.html [accessed 22 October 2012].

Aquinas, Thomas (1955) *Contra Gentiles* (New York: Hanover House), edited and updated by Joseph Kenny OP, at http://dhspriory.org/thomas/ContraGentiles.htm [accessed 22 October 2012].

Aquinas, Thomas (1963) *Commentary on Aristotle's Physics, Books I-II*, Lecture 1 (184a9–b14) trans. Richard J. Blackwell, Richard J. Spath, and W. Edmund Thirlkel (New Haven CT: Yale University Press, 1963), html edition by Joseph Kenny OP at http://dhspriory.org/thomas/Physics.htm [accessed 6 April 2013].

Aquinas, Thomas (2003) *On Evil*, trans. Richard Regan (New York: Oxford University Press).

Aquinas, Thomas 'Lectures on the Letter to the Romans', trans. Fr Fabian Larcher, ed. Jeremy Holmes (Ave Maria University Aquinas Center), at http://nvjournal.net/index.php?option=com_content&view=article&id=53&Itemid=62 [accessed 27 July 2012].

Aquinas, Thomas, *Commentary on the Sentences*, trans. Joseph Kenny OP, at http://dhspriory.org/thomas/Sentences2.htm [accessed 22 October 2012].

Aristotle (1995) *The Complete Works of Aristotle: The Revised Oxford Translation, Vols. 1 and 2*, ed. Jonathan Barnes (Princeton NJ and Chichester UK: Princeton University Press).

Armstrong, Karen (1999) *A History of God* (London: Vintage).

Arraj, James (1996) *The Mystery of Matter: Nonlocality, Morphic Resonance, Synchronicity and the Philosophy of Nature of Thomas Aquinas* (Midland OR: Inner Growth Books, 1996).

Arrivé, Michel (1992) *Linguistics and Psychoanalysis: Freud, Saussure, Hjelmslev, Lacan and others*, trans. James Leader (Amsterdam and Philadelphia PA: John Benjamins).

Augustine, *Enarrationes in Psalmos*, XLV, 7 (PL 36,518).

Augustine (2003) *Concerning the City of God against the Pagans*, trans. Henry Bettenson (London and New York: Penguin Books).

Augustine (2008) *Confessions*, trans. Henry Chadwick (Oxford and New York: Oxford University Press).

Battersby, Christine (1998) *The Phenomenal Woman: Feminist Metaphysics and the Patterns of Identity* (Cambridge: Polity Press).

Beattie, Tina (1996) 'Sexuality and the Resurrection of the Body: Reflections in a Hall of Mirrors', in Gavin D'Costa (ed.), *Resurrection Reconsidered* (Oxford: Oneworld Publications), pp. 135–49.

Beattie, Tina (2002) *God's Mother, Eve's Advocate: A Marian Narrative of Women's Salvation* (London and New York: Continuum).

Beattie, Tina (2006) *New Catholic Feminism: Theology and Theory* (London and New York: Routledge).

Beattie, Tina (2007, 2008) *The New Atheists: The Twilight of Reason and the War on Religion* (London: Darton, Longman and Todd; Maryknoll NY: Orbis Books).

Beattie, Tina (2008) '"Justice enacted not these human laws" (Antigone): Religion, Natural Law and Women's Rights', *Religion and Human Rights*, Vol. 3, No. 3, pp. 249–67.

Beattie, Tina (2012) 'How To Believe—Thomas Aquinas', *The Guardian—Comment is Free*, at http://www.guardian.co.uk/commentisfree/belief/2012/jan/30/thomas-aquinas-modernity [accessed 13 July 2012].

Beattie, Tina (2013) '"The Touch that Goes Beyond Touching": a reflection on the touching of Mary of Magdala in Theology and Art', in Reimund Bieringer, Barbara Baert, and Karlijn Demasure (eds), *Noli me tangere: New Interdisciplinary Perspectives*, Bibliotheca Ephemeridum Theologicarum Lovaniensium (Leuven, Paris and Dudley MA: Peeters).

Beauvoir, Simone de (1986) *The Second Sex* (Harmondsworth: Penguin Books).

Becker, Ernest (2011) *The Denial of Death* (London: Souvenir Press).

Bell, Rudolph M. (1987) *Holy Anorexia* (Chicago and London: University of Chicago Press).

Bem, Sandra Lipsitz (1993) *The Lenses of Gender: Transforming the Debate on Sexual Inequality* (New Haven CT: Yale University Press).

Benslama, Fethi (2009) *Psychoanalysis and the Challenge of Islam*, trans. Robert Bononno (Minneapolis MN: University of Minnesota Press).

Berthold-Bond, Daniel (1995) *Hegel's Theory of Madness* (Albany NY: State University of New York Press).

Bettelheim, Bruno (2001) *Freud and Man's Soul* (London: Pimlico).

Bjelić, Dušan I. (2003) *Galileo's Pendulum: Science, Sexuality, and the Body–Instrument Link* (Albany NY: State University of New York Press).

Boeve, Lieven (2010) 'Richard Kearney's Messianism: Between the Narrative Theology of Hermeneutics and the Negative Theology of Deconstructionism', in Lieven Boeve and Christophe Brabant (eds), *Between Philosophy and Theology: Contemporary Interpretations of Christianity* (Farnham Surrey and Burlington VT: Ashgate Publishing), pp. 7–17.

Boff, Leonardo OFM (1989) *The Maternal Face of God: The Feminine and Its Religious Expressions*, trans. Robert R. Barr and John Diercksmeier (London: Collins).

Børresen, Kari Elisabeth (1995) *Subordination and Equivalence: Nature and Role of Women in Augustine and Thomas Aquinas* (Lanham MD and Plymouth UK: Rowman & Littlefield Publishers).

Boss, Sarah Jane (2000) *Empress and Handmaid: On Nature and Gender in the Cult of the Virgin Mary* (London and New York: Cassell).

Boss, Sarah Jane (2004) *Mary*, 'New Century Theology' (London and New York: Continuum).

Bourke, Vernon Joseph (1965) *Aquinas' Search for Wisdom* (Milwaukee: Bruce Publishing Co.).

Bowie, Malcolm (1991) *Lacan* (London: Harper Collins).

Boyarin, Daniel (2003) 'On the History of the Early Phallus', in Sharon Farmer and Carol Braun Pasternack (eds), *Gender and Difference in the Middle Ages* (Minneapolis MN: University of Minnesota Press).

Brennan, Teresa (1993) *History After Lacan* (London and New York: Routledge).

Brophy, Don (2011) *Catherine of Siena: A Passionate Life* (London: Darton, Longman and Todd).

Brower, Jeffrey E. (2009) 'Simplicity and Aseity', in Thomas P. Flint and Michael Cannon Rea (eds), *Handbook of Philosophical Theology* (Oxford and New York: Oxford University Press), pp. 105–28.

Burns, Tony (2000) 'Aquinas's Two Doctrines of Natural Law', *Political Studies*, Vol. 48:5, pp. 929–46.

Burrell, David B. (2008) *Aquinas: God and Action* (Chicago IL: University of Scranton Press).

Bynum, Caroline Walker (1987) *Holy Feast and Holy Fast: The Religious Significance of Food to Medieval Women* (Berkeley CA: University of California).

Bynum, Caroline Walker (1991) *Fragmentation and Redemption: On Gender and the Human Body in Medieval Religion* (New York: Zone Books).

Bynum, Caroline Walker (1995) *The Resurrection of the Body in Western Christianity, 200–1336* (New York: Columbia University Press).

Bynum, Caroline Walker (2007) *Wonderful Blood: Theology and Practice in Late Medieval Northern Germany and Beyond* (Philadelphia: University of Pennsylvania Press).

Bynum, Caroline Walker (2011) *Christian Materiality: An Essay on Religion in Late Medieval Europe* (New York: Zone Books).

Capps, Donald (1995) 'Enrapt Spirits and the Melancholy Soul: The Locus of Division in the Christian Self and American Society', in Richard K. Fenn and Donald Capps (eds), *On Losing the Soul: Essays in the Social Psychology of Religion* (Albany NY: State University of New York Press), pp. 137–69.

Caputo, John D. (1997) *The Prayers and Tears of Jacques Derrida: Religion Without Religion* (Bloomington IN: Indiana).

Caputo, John D. (2002) 'Richard Kearney's Enthusiasm: A Philosophical Exploration on the God Who May Be', *Modern Theology*, 18:1 (January), pp. 87–94.

Caputo, John D. and Gianni Vattimo (2007) *After the Death of God*, ed. Jeffrey W. Robbins (New York: Columbia University Press).

Carey, Peter (2012) *The Chemistry of Tears* (London: Faber and Faber).

Catherine of Siena (1980) *I, Catherine: Selected Writings of Catherine of Siena*, ed. and trans. Kenelm Foster OP and Mary John Ronayne OP (London: Collins).

Catherine of Siena (1980) *The Dialogue*, trans. Suzanne Noffke OP (New York and Mahwah: Paulist Press).

Catherine of Siena (2000, 2001, 2007, 2008) *The Letters of St Catherine of Siena*, Vols I–IV, trans. Suzanne Noffke (Tempe: Medieval and Renaissance Texts and Studies).

Cavanaugh, William T. (2008) *Being Consumed: Economics and Christian Desire* (Grand Rapids MI and Cambridge UK: William B. Eerdmans Publishing Co.), p. 48.

Chaitin, Gilbert D. (1996) *Rhetoric and Culture in Lacan* (Cambridge, New York and Melbourne: Cambridge University Press).

Clark, Mary (ed.) (2003) 'Introduction', in *An Aquinas Reader: Selections from the Writings of Thomas Aquinas* (New York: Fordham University Press), revised edition.

Clemens, Justin (2007) 'Love as Ontology: Psychoanalysis against Philosophy', in Christine Kerslake and Ray Brassier (eds), *Origins and Ends of the Mind: Philosophical Essays on Psychoanalysis* (Leuven: Leuven University Press), pp. 185–200.

Clément, Catherine (1994) *Syncope: The Philosophy of Rapture*, trans. Sally O'Driscoll and Deirdre M. Mahoney (Minneapolis MN: University of Minnesota Press).

Coakley, Sarah (1988) '"Femininity" and the Holy Spirit?', in Monica Furlong (ed.), *Mirror to the Church: Reflections on Sexism* (London: SPCK), pp. 124–35.

Cohen, Arthur A. and Paul Mendes-Flohr (eds) (1972) *Contemporary Jewish Religious Thought* (New York: Macmillan).

Cohen, Sheldon M. (1996) *Aristotle on Nature and Incomplete Substance* (Cambridge and New York: Cambridge University Press).

Connolly, Pamela Stephenson (2012) '*Fifty Shades of Grey* is bad for bondage', *The Guardian: Shortcuts Blog—A Sideways Look at the News*, at http://www.guardian.co.uk/theguardian/shortcuts/2012/jul/08/fifty-shades-grey-bad-bondage [accessed 13 July 2012].

Copleston, Frederick (2003) *A History of Philosophy, Vol. 1: Greece and Rome* (London and New York: Continuum).

Corbari, Eliana (forthcoming) *Vernacular Theology: Dominican Sermons and Audience in Late Medieval Italy* (Berlin and Boston MA: Walter de Gruyter GmbH & Co. KG).

Costen, Michael D. (1997) *The Cathars and the Albigensian Crusade* (Manchester and New York: Manchester University Press).

Coudert, Allison P. (2011) *Religion, Magic and Science in Early Modern Europe and America* (Santa Barbara CA: ABC-CLIO, LLLC).

Crockett, Clayton (2007) *Interstices of the Sublime: Theology and Psychoanalytic Theory* (New York: Fordham University Press).

Crockett, Clayton, Creston Davis, and Marcus Pound (eds) (forthcoming) *Theology After Lacan* (Eugene OR: Wipf and Stock, forthcoming).

Daggers, Jenny (2011) 'On Playing with the Boys', ESWTR Journal Conference Papers for the 14th International Conference, Salamanca, 24–28 August, *Feminist Theology: listening, understanding and giving answer in a secular and pluralist world*.

Daly, Mary (1986) *Beyond God the Father: Towards a Philosophy of Women's Liberation* (London: The Women's Press).

Daniel, Arnaut and Paul Blackburn (1980) 'Sirventes', *Boundary* 2, Vol. 8, No. 3 (Spring), pp. 147–50.

Davies, Brian (1993) *The Thought of Thomas Aquinas* (Oxford and New York: Oxford University Press).

Dawkins, Richard (2006) *The God Delusion* (London: Bantam Press).

D'Costa, Gavin (2000) *Sexing the Trinity: Gender, Culture and the Divine* (London: SCM Press, 2000).

DeHart, Paul (2012) *Aquinas and Radical Orthodoxy: A Critical Inquiry* (London and New York: Routledge).

Descartes, René (1985) *The Philosophical Writings of Descartes*, Vol. 1, trans. John Cottingham, Robert Stoothoff, and Dugald Murdoch (Cambridge: Cambridge University Press).

Descartes, René (1993) *Meditations on First Philosophy*, 3rd edn, trans. Donald A. Cress (Indianapolis IN: Hackett Publishing Co.).

Desmond, William (2003) *Hegel's God: A Counterfeit Double?* (Aldershot and Burlington: Ashgate Press).

Dillard, Annie (1994) 'The Book of Luke', in *The Annie Dillard Reader* (New York: HarperPerennial), pp. 263–77.

Duffy, Eamon (2005) *The Stripping of the Altars: Traditional Religion in England c.1400–c.1580* (New Haven CT: Yale University Press).

Eliot, George (1994) *Middlemarch* (London: Penguin Books).

Elshtain, Jean Bethke (1993) *Public Man, Private Woman: Women in Social and Political Thought* (Princeton NJ: Princeton University Press).

Emery, Gilles OP (2003) *Trinity in Aquinas*, trans. Heather Buttery, Matthew Levering, Robert Williams, and Teresa Bede (Ypsilanti MI: Sapientia Press of Ave Maria University).

Ensler, Eve (2001) *The Vagina Monologues* (London: Virago, 2001).

Ernst, Cornelius (1979) 'Metaphor and Ontology in *Sacra Doctrina*', in Fergus Kerr and Timothy Radcliffe (eds), *Multiple Echo* (London: Darton, Longman and Todd).

Father of the Order of Friar Preachers (1881) *The Life of the Angelic Doctor, St. Thomas Aquinas* (New York: P. J. Kenedy and Sons), at http://www.archive.org/stream/lifeofangelicdoc00cavauoft/lifeofangelicdoc00cavauoft_djvu.txt [accessed 27 July 2012].

Felman, Shoshana (1987) *Jacques Lacan and the Adventure of Insight: Psychoanalysis in Contemporary Culture* (Cambridge MA: Harvard University Press).

Fenn, Richard K. (1995) *On Losing the Soul: Essays in the Social Psychology of Religion* (Albany NY: State University of New York Press), pp. 138–40.

Fiddes, Paul S. (2002) *The Creative Suffering of God* (Oxford and New York: Oxford University Press).

Fisher, David H. (1989) 'Introduction: Framing Lacan?', in Edith Wyschogrod, David Crownfield, and Carl A. Raschke (eds), *Lacan and Theological Discourse* (Albany NY: State University of New York Press).

Foster, Kenelm (ed.) (1959) *The Life of St Thomas Aquinas: Biographical Documents* (London and Baltimore: Longmans, Green).

Foucault, Michel (1990) *The History of Sexuality: An Introduction*, trans. Robert Hurley (New York: Vintage Books).

Frankenberry, Nancy (2004) 'Feminist Approaches: Philosophy of Religion in Different Voices', in Pamela Sue Anderson and Beverley Clack (eds), *Feminist Philosophy of Religion: Critical Readings* (London and New York: Routledge), pp. 3–27.

Freud, Sigmund (1913) 'Totem and Taboo', in SE Vol. 13 (London: Hogarth Press), pp. 1–161.

Freud, Sigmund (1920) 'Beyond the Pleasure Principle', in SE Vol. 18 (London: Hogarth Press), pp. 7–66.

Freud, Sigmund (1927) 'The Future of an Illusion', in SE Vol. 21 (London: Hogarth Press), pp. 3–58.

Freud, Sigmund (1937) 'Analysis Terminable and Interminable', in SE Vol. 23 (London: Hogarth Press), pp. 209–53.

Freud, Sigmund (1939) 'Moses and Montheism', in SE Vol. 23 (London: Hogarth Press), pp. 1–137.

Freud, Sigmund (1953–74) *The Standard Edition of the Complete Psychological Works of Sigmund Freud*, 24 vols, ed. and trans. James Strachey, in collaboration with Anna Freud, assisted by Alix Strachey and Alan Tyson (London: Hogarth and the Institute of Psychoanalysis).

Funkenstein, Amos (1986) *Theology and the Scientific Imagination from the Middle Ages to the Seventeenth Century* (Princeton NJ and Chichester UK: Princeton University Press).

Gallop, David (1984) *Parmenides of Elea: Fragments*, trans. David Gallop (Toronto: University of Toronto Press).

Gilligan, Carol (1982) *In a Different Voice: Psychological Theory and Women's Development* (Cambridge MA: Harvard University Press).

Gilson, Étienne (1941) *God and Philosophy*, ed. W. Harry Jellema (New Haven: Yale University Press).

Gilson, Étienne (1955) *History of Christian Philosophy in the Middle Ages* (London: Sheed and Ward).

Gilson, Étienne (1961) *The Christian Philosophy of St. Thomas Aquinas*, trans. L. K. Shook (London: Victor Gollancz Ltd).

Grant, Edward (2010) *The Nature of Natural Philosophy in the Late Middle Ages* (Washington DC: The Catholic University of America Press).

Gratton, Peter and John Panteleimon Manoussakis (eds), *Traversing the Imaginary: Richard Kearney and the Postmodern Challenge* (Evanston IL: Northwestern University Press, 2007).

Gray, Frances (2002) 'Review of Richard Kearney, *The God Who May Be: A Hermeneutics of Religion* (Indiana University Press, 2001)', *Notre Dame Philosophical Review*—an electronic journal published by University of Notre Dame (3rd March) at http://ndpr.nd.edu/news/23362-the-god-who-may-be-a-hermeneutics-of-religion/ [accessed 31 July 2012].

Gray, John (2008) *Black Mass: Apocalyptic Religion and the Death of Utopia* (London and New York: Penguin Books).

Grigg, Russell (2008) *Lacan, Language and Philosophy* (Albany NY: State University of New York Press).

Grosz, Elizabeth (1990) *Jacques Lacan: A Feminist Introduction* (London and New York: Routledge).

Hall, Pamela M. (1994) *Narrative and the Natural Law: An Interpretation of Thomistic Ethics* (Notre Dame and London: University of Notre Dame Press).

Hampson, Daphne (1990) *Theology and Feminism* (Oxford UK and Cambridge MA: Blackwell).

Hankey, Wayne John (2012) 'Aquinas, Plato, and Neoplatonism', in Brian Davies and Eleonore Stump (eds), *Entry in the Oxford Handbook of Aquinas* (Oxford and London: Oxford University Press), pp. 55–64.

Harding, Sandra G. (1986) *The Science Question in Feminism* (Ithaca NY: Cornell University Press).

Harmless, William (2010) *Augustine in His Own Words* (Washington DC: The Catholic University of America Press).

Hegel, G. W. F. (1977) *Phenomenology of Spirit*, trans. A. V. Miller (Oxford, New York, Toronto, Melbourne: Oxford University Press).

Hegel, G. W. F. (2005) *Philosophy of Right*, trans. S. W. Dyde (Mineola NY: Dover Publications, Inc.).

Heidegger, Martin (1974) 'The Onto-theo-logical Constitution of Metaphysics', in *Identity and Difference*, trans. Joan Sambaugh (San Francisco: Harper & Row).

Hollywood, Amy (2002) *Sensible Ecstasy: Mysticism, Sexual Difference, and the Demands of History* (Chicago and London: The University of Chicago Press).

Holquist, Michael (2002) *Dialogism*, 2nd edn (London and New York: Routledge).

Holsinger, Bruce W. (2005) *The Premodern Condition: Medievalism and the Making of Theory* (Chicago and London: University of Chicago Press).

Irigaray, Luce (1985) *Speculum of the Other Woman*, trans. Gillian C. Gill (Ithaca NY: Cornell University Press).

Irigaray, Luce (1985) *This Sex Which Is Not One*, trans. Catherine Porter with Carolyn Burke Porter (Ithaca NY: Cornell University Press).

Irigaray, Luce (1993) *An Ethics of Sexual Difference*, trans. Carolyn Burke and Gillian C. Gill (London: The Athlone Press).

Irigaray, Luce (1993) *Sexes and Genealogies*, trans. Gillian C. Gill (New York: Columbia University Press).

Irigaray, Luce (1996) *i love to you: Sketch of a Possible Felicity in History*, trans. Alison Martin (New York and London: Routledge).

Jacob, Margaret C. (1993) 'The Materialist World of Pornography', in Lynn Hunt (ed.), *The Invention of Pornography: Obscenity and the Origins of Modernity, 1500–1800* (New York: Zone Books), pp. 157–202.

Jambet, Christian (1983) *La Logique des Orientaux* (Paris: Seuil).

James, E. L. (2012) *Fifty Shades of Grey* (London: Arrow Books).

James, E. L. (2012) *Fifty Shades Darker* (London: Arrow Books).

James, E. L. (2012) *Fifty Shades Freed* (London: Arrow Books).

Jantzen, Grace M. (1995) *Power, Gender and Christian Mysticism* (Cambridge: Cambridge University Press).

Jantzen, Grace M. (1998) *Becoming Divine: Towards a Feminist Philosophy of Religion* (Manchester: Manchester University Press).

Jenson, Robert W. (1997) *Systematic Theology, Vol. 1, The Triune God* (Oxford: Oxford University Press).

Johnson, Elizabeth (1992) *She Who Is: The Mystery of God in Feminist Theological Discourse* (New York: Crossroad).

Jones, Serene (2006) 'Women's Experience Between a Rock and a Hard Place: Feminist, Womanist, and *Mujerista* Theologies in North America', in Seth Kunin (ed.), *Theories of Religion: A Reader* (New Brunswick NJ: Rutgers University Press), pp. 397–410.

Jordan, Mark D. (2007) 'God's Body', in Gerard Loughlin (ed.), *Queer Theology: Rethinking the Western Body* (Malden MA and Oxford UK: Blackwell Publishing), pp. 281–92.

Kant, Immanuel (1960) *Religion within the Limits of Reason Alone*, trans. Theodore M. Greene and Hoyt H. Hudson (New York: Harper Torchbooks).

Kant, Immanuel (1983) *Immanuel Kant's Critique of Pure Reason*, trans. Norman Kemp Smith (second impression of 1st edn; London and Basingstoke: The Macmillan Press Ltd).

Kant, Immanuel (1987) *Critique of Judgment*, trans. Werner S. Pluhar (Hackett).

Kant, Immanuel (1996) *The Metaphysics of Morals*, trans. and ed. Mary Gregor (Cambridge and London: Cambridge University Press).

Kant, Immanuel (1998) *Groundwork of the Metaphysics of Morals*, trans. and ed. Mary Gregor (Cambridge and London: Cambridge University Press).

Kant, Immanuel (2005) *Perpetual Peace*, trans. Mary Campbell Smith (New York: Cosimo Inc.).

Kant, Immanuel (2008) *Critique of Practical Reason, and Other Works on the Theory of Ethics*, trans. Thomas Kingsmill Abbott (Forgotten Books), at http://www.for-gottenbooks.org/info/Critique_of_Practical_Reason_and_Other_Works_on_the_Theory_of_Ethics_1000308607.php [accessed 26 July 2012].

Kearney, Richard (1998) *Poetics of Imagining: Modern to Post-modern* (New York: Fordham University Press).

Kearney, Richard (1998) *The Wake of Imagination* (London: Century Hutchinson; New York: Routledge).

Kearney, Richard (2001) *The God Who May Be: A Hermeneutics of Religion* (Bloomington IN: Indiana University Press).

Kearney, Richard (2002) 'God Who May Be: A Phenomenological Study', *Modern Theology*, 18:1 (January), pp. 75–85.

Kearney, Richard (2003) *Strangers, Gods, and Monsters: Interpreting Otherness* (London and New York: Routledge).

Kearney, Richard (2006) 'Poetics of a Possible God', in Lieven Boeve, Joeri Schrijvers, Wessel Stoker, and Hendrik M. Vroom (eds), *Faith in the Enlightenment? The Critique of the Enlightenment Revisited* (Amsterdam and New York: Editions Rodopi B. V.), pp. 305–23.

Kearney, Richard (2012) 'Diacritical Hermeneutics', in Maria Luísa Portocarrero, Luis António Umbelino, and Andrzej Wierciński (eds), *Hermeneutic Rationality—La rationalité herméneutique* (Berlin: Lit Verlag Dr. W. Hopf), pp. 176–92.

Kearney, Richard (2013) *Re-imagining the Sacred: the Anatheist Debate* (New York: Columbia University Press).

Kennedy, Helena (2005) *Just Law: The Changing Face of Justice, and Why It Matters to Us All* (London: Vintage).

Kenny, Anthony (1980) *Aquinas* (Oxford: Oxford University Press).

Kerr, Fergus (1988) *Theology After Wittgenstein* (Oxford and New York: Basil Blackwell).

Kerr, Fergus (2002) *After Aquinas: Versions of Thomism* (Malden MA and Oxford: Blackwell Publishers).

Kerr, Fergus (2007) *Twentieth-century Catholic Theologians: from Neoscholasticism to Nuptial Mysticism* (Oxford and New York: Blackwell Publishing).

Kerr, Fergus (2009) *Thomas Aquinas: A Very Short Introduction* (Very Short Introductions; Oxford: Oxford University Press).

Kilby, Karen (2005) 'Aquinas, the Trinity and the Limits of Understanding', *International Journal of Systematic Theology*, 7 (4), pp. 414–27.

Koerner Joseph Leo (2008) *The Reformation of the Image* (Chicago: University of Chicago Press).

Korsak, Mary Phil (1992) *At the Start . . . Genesis Made New: A Translation of the Hebrew Text* (Louvain: European Series, Louvain Cahiers, No. 124).

Koyré, Alexandre (1943) 'Galileo and the Scientific Revolution of the Seventeenth Century', *The Philosophical Review*, Vol. 52, No. 4, pp. 333–48.

Kristeva, Julia (1982) *Powers of Horror: An Essay on Abjection*, trans. Leon S. Roudiez (New York: Columbia University Press).

Kristeva, Julia (1987) *Tales of Love*, trans. Leon S. Roudiez (New York: Columbia University Press).

Kristeva, Julia (1991) *Strangers to Ourselves*, trans. Leon S. Roudiez (Hemel Hempstead: Harvester).

Kristof, Nicholas D. and Sheryl Wudunn (2010) *Half the Sky: How to Change the World* (London: Virago).

Labbie, Erin Felicia (2006) *Lacan's Medievalism* (Minnesota: University of Minnesota Press).

Lacan, Jacques (1975) *Le Séminaire Livre XX: Encore* (Paris: Éditions du Seuil).

Lacan, Jacques (1981) *The Four Fundamental Concepts of Psychoanalysis: The Seminar of Jacques Lacan, Book XI*, trans. Alan Sheridan (New York and London: W. W. Norton).

Lacan, Jacques (1999) *The Ethics of Psychoanalysis 1959–1960: The Seminar of Jacques Lacan, Book VII*, trans. Dennis Porter (London and New York: Routledge).

Lacan, Jacques (1999) *On Feminine Sexuality—the Limits of Love and Knowledge: The Seminar of Jacques Lacan, Book XX, Encore, 1972–1973*, ed. Jacques-Alain Miller, trans. Bruce Fink (New York and London: W. W. Norton & Company).

Lacan, Jacques (2005) *Le Séminaire livre XXIII, Le sinthome* (Paris: Éditions du Seuil).

Lacan, Jacques (2005) *Le Triomphe de la Religion précédé de Discours aux Catholiques* (Paris: Éditions du Seuil).

Lacan, Jacques (2006) *Écrits*, trans. Bruce Fink (New York and London: W. W. Norton).

Lacan, Jacques (2007) *The Other Side of Psychoanalysis: The Seminar of Jacques Lacan, Book XVII*, ed. Jacques-Alain Miller, trans. Russell Grigg (New York and London: W. W. Norton & Co. Ltd).

LaCugna, Catherine Mowry (1993) *God for Us: the Trinity and Christian Life* (San Francisco: HarperSanFrancisco).

Lang, Bernhard (2002) *The Hebrew God: Portrait of an Ancient Deity* (New Haven CT: Yale University Press).

Laqueur, Thomas (1990) *Making Sex: Body and Gender from the Greeks to Freud* (Cambridge MA: Harvard University Press).

Lash, Nicholas (2004) *Holiness, Speech and Silence: Reflections on the Question of God* (Aldershot UK and Burlington VT: Ashgate Publishing Ltd).

Leclerc, Ivor (1972) *The Nature of Physical Existence* (London: George Allen & Unwin Ltd).

Leupin, Alexandre (2004) *Lacan Today: Psychoanalysis, Science, Religion* (New York: Other Press), p. 106.

Lindberg, David C. (2008 (2nd edn, first published 1992)) *The Beginnings of Western Science: The European Scientific Tradition in Philosophical, Religious, and Institutional Context, Prehistory to A.D. 1450* (Chicago: University of Chicago Press).

Lloyd, Genevieve (1993) *The Man Of Reason: 'Male' and 'Female' in Western Philosophy* (London and New York: Routledge).

Loughlin, Gerard (ed.) (2007) *Queer Theology: Rethinking the Western Body* (Malden MA and Oxford UK: Blackwell Publishing).

Lubac, Henri de SJ (1995) *The Drama of Atheist Humanism*, trans. Edith M. Riley, Anne Englund Nash, and Mark Sebanc (San Francisco: Ignatius Press).

Luepnitz, Deborah (2003) 'Beyond the Phallus: Lacan and Feminism', in Jean-Michel Rabaté (ed.), *The Cambridge Companion to Lacan* (Cambridge and New York: Cambridge University Press), pp. 221–36.

Lynch, Thomas (forthcoming) 'Making the Quarter Turn', in Clayton Crockett, Creston Davis, and Marcus Pound (eds), *Theology After Lacan* (Eugene OR: Wipf and Stock).

Machamer, Peter (1998) 'Galileo's Machines, his Mathematics, and his Experiments', in Peter K. Machamer (ed.), *The Cambridge Companion to Galileo* (Cambridge and New York: Cambridge University Press), pp. 53–79.

MacIntyre, Alasdair (2009) *God, Philosophy, Universities: A Selective History of the Catholic Philosophical Tradition* (Lanham Maryland and Plymouth UK: Sheed & Ward).

MacLachlan, James (1990) 'Drake Against the Philosophers', in Trevor H. Levere and William R. Shea (eds), *Nature, Experiment, and the Sciences: Essays on Galileo and the History of Science*, Essays in Honour of Stillman Drake (Dordrecht: Kluwer Academic Publishers), pp. 123–46.

Manoussakis, John P. (2002) 'From Exodus to Eschaton: On the God Who May Be', *Modern Theology*, 18:1 (January), pp. 95–107.

Maritain, Jacques (1952) *The Range of Reason* [online text], Charles Scribner's Sons <http://maritain.nd.edu/jmc/etext/range.htm> [accessed 9 May 2012].

McCarthy, David Matzko (2011) *Sex and Love in the Home: A Theology of the Household* (Eugene OR: Wipf Stock Publishers, 2011).

McDermott, Timothy (ed.) (1992) *Summa Theologiae: A Concise Translation* (London: Methuen).

McGilchrist, Iain (2010) *The Master and His Emissary: The Divided Brain and the Making of the Western World* (New Haven CT: Yale University Press).

McGinn, Bernard (1994) *Meister Eckhart and the Beguine Mystics* (New York: Continuum).

McGinn, Bernard (2013) *The Varieties of Vernacular Mysticism: 1350–1550* (New York: Crossroad Publishing Company).

McInerny, Ralph (1993) *Aquinas Against the Averroists: On There Being Only One Intellect* (West Lafayette IN: Purdue University Press).

Merchant, Carolyn (1990) *The Death of Nature: Women, Ecology and the Scientific Revolution* (San Francisco: Harper & Row).

Meyerowitz, Rael (1995) *Transferring to America: Jewish Interpretations of American Dreams* (Albany NY: State University of New York Press).

Meynell, Alice (1913) *Collected Poems of Alice Meynell* (New York: Charles Scribner's Sons).

Milbank, John and Catherine Pickstock (2001) *Truth in Aquinas* (London and New York: Routledge).

Miller, Jacques-Alain (2002) 'Elements of Epistemology', in Jason Glynos and Yannis Stavrakakis (eds), *Lacan and Science* (London: Karnac Books), pp. 147–66.

Mills, Jon (2004) 'The I and the It', in Jon Mills (ed.), *Rereading Freud: Psychoanalysis through Philosophy* (Albany NY: State University of New York Press, 2004), pp. 127–64.

Mitchell, Juliet and Jacqueline Rose (eds) (1982) *Feminine Sexuality: Jacques Lacan and the École Freudienne* (Basingstoke and London: Macmillan Press).

Moltmann, Jürgen (1993) *The Trinity and the Kingdom: The Doctrine of God* (Philadelphia: Fortress Press).

Murdoch, Iris (1985) *The Sovereignty of Good* (Boston: Ark).

Neill, Emily R., Marla Brettschneider, Regula Grünenfelder, et al. (1999) 'Roundtable Discussion: From Generation to Generation: Horizons in Feminist Theology or Reinventing the Wheel?', *Journal of Feminist Studies in Religion*, Vol. 15, No. 1, pp. 102–38.

Nelson, Lynn Hankinson and Jack Nelson (eds) (1997) *Feminism, Science, and the Philosophy of Science* (Dordrecht, The Netherlands: Kluwer Academic Publishers).

Newman, John Henry (1996) *The Idea of a University*, ed. Frank Turner (New Haven CT: Yale University Press).

Nobus, Dany (2002) 'A matter of cause: reflections on Lacan's "Science and truth"', in Jason Glynos and Yannis Stavrakakis (eds), *Lacan and Science* (London: Karnac Books), pp. 89–118.

Noffke, Suzanne OP (1996) *Catherine of Siena: Vision of a Distant Eye* (Collegeville MN: Liturgical Press, Michael Glazier).

Nolan, Michael 'The Defective Male: What Aquinas Really Said', at http://www.womenpriests.org/theology/nolan.asp [accessed 1 June 2011].

Norberg, Kathryn (1993) 'The Libertine Whore: Prostitution in French Pornography from Margot to Juliette' in Lynn Hunt (ed.), *The Invention of Pornography: Obscenity and the Origins of Modernity, 1500–1800* (New York: Zone Books), pp. 225–52.

Nordling, Cherith Fee (2010) *Knowing and Naming the Triune God: A Conversation Between Elizabeth A. Johnson and Karl Barth* (New York: Peter Lang Publishing, Inc.).

Novak, Michael (1995) 'Aquinas and the Heretics', *First Things* 58 (December), pp. 33–8, at http://www.firstthings.com/article/2008/09/003-aquinas-and-the-heretics-17 [accessed 27 July 2012].

Oberman, Heiko A. (2006) *Luther: Man between God and the Devil*, trans. Eileen Walliser-Schwarzbart (New Haven: Yale University Press, 2006).

O'Connor, Timothy (July 1999) 'Simplicity and Creation', *Faith and Philosophy*, 405–12.

O'Malley, John (2012) 'Were Medieval Universities Catholic Universities?', *American Magazine*, 14 May at http://www.americamagazine.org/content/article.cfm?article_id=13417 [accessed 25 July 2012].

Palmerino, Carla Rita (2006) 'The Mathematical Characters of Galileo's Book of Nature', in Klaas van Berkel and Arjo Vanderjagt (eds), *The Book of Nature in Early Modern and Modern History* (Leuven: Peeters), pp. 27–44.

Pangle, Lorraine Smith (2002) *Aristotle and the Philosophy of Friendship* (Cambridge: Cambridge University Press).

Pascal, Blaise (1995) *Pensées and Other Writings*, trans. Honor Levi (New York: Oxford University Press).

Pasnau, Robert (2002) *Thomas Aquinas on Human Nature: A Philosophical Study of Summa theologiae Ia 75–89* (Cambridge: Cambridge University Press).

Patterson, Dennis Michael (ed.) (2003) *Philosophy of Law and Legal Theory: An Anthology* (Oxford: Blackwell Publishing).

Paul VI, Pope (1968) *Humanae Vitae*, 'Encyclical Letter on the Regulation of Birth', 25 July, at http://www.vatican.va/holy_father/paul_vi/encyclicals/documents/hf_p-vi_enc_25071968_humanae-vitae_en.html [accessed 8 December 2012].

Pegis, Anton C. (ed.) (1997 [1945]) *Basic Writings of Saint Thomas Aquinas: God and the Order of Creation* (One; Indianapolis IN: Hackett Publishing Company).

Pierce, Christine (2000) *Immovable Laws, Irresistible Rights: Natural Law, Moral Rights, and Feminist Ethics* (Lawrence KA: University Press of Kansas).

Plato (1997) *Complete Works*, ed. John M. Cooper (Indianapolis IN and Cambridge UK: Hackett Publishing Co.).

Plato (2003) *Gorgias and Timaeus*, ed. Paul Negri (Dover Thrift Editions; Mineola NY: Dover Publications, Inc.).

Plowman, Max (1944) *Bridge into the Future: Letters of Max Plowman* (London: Andrew Dakers).

Polis, Dennis F. (1991) 'A New Reading of Aristotle's *Hyle*', *The Modern Schoolman*, LXVIII (3), pp. 225–44.

Porter, Jean (1999) *Natural and Divine Law: Reclaiming the Tradition for Christian Ethics* (Grand Rapids MI and Cambridge UK: William B. Eerdmans Publishing Co.).

Porter, Jean (2005) *Nature as Reason: A Thomistic Theory of the Natural Law* (Grand Rapids MI and Cambridge UK: William B. Eerdmans Publishing Co.).

Pound, Marcus (2007) *Theology, Psychoanalysis and Trauma* (London: SCM Press).

Pound, Marcus (2011) 'Lacan's Return to Freud: A Case of Theological *Ressourcement?*', in Gabriel Flynn and Paul D. Murray (eds), *Ressourcement: A Movement for Renewal in Twentieth-Century Catholic Theology* (Oxford: Oxford University Press), pp. 440–56.

Quinn, Patrick (1996) *Aquinas, Platonism, and the Knowledge of God* (Aldershot: Avebury).

Rabaté, Jean-Michel (ed.) (2003) *The Cambridge Companion to Lacan* (Cambridge, New York, Port Melbourne, Madrid, Cape Town: Cambridge University Press).

Raymond of Capua (1980) *The Life of Catherine of Siena*, ed. and trans. Conleth Kearns OP (Dublin and Wilmington: Dominican Publications and Michael Glazier, Inc.).

Regnault, François (1985) *Dieu est Inconscient: Études Lacaniennes autour de Saint Thomas d'Aquin* (Paris: Navarin)—all translations are my own.

Reinhard, Kenneth and Julia Reinhard Lupton (2000) 'Revelation: Lacan and the Ten Commandments', at http://www.jcrt.org/archives/02.1/reinhard_lupton.shtml [accessed 30 July 2012].

Reinhard, Kenneth (2005) 'Toward a Political Theology of the Neighbor', in Slavoj Žižek, Er L. Santer, and Kenneth Reinhard, *The Neighbour: Three Inquiries in Political Theology* (Chicago IL and London: University of Chicago Press), pp. 11–75.

Reinhard, Kenneth and Julia Reinhard Lupton (2003) 'The Subject of Religion: Lacan and the Ten Commandments', *Diacritics*, 33 (2), pp. 71–97.

Ricoeur, Paul (1974) 'Fatherhood: From Phantasm to Symbol', trans. Robert Sweeney, in *The Conflict of Interpretations* (Evanston IL: Northwestern University Press), pp. 468–97.

Roazen, Paul (2002) *The Trauma of Freud: Controversies in Psychoanalysis* (New Brunswick: Transaction Publishers).

Robinson, Edward 1987) *The Language of Mystery* (London: SCM Press, 1987).

Rocca, Gregory P. OP (1993) 'Aquinas on God-Talk: Hovering over the Abyss', *Theological Studies*, 54, pp. 641–61.

Rogers, Eugene F. Jr (1995) *Thomas Aquinas and Karl Barth* (South Bend IN: University of Notre Dame Press).

Ross, Maggie (2011) *Writing the Icon of the Heart: In Silence Beholding* (Abingdon: The Bible Reading Fellowship).

Roudinesco, Élisabeth (1990) *Jacques Lacan and Co: A History of Psychoanalysis in France, 1925–1985*, trans. Jeffrey Mehlman (Chicago: University of Chicago Press).

Roudinesco, Élisabeth (1999) *Jacques Lacan: An Outline of a Life and History of a System of Thought*, trans. Barbara Bray (Cambridge: Polity Press).

Rowland, Tracey (Fall 2008) 'Natural Law: From Neo-Thomism to Nuptial Mysticism', *Communio: International Catholic Review* 35, pp. 374–96.

Rubenstein, Richard E. (2003) *Aristotle's Children: How Christians, Muslims, and Jews Rediscovered Ancient Wisdom and Illuminated the Dark Ages* (Orlando, Austin, New York, San Diego, Toronto, London: Harcourt Brace International).

Ruderman, Zoe 'The Scary New Butt Beauty Trend', *Cosmopolitan* website: http://www.cosmopolitan.com/advice/health/anal-bleaching-trend [accessed 30 July 2012].

Rüegg, Walter (2003) 'Chapter 1: Themes' in Hilde de Ridder-Symoens (ed.), *A History of the University in Europe, Volume 1: Universities in the Middle Ages* (Cambridge and New York: Cambridge University Press).

Ruether, Rosemary Radford (1993) *Sexism and God-Talk—Towards a Feminist Theology* (London: SCM Press).

Rundell, John (2007) 'Imaginings, Narratives, and Otherness: On Diacritical Hermeneutics', in Peter Gratton and John Panteleimon Manoussakis (eds), *Traversing the Imaginary: Richard Kearney and the Postmodern Challenge* (Evanston IL: Northwestern University Press), pp. 103–16.

Sarat, Austin (ed.) (2001) *Law, Violence, and the Possibility of Justice* (Princeton NJ: Princeton University Press).

Schroeder, Jeanne Lorraine (2008) *The Four Lacanian Discourses, or, Turning Law Inside-Out* (Abingdon UK and New York: Birkbeck Law Press, Routledge-Cavendish).

Schwartz, Daniel (2007) *Aquinas on Friendship* (Oxford and New York: Oxford University Press).

Scott, Karen (1999) 'Mystical Death, Bodily Death: Catherine of Siena and Raymond of Capua on the Mystic's Encounter with God', in Catherine M. Mooney (ed.), *Gendered Voices: Medieval Saints and Their Interpreters* (Philadelphia PA: University of Pennsylvania Press), pp. 136–67.

Seidel, George Joseph (2000) *Knowledge as Sexual Metaphor* (Cranbury NJ, London, Mississauga, Ontario: Associated University Presses Inc.).

Shepherdson, Charles (2003) 'Lacan and Philosophy', in Jean-Michel Rabaté (ed.), *The Cambridge Companion to Lacan* (Cambridge, New York, Port Melbourne, Madrid, Cape Town: Cambridge University Press), pp. 116–52.

Simons, Walter (2001) *Cities of Ladies: Beguine Communities in the Medieval Low Countries, 1200–1565* (Philadelphia PA: University of Pennsylvania Press).

Singer Irving (2009) *The Nature of Love: Courtly and Romantic* (Chicago: University of Chicago Press).

Smith, Mark S. (2001) *The Origins of Biblical Monotheism: Israel's Polytheistic Background and the Ugaritic Texts* (Oxford and New York: Oxford University Press).

Sölle, Dorothee (1990) *Thinking about God: An Introduction to Theology* (London: SCM Press).

Soskice, Janet Martin (2007) *The Kindness of God: Metaphor, Gender, and Religious Language* (Oxford and New York: Oxford University Press).

Soskice, Janet Martin and Lipton, Diana (eds) (2003) *Feminism and Theology* (Oxford: Oxford University Press).

Stump, Eleonore (2003) *Aquinas* (Arguments of the Philosophers Series; London and New York: Routledge).

Surin, Kenneth (1989) *The Turnings of Darkness and Light: Essays in Philosophical and Systematic Theology* (Cambridge: Cambridge University Press).

Swinburne, Richard (1977) *The Coherence of Theism* (Oxford: Clarendon Press).

Taylor, Charles (2007) *A Secular Age* (Cambridge MA: Harvard University Press).

Taylor, Mark C. (1989) 'Refusal of the Bar', in Edith Wyschogrod, David R. Crownfield, and Carl A. Raschke (eds), *Lacan and Theological Discourse* (Albany NY: State University of New York Press), pp. 39–53.

Toulmin, Stephen (1992) *Cosmopolis: The Hidden Agenda of Modernity* (Chicago: The University of Chicago Press).

Traina, Cristina L. H. (1999) *Feminist Ethics and Natural Law: The End of the Anathemas* (Washington DC: Georgetown University Press).

Turner, Denys (2004) *Faith, Reason and the Existence of God* (Cambridge: Cambridge University Press).

Tylus, Jane (2009) *Reclaiming Catherine of Siena: Literacy, Literature, and the Signs of Others* (Chicago and London: University of Chicago Press).

Vanhoozer, Kevin J. (ed.) (2003) *The Cambridge Companion to Postmodern Theology* (Cambridge and New York: Cambridge University Press).

Waller, Gary (2011) *The Virgin Mary in Late Medieval and Early Modern English Literature and Popular Culture* (Cambridge and New York: Cambridge University Press, 2011).

Ward, Graham (ed.) (2005) *The Blackwell Companion to Postmodern Theology* (Malden MA and Oxford: Blackwell Publishing).

Weber, Max (2003) *The Protestant Ethic and the Spirit of Capitalism*, trans. Talcott Parsons (Mineola NY: Dover Publications Inc.).

Weil, Simone (1950) *Waiting on God*, trans. Emma Craufurd (London: Fontana Books).

Weinandy, Thomas Gerard, Daniel A. Keating, and John Yocum (eds) (2005) *Aquinas on Scripture: An Introduction to His Biblical Commentaries* (London and New York: T & T Clark International).

Weisheipl, James A. (2008) 'Thomas d'Aquino and Albert his Teacher', *The Gilson Lectures on Thomas Aquinas* (Toronto: Pontifical Institute of Mediaeval Studies), pp. 1–18.

Whitehead, Alfred North (1985) *Process and Reality: An Essay in Cosmology* (corrected edition) (New York: The Free Press).

Wiesner, Merry E. (2000) *Women and Gender in Early Modern Europe* (Cambridge: Cambridge University Press).

Williams, A. N. (1999) *The Ground of Union: Deification in Aquinas and Palamas* (Oxford and New York: Oxford University Press).

Williams, Zoe (2012) 'Why Women Love Fifty Shades of Grey', in *The Guardian*, Friday, 6 July, at http://www.guardian.co.uk/books/2012/jul/06/why-women-love-fifty-shades-grey?newsfeed=true [accessed 9 July 2012].

Wiseman, Eva (2012) 'The Body Image Report: Uncomfortable in our Skin', *The Observer Magazine*, 10 June, pp. 14–23.

Witte, John Jr (2006) *God's Joust, God's Justice: Law and Religion in the Western Tradition* (Grand Rapids MI: William B. Eerdmans Publishing Co.).

Wolcher, Louis (2008) *Law's Task: The Tragic Circle of Law, Justice and Human Suffering* (Aldershot UK and Burlington VT: Ashgate Publishing).

Wolf, Arthur P. and William H. Durham (eds) (2004) *Inbreeding, Incest, and the Incest Taboo: The State of Knowledge at the Turn of the Century* (Stanford CA: Stanford University Press).

Wyrwa, Dietmar (2004) 'Augustine and Luther on Evil', in Henning Graf Reventlow and Yair Hoffman (eds), The Problem of Evil and Its Symbols in Jewish and Christian Tradition (London and New York: T & T Clark), pp. 124–46.

Wyschogrod, Edith, David R. Crownfield, and Carl A. Raschke (eds) (1989) *Lacan and Theological Discourse* (Albany NY: State University of New York Press).

Žižek, Slavoj (2000) *The Fragile Absolute—or, why is the Christian legacy worth fighting for?* (London and New York: Verso).

Žižek, Slavoj (2000) *The Ticklish Subject: the absent centre of political ontology* (London and New York: Verso).

Žižek, Slavoj (2002) 'The Real of Sexual Difference', in Suzanne Barnard and Bruce Fink (eds), *Reading Seminar XX: Lacan's Major Work on Love, Knowledge, and Feminine Sexuality* (Albany NY: State University of New York Press), pp. 57–76.

Žižek, Slavoj (2006) *How to Read Lacan* (London: Granta Books).

Žižek, Slavoj (2006) *The Silent Partners* (London and New York: Verso).

Žižek, Slavoj (2008) *For They Know Not What They Do: Enjoyment as a Political Factor*, 2nd edn (London and New York: Verso).

Zupančič, Alenka (2000) *Ethics of the Real* (London: Verso).

Index